iPhone Hacks

First Edition

David Jurick, Adam & Damien Stolarz

O'REILLY®

BEIJING • CAMBRIDGE • FARNHAM • KÖLN • SEBASTOPOL • TAIPEI • TOKYO

IPHONE HACKS

by David Jurick, Adam & Damien Stolarz

Printed in U.S.A.

Published by Make:Books, an imprint of Maker Media, a division of O'Reilly Media, Inc., 1005 Gravenstein Highway North, Sebastopol, CA 95472.

O'Reilly books may be purchased for educational, business, or sales promotional use. For more information, contact our corporate/institutional sales department: 800-998-9938 or *corporate@oreilly.com*.

Print History
April 2009: First Edition

Publisher: Dale Dougherty
Associate Publisher: Dan Woods
Executive Editor: Brian Jepson
Editor: Adam Flaherty
Creative Director: Daniel Carter
Designer: Gretchen J. Bay
Production Manager: Terry Bronson
Copy Editor: Nancy Kotary
Indexer: Patti Schiendelman
Cover Photograph: Michael James Smith
(www.myspace.com/genericamericanphoto)

Important Message to Our Readers: The technologies discussed in this publication, the limitations on these technologies that technology and content owners seek to impose, and the laws actually limiting the use of these technologies are constantly changing. Thus, some of the hacks described in this publication may not work, may cause unintended harm to systems on which they are used, or may not be consistent with applicable user agreements.

Your safety is your own responsibility, including proper use of equipment and safety gear, and determining whether you have adequate skill and experience. Electricity and other resources used for these projects are dangerous unless used properly and with adequate precautions, including safety gear. These projects are not intended for use by children.

Use of the instructions and suggestions in *iPhone Hacks* is at your own risk.
O'Reilly Media, Inc. and the authors disclaim all responsibility for any resulting damage, injury, or expense. It is your responsibility to make sure that your activities comply with applicable laws, including copyright.

ISBN-13: 978-0-596-51664-2

To Steve Jobs

CONTENTS

PREFACE

How important is mobile telephony? Over 2 billion people on Earth—over 1/4 of the world's population—have mobile phones. And apparently half of those upgrade frequently—over a billion mobile phones are sold each year. But calling the iPhone a "telephony" device is shortsighted. The iPhone is a mobile computing device. And really, if you study computing trends, you'll soon realize the iPhone is simply a computer.

The story of the iPod—Apple's previous great personal device play—is a story that will be studied at business schools for the next hundred years. Apple sat back for several years, watching the MP3 and portable media player market. They let things mature a bit, and then entered the market with what became a "category killer," a media player that outsold everything and became the very definition of portable music. Then they launched a digital music marketplace, that as of this writing is the #1 music store in the U.S.—beating every brick-and-mortar CD outlet.

Can they do it again? With the potential size of the emerging smartphone market, it's hard to predict a world where the iPod is as wildly successful, in terms of market share, as the iPod was. Still, Apple's numbers are impressive. In 2008 they sold about 10 million iPhones[1]. Compared to the billion phones sold worldwide[2] each of the last two years, that's close to 1% of all phones sold—not just smartphones. Not bad for a new entrant with a high-priced gadget. Apple beat RIM (Blackberry) sales in 2008 as well and has become the third largest mobile phone supplier by revenues[3].

But this isn't an investment book, this is a book about hacking the iPhone.

Computing and Communication

Since the dawn of smartphones, journalists have been bemused about mobile convergence: "This phone can take pictures, check your email and—surprise—even make phone calls." But their sarcasm belies a lack of foresight and perspective on telephony. The multimodal nature of mobile communication encompasses voice, text, pictures, and video in a myriad of combinations. Conference calling, voice mailing, multiparty calling, hunt groups, broadcast texting, email reading, picture and video broadcasting, social networking, picture texting, microblogging, podcasting, videoblogging, reading, conferencing, real-time language translation, and telepresence are just a few of the ways that communication is being transformed by the emergence of the computerized phone.

The points we're trying to make, with exclamation marks, are:

- Mobile phones are permeating the global culture
- Everyone will soon have a smartphone
- Mobile phones are the future of computers
- Mobile phones will fuel the next Internet boom

1. Apple: www.apple.com/pr/library/2009/01/21results.html
2. Gartner research
3. Jobs, Q3'08 Earnings call

Why is this? One theory we're presenting is that anything that makes communication more "telepathic"—transcending time and space—is likely to find universal affinity with humans. Thus, any device or technology that fundamentally enhances human communication will expand far beyond general expectations until everyone on Earth uses it.

Artists envision the future of culture in general. Science fiction writers envision the future of culture and technology, specifically.

But who prototypes that future? Hackers.

Please enjoy the book.

How to Use This Book

You can read this book from cover to cover if you like, but most hacks stand on their own, so feel free to browse and jump to the different sections that interest you most. If there's a prerequisite that you need to know about, a cross-reference will guide you to the right hack.

How This Book Is Organized

This book is intended to be a compendium of hacks for both the iPhone and the iPod touch. While there are numerous books and sites that re-present the features inherent in the iPhone, this book collects many of the cleverest and least obvious innovations and presents them for easy application.

Chapter 1, iPhone and iPod touch Hacking Basics
There's a lot of information out on the Web about "hacking" the iPhone and iPod touch, but it isn't well sorted and not all of it is reliable. In Chapter 1 you'll quickly learn the lingo so you can make immediate sense of the wealth of iPhone literature online. You'll also learn how to simply, safely, and reliably "jailbreak" your phone to access a whole world of features and applications.

Chapter 2, Troubleshoot Your iPhone or iPod touch
Some people are concerned that hacking puts them outside the reaches of tech support unless they have a "hacker" friend at close hand. Far from it! If you have the right skills and the right support, you can hack with security and peace of mind. In Chapter 2 you'll learn the basic iPhone "CPR" techniques cold. You'll even learn how to get a referral to an online specialist if complications arise.

Chapter 3, Messaging and Communication
The iPhone is an unusually capable communication device, but Apple hasn't satisfied every communication need. Chapter 3 shows you how to expand the iPhone to use a wide range of multimedia messaging, email, and Internet chat systems.

Chapter 4, Media and Data
The days of physical media, such as CDs and DVDs, are fading. Many people have already made the transition, and most of their personal and entertainment media is only in digital form on their hard drive, or "in the cloud" online. In Chapter 4 you'll import your DVD collection and convert it for the iPhone, and then start getting your information diet—RSS feeds, news, and books—on your phone.

Chapter 5, Game Emulation
The power of the iPhone is such that it can emulate almost every classic video game system since Pong. In Chapter 5 you'll learn how to take all the arcade games you have, from Nintendo, Sega, GameBoy, and original Playstation, and make them run on the iPhone or iPod touch.

Chapter 6, Telephony
Now that voice is just data, everything we've learned from the Internet can be applied to our telephone calls. Chapter 6 will show you how to use beyond Voice over IP on the iPhone and then cleverly combine voicemail, SMS, and voice-to-web technologies and make the most of the phone as a communication tool.

Chapter 7, Unlocking and Activation
The iPhone is designed to work on any GSM carrier in the world. And with some coaxing, it really can. In Chapter 7 you'll learn all the techniques for unlocking the iPhone to work with a SIM card from the carrier of your choice.

Chapter 8, Customization
From background images to skins to system sounds to ring tones, customization has long been a mainstay of operating systems and mobile phones. In Chapter 8 you will learn how to make your iPhone *your* iPhone.

Chapter 9, Network Hacks
With Wi-Fi and 3G Internet access, the iPhone has better network connectivity than most laptops on the market today. In fact, in good 3G coverage areas, it's as if the iPhone had a portable T1 Internet connection. The vast possibilities of this always-on networked pocket device are not lost on hackers. In Chapter 9 you'll learn dozens of clever applications of near-ubiquitous connectivity, such as network remote control, GPS tracking, web serving, and laptop tethering. You'll also learn how to bend a few rules, like running programs in the background on your iPhone and using VoIP over your 3G connection.

Chapter 10, Application Hacks
While the App Store application count has reached some astronomical number, only a handful of applications are innovative enough to be considered hacks. In Chapter 10 you'll learn how to make music, measure, and manage media with your phone. You'll also meet a group of App Store rejects that were too clever for their own good.

Chapter 11, Development Hacks
Computer programmers around the world are thinking to themselves "Maybe I should learn a bit about mobile application development." But for many, the learning curve of getting used to the Mac and Objective-C has deterred them from pursuing iPhone development. In Chapter 11 you'll learn that programming the iPhone is far easier than it seems. Any casual shell scripter will find they can make and distribute a useful and functional application in less than an hour. Professional developers will get a crash-course in iPhone development options.

Chapter 12, Hardware & Accessories
Today, the mobile phone is the computer. And computers beget accessories. Chapter 12 introduces the wide range of hardware connectivity possible with the iPhone and iPod touch. In this chapter you'll learn how to hook an iPhone to a car and to a large screen television. You'll learn how to perform surgery on the iPhone; how to wire it up to any serial device; and how to make it control an R/C car. You'll even learn how to build what is for some the "holy grail" of iPhone connectivity—an external keyboard. Remarkably, for most of the hacks in this chapter, no jailbreaking is required.

Conventions Used in This Book

This book uses the following typographical conventions:

Italic

Used to indicate new terms, URLs, filenames, file extensions, directories, and folders.

$

The Unix/Linux shell prompt you see when logged as a normal (mortal) user.

#

The Unix/Linux shell prompt you see when logged as root (the superuser).

`Constant width`

Used to show code examples, verbatim searches and commands, the contents of files, and the output from commands.

`Constant width bold`

Used in examples and tables to show commands or other text that should be typed literally.

`Constant width italic` and ***`bold italic`***

Used in code and commands to show text that should be replaced with user-supplied values.

Pay special attention to notes set apart from the text with the following icons:

 This icon indicates a tip, suggestion, or general note. It contains useful supplementary information or an observation about the topic at hand.

 This icon indicates a warning or note of caution.

The slider icons, found next to each hack, indicate the relative complexity of the hack:

Easy:
Intermediate:
Expert:

 Also, unique to this book, is the "jailbreak" icon:

While some hacks can be done with a stock iPhone, many require the factory firmware to be altered ("jailbroken") to allow new software on the device, as explained in [Hack #1.03]. The jailbreak icon indicates whether jailbreaking is needed.

Using Code Examples

This book is here to help you get your job done. In general, you may use the code in this book in your programs and documentation. You do not need to contact us for permission unless you're reproducing a significant portion of the code. For example, writing a program that uses several chunks of code from this book does not require permission. Selling or distributing a CD of examples from O'Reilly books does require permission. Answering a question by citing this book and quoting example code does not require permission. Incorporating a significant amount of example code from this book into your product's documentation does require permission.

We appreciate, but do not require, attribution. An attribution usually includes the title, author, publisher, and ISBN. For example: *iPhone Hacks*, by David Jurick, Adam Stolarz & Damien Stolarz. Copyright 2009 O'Reilly Media, Inc., ISBN: 978-0-596-51664-2.

If you feel your use of code examples falls outside fair use or the permission given here, feel free to contact us at *permissions@oreilly.com*.

Acknowledgments

Thanks to everyone at O'Reilly Media who helped make this book happen, including Brian Jepson and Adam Flaherty for their editing; Nancy Kotary, copyeditor; Terry Bronson, production manager; Gretchen Bay, designer; Patti Schiendelman, indexer; and Ed Stephenson, cover copywriter.

We'd like to specifically thank Brian Jepson and Adam Flaherty for their unique contributions. Brian exhibited unflappable patience while managing what seemed like an interminable project. His mentoring on writing craft and geek credibility were invaluable. Adam Flaherty's decisive editing tremendously improved the quality of the book, and his "give me three never-been-done-before hacks" challenge pushed the team to far exceed their original goals. And for the whole team, the care, professionalism, craft, and disciplined crunch-time effort that went into finishing this book is deeply appreciated by the authors.

David Jurick: I'd like to thank my parents for their unconditional support; my brother and sister; Damien Stolarz for all the mentoring he's given me while growing up; Aaron Kinney; Jason Levine; Kyle Culkin; Illian McJohnson; all of the 40zoners (Chang, Eric, Peter, Ross, Allison, Micah, Karen); Amanda Scharpf; Kappa Sigma; Christian Sanz for having so much faith in my abilities; everyone at Deca for always laughing at my jokes; and last but not least, the all powerful creator of the universe—Science.

Adam Stolarz: Thanks to my mom for support, encouragement, and the sharing of pains; thanks to my dad for the work ethic; Damien for business and travel; Matthew for music and movies; and Jenny for art and humor. Additional thanks, in no particular order, to the Dodge Stealth, the Chariot, Rims, Lucky 13, the Lawltima, the Honda Civic, Verwend, and of course, the NQN. Shout outs to Team Entropy, Perdition Gaming, Phono, Jtubez, Jookasaurus, Augury, Brea/Lorea, and Halik/Kilah/Zikah. And a very special thanks to Luke: it's complicated.

Damien Stolarz: The writing of this book has been an intense, watershed experience for me personally. I would like to thank Stephen Brown, James Rossfeld, and Steve Waterhouse for supporting me all these many months that I've slaved away on this book. I'd like to also thank my brothers Adam and David for tolerating my zeal. I'd like to thank Steve Jobs for being so on his game. And I must thank my wife, to whom I now owe 1.5 years of evenings and weekends. I *will* paint the trim on the front of the house now.

We'd Like to Hear from You

Please address comments and questions concerning this book to the publisher:

O'Reilly Media, Inc./Maker Media, Inc.
1005 Gravenstein Highway North
Sebastopol, CA 95472

(800) 998-9938 (in the United States or Canada)
(707) 829-0515 (international or local)
(707) 829-0104 (fax)

We have a web page for this book that lists errata, examples, and any additional information. You can access this page at: www.makezine.com/go/iphonehacks.

To comment or ask technical questions about this book, send email to *bookquestions@oreilly.com*.

Maker Media is a division of O'Reilly Media devoted entirely to the growing community of resourceful people who believe that if you can imagine it, you can make it. Consisting of MAKE magazine, CRAFT Magazine, Maker Faire, and the Hacks series of books, Maker Media encourages the Do-It-Yourself mentality by providing creative inspiration and instruction.

For more information about Maker Media, visit us online:
MAKE: www.makezine.com
CRAFT: www.craftzine.com
Maker Faire: www.makerfaire.com
Hacks: www.hackszine.com

CREDITS

About the Authors

David Jurick (www.davidjurick.com) is the IT manager at a digital entertainment/new media company based in Santa Monica, California. He has extensive experience in networking, computer hardware, software, scripting, and Unix/Linux-based operating systems. He holds a bachelor of science degree from the University of California, Santa Barbara.

Adam Stolarz (www.adamstolarz.com) is an avid PC gamer and computer expert with an electronics background. As a teenager he was a contributing author to *Car PC Hacks* (O'Reilly). He is currently studying political science and Japanese at California State University, Northridge.

Damien Stolarz is a partner at Perceptive Development (www.perceptdev.com), a Los Angeles–based software consultancy that develops iPhone applications. He is an inventor, author, and entrepreneur who loves making machines talk to each other. He has authored several books including *Mastering Internet Video* (Addison-Wesley), *Car PC Hacks* (O'Reilly), and *Hands-On Guide to Videoblogging and Podcasting* (Focal Press). He holds a B.S. in computer science and engineering from the University of California, Los Angeles. His personal blog is www.damienstolarz.com.

Contributors

The following people contributed to this book in the form of hacks:

George Dean IV is a software developer at Perceptive Development in Los Angeles (www.perceptdev.com). Dean has a broad range of experience with nearly a dozen programming languages on a variety of platforms. He remains interested in a wide range of disciplines including mathematics and all manner of sciences. His artistic pursuits include film scoring and screenwriting. He holds a B.S. in computer science from the University of California, Los Angeles. His personal site is www.georgedeaniv.com.

Matthew Drengler is currently a senior at the University of Toledo studying electrical engineering. After graduating he plans to go to Ohio State University to pursue a master's in business administration. When Drengler isn't studying for classes he enjoys playing golf, guitar, pool, Xbox 360, and cooking. You can find his blog at http://matthewdrengler.com/blog.

Zack Gainsforth is a physicist with the University of California, Space Sciences Laboratory, studying comet samples returned from the Stardust NASA mission as well as other astromaterials. He was a successful computer programmer working for Diskeeper Corporation, and software he worked on is on tens of millions of computers worldwide. His real love is physical science, a career he started out with a home-built lab supported by his very tolerant parents. He eventually went on to attend the University of California at Berkeley to study physics from whence he went on into his current research. He has contributed to several scientific publications and co-authored an article for *Science*. He is happily married to what he believes to be the smartest gem in the Eastern Hemisphere, Cindy. His website is www.thetalab.com.

iFixit is the Mac+iPod do-it-yourself company. It has the goal of empowering people to do repairs themselves by giving them the knowledge, tools, and parts to do so. So far, they've helped over 30,000 people repair their computers and iPods. iFixit was started in 2003 by students at Cal

Poly, San Luis Obispo. They're now the largest Mac laptop parts store in the world, and introduced iPod parts in 2006 and iPhone and iPod touch parts in 2007. iFixit is a for-profit, Christ-centered company. They can be contacted at www.iFixit.com or 1-866-61-FIXIT.

Mathias Kettner has been working with Linux since the 0.99 kernel, when a complete installation fit on six floppy disks. In the many years since then his passion for Linux has remained. Today he is a Linux consultant, trainer, and author of the bestselling book Fehlerdiagnose und Problembehebung unter Linux (SUSE Press). He holds a diploma in computer science from Ludwig-Maximilians-Universität München. His website is http://mathias-kettner.com.

Christopher "karp" Kurpinski fell short of his boyhood aspirations to become a mad scientist and settled for a career as a cynical engineer. Despite his best efforts to sleep through every class, he somehow received a masters in electrical engineering from UCLA. Kurpinski currently resides in suburban Detroit where he attends law school at the University of Michigan and works as a technical patent analyst on the side. Taking an almost perverse joy in using things in ways they were never intended, he once climbed a church just for the hell of it. One day, he hopes to have all of his vintage scooters running at the same time. His website is www.kurpinski.net.

Patrick Ng is a photographer who works in Hong Kong as a stationery and gift buyer for a retail chain store called city'super. Patrick thinks like a man of action, but acts like a man of thoughts. He keeps a journal of hacks and interesting things on his personal blog Scription (http://moleskine.vox.com).

Josef Průša is a young, unconventional DJ from Czech Republic. He started DJing when he was only 15 years old. He likes new technologies and loves hacking new functionality into them, whether the results are interesting, useful, or merely funny. His interests are programming, electronics, music, cars, and economics. In addition to R/C car control, he's recently been using an iPhone to control music for his DJ performances. You can check out his new projects on his website http://josef-prusa.eu.

Erica Sadun holds a Ph.D. in computer science from the Georgia Institute of Technology. She has written, co-written, and contributed to over two dozen books about technology, particularly in the areas of programming, digital video, and digital photography. An unrepentant geek, Sadun has never met a gadget she didn't need. Her checkered past includes run-ins with NeXT, Newton, and a vast myriad of both successful and unsuccessful technologies. When not writing, she and her geek husband parent three adorable geeks-in-training, who regard their parents with restrained bemusement. Her site is http://ericasadun.com.

Devananda Van der Veen is a MySQL DBA and the author of the open source database and server management tools MyCAT. He currently works for Hydra Network, telecommuting from his home on the Olympic Peninsula where he enjoys playing the Shakuhachi and living in the great outdoors. He maintains a blog at http://blog.dbadeva.com.

Joe Vennix is a teenager from Houston, Texas, who has been hacking away at the iPhone since its launch. He sells apps on the iTunes store and maintains an iPhone news and apps listings site at www.iphonexe.com. His musical tastes vary from Pink Floyd to Buckethead to Funkadelic, and he's pretty psyched about being published in a book. Shoot him an email via joe@iphonexe.com.

ZodTTD is very scarce on details of his origin. He began his journey through software development at a very young age. He learned to program homebrew games on the Gameboy Advance using makeshift flashcarts. He worked on Open Transport Tycoon Deluxe for the Tapwave Zodiac—hence the moniker "ZodTTD." He's worked on porting all the major game emulators—PSX, Sega, SNES, GBA, MAME, and more—to the iPhone. He works full-time maintaining game ports and developing iPhone applications. His website is www.zodttd.com.

iPhone Hacks

First Edition

David Jurick, Adam & Damien Stolarz

01 IPHONE AND IPOD TOUCH HACKING BASICS

There are a lot of reasons to hack your iPhone or iPod touch.

There's this myth that hacking will go away "once Apple adds that one killer feature." But it's unlikely, because the iPhone is unlike the earlier iPods or any phone on the market before it. It is a full-featured personal computer.

The iPhone is a global device that uses the international standard GSM protocol. Unlocking the phone so that it can use SIM cards anywhere is a major industry, and will probably continue to be so even after Apple's exclusive contracts with mobile carriers are gone.

The iPod touch is the heir apparent of the iPod, and once flash memory sizes surpass hard drives, the iPod touch will be the iPod. But this iPod surfs the Web, gets email, and maps your location, and new applications are constantly being developed for it. The impulse to get the iPod—already the de facto standard MP3 player—to do even more is irresistible.

No matter what Apple adds to its Software Development Kit (SDK), there will always be something important that they left out. It might just be the future killer application. And thus, the hacking community will continue to push the boundaries of what can be done with the phone.

It's important to realize that the iPhone is as powerful as a top-of-the-line late-'90s computer. Late-'90s computers were fast enough to use broadband and to fuel the first Internet boom.

But this computer fits in a shirt pocket, and can be controlled with one finger.

Now imagine a world where everyone is holding a broadband-connected, Unix-based personal computer in their hand.

Can you think of anything that Apple just might not have thought of?

We can.

HACK 1.01: Learn the Language of iPhone Hacking

Bypass the iPhone learning curve with this quick tutorial.

It's easy to get overwhelmed with a flood of new terminology when learning a new topic, especially when it comes to computers and hacking. The iPhone has an unusually steep learning curve. This hack will quickly get you "talking the talk" so you can get past the *n00b* ("newbie") phase quickly and make sense of the online discussions.

The iPhone Cellular Standard

Apple's iPhone was originally released in the United States exclusively on the AT&T network. There are a number of different cellular phone standards, but the technology in widest use around the world and standard in Europe is called *GSM* (Global System for Mobile communications). GSM describes the technology for providing voice services, but the GSM system includes several levels of wireless data service as well. *GPRS* (General Packet Radio Service) is the slowest of these protocols, providing speeds up to 40Kbps—similar to a dial-up modem. *EDGE* (Enhanced Data rates for GSM Evolution) is a data transmission protocol capable of speeds up to 180Kbps, with a theoretical maximum of 230Kbps, like the now painfully slow broadband Internet from the late '90s. Generally, this speed makes EDGE a *2.5G* (between second- and third-generation) wireless protocol, as contrasted with the *3G* phones, which use *HSDPA* (High-Speed Downlink Packet Access, the fastest current data standard used with GSM networks), which is comparable to a slow DSL connection. GSM phones are characterized by their use of a *SIM* (Subscriber Identity Module) card, and the ability for users to switch phones by simply moving a SIM card from one phone to another (Figure 1-1). Once Apple's exclusive contract with AT&T has run out, they may create an iPhone that runs on other mobile standards such as the *CDMA* (Code Division Multiple Access) and *EVDO* (Evolution-Data Optimized) standards used by Verizon and Sprint in the United States.

Figure 1-1.
The iPhone's SIM card on its tray

iPhone Applications

The iPhone runs an *embedded* (for a device, not a computer) form of Mac OS X for its *system software*, a thinned-down version of the same code that runs on Macintosh computers. *Native applications* are programs that are installed on the iPhone, as opposed to *web applications*, or *iPhone-optimized web pages*, that run in the Mobile Safari web browser, using technologies such as *AJAX* (Asynchronous JavaScript and XML), and which require a working Internet connection to operate. The many built-in applications on the iPhone, such as Calendar, Photos, YouTube, and Safari, are native applications; there are also native *third-party applications*. The applications on the iPhone are all launched by *SpringBoard*, an application that controls the home screen. Figure 1-2 shows a jailbroken (hacked to be freed from restrictions) phone with some third-party apps.

Figure 1-2.
A number of installed third-party native applications on a jailbroken phone

The iPhone's Unix Heritage

Unix is a cross-platform, multiuser, server operating system with a long history. It was first developed at AT&T in 1969. It was one of the first open source operating systems. It has heavily influenced every operating system since then. Over the last 40 years, it has split into a large family tree with dozens of competing versions and several prominent clones, such as Linux. It has long been a programmer's operating system (OS) as well as the ancestral home of computer hackers. Unix and Unix-like servers such as Linux represent a substantial portion of the servers on the Internet. Mac OS X is a Unix operating system.

One of the interesting things about the iPhone—and an interesting full circle for AT&T—is that upwards of 10 million people are now running a Unix-based operating system on their iPhone.

Chroot, Jails, and Jailbreaking

As we just mentioned, Unix is a multiuser system. Different accounts (login names) can be given different privileges. For instance, the superuser administrator named *root* can change any file on the system. The iPhone normally runs applications as a user named *mobile*, who has more limited access.

The word "root" in Unix systems is also used to describe the top of a hard drive hierarchy, in which the uppermost folder is the "root" directory (like the root of a plant or tree). If you see the slash symbol (/), this signifies the root of the hard drive.

One method of enforcing security on Unix systems is called *chroot()*. Normally, any user on Unix can potentially see the whole hard drive. What *chroot()* does is change the root directory so that a user can access only his or her own home directory. For instance, if Joe's home directory is */Users/joe*, chroot makes it so that / points to */Users/joe* on the hard drive. Now Joe can't access parts of the system that he shouldn't. This security measure puts Joe in what is called a *chroot() jail*.

The term *jail* has come to encompass any metaphorical padded cell or "jail" that restricts access to certain directories and limits which programs can be run.

On the iPhone, the flash drive has two partitions—about 300 megabytes (MB) for the OS (operating system) and Applications (partition */dev/disk0s1*), and the rest of the phone's total storage for user data such as pictures, music, and movies (partition */dev/disk0s2*). As shipped, there are two major restrictions: the user can't write to the OS partition, and the iPhone won't run (execute) any programs stored on the data partition. If you install an App Store application, it can run because it is stored on the OS partition.

On the iPhone, the process of *jailbreaking* removes both of these restrictions. By changing the file */etc/fstab*, you:

- Make the OS partition writable
- Enable execution of programs on the data partition

The iPhone ships with many software and hardware security features to ensure that it is not easily cracked by malicious interlopers, and to create a chain of accountability so that an insidious or destructive program can be traced to its creator if it does manage to get onto the phone. Because of this thick layer of security, it is necessary to jailbreak the iPhone **[Hack #1.03]** to install programs and access features that aren't available through the App Store.

Most software for jailbreaking adds package management for installing new applications directly to the device. Jailbreaking adds a wide variety of common Unix/Linux tools, including *Secure Shell (SSH)*, so that you can connect to your iPhone with a terminal program and configure it.

Significantly, because a jailbroken iPhone is a full-featured Unix server, just about every major Internet service and development technology—MySQL, Apache web servers, PHP, Python, Perl, Ruby, and Java, to name just a few—are available for the iPhone. That means that porting existing code—especially open source code—to the iPhone is trivially easy. Thus, many of the hacks in this book depend on jailbreaking the phone.

The SDK and the App Store

In February 2008, Apple announced a *Software Development Kit (SDK)*, allowing the creation of third-party applications that could be installed on the phone. For the eight months prior to that date, creating native iPhone applications required a reverse-engineered development environment commonly referred to as the *toolchain* (a set of software tools used to create new applications). This is because SDK applications run in a *sandbox* (another word for "jail") that limits their ability to do harm, but also limits their ability to do good. Thus, there are *SDK applications* (developed with Apple's Mac-based development tools, sold in Apple's App Store, and complying with Apple's restrictions and distribution policies), and *toolchain applications*, developed using these reverse-engineered software development kits. Toolchain apps can use any feature on the phone that is available. In contrast, the SDK is limited to the features that Apple has exposed in its SDK. For instance, an SDK application cannot take pictures without the user's permission, and cannot dial a phone number or send a text message without the user being notified, and generally cannot keep running in the background when the user switches to another program. Toolchain applications have none of these restrictions. For extensive information on programming toolchain applications, see *iPhone Open Application Development*, 2nd Edition (O'Reilly, 2008) by Jonathan Zdziarski.

Unlocking

Understanding the various methods of hacking the iPhone depends on an understanding of its different parts. As mentioned earlier, the iPhone is very similar to a conventional desktop PC, with computing power easily comparable to systems from the late 1990s. Its main CPU runs around 400Mhz, and it has a screen, an onscreen virtual keyboard, a touch screen that functions as a mouse, and 4GB or more of flash storage for its filesystem (file storage). It runs an operating system—which is actually Mac OS X. Unlike most personal computers, however, the iPhone has two "brains"—one is the ARM processor (ARM11 specifically), the CPU that runs the Mac OS X system software and the *GUI* (graphical user interface), and the other is a chip that handles communication with the cellular network, called the *baseband chip* (an Infineon GSM processor).

Every mobile phone in the market has a baseband chip. On most phones (non-"smart" phones) this baseband chip is the only processor for the phone. This chip contains a simple central processing unit, as well as a wireless modem, and is responsible for all GSM/EDGE/HSDPA cellular communication. Jailbreaking an iPhone hacks only the Mac OS X that runs on the ARM processor. The iPhone's baseband chip is a "second brain" that must be reprogrammed—often against its will—if you want to unlock the phone.

Some people wonder why the phone chip is called a "baseband." The name is related to the more familiar term *broadband*, which describes a wired or wireless transmission carrying many different channels (bands or frequencies), such as a cable modem connection shared by everyone in a given neighborhood. By contrast, baseband is when a wired or wireless transmission has one base (low) band that transmits only one signal, such as a single wireless phone call.

One of the most popular terms that you will run into in hacking the iPhone is *bricking*, which means rendering your iPhone as useless as a brick because of hacking gone awry. Example: "Oh, no! I think I bricked my iPhone trying to unlock it." To be precise, bricking should describe a state that is permanent and irreversible, but the iPhone community often uses this term loosely for a temporary state that is relatively easy to reverse. And some users have even had "hard" (seemingly permanently) bricked phones come back to life with later iPhone firmware—new versions of Apple's firmware resurrected a lot of previously "bricked" phones. Typically, there are many options (such as forcing a full restore on your iPhone) that can fix the many seemingly incurable ills of carelessly hacked phones. (See Chapter 2, "Troubleshoot Your iPhone or iPod touch.") Hardware hacking (that is, opening up the phone, as described in Chapter 12, "Hardware") creates the highest risk of bricking phones. Next to that, trying to do a SIM unlock (modifying the phone to use a different mobile carrier than it was designed to use) is the most fruitful source of bricks (see Chapter 7, "Unlocking and Activation"). Easy-to-use one-click SIM unlocking applications **[Hack #7.02]** became popular because they ran a lower risk of bricking an iPhone for novice users.

iPhone OS and Firmware

Whereas PCs run software, the preferred term for embedded software—that is, software that runs on devices instead of computers—is *firmware*. When used in iPhone-speak, "firmware" is used loosely to describe each successive version (1.1.1, 1.1.2, 1.1.3, 1.1.4, 2.0, 2.1, 3.0, and so on) of new software for the iPhone. These files usually come in the form of an *IPSW* (iPhone software) file, such as *iPhone1,1_2.0_5A347_Custom_Restore.ipsw*. These files usually contain an update for Mac OS X as well as the *baseband firmware*, the software that runs the modem, which is independent of the version of system software on the phone. The baseband firmware is essential for the proper functioning of EDGE, HSDPA, Wi-Fi, Bluetooth, and phone calls. When you activate an iPhone for the first time in iTunes, or when you unlock the phone for use on any GSM service provider, you are modifying the baseband firmware.

Just like a conventional computer has a BIOS (which is in control of the computer before Windows, Linux, or Mac OS X is loaded, and is built into the hardware of the machine), the iPhone has a *bootloader*, or bit of software that runs before the operating system and determines which software to use during bootup. In fact, the iPhone has two of them. The main CPU has a bootloader called iBoot, also known as the *recovery bootloader*. This software tries to load the system software. If it cannot, or if the phone is in recovery mode **[Hack #2.04]**, then it asks to be connected to iTunes. The *baseband bootloader* is the software that runs on the baseband and loads the baseband firmware. Figure 1-3 shows the different operating software on the iPhone.

Figure 1-3.
The various parts of the iPhone's operating software

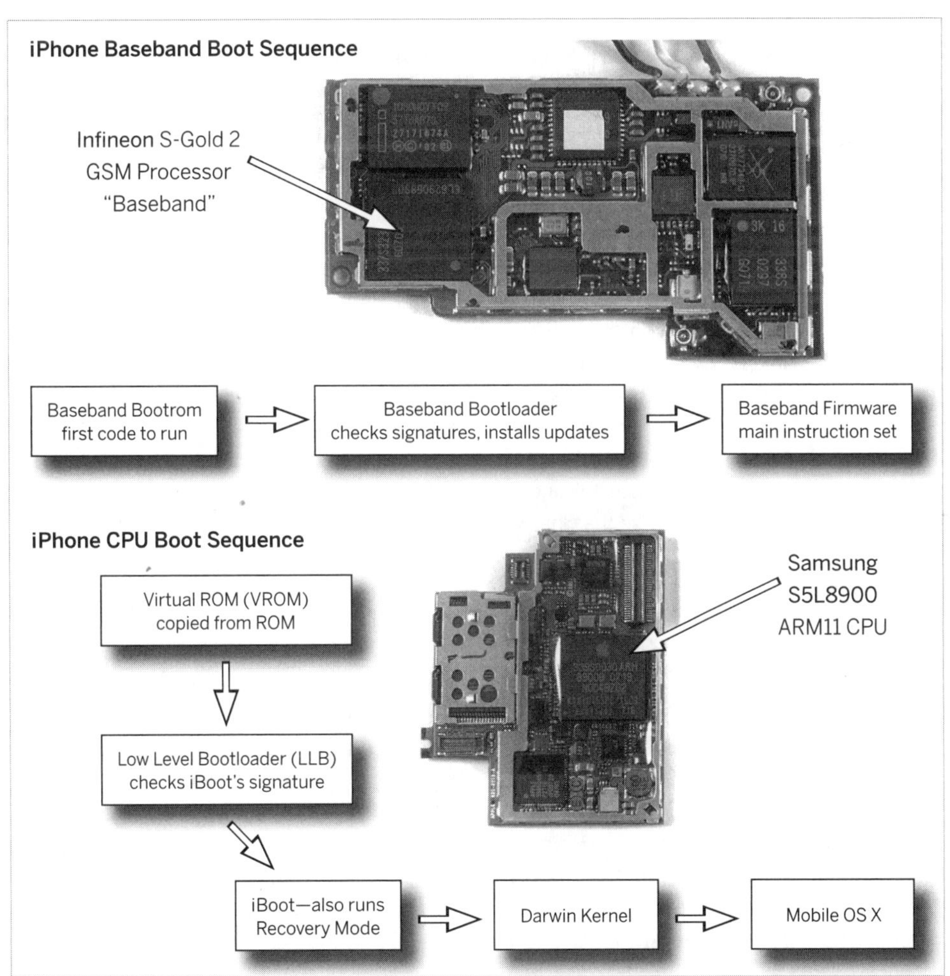

OOB or *OOTB* means out-of-box or out-of-the-box; it describes a phone that is brand new, not activated, jailbroken, unlocked, or otherwise molested. The term is used to describe models of phones that ship with particular software version. For instance, "OOB 1.1.2" phones shipped with a baseband bootloader (Version 4.6) that was more resistive to baseband firmware updates than earlier versions. Thus, some earlier phones were coveted because of their flexibility in downgrading and upgrading to different system versions and unlocking.

Apple's iTunes program frequently prompts users to upgrade their phone to the latest software. *Upgrading* your iPhone upgrades the software to Apple's current version but keeps the user data (leaving the user partition of the flash drive intact), whereas *restoring* **[Hack #2.04]** your iPhone's software erases user data and reinstalls the system software. However, restoring does not reset any baseband (firmware) alterations. *Virginizing* your iPhone **[Hack #2.05]** puts it in the exact same software state that it was in when you bought it, including resetting your baseband firmware back to factory settings by relocking it. Virginizing is a prudent choice for those returning their phones under warranty, as phones that are serviced in a hacked state may be denied warranty service.

HACK 1.02: Discover Your iPhone's Hackability

Which hacks you can do? It depends on what software version your iPhone is running.

The brief history of iPhone hacking is a game of cat-and-mouse between Apple's patches and the iPhone user community's cracks.

A software update from Apple can include a number of things: updates to the operating system (Mobile OS X), new baseband firmware, and updates to the iBoot bootloader **[Hack #1.01]**. Each update brings new features, bug fixes, and—in some cases—a little more resistance toward the hacks you'll find in this book. So, before you can make your iPhone do new tricks, you need to know your firmware version and whether the hack you intend to apply will work with that version.

The most common first hack after opening your iPhone is jailbreaking, which lets you reconfigure the iPhone operating system and install unsigned third-party applications. However, some people may want to unlock their phone so that they can use it with any GSM carrier. These two hacks, jailbreaking and unlocking, depend on the firmware and the baseband, respectively. As time goes by, each new version will close some doors to hacking and open some others. Trying to hack one version with a procedure that was designed for a different version will result in an unsuccessful hacking attempt. In the worst case, this mistake could cause technical difficulties that require a full restore **[Hack #2.04]** and/or virginization **[Hack #2.05]**.

When Apple releases a firmware update, it's often to add or update a feature—such as the iTunes Music Store app—or to fix a security issue, like a vulnerability in the web browser. Chances are good that the upgrade will, intentionally or unintentionally, temporarily render various hacks inoperable. So don't rush to install each new update; instead, give the hacking community time to catch up so that you won't have to struggle with the inevitable incompatibilities that arise with new firmware. And once it's safe to proceed, perform a restore before you update to prevent any possible conflicts between your hacked iPhone and the new version.

Taking Inventory

Here's what you should know about your device:

- Device type (iPhone / iPod touch, and which generation)
- OS firmware version and baseband (modem firmware) version
- (Optional) Bootloader versions (iBoot, the OS bootloader, and the baseband bootloader)

Step 1: Identify your phone model.
As of this writing, there are four models: the original iPhone (released June 2007) and iPod touch (released September 2007), the iPhone 3G (released July 2008), and the second-generation iPod touch (released September 2008).

This information is the easiest thing to identify.

- Look at the back of the device and see whether it says iPod or iPhone. That's your first clue.
- The original iPhone has a mostly aluminum backing with a small black plastic area. The iPhone 3G has a shiny black or white plastic back.
- The original iPod touch has no volume controls on the top left (facing the device). The second-generation iPod touch has volume controls.

Step 2: Identify your firmware and baseband version.
The firmware version can be found either using iTunes or directly on your iPhone. In iTunes (with your iPhone connected to your computer), go to your iPhone's summary tab and locate "Version." To right of it is the firmware version, listed as a version number such as 2.1, followed by a hexadecimal number in parentheses. On your iPhone, open the Settings menu and scroll down until you see General. Tap on General and select About from the top of the list. On the About screen, about halfway down the list, you will see your firmware version number, as well as your "Modem Firmware" (a.k.a. baseband version), as shown in Figure 1-4.

The easiest way to do this is by selecting Settings→General→About. The Version field will give the version of your software (i.e., Mobile OS X), and the baseband (labeled "Modem Firmware").

A comprehensive list of firmware and baseband versions can be found at www.theiphonewiki.com/wiki/index.php?title=System. You can see some of these in the tables on the following pages.

Figure 1-4.
The About screen

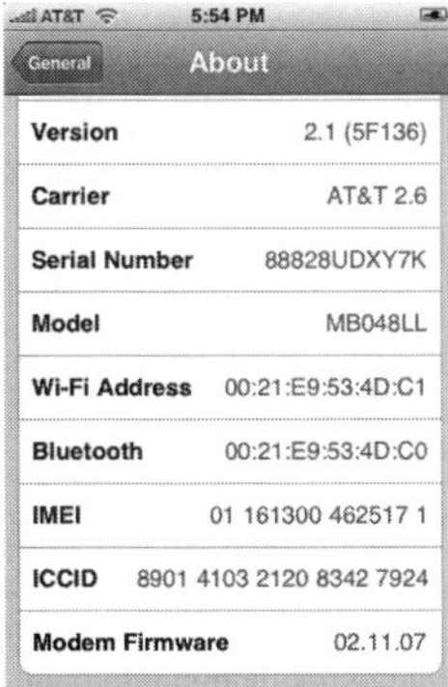

Step 3: Identify your bootloaders.
As mentioned in **[Hack #1.01]**, there are actually two bootloaders: one is iBoot, which boots Mobile OS X. The other is the baseband bootloader that runs before the baseband firmware; it is responsible for security checking and updating the baseband. Because the iPod touch doesn't include the EDGE, Bluetooth, and phone features of the iPhone, it does not use baseband firmware, so this hack applies only to the iPhone. Programs such as BootNeuter **[Hack #7.02]** unlock the iPhone by hacking

the baseband firmware. Programs such as Pwnage **[Hack #1.03]** hack the iPhone's OS bootloader. The main reason to identify your bootloader is for situations where you need to virginize your phone and return it to factory condition. Table 1-1 shows several of the factory bootloader versions.

Table 1-1
Baseband bootloader versions.

3.9	Original iPhones phones that came out of the box with Version 1.1.1 and older had this bootloader.
4.6	Original iPhones with OTB Version 1.1.2 and later iPhones prevented former unlock methods from working.
5.8	iPhone 3G comes with this bootloader.

Generally, the tools that modify your bootloader will tell you what version you have. If you get a secondhand phone and you need to take inventory of your versions, however, there are several utilities that will tell you what you have. Finding out your bootloader version is slightly more complex than finding your firmware or baseband version. It requires use of SSH **[Hack #9.04]**. Using techniques gleaned from that hack and others in the same chapter, find the program called bbupdater through Google or other sources and upload it to the */usr/bin/* directory on your device. Next, using either Mobile Terminal **[Hack #9.05]** or an SSH terminal program, run bbupdater with an argument of `-v`. You should receive output like this:

```
Resetting target...
pinging the baseband...
issuing +xgendata...
firmware: DEV_ICE_MODEM_04.02.13_G
eep version: EEP_VERSION:208
eep revision: EEP_REVISION:1
bootloader: BOOTLOADER_VERSION:4.6_M3S2
```

As you might have gathered already, the entry for **`BOOTLOADER_VERSION`** is your bootloader version.

An alternative and slightly easier method to determine your bootloader involves using the BBinfo from www.trejan.com/projects/ipod/#BASEBANDFIRM. You download the application from www.trejan.com/projects/ipod/bbinfo-1.1.zip and copy it over to the */Applications/* folder on your phone **[Hack #1.05]**. Alternately, add www.trejan.com/irepo as an Installer.app source **[Hack #1.04]**.

Tables 1-2 and 1-3 show some of the iPhone firmware and baseband versions throughout the ages.

Table 1-2
A historical account of iPhone firmware versions

1.0	This was the first iPhone firmware version. When the iPhone was first made available to U.S. consumers on June 29, 2007, Version 1.0 was preinstalled on every unit.
1.0.1	This update was released on July 31, 2007. It aimed to fix a security vulnerability in of the Safari web browser, which allowed a malicious breed of hackers to take complete control of someone else's iPhone via its Wi-Fi connection. These hackers were able to exploit this vulnerability to make phone calls and even view the personal data on the victim's iPhone. Although this update was designed to increase security against outside hackers, ironically it opened up new doors to the benevolent hacking of the type you'll find in this book. New iPhone hacks and ideas began appearing everywhere on the Web, giving owners myriad ways to customize their iPhones beyond what its factory settings had to offer.
1.0.2	This update was released on August 21, 2007. It provided a few minor bug fixes to help the iPhone function a little better. Luckily, 1.0.2 did not put a damper on the hacking opportunities offered by 1.0.1. New hacks began emerging at a jaw-dropping rate as more and more computer-savvy owners took interest in unleashing the full potential of the iPhone. As a result, 1.0.2 became one of the most popular firmware versions to hack, and when 1.1.1 hit the scene, unlocked phones running 1.0.2 proved to be a hot commodity.
1.1.1	Apple's first full update was released on September 27, 2007. A wide array of new features and improvements was offered in this update. The most notable new feature was the iTunes Wi-Fi Music Store application, which allowed users to purchase new songs from iTunes right from their iPhones. Other improvements included better interaction with Bluetooth headsets, support for TV output, and the ability to turn EDGE/GPRS data service on and off when roaming internationally. However, these improvements came with a price. Upon updating to 1.1.1, iPhones that had previously been unlocked to work with other service providers were hit with a software conflict that crippled many functions, including the ability to make and receive calls. Fear that the damage was permanent sent the iPhone hacking community into a panic. Fortunately, a solution was devised by the collaborative efforts of a number of brilliant hackers, and crisis was averted. Although this success brought a glimmer of hope for hackers, there was still one big problem with the 1.1.1 update—it was extremely difficult to hack. A temporary stalemate was in effect between Apple and the hacking community. Nevertheless, this hindrance just forced hackers to come up with more clever approaches. A way to jailbreak was found by using a vulnerability in how the iPhone processed *.tiff* images, allowing the phone to be taken over and to grant full filesystem access. The pinnacle of this effort was the iconic www.jailbreakme.com, which allowed most iPhone owners to hack their phones in less than 30 seconds.
1.1.2	November 12, 2007 saw the official release of Apple's next firmware version. This update fixed a few "issues"—most notably 1.1.1's aforementioned *.tiff* vulnerability. This fix built yet another brick wall in the development community's path. In addition, unlocked iPhones experienced the same difficulties as they did with the previous update. Despite the inconveniences caused by 1.1.2, the hacking community experienced only a brief hiccup in its progress, because dealing with 1.1.1's problems had prepared them for just about anything. In the following months, a way was found to preserve jailbreaks performed on a 1.1.1 iPhone and allow them to survive the firmware upgrade process.
1.1.3	To kick off the new year, Apple released yet another update on January 15, 2008. As with Versions 1.1.1 and 1.1.2, this new update caused a headache for users with hacked iPhones. Aside from this expected inconvenience, this update added a number of useful new features.

1.1.4	Released February 26, 2008, this update added a few subtle things to the 1.1.3 version. The Bluetooth and camera features were slightly improved. Unlike many of the previous firmware versions, 1.1.4 didn't really cause too much trouble in the iPhone hacking community. Most of the hacks used on previous versions still worked on 1.1.4.
2.0	Accompanying the release of the new 3G iPhone on July 11, 2008, this new firmware version added many useful features. One of the most notable was the highly anticipated iTunes App Store, which allowed users to add third-party apps **[Hack #1.04]** to their iPhones without having to perform a jailbreak **[Hack #1.03]**. Other features included Microsoft Exchange email support as well as support for Apple's new MobileMe calendar, contact, and email services. However, this version also basically reset the jailbreaking progress—the hacked Installer.app no longer worked with 2.0, and all the third-party applications written before the Apple SDK no longer ran on this version of the iPhone/iPod operating system.
2.0.1	Apple released this update on August 4, 2008. This new update fixed some minor bugs and sped up the software.
2.0.2	Apple released this update on August 18, 2008. Like its predecessor, 2.0.2 targeted a number of minor software bugs.
2.1	Released September 12, 2008, this release required and was released with iTunes 8. It added features like Genius (automatic smart playlists) and increased speed and stability of applications across the board.
2.2	Released November 21, 2008, this added bug fixes, Google Street View, and over-the-air podcast downloads.
2.2.1	Released January 27, 2009, this update made Safari more stable, fixed some Mail bugs, and upgraded the firmware to resist YellowSn0w, the 3G unlock application.

Table 1-3.
Baseband firmware versions

03.11.08_G through 03.14.08_G	These baseband versions were for the most part unnoticed, as they were released before an unlock was reached. It was with 1.0.2/03.14.08_G that SIM-unlocking was achieved.
04.01.13_G	When this version came, alongside firmware 1.1.1, it disabled many phones that had been unlocked on firmware 1.0.2. Furthermore, this new version added extra dependencies on a portion of the baseband called the *seczone*, which prior unlocking methods had simply erased to perform the unlock. This change made the hacking community realize that there was more than the iPhone's firmware version working against them with each update.
04.02.13_G	Firmware 1.1.2 brought with it another version of the baseband, which disabled unlocks. As time went by, this obstacle was overcome, too. Unfortunately, new-in-box 1.1.2 iPhones with the 4.6 bootloader (Table 1-1) could not be unlocked.
04.03.13_G	Firmware 1.1.3 added some interesting features, including support for the "locate me" feature in Google Maps (a fairly effective GPS alternative). On new phones, this firmware was combined with bootloader 4.6, creating a double-strength wall against unlocking efforts.
04.04.05_G	Accompanying 1.1.4 firmware was yet another baseband version. As always, it thwarted unlocking techniques for previous baseband versions.

04.05.04_G	This new baseband version was designed for first-generation iPhones (which were non-3G) to run alongside firmware Versions 2.0, 2.0.1, and 2.0.2.
01.45.00	This was the first baseband version designed to run on the 3G iPhone. It was used only with the 2.0 firmware.
01.48.02	Like the Version 01.45.00 baseband update, this version worked only with the 3G iPhone. It was used with firmware Version 2.0.1.
2.04.03	Accompanied firmware 2.1.
2.08.01	Accompanied firmware 2.0.2
2.11.07	Accompanied firmware 2.1
2.28.00	Accompanied firmware 2.2
2.30.03	Accompanied firmware 2.2.1; disabled YellowSn0w SIM unlock.

Anxious to update the firmware on your hacked phone to Apple's latest and greatest release? Just follow these simple guidelines:

Wait before you update the firmware.

When Apple releases a new firmware version, you should wait to update until you have more information about it. Knowing how the update will affect the hacks that you've already done to your iPhone, as well as the hacks you still plan to do, could help you avoid catastrophe. Updating erases any hacks you've already performed, which should provide you with plenty of motivation to wait. To help prevent any unwanted updates while you're still waiting, when iTunes shows you a window like the one shown in Figure 1-5, check the "Do not ask me again" box before you hit Cancel, so that iTunes will leave you alone until you explicitly tell it to update by pressing Update on the iTunes iPhone information screen.

Step back to a previous firmware version.

If you've already updated your firmware and can't get your favorite hacks to work, you can sometimes reverse the update. Read the documentation for your jailbreaking program.

Figure 1-5.
iTunes offers frequent updates

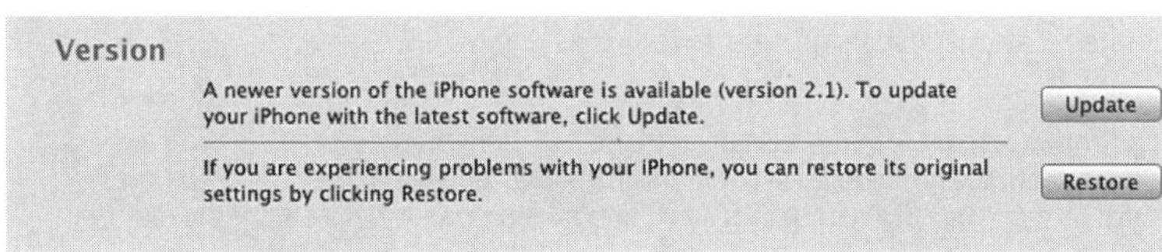

The ramifications of a misapplied hack are rarely fatal, but some are irreversible and many of them can be difficult and time-consuming to repair. Thus, the method by which you can hack your iPhone is very specifically dictated by the software version currently installed. So, just say "No!" to unsolicited firmware upgrades until the iPhone hacking community says they're ready. Caveat hax0r.

HACK 1.03: Open Your iPhone or iPod touch to Customization by Jailbreaking

Free your iPhone or iPod touch from the shackles of its proprietary prison.

The iPhone is very closed when it comes out of the box. Unlike a personal computer, the filesystem is not designed to be visible to the end user, and end users are not free to install any program they choose. Although it has a number of great built-in applications, and although many third-party applications are available through the App Store, there will always be customizations and new applications that cannot be implemented through Apple's sanctioned methods. These features are possible only when the iPhone is freed from its shackles, and the process of opening up the iPhone in this way is called *jailbreaking*.

Why Jailbreak?

Jailbreaking a phone is like logging in as "Administrator" or "root" on a Windows or Unix machine. It gives the user complete control—and of course, complete responsibility if something goes wrong. A jailbroken phone can run any application developed for the iPhone—including badly written applications or even viruses. Your jailbroken iPhone is unprotected and it's now your job—not Apple's—to keep it from getting hurt or sick.

When we speak about "hacking an iPhone," jailbreaking is the basis of most hacks. After jailbreaking, you've taken your first step into a larger world.

The benefits of jailbreaking are numerous. Just a few examples are:

- Perform system-wide skinning of the phone **[Hack #8.02]**
- Run community and third-party applications from outside the App Store **[Hack #1.04]**
- Run background applications **[Hack #9.14]**
- Run your iPhone as a web server **[Hack #9.10]** or file server **[Hack #9.06]**
- Develop iPhone applications on the phone itself **[Hack #11.12]**
- Carrier-unlock your phone (Chapter 7)
- Use your iPhone as a general-purpose computer **[Hack #12.23]**

As time goes by and firmware updates come, certain paths to unlocking may be blocked, or new options opened. As such, the procedures listed in this hack may change or become outdated, and your mileage may vary. You can always check forums and the community **[Hack #2.06]** to learn the most up-to-date method.

A Brief History of Jailbreaking Applications

Due to unprecedented, fervent passion for the iPhone platform, combined with the opportunity for tremendous profits from unlocking iPhones for use with alternate GSM carriers, there have been a number of competing unlocking applications. Because jailbreaking is the first step of running any third-party software to perform an unlock, most unlocking applications have jailbreak as their primary feature.

Numerous applications have come and gone in the fast-paced game of one-upmanship that is iPhone hacking. iBrickr, iFuntastic, iLiberty (shown in Figures 1-6 and 1-7), ZiPhone (Figure 1-8), and iPHUC are just a few examples. What may not be obvious to the end user is that each of these applications relied on the same basic code—and cracks—mostly discovered and developed by members of the iPhone Dev Team (http://wikee.iphwn.org) or **GeoHot** (http://iphonejtag.blogspot.com). Each time Apple released new firmware, they tended to patch all the publicly known cracks, rendering all existing hacking software useless for the new phones and software. Thus, there would be a period of days or weeks when the hacking community would pore over the new firmware, looking for new, unexploited cracks. As soon as they were found, a new version of complex command-line tools and dissertation-length step-by-step tutorials would be posted, showing how to manually jailbreak or unlock the new versions, followed by a slew of cute, end-user-oriented GUI applications to do the same thing.

These applications differed mostly in their fee model (most of the good ones being free), their ease of use, and how well they dealt with the numerous combinations of firmware and software. Also, because some versions of these apps implemented the hacks in an inconsistent or outright buggy way, and because Apple's own updates would often scramble previously hacked phones into an unstable state, even more features had to be developed to repair these ravages.

Figure 1-6.
iLiberty (Windows)

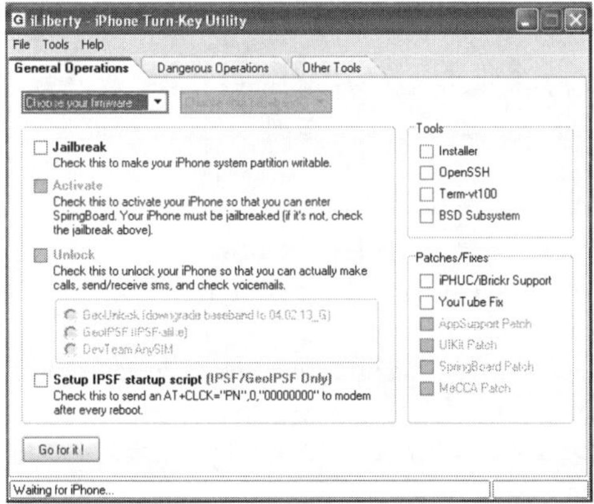

Figure 1-7.
iLiberty (Mac OS X)

Figure 1-8.
ZiPhone 3.0 (Mac OS X)

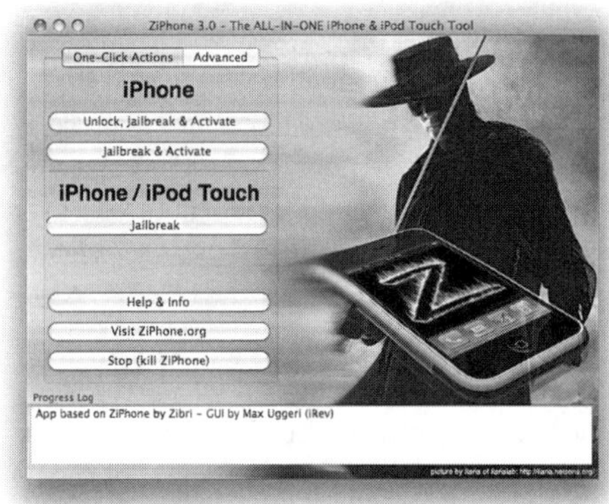

Through these applications, perhaps millions of people have had their 1.x.x firmware phones successfully hacked and their phones unlocked. However, there were still problems:

- People who unlocked their phones—for instance, to run them on T-Mobile in the United States—were generally stuck on the firmware version they had upon unlocking (such as 1.1.1), afraid to mess up their unlock through further hacking.
- People would blindly update their phones when iTunes suggested it and wind up with temporarily "bricked" phones—and would swear off hacking because of the bad experience.
- People got tired of erasing their phone over and over and having to wait every time Apple released new firmware.
- Many of these programs, in their race to market, were buggy, and unwittingly performed (at the time) irreversible changes, such as changing bootloaders.
- Some of the programs might have contained copyrighted software not owned by the authors. Although this rarely deterred end users, who knew they were in a sort of a digital "back alley" anyway, it violated the spirit of the iPhone hacking community, who were trying to use completely legitimate, legal, and moral means to hack the iPhone.

For a while, iLiberty and ZiPhone were all the rage, and these applications—though effective for the vast majority of users—left a few casualties in their wake. Specifically, ZiPhone downgraded the firmware on phones in such a way that it was difficult to "virginize" them **[Hack #2.05]** if they needed to be taken to an Apple store for hardware warranty service. And a major blow was dealt to the first-generation unlocking applications when Apple released its 2.0 firmware and its own App Store, replacing (and for a while, effectively disabling) the popular 1.x firmware Installer.app store. As usual, there was no immediately effective jailbreak for the new firmware.

However, a culmination of efforts by the iPhone dev team came up with an elegant, consistent, and very stable solution to both 2.x firmware jailbreaking and unlocking. By consolidating all the still-working exploits from the 1.x era, and adding a discovered exploit that could not be disabled by any Apple software patch, the Pwnage (expert) and QuickPwn (quick and easy) applications were created. Part of their elegance lies in how they do not directly jailbreak the phone. Rather, they patch Apple's own firmware packages—adding jailbreaking and unlocking code as needed—and then the user simply patches their phone using iTunes.

As of this writing, these programs are the best way to jailbreak an iPhone. To learn about the latest methods, you can follow developments in the hacking community **[Hack #2.06]**.

Jailbreaking with Pwnage and QuickPwn

Developed by or in coordination with the iPhone dev team, Pwnage can be downloaded from http://wikee.iphwn.org or http://blog.iphone-dev.org. Both Mac (Figure 1-9), and Windows (Figure 1-10) versions are available. Along with the Pwnage tool, you'll need to download the correct restore image for your phone and the appropriate bootloader files—but Pwnage will assist you with this.

Figure 1-9.
Pwnage for the Mac

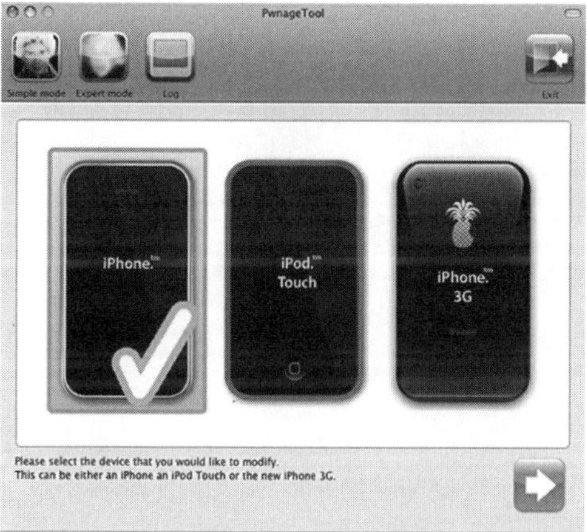

Figure 1-10.
Pwnage for the PC (winpwn)

Select your device, then select the firmware (*.ipsw* file) that you (or Pwnage) downloaded. For both platforms, select the appropriate bootloader files when prompted. For first-generation iPhones, these files will be called *BL-39.bin* and *BL-46.bin*, and can be found through a Google search on the iPhone. Once you have selected all the options you want, build your custom *.ipsw*. If you're also unlocking, be sure to choose "NO" when Pwnage asks if you are a legit user, make sure that the options Activate Phone, Enable Baseband Update, Neuter Bootloader, Unlock Baseband, and Autodelete Bootneuter.app are all checked. If you've already unlocked your phone, you shouldn't have to unlock it again, but it also won't hurt anything if you do. Once your custom *.ipsw* file has been built, you're almost done! If you're running winpwn, go back to the main screen and click "iPwner," then select the custom *.ipsw* file that you just built. On both systems, you will need to enter DFU mode at this point **[Hack #2.05]** to allow iTunes to install the *.ipsw* file on your phone. Once again, the application will guide you through this process.

Launch iTunes. If you're on Mac OS X, hold down the Option key while you press the Restore button in iTunes. On Windows, hold down the Shift key as you click Restore. Select the custom *.ipsw* file that you made, and wait for the restore to finish. Congratulations—you're done!

Pwnage has a number of conditional steps—and uses iTunes to do the deed. If you want an even simpler jailbreaking experience and you have a fresh iPhone with no complicated prehacking history, then QuickPwn (Figure 1-11) is a good choice (www.quickpwn.com).

Figure 1-11.
QuickPwn

Jailbreaking the Latest Firmware

With your iPhone jailbroken, you are now free to manipulate it as you see fit. Or, as iFuntastic says, to make your iPhone *your* iPhone.

Apple's intent to lock down its phone is strong. But an army of curious hackers seems to be able to keep finding exploits that give it control over the iPhone. Because any code made by man can be broken by man, and because software is very complex and always seems to have some bugs in it, it stands to reason that any new firmware will eventually be broken.

When no exploits could be easily found for later firmware versions, a clever approach was found—simply roll back the version. Apple then patched the firmware so that users couldn't roll back the firmware—at least, not yet. So even if at some point in the future, it seems that all hope is lost for software jailbreaking methods, it's probably just a matter of time before the hack is found. And if the iPhone ever gets really, really impenetrably secure, there's always the hardware approach—such as the famous hardware hack by GeoHot (http://iphonejtag.blogspot.com/2007_08_01_archive.html) and methods derived from it.

The iPhone dev team has been the most consistent and reliable force for responsible iPhone hacking since the iPhone's release, so before you download a payware application from some glossy site, seek out the iPhone dev team sites http://wikee.iphwn.org and http://blog.iphone-dev.org to see what they have to say.

HACK 1.04: Install Third-Party Apps

Open your iPhone to a whole new world of applications!

Although Apple's App Store is certainly the easiest out-of-the-box way to get new applications, things weren't always this easy. In the beginning, there were no third-party applications. Then there were ways to copy applications manually to the iPhone over SSH/SCP, SMB, or AppleTalk. A format called "PXL" (Package and eXtension Library) for downloading applications through web downloads briefly appeared and then fell into disuse. But then the company NullRiver brought out Installer.app (Figure 1-12). This application—which set an example for Apple to follow—allowed for incredibly easy discovery and instant installation of new programs. The best part about it is that it runs directly from your iPhone and downloads new applications over Wi-Fi or EDGE, which is great for people who are always on the go and don't always have access to a computer. iPod touch owners could use Installer.app as well via Wi-Fi.

Figure 1-12.
Installer.app

Enter Installer.app

Since its introduction shortly after the iPhone's initial release, Installer.app has become the most popular way to install third-party apps and utilities. Thousands of third-party applications existed before Apple had even announced their App Store efforts. And for those original iPhone users still running a pre-2.0 firmware, Installer.app is still their only source of applications.

When Apple's 2.0 firmware came out—in conjunction with the App Store and around the time of the iPhone 3G—most of the third-party "toolchain" applications would not work on the new firmware. This was not so much an intentional result from Apple, but simply the side effect of Apple completely revising its SDK. (The same thing happens with new versions of Mac OS X or Windows; the tools to develop software changes frequently.) But none of the applications on Installer.app had a polite "Sorry, I don't support the 2.0 firmware" message and thus there was general confusion.

The Install tab takes lists of apps from various privately operated sources and sorts them into a list that you can choose from. From the Install screen, tap an app to get a basic description of the app. On this page there is also an Install button, which will download and install this package on your iPhone, and a More Info button, which sends you to a website with more information on the app.

After you install a package, if it's an application, it will simply appear on your home screen, and if it's something else, like a skin pack or theme or ringtone, it should appear in the appropriate place. If not, try restarting your iPhone.

The Update tab shows whether there are any newer versions of apps that you have already installed through Installer.app. If there are, you can read about them and install them through the same procedure for installing apps.

The Uninstall tab shows all of the packages that you've installed through Installer.app. Selecting one and tapping "Uninstall" will get rid of it.

The Sources tab shows where your list of packages is coming from. You can tap any of the sources to get more information about them, including contact information for the maintainer. You can get additional sources through packages in the Install tab.

Nonetheless, when the 2.0 firmware was released, and people started to port their 1.x toolchain applications to the 2.0 SDK, NullRiver came out with a new version of Installer and that version remains the de facto Installer solution for third-party application installation on jailbroken phones.

Enter Cydia

There were several major critiques of the NullRiver Installer application. First and foremost was that it was closed source and operated by a private company—thus, whenever it had trouble there was little recourse (of course Apple's App Store is also closed source and proprietary, but they also happen to make the iPhone, so there's some chance that they'll be responsive to change requests). And one of the noted problems was the immature installer/uninstaller management provided in NullRiver's Installer. Thus, Jay Freeman (known online as **saurik**) ported APT, the extremely well-supported open source package manager from Debian Linux. The project is here: www.telesphoreo.org. Cydia is a GUI front end for the Telesphoreo port of APT created by saurik.

To quote the author: "In order to provide some relief for these issues, I have decided to start a project called Telesphoreo with the goal of creating a distribution of GNU and BSD's userspace for the iPhone as a collaborative, open source project. The name is an ancient Greek word meaning "to bring fruit to perfection or maturity," which I feel is what needs to be done to Apple's product: it's passable as a phone, but as a portable workstation it is almost unmatched...with the right software."

The Cydia application, shown in Figure 1-13, accesses these new, well-documented installation sources, and has become the alternative to Installer.app for application installation; many of the same applications are available from both Cydia and Installer.app (Figure 1-14).

Figure 1-13.
Cydia

Figure 1-14.
Cydia and Installer.app

Repositories

Both Installer.app and Cydia share the concept of *repositories*, which are additional sources of programs. Apple's App Store can be considered one large repository—there's only the App Store, and only Apple can decide whether a program goes on the list. In contrast, Installer and Cydia allow you to add any sources you want. Some companies that provide a number of iPhone applications maintain their own sources. More often, developers submit their applications to another popular repository. If you develop your own iPhone applications, you may want to create your own source repository.

A repository is included by adding its URL, such as "http://installer.iclarified.com", to the sources page, as shown in Figures 1-15 and 1-16.

Figure 1-15.
Adding source repositories to Installer.app

Figure 1-16.
Adding source repositories to Cydia

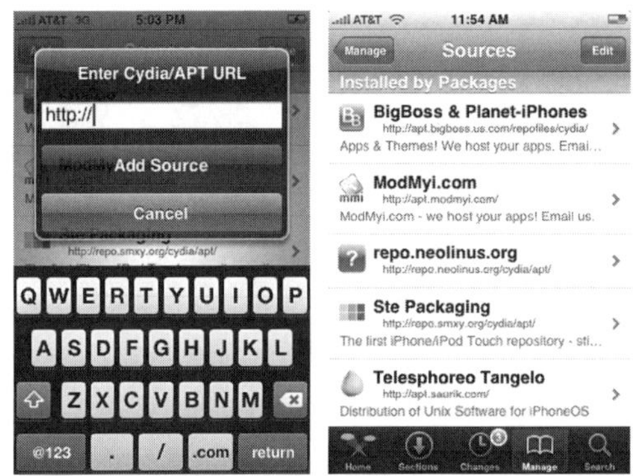

You can also install additional repositories by searching for them in the Sources category, which in turn will add them to the source list. For instance, to get a larger selection of applications to chose from, locate Community Sources in the Community section of the list and install it. With Community Sources installed, the list of applications becomes much longer, offering you more choices to customize your iPhone. Figure 1-17 shows the procedure.

Figure 1-17.
Adding Community Sources

Trusting Sources

Two reasons Apple has carefully controlled the App Store—besides any financial, business, and brand protection reasons—are quality control and trust. By vetting applications and ensuring that they look good, work well, and have no viruses, spyware, or unrevealed side effects, Apple provides a meaningful service.

It's important to note that by jailbreaking your phone and then running Installer or Cydia, you're leaving the walled garden of the Apple App Store, and entering a large and potentially—but not usually—cruel world. However, people download and install applications all the time for Windows, Mac OS X, and Unix platforms, and intelligent users generally know how to detect bad software. So if an application—or app source—seems fishy, ask around before you install it on your phone.

You're not on completely your own, as there is a lively community that may be able to help you. And the more you participate, the larger that community becomes **[Hack #2.06]**.

 HACK 1.05: Manipulate Your iPhone's Filesystem

Now that your iPhone or iPod touch has been jailbroken and freed from the shackles of conformity **[Hack #1.03]**, it's time to learn how to navigate the files and folders of its file directory. Being able to find your way around the iPhone's filesystem is absolutely mandatory for mastering the full customization capability of your iPhone or iPod touch.

If you're familiar with the hierarchical storage system on hard drives, where files are sorted into nested containers called folders or directories, then you'll find that underneath the glossy user interface, the iPhone is no different. And if you're familiar with the directory structure of Unix-like operating systems such as Linux, BSD, and Mac OS X, you'll have an even better sense of where things are stored on the iPhone.

There are as many ways to look at iPhone files as there are ways to access any computer. Depending on what server software you install on the iPhone, you can use FTP, HTTP, AFP (Apple file sharing), or techniques like the Unix SCP (secure copy protocol). But most of these techniques use the wireless network connection on the iPhone. But if you want to move files the quickest, you can use a copy utility that works over the iPhone's USB connection.

The first step of familiarizing yourself with the file directory is to get good browsing software for your computer. DiskAid is an excellent choice. The user-friendly interface of this program makes it perfect for beginners. Yet the ability to modify files and folders in the iPhone's file directory makes this same program highly useful for even the most advanced hackers as well.

Access iPhone Files from Your Computer

As mentioned earlier, the ideal file-management software for both Mac and PC is DiskAid, available from www.digidna.net/diskaid. It's free, and it can be used with or without jailbreaking. Once your file-management software has been installed, start it up while the iPhone is connected to your computer. Figure 1-18 shows the interface of DiskAid. Once the software is loaded, you'll see the basic, "safe" media directory. The drop-down menu in the lower left will allow you to access the root directory, which has the guts of the device.

Figure 1-18.
DiskAid

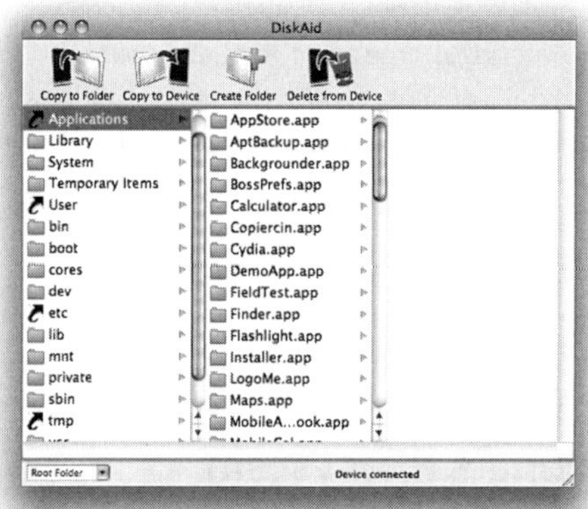

Understand the Hierarchy

Try opening up each folder and taking a look around. However, be careful not to modify any of the files until you know what they are, as you could do unnecessary damage to your phone. Of the folders, the main ones to spend some time browsing through are *Applications*, *System*, and */var/mobile*. Remember that your root directory, /, is the origin of the main folders.

An important lesson in iPhone file directory browsing is to understand folder path addresses. When you see the phrase */private/var/tmp*, it will help you to know that this phrase actually means to look in your / (root) directory for the *private* folder. Once you find the *private* folder, open it to be greeted by another group of folders. Look down this list to find the *var* folder, and open it up to see even more folders. Look through this new list to find the *tmp* folder, and open it. You've now arrived at your destination, as in Figure 1-19. All the mysterious phrase */private/var/tmp* was trying to say was to just look inside the *tmp* folder by following the path from */private*, through *var*, and into *tmp*.

Figure 1-19.
The */private/var/tmp* folder

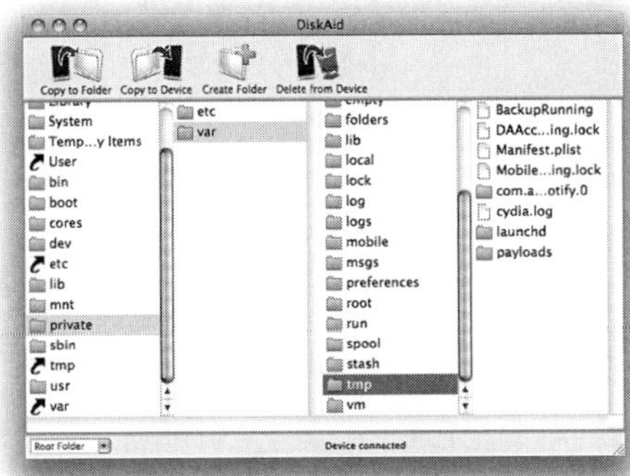

Also note that in Unix, there is a feature called "symbolic links," which is similar to aliases on Mac OS X or shortcuts on Windows. On Unix filesystems you can refer to the folder by any of its symbolic links, so */private/var* and */var* are effectively synonymous. In DiskAid these are symbolized by the "curved arrow" icon for directories.

Here are some brief explanations for each of the main folders in the *Home* or (root) directory.

/

This "slash" symbolizes the top of your filesystem, the root directory, simply called "*root*." Pathnames (folder/directory paths) are symbolized with this forward slash, such as */var/mobile*.

Applications

Contains—you guessed it—applications. In addition to the stock iPhone applications, some of the third-party applications that you may install will be placed in this folder. This is where you'll typically go for such things as customizing application icons or even modifying the program code. User-installed applications from the App Store will be installed in */var/mobile/Applications/*.

Library

Contains various preferences and frameworks, as well as the ringtone and wallpaper folders.

System

This is where a lot of the Mobile OS X system files can be found. The programs that customize your phone with custom graphics, carrier logos, and skins change many graphics files in this folder.

bin

bin is short for binary, meaning simply a program you can run, usually command-line based. On an iPhone, you'll find the various essential shell utilities and command-line programs here.

cores

This is where core dumps are stored. When a program crashes, the OS sometimes writes a file to disk showing the memory state of the program just before it crashed, for the purposes of debugging.

dev

dev stands for device. In Unix, almost everything is treated as a file from the programmer's perspective—the hard disk, network cards, and Bluetooth can all be accessed with files such as */dev/disk0*.

etc

A shortcut to */private/etc*, the *etc* directory is traditionally where configuration files—the text files that define settings for programs—are stored.

private

Contains a lot of important files, including music, photos, and some email data.

sbin

This is the place for superuser binaries—programs for system administration.

tmp

The *tmp* directory is where temporary files used by programs are written. The expectation is that the contents of this directory are frequently deleted, like a "trash can."

usr

usr is intended to be for shareable, read-only data. Folders such as */usr/sbin* and */usr/bin* contain additional commands, and */usr/lib* contains libraries of software code shared by the whole system.

var

A shortcut to */private/var*, *var* stands for variable and is intended to contain variable data, such as logs, news, mail spool files and so on, which is constantly being modified by various programs running on your system. On the iPhone, it also happens to be the directory that contains much user data, originally in the */var/root* directory but now stored in the */var/mobile* directory.

/var/mobile

A lot of the iPhone user's personal data is stored here, including music, pictures, and more.

/var/root

Prior to firmware 1.1.3, user data was stored here. It has moved to */var/mobile*.

As you gain more experience navigating through your directory, you can begin using the other main ability offered by your browser software: modification of files and folders. DiskAid allows you to add, replace, or delete any file or folder in your directory. These abilities open your iPhone up to an all-new breed of customization options, from changing icons and backgrounds **[Hack #8.02]** to modifying the files that an application is based on.

Browse Your iPhone Directory on the iPhone Itself

Because your iPhone is probably with you far more than your personal computer, you will probably want to be able to access the filesystem on the go. There are a few utilities that make this easy as well.

MobileFinder

You can find MobileFinder in Cydia. Once installed, you'll see the icon for MobileFinder on your SpringBoard. Just tap it to start the application (Figure 1-20). Once the application starts, you'll be greeted by a screen like that in Figure 1-21.

Figure 1-20.
MobileFinder icon

Figure 1-21.
Browsing the root file directory with MobileFinder

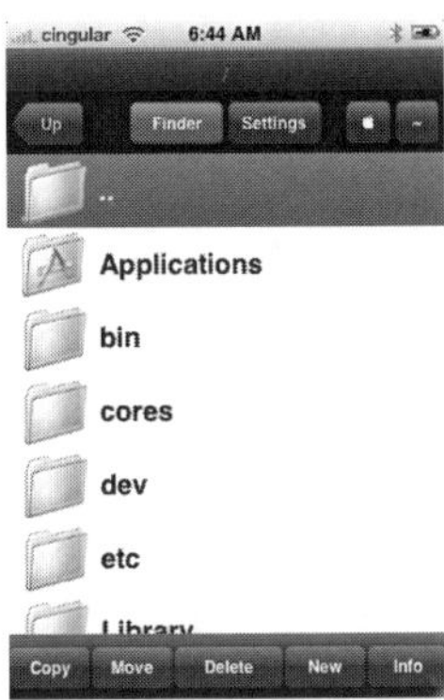

MobileFinder has started you at your root directory. To open a folder, just tap it. If you need to go back to the previous list of folders, just hit the Up button at the top left of the screen. MobileFinder displays the folder you're currently in at the top of the screen to help prevent you from getting lost. These convenient features can be seen in Figure 1-22.

Figure 1-22.
Pressing the Up button at the top left displays the previous directory; the current directory is shown at the top.

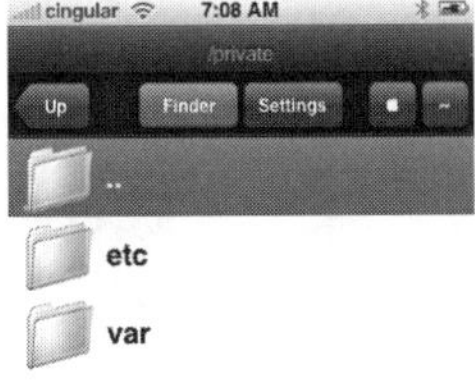

If you ever find yourself lost in a sea of folders, and wish to return to the root directory, just repeatedly press the Up button at the top left of the screen until you get back. Alternatively, you can press the folder icon with trailing dots at the top of the folder list, which serves the same function as the Up button.

To customize your MobileFinder experience, press the Settings button at the top of the screen. You'll be able to change numerous attributes affecting the file directory and its appearance, as shown in Figures 1-23 and 1-24. When you are done with the Settings screen, press the Finder button to resume browsing.

Figure 1-23.
The top half of the Settings screen

Figure 1-24.
The bottom half of the Settings screen

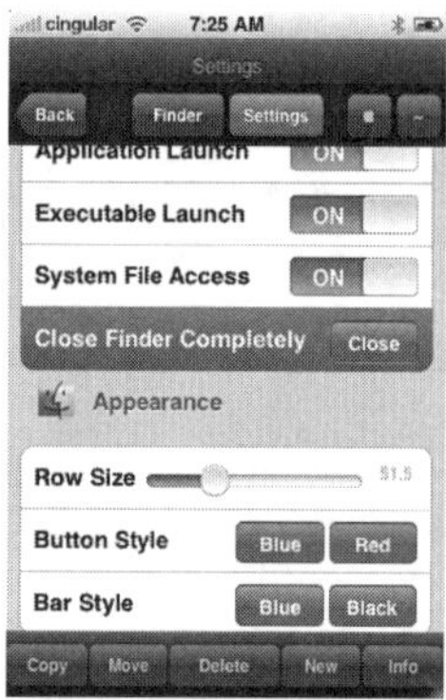

The bottom five buttons on the MobileFinder screen help you with file operations: you can copy, move, and delete files with the three buttons on the left. The New button creates a new file, folder, or bookmark. The Info button provides any available information about a selected file. In addition to modifying files, MobileFinder can launch applications. Just tap an Application, and it will launch.

Although MobileFinder may not be as easy to use as DiskAid, it makes up for this by eliminating the need for a computer to do this type of work. For more information about MobileFinder, simply read the release notes for the app in Cydia. Note that there's a version of MobileFinder on the App Store—but it lacks the features of the jailbroken version.

Mobile Safari

Did you know that most web browsers can also be used to browse your filesystem? For example, if you type `File:///C:/` into Windows Explorer on a PC, you can browse your hard drive.

Unfortunately, this behavior is stripped out of Mobile Safari, but you can set up a web server on the device to solve the problem.

On a jailbroken device, install lighttpd **[Hack #9.10]**. Also, make sure that OpenSSH is installed (preferably with Cydia).

Once lighttpd is installed, you'll need to create a configuration file before it will run. SSH to your phone **[Hack #9.04]**. Navigate to */etc* and type nano `lighttpd.conf`, then press Enter. This step opens up a new file in the nano editor.

Enter the following lines:

```
dir-listing.activate = "enable"
server.document-root = "/"
```

The document root in the second line, inside the quotes, can be any directory you want. We're using "/" or the root directory, so that everything on the phone can be viewed. There are plenty of other options that you can set for your web server as well. We'll just add one more for security:

```
server.bind = "127.0.0.1"
```

This line makes sure that only the phone browser can view our files. You can also add your home network prefix to allow other computers on your network to see the files, or you can leave the line out altogether.

To start up your web server, type `lighttpd -f /etc/lighttpd.conf` and make sure that there are no error messages. Go to Safari, and navigate to localhost or 127.0.0.1 (Figure 1-25).

Now you can browse the files on your iPhone! This hack has the added benefit that any file that Mobile Safari can handle—such as audio/video files, PDFs, and so on—can be accessed and viewed.

Figure 1-25.
Browsing your iPhone's filesystem on your iPhone using Mobile Safari

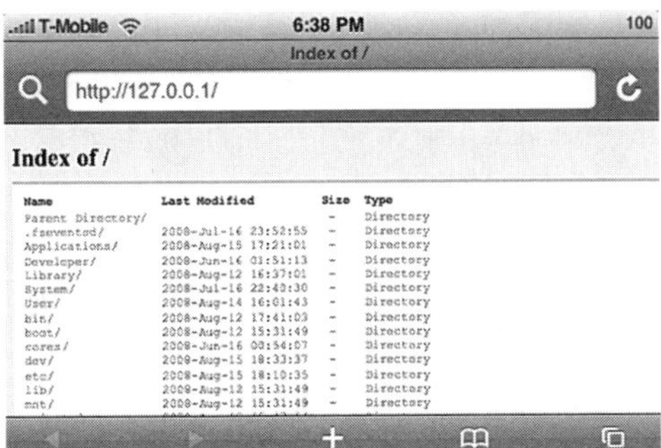

There are thousands of files on your iPhone that might hold the key to the hack you wish to accomplish, so getting to know your filesystem is a good first step.

— Adam Stolarz, Christopher Kurpinski & David Jurick

HACK 1.06: Back Up Your iPhone's Files

You'll kick yourself later if you don't!

Your iPhone most likely contains valuable information that would be tragic to lose. In fact, many people rarely connect their iPhones—or iPods, for that matter—to their computer—once they do the initial load of contacts, music, and pictures. Plus, with the iPhone's own 3G/Wi-Fi connectivity, integrated iTunes and App Store, and now, push email features, there's almost no reason to plug the iPhone back into the computer.

Except for one reason: backups.

Unlike in a corporate IT environment, you probably don't have a system administrator backing up your phone each night. And if you're like millions of iPhone users, your techie friend helped you unlock it so that you could use T-Mobile about six months ago and you've been afraid to mess with it, but you want to make sure you don't lose your chat history and your pictures.

The moral of this story is this: it's never too late to back up.

Actually, that's wrong! It's often too late to back up. So keep reading.

There are several major ways to back up the files on your iPhone:

iTunes

Apple provides a thorough backup procedure for all the Apple-sanctioned features of your phone. However, it's currently an all-or-nothing proposition: there's no way to selectively back up certain features more frequently, so you often have to wait several minutes for it to go through all its different backups. And if the sync fails or stops working for any reason, you may think that you've backed up when you haven't.

The cloud

With Apple's new push email and push contacts, you really won't have to worry about losing any important emails, calendars, or contacts. (Getting duplicate entries might be a new problem, however.) And simply by using Exchange, or Gmail, or any IMAP-based email server, you'll ensure that your email stays unharmed in the event of iPhone damage or replacement.

Manual copies

On a jailbroken phone, you can browse the filesystem **[Hack #1.05]** and copy the most important files back.

You can easily back up your files on your computer using iTunes so that if disaster strikes, all will not be lost. The problem is, what do you back up? The simplest solution is everything—but just like a full PC or Mac backup, you'll still need an expert to help you sift through those 16 MB of who-knows-what to find the exact file you need to get your chat logs or address book back.

Fortunately, there are solutions to most of these problems. We'll detail them here.

Strategy 1: Use iTunes

The simplest solution for any phone, jailbroken or not, is to back it up with iTunes. The bacon-saving feature of iTunes allows you to protect all these files:

- Text messages
- Notes
- Call history
- Contact favorites
- Sound settings
- Widget settings
- Certain network settings
- App Store settings

To back up your files, first start iTunes with your iPhone connected to your computer. From the Devices section, click on your iPhone so that it's highlighted and its information is displayed in the main iTunes pane, as shown in Figure 1-26. Finally, click the sync button at the bottom right of the iTunes window. Your files will be backed up on your computer.

Technically, syncing and backing up are not the same, but if you sync the iPhone, it will also back it up. The Apple article at http://support.apple.com/kb/HT1766 explains the difference. Basically, a full sync or an update will trigger a backup. During a restore, you'll be offered the chance to back up the iPhone as well.

To verify that files have been backed up on your computer (or just to find the date on which it was last backed up), go to the iTunes Preferences menu. After the Preferences window appears, click on the Devices tab. You'll see your iPhone's preferences, as shown in Figure 1-27. On the Devices tab, locate your iPhone in the box that says "The following iPhones are backed up on this computer." The date on the right is the last time it was backed up.

To set iTunes so that it will back up your iPhone every time you connect it to your computer, just check the box next to "Automatically sync when this iPhone is connected" in the Options section at the bottom of the iTunes window. Now, whenever you start iTunes with your iPhone connected to your computer, it will automatically sync and back up your files. (However, if your phone is jailbroken, make sure that you choose "No" when it offers you a firmware update.)

Backing up your important iPhone files on your computer will save you a great deal of frustration if you ever have to restore your iPhone **[Hack #2.04]**. With the simplicity of iTunes syncing function to back up your files, you'll be up and running much more quickly with your global iPhone settings fundamentally intact.

Figure 1-26.
The iTunes main iPhone screen

Figure 1-27.
Device backups

On the Mac, these backups are actually stored in *~/Library/Application Support/MobileSync/Backup/* (where ~ is your home directory: */Users/you*). Erica Sadun has created an extremely useful command-line program called *mdhelper* (available from http://ericasadun.com/ftp/Macintosh/mdhelper-universal.zip) that can be used to crack open these backups and get the goodies out of them. Sometimes, for a variety of reasons, iTunes doesn't offer you to restore your iPhone to an earlier backup, or you want only part of the backup. With mdhelper, you can extract just the parts you need. To use it, run Applications→Utilities→Terminal and change to the directory where mdhelper resides. Run it using this command:

```
./mdhelper
```

and you'll get these options:

```
Usage: mdhelper options
-h         Print this message and exit
-d         Show the backup directory
-l         List contents for each platform
-L         List the summary for each platform
-f         List all files and mdbackup names for each platform
-m         Extract all available manifests
-X phrase  Extract all files where the device name starts with the match phrase
-C phrase  Extract all files containing the phrase in the original filename
-M phrase  Extract all mdbackups whose name contains the match phrase
-x files   Extract each mdbackup file listed by path
```

Here are some example usages. To extract databases for SMS (to be placed back in */var/mobile/Library/SMS/sms.db*) and notes (*/var/mobile/Library/Notes*):

```
./mdhelper -C sms.db
```

The following commands extracts all the property lists, which contain bookmarks (*/var/mobile/Library/Safari/Bookmarks.plist*) and map bookmarks.

```
./mdhelper -C .plist
```

The following command extracts SQLite databases, which contain Address Book (*/var/mobile/Library/AddressBook/AddressBook.sqlitedb*) and Calendar (*/var/mobile/Library/Calendar/Calendar.sqlitedb*) data:

```
./mdhelper -C .sqlitedb
```

There are dozens of other settings; if you explore */var/mobile* and */var/mobile/Library*, you should be able to see what is what.

Strategy 2: Use the Cloud

There are several core features—namely email, contacts, and calendars—that have been pushed into what is called "the cloud." The cloud is a cute way of describing servers that are somewhere on the Internet. If you're using Gmail or another IMAP-based email server, or Exchange, you're already using the cloud. Thus, if you (gasp) had to get a new iPhone, your email would be intact—it's not only on the iPhone—it's also on a remote server.

Another feature with cloud data storage is the *push* feature. With push, changes made on the Web or on computers to calendars, contacts, and email are instantly pushed over the EDGE or 3G or Wi-Fi Internet connection to your iPhone. This feature ensures that there is a copy of all this data securely stored on Apple's servers, as well as on your Phone, and probably on your computers that are syncing to MobileMe as well (Figure 1-28).

Figure 1-28.
Apple's MobileMe "cloud" syncing

Many of the iPhone applications that accessorize existing online services—eBay, Amazon, PayPal, WordPress, Jott—rely on accounts that you already have online. So saving data to the cloud is built into these applications, and all you need to do to get running on a new phone is reinstall the applications and reenter your login information.

[Hack #11.01] and **[Hack #11.03]** show you how you can create scripts and applications to back up anything not covered here to the cloud.

Strategy 3: Manually Back Up

Some files can be manually backed up with no jailbreaking funny business. For instance, the iPhone shows up in Windows and on the Mac as a digital camera, in addition to being a phone.

Photos

To back up photos, you can simply drag the pictures off the phone on Windows or slurp them off using iPhoto or Image Capture on the Mac. If you leave them on the iPhone or iPod touch (assuming that you have room) then you'll have two copies—one on the computer, one on the device—and thus you'll have options if one or the other of those machines eventually crashes.

Music and photos

But what if, Jobs forbid, you should lose your desktop computer, and some of your movies, music, and photos are now only on your iPhone or iPod touch? If you've jailbroken it, you should have no problem pulling them out of */var/mobile/Media* using **[Hack #1.05]**.

Desktop files

Now that your iPhone has become your primary computer, and your desktop is falling into disuse, you'd better back up your critical files onto your phone. An App Store application called Air Sharing makes this easy and smooth, even if you haven't jailbroken your phone. If you have a Mac see **[Hack #9.06]** to learn how to mount the iPhone filesystem using AppleTalk or SSH.

App Store applications

Even if you use App Store applications, you may not sync to iTunes that frequently. And if you're concerned that iTunes isn't backing up some really important data for you, or you want to make a backup on a different computer, then AppBackup (www.scott-wallace.net/iphone/appbackup) is for you. Ironically, AppBackup requires jailbreaking, even though its purpose is to back up App Store apps. Each App Store app has its own sandbox, a private file area where its data is stored. AppBackup can zip up these data files—on an app-by-app basis, or for all applications—and then store them in */var/mobile/Library/AppBackup/tarballs* (Figure 1-29). You can find AppBackup on Cydia, under Utilities, in the "BigBoss" repository.

If you use MobileFinder **[Hack #1.05]**, you can actually back up all the app data without using a computer. Navigate to the */var/mobile/Library/AppBackup/tarballs* folder and click Send→E-Mail. Then send the file to yourself—you now have an online backup of that data. To restore it later, copy the file back into the same directory, run AppBackup, and restore.

Figure 1-29.
Backing up an App Store file to email

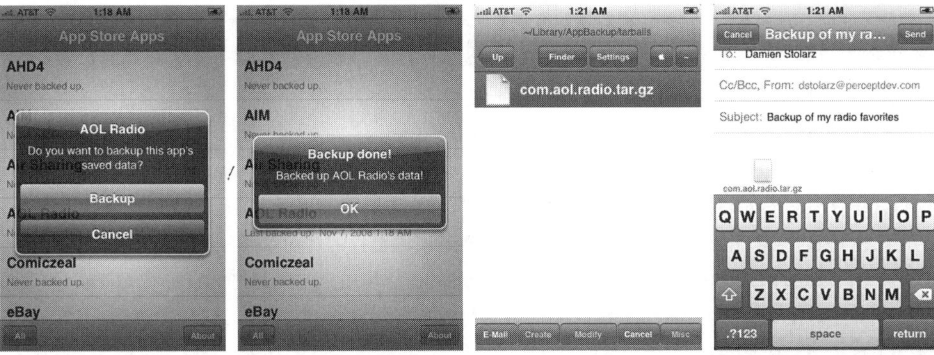

Jailbroken applications

Sometimes the data that you want to back up just isn't backed up by iTunes or the cloud, and you're going to have to go hunting for it. For instance, a fantastic application by saurik called Cycorder **[Hack #4.09]** allows you to record great, high-quality video on your iPhone. Unfortunately, the files aren't automatically backed up by iPhoto or iTunes. Luckily, the video is stored in */var/mobile/Media/Videos*. Using any of the techniques in **[Hack #1.05]** or **[Hack #9.06]**, you can copy these files to your desktop, or email them to yourself one by one using MobileFinder.

Fortunately, many jailbroken applications do sensible things, such as storing user data in */var/mobile*, like many of Apple's native applications do. Thus, a full backup of the */var/mobile* directory may not capture every custom setting and all user data on the phone, but it will get most of it.

Each time you upgrade the firmware on your jailbroken iPhone, you have to reinstall all your applications. **[Hack #10.10]** shows how to back up those applications as well.

If you have an iPhone with numerous App Store and jailbroken applications and lots of custom data, you owe it to yourself to back them up.

02 TROUBLESHOOT YOUR IPHONE OR IPOD TOUCH

Troubleshooting is more of an art than a science. That's a polite way of saying that troubleshooting involves a lot of trial and error and doesn't always work. By the time you're troubleshooting, something's already broken and it's not working the way it should. If you ask for advice, you'll probably get some obvious suggestion, even the one you've already tried, and your would-be savior may shrug and say, "That should have worked."

If you've ever owned a luxury car, you've experienced "platinum service"—and the price that goes with it. But if you've extensively modified your car with aftermarket parts and you take it to the dealer for engine work, you will find it hard to get warranty service on your customizations.

The same goes for the iPhone. Walk into an Apple Retail Store Genius Bar and ask them if you can upgrade the firmware on your stock iPhone, and you'll have no problem. Ask them how to rejailbreak your phone so you can continue to use it on T-Mobile after you upgraded to the Beta 3.1b firmware with cut-and-paste that you got off Pirate Bay, and you'll get the iColdShoulder.

This chapter presents the self-help and community support that you can get for your hacked iPhone. Some of these tools are basic—and similar to what you'll get if you step through the troubleshooting steps on Apple.com. But Apple's advice doesn't take into account the system-wide skinning you've done—not to mention other wild things you might have done, such as downgrading your firmware and patching the bootloader so that you could dual-boot iPhone Linux.

To continue the car metaphor, the first couple of hacks are like checking fluid levels and changing a tire. These quickly move into changing spark plugs and maybe even the brakes. Later in the book, you'll be swapping out the engine—so this chapter also shows you how to call AAA for your hacked iPhone.

The main things to know about iPhone debugging are:

1. Millions of iPhones have been successfully hacked.
2. iPhone hacking applications are constantly improved.
3. The earliest hacks are the flakiest, and waiting often pays off. However, guinea pigs are necessary.
4. You can usually unhack your phone, and it's a good idea to do this if you need to get hardware-related warranty support.

HACK 2.01: Triage Your iPhone

Remain calm.

The iPhone (or iPod touch) is a well-designed, complicated computer. Despite looking like a single unit, it actually has a number of peripherals—just like a PC. An iPhone's performance can be reasonably compared to a top-of-the-line consumer PC from around 1998–1999, except with a more modern OS and applications. Therefore, we can approach repair of the iPhone (or iPod touch) like we would a conventional PC. Here's an example of the specs for this "PC":

- Operating System: Mac OS X
- CPU: 400Mhz
- Peripherals: touch screen, Wi-Fi, Bluetooth, wireless broadband modem, sound card, built-in microphone, GPS receiver, 4–32GB hard drive, accelerometer, 3D video card, 2 megapixel camera, 480x320 LCD screen.

If you have experience debugging PCs, debugging the iPhone is actually not that hard. The usual checklist (Figure 2-1) for debugging a PC involves finding out which of the areas the problem is in.

1. Applications: is a specific application having or causing trouble?
2. Operating system: does it lock up on boot and never get to the application launching screen? If not, can you launch applications?
3. BIOS: is the computer getting through its power-on self-test and finding something to boot from?
4. Hardware: is the hardware plugged in and working?

Figure 2-1.
Four areas to debug

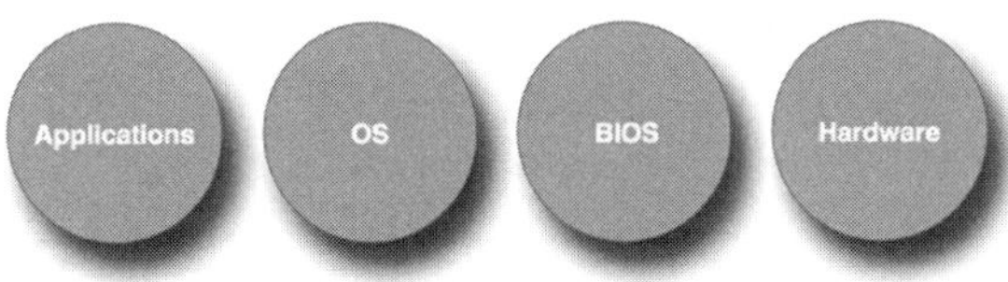

A lot of the same techniques can be applied to the iPhone. Here are some of the common-sense approaches that still apply, translated into iPhone-speak.

Applications

If you have a working iPhone that can make calls, but the phone is laggy or just acting weird, it could just be application trouble. The following are some ways to diagnose application trouble.

Problems:

- You get stuck in an application and can't get out.
- Battery life is draining faster than you expect due to background processes.
- Applications crash as soon as you launch them.

Solutions:

1. Force-quitting the running program may fix problems with a single application **[Hack #2.02]**.
2. Rebooting the iPhone gets you to a known state **[Hack #2.03]** and may fix whatever temporary problem was occurring.
3. Uninstalling or disabling bad, broken, or conflicting programs—especially background processes **[Hack #2.04]**—can help.
4. Get an updated version of the application that's compatible with your firmware.
5. It could be bad application settings. Go to Settings→General→Reset→Reset All Settings, which will reset most applications as well as system configuration settings.

Operating System

On a conventional PC, problems with the OS are more severe. DLL conflicts, missing drivers, or overall system instability leads us to believe that not just one program is giving us trouble but the whole operating system is having a problem.

Problems:

- You have similar problems with any application you run.
- Major system services aren't working at all—sound, Bluetooth, and so on.
- The whole system is lagging.
- You can't even get past the Apple logo, or to the application launching screen.

Solutions:

1. It could be bad application settings. Go to Settings→General→Reset→Reset All Settings, which will reset most applications, as well as system configuration settings.
2. If the iPhone crashes or hangs on boot up, the OS may need to be repaired **[Hack #2.04]** or reinstalled from scratch **[Hack #2.05]**.
3. Make sure to back your iPhone up before the trouble **[Hack #1.06]**, in case it crashes and must be reformatted.

BIOS

On a PC, you'd suspect BIOS problems when you can't even get to an OS boot screen. On an iPhone, the symptom would be that you never see the Apple logo when you turn it on.

Solutions:

If you can't even get the OS to boot, your boot loader may be broken, or the BIOS may be misconfigured. In the iPhone's case, this is usually the result of repeated firmware upgrades with various back-alley unlocking programs. Upgrading the firmware with the Pwnage application, which should in turn repair the firmware bootloader with Bootneuter, may fix these problems **[Hack #1.03]**.

Hardware

Don't rule out that your iPhone might be wigging out due to hardware troubles such as bad memory, corrupted firmware, or device malfunction.

Problems:

- Your iPhone won't boot at all—it seems dead.
- Your iPhone tries to boot and then crashes.
- Your iPhone says "Repair Needed."

Solutions:

1. If your PC is unplugged, it won't turn on. Similarly, if your iPhone has a dead battery, it won't turn on. Plug it into a wall or your computer and let it charge for a while (longer than 10 minutes) and see if it "wakes up." Figure 2-2 shows an iPhone that's hungry for power.
2. Reinstall everything from DFU mode **[Hack #2.05]**, cross your fingers, and hope it's not hardware. This approach works more often than not. The iPhone is a robust device.
3. If your phone says "Repair Needed" (Figure 2-3), it could mean hardware, firmware, or software. Apple may recommend that you take the phone to the Genius Bar for diagnosis. However, one glance at your hacked boot logo may eliminate their sympathy (and your warranty). Thus, you may want to virginize **[Hack #2.05]** your phone, if you can, before you bring it in for service.

Figure 2-2.
iPhone needs food, badly

Figure 2-3.
Repair Needed

Summary

There's very little to fear with a "broken" iPhone. Except for accidental hardware damage, like cracked screens, the iPhone is unusually durable. The "body count" of truly bricked iPhones is so low that it shouldn't be a concern.

HACK 2.02: Force Quit an iPhone Application

The fastest way out of a hung situation.

If you're a PC user, you might not be used to Apple's habit of making one button do many things. And even though technically the iPhone has four buttons, if you include the volume controls, pretty much all the resetting, rebooting, and reprogramming of the iPhone uses just two buttons—Home and Power.

The first hack of note is Force Quit. This is the equivalent of Command-Option-Esc/Force Quit on a Mac, or Ctrl-Alt-Del/End Process on a Windows PC. If you're in an application on the iPhone that is hung or isn't responding quickly enough because of network access or some other problem, you can get out to the Home screen.

To force quit an application that's frozen, press and hold the Home button for at least 6 seconds to close the frozen application (Figure 2-4).

Figure 2-4.
Hold down Home for 6 seconds to Force Quit

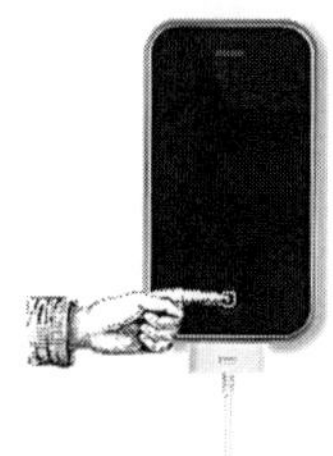

There are other applications that capture this button push and may make it do something different. For instance, if you're using Lance Fetter's backgrounder application **[Hack #9.14]**, you might see a "Backgrounding Enabled" message (Figure 2-5). In this case, just continue to hold the button and the app will quit.

Figure 2-5.
Backgrounding Enabled

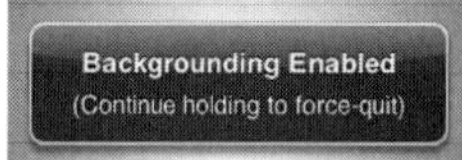

If your iPhone is still sluggish or unresponsive after you force quit the application, the next thing to try is rebooting **[Hack #2.03]**.

HACK 2.03: Reboot Your iPhone

What to do when it just isn't working right.

If you're stuck in a program and force quitting [Hack #2.02] didn't do the trick, your phone may be totally frozen. Sometimes you can't get anything to work—or work right. Flaky apps may have put your operating system into an indeterminate state—or those Apple-forbidden background apps that you bravely ran may have slowed your phone to a plodding crawl.

Power Off Normally

The first step to rebooting your phone is to simply try to turn it off. Hold down the Power button on the top (Figure 2-6) until you see the "slide to power off" graphic. If your touchscreen is responding, and you can slide it, whew. Let it turn off, then press the Power button. You're back in business.

Figure 2-6.
Hold down the Power button

If that doesn't work, your next option is a "hard" reset. To perform this, press both buttons (Home and Power, as shown in Figure 2-7) at the same time for about 10 seconds—the phone will reboot.

Figure 2-7.
Hard reset: press and hold both Power and Home buttons

Then, when you see the boot logo, let go (Figure 2-8).

Figure 2-8.
Time to let go

If this doesn't fix things, a good idea is to ensure that your phone is charged. Your next step might be to restore [Hack #2.04] your phone. (Screenshots shown are from the iPhone Dev Team's Pwnage Tool.)

HACK 2.04: Restore and Recover Your iPhone

Reinstall Mac OS X on your device with recovery mode.

Ordinarily, if you want to reinstall OS X on your iPhone, you just plug it into your computer and click "Restore" in iTunes (Figure 2-9).

Figure 2-9.
Restoring an iPhone

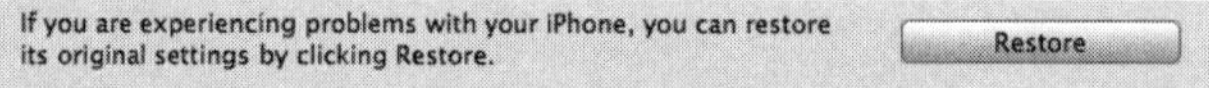
If you are experiencing problems with your iPhone, you can restore its original settings by clicking Restore.
Restore

Restore

However, restoring works only if iTunes recognizes your iPhone. If that's not happening, then recovery mode is the answer. Recovery mode lets iTunes know that the iPhone is ready to be restored.

Restoring your iPhone puts it into an almost completely factory-fresh state that includes the erasure of all data, including songs, videos, contacts, photos, calendar information, and any other data that was added to your iPhone after its purchase. Because the loss of all your data can be inconvenient at best, restoring should be your last resort after trying any applicable troubleshooting techniques.

The only more drastic restoration beyond restoration is DFU (Device Firmware Upgrade) mode [Hack #2.05].

At times, you might want to use restore mode even when you're not restoring. For example, you may also be asked to enter restore mode by some hacking applications, because it puts the iPhone in a state where it waits for an application to talk to it, whether that's iTunes or a less official app. And you can back out of restore mode easily.

Entering Recovery Mode

There are a couple of ways to get into recovery mode:

1. Make sure that your phone is off. If your phone is working normally, just hold down Power for five seconds and then slide to turn off. If your device can't boot or is hung, you'll turn it off by holding Power and Home until it powers off.
2. Hold down the Home button (Figure 2-10).
3. Connect it to your computer via USB.
4. Keep holding the Home button until your phone displays a screen similar to Figure 2-11, then let go.

Figure 2-10.
Hold down Home until you are told to let go

Figure 2-11.
A device in recovery mode

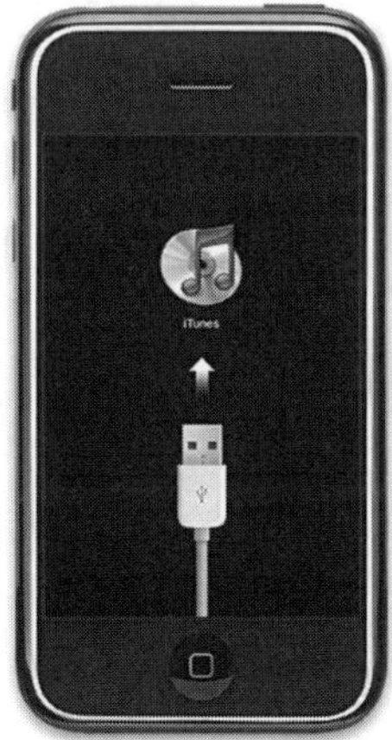

Restoring the Firmware

If iTunes is running, it'll restore your device, as shown in Figure 2-12.

Figure 2-12.
iTunes notifying you that it's found a device in recovery mode

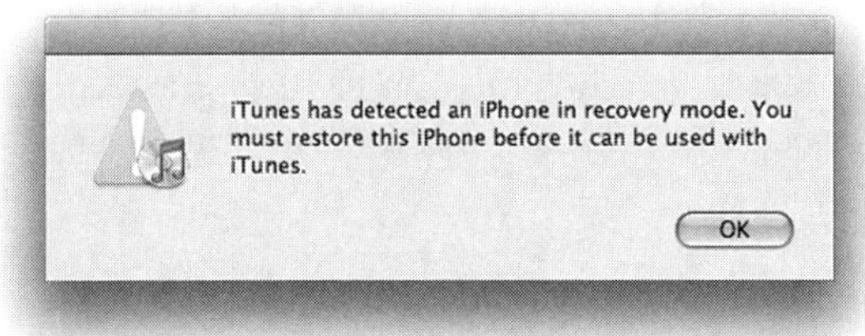

The next step, if you're going through with it, is to click Restore (Figure 2-13).

Figure 2-13.
iTunes has made the Restore option available

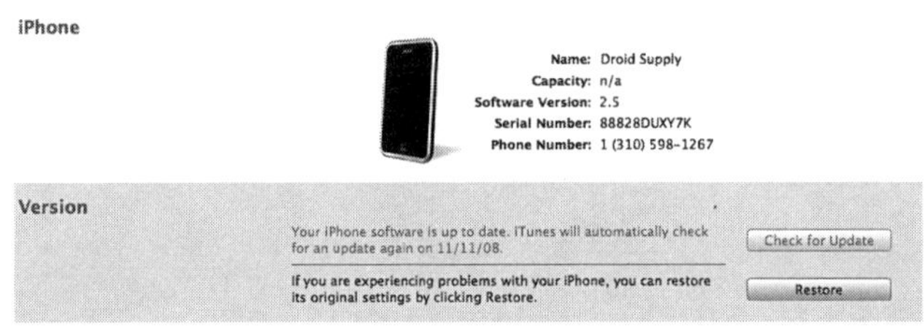

In many cases, you will be option-clicking (Mac) or shift-clicking (Windows) the Restore button. This will allow you to restore to the firmware of your choice. A link to all of Apple's firmware files can be found in **[Hack #1.02]**, and you can either download a custom firmware online or create your own with jailbreaking tools like Pwnage **[Hack #1.03]**. Figure 2-14 shows the firmware selection dialog.

Figure 2-14.
Loading a firmware image

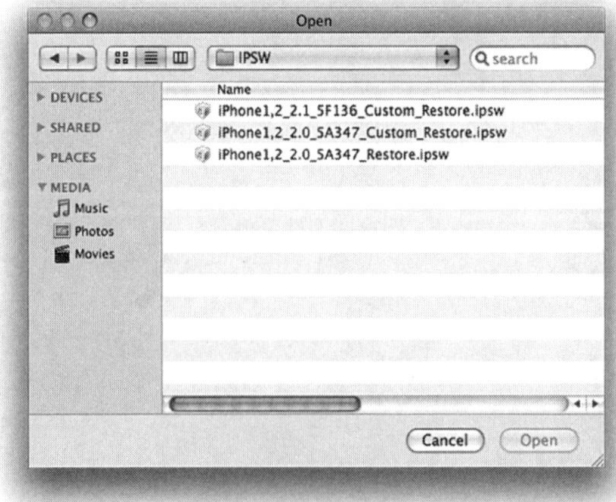

Exiting Recovery Mode

If you change your mind about recovery mode, it's easy to get out of with a hard reset. If you just leave the device for a while, it will power down, at which point you can simply turn it back on. To speed things up:

1. Disconnect the iPhone or iPod from the computer.
2. Hold down the Power and Home buttons until you see the boot logo (Figure 2-15).
3. When you see the boot logo, let go (Figure 2-16).

Figure 2-15.
Hard reset: press and hold both Power and Home buttons

Figure 2-16.
Let go of both buttons

It's almost guaranteed that within your first week of iPhone hacking you will think you've "bricked" your phone. Luckily, it is very easy to fix. When all else fails to bring back your iPhone's functionality, look to the Restore function, either in recovery mode or DFU mode **[Hack #2.05]** to solve your problem. This trusty technique should fix almost any imaginable hacking- or non-hacking-related iPhone issue.

Fully restoring your iPhone to a factory state (including firmware) is called *virginizing*. Restoring an iPhone, iPhone 3G, or iPod touch in DFU mode with an Apple-provided firmware image is all you usually need to do to virginize your phone.

HACK 2.05: Enter DFU Mode

Reinstall everything with Device Firmware Upgrade Mode.

In the process of hacking your phone, you may get into a state where you just can't get the OS to boot. Or you may get errors when attempting to restore your device. Or you may be trying to unlock your phone (Chapter 7) and you need to replace not just the OS (as in jailbreaking) but the bootloader firmware as well. DFU mode performs a similar function to restore mode, except that in DFU mode, the iPhone never even tries to boot OS X. It's kind of like booting a PC off a restore disc, which then replaces your OS with a pristine installation.

More likely, though, you'll be trying to do something clever with your phone, and the instructions for that clever feat will ask you to enter DFU mode.

For all of these situations, DFU mode is the troubleshooting mode you seek. In DFU mode, your iPhone never gets to boot to Mac OS X. Instead, it sits there waiting to have its memory—and BIOS—completely erased and rewritten.

Entering DFU Mode

Here are the basic steps to get into DFU mode. You have to get the timing right.

If you have any trouble following the instructions here, you can use the Pwnage application (available at http://blog.iphone-dev.org), which will guide you through the process. The screen shots given here and throughout this chapter came from this excellent application.

1. Turn off your phone (Figure 2-17).
2. Hold down both the Home and Power buttons for exactly 10 seconds, then release the Power button and keep holding the Home button (Figure 2-18).
3. After another 10 seconds, let go of the Home button as well (Figure 2-19).

Figure 2-17.
Power down the phone

Figure 2-18.
Hold both for 10 seconds, then release the Power button

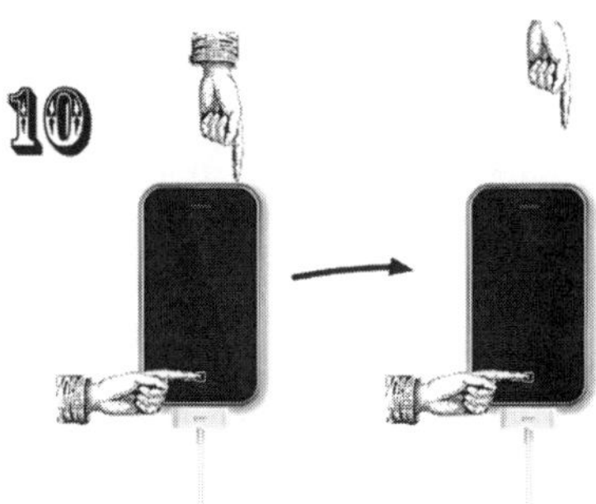

Figure 2-19.
Hold Home button for another 10 seconds, then release

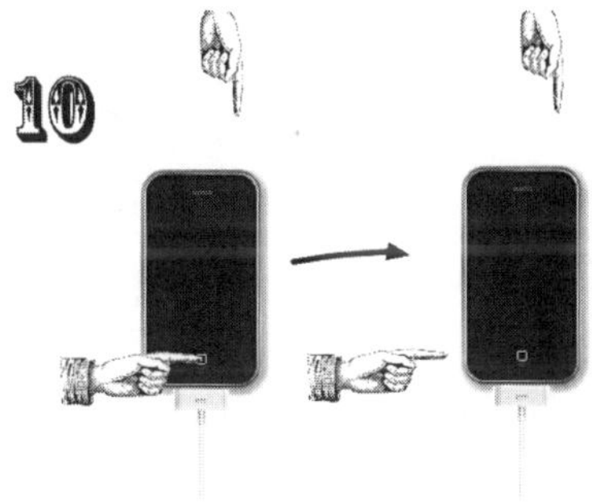

In DFU mode, there should be nothing on the iPhone screen except backlit blackness, as shown in Figure 2-20.

Figure 2-20.
DFU Mode: screen is lit, but black

On Windows, you should hear two USB beeps—one "device disconnected" beep after the first 10

seconds, then one "device connected beep" once you enter DFU mode. On Windows XP, you should also see a device identification bubble in the taskbar (Figure 2-21).

Figure 2-21.
Taskbar notification in Windows XP

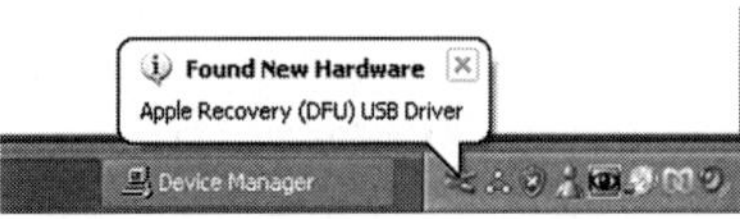

Once you're in DFU mode, iTunes should give you the same recovery mode message it gives with the normal recovery mode **[Hack #2.04]** (Figure 2-22).

Figure 2-22.
iTunes detecting the iPhone in DFU mode

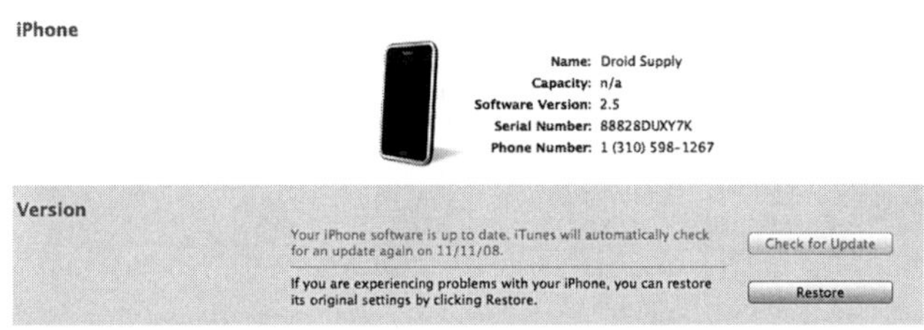

Next, option-click (Mac) or shift-click (Windows) the Restore button. This will allow you to restore to the firmware of your choice. A link to all of Apple's firmware files can be found in **[Hack #1.02]**, and you can either download a custom firmware online or create your own with jailbreaking tools like Pwnage **[Hack #1.03]** (Figure 2-23). If you simply click "Restore" and allow iTunes to choose the firmware, you will virginize your phone.

Figure 2-23.
Loading a firmware image

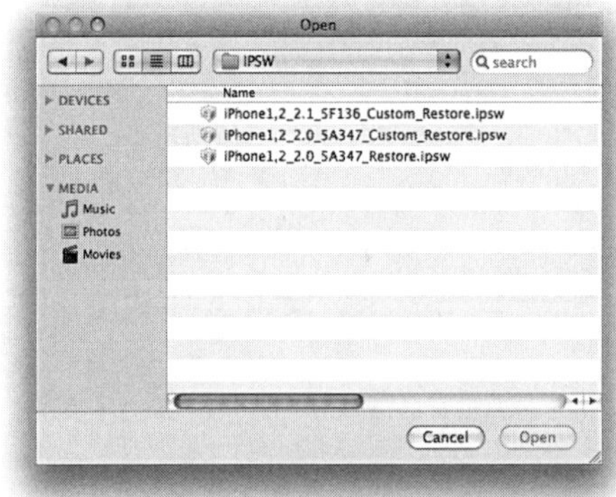

Exiting DFU Mode

You can back out of DFU mode as long as you haven't started loading a new firmware image.

The steps are:

1. With the phone plugged into your computer, hold down both the Power and Home buttons for 10 seconds or longer—until the screen changes.
2. On Windows, you may hear a beep or get a USB device notification as your iPhone comes out of DFU mode.
3. Your phone should boot as normal. If it's still off after 10 seconds, you should be able to turn it on by pressing the Power button briefly.

HACK 2.06: Get Quality Support with iPhone Hacking

Courteous, experienced hacking support is available 24/7.

Although this book attempts to address as many issues as possible, it is still likely that you may encounter a completely new and unique situation with your iPhone. Luckily, the Internet is full of great resources that can help you determine a solution to the problem.

The big problem is that iPhone hacking is, by definition, unofficial and mostly unauthorized. And even when hacking is tolerated, or even privately encouraged, it is unreasonable to expect a large corporation to support not only its own software, but the broad scope of possible hacked variants of that software. Thus, it's necessary to go elsewhere for support. Fortunately, support is available—in fact, the organized support available for iPhone hacking surpasses that of most software companies, and is free.

For those unfamiliar with the open source software movement, it is quite a cultural shock to find that they can often contact the real author of a piece of free software—and get courteous and helpful email support. In an age of self-help forums and pay-per-incident support calls, the accessibility and, for lack of a better word, the humanity shown by open source software developers is legendary.

The Community

Although there are hundreds—if not thousands—of websites, forums, portals, and blogs dedicated to the iPhone, the actual core of hackers who do the real work are few in number. Perhaps several dozen key contributors do the intellectually stimulating but long and painstaking work of discovering the exploits, creating stable, well-tested software to open up the iPhone and iPod touch, and packaging it so that anyone can use it.

In the flurry to monetize the iPhone phenomena in every way possible, some application vendors have taken open, free work and software from a core iPhone hacking team, wrapped it in a proprietary application, passed it off as their own work (or given perfunctory acknowledgement) in order to make money through licensing, advertising, and "Please Donate" online tip jars.

Arguably, these carpetbagging "script kiddies" have added some value—perhaps in packaging up hard-to-use command-line tools into a friendly "click here to jailbreak" application. But as they did not develop the original hacks themselves, they are not necessarily capable of fixing the bugs, or reversing any damage that their one-trick applications may cause.

The best people to support a hack—and to accurately represent what it's capable of doing—are the authors themselves.

The iPhone Dev Team

We keep speaking about the iPhone hacking community. Specifically, the iPhone hacker community consists of several dozen core individuals who have enabled or created most of the innovations you will see in this book. The largest group has associated under the banner of the iPhone Dev Team. Their website and blogs have moved around a bit, but at the moment their main portal can be found at http://wikee.iphwn.org (Figure 2-24) and their blog at http://blog.iphone-dev.org (Figure 2-25).

Figure 2-24.
iPhone Dev Team Portal

Figure 2-25.
iPhone Dev Team Blog

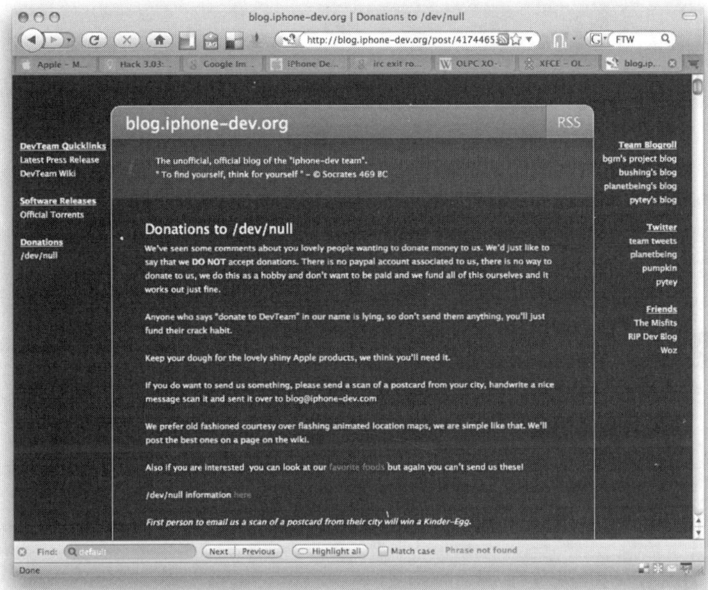

Hackint0sh

The Hackint0sh forum (www.hackint0sh.org) is a huge community of more than 80,000 members and covers a wide range of Apple hacks including iPods, iPhones, Apple TVs, and Mac OS X in general. This is the primary forum for support on iPhone Dev Team hacks and an excellent resource for new and experienced hackers (Figures 2-26 and 2-27).

Figure 2-26.
Hackint0sh welcome

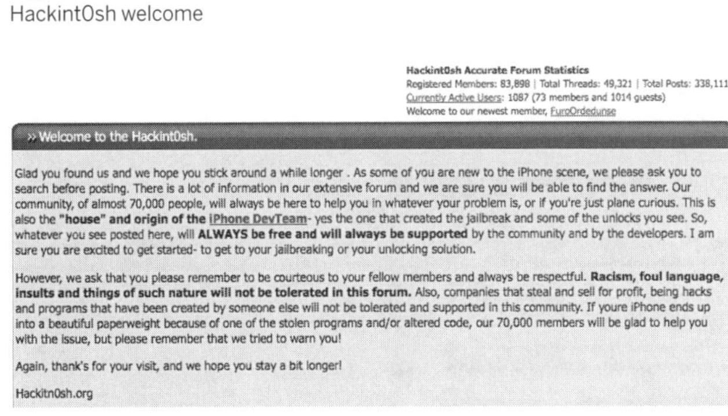

Figure 2-27.
HackintOsh forum

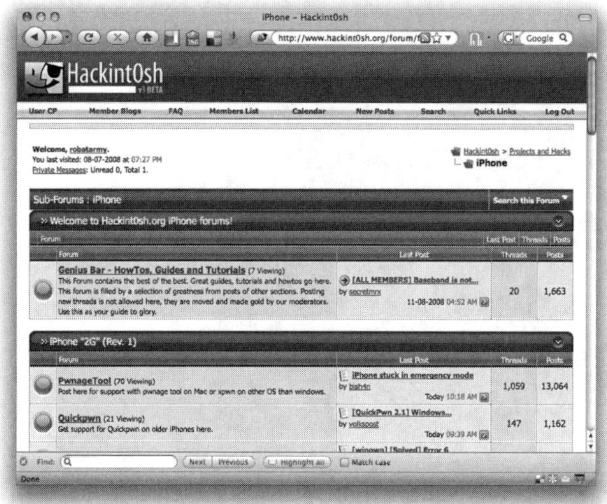

The iPhone Wiki

Another fantastic, ad-free, real-deal site is www.theiphonewiki.com (Figure 2-28), started and maintained by **GeoHot** (George Hotz), who was first to unlock an iPhone and who continues to make major breakthroughs on iPhone hacking. The wiki has the clearest, most concise, just-the-facts analysis of all the known exploits on the iPhone and iPod touches. Although sometimes hard to read for nonengineers, this is a warm respite from the biased shilling and link posting that pervades the gadget blogosphere. Hotz's own very technical blog can be found at http://iphonejtag.blogspot.com.

Figure 2-28.
The iPhone wiki

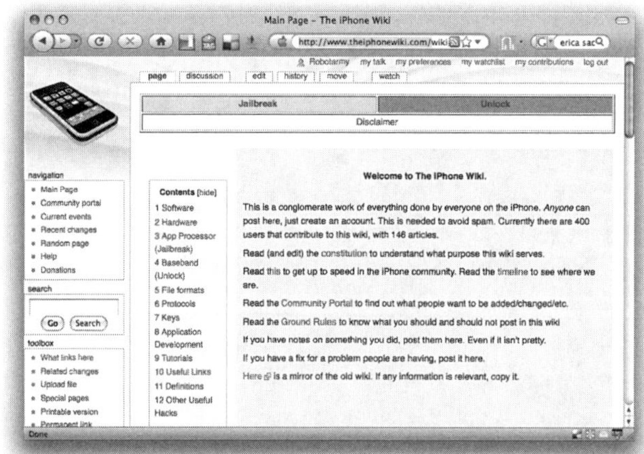

iClarified

Another great resource that is well edited, well maintained, and easy to use is http://iclarified.com (Figure 2-29). This site is clean and concise; they also operate their own iPhone application repositories for both Installer.app and Cydia **[Hack #1.04]**.

Figure 2-29.
iClarified's website

modmyi.com

Another well-established site supporting iPhone hacking is www.modmyi.com (Figure 2-30). Although their site is cluttered, their content is good. Like iClarified, they provide iPhone application repositories and hosting for user-created applications and skins.

Figure 2-30.
The modmyi site

Real-Time Tech Support: IRC

Sometimes the wikis, forums, and step-by-step tutorials just don't have the answer. And no matter how much searching you do, sometimes it helps to have a human being point you in the right direction.

If you still can't find what you're looking for on any iPhone hacking websites, then this is your solution: IRC (Internet Relay Chat) connects users from all over the world. IRC servers provide chat rooms called *channels* where you can get help day or night.

To start chatting, you must first install an IRC client on your computer or iPhone. Mac users can download Colloquy from http://colloquy.info. PC users can download mIRC from www.mirc.com. To get an IRC client on your iPhone, you can search for IRC in Cydia or Installer; Mobile Colloquy and iRCm are two applications available as of this writing.

Once you have your IRC client running, add this server: *irc.osx86.hu* with the port set to *6667*. If you already have IRC properly configured, you can just type this URL into your browser: irc://irc.osx86.hu/iphone. See Figure 2-31.

Although this is by no means a minitutorial on IRC, you can get a list of channels to join by typing:

```
/list
```

And you can join a channel by typing `/join <name of channel>`, such as:

```
/join #iphone
```

Several useful channels are #iphone, #iphone-dev, and #itouch.

If you're not familiar with IRC, the basic rules are: don't post too much; don't harass; be polite; follow the directions you see when you join the room. Once you've joined one of the channels, you can ask your questions. You're likely to get your answers, as many of the iPhone Dev Team developers inhabit these rooms whenever they're online, which is most of the time.

Figure 2-31.
IRC client in the #iphone channel

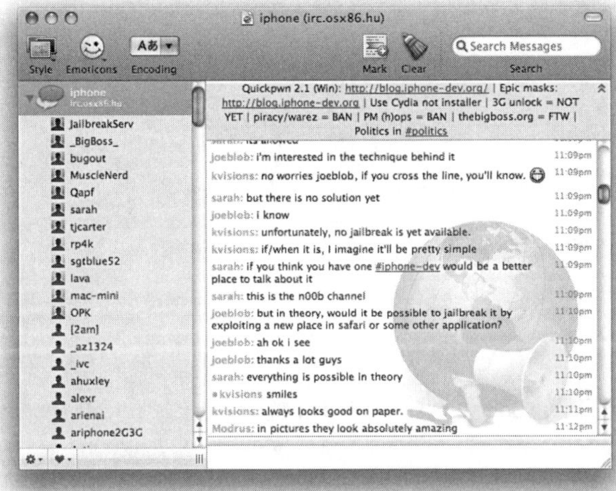

Some Favorites

One of the best ways to find reputable, primary sources of information on iPhone is to seek out the websites of your favorite application authors.

For instance, a prolific contributor to the community, Erica Sadun, has created a number of indispensable command-line utilities and provided source code as a starting point for iPhone development, and she's even written a very popular book on the subject: see http://ericasadun.com (Figure 2-32).

Figure 2-32.
Erica Sadun's website

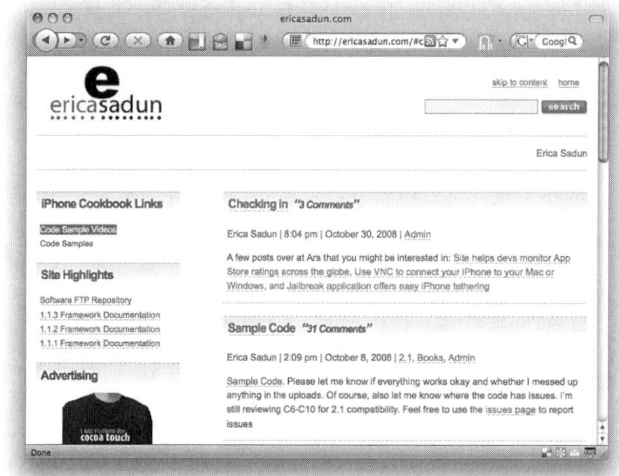

Jay Freeman (**saurik**) is a Dev Team member and software master who single-handedly developed Winterboard (for iPhone skinning), ported Java to the iPhone, and created the open iPhone distribution application Cydia. He also completely simplified development of jailbroken applications so that you can do iPhone development right on the iPhone itself! See www.saurik.com (Figure 2-33).

Figure 2-33.
Jay Freeman's website

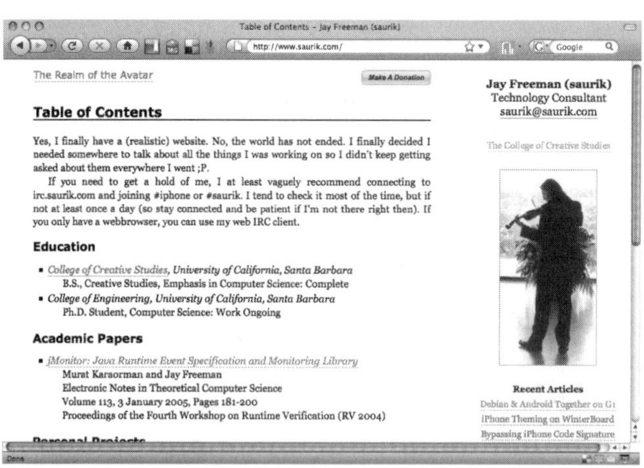

BigBoss, a Dev Team member and early repository hoster, created the popular and tremendously useful BossPrefs application used to configure many of the system-wide settings on jailbroken phones. BigBoss's site at http://thebigboss.org has great resources and is one of the biggest application repositories (Figure 2-34).

Figure 2-34.
BigBoss's website

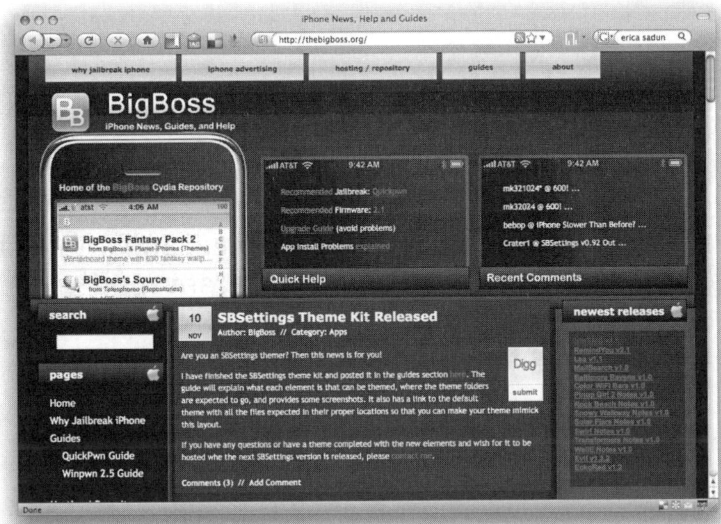

Some forums have pleas for donations, with comments like "Help keep applications like this in development," despite the fact that they have no relationship to the developers. If you feel compelled to donate in order to support the iPhone hacking community, consider donating directly to the individual hackers and developers who create the applications you use. You can usually find their personal blog or website with a little searching.

03 MESSAGING AND COMMUNICATION

Over the last several decades, computers, phones, and Internet platforms have provided us with dozens of different modes for text-based multimedia communication: email, chat, text messaging, instant messaging, and multimedia messaging.

The iPhone and iPod touch support email exceptionally well, providing high-fidelity support for many common email attachments. The addition of near-instant "push" email support to the iPhone—for free—has enhanced real-time communication.

This chapter introduces the iPhone email system and various clever ways to use it. It also covers the other must-have communication tools—SMS, IRC, and IM—and ways to get the most out of these protocols. Finally, it presents several workarounds to solve the iPhone's remaining deficiencies in these areas.

HACK 3.01: Get the Most from iPhone Email

You can use a free Yahoo! push email account as extra "cloud" storage for your iPhone.

Sure, the iPhone is a "computer in the palm of your hand." But it lacks a few key features that desktops have. The iPhone has a tiny keyboard, making it difficult to enter long URLs. Frustratingly, the iPhone still lacks (as of this writing) copy-and-paste functionality, making the manipulation of URLs—a key part of Internet power surfing—a difficult task. And the iPhone has resisted the urge to provide system-wide filesystem access, preferring to keep data (pictures, videos, podcasts, and notes) in their own application "silos."

Fortunately, the iPhone does have a feature that can be leveraged into a makeshift copy-and-paste and filesystem—email. Many of the built-in iPhone applications have an integrated "email this" feature that allows URLs and picture attachments to be emailed. And because the iPhone can connect to the many free mail servers, saving files and URLs is easier than it seems.

iPhone Email Support

The iPhone's email application is probably the easiest to set up of any phone-based email. It has flexible support for IMAP, POP, Exchange, and AOL. One of the ways that iPhone email excels is in its ability to preview HTML email, display most common attachments (*.pdf*, *.doc* files, and *.xls* files), as well as to follow the links in emails.

One of the main complaints about early versions of the iPhone was its lack of "push" email—the iPhone "pulled" email on a schedule and the shortest interval that you could set for updates was every 5 minutes. That was resolved with firmware Version 2, putting the iPhone on an even playing field with the ubiquitous BlackBerry. You can get push email from an Exchange server, from Apple's MobileMe service, or even from a free Yahoo! email account (Figure 3-1). iPhone (and iPod touch) email is easy to set up even without being connected to a computer.

Figure 3-1.
Yahoo! push email

Email as a Clipboard and Hard Drive

Although there was a time, long ago, when large email attachments were a burden, for most of the free email services, those times are past. Yahoo! and Google both provide free IMAP accounts with tremendous storage (Google calls their plan "Infinity+1," as they are continually increasing the amount of storage available to each user). Therefore, it's quite easy to set up an additional email account that's only for private use for your own personal storage.

Anything that the iPhone can play can be attached to an email. Most graphic image formats, MP3 and AAC music, MP4 videos, Microsoft Office (Word, PowerPoint, and Excel files), and PDF files can be viewed. As mentioned, Yahoo!'s email even supports push on the iPhone, so it's an ideal candidate for this use, as there will be almost no delay between sending yourself a file or link—from your desktop—and having it show up on the phone.

Setting Up

The first step is to create a free account at Yahoo! (Figure 3-2).

Figure 3-2.
Yahoo! Email signup—you know the drill.

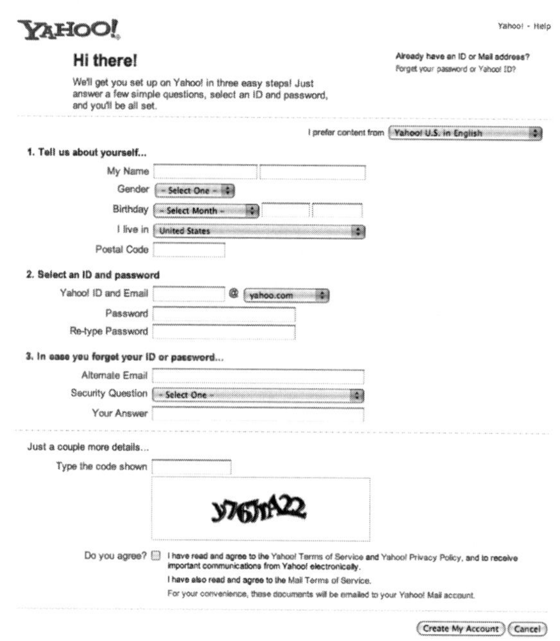

Go to Settings→Mail→Accounts→Add Account and choose Yahoo! Mail (Figure 3-3). Fill out the required information in the new window (Figure 3-4). Once you're done, just hit the Save button at the top right. Your iPhone will then connect with Yahoo! to verify the information. Once it finishes verifying, your additional account(s) will be saved and visible in the Accounts section of the Mail screen. If you click Advanced, you can verify that push mail is enabled.

Figure 3-3.
So many mail options!

Figure 3-4.
Yahoo! free push email storage

You can send any reasonably sized files—including multimegabyte MP3s and movies—to this email "hard drive" (Figure 3-5).

Figure 3-5.
Sending files to the private email account

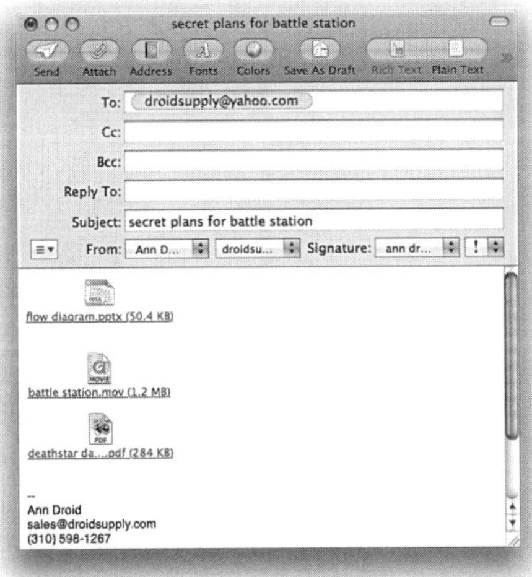

Once these notes-to-self get pushed to your iPhone, you can access any of the documents for view or playback by clicking their icons in the message (Figures 3-6 and 3-7).

Figure 3-6.
Email storage

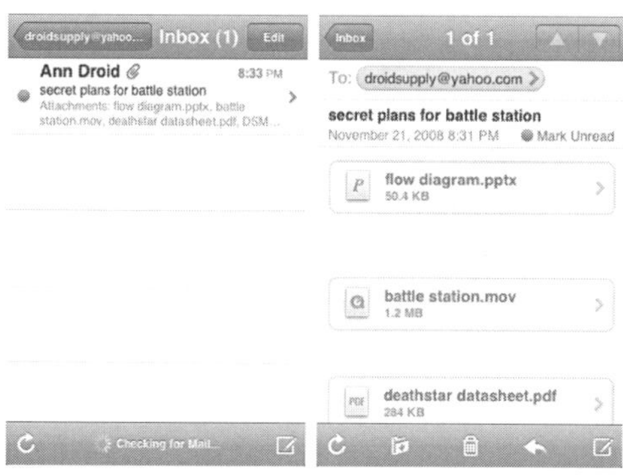

Figure 3-7.
Viewing an attachment

If you ever need a hard copy, you can quickly and easily forward them to someone who has a printer. You can even create "folders"—a very filesystem-esque concept—via the Yahoo! Webmail page or the iPhone and organize your various "files" (attachments) just like you might on your hard drive. The great thing is that these will be cached (downloaded) onto your iPhone, be web-accessible, so if you should need to restore your iPhone, you won't lose any of them.

Another useful trick is to bookmark links on websites. Many websites have a "recommend this" or "email this link" feature for articles. You can use this private iPhone email address for those kinds of messages, so they don't clutter up your normal inbox.

While we're on the subject of free "push" services, it's important to note that Google offers free Calendar and Contact syncing. Check out www.google.com/mobile/apple/sync.html.

Copy and Paste

As mentioned before, the closest the iPhone comes to copy-and-paste is the inclusion of an "email this" in many iPhone applications, allowing one to send web URLs, notes, pictures (Figures 3-8 and 3-9), and on jailbroken phones, movies, and any other file accessible on the phone.

Figure 3-8.
"Copying" a URL to the "clipboard"

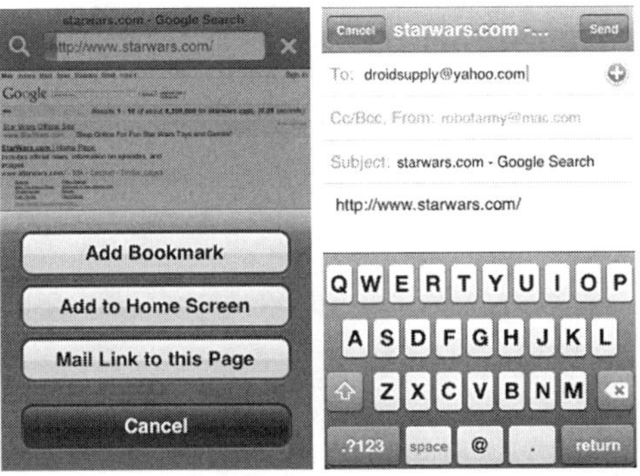

Figure 3-9.
"Copying" a photo to the "clipboard"

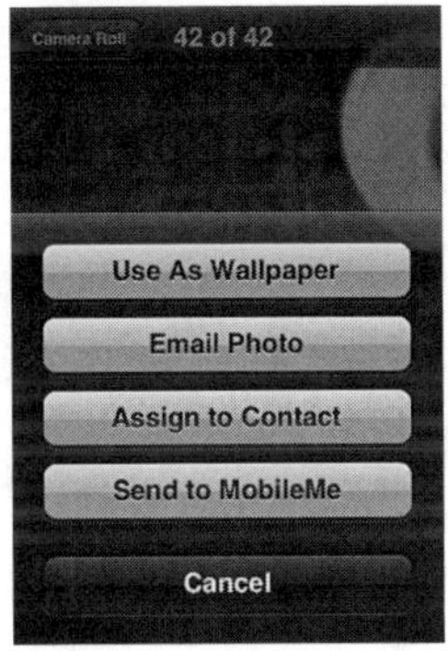

If your phone is jailbroken, installing MobileFinder (found in Cydia **[Hack #1.04]** and shown in Figure 3-10) will allow you to attach any file in the entire filesystem to an email. This is very convenient for backups and for sending movies, audio files, or other content that is on the iPhone and needs to be backed up, shared, or saved in the inbox for convenient access. Using MobileFinder **[Hack #1.05]**, navigate to the file you want, as in Figure 3-11, then click the "E-Mail" button on the bottom left. This will launch your default email account with the selected file attached.

Figure 3-10.
MobileFinder Icon

Figure 3-11.
Backing up the Address Book via email with MobileFinder

HACK 3.02: Unleash the Full Power of Texting

Go beyond Apple's barebones SMS application.

The Mobile SMS application that comes on the iPhone is functional, but it lacks many of the text messaging features that people have grown used to on other phones. An initial lack of multiple-recipient texting was remedied in firmware Version 1.1.3, but some serious limitations remained. Multimedia Messaging Service (MMS), also known as *picture messaging*, provided by every mobile carrier and supported by most camera phones, is completely missing from the iPhone.

There are other reasons the built-in SMS just doesn't cut it. Many people want to send canned messages from a message template—"I'm going to be late, please have the call without me"—without having to type it all. And even though the iPod touch, not being a phone, doesn't have any built-in texting support, people want to send messages with it as well.

Luckily, there are some useful tricks and third-party applications to help you get around the SMS and MMS limitations. Many of these solutions use built-in features of the iPhone or are App Store apps and thus don't require jailbreaking.

Send Multiple Text Messages via Email

Prior to firmware 1.1.3, sending a SMS to multiple recipients was impossible. Even if your iPhone has 1.1.3 or later, the SMS that you send to multiple recipients still diminishes your plan's monthly allowance of text messages. Sending text messages via email conserves your valuable text message allotment and allows iPhone owners to use email groups to still send SMS to multiple recipients.

The only requirements for accomplishing this are that you know what cellular service provider each of your recipients uses, and that you are connected to the Internet with either Wi-Fi, 3G, or EDGE. No jailbreak is required! As long as you know this information, the rest of this process is a piece of cake.

First, write down the 10-digit cellphone numbers of the contacts that you would like to send the SMS message to. Next, open your email account and compose a new email. In the *To* field, type in the 10-digit phone number followed by an "@" sign and the domain address associated with that person's cellular service provider. The domain addresses and character limits of major U.S. cellular service providers are listed here:

- Older AT&T Wireless: xxxxxxxxxx@mmode.com (110- and 160-character limits for TDMA subscribers and mMode/Next Generation network users, respectively)
- Cingular: xxxxxxxxxx@mobile.mycingular.net (160-character limit)
- Newer AT&T Wireless: xxxxxxxxxx@txt.att.net
- T-Mobile: xxxxxxxxxx@tmomail.net (140-character limit)
- Verizon: xxxxxxxxxx@vtext.com (160-character limit)
- Sprint PCS: xxxxxxxxxx@messaging.sprintpcs.com (160-character limit)

Say, for example, that you wanted to send messages to the recipients whose numbers are (619) 123-4567, an AT&T Wireless subscriber, and (818) 123-4567, a Verizon subscriber. You would write them as 6191234567@txt.att.net and 8181234567@vtext.com, pressing the blue plus sign button to add additional recipients. Characters written in the subject and message fields of the email will be included in the text messages as "*(subject)message*". Figure 3-12 shows the completed message.

Figure 3-12.
Entering multiple numbers into a new email to send as SMS

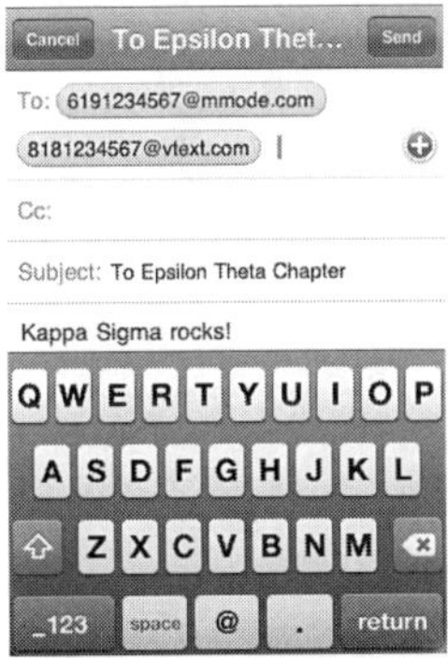

Because you are sending the SMS messages via email, it won't be billed as a text message, and it won't count against your monthly allowance of text messages. However, it will still count as an incoming SMS message for the recipient, which could count against *their* monthly text message allowance and/or incur a charge, depending on their service provider.

In addition to multiple SMS recipients, this email technique will work for a single recipient. By sending SMS text messages to one or more recipients using your email, you'll be saving money, as these won't be billed as normal outgoing SMS text messages.

A similar approach is taken by several of the App Store SMS messaging applications, such as Maildash by PureBlend Software (Figure 3-13) and Quicksend from Absolute Apps. These applications use SMS gateways to forward emails to SMS clients.

Figure 3-13.
Using Maildash

Send SMS Through Your Instant Messenger

A second way to get text messages out of your iPhone or iPod touch is through instant messaging. Both Yahoo! and AIM use SMS gateways that allow you to text directly from an IM client. To send text messages via IM, just add a "buddy" using the recipient's phone number with a plus before it, as shown in Figure 3-14. You'll get responses to this SMS in your IM chat.

Figure 3-14.
Adding a mobile number in Mac AIM

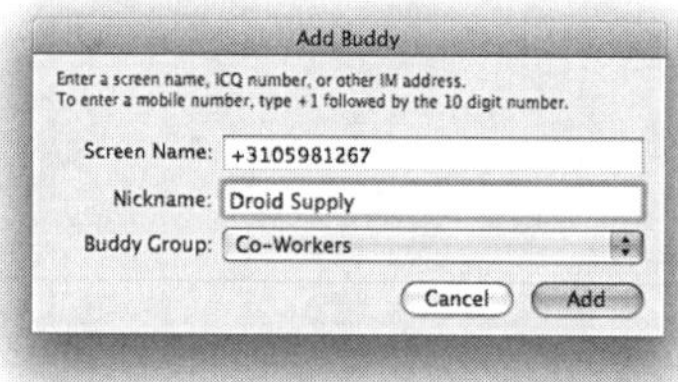

Although AIM can text only domestically, Yahoo! has some worldwide texting capability. You can see a list of supported locations here: http://messenger.yahoo.com/features/sms.

There's an App Store app called beejive (Figure 3-15) that also sends SMS through AIM or Yahoo! messaging, and integrates with your iPhone address book so you don't have to manually add the recipient phone numbers.

Figure 3-15.
Sending SMS with beejive

Sending MMS Messages

Here is a way for you to send and receive MMS without any jailbreaking whatsoever. As with SMS, to send a picture message, you must first know what cellular service provider the recipient uses. Once you know this information, use one of following MMS email addresses, replacing xxxxxxxxxx with the recipient's 10-digit mobile number:

- AT&T Wireless: xxxxxxxxxx@mms.att.net
- Cingular: xxxxxxxxxx@mms.mycingular.net
- Sprint PCS: xxxxxxxxxx@messaging.sprintpcs.com
- T-Mobile: xxxxxxxxxx@tmomail.net
- Verizon: xxxxxxxxxx@vzwpix.com

Once you have the recipient's information ready, open the picture from your iPhone's Camera Roll, and click the icon at the bottom left to pull up a menu (Figure 3-16). Select Email Photo, and you'll be brought to the email composition screen with your picture attached to the email. On the first line, enter the recipient's cell number followed by the appropriate MMS email address as shown in Figure 3-17. If you want to send it to more than one person, just add an additional email address in the *To* field. Then press Send, and the recipient will receive the picture as a normal MMS message.

 Although sending this MMS via email is free for you, the recipient will still be charged by their service provider for an incoming MMS message.

 If the recipient has an iPhone that does not support MMS, you will have to send the picture to their regular email address instead of the previously described MMS email addresses.

 Once you know this process will work, you can add a "phone-email" to your contacts' email listings in your Address Book. You could also do this in advance on your computer's address book and sync it over to your iPhone.

Figure 3-16.
The email Photo button

Figure 3-17.
Sending an MMS message to a recipient using Verizon Wireless

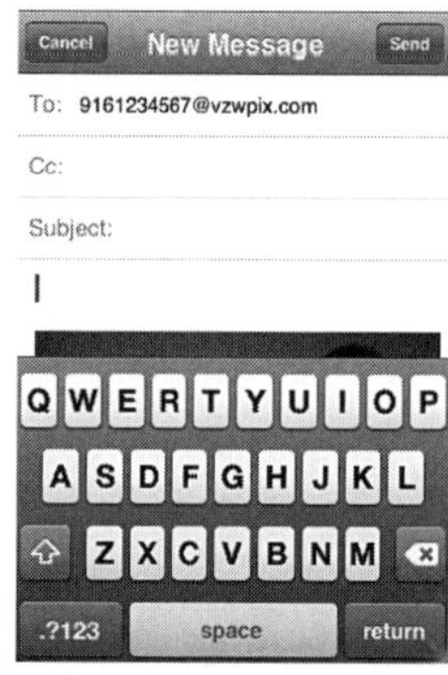

Receiving Multimedia Message Service (MMS) on the iPhone

Unfortunately, the iPhone does not support Multimedia Messaging Service (MMS). Some carriers implement an alternate method of receiving the message via the Web. In the U.S. market on AT&T, when you receive an MMS, you may get an email message such as the one in Figure 3-18, telling you to log into a web page. Without copy-and-paste functionality, accessing this message is a pain, but it can be done.

Figure 3-18.
The email

Enter this data into the form they send you (Figure 3-19).

Figure 3-19.
Retrieving an image

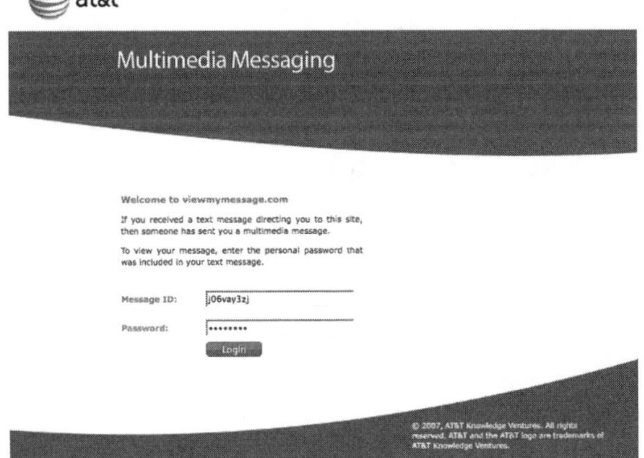

This allows the message to show up, as you can see in Figure 3-20.

Figure 3-20.
The picture retrieved

Because of this inconvenience, it's best to have your would-be senders find an alternative way to send you multimedia messages. Some options are:

1. Have the sender attach the media via email to any email address you can check on your iPhone. If you have a lot of friends who send you messages, you can set up a separate email account **[Hack #3.01]**. As long as the media is in an iPhone-compatible format (JPEG, PNG, TIFF, MP3, and so on), you'll be able to play it back or view it on the iPhone. And because this process is done completely by email, neither you nor the sender will incur any MMS charges from your service providers. If the sender is on an iPhone as well, the solution is obvious—have them email the picture.
2. Alternatively, if the sender only knows your cell number, they can host the picture on a web page (if it's not already hosted), and send an SMS message containing a link to the web page. Depending on their phone, they may have a feature that allows them to send a link as a text message, or to copy and paste the URL from their phone's web browser into an email.

[Hack #3.04] shows how to receive MMS natively—but requires jailbreaking.

HACK 3.03: Text Your iPhone with Your Desktop Instant Messenger

Texting is a fast way to get data to your iPhone.

Email is a great way to send messages to your phone **[Hack #3.01]**, but often, tiny ephemeral to-dos or URL messages get lost in the morass of distracting email messages. And if you don't have push email configured just right, the message might not arrive right away. The sheer inconvenience of booting up an email program, typing in your iPhone email address, and waiting for it to send begs for another solution.

Fortunately, there's a way to get important notes onto the iPhone: text messaging. Using an IM-to-SMS gateway such as those provided by the AOL Instant Messaging (AIM) or Yahoo! Messenger desktop clients, you can very easily send URLs and short messages to your phone. This gives you prominent notification on your phone's screen, as well as an audible alert, so if the message is "don't forget to buy milk," you've got a good chance of noticing it before you get home.

Depending on the text message option attached to your cellular plan, you may pay extra to send or receive text messages.

Add Your Phone to Your Instant Messenger

First, create an account on either AIM or Yahoo!; for this example, we use an AIM user called "iphonehacks." The look of the screen varies by client (we're using a Mac here) but the approach is the same in most clients: add a user using the plus sign and the 10-digit number (Figure 3-21).

Figure 3-21.
Cell phone numbers in AIM

Note to Self

Sending a note to yourself is quite fast due to the fast-delivery design of the text messaging system (that's part of what your text message plan is paying for). Typing phone numbers into the IM is probably the quickest way to get them from the desktop to the phone and not lose it, which is especially useful if someone is reading a number to you (Figure 3-22). The number will be converted to a text message through AOL's IM-to-SMS gateway, and sent to the iPhone. The iPhone recognizes it as a phone number, so you can click it and quickly dial it.

Figure 3-22.
Sending a phone number

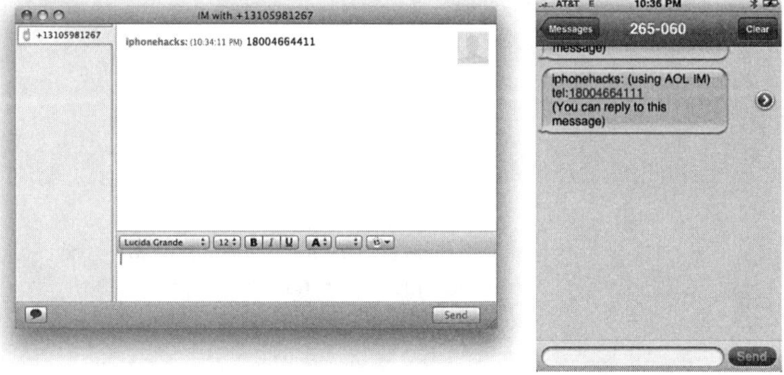

Now your small bits of information—shopping lists, to-do lists, and the like—won't get lost in your email inbox when sent via SMS.

Shrinking URLs for Text Messages

Let's say you needed to note down an address for the Apple Store (Figure 3-23) and you wanted to send that map URL to your phone.

Figure 3-23.
Selecting a Google Maps URL

Print
Send
Link
Paste link in email or IM
Paste HTML to embed in website
Customize and preview embedded map
Get directions - Search nearby -
Save to My Maps - Send
Edit
Topanga Plaza

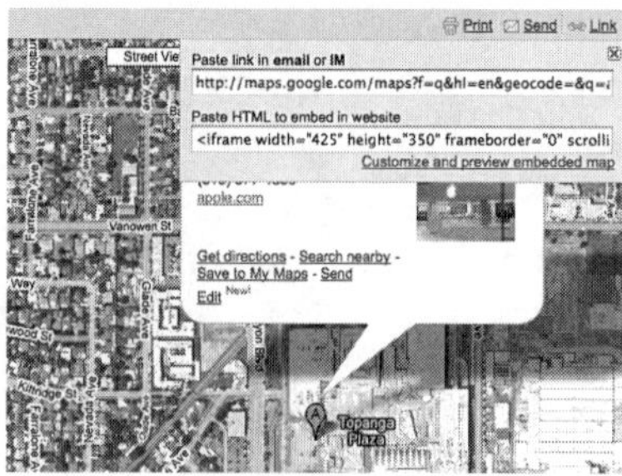

Because URLs can be very long, if you send them via SMS, they're going to be chopped into multiple text messages, may cost more to send, and won't be clickable when you receive them anyway (Figure 3-24).

Figure 3-24.
A long URL broken into two messages

AT&T
11:08 PM
Messages
265-060
Clear
http://maps.google.com/maps?f=q&hl=en&geocode=&q=apple+store+topanga&sll=34.18834,-118.607175&sspn=0.010969,0.017896&ie=UTF
iphonehacks: (using AOL IM) -2/2- 8&ll=34.191198,-118.607175&spn=0.010969,0.017896&t=h&z=16&iwloc=A
(You can reply to this message)
Send

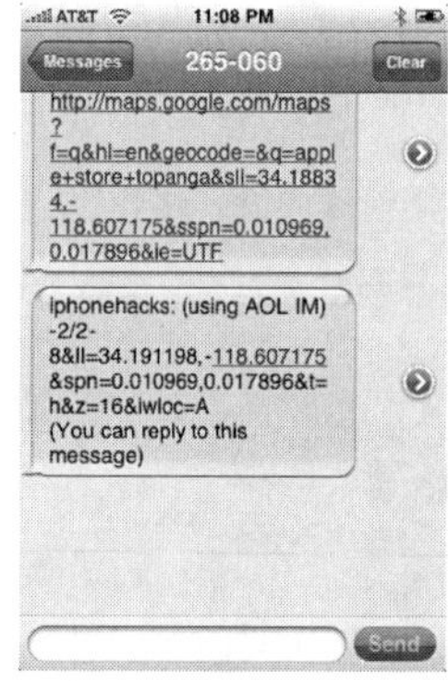

The trick is to go to http://tinyurl.com. There you will find a form where you can paste in the URL. TinyURL hosts a link to your URL that is much shorter—just a few characters (Figure 3-25).

Figure 3-25.
TinyURL makes URLs tiny

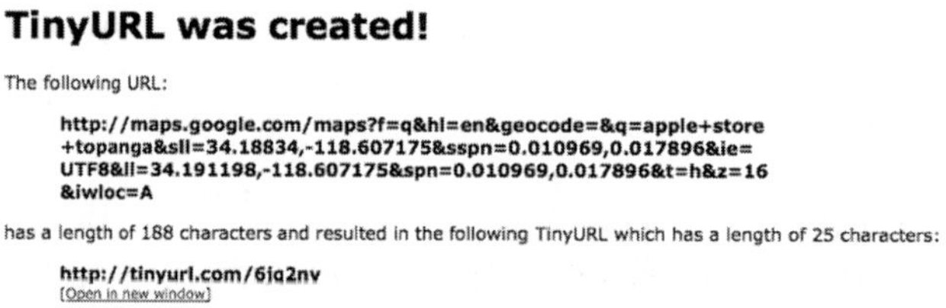

TinyURL was created!
The following URL:
http://maps.google.com/maps?f=q&hl=en&geocode=&q=apple+store+topanga&sll=34.18834,-118.607175&sspn=0.010969,0.017896&ie=UTF8&ll=34.191198,-118.607175&spn=0.010969,0.017896&t=h&z=16&iwloc=A
has a length of 188 characters and resulted in the following TinyURL which has a length of 25 characters:
http://tinyurl.com/6jq2nv
[Open in new window]

These tiny URLs fit clickably into a single SMS (Figure 3-26).

Figure 3-26.
Clickable tiny URL

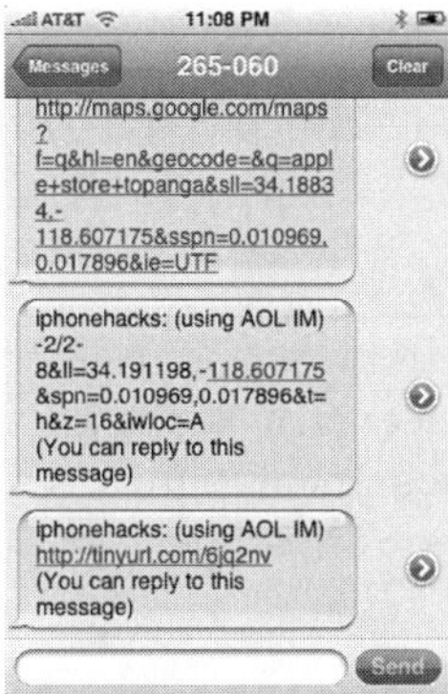

It's worth noting that Google already provides another way to send the URL via its own SMS gateway, as shown in Figure 3-27. A number of websites are incorporating features that allow you to send bits of information to your mobile via SMS, so look for them.

Figure 3-27.
Google offers send-to-phone

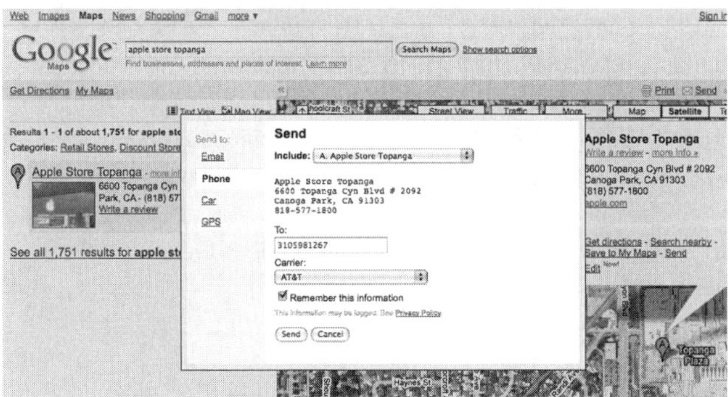

HACK 3.04: Enable MMS Picture Messaging on Your iPhone

A little change to your iPhone's messaging plan lets you send and receive MMS messages with SwirlyMMS on jailbroken phones.

The iPhone does so many things quite well, making it all the more frustrating when the iPhone fails to perform some normal task. Tethering, copy-and-paste, forwarding SMS…the list goes on. And sending and receiving MMS picture messages, just like on any normal phone, is another one of those frustrations.

Some people don't want to work around their phone's inability to receive MMS, as in **[Hack #3.03]**—they want it to "just work." The good thing is that the iPhone is very capable of it. It just takes some software—and a change to the texting plan—to make it work. Specifically, it requires:

1. Changing your cellular plan to enable Multimedia Messaging (a.k.a. Picture Messaging)
2. Jailbreaking the phone **[Hack #1.03]**
3. Installing SwirlyMMS

Picture Messaging, WAP, and WAP Push

Wireless Application Protocol, or WAP, is a standard allowing phones to access the Internet. WAP is used extensively on most phones that have a "wireless Internet" feature. Because most phones have far less computing power than a desktop computer, this set of standards allowed web pages to be formatted for the small screen and to reduce the bandwidth necessary to deliver them.

For the protocol-minded, WAP could be considered a sort of "TCP/IP" for phones, providing TCP-like streams through the Wireless Transaction Protocol (WTP), UDP-like data delivery through the Wireless Datagram Protocol (WDP), and a sort of "compressed HTTP" through the Wireless Session Protocol (WSP).

WAP Push is a network-to-phone push protocol that sends a WAP URL to the phone for it to then retrieve automatically without user intervention—sort of like texting a web address directly to the phone. The iPhone was promoted as the first phone with "real Internet" and, like many advanced smartphones, was able to use the Internet TCP/IP protocols directly. Subsequently, Apple developed a separate push architecture for MobileMe and Exchange on the iPhone.

As a result, most iPhone data plans do not have the "WAP Push" feature enabled by default. Before you can add support for MMS, you must add WAP Push to your plan, without removing access to the normal WAP gateway that the iPhone uses. Typically, you can call your provider and request that it be added to your plan if you don't already have it. If they offer to transfer you to "iPhone technical support," don't let them, because you're asking for a very un-iPhonic thing.

The technical changes that need to be made, once you get hold of your carrier's technical sales representative (see following section), are:

1. Enable WAP Push.
2. Preserve both the old and new WAP gateway (i.e., don't disable the iPhone features).
3. Change the texting plan to a non-iPhone plan (i.e., a texting plan that supports Picture messaging).
4. Leave the iPhone data plan intact (allows visual voicemail to work).
5. Resend over-the-air activation messages, or OTAs, to the phone.

The forums at www.swirlyspace.com have lots of data on how to configure various worldwide GSM carriers to allow MMS.

Adding WAP Push to a U.S. AT&T Account

Although your carrier may vary, the majority of U.S. domestic iPhones are on AT&T, so this hack will show you how to get it working on AT&T.

1. Call 888-892-9760. Navigate through the responses until you reach an operator. Validate your account credentials to their satisfaction.
2. Ask to speak to a technical sales representative.
3. Ask if you can please remove your iPhone text messaging plan, and add the normal text messaging plan with MMS features (WAP Push).

Sometimes, depending on the level of expertise of the tech support person, they may not understand the goal. One way to make it clear is to say that you want the ability to use the SIM card in both an iPhone and in another phone that supports Picture Messaging (MMS). That way, they will know that they need to keep the iPhone features working (iPhone data plan, visual voicemail, and access to the iPhone-specific WAP gateways that allow WAP traffic to go to the iPhone) as well as the new WAP gateways that will enable the WAP push. As an added bonus, you can now swap your SIM card into other phones, as long as they are unlocked or locked to AT&T's network.

Figures 3-28 and 3-29 show screenshots of an AT&T plan configured to allow MMS. The texting plan is "Messaging 200."

Figure 3-28.
Data plan before

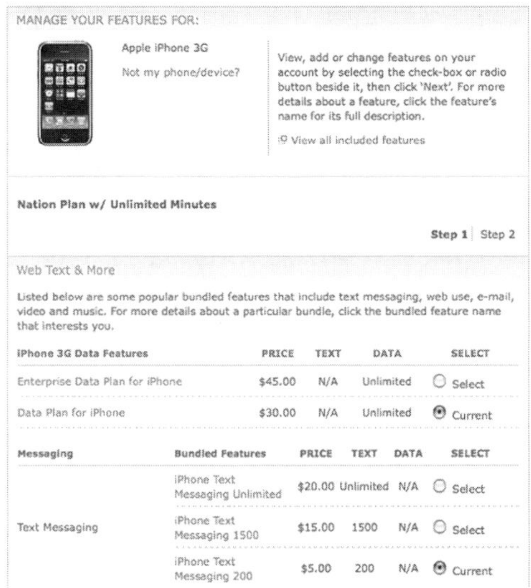

Figure 3-29.
Data plan after

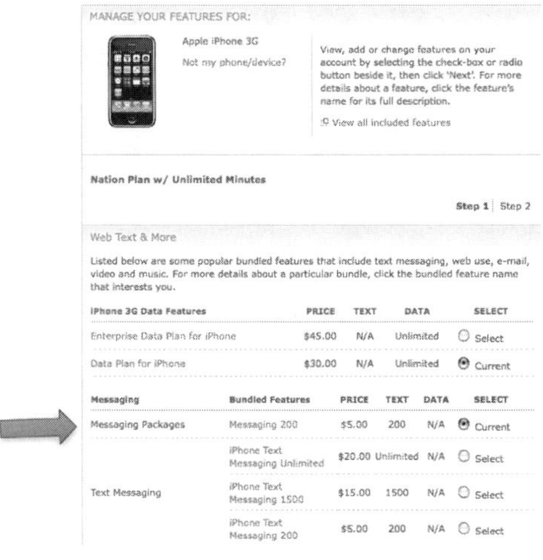

Using SwirlyMMS

SwirlyMMS (www.swirlyspace.com) can be installed with Cydia on a jailbroken **[Hack #1.03]** phone. This app allows you to send MMS pictures to phones capable of receiving them, and to receive MMS as well.

Launch SwirlyMMS, and you'll see a screen with a couple of buttons. Click the Settings button and enter your MMS information (Figure 3-30). You will need to contact your cellular provider, or the SwirlyMMS forums, to determine the appropriate information. Settings for a number of popular providers can be found on www.swirlyspace.com.

Here are settings that worked for SwirlyMMS on the U.S. AT&T network:

> MMSC: http://mmsc.cingular.com
> Proxy: wireless.cingular.com:80
> APN: wap.cingular
> Username: <blank>
> Password: <blank>

Figure 3-30.
SwirlyMMS

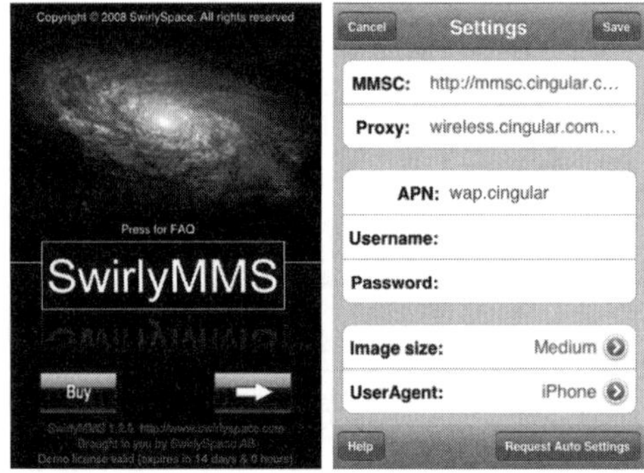

Sending MMS

After you fill out the settings, click the Save button at the top left. Click the New MMS button at the bottom right, and you'll see a screen where you can compose the MMS message, as in Figure 3-31. You can give the message a title if you like. Click the Plus button to the right of the *To* box to select from your contacts or just type in a phone number. Next, click the Plus button to the right of the File: box to select a picture to send, or to take a new picture. Finally, press the Send button to send the message.

Figure 3-31.
Composing a picture message

Receiving MMS

Receiving MMS is just as easy. Just like the other message-related applications, SwirlyMMS will tell you when a picture message has come in (Figure 3-32). At that point, MMS works just like it would on other phones. When you receive a message and click on it, Swirly will fetch it and display it (Figure 3-33). From there you can use the buttons on the bottom to save the image somewhere on your iPhone's filesystem (it's automatically copied to your photos as well), or forward it to another recipient.

Figure 3-32.
SwirlyMMS in the launch bar

Figure 3-33.
Receiving a picture message

HACK 3.05: Increase the Duration of Your iPhone's SMS Alert

Really feel the message.

This is a simple but useful hack. The iPhone is configured to vibrate for 0.4 seconds whenever you receive a new message, and there's nowhere in the Settings menu where you can change that. Such a short alert duration can make it easy to miss the announcement of a new SMS message. Luckily, there is a way to change this duration on jailbroken iPhones **[Hack #1.03]** so that it vibrates for longer (or shorter, if you prefer) when you receive a new SMS.

Most settings on an iPhone are stored in files called *Property Lists* or *plists* for short. You can find out how to edit plists in **[Hack #11.02]**.

You will need to access the */System/Library/Frameworks/Celestial.framework* directory of your iPhone **[Hack #1.05]**. Find the file called *SystemSoundVibrationPatterns.plist* in this directory (Figure 3-34) and copy it to your computer.

Figure 3-34.
Finding *SystemSoundVibrationPatterns.plist*

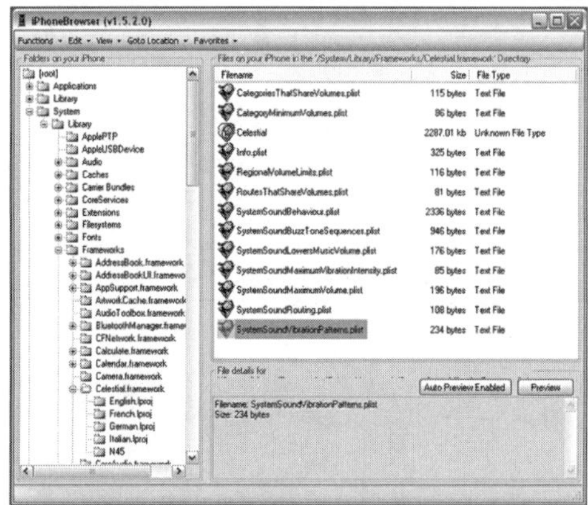

Find the section of the file beginning with the line Default, as in Figure 3-35. The numbers 0.4000... and 0.5000... that are wedged between the phrases are the values for OnDuration and TotalDuration, respectively. The value for OnDuration represents 0.4 second duration of your iPhone's default SMS vibration alert. To prolong the duration to 1.4 seconds, change OnDuration to 1.4, and TotalDuration to 1.5, as demonstrated in Figure 3-36. You can use a different duration if you prefer, but just make sure that TotalDuration is 0.1 greater than OnDuration.

Figure 3-35.
Original values of OnDuration and TotalDuration

```
<?xml version="1.0" encoding="UTF-8"?>
<!DOCTYPE plist PUBLIC "-//Apple Computer//DTD PLIST 1.0//EN"
<plist version="1.0">
<dict>
	<key>ConnectedToPower</key>
	<dict>
		<key>Intensity</key>
		<real>1</real>
		<key>OffDuration</key>
		<real>0.10000000000000001</real>
		<key>OnDuration</key>
		<real>0.40000000000000002</real>
		<key>TotalDuration</key>
		<real>1</real>
	</dict>
	<key>Default</key>
	<dict>
		<key>Intensity</key>
		<real>1</real>
		<key>OffDuration</key>
		<real>0.10000000000000001</real>
		<key>OnDuration</key>
		<real>0.40000000000000002</real>
		<key>TotalDuration</key>
		<real>0.5</real>
	</dict>
```

Figure 3-36.
New values of OnDuration and TotalDuration

```
<?xml version="1.0" encoding="UTF-8"?>
<!DOCTYPE plist PUBLIC "-//Apple Computer//DTD PLIST 1.0//EN"
<plist version="1.0">
<dict>
	<key>ConnectedToPower</key>
	<dict>
		<key>Intensity</key>
		<real>1</real>
		<key>OffDuration</key>
		<real>0.10000000000000001</real>
		<key>OnDuration</key>
		<real>0.40000000000000002</real>
		<key>TotalDuration</key>
		<real>1</real>
	</dict>
	<key>Default</key>
	<dict>
		<key>Intensity</key>
		<real>1</real>
		<key>OffDuration</key>
		<real>0.1</real>
		<key>OnDuration</key>
		<real>1.4</real>
		<key>TotalDuration</key>
		<real>1.5</real>
	</dict>
```

Once you're done editing the file, save it and copy it back to the */System/Library/Frameworks/Celestial.framework* directory of your iPhone. This will replace the original file with the altered file that you created. Finally, reboot your iPhone to apply the changes.

HACK 3.06: Use Instant Messaging on Your iPhone

Instant messaging is one of the iPhone feature set's most glaring omissions. These apps will let you fill the void.

Instant messaging is a very common and quick way for people to communicate. Many people "live" in their IM client. Most smartphones have third-party applications that enable you to use IM, and many if not most Internet-connected phones have added AOL Instant Messenger (AIM) support as a standard function. Every Macintosh computer comes with the AIM-compatible iChat program, so the lack of iChat on the iPhone was somewhat surprising. Thankfully, the iPhone developer community has produced a number of solutions for this IM dilemma.

Solutions to this problem fall into several major categories. App Store applications—such as AOL's own AIM client—work predictably: they have the annoying feature of logging you out when you quit them, due to the "no background app" policy for App Store apps. Web-based solutions have the worst integration with the phone and are a bit sluggish, but they work, and at least they stay connected when you quit them. Some jailbroken IM clients offered persistent connectivity but then decided to "go legit" and get into the App Store, losing this feature in the process. Finally, a couple of hacks based on push email and backgrounding have created somewhat of a solution.

As of this writing, it is anticipated that Apple will be releasing a more comprehensive push architecture for application developers that will accommodate the needs of IM apps.

Web-based IM Applications

FlickIM

FlickIM (www.flickim.com) is a web-based AIM application (Figure 3-37) representative of a variety of web-based IM products. It remembers your login information and reconnects automatically when you navigate to it. It has corner message windows that pop up when you receive a message in a conversation you're not looking at, which you can tap to go right to that chat. It also has full support for landscape mode (of course the large widescreen keyboard prohibits reading the chat, but if you're more comfortable typing with the larger keys, you're good to go). Also you can configure it to notify you via email or SMS when you receive a new IM. Also, it has a variety of skins to match your personal preference. If all you use is AIM, you're good to go quickly with this client.

Figure 3-37.
FlickIM's main screen and an IM

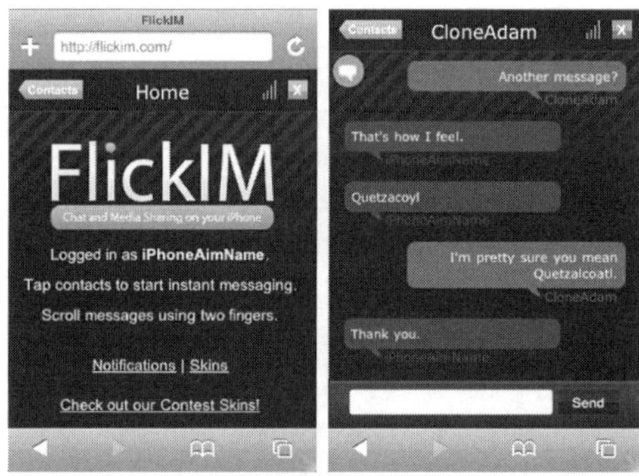

beejive's Jivetalk

Jivetalk is available both as an App Store application and a web application (http://iphone.beejive.com) (Figure 3-38). It supports AIM, ICQ, MSN, Y!IM, Jabber, and Google Talk, and you can store multiple accounts for each protocol. By default, the keyboard closes every time you send a message. If you click the gear in the top-right on your buddy list, you can correct that and set other options. For a web app, it works quite well. The web app uses the same servers as their flagship App Store product.

Figure 3-38.
beejive's Jivetalk web application

App Store Apps

Although there were several excellent native IM applications on jailbroken phones, the siren song of App Store riches made everyone "go legit." As a result, there is little left in the Installer/Cydia world for free or shareware IMing.

As of this writing, MobileChat (Figure 3-39), IM+ Chat (Figure 3-40), and beejive's Jivetalk (Figure 3-41) are the main options for multi-IM messaging. MobileChat is relatively inexpensive, but IM+ Chat is almost $10 and beejive is almost $15. However, they both operate services that act as an intermediary between you and the IM network, keeping you logged in, so they have real ongoing service costs to support the features of their application. IM+ has a free version with reduced features that you can try out. beejive can even email you or text message you when new messages come in, which can help notify you if you're doing something else on the device and close it to create a "background" experience.

Figure 3-39.
MobileChat

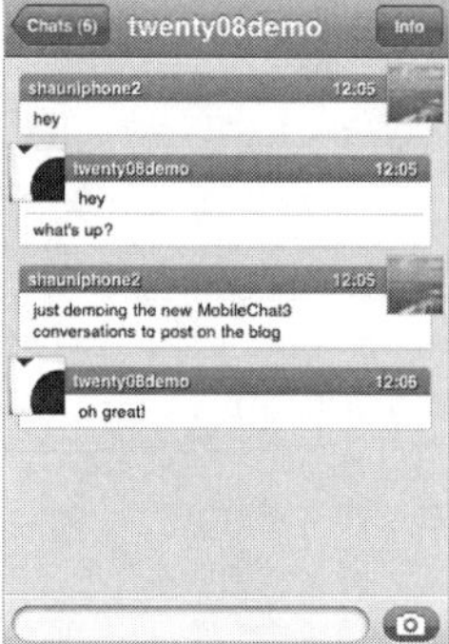

Figure 3-40.
IM+ Chat

Figure 3-41.
beejive's Jivetalk App Store application

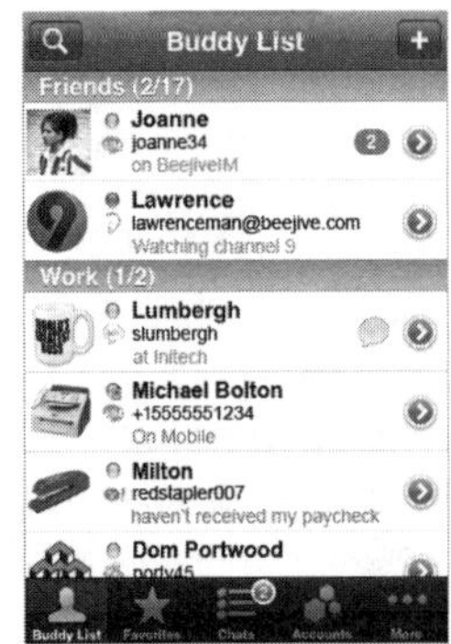

Free Apps

The various instant messaging apps are categorized in the "social networking" section of the App Store, and the major social networks (Facebook, LinkedIn, etc.) tend to supply some sort of iPhone application. In addition, both AOL (Figure 3-42) and Yahoo! (Figure 3-43) provide a free instant messaging application that works with their particular IM system.

Figure 3-42.
AOL's AIM application

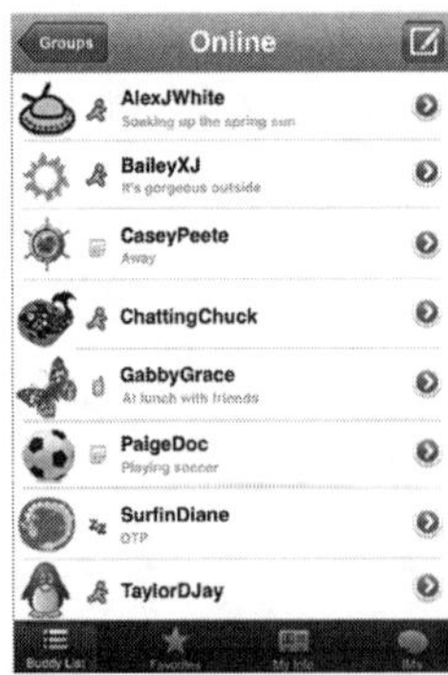

Figure 3-43.
Yahoo!'s IM application

Jailbreak Solutions

Instant messaging is supposed to be instant, not delayed until you run the IM app. And if your phone doesn't beep or buzz to let you know that you have a message, messaging isn't very effective, either.

If you have a jailbroken phone, you have a couple of additional options for using IM products in a way that works like it should.

Backgrounder **[Hack #9.14]** can be used to let an IM client run in the background, so that you can go on to run other applications and remain logged in. It's easy to use—simply hold down the Home button slightly longer than normal, and you'll get a "Backgrounding Enabled" message (Figure 3-44). If you have your ringer switch set to silent, AIM will vibrate the phone briefly whenever an IM comes in, and it will continue to be logged in in the background. You can run any other app—play video, take calls, and so on—and your instant messaging session will still work.

Figure 3-44.
AIM in the background

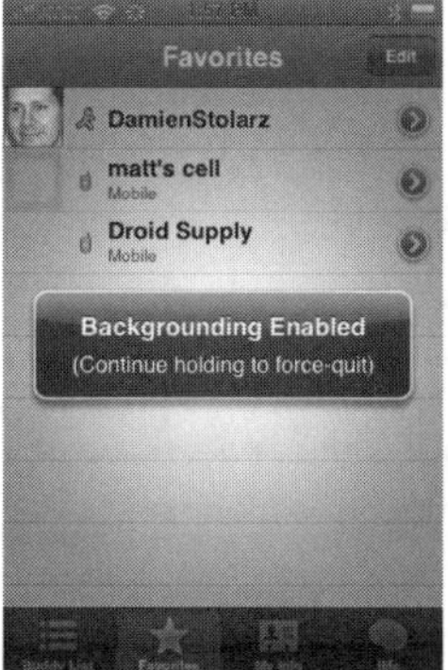

 HACK 3.07: **Connect to IRC on Your iPhone**

Stay logged into IRC—no matter where you are.

The decades-old IRC protocol remains one of the most popular communication methods, especially for those "in the know" in the computing world. And it's a great way to get support for iPhone hacking **[Hack #2.06]**. This hack covers two ways to IRC on your iPhone or iPod touch.

Remote IRC to Your Mac

If you have a Mac, and you chat on IRC, chances are you've used Colloquy—a powerful and flexible OS X IRC client. And now, thanks to a new plug-in, you can monitor your Mac-based IRC connection from your iPhone/iPod touch's Safari browser. Here's how:

1. The first step is getting Colloquy installed on your computer. The latest version can be found at www.colloquy.info/downloads.html.
2. After Colloquy is installed, you will need to install the Web Interface plug-in, which can be downloaded from www.colloquy.info/downloads/colloquy-web-interface.zip. Put the plug-in into */Library/Application Support/Colloquy/PlugIns*.
3. Set the password that you have to type in when you fire up the connection on your iPhone. Fire up Terminal in your */Utilities* folder, and type in the following:
   ```
   defaults write info.colloquy WebInterfacePassword yourpassword
   ```
4. Start Colloquy, or restart it if it was already running.
5. If your iPhone is connected to the same Wi-Fi network as your Mac, you can go to http://*ipaddress*:6667 (where *ipaddress* is the IP address of your Mac), type in the password you set earlier when prompted, and you're good to go. However, if you want to connect to it from EDGE or from a remote network, you'll need to make sure that port 6667 is properly forwarded to your Mac. This process is a bit different for each router. You can refer to your router's manual or use www.portforward.com to set this up. Once that's all straightened out, head to http://ipaddress:6667. If you don't know your IP off the top of your head, finding out is as simple as visiting www.whatismyip.com.

Now your iPhone will be controlling your Mac's Colloquy remotely. It will let you talk in whatever rooms you've currently joined on your Mac. (You won't be able to configure your connections using your iPhone.) You can scroll through your list of rooms or the messages in a room by scrolling with two fingers. If you tilt your iPhone to landscape view, you can read the IRC log in widescreen. You can't type this way however, as the keyboard would've eaten 80% of the screen, so they didn't bother adding it.

You'll see the same chat on both your iPhone and your Mac, so you can jump seamlessly from your iPhone to your Mac and back without losing track of the conversation. Also, if your connection dips out for a minute or more, the messages will be sent to your phone when your connection comes back on, so there are no messages lost in the void.

Any other details, updates, or answers to questions you might have can be found at www.colloquy.info/iphone.

IRC Out and About

If you want to IRC on the go—away from your home wireless network—you can do so by using one of the following apps.

Rooms

If you're looking for a commercial, easy-to-use GUI IRC client, Rooms (Figure 3-45) is available from the App Store.

Figure 3-45.
Some of the screens of Rooms

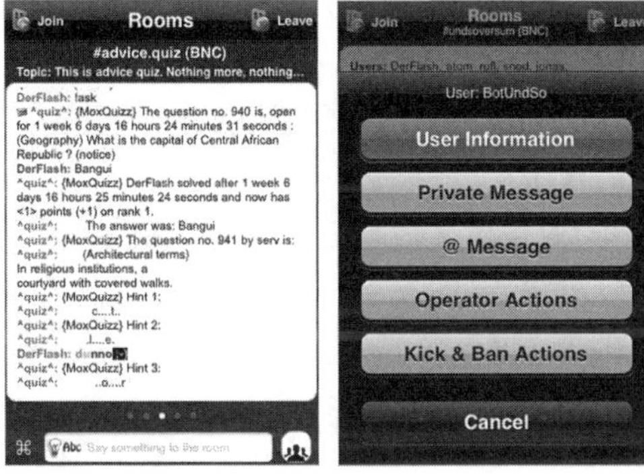

iRCm

If you're just looking to get connected and know your way around IRC already, the quick, free way to get onto IRC is to install iRCm, which can be found in Cydia on a jailbroken phone (Figure 3-46).

Figure 3-46.
iRCm

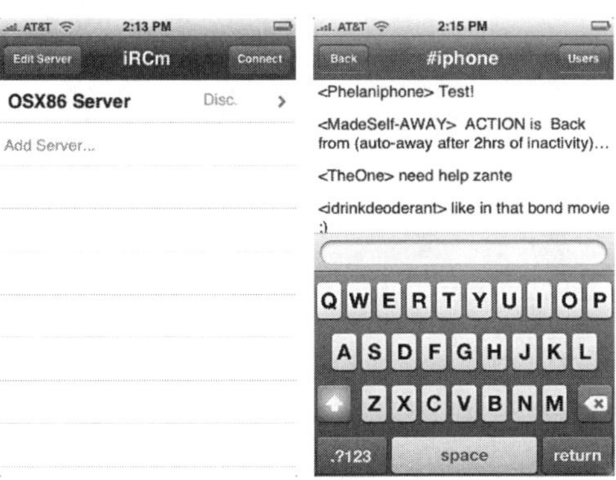

iRCm is very simple. Add servers with Add Server, type in the server information, tap back, tap server, and tap connect. It shows a bit of the behind-the-scenes connection log. The double-spaced chats might make it more readable, but in essence they function the same. iRCm also has support for IRC slash commands (e.g., `/join` and `/raw`, for those who know what they're doing).

04 MEDIA AND DATA

The iPhone is a media powerhouse, but there are ways to make it even more powerful.

Unlike other smartphones, the iPhone builds directly on a rich iPod heritage. This means that it has best-of-breed audio and video performance and compatibility with the widely used tools for preparing content for video-enabled iPods. Also unlike most smartphones to date, it runs Unix; specifically, Mac OS X, which means that many of the open source, Linux, or BSD projects that could be compiled for the Mac can also run on the device. Both the iPhone and iPod touch have extensive networking support—and more wireless connectivity options than most laptops. When you put it all together, you have a portable iPod successor that is for all intents and purposes always connected to the Internet, combined with gigabytes of high-speed solid-state storage.

If you're a news junkie or RSS fiend, the iPhone is your friend. If you're obsessed with music, your new iPod connects you to others just as obsessed as you. If you're a bookworm, you'll be able to overfill your iPhone's digital bookshelf. And if you're a videophile, you can carry dozens of feature-length movies on your iPod or remotely stream hundreds of DVD rips from home—this chapter will show you how.

HACK 4.01: Carry a Portable File Server

Make your iPhone into the wireless successor to the thumb drive.

In [Hack #1.05] we discussed looking at files anywhere on your filesystem. Although there are now hundreds of ways to push your data into the "cloud"—email, FTP accounts, WebDAV, Amazon S3—sometimes you don't want your data hosted out there on the Internet. Sometimes you're not online, but you just need a way to carry your files with you and get them onto another computer easily.

Part of the reason for the popularity and ubiquity of thumb drives is the need for a *sneakernet*—the term for "networking" by walking files from one computer to another. But using the iPhone as a physically connected thumb drive alternative is somewhat inconvenient—you must have your cable with you, you may need to install iTunes, and often a photo application will pop up. And it's just not as cool.

But it's also silly that you have to carry around your iPhone *and* a thumb drive, and that you can't peek into your thumb drive and check which files are on it without plugging it into the computer.

Luckily, several App Store apps solve both of these issues by turning the iPhone into a convenient portable file server.

Air Sharing

Air Sharing is a clean, feature-filled app that makes the iPhone or iPod touch into a temporary WebDAV server. WebDAV (Web-based Distributed Authoring and Versioning) is a file-serving protocol that allows you to share a hard drive over HTTP. You launch the app, and right on the bottom of the screen you'll find a WebDAV URL (Figure 4-1): in the example, http://10.0.1.190:8080.

Here are operating-system-specific instructions:

- Mac OS X: Finder→Go→Connect to Server, then type in the URL.
- Windows Vista: Start→right-click My Computer→Map Network Drive, select a drive letter, type in the URL.
- Windows XP: Start→My Network Places→Add a Network Place→Next→Choose another network location→Type in the URL.
- Linux GNOME: Use the Nautilus File browser, but change the URL prefix from http:// to dav://
- Linux KDE: Konquerer expects the URL to be changed to webdav:// instead of http://
- Any web browser: Type in the URL. You'll be able to browse and download files (but not upload).

One of the nicest things about Air Sharing is that it allows convenient previews of any file that you upload and that the iPhone is capable of previewing, which includes any multimedia like MP3s and MOVs. So if you have a set of movies or music that you don't want to go through the whole sync-to-iTunes process with, or if they're work- or demo-related and not intended to be part of your personal listening library, this application is a great way to play them back outside of the iPod application.

Figure 4-1.
Air Sharing serves WebDAV

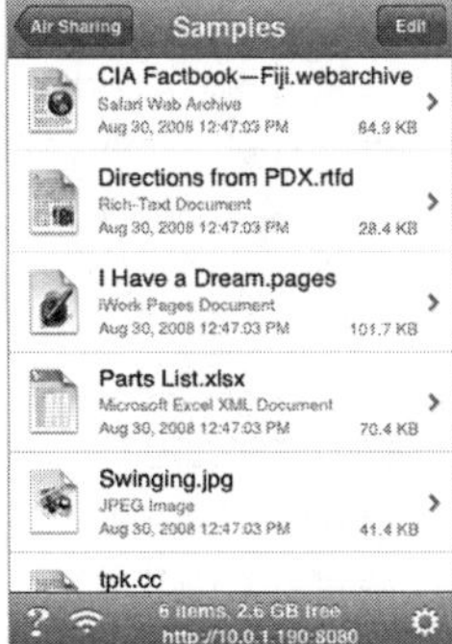

Mobile Studio

Another very similar application is Mobile Studio. Its heritage is in the MobileFinder group of applications **[Hack #1.05]** but it's been completely sanitized for the App Store. Nonetheless, it is a very effective FTP server for the iPhone, with features similar to Air Sharing. The good thing about FTP is that it's ubiquitous—every computer has an FTP client, if only a command-line one—and thus it's less clunky than mounting a WebDAV share if you know what you're doing. Mobile Studio presents the URLs that can be entered into most web browsers if you just want to view the files, or can be connected to by any FTP client on your machine. Mobile Studio also provides tutorials within the app on how to get connected from the various OSs you might be on. And if you're inclined to use the command line, typing `ftp <IP address of your phone>` will get you in.

Figure 4-2.
Mobile Studio serves FTP

Bonjour

Both of these applications offer the ability to use a Bonjour address. Bonjour is Apple's fun name for Zeroconf, a "zero configuration" network addressing standard that allows local IP network devices to be discovered by name. You can read about its details at www.zeroconf.org. More importantly, if you're on XP, Vista, Windows 7, or a Linux distribution, you can make your discovery of these servers easier, and set it up so you can use the same name (the name of your device) each time you connect, instead of an ever-changing IP address. You can get Bonjour for Windows from www.apple.com/macosx/technology/bonjour.html. Most Linux distributions come with Bonjour compatibility.

Limitations

Because of the App Store restrictions, applications can access files only in their own private storage area, so you'll be able to download only files that you upload to these servers. It's also worth noting that these apps act as a server only while they're running—which can be considered both a bug (no sharing if you quit) and a feature (if it ran all the time, you'd be advertising your files to anyone). By default, these servers have no passwords set. If you're concerned about security, set a password.

Going Beyond

[Hack #9.06] discusses using AFP and SSH, and if you've jailbroken your phone, you can easily install those applications in Cydia, mount your entire iPhone filesystem on a Mac, and access it using a free SCP program on Windows or Linux. But with these apps you get the cute file previews, the tidy isolation of your files, and the ability to connect quickly without a password. So even if you're jailbroken, you will probably find these apps useful.

HACK 4.02: Convert Videos, DVDs, and Blu-Ray Discs to iPhone- and iPod touch–Ready Formats

Not everything is on the iTunes store, and much of it is already in your collection. But you can put media from any source on your device.

There's a lot of video out there, and not all of it comes in tidy iPod-compatible formats. In fact, before the iPod with video and the Sony PlayStation Portable (PSP) came along, the DivX/XviD formats (technically, MPEG-4 part 2 in an AVI container) had pretty much wrapped up the harddrive-based video space. But now, because of Apple's commanding presence in downloadable video distribution, we find a large amount of content in MOV. To get content to work on the iPod touch or the iPhone, it's necessary to compress it into an iPod-compatible format.

Video Compression 101

If you're familiar with online video, you've probably downloaded AVI files, WMF files, and perhaps MOV files. You may have downloaded files that ended in *.xvid* or *.divx*. The irony of this alphabet soup is that most of these file formats share the same basic compression technique—MPEG-4. Yet you can't just put them on your iPod touch and hit play. Why must the world be like this? Read on.

Here's a quick list of the main things you need to know about video compression:

Media container *(file formats)*
Video is stored in a digital "box" or container. Examples are *.mov*, *.mp4*, *.avi*, *.wmv*, *.m4v*, and *.mkv*. You can store all kinds of codecs (see the next list item) in an MOV; thus, the mere presence of an MOV extension doesn't mean that it will play on an iPhone. Similarly, you might have perfect iPhone compatible data in an AVI container, but the iPhone isn't going to understand it, because it's in the wrong "box."

Codecs *(compressor-decompressors)*
The *codec* is the technique used to squish gigabytes of video into mere tens or hundreds of megabytes. Examples include DivX/XviD (MPEG-4 part 2), WMV (Microsoft's VC-1 codec, similar to MPEG-4), H.264/AVC (advanced video codec; basically, MPEG-4 part 10, a more recent version of MPEG-4), and MPEG-2 (DVD "VOB" files; also digital broadcast television, satellite, TiVo, and most set-top boxes encode to MPEG-2).

Resolution
Resolution refers to how many dots are in the picture. *Aspect ratio* is the ratio of horizontal dots to vertical dots. Not all dots are square, because video is often stored at a small resolution and then blown up—or on the iPhone, shrunk—to fit the screen. Video can be high-definition (i.e., 1280x720 pixels or 1920x1080 pixels). Standard-definition video is in the range of 640x480 or 720x480. The iPhone screen is exactly 480x320, so widescreen (letterboxed) movies can be encoded at 480x270.

Frame rate
Movies usually run at 24 frames per second (fps). TV shows usually run at 30fps or 29.97fps, or 25fps in Europe. Sometimes for Internet this frame rate is cut in half to 15fps or 12fps.

Codec profiles and levels

In the MPEG-4 standard, there are profiles and levels. *Profiles* are bundles of audio and video codec settings that target a particular class of devices. You'll hear of "Main," "Baseline," and "Simple" profiles. Within a profile are levels—how much computation it takes to encode video in that format.

Bit rate

The *bit rate* specifies how much data the device can decode, and how fast. A studio DVD might have anywhere from 6 megabits per second (Mbps) to 10 Mbps of MPEG-2 data, meaning how fast the firehose of data flows. Blu-Ray sends tens of megabytes of MPEG-4 data. Your Internet connection might support from 1 Mbps up to 20 Mbps. A portable device like the iPhone or the PSP might take video that's only 1-2 Mbps or less.

So with all that knowledge, you should have no trouble understanding Apple's iPhone specifications:

- H.264 video, up to 1.5 Mbps, 640x480 pixels, 30 fps, Low-Complexity version of the H.264 Baseline Profile with AAC-LC audio up to 160 Kbps, 48kHz, stereo audio in *.m4v*, *.mp4*, and *.mov* file formats
- H.264 video, up to 2.5 Mbps, 640x480 pixels, 30 fps, Baseline Profile up to Level 3.0 with AAC-LC audio up to 160 Kbps, 48kHz, stereo audio in *.m4v*, *.mp4*, and *.mov* file formats
- MPEG-4 video, up to 2.5 Mbps, 640x480 pixels, 30 fps, Simple Profile with AAC-LC audio up to 160 Kbps, 48kHz, stereo audio in *.m4v*, *.mp4*, and *.mov* file formats

What does it all mean? Basically, the iPhone supports two flavors of MPEG-4: H.264 (the new stuff) and MPEG-4 (the old stuff). But it supports them only with particular settings. So getting video into an iPhone compatible form isn't hard, but getting the best possible compression and best possible picture for the best possible storage is, as always, a series of tradeoffs. The best-looking file for your iPhone may not be the best format for your Apple TV or, especially, your non-Apple home theater PCs. Thus, you have to choose—do you want a lowest-common-denominator (which Apple has attempted to provide with its downloadable standard-definition movies), or do you want to have several versions of your library—one in portable MP4, and one in a higher-resolution Xvid format?

The choice is yours; here, we'll present a couple of the easiest tools to get started.

HandBrake

Probably the leading free, open source, cross-platform (Windows, Linux, and Macintosh) tool for encoding videos for the iPhone/iPod family of devices is HandBrake, available for download at handbrake.fr. This tool has come a long way. Originally it was primarily a DVD ripping program, but with the recent integration of the famous open source video codec ffmpeg libraries (ffmpeg.mplayerhq.hu), it can now convert almost any file into an iPhone format.

Figures 4-3 and 4-4 show HandBrake on Mac OS X and Windows XP, respectively. A Linux version with GUI is also available. To use it, select the file to convert using the "Source" button in the top left. On the right-hand side of the main window (the presets drawer) are a variety of settings, and under the Apple tab are presets for the Apple family of devices and computers.

The "Universal" setting is designed to produce a file that will give good results and be compatible across the full line of devices, from Apple TV to older iPods. If you're trying to optimize for size and quality on an iPhone or iPod touch for solely handheld viewing, you can make smaller files to fit the 360x480 screen. However, if you plan to watch these files on a television on computer screen, Universal is best.

Figure 4-3.
HandBrake (Mac OS X)

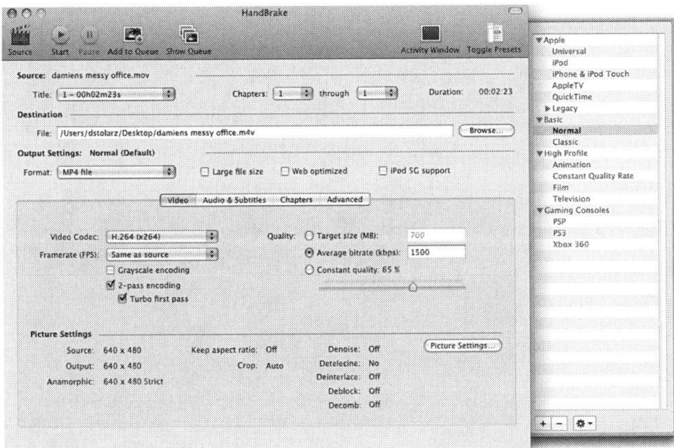

Figure 4-4.
HandBrake (Windows XP)

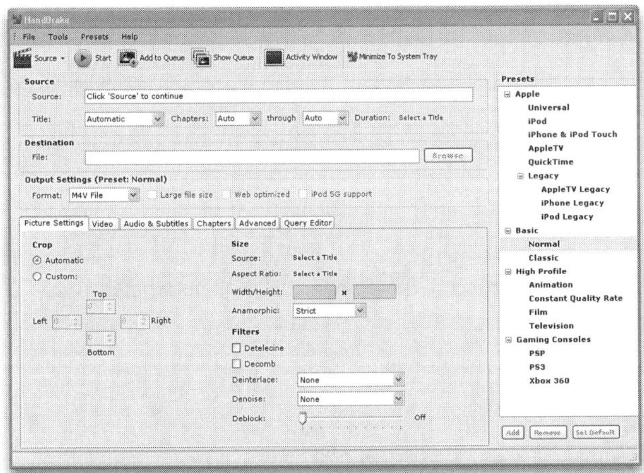

Command-Line HandBrake

If you're more into command-line utilities, perhaps for creating batch encoding workflows for your voluminous library, HandBrake has a command line interface. You can download it separately at http://handbrake.fr, and read the documentation at http://trac.handbrake.fr/wiki/CLIGuide.

The command line is quite easy to use, and allows you to set any minute parameter for tweaking. In its most basic form, it looks like this:

```
HandBrakeCLI -i inputFile -o outputFile
```

which uses the default settings to create a 1Mbps MP4 file.

More complicated options can also be set, such as:

```
HandBrakeCLI -i inputFile.avi -o outputFile.m4v -e x264 -b 1500 -B 160
```

which will create an H.264-encoded, 1.5Mbps MP4 file with 160kbps audio.

To see all the available options, enter this command:

```
HandBrakeCLI -h
```

QuickTime Pro

If you have to convert a file quickly, you have a couple of options. If you have a registered copy of QuickTime Pro on the Mac or PC, then you can export (slowly) MOV and H.264 files with easy save-for-iPhone presets (Figure 4-5).

Figure 4-5.
QuickTime Pro export settings

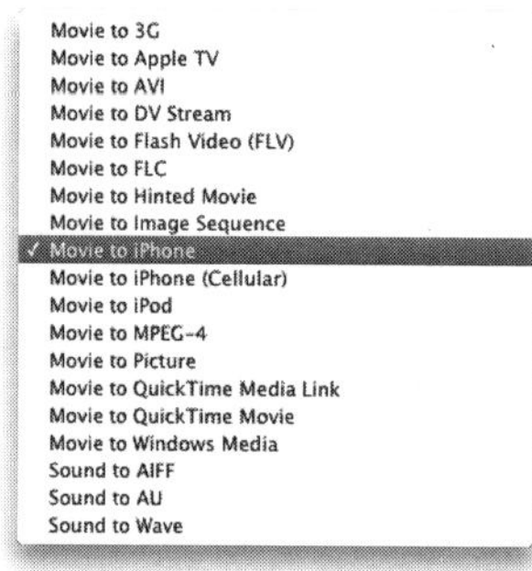

However, on a PC, although QuickTime Pro can export to the iPhone, the likelihood that it will be able to open your format in question is low, as it prefers to open MOV files. So you're better off using another tool.

iMovie (OS X)

iMovie HD, bundled with most Macs, lets you export to a variety of different formats, including one especially for the iPod (which, in turn, works just great on the iPhone). iMovie has built-in support for many MPEG-2, MPEG-4, and MOV files, so it can load things that even the QuickTime player won't load. The downside is that it takes a while to import the file, and it translates the resolution to an iMovie HD format, which is then reduced down for the device. The upside is that you can edit the movie and import a variety of formats. Once that's done, go to File→Export, click the Mobile button (Figure 4-6), and let 'er rip. After the conversion is done, your new video will be sent straight to your iTunes library.

Figure 4-6.
iMovie export settings

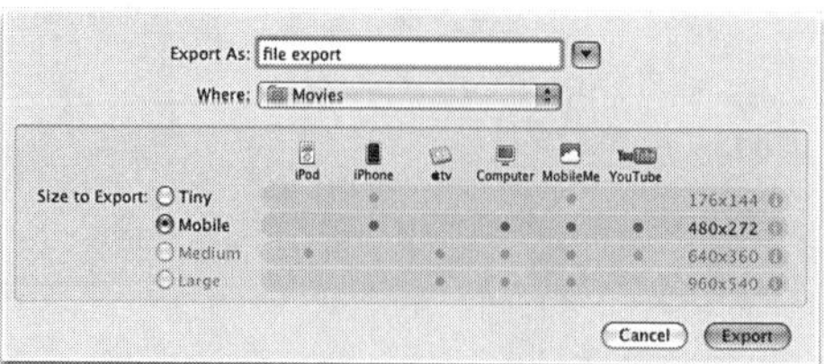

Photo-JPEG

It's worth noting that the iPhone codecs listed previously are the main ones that Apple specifies as supported. Although iTunes will refuse to transfer them to your iPhone, you can also save files as Photo-JPEG—a video format where each frame is simply a JPEG file, with no fancy MPEG-4 stuff going on. This format is excellent for exporting files like PowerPoint, in which there are lots of high-resolution stills that need to be played back **[Hack #4.03]**.

As an example, the QuickTime Pro export settings shown in Figure 4-7—30fps Photo-JPEG with Apple Lossless audio—produced a file playable on the iPhone. The file won't transfer in iTunes, but when copied to the device and played in AirSharing **[Hack #4.01]** or emailed as an attachment, it works just fine.

Figure 4-7.
QuickTime Pro export settings

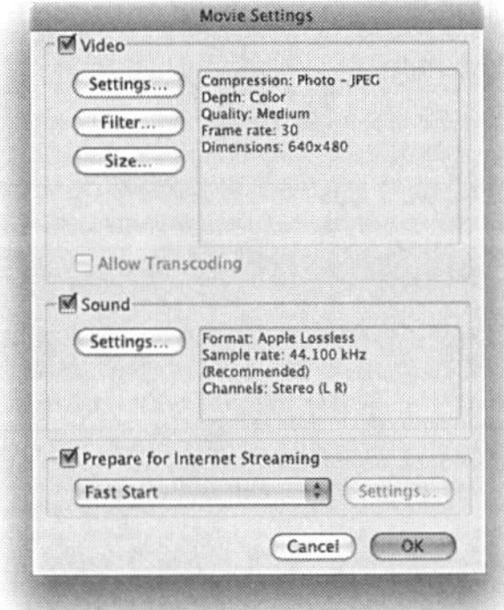

Hardware Assist

One of the first things that is apparent when converting movies is that it takes a long time. Although "real-time" conversion sounds fast, in fact it simply means that it takes two hours to convert a two-hour movie. Converting a whole library could take weeks or months. Although dedicating a quad-core or 8-core machine to the task is one option, if you have a Mac, there is a cheaper option that will save a tremendous amount of CPU time and increase encoding performance.

Elgato (www.elgato.com) makes a device called Turbo.264 that is a USB-connected MPEG-4 encoding accelerator (Figure 4-8). For $100, it adds an MPEG-4 encoder chip to your Mac that when used with special software, allows the Mac to do encoding without using much CPU time at all. If you have an older Mac (such as a Power PC), the speed increase can be ten times faster, and even on dual-core Intel Macs, the performance is increased several times over.

Figure 4-8.
The Elgato Turbo.264

Videora (Windows)

If your videos sit on a Windows-based machine, most of your choices involve some $25–$50 shareware app from a company that you've likely never heard of.

However, there's a freeware alternative called iPhone Converter from Videora at www.videora.com/en-us/Converter/iPhone. It converts video to a suitable iPhone format almost too easily (and all without spy- or adware). It's a small download and a quick install, and it converts files quickly.

Launch the app and flip over to the Convert tab, then click the Video File tab. When you're prompted to Select Mode, pick Normal. You'll have to go through a couple simple steps by pressing the orange Next button a couple times. Once you reach the Video Settings page (Figure 4-9), make any changes to the video quality, but leave the Video Format and Video Size settings the same. Scroll down and click the Start Converting button.

When a file is done converting, it will go into both your Library tab as well as be placed automatically into your iTunes library. If you get an error when it tries to transfer it to iTunes, you may have to just browse for the video file and drag it into iTunes. From there, of course, you can sync it onto your iPhone and enjoy.

Figure 4-9.
Videora settings

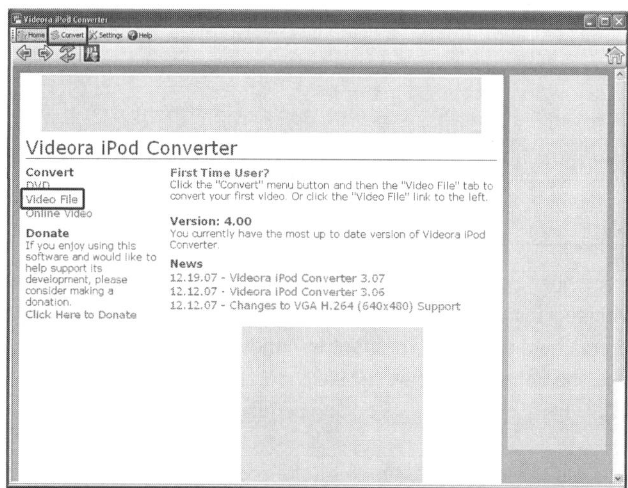

Web-based Conversions

If you don't want to download or install anything, and your video is under 100 MB, a simple service called Zamzar (www.zamzar.com), shown in Figure 4-10, can convert all manner of files to different formats, including converting non-iPhone video to H.264 (and it's watermark-free!). You simply go on, select a file, choose a resulting format, punch in your email, and start it. After your movie is uploaded, it will be converted. Once it's done, Zamzar will send you an email with the link to the file, what file it was, what format it was, and what you converted it to. The file will stay available for one day.

This service is perfect for any sort of small files, or if you're traveling and your laptop doesn't have a conversion program. If iTunes rejects a video converted using the "iPhone" format, you could try using the "iPod" format, which often can solve the problem.

Figure 4-10.
The Convert Files tab on Zamzar, which allows a video on your computer to be uploaded and converted

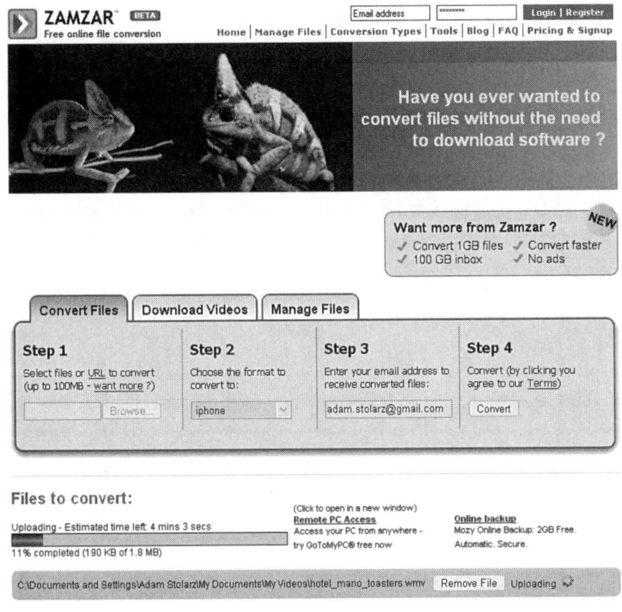

DVD and Blu-Ray on Your iPhone

If you don't know what an MP3 is, you probably aren't reading this book. And if you aren't reading this book, you probably don't know that the way to make an MP3 is to "rip" a CD by simply inserting the CD in a drive and clicking Import in iTunes.

With us so far? Well, you may be surprised to find that it's not as easy with DVDs. Basically, though CDs are (for the most part) not copy-protected or encrypted, DVDs are. Therefore, most of the mainstream "ripping" programs for audio don't import DVD video. Yet there are many reasons that you might want to convert and back up DVDs:

Scratch prevention
Children scratch their DVDs. It's cute to watch them try to insert them in computers and DVD players, and it's a good "teachable moment"—but it rapidly makes them unplayable.

Mobility
Physical DVDs, though small, aren't small enough. If you're going on a trip and want to bring some of your DVD library with you, a copy on your iPhone takes up even less space than a DVD.

Convenience
It's unlikely that you'd get to enjoy all four seasons that you bought of your favorite show on DVD unless they were there whenever you had a bit of downtime—on the plane, in a hotel, at a family gathering, on a date.

Security
If your house burns down or gets robbed, do you really want to have to buy all your DVDs again?

DVD and Blu-Ray Ripping

Putting DVD video on your iPhone can be accomplished in two steps. First, you need to extract (a.k.a. *rip*) the video content from the DVD. Then, you convert the video content to an iPhone-compatible MP4 format that can be synced with iTunes. This is hard to accomplish because of copy protection, also known by the fancy name of Digital Rights Management (DRM). Copy protection for DVD and Blu-Ray comes in the following various flavors.

Content Scrambling System (CSS)

This is the form of encryption used by DVD players. There are many codes and each DVD may use a different code. Compliant DVD players know all the codes. It was cracked in the late 1990s by the reverse-engineering of a software player.

AACS

This protection is like CSS, but for Blu-Ray. Every Blu-Ray disc has a key to playing it back. Thousands of unique keys are then used to lock a copy of this key. Every authorized Blu-Ray player uses one of these keys. If that player ever gets hacked, it will get excommunicated, and all future discs will have that key disabled and the player won't be able to play new Blu-Ray releases. It was cracked shortly after Blu-Ray was released.

BD+

This is an extra form of protection on top of AACS. Even after it's decrypted, the content of a Blu-Ray won't look right, because it's scrambled. Each Blu-Ray title has a tiny program on it that the Blu-Ray player must run to descramble the content. This step slows down the speed of cracking new DVD titles, because each disc has to be carefully analyzed to see how its unique descrambling code works.

DVDs consist of 4–9 GB of VOB (video object) files. These are basically MPEG-2 video files with audio interleaved either in a PCM (uncompressed) or AC3 (Dolby surround) format. If you just insert a DVD in a drive and try to copy the files off, they either won't copy, or they won't work once copied off. They are encrypted. To defeat the encryption, you need a decryption program.

The DVD has a specific file structure. The video is stored in a folder called *VIDEO_TS* on the DVD.

Blu-Ray discs can be as big as 50 GB. The video is stored in high-definition 1920x1080 resolution, and encoded with MPEG-2, MPEG-4 AVC, or sometimes Microsoft's VC-1 (WMV 9-ish) codec.

The Blu-Ray disc has a specific file structure. The movie is stored in a folder called *BDMV*. Home-burned discs have a different folder, *BDAV*.

There are two basic approaches to ripping:

1. Get an all-in-one program that rips a DVD or Blu-Ray and converts it to iPhone-compatible formats.
2. Archive your movies by saving the *VIDEO_TS* folder or *BDMV* contents on your hard drive. Then, use a program such as those described earlier in this hack to encode for iPhone.

 The most definitive resource online for DVD backups is www.doom9.org.

Why Is It So Hard?

Generally, the copyright owners of DVDs and Blu-Ray discs have done their best to keep DVD ripping software off the market. It persists in two forms: open source projects, often hosted internationally, where there is no financial motive and, thus, no one to sue; and off-shore corporations in countries that aren't under a reachable jurisdiction. Proponents of these tools contend that the software has substantial legal, noninfringing use—under the fair-use or fair-dealings laws of the countries that it is used in. Opponents contend that it violates laws about defeating encryption.

Ripping on a Mac

To rip a DVD, you can use either MacTheRipper (www.mactheripper.org) or FairMount (www.metakine.com/products/fairmount). FairMount requires the VLC Media Player from www.videolan.org to function. But it's not necessary to have VLC Media player running when you're using FairMount. You can see FairMount mounting a DVD in Figure 4-11. MacTheRipper can be seen ready to rip a DVD in Figure 4-12.

Figure 4-11.
FairMount (Mac OS X)

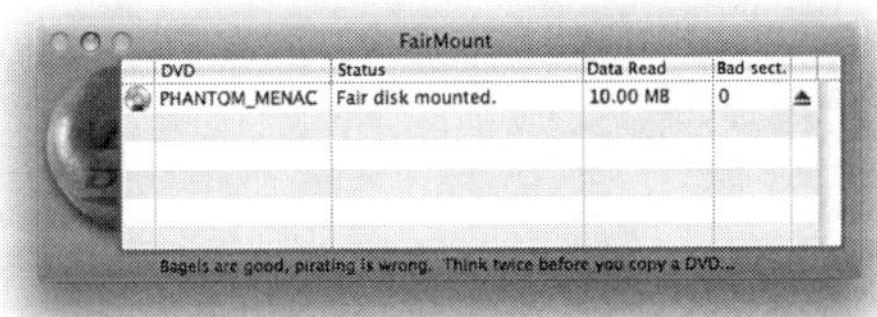

With a DVD inserted in your computer's drive, start up FairMount; it will automatically mount the disc. In Finder, the DVD should now show up as a removable drive, instead of as a disc. When you click on it in Finder, you'll see that it contains a folder titled *VIDEO_TS*. You could rip this folder to your hard drive, and then convert the video, or you can just select (or drag) this folder with your video conversion program.

Figure 4-12.
MacTheRipper

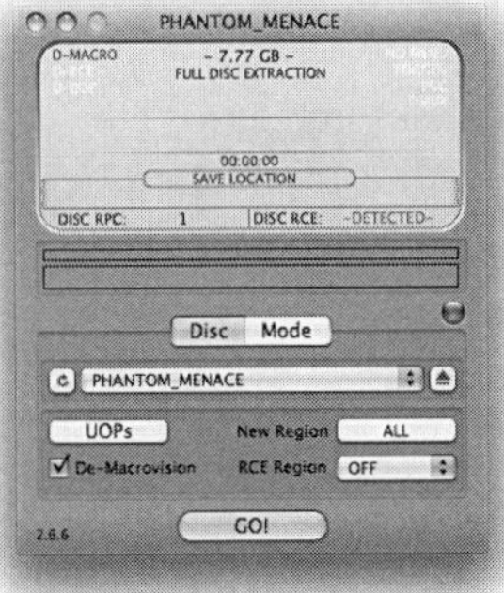

Occasionally, you may run into a title that doesn't rip in either MacTheRipper or through FairMount. Two other Mac ripping programs that handle a wider range of encryption methods are http://ripitapp.com and OSEx (www.macupdate.com/info.php/id/9830). If that still doesn't work, and if you have Boot Camp on your Mac, you can boot to Windows and try one of the PC-based ripping programs, which should do the trick.

PC Ripping

There are a couple of options for PC ripping. Some are free, and many are free for a while but later start charging. Some free options are:

DVDFab HD Decrypter

A free, simplified version of this program can be found at www.dvdfab.com/free.htm. This version gives you the basic tools—which are enough. The Full Disc option rips the entire disc. The Main Movie option, shown in Figure 4-13, allows you to select which parts of the DVD to rip. Because you probably just want the main movie, select Main Movie and start ripping the DVD. DVDFab will output a folder containing two folders titled *AUDIO_TS* and *VIDEO_TS*. *VIDEO_TS* will contain a file ending with *.VOB*, which you'll need to convert. The "HD" in DVDFab HD Decrypter is telling you that it can extract some HD titles on HD-DVD and Blu-Ray. You'll see when you insert your disc (assuming that you have the appropriate drive on your PC) whether those discs can be extracted.

Figure 4-13.
DVDFab

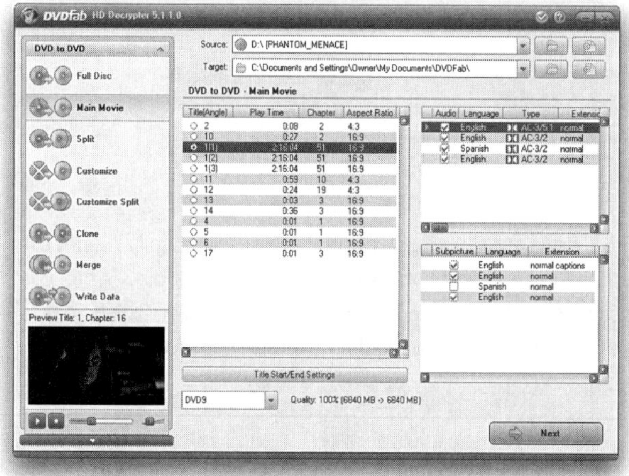

ImgBurn

Another classic DVD decryption tool is ImgBurn (www.dvddecrypter.org.uk). ImgBurn is the successor to DVD Decrypter, a favorite at the Doom9.org forums. It's ready to rip in Figure 4-14.

Figure 4-14.
ImgBurn

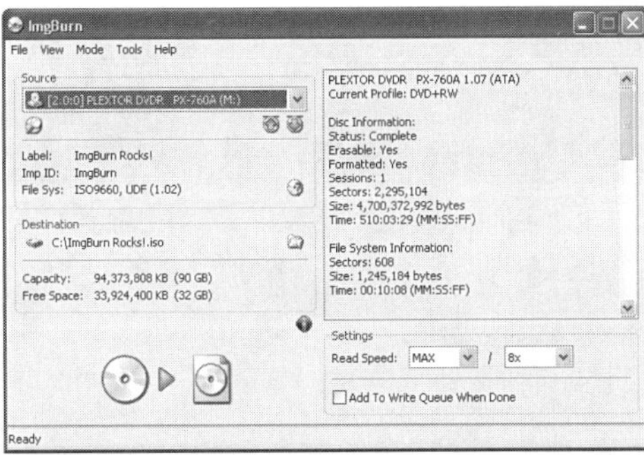

A payware solution on the PC for DVD and Blu-Ray ripping is AnyDVD from SlySoft (www.slysoft.com/en). Although it costs money, they have a development team actively working to play catchup with the ever-changing Blu-Ray title encryptions. At the time of this writing it's the most workable solution for Blu-Ray ripping. You can see it ready to go in Figure 4-15.

Figure 4-15.
AnyDVD

Encoding and Conversion

Once you have extracted your DVD or Blu-Ray disc via one method or another and have the video ready for encoding, you'll need to use a tool to get it onto your iPhone. If you're going to hook your iPhone up to a television or use this file on your Mac or PC in addition to the iPhone or iPod touch, you may want to encode it in 640x480 or similar resolution, instead of the native iPhone resolution. And while you're at it, you'll probably want to encode it with chapters. This recent addition to the various encoding tools gives you a similar experience to what you would get buying movies from the iTunes store, with chapter markers corresponding to the normal chapters in the DVD.

As mentioned earlier in this hack, HandBrake is the best free, cross-platform (Macintosh/Windows/Linux) tool for DVD encoding. Figure 4-16 shows HandBrake with a DVD:

Figure 4-16.
HandBrake creating chapters

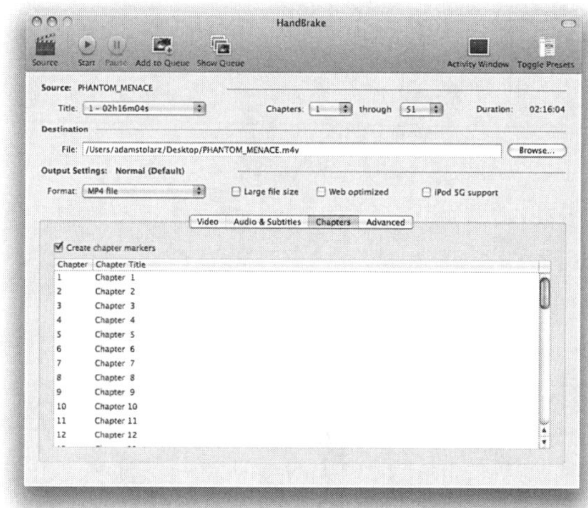

Mac Encoding

On the Mac, there are a few other programs of note. As mentioned earlier, Elgato's Turbo.264 hardware accelerator works with their encoding software, which you can download and check out from their website (www.elgato.com). It presents a very clean interface (Figure 4-17), and when encoding a main title, automatically creates chapters.

Figure 4-17.
Elgato's Turbo.264

RoadMovie (Figure 4-18) from Bitfield software (www.bitfield.se) has excellent support for subtitles and enhanced metadata, allows you to edit and create your own chapters if your DVD lacks them or you want to put in your own, and can also use the Elgato Turbo.264 encoder.

Figure 4-18.
RoadMovie creating chapters

All-in-one Programs that Rip and Convert

If you want a simple one-click way to put DVD video on your iPhone, there are a number of programs for both PC and Mac that do both the ripping and converting. You may be able to get a trial version of the program, but it may not be fully functional until you purchase it. A couple of the most popular all-in-one programs that offer trial versions are:

- For the Mac: DVD to iPod Converter for Mac (www.iphone-tool.com/tool/dvd-to-ipod-converter-for-mac.html)
- For the PC: Cucusoft iPod Video Converter Suite (www.top5soft.com/video/cucusoft-ipod-video-converter-dvd-to-ipod-suite.html)

It's worth noting, however, that some of the best DVD ripping tools in life are free.

HACK 4.03: Present PowerPoint on a Projector or TV Using Your iPhone or iPod touch

You can use an iPhone or iPod touch to show presentations on most projectors.

Apple provides two video output cables: the composite AV cable (Figure 4-19) and a component AV cable. These allow the iPhone to send movies and slideshows to an external television. If you're trying to display video on an older television that doesn't support composite or component connectors, then **[Hack #12.05]** will show you how to hook up to coaxial input. Because many projectors also accept composite and component signals, an obvious application is to ditch the laptop and show your PowerPoint presentations with your phone. Alas, though this works, you lose much of the fidelity of your presentation because PowerPoint's movie exporter does not preserve the transitions, slide-in-text, or other animations that may be part of a presentation.

Figure 4-19.
Composite AV cable (from the Apple Store)

There are actually three built-in Apple programs that can output to the TV screen: YouTube, the built in movie player, and the Pictures application—if you connect the cable to the television. But until recently, App Store applications could not access the video output. And until Apple releases a Keynote player for the iPhone, we're going to have to take other measures.

 [Hack #12.06] shows how to enable video out for almost any application.

Simple Slide Export

If your PowerPoint presentation makes minimal use of animations and transitions, the basic trick of exporting each slide to a JPEG file and storing them in your photo library will do the trick. PowerPoint on both Mac and PC has a feature to "Save as Pictures" or "Save as Movie" (Figure 4-20).

Figure 4-20.
Save as Pictures

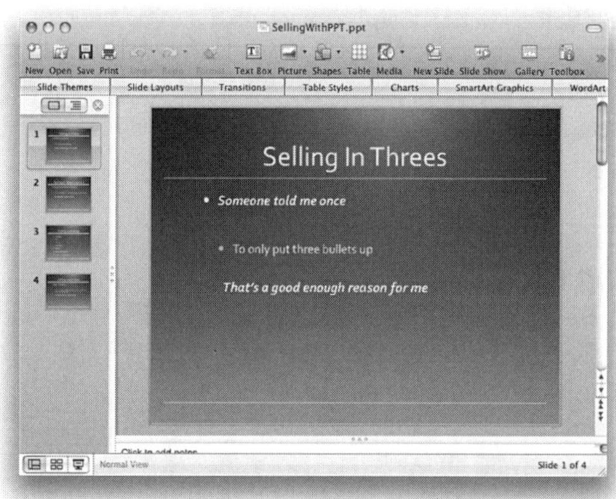

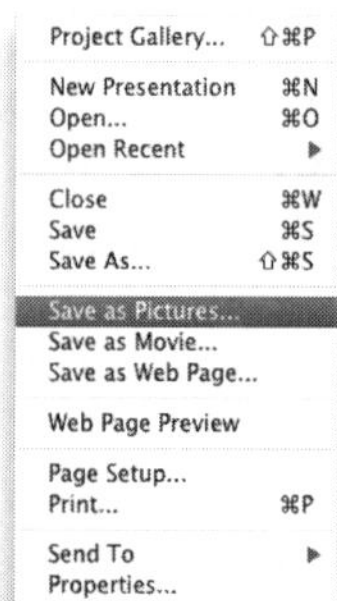

The "Save as Pictures" option will save files to a folder (Figure 4-21) that you can drag to iPhoto, create an album, and then sync to the iPhone or iPod touch with iTunes (Figure 4-23).

Figure 4-21.
A folder full of pictures

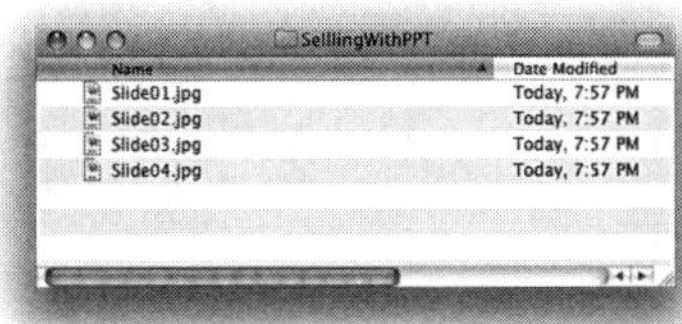

On Windows PowerPoint, choose "Save As..." and choose JPEG. Then choose to save Every Slide (Figure 4-22).

Figure 4-22.
Saving all the slides

Figure 4-23.
Syncing with iTunes

Once you've got the files onto your iPhone or iPod touch, go into Photo Albums, select your presentation, and press the play triangle. If your video cable is connected, the presentation will play on your projector or TV (Figure 4-24).

Figure 4-24.
Playing the presentation

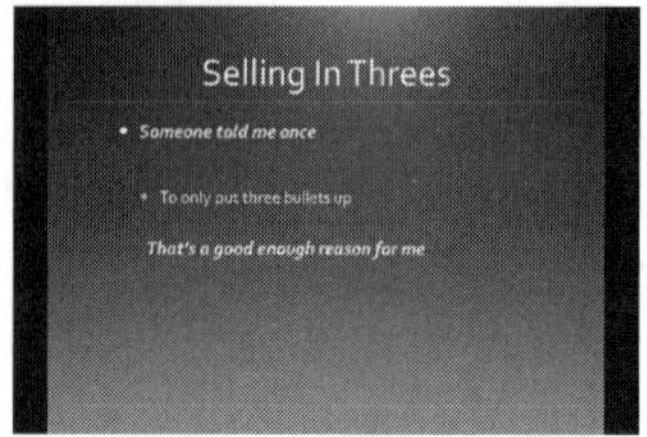

Exporting with Animation

If you are on a Mac, or are a PC user with access to a Mac, you can use Apple's Keynote package (if you have it) to open the PowerPoint document and export it as a movie (Figure 4-25).

Figure 4-25.
Exporting with Keynote

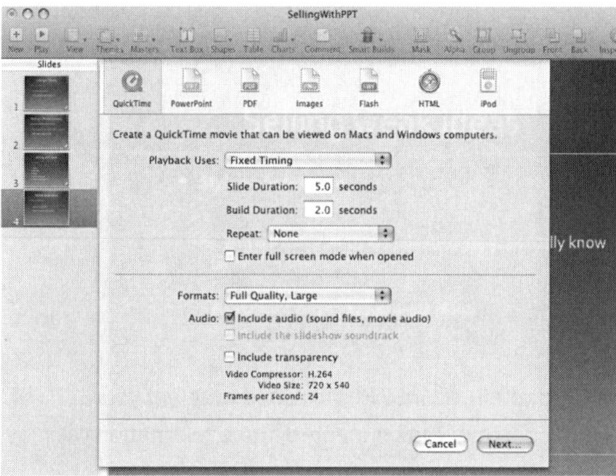

If you're already doing your presentations with Keynote, then this is a good option for you. However, if you've carefully constructed a complex animation, your presentation embeds additional movies and sounds, or it plays back correctly only on your machine, then you'll need to try another option.

Hack It with Screen Capture

There are dozens of applications for screen capture and "screencasting." By using screen capture software, you can run through your presentation—at the speed you want to, as if you were delivering it—and turn it into a video file. A few of them are free, but record only video, not audio. For a lot of presentations, that's sufficient.

A good free option for screen recording on Mac and PC is Jing (www.jingproject.com; Figure 4-26).

Figure 4-26.
Jing

Using Jing is straightforward. Although it's oriented towards uploading your videos, it can just as easily save them to disk, as a SWF format (which you'll need to convert to MP4 using **[Hack #4.02]**). To get it working, follow these steps:

1. Make sure that PowerPoint is set to display in an individual window, not as a full screen. Go to Slide Show→Set Up Show to change this setting (Figure 4-27).
2. When you present your movie, you'll have it in a window. Choose your size—640x480 is good, and that's as high-res as you can play back on the iPhone, but you may need to go higher if fonts are too grainy (and then size it down when you convert). Jing helps you set a precise window size, such as 640x480. You can pause the recording right after it starts, adjust your PowerPoint window, and then resume recording.
3. Once you start the slideshow, use Jing to wrap a capture window around your presentation (Figure 4-28), start the recording, and go through your presentation at your own pace so that you'll know the timings—and when to pause, if necessary—when you finally present it.

Figure 4-27.
Slideshow setup on Mac OS X and Windows

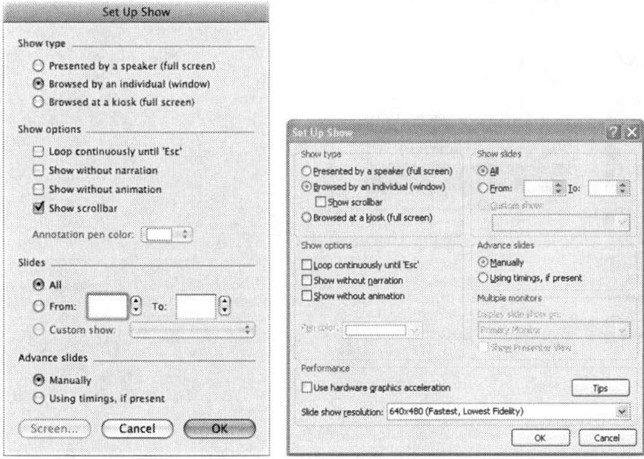

Figure 4-28.
Capturing the slideshow

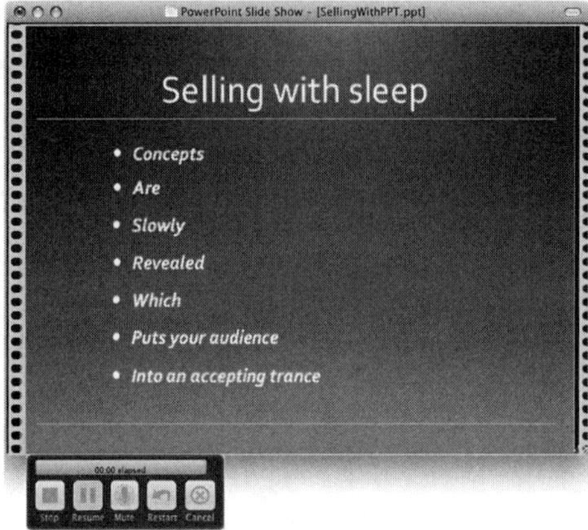

Capturing Audio and Video

If you're on a PC, another free option that does capture audio is CamStudio (http://camstudio.org; Figure 4-29). You'll need to download the 2.0 version or newer to get the audio capture feature. It will save the file as an AVI, and it gives you the option of saving it as an SWF (Flash video). Don't bother; you'll need to convert that AVI to a file that can play on your iPhone **[Hack #4.02]**, and Flash is no help there.

Photo-JPEG videos **[Hack #4.02]** can play on an iPhone, making for great still frames when the content is paused.

Figure 4-29.
Capturing with CamStudio

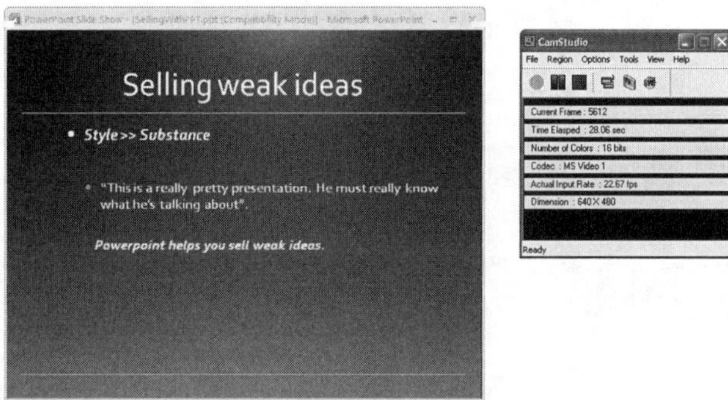

If you need to record audio on the Mac, you'll find some options in the $30–$70 range with iShowU (http://store.shinywhitebox.com) and SnapzProX (www.ambrosiasw.com/utilities/snapzprox).

Presenting

Once you've converted your file, drag it to iTunes, sync your device (Figure 4-30), hook it up to the TV or projector, and play (Figure 4-31).

Figure 4-30.
Syncing an exported slideshow

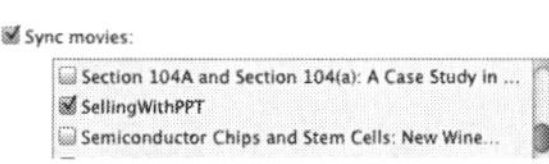

Because you had the chance to rehearse the timings when you made the video, you should have a pretty good sense of when things happen. If you need to pause, perhaps to answer an audience question or because you're talking longer, you can just tap on your iPhone to pause and the image will remain on the screen. And using the seek slider, it's pretty easy to go back to any part of your presentation.

Figure 4-31.
Viewing the slideshow

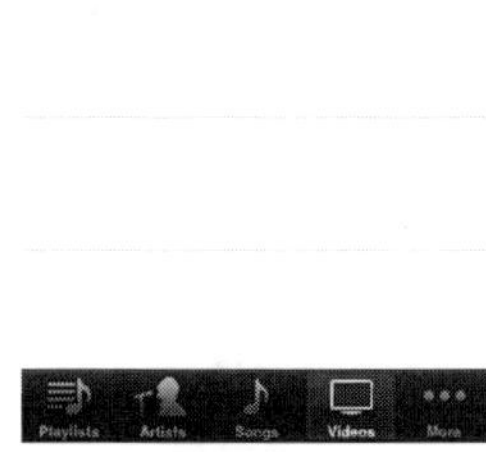

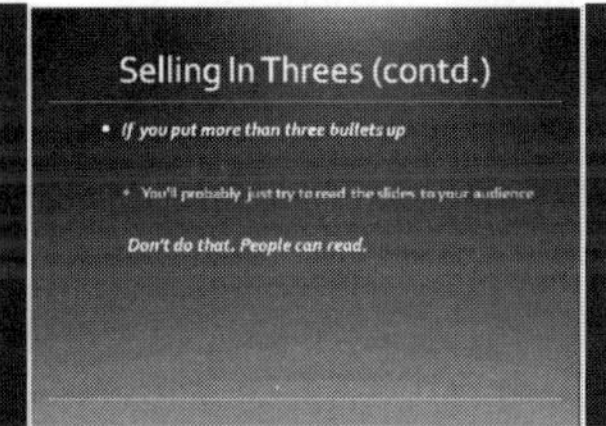

As low-tech as this may sound, you're going to need to stretch a video cable from your iPhone adapter over to the projector, and if you have audio and video, you'll need to extend both of them. Luckily, the low-tech solution is easy to find. At any RadioShack or comparable store, you should be able to find an RCA female-to-female adapter (also known as a *coupler*) to connect to your Apple composite AV cable (Figure 4-32). Then you can use any long RCA cable to reach the projector. It's possible that the A/V staff at your venue will have the cable you need, but just in case, you can pick up any thin 25-foot video cable as well.

Figure 4-32.
RCA extender and Apple composite AV cable

But you don't have to go with the 50-foot wires. Apple does provide a remote control for your iPhone and iPod touch (Figure 4-33): the Apple Universal Dock.

Figure 4-33.
Apple Universal Dock

You can dock your device, plug in the Apple composite AV cable to the dock, plug the cable into the projector, and control your presentation from anywhere in the room.

Even with all the accessories, this solution is much smaller than your laptop, and you could carry enough gear in your pockets to deliver impromptu presentations.

One More Thing

If you really want to stay light while you present on the road, you'll need a tiny projector, like the Optomo Pico pocket projector (www.optoma.co.uk/optomapico/PicoIntro.aspx, Figure 4-34).

Figure 4-34.
Now you're presentable!

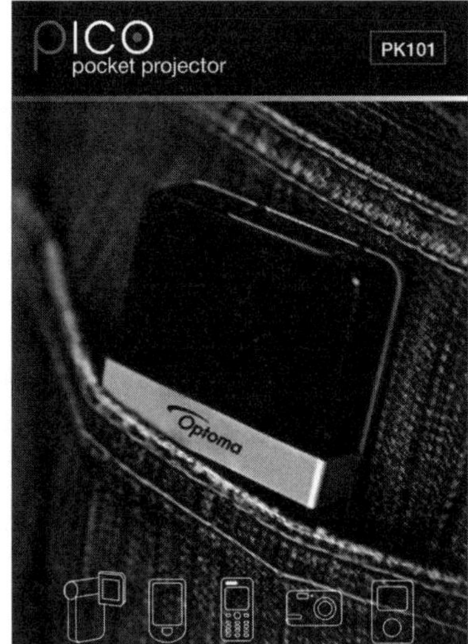

HACK 4.04: Sync Music and Videos from Multiple Computers to Your iPhone

Your device can be friends with more than one iTunes.

Normally, if you try to sync your iPhone with multiple computers, the music and videos that you synced from the previous computer will be overwritten by the media on the new computer. Luckily, there is a native app called SwapTunes that solves this problem by creating two separate media libraries on your iPhone. SwapTunes allows you to sync between two different computers.

SwapTunes can be downloaded from Installer or Cydia **[Hack #1.04]**. After you sync with iTunes on the first computer, click on the SwapTunes icon on your springboard, and a screen that says "Swapping your Music/Video Library..." will open, as in Figure 4-35. After about five seconds, the screen will automatically close to signal that it has finished swapping libraries. Now when you open your iPod, you won't have any music or videos in it.

You can now sync with iTunes on the other computer without your previous media getting erased. Just run SwapTunes whenever you want to switch between the two media libraries on your iPhone.

Figure 4-35.
SwapTunes switching between libraries

Normally, whenever you connect your iPhone to iTunes, the capacity bar at the bottom will be multicolored to show amount of memory taken up by Audio, Video, Photos, Other, and Free Space, as shown in Figure 4-36. After you swap libraries with SwapTunes, iTunes on the same computer will show your iPhone's memory as being solely composed of other media, as in Figure 4-37. Because iTunes doesn't recognize there are any songs or videos on your iPhone, you can now sync it with another computer's library without the older library getting erased.

Figure 4-36.
Prior to using SwapTunes, iTunes displaying the individual Audio, Video, Photos, and other components of the iPhone's capacity at the bottom of the program's window.

Figure 4-37.
After using SwapTunes, iTunes will not recognize the different categories of the iPhone's media Library, and the media will just be recognized as Other.

HACK 4.05: Stream Music and Videos from Your Computer to Your iPhone

You're never too far away from your media.

Although the iPhone's multigigabyte capacity allows a significant amount of media to be stored on it, it probably isn't big enough to hold your entire collection of music and videos. To still be able to access your computer's vast media collection, you will have to stream it over the Internet. The good thing is that you can access your desktop computer anywhere in the world from your iPhone, as long as you have Internet access. Whether you use a Mac or PC, setting up a media stream from your computer is very easy—and free!

Mac

For streaming on Macs, you will be using a system called Telekinesis that allows for (appropriately) remote control of your Mac using your iPhone. Telekinesis uses AppleScript to manipulate your Mac in many ways, differently from VNC **[Hack #9.02]**.

Download the iPhone Remote application from http://code.google.com/p/telekinesis. The first time you run it, it will ask you to set up a username and password for logging in to your computer.

To stream videos over Telekinesis, go into iPhone Remote's configurations, shown in Figure 4-38. If you enable "Share media insecurely," you won't need a password, but it also allows anyone who contacts that port and knows the direct path of your files to download them.

Figure 4-38.
Check this box, if you dare (you dare)

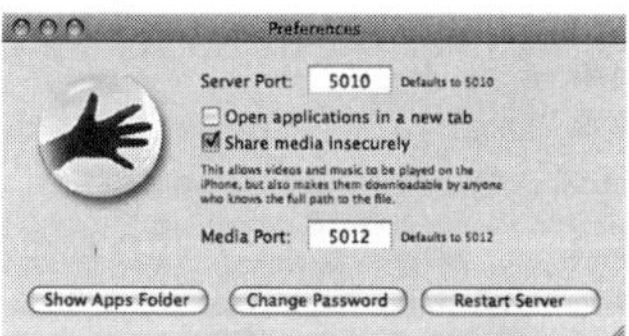

Make sure that iPhone Remote is running. On your iPhone, open up Safari and type in the IP for your Mac, starting with https://. The example in Figure 4-39 displays https://192.168.1.101:5010.

Figure 4-39.
The login screen

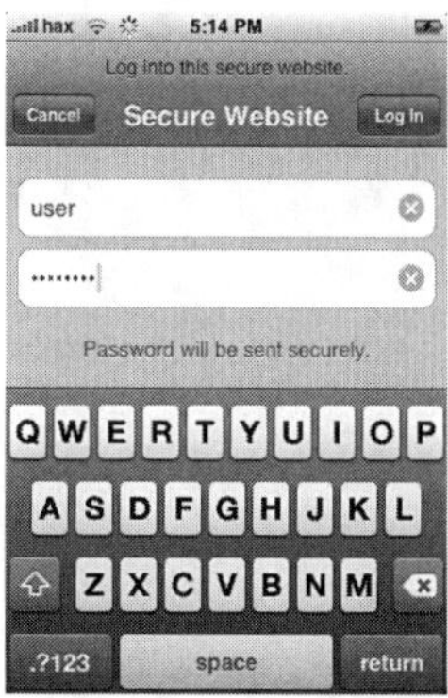

Accept the certificate, and log in with the account that you created when you first ran iPhone Remote. This will bring you to the main screen, as shown in Figure 4-40.

Figure 4-40.
Telekinesis main screen

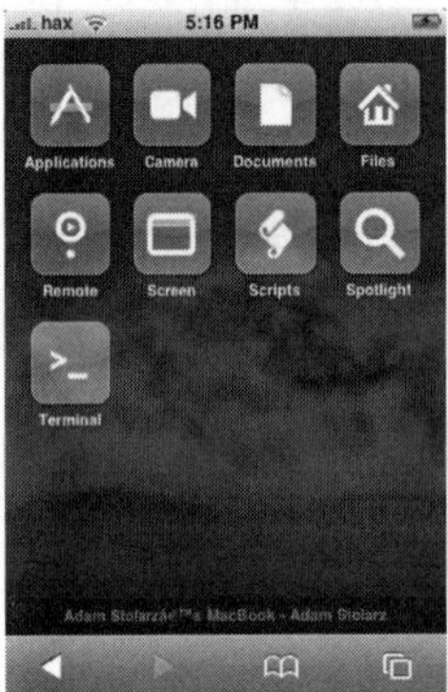

As you can see, there are many different applications that you can use with Telekinesis, but for now we will concern ourselves only with Media. Tap Media to open a browser of your filesystem, shown in Figure 4-41.

Figure 4-41.
Navigating the hard drive

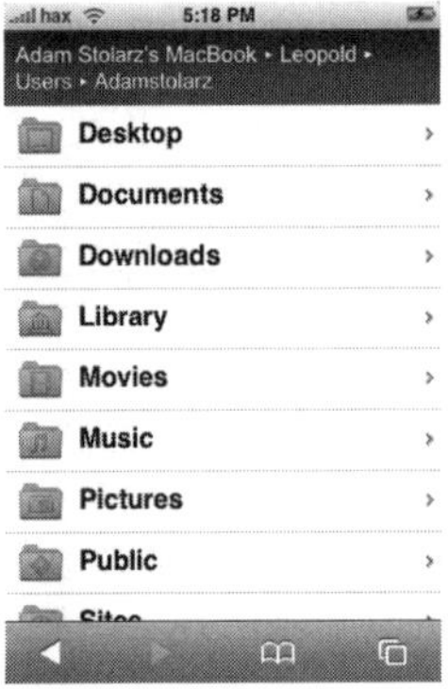

The movie in this example is appropriately in the *Movies* folder. So a tap will bring you to that folder and display the contents as in Figure 4-42.

Figure 4-42.
Playing a movie

Now that you have it all working on your local LAN, you need to get it working through your firewall. The basic procedure is to set a static IP on your Mac, use a dynamic DNS service so that you can attach a name to your home IP address, and then configure your Internet gateway for port forwarding. Once you know the URL to your home PC, you can connect from anywhere. **[Hack #9.11]** has more information on this common but sometimes complicated task.

If your media is elsewhere, it's easy enough to find with Telekinesis's browser. Now just tap to open the video or song, and it will begin streaming. It will continue to play if you go into another iPhone app, but not if you switch Safari pages.

PC

If you're a PC user, or you'd rather use a PC to set up your iPhone media server, there's an even easier solution to your remote-media needs. Orb is a software + service that helps you access your media anywhere. And naturally, they've added support for the iPhone.

Go to http://corp.orb.com/download_orb, create a user account, download Orb, and then install it. Once it is installed on your computer, start the program and you'll see a new icon for Orb at the bottom right of your monitor. Right click the icon, and select Configuration. In the configuration menu, click on the Media tab to select which media folders on your computer will be streamed by Orb, as shown in Figure 4-43.

Figure 4-43.
Configuration of the media to stream in Orb

Whenever the Orb application is running on your computer, your media is being streamed, and is accessible from anywhere. The Orb software and website handles all the complicated parts of firewalls and transcoding.

Once you have Orb configured correctly, you can access it from any browser, not just your iPhone, via http://mycast.orb.com. Log into your account, and you now have access to all the media on your computer, even if you're thousands of miles away from it! Figure 4-44 shows the iPhone app.

Figure 4-44.
The Orb client on iPhone

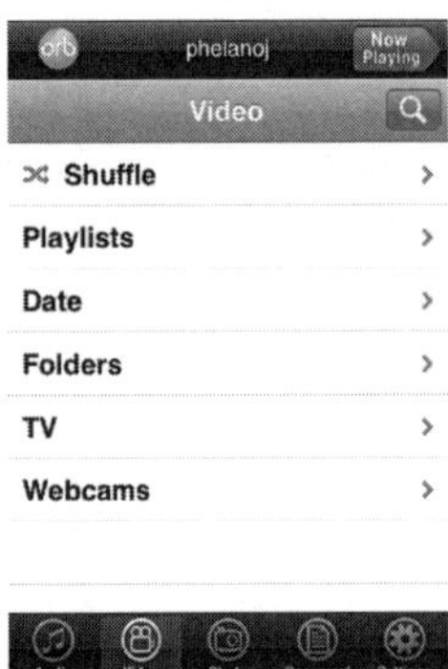

The Orb application costs $10, but the good thing is that you can run the free version of their App Store app and connect to your server to see whether the service works for you before you buy.

Linux: MythTV

The Linux-based DVR project MythTV is a powerful system for viewing and recording TV. With a lot of hard work and a little luck, you can stream recorded shows from your MythTV computer to your iPhone.

For the purposes of this hack, we'll assume that you have to get MythTV set up and running on a computer. If not, instructions can be found on the MythTV wiki (www.mythtv.org) and support pages for your specific Linux distribution.

1. Make sure that you have the MythWeb package installed, and that you can view your MythTV web page from another computer.
2. The next step is to transcode the recordings into MP4 format. Detailed instructions can be found on the MythTV wiki (http://mythtv.org/wiki/index.php/Streaming_to_iPod_touch_or_iPhone). The basic process is to create a script that uses ffmpeg to transcode into an iPod-friendly format. Make sure to test this on your MythTV system before continuing. From a terminal, run the script on a recording, and confirm that the output can be played by mplayer, or any other media player. *lib-faac* is a common source of issues, and depending on the Linux distribution you're using, you may need to compile *lib-faac* from its source.
3. After confirming that transcoding works, load *mythtv-setup* and create a user job to call the transcoding script that you created. In this case, the user job is named "ipod transcoding."
4. Enter MythTV frontend, and set the user job to run automatically after a recording is finished.
5. Confirm that MythTV can run the user job correctly by selecting a recording, then click "run ipod transcoding."
6. Wait a few seconds, then open a terminal and enter `ps -ef|grep ffmpeg`. Confirm that ffmpeg is running. If the only output is only "grep ffmpeg" or blank, go back to the "System Information" screen in MythTV, and confirm that the user job status is "running" and not "queued." If MythTV lists it as running, and there is still no ffmpeg process, then the syntax of the user job is probably incorrect. Double-check it in *mythtv-setup* and confirm that it is correct.
7. Because MythTV can't manage the transcoded files, you will need to create a cron job to delete the MP4 files after the associated recording has been deleted.
8. The MythTV-for-iPhone project is available on Google Code, (http://code.google.com/p/mythtv-for-iphone/wiki/InstallationGuide) and provides an iPhone-formatted web interface to the recorded MythTV programs.
9. Download the MythTV-for-iPhone files, and install *smarty* and *php-curl*. The *smarty* directories should go in the root web folder. For example, if the *mythweb* folder is under */var/www/mythweb*, then the smarty folders would go into */var/www/smarty*. Smarty templates would be installed into */var/www/smarty/templates*.
10. Create a *mythiphone* directory (*/var/www/mythiphone*) and copy the MythTV-for-iPhone PHP files into it. Copy *i_settings.php.dist* to *i_settings.php* and edit it based on the settings of your MythTV server.
11. Update *apache2.conf* and add the line: `Alias /recordings <mythtv recording folder>` at the end of the file.

The MythTV-for-iPhone project references the */recordings* folder, and without this alias, the recordings won't show up.

At this point, everything should be installed. On the iPhone, open Safari and navigate to the *iPhone* folder on your MythTV server. For example, *192.168.2.101/mythiphone*. Any recordings that are green should be viewable on the iPhone.

If you want to access the recordings from a remote location, you will need to assign your MythTV server a static IP **[Hack #9.11]**. If you want to password protect the *mythiphone* folder, you should configure Apache's basic authentication feature (see http://httpd.apache.org/docs/2.0/howto/auth.html).

Cross-Platform: Simplify Media

One last candidate that has support for Linux, Windows, and Mac is Simplify Media (www.simplifymedia.com). Although it works only for audio, it has some features that Orb does not, like the ability to share within a small group so that all your media—from multiple computers—is shared to any of your devices. You can even share within a small group of friends and let them access your media library as well. A trio of media lists can be seen in Figure 4-45.

Figure 4-45.
Simplify Media source lists on Mac, Windows, and the iPhone

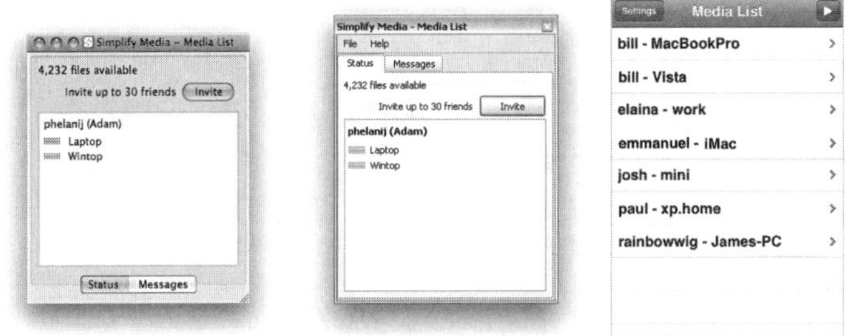

Other Options

It seems like pretty much every home theater system (except maybe Windows Media Center) is adding support for remote iPhone connectivity.

- TVersity: http://tversity.com
- EyeTV: www.elgato.com

— Christopher Kurpinski & Adam Stolarz

HACK 4.06: Read News, RSS, and Websites Quickly

Consume your feeds efficiently.

One of the most interesting evolutions over the last decade of the Web has been syndicated content. Although not everyone is a "news junkie," almost everyone has a daily ration of information that they need to get. However, the excessive load times experienced on even the fastest devices and networks can make accessing this content difficult.

There are dozens of ways to get concise, cleanly formatted, and edited information to your device, and more App Store apps are appearing all the time. This hack will cover a few of the basic ways of maximizing information consumption while minimizing load time.

Really Simple Syndication (RSS)

RSS is a protocol for syndicating content, and is used by weblogs, news sites, and others. The little orange icon you see on many websites (Figure 4-46) indicates a link to an RSS feed. You can read it on a web page, or you can read it more efficiently in an RSS reader.

Figure 4-46.
The universal RSS feed icon

For the purposes of this hack, find a site that has news you care about, find its RSS icon, click on it, and you'll be redirected to the RSS address. Copy or write down this web address, because you'll need it soon.

As examples we'll use Slashdot, WoW Insider, and the update feed for webcomic XKCD.

View RSS Feeds on Your iPhone's Web Browser

The easiest way to view a feed is to just enter it in Safari. If you get to the feed on your computer, you can quickly get it onto your phone by emailing it, texting it **[Hack #3.03]**, or bookmarking it and synchronizing your bookmarks.

In Safari, it will appear like Figure 4-47.

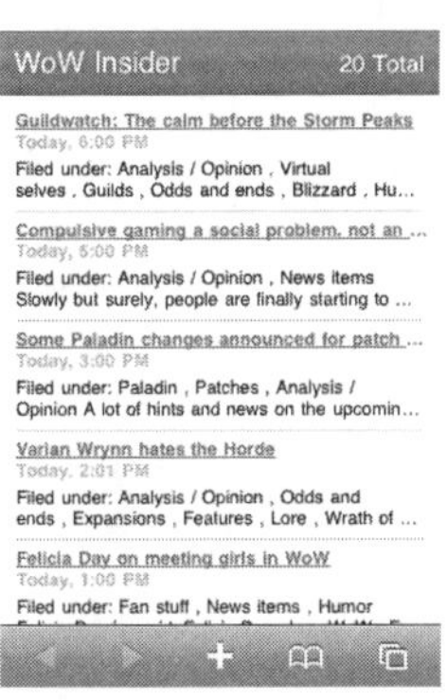

Figure 4-47.
WoW Insider on Safari

Usually people subscribe to several (or a lot) of RSS feeds. An RSS reader aggregates these various feeds into one customized diet of news.

Google News

Google provides one popular RSS aggregator that's optimized for the iPhone. There are dozens—if not hundreds—of these web-based aggregators for the iPhone, so take this as more of an example than a preference.

To view your feeds on your iPhone, just open up your Safari browser, and go to www.google.com/reader. Log in, and you'll see your RSS feed subscriptions that you can select to view (Figure 4-48).

Figure 4-48.
Google Reader showing several feeds

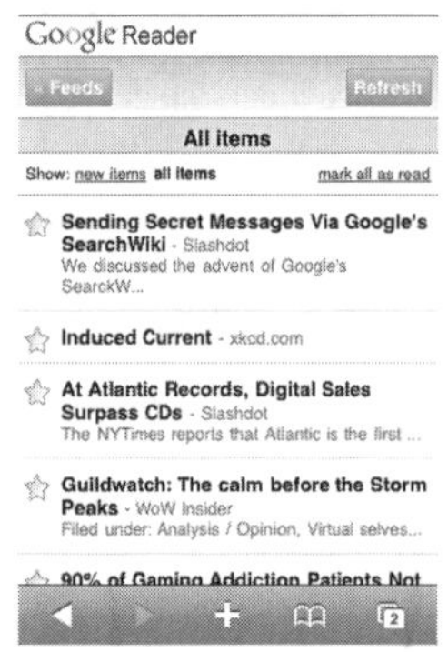

View RSS Feeds on Your iPhone with App Store Apps

Searching for RSS in the App Store will give you more than enough applications to try out. Free RSS Reader by Simon Oulid (Figure 4-49) is a solid, basic offering. The paid version enables automatic caching of pictures.

Figure 4-49.
Free RSS Reader (also works in English)

If you're looking for a more polished interface, you can spend a few bucks more and get iPhoneNewsreader (www.iphonenewsreader.com). Figure 4-50 shows the navigation interface and Figure 4-51 shows nice reading presentation.

Figure 4-50.
Newsfeeds as a stack of magazines

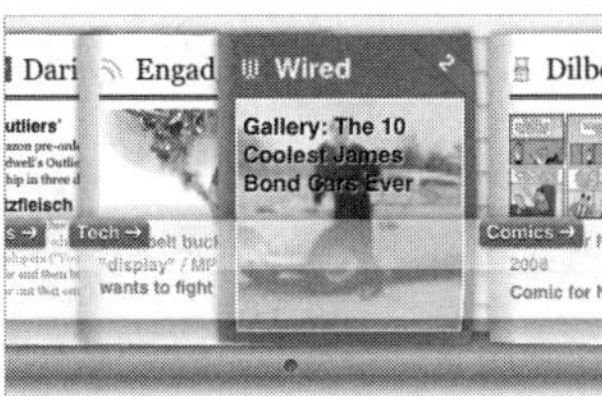

Figure 4-51.
Headlines on the left, articles on the right

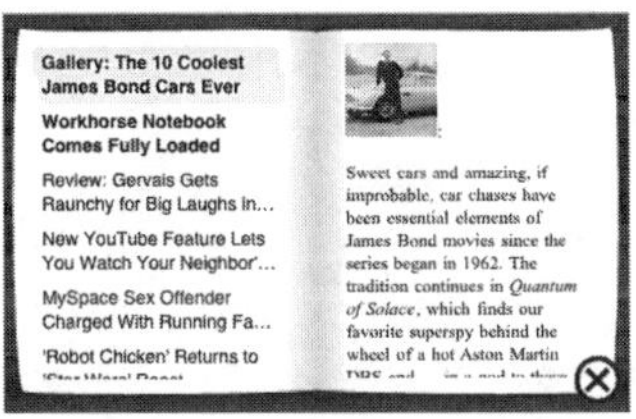

More than RSS

If it's not just RSS feeds you need to keep up with but websites of any variety, check out Instapaper. Like many of the social bookmarking tools, it allows you to mark pages of interest while you're on your PC with the use of a simple bookmarklet. The killer feature, however, is that these bookmarked pages are automatically downloaded and cached for rapid offline reading when you launch the app (Figure 4-52).

A key low-tech-is-better feature of this app is that you can go into a "text-only" mode and enjoy the words without all of the website noise (Figure 4-53).

Figure 4-52.
Ready-to-read whenever you're bored

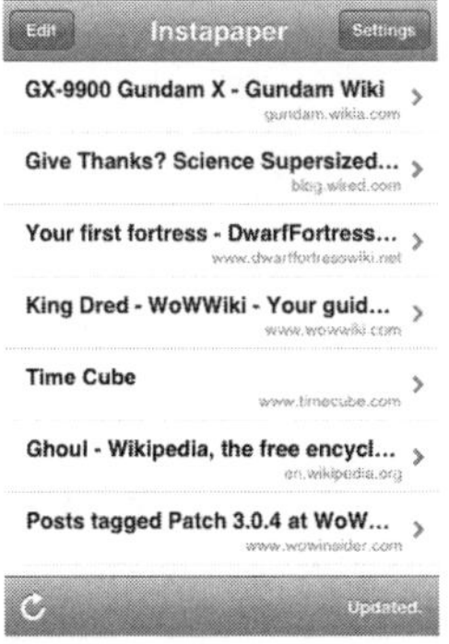

Figure 4-53.
Simple and clean

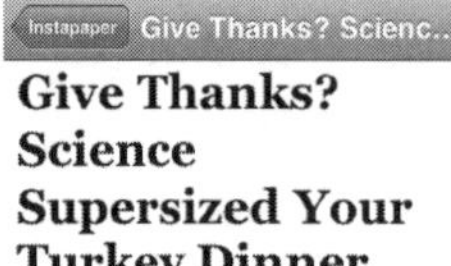

Intelliscreen

The jailbroken phones always get something a little cooler. You can install Intelliscreen using Cydia on a jailbroken device. If you're familiar with Windows Mobile devices, you know that one nice feature they have is useful, at-a-glance information on the screen when the phone is locked. The iPhone tells you only the time and the date and what network you're on. With Intelliscreen, you have a variety of configurable available data—including your RSS feeds. A news-centric screen is shown in Figure 4-54.

Figure 4-54.
Intelliscreen can show RSS feeds and more

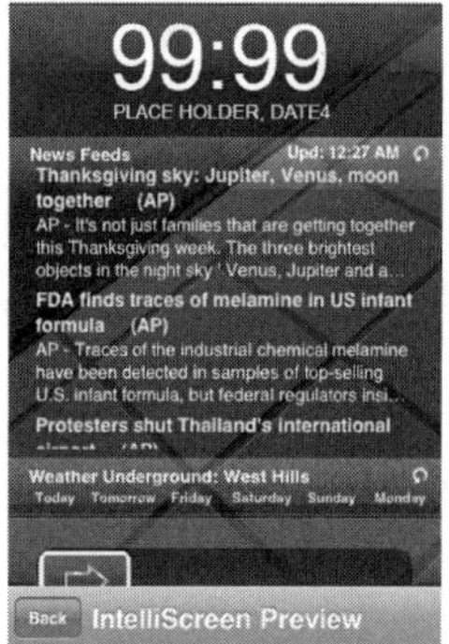

HACK 4.07: Read e-Books on Your iPhone

Be well read.

The term "e-book" in the general sense describes any method by which one could read something approximating a physical book (sequential chapters of text) on an electronic device (hence the "e"). The problem is that due to the vagaries of reader devices and the unproven financial and security models, no single dominant e-book standard has emerged. (You can look at a laundry list of e-book formats here: http://en.wikipedia.org/wiki/Comparison_of_e-book_formats.)

Nonetheless, a number of workable standards have emerged. You may be amused that text (*.txt*) and HTML (*.html*) are two of the most common standards, which shows how hard it is to improve upon the basics. A variety of iPhone applications will allow you to experience the joy of reading literature on what is probably your most handy reading device.

An e-Book Reader Anthology

At the moment, books are handled rather inconsistently in the App Store. Because Apple didn't want to go into the e-book distribution business and compete with Amazon (yet?), there is no "books" option that allows you to buy titles to read with some one-and-true Apple e-book program.

Instead, you have several options: download one of several e-book readers that work with a motley crew of DRM-free formats, or download one of dozens of books, such as *iPhone: The Missing Manual* (O'Reilly), that are packaged individually. A gallery of these is shown in Figure 4-55.

Figure 4-55.
e-books and e-book readers

QUICK TIP 

KINDLE FOR IPHONE

As this book was going to press, Amazon released its Kindle iPhone application, which allows you to read Kindle books on your iPhone. If you have a Kindle, Amazon's WhisperSync keeps your Kindle books in sync across devices (on your iPhone, you can pick up reading where you left off on your Kindle and vice-versa). If you don't own a Kindle, you can still buy books and read them on your iPhone with Kindle for iPhone.

Stanza

The most popular App Store e-book application is the free Stanza, from Lexcycle (www.lexcycle.com). Stanza works with the desktop application of the same name, which can work with HTML, PDF, Microsoft Word, RTF, as well as all the major e-book standards:

- Mobipocket
- Microsoft LIT
- Palm doc
- The epub Open e-book standard
- Unprotected Amazon Kindle

This desktop app (Figure 4-56) lets you easily view and copy your e-books wirelessly over to your iPod. The iPod app also lets you browse from thousands of free e-books and download them straight to your device.

Figure 4-56.
An e-book open in Stanza

With an e-book open in Stanza, you can share it to your device over a wireless network by enabling sharing. Now from your device you can find all the books that you currently have open in Stanza and download them (Figure 4-57). And you're ready to read!

Figure 4-57.
How to steal your own free e-books from yourself

One interesting feature of Stanza is an experimental feature to export books as MP3 audiobooks, so you can listen to them instead of reading them—especially useful if you are driving.

eReader

eReader (www.ereader.com), which you can see in Figures 4-58 and 4-59, is an application provided by fictionwise.com and ereader.com e-book store websites, and is the only one so far to support a form of DRM tolerable to a wider range of commercial publishers. The reader supports convenient direct downloads of eReader-formatted PDB books from these two stores. (Note that PDB is a container format, and not all PDB books work with the program, so make sure that it matches eReader.)

Figure 4-58.
eReader

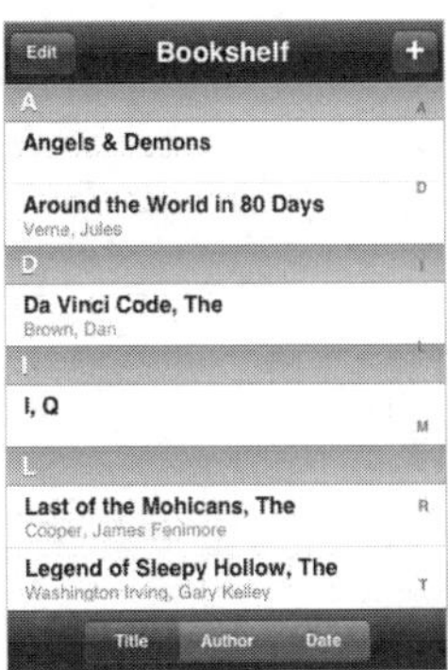

Figure 4-59.
Reading a book in eReader

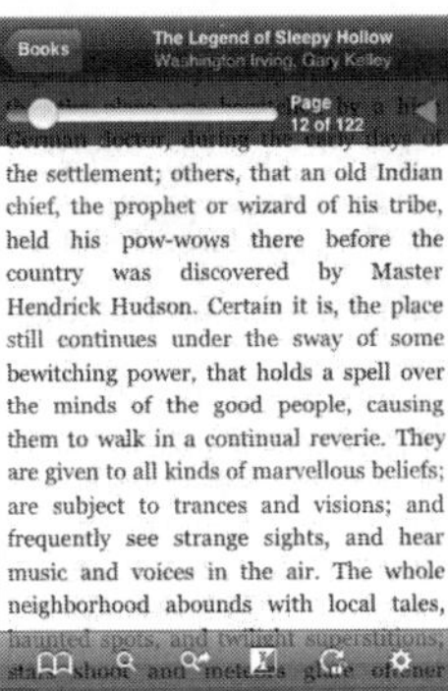

When you purchase a DRM-protected title, you'll have to enter your credentials at least once to make eReader unlock these files (Figure 4-60). You have to get the name you registered with when you made your account online just right, and you have to type in the credit card you used for the purchase. It's best to use the same credit card for all your purchases, as that is your DRM "key."

Figure 4-60.
Logging in to eReader

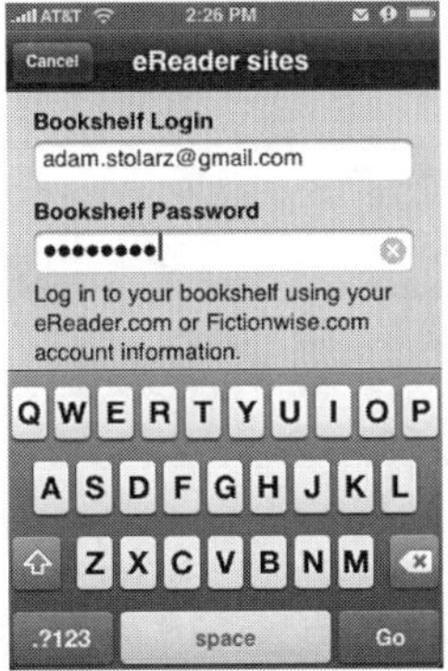

Also, you can feed eReader-formatted PDB books you download from other sites, or PDB files you've created yourself, by serving them from a local web server or uploading them to your eReader.com or Fictionwise.com account and then downloading them to your device (www.ereader.com/personal-content).

BookShelf

BookShelf (www.iphonebookshelf.com) is an App Store application (Figure 4-61) that supports several e-book formats, as long as they aren't DRM-encrypted, including text, HTML, a variety of Palm formats (Plucker, PalmDoc, Mobi), and a few others. To feed it books, run the ShelfServer application on your computer desktop (PC, Mac, and Linux are supported; Figure 4-62). ShelfServer can also slurp the text out of PDFs to convert them for ingestion as an e-book.

Figure 4-61.
BookShelf means books

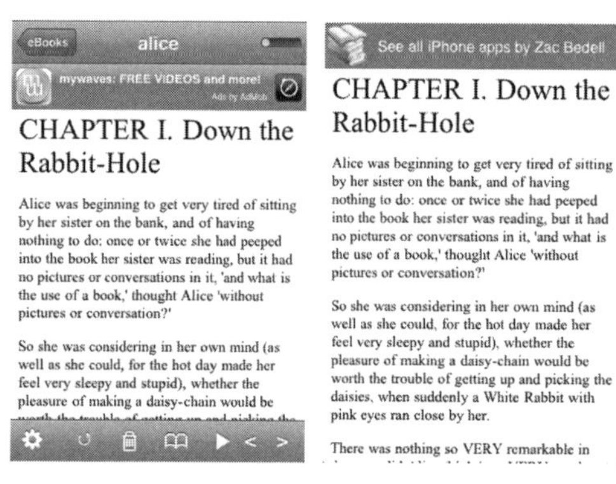
eBooks
alice
mywaves: FREE VIDEOS and more!
CHAPTER I. Down the Rabbit-Hole
Alice was beginning to get very tired of sitting by her sister on the bank, and of having nothing to do: once or twice she had peeped into the book her sister was reading, but it had no pictures or conversations in it, 'and what is the use of a book,' thought Alice 'without pictures or conversation?'
So she was considering in her own mind (as well as she could, for the hot day made her feel very sleepy and stupid), whether the pleasure of making a daisy-chain would be
See all iPhone apps by Zac Bedell
CHAPTER I. Down the Rabbit-Hole
Alice was beginning to get very tired of sitting by her sister on the bank, and of having nothing to do: once or twice she had peeped into the book her sister was reading, but it had no pictures or conversations in it, 'and what is the use of a book,' thought Alice 'without pictures or conversation?'
So she was considering in her own mind (as well as she could, for the hot day made her feel very sleepy and stupid), whether the pleasure of making a daisy-chain would be worth the trouble of getting up and picking the daisies, when suddenly a White Rabbit with pink eyes ran close by her.
There was nothing so VERY remarkable in

Figure 4-62.
ShelfServer serving up a folder of e-books

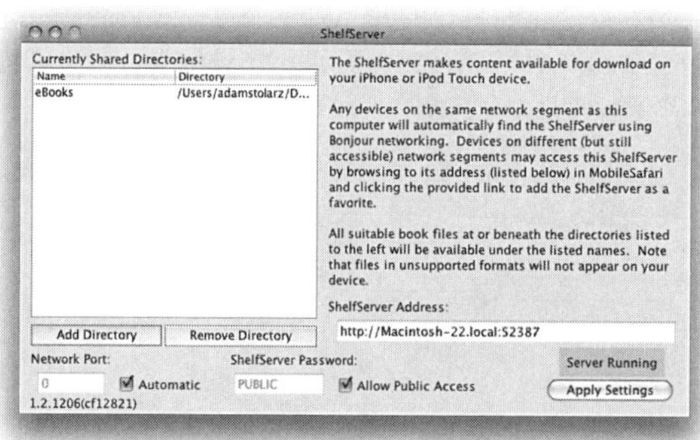
ShelfServer
Currently Shared Directories:
Name
Directory
eBooks
/Users/adamstolarz/D...
The ShelfServer makes content available for download on your iPhone or iPod Touch device.
Any devices on the same network segment as this computer will automatically find the ShelfServer using Bonjour networking. Devices on different (but still accessible) network segments may access this ShelfServer by browsing to its address (listed below) in MobileSafari and clicking the provided link to add the ShelfServer as a favorite.
All suitable book files at or beneath the directories listed to the left will be available under the listed names. Note that files in unsupported formats will not appear on your device.
ShelfServer Address:
http://Macintosh-22.local:52387
Add Directory
Remove Directory
Network Port:
ShelfServer Password:
Server Running
Automatic
PUBLIC
Allow Public Access
Apply Settings
1.2.1206(cf12821)

You can also download from online book sites that support the ShelfServer protocol, listed at www.iphonebookshelf.com.

PDFs

For reading e-books that are PDF format, there's not much to do—you just email the PDF to yourself. The problem is that most PDFs are unreadable on small devices and require much scrolling and clicking when zoomed in to a readable magnification. This is not so much a fault of the iPhone as a known fault of PDF, which was designed to preserve, with high fidelity, the look and dimensions of a conventional book. If you're in a pinch and need to read a large PDF, one trick is to email it to a Gmail account—Gmail lets you read the PDF attachment as a text file, which can make a single-column view in Safari a better experience.

Classics

One e-book offering available in the App Store that has to be mentioned is Classics. A model of user interface design, this application packages up nine classic books into a classy and fun-to-read interface (Figure 4-63). A bookshelf presentation, followed by 3D effects for page turns (Figure 4-64) and attention to hyphenation, spacing, fonts, and readability, this application sets a high bar for e-books on the iPhone. Unfortunately, as of now there's no way to add books to this handsome bookshelf.

Figure 4-63.
Classics

AT&T
4:04 PM
CALL OF THE WILD
Paradise Lost
The Jungle Book
The TIME MACHINE

Figure 4-64.
Classics: turning the page

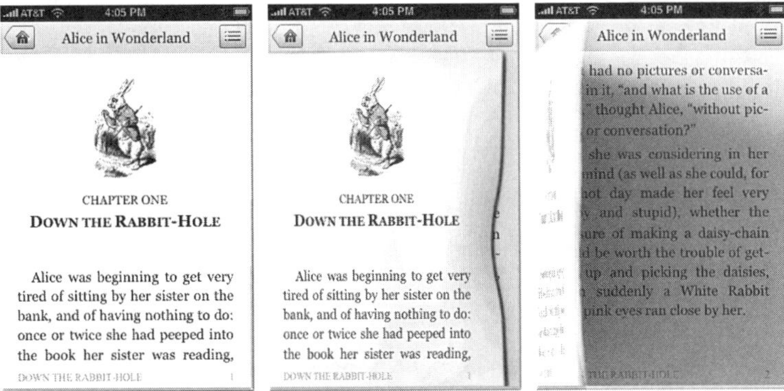
AT&T
4:05 PM
Alice in Wonderland
CHAPTER ONE
DOWN THE RABBIT-HOLE
Alice was beginning to get very tired of sitting by her sister on the bank, and of having nothing to do: once or twice she had peeped into the book her sister was reading,
DOWN THE RABBIT-HOLE
1

ComicZeal

If you like comics, then there's another app for you—ComicZeal (www.bitolithic.com/ComicZeal/comiczeal.htm). This application provides excellent features for reading comics (Figure 4-65).

Because most of the CBR/CBZ comic files that are downloadable from the Internet are of too high a resolution for the iPhone's screen, Bitolithic provides the ComicZealCreator for Mac and

Windows to convert comic files to the ComicZeal *.cbi* format (www.bitolithic.com/ComicZeal/comiczealcreator/comiczealcreator.htm). These reduced-size files are easier on the iPhone's CPU, which translates to longer battery life and thus longer readability. The program even starts up a mini web server, so you can type the address into ComicZeal and download your files.

Figure 4-65.
ComicZeal doing its thing

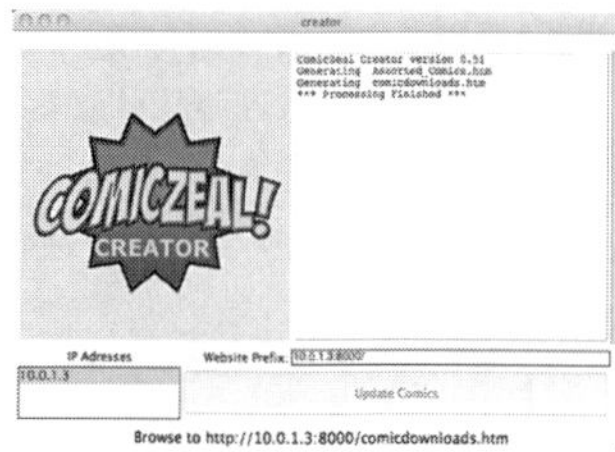

Finding Professional-Quality Content

The problem with e-books is that no one has created the "iTunes of e-books" (not that Amazon.com isn't trying), in the sense that the majority of new books are not available in a digital format. Music CDs are inherently digital; books, using "dead-tree technology," are still primarily analog media, despite their digital production process.

Like iTunes Plus and the variety of music options available on the market without DRM, there are some places where you can purchase unencumbered e-books of twentieth- and twenty-first-century content (i.e., content still under copyright).

 A good resource for e-book sources is http://wiki.mobileread.com/wiki/E-book_stores.

Examples include:

- Feedbooks (http://feedbooks.com)
- eReader (www.ereader.com)
- Fictionwise (http://fictionwise.com)
- ManyBooks (http://manybooks.net)
- PanMacmillan (www.panmacmillan.com)
- CyberRead (www.cyberread.com)
- Project Gutenberg (http://gutenberg.org)
- Safari Books (http://safari.oreilly.com)

Dictionaries

If you're going to read, you'll often want a dictionary nearby. Fortunately, there are a number of great options for iPhone-based dictionaries.

WeDict (free)

Of key import for college students, writers, and people learning another language is a portable knowledge base for all things linguistic. That's what you get with WeDict, a flexible dictionary for the iPhone and iPod touch. One of the cleverest things about WeDict is that you can download it from the App Store, but then enhance it (on a jailbroken phone) via Cydia.

1. Download WeDict from the App Store
2. Add the Merriam-Webster dictionary via Cydia (Figure 4-66).

Figure 4-66.
Blurring the line between SDK and jailbroken apps

Open WeDict, type in the word you want defined, and then hit the Search button at the top right to get your results. A gallery of different dictionary results is displayed, as in Figure 4-67.

Figure 4-67.
Seen here: entries from Merriam-Webster, English Etymology, and English-German

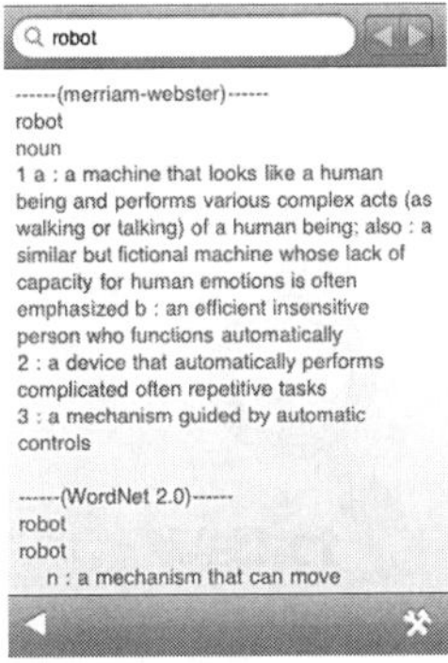

AHED

One of the remarkable things about the iPhone and iPod touch is that you can get full, unabridged dictionaries. Figure 4-68 shows the *American Heritage Dictionary*, available for a hefty $30—but worth it all. This is the real deal—it's a standard for many writers and editors, rather than a cheap knockoff, and you won't be left scratching your head for a missing definition.

Figure 4-68.
American Heritage Dictionary

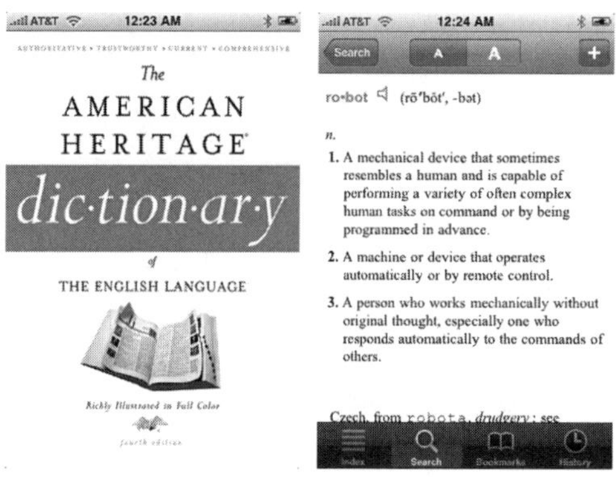

Despite the early, disorganized state of the iPhone/iPod e-book economy, there are real gems to be found in the hundreds of thousands of books available in e-book format. Your iPhone or iPhone touch just became your walking dictionary (and more). It just goes to show that the more you put into the iPhone, the more you get out of it!

HACK 4.08: Take Panoramas and Nightshots with Your Built-in Camera

Two megapixels is plenty!

The iPhone's built-in camera is unable to compete with dedicated cameras for image quality. However, you have it with you everywhere you go, and chances are good that you don't carry your camera except to special events. Therefore, there are many times when you want to milk the last bit of image quality out of your camera.

Two areas where you may want to enhance your iPhone camera are:

1. Low light conditions (night shots)
2. Resolution and field of view

Resolution and Field of View Enhancement

A 2-megapixel resolution isn't too shabby for a tiny camera hiding in the corner of your iPhone. If you where you want a much bigger image, you may be missing your 8-megapixel dedicated camera. The solution is to stitch your photos together to create a larger frame. One common application for this is when you want to photograph a large poster at a conference, so you can read the text later, but the fonts are too small to see in one frame.

If you have a Mac, you can use software called Calico Panorama, manufactured by Kekus Digital (www.kekus.com). It is relatively cheap: $39 as of this printing. On a PC, you can use freeware software called AutoStitch that uses a prior version of the same code engine (www.cs.ubc.ca/~mbrown/autostitch/autostitch.html).

First, take a "panorama set" of photos, that is, a series of photos, making sure to overlap them generously. When going from side to side, I find it useful to move the camera just enough to put the right half of the screen onto the left half. Therefore, for a total image width of three fields of view, you will take five side-by-side photos. If you wish, you can do multiple rows as well.

Figure 4-69 shows an example I made at the Getty museum in Los Angeles (www.getty.edu), starting with several side-by-side images.

Figure 4-69.
Three photos

Run these through the panorama software (in this case, I used AutoStitch), shown in Figure 4-70.

Figure 4-70.
Stitched results

The result is the maximum field of view that the software can produce from the images you gave it. It will automatically align them and adjust contrast and color settings to make the result seamless. The last thing you'll need to do is crop the edges to produce a finished product, as shown in Figure 4-71.

Figure 4-71.
Cropped image

Low Light Conditions

The iPhone camera is pretty smart about auto-adjusting contrast when bright and dim objects are both in the field of view. Nevertheless, it requires a minimum light intensity in order to form an image. At night, for example, there often is insufficient light to create a nice photo. However, if you can distinguish *any* shapes in your image, then you can merge dozens of photos in order to produce a single higher-contrast image. You need to have one well-defined visible object in the image. This can be a penlight, street lamp, or whatever. This provides a single object that is visible in each image and allows you to align the images. Next, you will need an open source software package available (for Macs only!) called Lynkeos. Generally, it is used by astronomers to improve the quality of images taken through telescopes—but there's no reason that you can't use it to create images of the beautiful city lights taken from your drive home after skiing (when you had only your iPhone).

First, you need to obtain images. Set your camera against an object so that it is very still. Even a slight shake of your hand will introduce blurring in the final image. This means you can set your iPhone on its side on a rock, table, against a tree, or something like that. You can even use a shoe as a tripod. Shoes and socks are handy because you (hopefully) always have them with you and they won't scratch your iPhone.

Adjust your iPhone position so that you can both reach the snapshot button and so that your frame contains at least one sharp, bright object. You should see it well in your camera roll on every photo. This is critical or Lynkeos will not be able to squarely align the images.

Take as many images as you can stand—you will probably need several dozen, and you won't know if you got enough until you go to process them. The more images you take, the better your final image becomes—assuming you are photographing a still environment. Unfortunately, this technique won't work for catching a moving object! (No photographing nocturnal panthers using your iPhone!)

When you get back home, download the images onto your computer, and use Lynkeos (http://lynkeos.sourceforge.net) to "stack" the images and produce one final high-quality frame (Figure 4-72). Note that Lynkeos is available only for Mac OS X.

Figure 4-72.
Stacking the images

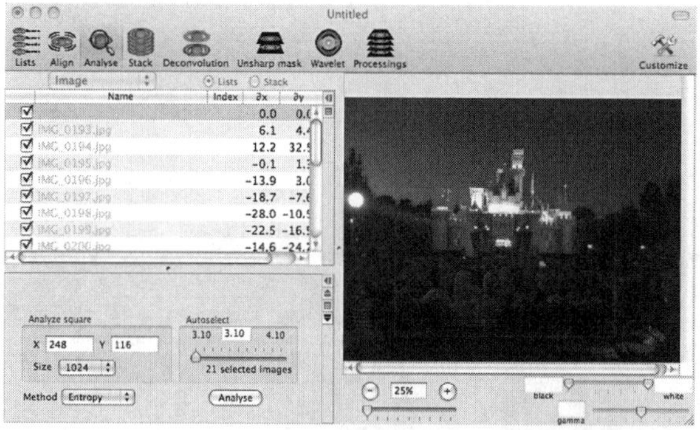

There is a very quick and easy tutorial for Lynkeos available from its Help menu. You should go through that tutorial, which takes less than 10 minutes.

Figure 4-73 shows an example of an image before processing; Figure 4-74 shows the results.

Figure 4-73.
Before

Figure 4-74.
After

It's like night and day!

PanoLab Pro

If you'd like to do your photo fixing and panoramas right on the phone, PanoLab (Figure 4-75) is an option. This inexpensive App Store app helps you align your panorama pictures as you take them (Figure 4-76), and lets you easily align the edges of the various pieces using your fingers and multitouch.

Figure 4-75.
PanoLab Pro

Figure 4-76.
Aligning the photo

PanoLab Pro also includes an exposure adjustment feature (Figure 4-77) that helps adjust for varying light conditions between shots.

Figure 4-77.
Adjusting the exposure

You can export your large panoramas at high resolutions to your computer so that they can be printed out or displayed in their full glory.

— Zack Gainsforth & Damien Stolarz

 HACK 4.08: Record and Upload Videos with Your iPhone

Surprise: Your iPhone is a great videocamera.

One of the most conspicuous missing features of the iPhone is out-of-the-box videocamera capability. Almost every other smartphone on the market is smart enough to record decent video clips for posterity. Until Apple adds video recording, there are several video camera alternatives for your jailbroken phone.

A Brief History of Consumer Filming

In the 1940s, we could really film only movies and wars. The 1950s and 1960s brought us 8 mm cameras, but only presidents and other wealthy elite could afford the film. It was the invention of the VCR in the 1970s that paved the way for the 1980s, when videocameras came to the mass market. Weddings, bar mitzvahs, birthday parties, and births were all preserved for time immemorial using boombox-sized cameras on the shoulder. The 1990s brought us smaller and cheaper cameras and we began branching out, stealthily capturing concerts, movie bootlegs, and police beatings. Once we finally went digital and solid-state in the 2000s, videocameras jumped onto phones—and now almost anyone can catch the ephemeral events of life and upload them for viewing by complete strangers.

Cycorder

Cycorder (www.saurik.com) by Jay Freeman (a.k.a. **saurik**), is a fantastic, responsive, and free (ad-supported) application for video capture. You can find it featured in Cydia.

Cycorder records at a little less than half of a normal TV's or videocamera's frames per second, taking a JPEG picture of each 384x288 frame. Because they're JPEG instead of MPEG-4, each frame is very clear when paused. You can see the specs in Figure 4-78.

Figure 4-78.
Specs of a Cycorder recording

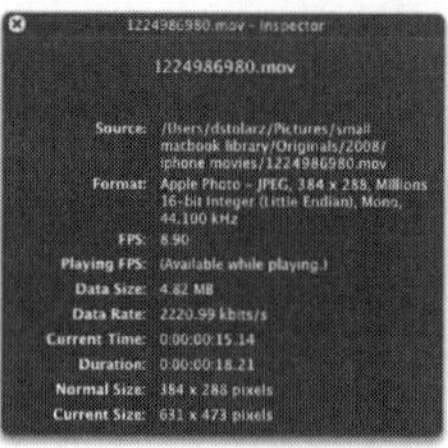

Because of the quality of the recording and the relatively light compression, the bit rate is very high (in this case, almost 2.5Mbps), so a 15-second movie takes almost 5 MB on disk.

iPhone Video Recorder

The payware solution, which still requires a jailbroken phone, is iPhone Video Recorder (www.iphonevideorecorder.com), shown in Figure 4-79. You can install it by adding the www.iphonevideorecorder.com source to Cydia. It allows you to capture either to JPEG MOVs in real time (like Cycorder) or to do a post-encode to MPEG-4, which is significantly smaller and thus easier to upload. The iPhone, as you might imagine, was never intended as a video encoding device (its MPEG-4 chip accelerates only playback, not recording).

Figure 4-79.
iPhone Video Recorder

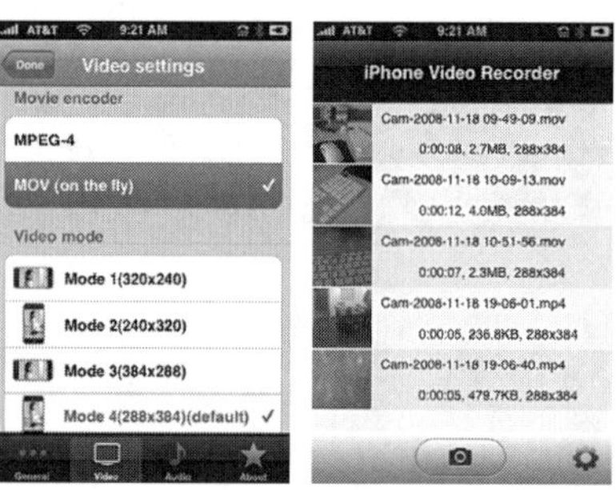

A remarkable feature of this software is the ability to upload videos directly to YouTube (Figure 4-80). Naturally, you'll need a YouTube account and you'll need to add your login and password in the application.

Figure 4-80.
Uploading to YouTube

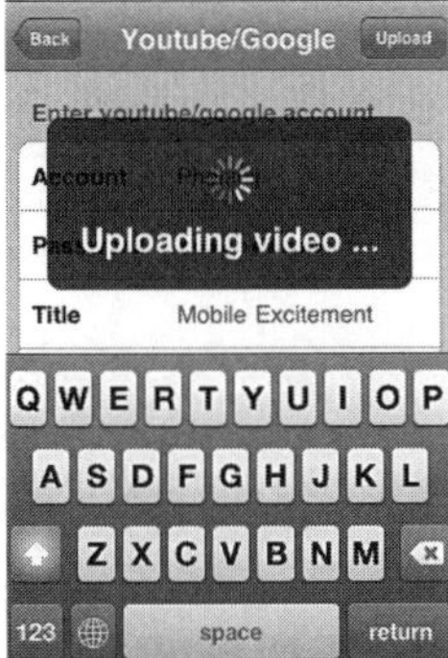

We can only speculate why the iPhone shipped without an integrated videocamera application, but it's easy to remedy on a jailbroken phone.

05 GAME EMULATION

No one imagined that Apple would ever go into the video game space. Macs have long been criticized for their lack of games, and Windows has long been the system of choice for advanced PC gaming. But if you believe the hype, Apple's iPhone is a potential "game changer" in video gaming.

The iPhone is both well suited—and hamstrung—with respect to games. Its lack of tactile buttons—depending entirely on multitouch for keypresses—makes it a less satisfying experience than, say, a Sony PSP. However, its inclusion of an accelerometer gives it some of the "outside-of-the-box" vision that made the Nintendo's Wii controllers (also accelerometer-enhanced) so popular.

Now, don't expect people to start swinging their iPods around to play virtual table tennis—at least, not yet. The lack of a high-speed video output capability and a standard method of attaching accessories prevents the iPhone from being an immediate replacement for your Wii. But the handheld personal nature of the device, its virtually unlimited offboard storage (i.e., the Internet), and its geoconnected features are already inspiring startups to go after location-enabled "social gaming" concepts. And the multitouch screen, though bad for buttons, is good for new control modalities—such as drawing lines or "chording" multiple touch points—and games built around these new control paradigms are in the offing.

But one of the unsung opportunities for the iPhone is not to go forward into the new, but to emulate the old. There is a rich, hackerish tradition in the computer world of making any new computer or video game system emulate those that came before it. Sony and Nintendo regularly allow their new consoles to play (when possible) older "classic" games, because just like an old movie, these games are just as playable now as they were 25 years ago.

The iPhone and iPod definitely break new ground enhancing "productivity," especially when "productivity" means producing high scores in your favorite video game.

HACK 5.01: Understand the Homebrew and Emulation Scene

Certain useful knowledge helps you get the most out of video game emulators.

If you're familiar with computer science, you may know about Moore's Law. Gordon Moore was one of the cofounders of Intel, and in the mid 1960s, he predicted that computer speed (actually, transistor density, or how many computing units fit on a chip) would double about every two years. Seemingly, in violation of Murphy's Law, Moore's Law has remained true, and we've seen a doubling of computing power (or a halving of size for equivalent power) about every two years. What this means is that in the 8 years from 1999 to 2007, the CPU power in commercially available handhelds multiplied by 16 times—actually quite a bit more, considering the 16MHz CPU that the Palm V was using at that time.

Emulation

Video game consoles have usually been made with CPU and speed similar to that available to their computer contemporaries. Even arcade machines are simply powered by custom computers. Thus, the latest computer can almost always emulate—with fair fidelity—the video games of a few years ago. The nice thing about game consoles—arcade, home, or portable—is that they are tremendously consistent in their construction. Compared to the variability of PC and even Macintosh hardware, a new version of which comes out every couple of months with new features (often at the cost of driver compatibility), game consoles are designed to last 5, 7, or even 10 years in the market before they are finally retired.

As a result of this consistency, and because game systems proliferate in the millions (the PlayStation has shipped 100 million units worldwide), the number of creative hackers paying attention to these platforms is tremendous. Sometimes this attention is for the nefarious purposes of software piracy, but often it is for the benign and even laudable purposes of implementing game modifications, cheats, creating new homebrew games, and general learning.

Usually, when a game system comes out, hardware hackers and cheat-system developers will study a platform and find methods for attaching peripherals—often to the same connections used by the original hardware designers for debugging or to ports built into the product for future expansion. At this time, the platform is usually on a par with computers of that era, making emulation infeasible. But gradually, as general community knowledge grows (especially since the 1990s, fueled by BBS communication, and later, by the Internet), the entire ROM (read-only memory) and BIOS (Basic Input/Output System) of the game system are extracted from a gaming system and carefully reverse-engineered and analyzed.

Because game PCs use the same kinds of CPU as computers (often Motorola chips, such as 6502s in the 1980s or Power PCs in the 1990s), and because full chip emulators are available for most of these chips on PC platforms, it's only a matter of time before the code extracted from the memory hardware of these systems runs completely "in vitro," in the test tube of the PC.

By the time these systems are fully understood, computer speed has advanced to a point at which a modern PC can easily emulate the full processor and graphics capabilities of the original gaming console, and they often do.

Homebrew

In the early days of video games, such as the Atari era, it was understood that computers and video games are related, and many game systems also had an optional programming cartridge, keyboard, and other tools for interacting with the system. The manufacturers were not too restrictive about modifications to their systems.

Later systems, such as Nintendo's, built a strong business around being a "gatekeeper" of titles, and it was difficult to create cartridges for this system without going through them. But by the 1990s, when games became epic in length, with sprawling levels, it became relatively straightforward to create new levels for games, because the border between a game engine and the data (levels) for that engine was easily distinguishable to reverse-engineers. These "mods" or modifications to games became possible through a variety of hardware tools such as GameGenie, GameShark, and a community built up around not only "cheating" games but also modifying them.

In the same fashion, people began trying to create their own entire games. In the 1990s, Sony actually embraced the idea of PlayStation hobbyist-coders and produced the Net Yaroze PlayStation—a more expensive PlayStation that included a method of connecting it to the PC and programming games, in C, on the console.

The hacking and game cloning community came up with their own workarounds that allowed independent creation of games and game hacks for these systems. Once the games could be completely emulated on a PC, the task of extending games or creating games became much easier, and homebrew games could be distributed via the Web to others with the emulator. For consoles like the Sega Dreamcast, Sony PSP, and Nintendo Game Boy Advance (GBA), convenient loading mechanisms made it straightforward to play homebrew games on the actual hardware.

A decade-strong website where you can find a lot of homebrew activity for all major mobile and gaming platforms is www.pdroms.de.

Running an Emulator

The punch line of all this is of course that the iPhone is fast enough to emulate a fair number of games, and that most of the major emulators have been already ported to the iPhone. Figure 5-1 shows the */var/mobile/Media/ROMs* folder on a jailbroken iPhone with all the major emulators installed.

Figure 5-1.
The */var/mobile/Media/ROMs/* folder

Name	Date Modified
GAMEBOY	Today, 9:33 PM
GBA	Today, 5:51 PM
GENESIS	Today, 2:50 PM
MAME	Today, 11:41 PM
NES	Today, 3:51 PM
PSX	Today, 11:38 PM
SCUMMVM	Today, 10:39 PM
SNES	Today, 11:15 PM

ZodTTD is the online name of the developer who has been behind almost every game emulator release for the iPhone. You can find his site, and a lot of info about his emulation exploits, at www.zodttd.com (Figure 5-2).

Figure 5-2.
ZodTTD's website (www.zodttd.com)

Probably the best way to get started with game emulation is to download some working emulation software for the PC so that you can try out various ROM files and make sure that everything is working before you transfer them to the somewhat slower iPhone.

There are only a few important terms that you'll run into:

- *Game cartridges* generally store programs in read-only memory, and when they are backed up on a PC, they are called *ROMs*. Downloading a ROM means downloading a memory dump of a game cart. In practice, a good emulator can run the majority of ROMs—homebrew and commercial—for a given game system.
- Some game consoles, such as the Sony PlayStation and GBA, require a memory dump of the BIOS contained in the system itself in order for the emulator to run. This code is not freely available separately from the console, but there are various hardware and software techniques used to get these files.
- Some game systems, such as the Sony PlayStation, use a CD instead of a cartridge, and game backups are stored in an *.ISO* file. This is sometimes referred to as a "ROM," as it is a copy of the game file.

For links on where to download game emulators, check out sites such as www.emulator-zone.com and www.zophar.net, or Google "game emulator."

— Damien Stolarz & ZodTTD

HACK 5.02: Play Nintendo Games on Your iPhone or iPod touch

With the native application NES, you can be playing Nintendo Entertainment System games on your iPhone within minutes.

The Nintendo Entertainment System (Figure 5-3) was released in 1985, and its 8-bit might brought the entire video game industry out of the confusing failing mess that it had been in two years prior. It set the standard for game design and controller layout for all future consoles. Many of the most memorable classic games were for this very console. It dominated the market until the release of the Sega Genesis a few years later.

Figure 5-3.
The Nintendo Entertainment System

Getting a Homebrew ROM

The page http://bobrost.com/nes details the results of a course taught at Carnegie Mellon University by Bob Rost in 2004 on programming for the NES, and provides a number of games developed by students in the class. They are good examples of entertaining homebrew games.

You can download the ROM for Sack of Flour, a platform game similar to the Mario series, to emulate on your iPhone from http://bobrost.com/nes/games.php.

It runs smoothly (Figure 5-4), as it should, given how much more powerful the iPhone is than the original NES. We were able to guide our jumping sack of flour past at least a few of the many perils contained in the game.

Installing NES

1. Install NES through Cydia **[Hack #1.04]**. The source is at www.zdziarski.com/projects/nesapp and if you don't find it in Cydia, you can download the game from that site, and copy it over to */var/mobile/Applications*. You'll need to install *respring* through Cydia **[Hack #1.03]** to make the icon appear.
2. Gather up the ROM(s) for the game(s) you want to play.
3. Copy these files to */var/mobile/Media/ROMs/NES/* (**[Hack #1.05]** explains how to copy files to your iPhone).

When you open the NES application, you'll see a list of any ROM files you've installed. Clicking the Settings button will allow you to change some of the gameplay options.

Figure 5-4.
Sack of Flour

Extracting Your ROMs

If you have a collection of Nintendo games and a Nintendo console that you don't mind soldering, you can get hardware to copy the ROM off your own carts here: http://tinyurl.com/copynes.

A pack of NES homebrew ROMs can be found here: http://xbox-emulation.dcemu.co.uk/nes-roms.shtml and you can always find something at www.pdroms.de/files/nes.

HACK 5.03: Play Sega Genesis Games on Your iPhone or iPod touch

With the native application genesis4iphone, you can be playing Sega Genesis games on your iPhone within minutes.

The Sega Genesis (Figure 5-5), known outside North America as the Sega Mega Drive, was released at the end of the 1980s. It was known for its many fast-paced action and platform games.

Figure 5-5.
The Sega Genesis/Mega Drive (photo by Bill Bertram)

Getting a Homebrew ROM

Pier Solar (Figure 5-6) is a role-playing game (RPG) with a turn-based battle system like Final Fantasy I, developed by Watermelon, juicy development. It's the first new Genesis RPG to be developed this millennium.

You can find the ROM file at www.piersolar.com (click the Media link at the top of the page and look for a link to the demo on the page).

Installing the Emulator

1. Install genesis4iphone through Cydia **[Hack #1.04]**. The source is www.zodttd.com; if you don't find it in Cydia, you can learn which Cydia repository to add by checking ZodTTD's site.
2. Gather up the ROM(s) for the game(s) that you want to play. We'll use Pier Solar as our example. Make sure that the ROM files end in *.SMD*.
3. Copy your ROMs to */var/mobile/Media/ROMs/GENESIS/* (**[Hack #1.05]** explains how to copy files to your iPhone).

When you open genesis4iphone, you'll see a list of the ROM files that you've installed. In this case, tap Pier Solar.

Figure 5-6.
Pier Solar

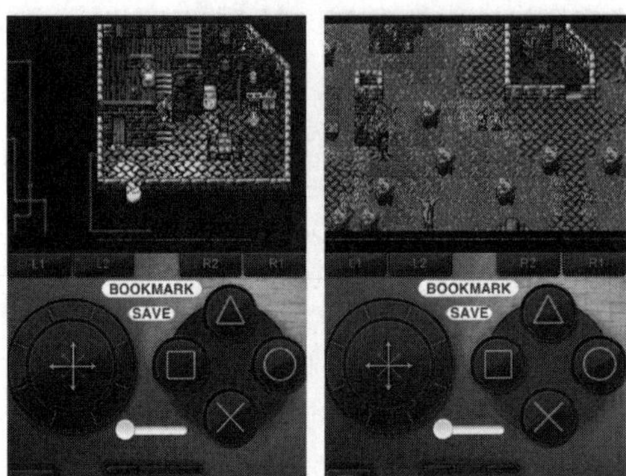

Extracting Your ROMs

If you have a collection of Sega Genesis games, you can extract your ROMs with products such as the Venus Multi Game Hunter. These products have been out of production for some time, so you'll have to hunt around on forums for someone selling this equipment.

You can find additional data about available backup systems at www.supermagi.com and http://tinyurl.com/gamebackup.

You can also find a few homebrew Genesis games at www.pdroms.de/files/genesis.

HACK 5.04: Play Nintendo Game Boy Games on Your iPhone or iPod touch

Your iPhone can emulate a Game Boy with a bigger, brighter screen.

It's fitting that the iPhone should pay homage to the device that originally put portable gaming on the map, Nintendo's Game Boy (Figure 5-7).

Figure 5-7.
The Nintendo Game Boy (image courtesy Boffy b)

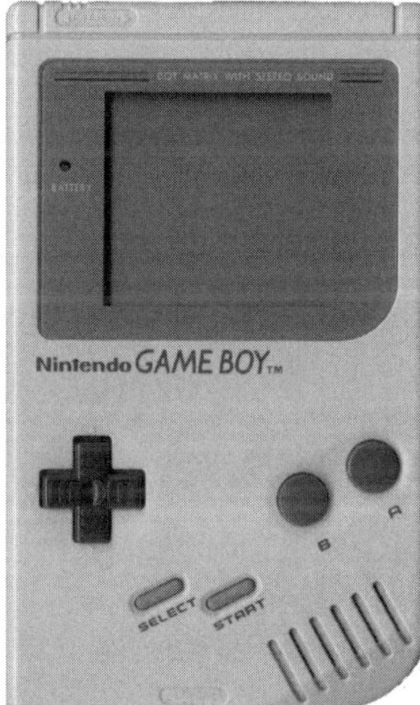

Getting a Homebrew ROM

Horrible Demon 4 (Figure 5-8) is a side-scrolling action/adventure game with many acrobatic features, created by homebrew developer Bertil Hörberg. It is similar to Castlevania 2, with the addition of RPG-style item collecting. You'll find the ROM at www.gambitstudios.com/freedom2001_entries.asp.

You can find Bertil's home page at http://beril.se.

Installing gameboy4iphone

1. Install gameboy4iphone through Cydia **[Hack #1.04]**. The source is www.zodttd.com; if you don't find it in Cydia, you can figure out which repository to add by checking ZodTTD's site.
2. Gather up the ROM(s) for the game(s) you want to play. Make sure that the file extension is *.GBC*.
3. Copy these files to */var/mobile/Media/ROMs/GAMEBOY/*.

When you open gameboy4iphone, you'll see a list of any ROM files that you've installed.

Figure 5-8.
Horrible Demon 4

Extracting Your ROMs

If you can find a used or new Bung GB Xchanger, you can copy your Game Boy games to the PC over a parallel port connection. Googling "GB Xchanger" comes up with several current vendors.

You can find homebrew games for the Game Boy at www.pdroms.de/files/gameboy.

HACK 5.05: Play Super Nintendo Games on Your iPhone or iPod touch

With the native application snes4iphone, you can be playing Super Nintendo (Super NES) games on your iPhone within a few minutes.

Nintendo's 16-bit Super Nintendo Entertainment System (Super NES; see Figure 5-9) came to the U.S. market in late 1991 and became the dominant video game platform for the first half of the 1990s, competing for some time even with the newer 32-bit systems and selling almost 50 million units worldwide.

Figure 5-9.
The Super Nintendo Entertainment System (Super NES)

Getting a Homebrew ROM

In the ROM pack found at http://tinyurl.com/snesroms, you'll find hundreds of homebrew ROM files, including Bio Worm (Figure 5-10) by developer Wani (www.uvlist.net/game-7144-Bio+Worm), a game reminiscent of Pac-Man, Bomberman, and Centipede.

Installing snes4iphone

1. Install snes4iphone through Cydia **[Hack #1.04]**. The Cydia source is www.zodttd.com.
2. Gather up the ROM(s) for the game(s) that you want to play. Make sure that the ROM file ends in *.SMC*.
3. Copy your ROMs to */var/mobile/Media/ROMs/SNES/*.

When you open snes4iphone, you'll see a list of any ROM files that you've installed.

Figure 5-10.
Super NES games on snes4iphone

Extracting Your ROMs

You can extract all your SNES ROMs with products such as the Venus Multi Game Hunter, which was mentioned under the discussion for the Sega Genesis. If you can't find one, you can find additional backup systems at http://en.wikipedia.org/wiki/Game_backup_device and www.supermagi.com under "Game Backup Units."

Check out www.pdroms.de/files/supernes for more homebrew SNES games.

HACK 5.06: Play Nintendo Game Boy Advance Games on Your iPhone or iPod touch

With the native application gpSPhone, you can play almost any Nintendo Game Boy Advance (GBA) game on your iPhone or iPod touch.

The Game Boy Advance (GBA; see Figure 5-11) was the third iteration of technological advancement of the Game Boy series of handhelds from Nintendo, released in 2001. It had technical specifications surpassing the SNES, and along with the many new games released for it, a number of SNES games were ported, which allowed people to play some of their favorite SNES games wherever they went. And a short-lived and little-known line of "video cartridges," which let you watch movies or cartoons, even came compressed on a cart.

Figure 5-11.
The Nintendo Game Boy Advance—GBA (photo by Christopher Down)

Getting a Homebrew ROM

You can find Anguna (Figure 5-12), a homebrew game by Nathan Tolbert and Chris Hildenbrand, at www.tolberts.net/anguna. It's an old-school, Zelda-esque dungeon game.

Installing gpSPhone

1. Install gpSPhone through Cydia **[Hack #1.04]**. The Cydia source is www.zodttd.com; if you don't find it in Cydia, you can figure out how to download it at ZodTTD's site.
2. The GBA emulator is unique in that you need a ROM for the cart you want to play and also need to extract the BIOS from the GBA and save it in a file called *gba_bios.bin*. You'll need to put this file directly into the *gpSPhone.app* folder. To do this, browse to your *Applications* folder **[Hack #1.05]**, go into *gpSPhone.app*, and put the file there. See the following section, "Dumping Your BIOS."
3. Gather up the ROM(s) for the game(s) that you want to play. Make sure that they end in *.GBA*
4. Copy your ROMs to */var/mobile/Media/ROMs/GBA*.

Figure 5-12.
Anguna

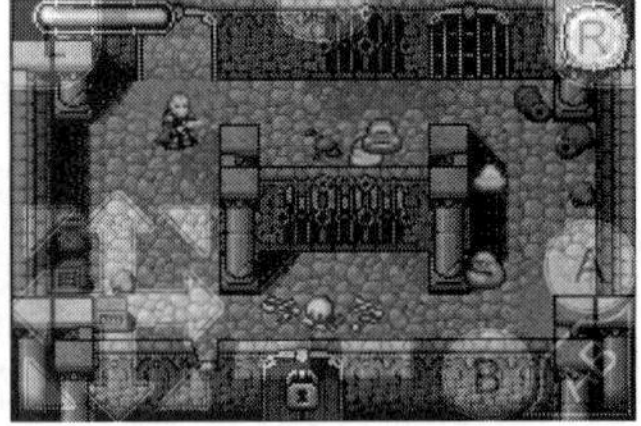

Dumping Your BIOS

The developer Darkfader (http://darkfader.net/gba) developed an application called DumpRom that backs up the GBA BIOS. The tutorial at http://wiki.pocketheaven.com/GBA_BIOS helps walk you through the process.

Extracting Your ROMs

A variety of tools can back up GBA ROMs. Devices like G-BANK can be found at www.gameboy-advance.net and a tutorial can be found here: www.gameboy-advance.net/gba_roms/make_gba_roms.htm.

You can find a pack of homebrew Game Boy Advance games here: http://gbaemu.dcemu.co.uk/gba_roms.shtml.

 HACK 5.07: Play PS1 Games on Your iPhone or iPod touch

With the native application psx4iphone, you can play many PlayStation games on your iPhone or iPod touch.

The original PlayStation (Figure 5-13), known as a PS1 or PSX, was a fun video game system from the mid-1990s, released about 10 years after the NES. It used a CD-ROM, instead of cartridges, which allowed for 700 MB of game storage, which at that time may as well have been limitless. Instead of filling the whole disc with games, sometimes the game would reside on track one, and the rest of the tracks were simply CD audio tracks, so you could play the audio tracks of some PS1 games in your CD player.

Figure 5-13.
The original PlayStation

Copying an ISO for the Game

CD-based games are the easiest to back up, because you can just copy the games that you own onto your computer. There are several ways to create an ISO file of the game CD that you want to play:

- If you're on a Mac, use Roxio Toast; choose File→Save as disk image, then rename the resulting *.toast* file to *.iso*.
- If you're on a PC, you can use Alcohol 52% (www.alcohol-soft.com), available in a trial version, and choose Datatype→Play Station in the Image Making Wizard (be sure to check "Read Sub-Channel Data;" see Figure 5-14).
- On a PC, you can also use the Delta software (http://tinyurl.com/deltapsx), which serves as a launcher for the PC-based PSX emulator ePSXe (www.epsxe.com), by going to Tools→Disk Imager and importing the disc (Figure 5-15).

Figure 5-14.
Making a disc image with Alcohol 52%

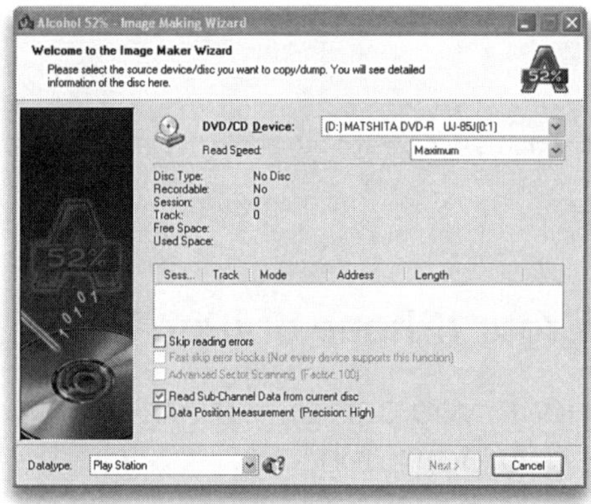

Figure 5-15.
Importing a disc with Delta

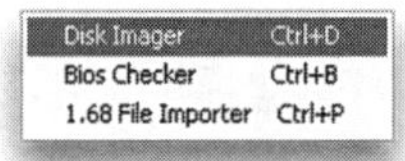

Extracting the PlayStation BIOS

Copying your game was too easy, so here comes the hard part: the PlayStation BIOS. Each game depends on software libraries provided by Sony on a ROM chip inside the U.S. (NTSC) or Europe (PAL) versions of the PlayStation. As a result, your game will not play without this file. Naturally, this software is copyrighted by Sony—and they don't provide it for general distribution. But the code is right there inside your PlayStation. So how do you get it out?

To extract the PlayStation BIOS, you need one of several "game cheat" or homebrew development devices that were available in the mid to late 1990s. Then you'll need to flash it with a replacement ROM that gives you, among other things, access to the PSX memory. Finally, you'll need to copy the PSX binary memory from 0x0bfc00000–0x0bfc7ffff into a file called *scph1001.bin* for the emulator to use.

A number of "carts" have been designed to plug into the early PSX parallel port:

- GameShark
- Action Replay
- Game Enhancer
- Game Wizard
- PlayStation Xplorer, also known as Xploder in the United States (see Figure 5-16)

If you can get a PlayStation 1 Xplorer/Xploder FX, parallel port version, that's probably your best bet, because these include an interface for connecting to your PC. This is old technology that you're dusting off, so you'll have to do things like set your parallel port to SPP mode in your PC's BIOS—assuming that you know what a parallel port is, and assuming your PC has one. You may need to pull a 486 motherboard off some shelf in your garage and install Windows 98 on it to get this hack going.

You may be able to purchase an Xploder at www.whitedog.co.uk (a direct link to the product shown in Figure 5-16 is http://tinyurl.com/5glhdv), or you can hunt around on eBay or on relevant message boards where people might be looking to unload one.

Figure 5-16.
PlayStation Xploder

Only the older, large gray PS1s have a parallel port; the newer PS1s don't, so you'll need to make sure that you have the original model. The PSX BIOS is usually saved in a file based on the PSX's model number. You can find a reference to the various versions of the model number on Wikipedia: http://en.wikipedia.org/wiki/Playstation. In Figure 5-17 are a SCPH-1002(left) and SCPH-9002 (right). Notice that the SCPH-1002 has a parallel port; you'll need that to plug into the Xplorer or any other connector such as the Action Replay.

Figure 5-17.
Comparing PlayStation models— (left) SCPH-1002 and (right) SCPH-9002 (photo by Niklas Sobieski Larsson)

You can find software for the old Xplorer/Xploder here: http://tinyurl.com/xploder. On that page you'll see *x-killer-v0.55.zip*. This utility lets you upgrade the ROM on your Xplorer, and allows you to access the PSX memory. As mentioned before, our goal is to create a file called *scph1001.bin* (or *scph1002.bin*, if your PSX is a 1002) by saving the memory from 0x0bfc00000–0x0bfc7ffff to disk. You can create a new binary file using the Memory Editor feature in X-Killer (Figure 5-18).

Figure 5-18.
X-Killer's Memory Editor menu option

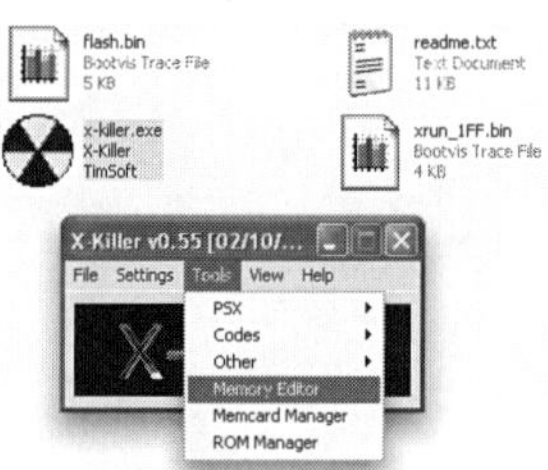

If you're using a different cart than the Xplorer, or even with Xplorer, you may want to flash the cart with the "Caetla .34" or "Caetla .35" ROMs that offer the most flexibility. You can find documentation and some of the historical tools used with various carts here: http://gsmcables.i12.com/xianaix.htm.

Testing Your BIOS and ISO

Given that the ePSXe software for Windows is a well-supported project, you may want to do a run-through with ePSXe (www.epsxe.com) to make sure that your ISO and the PSX BIOS file that you copied from your PlayStation are working correctly.

Figure 5-19.
Testing the BIOS in ePSXe

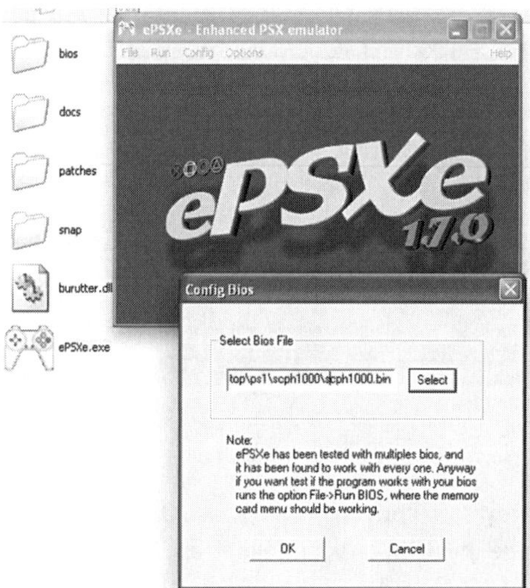

A very useful program for getting ePSXe working, which will help you figure out how to configure your emulator for running on XP, is Delta2 (http://delta.ngemu.com; Figure 5-20). In this test, we had to download and install the P. E. Ops Soft driver for the PSX Graphics tab, and that got our game running. You can also extract ISOs with Delta.

Figure 5-20.
Configuring an emulator with Delta2

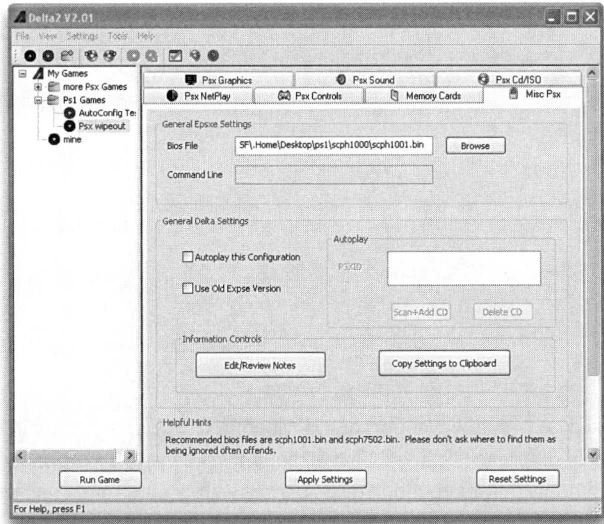

Installing psx4iphone

Now that your BIOS is ready, the final steps are:

1. Install psx4iphone through Cydia **[Hack #1.04]**. The Cydia source is www.zodttd.com; if you don't find it in Cydia, you can figure out which repository to add at ZodTTD's site.
2. Get together *scph1001.bin* and any ISOs for games you want to play. (Note that psx4iphone is case-sensitive.) If you have another BIOS file, such as *scph1002.bin*, you should be able to rename it to *scph1001.bin* with no problems.
3. Using a file transfer technique such as iPhoneBrowser or Netatalk **[Hack #1.05]**, copy these files to */var/mobile/Media/ROMs/PSX*.

Make sure that the BIOS file you copy from your PlayStation is named *scph1001.bin*. The filename is case-sensitive, so *SCPH1001.BIN* won't work.

When you open psx4iphone, you'll see a list of any ISO files that you've installed. The Settings screen is shown in Figure 5-21.

Figure 5-21.
The Settings menu of psx4iphone

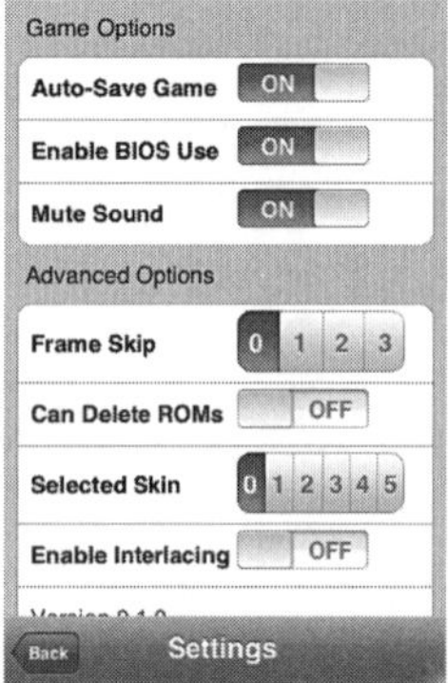

In the mid 1990s, my company worked on a multiplayer port of the Wipeout XL. I've spent hours in the source code debugging multiplayer differences caused by bad random seeds, and it's probably one of the games I've spent the most hours in (not counting RPGs). It has a great electronic/techno soundtrack, so naturally I wanted to play Wipeout on my iPhone.

After copying the CD to an ISO file (Figure 5-22) using Alcohol 52% in Parallels running Windows XP, I used iPhoneBrowser to copy it into the */var/mobile/Media/ROMs/PSX* folder on my iPhone.

Figure 5-22.
My original PSX Wipeout CD in front of my monitor

I was actually amazed to get this far (Figure 5-23), because Wipeout was an extremely demanding game and we even had trouble keeping it from skipping on our Pentium 200MMX PCs when we were developing it. The frame rate was too low to be truly playable in psx4iphone, but the game could load and run completely without crashing, and ZodTTD (the engineer who maintains the psx4iphone project) is working on optimization. When I read the compatibility list on the forums, it indeed said that Wipeout was one of the games that didn't run fast enough. But chances are one of the many discs in your collection will.

Figure 5-23.
Playing Wipeout

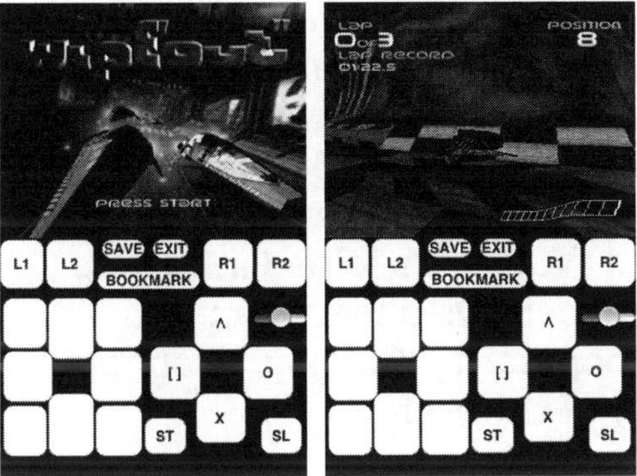

06 TELEPHONY HACKS

The iPhone has arrived, not coincidentally, at a time when the very meaning of telephony is being reinvented on all fronts. Telephone service is an utter commodity; it is already available domestically for flat fees and its cost is rapidly approaching zero. Mobile phones have all but eliminated the pay phone and are on their way to completely replacing terrestrial lines, and Voice over Internet Protocol (VoIP) has joined in to help finish the job. Now, relatively inexpensive all-you-can-eat cellular plans are increasing in popularity. Quickly, telephony is approaching the cost scalability of the Web.

In this interesting time for telephony, a number of new "Telephony 2.0" startups—too many to count, really—have sprung up. Following the successful patterns of their web counterparts, these companies give away interesting voice-based services for free in hopes of accumulating enough users to spur some large corporation to buy them out.

There's a lot you can do with a web page and nearly free inbound and outbound voice capability. You can create clever new voicemail services. You can create conference calls on the fly. You can give out additional phone numbers that dial your cell phone and home phone at the same time. And with Voice over IP, you can ignore your mobile phone minutes plan altogether and call anywhere on earth cheaply. You can block calls you don't want, and deliver custom greetings depending on who calls.

This chapter will cover some of these interesting new developments in web-connected telephony and show how they can be used on the iPhone.

HACK 6.01: Use GSM Codes to Configure Phone Features

The iPhone is a GSM phone, and there are a wide variety of not-so-secret GSM codes that you can use to configure your phone's behavior with the network.

Although the United States has several competing cellular transmission standards, most of Europe and many parts of the developed world have standardized on GSM. GSM phones are distinguished by their use of a Subscriber Identity Module (SIM) card, which allows for easy swapping of phones when batteries go dead or new phones come out. One of the interesting features of GSM phones is the ability to configure various carrier settings by entering a code directly on the phone (Figure 6-1). If you learn these codes and refer to them, you'll have one less reason to call customer service.

Some of these codes may not be supported on all carriers, or may be different in countries outside of the United States. Make sure to tap "call" after entering each code.

Current Account Balance

#BAL# show current account balance (on T-Mobile monthly)
*BAL# show current account balance (on AT&T monthly)
*777# show current account balance for prepaid phones

Figure 6-1.
Sample GSM code input and confirmation

Current Airtime Usage

#MIN# show current minutes used (on T-Mobile)
*MIN# show current minutes used (on AT&T)

Call Waiting

*43# enable the call waiting feature
#43# disable the call waiting feature
*#43# show current status (enabled/disabled)

Outgoing Caller ID

*31#<number to call> allow your caller ID number to be seen for this call
#31#<number to call> do not display the outgoing caller ID for this call
*#31# show outgoing caller ID status

Incoming Caller ID

*30# show caller ID for incoming calls
#30# do not display caller ID for incoming calls
*#30# show incoming caller ID status

Call Barring

You can use GSM codes to restrict the types of calls that can be made to or from your phone. The general format is:

*#<route>#	show current status (enabled means restricted)
#<route><network code>*<type>#	enable these calls (disable restriction)
#<route>*<network code>*<type>#	disable these calls (enable restriction)

Route

33	outgoing
331	outgoing international
332	outgoing international, except home
35	incoming
351	incoming if roaming

Network Code

You may need to check with your carrier to find out what the network code is. In some cases, the default code is 0000. To change your network code, you can use:

**03*330*<old password>*<new password>#

Type

10	all call types
11	voice calls
12	data calls
13	faxes
16	SMS
18	all data services except SMS
19	all services except SMS
25	all asynchronous data services

So for instance, to block SMS (for example, if you're getting SMS messages that you don't want), enter:

*35*0000*16#

0000 is the default call barring code; if you have changed it, enter yours.

To remove the call barring, enter:

#35*0000#

Don't forget to tap "call" after entering each code.

Call Forwarding

You can use GSM codes to set up call forwarding on your iPhone. The most common reason to do this is to forward calls to a landline when you are outside of cellular coverage. Make sure to check your carrier's billing policies on call forwarding before enabling this feature. Use the following format for call forwarding commands:

Show Status: *#<code>#
Set: *<code>*<number to forward to><option>#
Cancel: #<code><option>#
Reestablish: *<code><option># (set forwarding to the last number that was not forgotten)
Cancel & Forget: ##<code><option># (cancels and forgets the number that was set)

Code

002 all calls
004 busy, no answer, or out of coverage (useful for switching voicemail providers)
21 sets all options (all calls, busy, no answer, or out of coverage)
67 when busy
62 when out of coverage
61 when there is no answer

To set the length of time for the phone to ring before forwarding, add " *<time delay> " before # Time delay can be 5, 10, 15, 20, 25, or 30. If no time is specified, 15 seconds is usually the default.

Option

no option apply to all calls
*11 only apply to voice calls
*25 only apply to data calls
*13 only apply to fax calls
*89 only apply to line 2 calls

So for instance, to forward all missed calls (ignored, cancelled, call waiting) to voicemail (Figure 6-2), enter:

004<new number>#

Figure 6-2.
Forwarding all missed calls

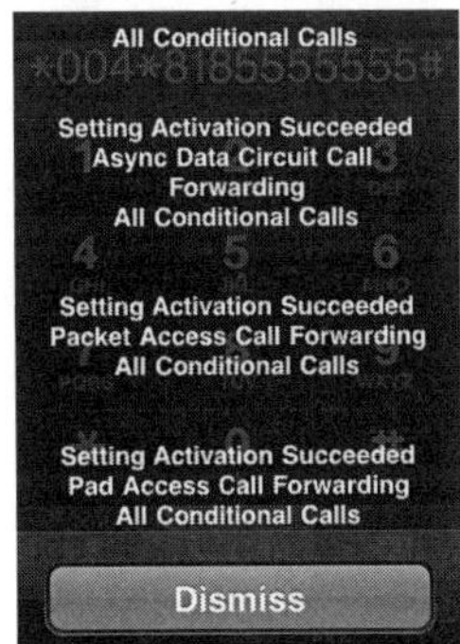

To check the status of redirection (Figure 6-3), enter:

*#61#

Figure 6-3.
Checking status of a redirection

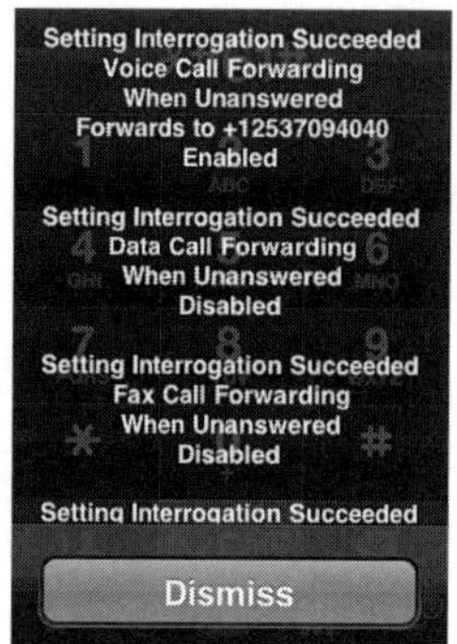

To cancel redirections, enter:

##002#

Enter *43# to activate call waiting; to deactivate, enter #43#.

QUICK TIP 

FIX THE VOICEMAIL BUTTON ON AN UNLOCKED PHONE

If your voicemail button doesn't work after unlocking your iphone, you can use the following procedure to set it up. Go to the "phone" screen, bring up the keypad, and enter the following: *5005*86*<your voicemail number> #. Press call, and wait a few seconds. When the wait screen disappears, your voicemail button will now be connected to the number you entered. Unfortunately, some carriers use SIM cards that have hardcoded voicemail numbers, and this method will not work on those carriers.

Enter Field Test Mode

Entering *3001#12345#* engages Field Test mode (Figure 6-4) to display more detailed technical information about the current cell network. You'll also notice that your signal strength indicator is now showing strength in dB, instead of bars.

 To understand some of the terms used in Field Test mode: www.tele-servizi.com/Janus/engfield1.html

Figure 6-4.
Field Test mode

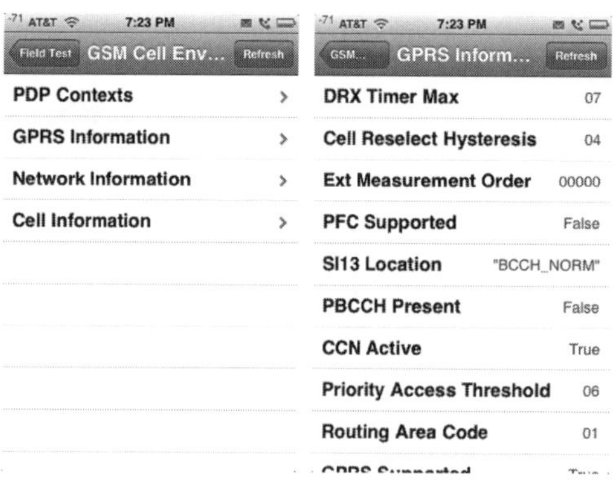

Display IMEI

Entering *#06# shows the IMEI number. This is also printed on the back of your phone.

Search Google for "GSM codes" to look for more codes that work with your particular carrier.

— Christopher Kurpinski & Damien Stolarz

HACK 6.02: Add Speed Dial with Custom Icons

You can create an icon on your home screen that dials a frequently used phone number.

Dialing numbers quickly and easily is a key feature of any mobile phone. But many iPhone dialing tasks take several more clicks than they need to. This hack will give you a one-click method of dialing from the home screen of your iPhone.

Pressing the home button twice will take you directly to your phone number favorites list on the iPhone. Try it.

Ever wonder why your phone calls voicemail when you hold down the 1 key? Basically, it looks for the voicemail number stored on your SIM card, and calls that. And even though you can't assign speed-dial numbers on the iPhone, that voicemail shortcut still exists (hold down the number one and it calls your voicemail center). If your SIM card allows you to change the voicemail number on your SIM card (some SIM cards, like the newer cards on T-Mobile America, do not), then you can use this to set up a single speed-dial number. Bring up the keypad on your phone, type the following code **[Hack #6.01]**, and press the Call button:

*5005*86*<phone number to assign>#

After the phone finishes processing, hold down the 1 key. If you're lucky, it will dial the number you just assigned. If not, make sure that you're entering the code correctly. If everything is correct, and it still doesn't work, you may be out of luck.

This hack can come in handy if you want to use an alternative voicemail provider **[Hack #6.06]**, or if you want a quick way to call your most frequently used number. Best of all, if your carrier supports the visual voicemail feature, this should not affect your voicemail button.

Set Up Speed-Dial Shortcuts

There are two basic methods for adding a speed-dial icon to your phone: creating a web clip and creating a new application.

Speed dial via Web Clip

The first method can be done without jailbreaking your phone and takes advantage of the Web Clip feature in Safari. Safari allows you to save bookmarks as an icon on your home page. This can be used to get one-touch access to frequently used websites, but in our case we'll use it to generate speed-dial bookmarks. Most modern phones recognize URLs that begin with "tel://" as telephone numbers. We can take advantage of this by creating a bookmark to a "tel://" URL on the home page. It's difficult to do this directly from Safari, so we'll need to use a web service. The downside of this method is that depending on the way the web service is implemented, it may not be totally secure. Also, some services may actually route the link through their server, which would require your browser to navigate to their site before placing the call.

Open Safari on your phone and navigate to <phone number>.tel.qlnk.net. Hit cancel, and then hit the bookmark button (Figure 6-5).

Figure 6-5.
Making a tel.qlnk.net Web Clip

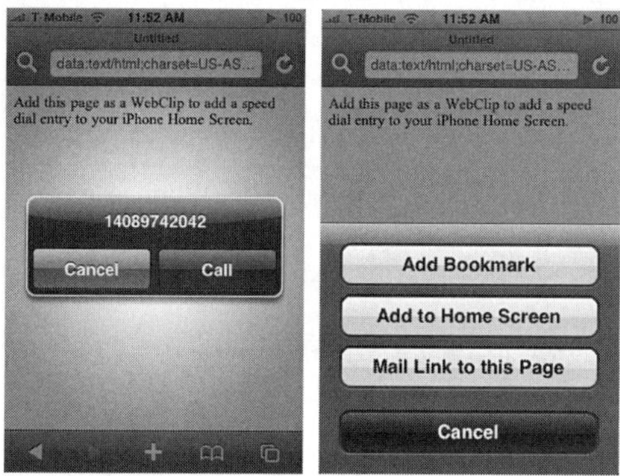

Instead of creating a bookmark, select "Add to Home Screen." Enter the name that you want to use and select "Add." You can also use "<phone number>.tel.qlnk.net/?picurl=http://path.to/photo" if you want to add a custom picture (Figure 6-6).

Figure 6-6.
A speed-dial Web Clip on the Springboard

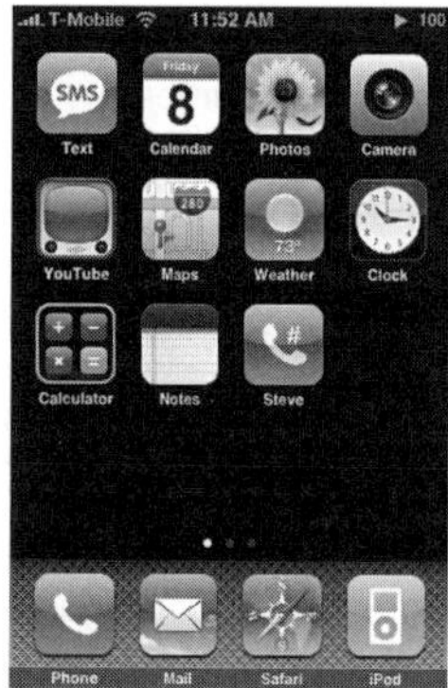

Another site that offers a similar service is www.soft-use.com/speeddial. Enter the name, phone number, and (optionally) a link to an online image. Press "Generate," and then "Tap for Shortcut" (Figure 6-7).

Figure 6-7.
Generating a soft-use.com speed-dial shortcut

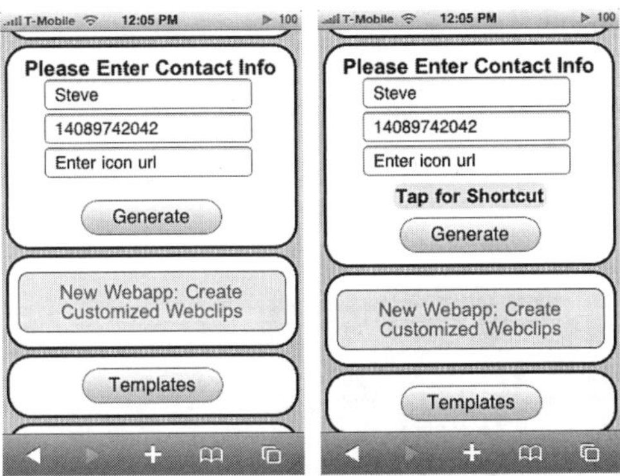

Like before, cancel the call, and select the bookmark icon, then "Save to Homepage." Both of these sites allow a custom image to be used, but it must exist on the Web. You cannot load an image from the phone, or a hard drive.

Both services will add a new Web Clip to your home page. When you want to place a call, tap the icon. A question box will pop up and ask you to confirm the call. Select "Call," and the phone number that you entered will be called. What's happening here is that a bookmark is created using the tel:// protocol. Safari opens the bookmark, sees the "tel://" indicator, and knows that it is a phone number. For security reasons, Safari always has to ask permission before making a call, which is why you have to select "Call" before the call is placed.

On a jailbroken phone, the process is even easier. Both of the previous methods still work, and you can also use urlclip (found in Erica Utilities) to directly add a Web Clip to your homepage. SSH **[Hack #9.04]** into your phone, or use the Terminal app, and type "urlclip <name> tel://<phone number>," where <name> and <phone number> are replaced with the name and phone number you want to use. This will add the speed-dial Web Clip to your home page, but with the default Safari icon displayed (Figure 6-8).

Figure 6-8.
A speed-dial button made with urlclip

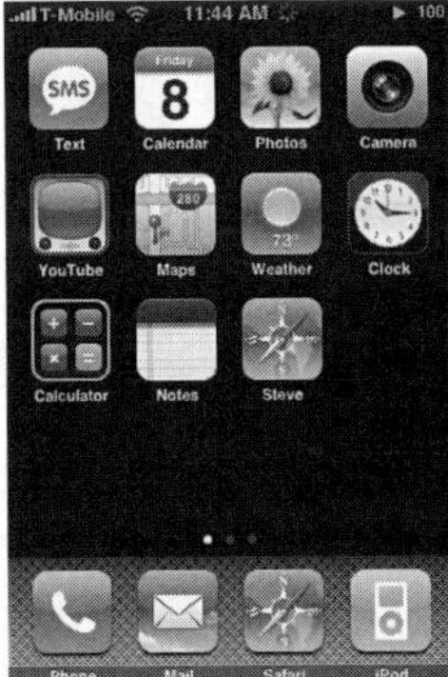

Speed dial via application

The second method (on jailbroken phones) is to use the application TapDial. After installing, run TapDial and enter the name and phone number that you want to use. Instead of a Web Clip, TapDial actually creates a new application for each speed-dial number. Unlike the Web Clip methods, this is a one-press solution and does not ask for confirmation before calling (Figure 6-9).

Figure 6-9.
Using TapDial

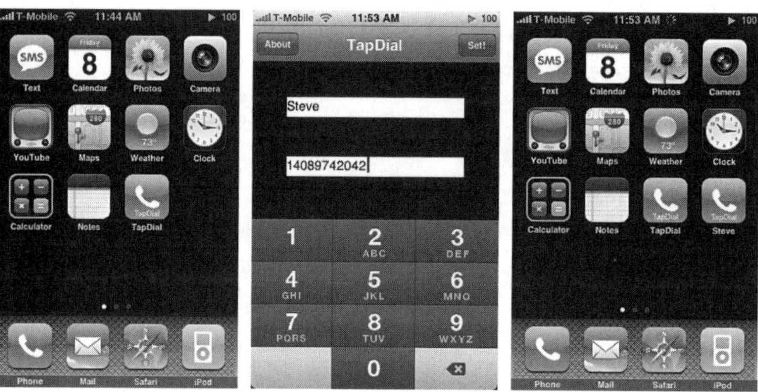

Making It Look Good

All of the demonstrated methods will add speed-dial icons to your phone, and some will even let you use custom pictures from the Web. But what if you want to use pictures from your laptop? Or the pictures already on your phone? Luckily, if your phone is jailbroken, there's a way to do just that:

1. Make sure that you have SSH installed on your phone **[Hack #9.04]**.
2. Create a 58x58 PNG icon for your speed-dial number.
3. Copy the icon(s) to your phone, using SCP or SFTP.
4. SSH to your phone, and find the speed-dial icon that you want to change.
   a. If you used a Web Clip method, use `find / -name "WebClips"` to locate your Web Clip directory. For this example (Figure 6-10), it was located at */var/mobile/Library/WebClips*. If you have multiple Web Clips, enter each directory, and type "cat Info.plist" to see the name and phone number for that clip.
   b. If you used TapDial, use `find / -name "<name>.app"`, where `<name>` is the title of your speed-dial icon, to find the app. For this example (Figure 6-11), it was under */Applications/*.
5. Back up the existing icon (optional). Use `cp icon.png icon.png.bak` to back up the current icon.
6. Copy your new icon to *icon.png*. For this example, we loaded the new icon into our home directory, which is the default. Simply type `cp ~/<new icon> ./icon.png`, where `<new icon>` is the name of your new icon.
7. Exit SSH.
8. The new icon (Figure 6-12) won't be used right away. You'll need to use the *respring* application or restart the phone to refresh the icon.

Figure 6-10.
Finding the Web Clips

```
192.168.15.166 - PuTTY
iPhone:~ root# cd /var/mobile/Library/WebClips/
iPhone:/var/mobile/Library/WebClips root# ls
...                                            icon.png
iPhone:/var/mobile/Library/WebClips root# cd 00D24ACB-BD77-4967-9610-2F094D6D442B.webclip/
iPhone:/var/mobile/Library/WebClips/00D24ACB-BD77-4967-9610-2F094D6D442B.webclip root# ls
Info.plist  icon.png
iPhone:/var/mobile/Library/WebClips/00D24ACB-BD77-4967-9610-2F094D6D442B.webclip root# cat Info.plist
<?xml version="1.0" encoding="UTF-8"?>
<!DOCTYPE plist PUBLIC "-//Apple//DTD PLIST 1.0//EN" "http://www.apple.com/DTDs/PropertyList-1.0.dtd">
<plist version="1.0">
<dict>
        <key>Scale</key>
        <real>1</real>
        <key>ScrollPoint</key>
        <string>0.000,1.000</string>
        <key>Title</key>
        <string>Steve</string>
        <key>URL</key>
        <string>tel://14089742042</string>
</dict>
</plist>
iPhone:/var/mobile/Library/WebClips/00D24ACB-BD77-4967-9610-2F094D6D442B.webclip root#
```

Figure 6-11.
Copying the icon into the Web Clip

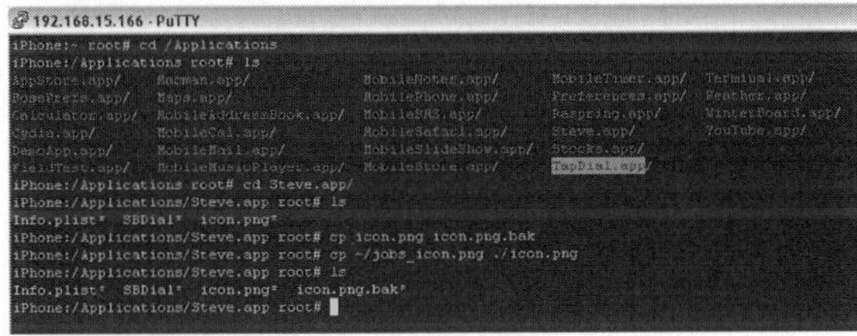

Figure 6-12.
Custom icon on a speed-dial button

Congratulations! You've got a personalized speed-dial icon. You can use this technique to create as many as you want.

A Quicker Way

An app called CallMe was released for jailbroken phones, and is the best method yet of creating a speed-dial icon with a custom picture. It uses your contact list and imports the picture for that contact (Figure 6-13). With this tool, it's easy to create and manage speed-dial icons. The only drawback is that sometimes you don't want to use the same picture for an icon. For example, when the contact picture is a body shot, it might look good for phone calls, but not for an icon, so the method of adding custom pictures is still applicable in those cases.

Figure 6-13.
CallMe using address book images

Can't decide which method to use? Consider this; the Web Clip method requires two taps before placing a call, but your shortcuts won't be lost if you upgrade your firmware. TapDial and CallMe are one-tap solutions, but if you upgrade your firmware, you'll lose all your speed-dial icons.

One More Thing

You can take icon customization one step further if you want to have flexible icon placement. The iPhone will not allow random placement of icons; it groups everything together. You can get around this by creating some blank icons. Here's how:

- Use one of the previously described methods to create a Web Clip.
- Edit the Web Clip *Info.plist* file, and delete the title and URL sections (this prevents the name from appearing).
- Create a 58x58 transparent *.png* image, and load it into your phone using the methods described earlier.
- Find the Web Clip on your iPhone, and copy the transparent PNG to *icon.png* for that Web Clip.
- Restart Springboard on your phone, and you should have a transparent icon. Pressing it will launch Safari to a blank page. You can create as many of these as you need, and use them as placeholders, to space out the icons on your phone (Figure 6-14).

— Christopher Kurpinski

Figure 6-14.
A couple examples of custom icon arrangement using blank Web Clips

HACK 6.03: Access Your Asterisk Voicemails on Your iPhone or iPod touch

Upgrade your Asterisk server with special iPhone/iPod touch functionality.

Asterisk is an open source engine for telephony. It often serves as a modern digital replacement for the traditional office PBX and can power a large internal company phone network. Many offices use Asterisk to implement their voicemail system. For more information on setting the server up for yourself, check out www.asterisk.org.

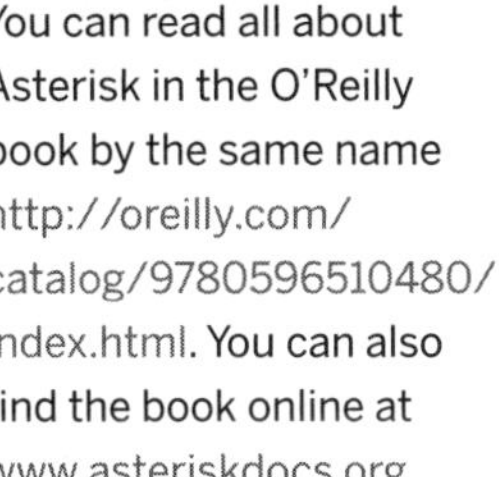

QUICK TIP

You can read all about Asterisk in the O'Reilly book by the same name http://oreilly.com/catalog/9780596510480/index.html. You can also find the book online at www.asteriskdocs.org.

The iPhone application is a plug-in to your existing Asterisk server that allows you to retrieve your voicemails easily over a web connection. It is implemented as a web application, served by Apache/PHP on the Asterisk server. You'll need to install a couple libraries to make sure that the plug-in can work: you'll need a running Apache, PHP, and the *lame* libraries (so that you can encode MP3s). You can find full and up-to-date instructions at http://tinyurl.com/asteriskinstall.

Once your server is configured to work with the Asterisk Voicemail for iPhone plug-in, you can access it by typing in the address into Safari. You'll see a screen like Figure 6-15.

Figure 6-15.
The main screen for Asterisk voicemail for iPhone

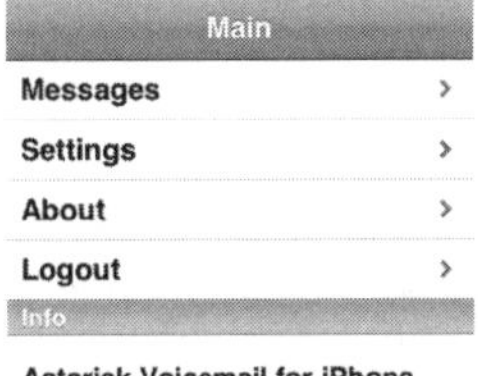

From this screen, you can access any of the voicemails in your mailbox to listen to, move, delete, or call back. Voicemails play back on your phone as an MP3 (Figure 6-16).

Figure 6-16.
Listen to, move, delete, or call back Asterisk voicemail

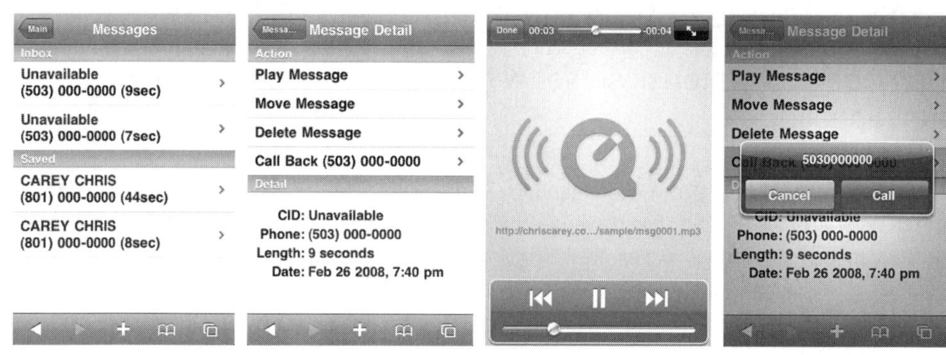

Having all your telephony on one device is very convenient, and this can bring your Asterisk-based desk voicemail conveniently to your phone.

HACK 6.04: Access Your Vonage Voicemails on Your iPhone or iPod touch

Vonagent lets you listen to your Vonage voicemails on your iPhone or iPod touch.

If you have Vonage and want to access your voicemails away from home, on your iPhone or iPod touch, the Vonagent application will give you an experience as convenient as visual voicemail.

The application is currently available for jailbroken phones, so you'll need to access it using Cydia, by adding the http://intelliborn.com/cydiav source. You can go to www.vonagent.com for a step-by-step guide to this.

Once you've got Vonagent installed and running, input your Vonage username and password. Hit Save, and the main screen should update with your information and preferences (Figure 6-17).

Figure 6-17.
Vonagent information filled in

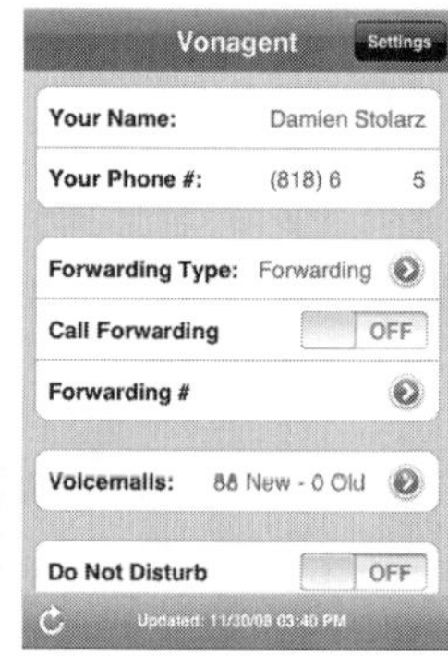

By tapping on voicemails, you can get to your Vonage voicemails and listen to them (Figure 6-18).

Figure 6-18.
Accessing and listening to a voicemail

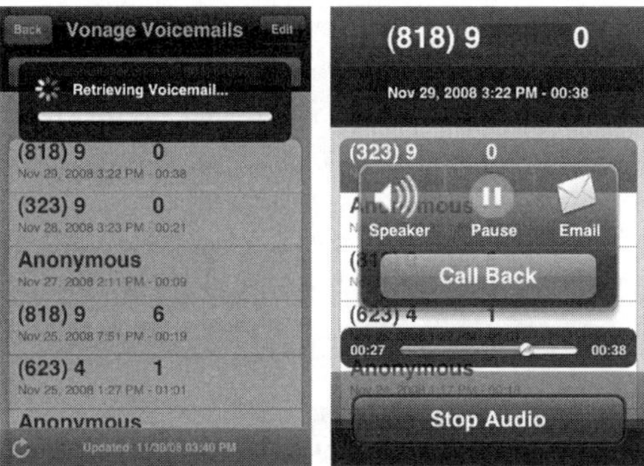

Vonagent goes beyond Apple's voicemail in that you can easily email a message if it needs to be forwarded to someone else to deal with, or if you want to save the information to your own inbox for later follow-up.

HACK 6.05: Use Voice over IP on Your iPhone or Second-Generation iPod touch

Several applications allow Voice over IP (VoIP) on your iPod touch or iPhone, allowing you to use your second-generation iPod touch as a phone or save your voice minutes on your iPhone.

One of the drawbacks of the gateway-drug iPod is that you start craving iPhone features. Sure, you can usually get twice the storage on your iPod than the current iPhone—and it's smaller—but you want to stay in touch and you don't know why you can't just make a phone call.

Fortunately, because the second-generation iPod touch supports the microphone input, if you have iPhone-style headphones, it can make phone calls just like an iPhone—as long as you're on a Wi-Fi network. Additionally, for iPhone users who want to use VoIP—either to save minutes, or because they are overseas and want to make cheap calls via Wi-Fi—there are several applications that allow you to accomplish this feat.

SIP

Session Initiation Protocol (SIP) is the language that VoIP applications use. So applications that support SIP allow you to hold voice conversations over the Internet. Usually, these applications can make free calls between SIP phones, and then, using a gateway, can make paid calls to traditional phone services.

You can make a SIP account with a variety of vendors, and most of the VoIP apps that are distributed for Windows, Linux, and Mac OS X are usually bundled with some sort of SIP account so that you can pay them money to reach the PTSN (public telephone switch network; i.e., landlines and mobile phones). SIP accounts generally provide extremely cheap per-minute rates and are purchased much like prepaid calling cards. A good stable SIP account vendor is http://gizmo5.com. They also have a desktop application and offer a few free minutes of calls (i.e., no up-front payment required) so you can see whether SIP is for you before making a commitment.

There are two features you can get with SIP gateways: call out, and call in. If you just have a SIP account, you can call to other SIP accounts essentially for free. If you want to make calls out to landlines, but you don't care about receiving calls (on that number, anyway), then you pay only for SIP-out minutes. If you become so enamored with SIP that you put it on your iPhone, your iPod, and your desktop, so that people can call you on your PC or on your handheld, depending on where you are, you'll need to get a phone number for incoming PTSN to SIP calls—a SIP-in number.

Because there's really no cost, it's good to experiment with SIP on your desktop and get everything working there, because it eliminates variables when debugging your iPhone or iPod SIP connection.

Fring

Fring (Figure 6-19) is an App Store application based around instant messaging, but it also supports SIP. Like the various other multi-IM programs, it lets you use MSN, Google, ICQ, Twitter, Yahoo!, and AIM, but it additionally supports voice—so you can use it to communicate with Skype users, other Fring users, and also use the voice chat features of several IM clients (Figure 6-20).

Figure 6-19.
Fring chat add-ons

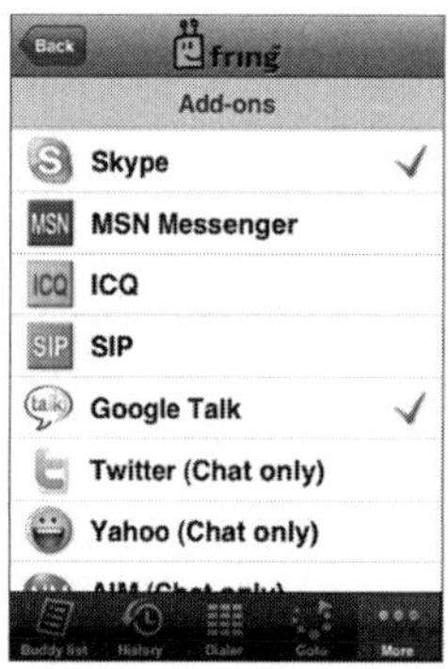

Additionally, Fring integrates a SIP account and gives you a number of options (Figure 6-21) of places to create an account, or you can add your preexisting SIP account. Fring's system tunnels the voice traffic through their servers (a hundred milliseconds away in Europe) and out to the SIP network, instead of your call going straight to the person you're calling, so this can sometimes add delay in the form of call latency.

Figure 6-20.
Fring VoIP add-ons

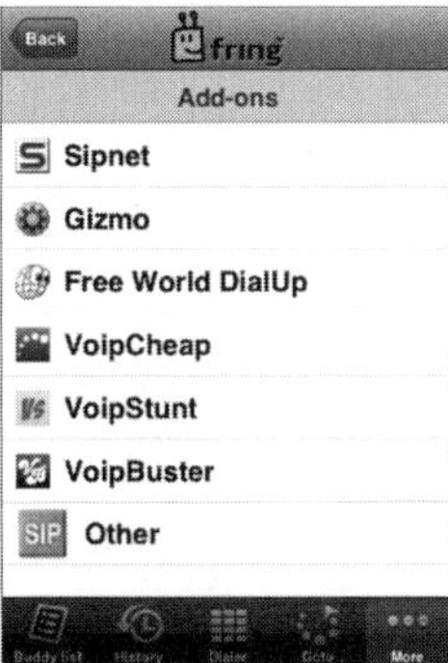

When used with an iPod touch, you have the option to call out using SIP or to chat with contacts (Figure 6-21).

Figure 6-21.
Fring iPod touch contact options

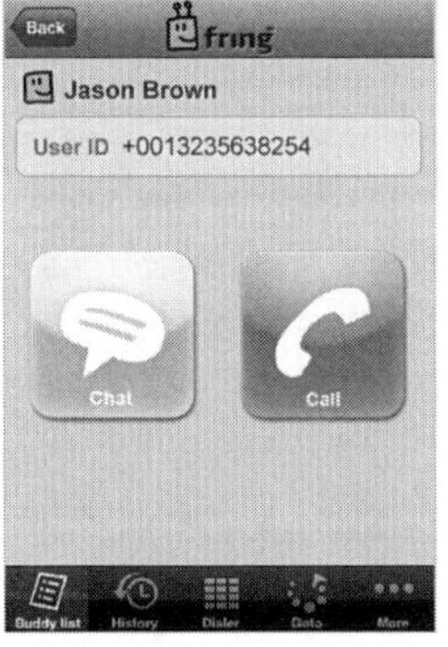

The more options that you have configured, the more options you have to call. Figure 6-22 shows options on an iPhone to make a call via SIP, Skype, or the iPhone's own GSM connection.

Figure 6-22.
Fring iPhone contact options

truphone

Another option for SIP calling and voice chat is the App Store app truphone (Figure 6-23).

Figure 6-23.
truphone call interface

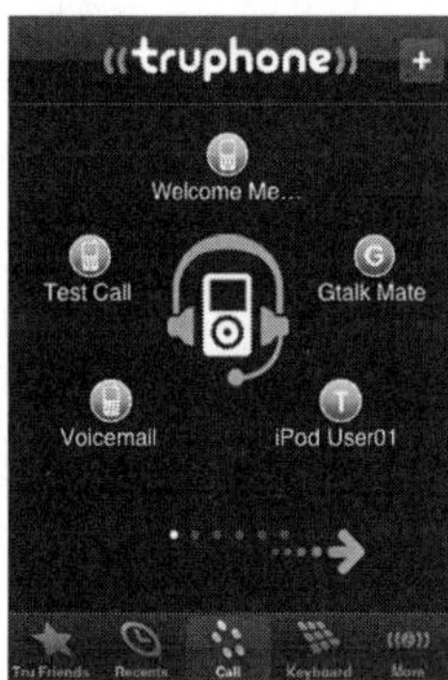

truphone has a similar feature set as Fring: voice chat with other IM clients, Skype voice support; it also features an integrated SIP service provided by truphone that simplifies configuration of VoIP features.

SiAX

For jailbroken phones, SiAX (Figure 6-24) is an option. It does not have the Wi-Fi-only limitations of the App Store applications (it will work over the iPhone's 3G network), and it has a few features that the previous applications lack, like the ability to use a STUN server (for getting through firewalls). SiAX also supports the Asterisk IAX protocol, so you can make calls through your Asterisk server.

Figure 6-24.
SiAX

Wi-Fi vs. 3G

The App Store VoIP applications generally do not support 3G connections and function only when on Wi-Fi. Although SiAX supports 3G, Fring and truphone do not.

VoIPover3G is a native application (Figure 6-25), available via Cydia, that can trick applications on an app-by-app basis into thinking they're on Wi-Fi. It works for truphone, Fring, and even the App Store and iTunes stores, so you can download larger items over 3G connections.

Figure 6-25.
VoIPover3G

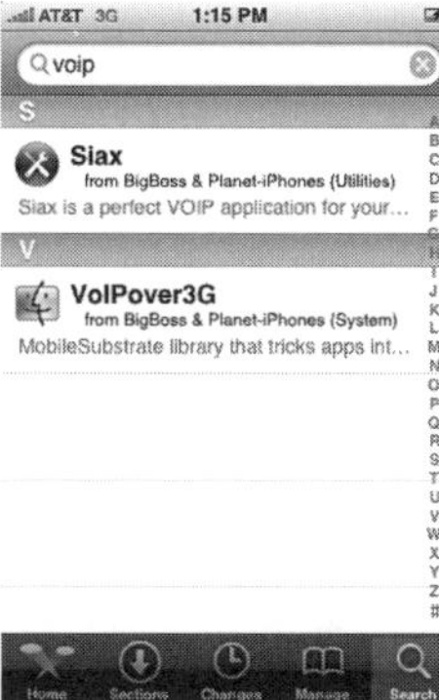

With SIP, Skype, and Asterisk options for your iPhone and second-generation iPod touch, you can set up flexible phone options so that you can make your calls cheaply from anywhere you want.

HACK 6.06: Get Visual Voicemail on T-Mobile or Other Carriers

You can simulate the visual voicemail feature on other carriers using a voicemail-to-email service and a push email account.

As great as visual voicemail is—and it is pretty cool—there are still some things that it can't do. It's also a carrier-dependent feature, so you'll lose the feature if you unlock your phone to use it on a carrier who doesn't support it. Luckily, there are some services available that you can use to improve your voicemail no matter what carrier you're on. Figure 6-26 shows Apple's built-in visual voicemail.

Figure 6-26.
Visual voicemail

The basic features of visual voicemail are:

1. Voicemail audio is pushed to your phone.
2. You can see which voicemails you've listened to and which you haven't.
3. Voicemails are automatically "pushed" to your phone; that is, they're usually ready to be listened to without making a phone call.

Visual Voice Email

There are three basic steps to getting your pseudo visual voicemail enabled:

1. Create a new push email account just for voicemails.
2. Forward your voicemail to a third-party voicemail service.
3. Have the service email your voicemails, attached as MP3s, to that email address.

Step 1: Create a new push email account for voicemails.

Yahoo! provides free email accounts that are fortunately push-enabled on the iPhone. **[Hack #3.01]** shows you how to set one up. You can set some obscure address that no one would want that includes your phone number, like my-5551212, and you can even create rules on the Yahoo! side that automatically trash any email that does *not* come from your voicemail provider. Make sure that push is enabled and that your phone is receiving email messages from this address before the next step.

Step 2: Subscribe to a free voicemail service.

There are probably hundreds, if not thousands, of voicemail systems that you could choose. If you already have some sort of voicemail-to-email solution, you could just forward your phone to that. But for the purpose of this hack, we'll use a nice free voicemail and digital fax service called K7.net (Figures 6-27 and 6-28). **[Hack #6.07]** discusses other voicemail options.

Choose the settings shown in Figure 6-27—PCM for the sound and "send to my email" for receiving messages. Obviously, you should enter the email address that you configured in Step 1.

Figure 6-27.
K7.net signup

Figure 6-28.
K7.net signup confirmation

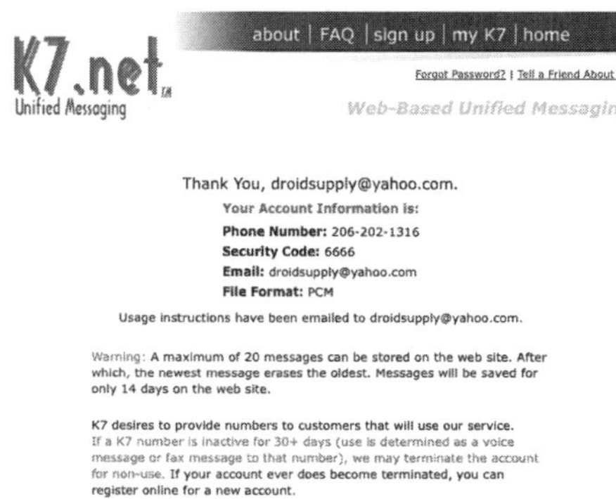

Step 3: Forward your voicemail to this new service.

Forward voicemails to your new voicemail service, instead of that provided by your cell carrier, such as T-Mobile or AT&T. You can select which kinds of calls to forward: call waiting calls, or ignored calls, or missed calls, or all of them. The exact codes to press vary by carrier **[Hack #6.01]**. For instance, to set up call forwarding on your U.S. iPhone on AT&T, open the keypad on the phone, and enter the following: *004*<new number># , then press "Call" (Figure 6-29).

Now, any missed calls you receive will be sent to your email system instead of your carrier's voicemail system. Make sure to check your carrier's billing policies on call forwarding before enabling this feature.

Figure 6-29.
K7.net forwarding confirmation

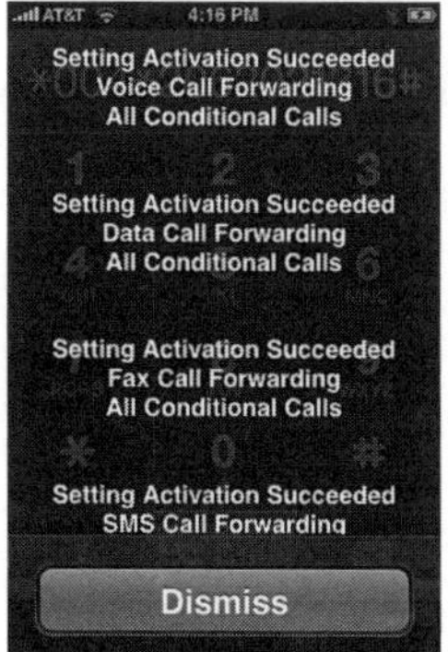

To clear this number and return to the original voicemail settings, type ##004#, then press "Call."

Your "visual voicemail"

To see how it works, go into your email and select the account you set up. After you receive a few phone calls and let them go to voicemail, you should see a screen like Figure 6-30.

Figure 6-30.
Forwarded voicemail listing

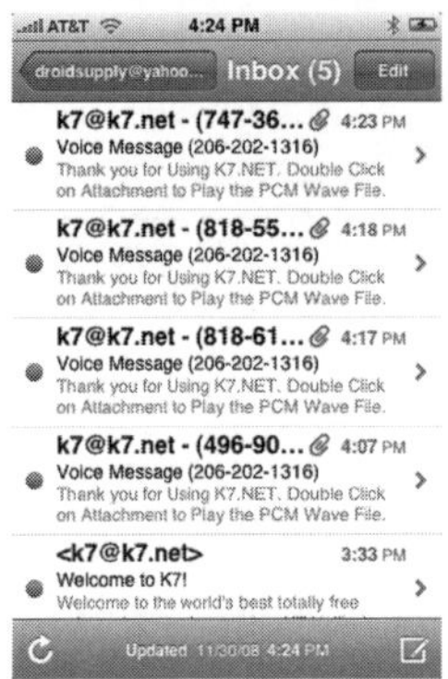

When you click on one of the messages, you'll be able to listen to it right away, as the voicemail has already been downloaded to your mail (Figure 6-31). Even if you go out of cell range, the voicemails are right there to be listened to—just like visual voicemail.

Figure 6-31.
Forwarded voicemail detail

The main drawback of using K7 in particular as a voicemail vendor is that they never show the number that called you in the body of the email—it's only in the sender field. Other voicemail services vary in the way they include caller ID in the message. Thus, you can't use the iPhone's number recognition feature and simply click the number to call back. Also, because the numbers are not integrated with the address book, you can't see your address book entry; you see only the number of who's calling.

On the other hand, this messaging approach has some advantages over visual voicemail. Because voicemails are on an email account, you can access your voicemails from a desktop computer, if your phone battery goes dead (Figure 6-32). And this gives you an archive as well. So if you're one of those people who likes to hold on to old voicemail messages for posterity or recordkeeping, you've got them. And if the voicemail would be better handled by someone else you work with, you can forward it on to them.

Figure 6-32.
Forwarded voicemail in desktop email client

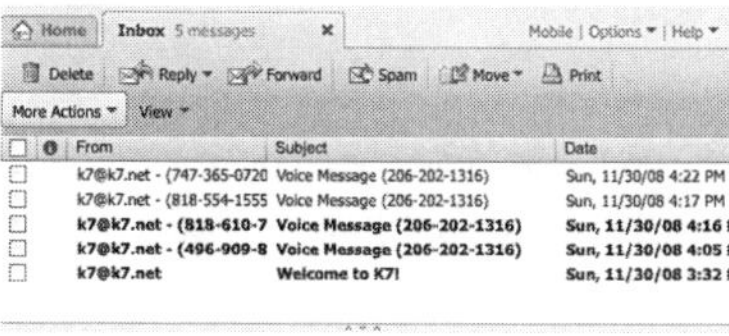

— Christopher Kurpinski & Damien Stolarz

HACK 6.07: Automatically Translate Your Voicemails to Text

A number of companies now offer the ability to translate your voicemails to text, so that you can easily read them instead of having to listen.

One of the recent features to appear in the telephony scene is automatic voicemail-to-text translation.

It works like this:

1. You forward your phone's voicemail service to the new service, and set your outgoing message.
2. When people leave you a voicemail, up to one minute of that message is transcribed by a combination of machine translation and anonymous human translation.
3. The translated message is then sent to you, either in an SMS, an email, or both.

The email usually comes with the audio message itself attached as a media file, so you can play back the full message or parts that the translator missed or misunderstood.

In an age of venture-funded free services, why does it cost so much? It's because they're actually paying people to do the translation. Computer-based translation just isn't advanced enough to handle speech-to-text. By using an army of workers who get paid per translation, they are able to scale. But because these translations cost real money, each of the companies offering this service still has to charge something, and thus there are limits on the length of messages (between 15 seconds and a minute) and how many messages they will translate in a month.

Various Services

It seems like a new telephony company starts up every 15 seconds, given the amount of competition in this area (theoretically, a good thing for consumers). Current providers of voicemail-to-text include:

CallWave	www.callwave.com
GotVoice	www.gotvoice.com
PhoneTag	www.phonetag.com
SpinVox	www.spinvox.com
VoiceCloud	www.voicecloud.com
YouMail	www.youmail.com

The services vary tremendously with regard to the quality of translations—even from day to day. They are also naturally affected by issues such as recording quality and the accent of the people who leave you messages.

In the U.S. market, the popular U.K.-based SpinVox (Figure 6-33) service is provided by another company, Ureach.com. For $10 a month, they offer about 40 translations. For some people, that's about three days of voicemail, so you'll definitely need to get on an all-you-can-eat plan. The problem is that there's a fixed cost for translations and the quality of the translations may suffer if you opt for this. Some of the other services, such as YouMail, offer (limited) "unlimited" translations, and even have options for translating only the first 15 seconds of the message—so you can get the gist of it and return the call if you need to.

Figure 6-33.
SpinVox

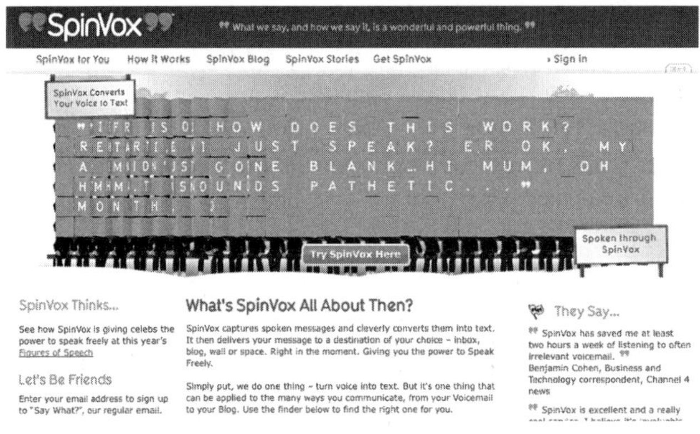

SpinVox/Ureach

Here are some examples of translations through SpinVox/Ureach:

Example 1: "Mrs. Dollards(?) it's....Anyway it's 8:48 and I'm gonna phone at 9:00 at Mike's office and then I'm gonna be prepared for that conference call. If you got the message and got my information from last night, I'd called and said to you I think you got an email coz it was sent out to both of us but don't know if you've had the information, if you don't I can give it you."

Sadly, Mr. Stolarz became "Mrs. Dollards."

Example 2: "Hi Bro I have a habit of writing text messages and sending them to the wrong people. That message was for, for Tina cos she wrote where are you, and I wrote working where are you? But, out of context, just you receiving it, you probably, it sounds like you were supposed to be here and you weren't and I'm like, where are you? Exclamation point. But it wasn't for you. So don't be alarmed. But it is a funny slip of some sorts cos I did wanna find out when you were next available to come over and stuff. So anyway give me a call. Ok bye"

As you can guess, the translations from SpinVox are very accurate; it's mainly names that give them trouble.

VoiceCloud

Here's another example of translations, this time from VoiceCloud:

Example 1: Hi, I just wanted to let you know that I sold the book case for a 140 dollars to a nice young couple who had just tried to go to Ikea yesterday and buy mine but Ikea was sold out so they were very happy to find the discounted one that they could come get today, that was brand new, so anyway that was a cute story, it all worked out nicely, I have a 140 dollars and the boxes are out of the house, yea, ok bye… Voice-to-Text by VoiceCloud

Other service features

A differentiating feature of one of the services—YouMail—is that in addition to transcription, you can have a custom greeting that's based on caller ID. So if you have a business greeting but you don't want to give the cold leave-a-message-I-can't-talk-right-now to friends and family, you can enter them into your address book and give them friendly customized greetings based on MP3s you upload. You can even implement blacklists, so you can outright refuse to take a message from numbers of people you don't like.

The main problem with all of these services is that if you have a *lot* of voicemails, you're just going to blow out most of their translation plans. And the few services that offer "unlimited" transcriptions aren't necessarily going to give you the same results. Figure 6-34 pretty much sums up how your translations get used up if you're playing cell-phone tag with bad reception.

Figure 6-34.
SpinVox sample text

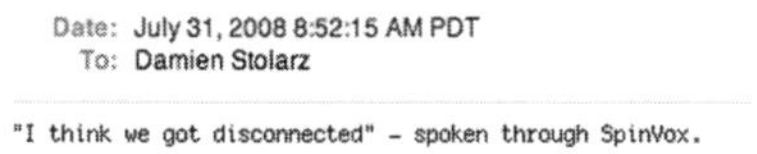

Date: July 31, 2008 8:52:15 AM PDT
To: Damien Stolarz

"I think we got disconnected" - spoken through SpinVox.

It's quite a remarkable fact that some fine gentleman or lady on the other side of the world stayed up late and got paid US$0.10 to memorialize AT&T's lack of cell coverage on the 405 by translating a message to that effect. It's also, to many, a bit eerie. Most people assume that voicemails are private messages, destined only for the listener, and the prospect that an angry or a flirty message will be faithfully typed in by a human agent, perhaps in India, is unnerving. But to a business user who only occasionally gets racy phone calls, the slight reduction in privacy may be worth it for the convenience of sifting through voicemails during a time-wasting meeting.

HACK 6.08: Update Twitter or Your Blog with a Phone Call

You can use several of the digital transcription services to speak short text updates sent directly to Twitter or a blog.

One of the more popular phenomena of late is *micro-blogging*—the posting of one- or two-sentence SMS-sized postings to Twitter or to a social network as "status messages." For one of the cool kids who used to have a *.plan* file just like John Carmack, leaving status messages is nothing new. But updates are expected much faster now, first with instant messaging, and now with Facebook and tweets—and sometimes you're not in a position to type.

Some of the services in **[Hack #6.07]** offer the ability to post directly to Twitter.

Jott (www.jott.com; Figure 6-35) is designed around the concept of to-do lists, allowing you to leave voice notes for yourself that get automatically translated to text to-do items in your lists.

However, this same microtranslation service can be used for free to speak 15-second updates to Twitter or a blog—just long enough to fill those 140 characters.

Figure 6-35.
Jott

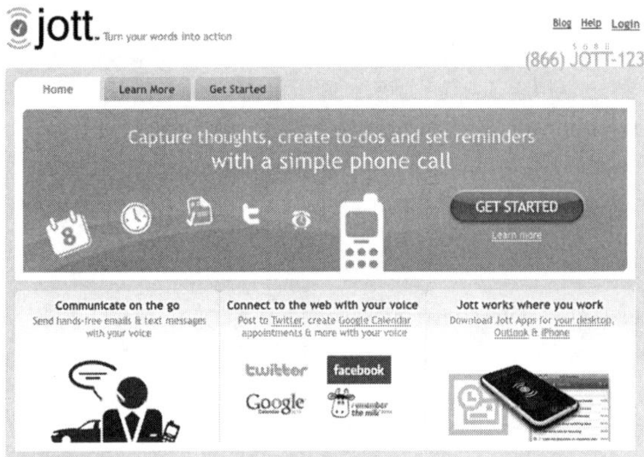

To use the Jott service, register for their free plan, enter your phone number, and then dial 866-JOTT-123. Jott knows who you are and asks "who do you want to Jott?" You say "twitter" and then speak your tweet. It will post it within a few minutes.

SpinVox offers a similar service, allowing you to post to Twitter, Jaiku, and Facebook. Once again, the service is free; you just sign up (Figure 6-36) and call the number they give you: +1-877-5-SPOKEN.

Figure 6-36.
SpinVox signup

The service recognizes your phone number, and voilà: your translated text shows up on Facebook and Twitter (Figure 6-37).

Figure 6-37.
SpinVox-rendered text on Facebook

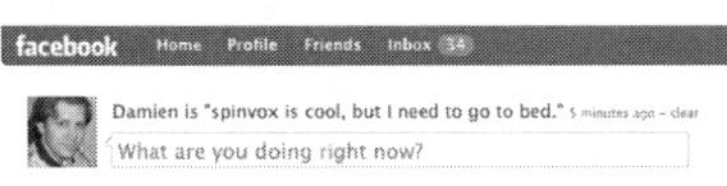

If you need to update more than just Facebook and Twitter, metaposting service called Ping.fm takes posts and then reposts them to any other service you can think of (Figure 6-38). It uses SpinVox as its speech-to-text engine and then posts the message simultaneously to whatever service you designate. Now, all your social networks will be updated with the minutiae—or brilliant and sudden insights—of your life. It gives you a number to call and greets you with a very short "leave a message," and thus is well suited to rapid impulse posting. You can even set up categories, so that your voice-based posts target specific subsets of your online services, and designate whether they constitute a "status update" (i.e., what you're doing) or a microblog of something that you wanted to say.

Figure 6-38.
Ping.fm supported services

Other Services

While you're trying these services out for blogging, you may find that their posting features are useful for other hands-free activities. For instance, the paid SpinVox features allow you to use your voice to send a text message or email to people—very useful when you need to email a colleague who isn't answering their phone, or when you need to get the thoughts out of your head and into their inbox. Because so many of these services offer free trials or services, there's no harm in trying them all. reQall (www.reqall.com) and Dial2Do (www.dial2do.com) compete with Jott and are worth a look.

HACK 6.09: Create a Podcast While Driving

You can create a podcast—a blog with downloadable MP3 files—just by making a phone call.

If you live in a major U.S. city, there's a good chance that you spend hours a day in a vehicle. That gives you lots of time to make hands-free cellular calls and listen to media on your iPhone. But once you've listened to all your books on tape once, all your music twice, and done every course on iTunes U, it's time to actually start creating content yourself on the go.

There are many different services that allow you to make a podcast using only your phone. For our purposes here, we will use Gcast (www.gcast.com; see Figure 6-39). It's fairly quick to get up and running.

Figure 6-39.
Gcast's main page

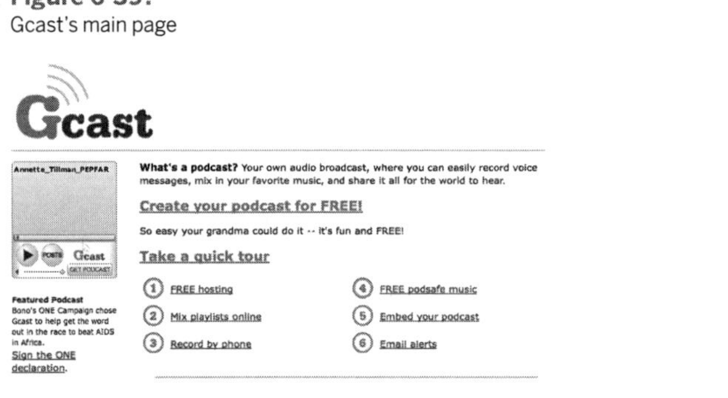

Creating a Gcast account is straightforward. Once you've created an account, you can call in to create your first podcast post.

Calling in a podcast is easy. Dial 1-888-654-2278 from the phone number that you entered during account creation. Then type in your chosen PIN on that same screen. The automated service will then start recording, and you can start producing content (by speaking words into your phone). When you're finished, press #. Then you can choose to scrap your recorded rambling and try again, or go ahead and save and/or post it online. Then hang up. In about five minutes time, the podcast should be posted online.

Like any good podcast, people can subscribe to your Gcast in many different ways. Although any RSS reader will work, one of the more popular ways to subscribe to a podcast is via iTunes (Figure 6-40).

Figure 6-40.
Current options for subscribing to a Gcast podcast

Get future podcast episodes
Option 1: SUBSCRIBE with iTunes
Option 2: add to your start page MY YAHOO! Add to Google MY MSN newsgator
Option 3: Enter email Get Free Alerts »

The Gcast Subscribe with iTunes link gives you an XML link that you can use to add your podcast to your iTunes. The link should look something like this:

www.gcast.com/u/iphonehacks/main.xml

You can put this link on your website or email it to people; they should be able to read it in any RSS reader or podcast client. If you specifically want to target iTunes, use a special "launch iTunes" URL:

itpc://www.gcast.com/u/iphonehacks/main.xml

You can see how the podcast looks in iTunes in Figure 6-41.

Figure 6-41.
A Gcast podcast in the context of iTunes

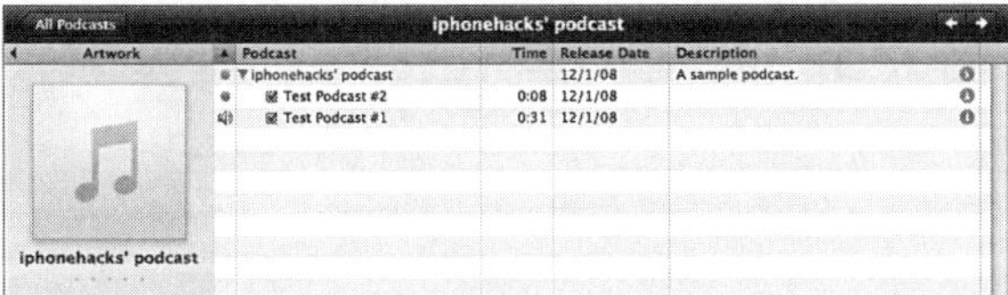

Other Options

Gcast is a great option if you want a simple podcast that you are going to promote on your own, through your website, or on your text blog. If you'd like other options, such as systems that allow you to do multiparty calls or that promote your blog to an audience, there are a number of other options, including these:

Hipcast	www.audioblog.com
TalkShoe	www.talkshoe.com
Gabcast	www.gabcast.com
Yodio	www.yodio.com

07 UNLOCKING AND ACTIVATION

In the world of GSM-based cellular providers, it is the SIM card, not the phone, that determines what network you connect to. Some people have a collection of GSM phones and swap their SIM card between them (Figure 7-1). It is even a good backup strategy for the mobile businessperson to have two phones, in case one breaks or runs out of battery charge.

Figure 7-1.
SIM card

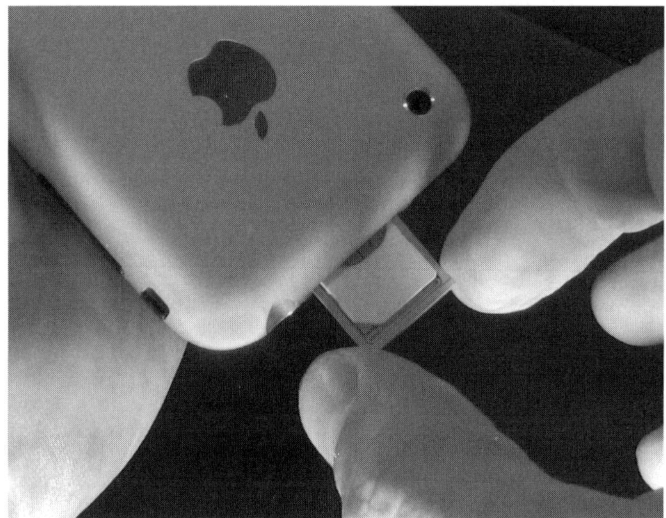

Because the iPhone is a GSM phone, it is physically capable of connecting to most GSM networks.

Many mobile phones around the world are subsidized. The manufacturer expects to make $300USD, $500, or more on the phone. Instead, it is sold for $100, $200, or given away "free" for consumers who agree to be locked in to a contract for a year or longer. You pay for part of your phone, and your mobile carrier pays for part of it, in exchange for having you as a customer for a while. And if you leave early, you have to pay to break your contract.

You'd think that this would be enough for people to stick with a carrier. But there's also exclusivity. Any mobile phone vendor is free to make exclusive deals with carriers, so that they can have a limited-time "exclusive" on a hot new phone. Yet even when they sell the same phone to all carriers in a market, they still have a habit of locking the phones, so that phones sold by a given carrier will work only with SIM cards from that carrier.

Methods of Unlocking

The goal of unlocking is to remove or change the code that prevents a phone from working on any GSM carrier. The most common methods include the following:

1. A sanctioned software unlock. This is the cleanest method. In this approach, the carrier or manufacturer does something to release the phone from its GSM bonds **[Hack #7.01]**.
2. A hacked software unlock. In this approach, the method of locking is reverse-engineered, and some exploit is used to bypass or defeat it. Some of these changes can be permanent and resistant to new upgrades, but some are brittle, dependent on software versions, and break whenever the phone's software is updated (which, for iPhones, is often) **[Hack #7.02]**.
3. SIM cloning hacks, which replace the SIM with a SIM that has been copied, with alterations, to satisfy the phone's need for carrier X while letting it communicate with carrier Y **[Hack #7.03]**.
4. "Turbo-SIM" hacks, which work by inserting a small shim circuit between the carrier SIM card and the phone tricks the phone, the SIM, and the carrier network into thinking everything is normal **[Hack #7.04]**.

General Unlocking Advice

If you have a sanctioned unlock from Apple **[Hack #7.01]**, there's nothing to do. Your iPhone will work with any SIM card worldwide, and you can upgrade your firmware at will.

For any of the various other methods of unlocking, you're playing a game of cat-and-mouse with Apple. And although the first-generation iPhones are thoroughly unlockable, the 3G iPhone have been increasingly harder to unlock, as will, presumably, future iPhones.

 If you have unlocked your iPhone, don't upgrade your firmware when a new version is released!

As new firmware versions are released, Apple clamps down on existing unlocking methods, causing them to break. It's best to wait until more information pertaining to each new release has been gathered by the iPhone hacking community. With more knowledge about the firmware, you'll have a better idea about what steps should be taken to assure that the upgrade goes smoothly.

Initially, all the simple unlocking hacks used prior to the update may not work on the new firmware version. At first, the only unlocking method may be a complicated command-line hack that requires many steps. Even if the procedure goes flawlessly, these early unlocking hacks may still have a low success rate. These hacks may be too complex for the average user, thus limiting the number of iPhone owners who can benefit from such a method.

Once the iPhone hacking community has had sufficient time to examine the details of the new firmware version, simple, easy-to-use applications for unlocking will slowly begin to emerge, and will phase out the complicated hacks that were developed initially. Around that time, the usual suspects **[Hack #2.06]** start to come to a consensus about which unlocking solution works with the latest firmware.

All hail those intrepid volunteers devoted to the noble cause of testing cutting edge, untested, and possibly dangerous unlocking techniques!

HACK 7.01: Buy an Unlocked iPhone from Apple

If money is no object, you can purchase an unlocked iPhone.

If you have enough money, in some regions, such as Hong Kong, Belgium, Italy, and Australia, you can purchase an unlocked iPhone. Insert your SIM chip from any carrier, activate, and you're done (Figure 7-2).

Figure 7-2.
Unlocking in iTunes (screenshot courtesy of Iain Rauch)

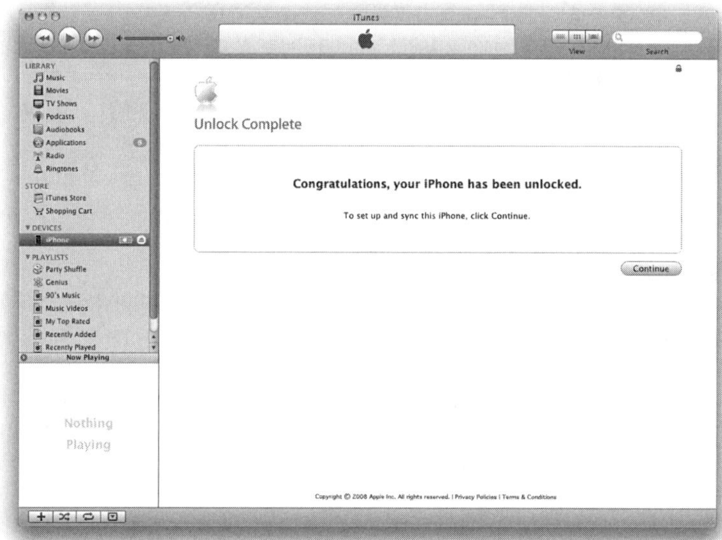

This is by far the best and potentially the easiest unlocking solution. You'll pay a full, unsubsidized list price, which may be shocking, but not much more shocking than the original price of the iPhone at $600USD at release. In Hong Kong for instance, phones range between $700–$800USD for the 8GB and 16GB 3G models.

Depending on exchange rates, you may do better. For instance, Figure 7-3 shows an unlocked 8GB iPhone 3G for approximately $634 plus another $55 or so for shipping.

Figure 7-3.
eBay sells unlocked iPhones

There are a few drawbacks to this approach:

1. You're buying something with potentially less protection under domestic trade law, that takes a while to arrive, and that is subject to the vagaries of international commerce.
2. Your warranty situation may be uncertain. If you walk into an Apple store in California with a new phone from Australia with a problem, will they cover it under warranty? And even if the answer is yes, if you have to swap phones, they are unlikely to have an unlocked replacement on hand and will probably refer you to the Apple office in the country the phone came from.
3. These phones are expensive.

However, the advantages of having an Apple-unlocked phone are numerous. For one thing, you can be certain that no future Apple software upgrade is going to be designed to disable your unlock. Thus, you don't have to fear upgrades, and you can stay current with the rest of the iPhone software world. Also, your phone may have excellent resale value should you want to upgrade—unlocked phones have a brisk trade online.

 HACK 7.02: Unlock Your iPhone with Software

Free your phone with free software—and a little free time.

For the original iPhone and 3G iPhone, there have been many exploits that have led to a number of software-based unlocking solutions. Although all of these techniques eventually reduce to "run this program and click unlock," the tremendous amount of mental gymnastics and brilliant reverse engineering that go into them is admirable. It's possible that the world's most hyped phone has become the world's most hacked phone, because whether you're looking for fame or fortune, both can be found in the iPhone unlocking arena.

The very first iPhone unlock was achieved through hardware **[Hack #7.03]**, but almost immediately a number of software solutions came out. Usually, jailbreaking and unlocking go hand in hand, and the graphical applications used for jailbreaking **[Hack #1.03]** are usually used for unlocking.

Jailbreaking and unlocking both depend on exploits, which are essentially bugs or features with side effects that can be used to gain control of parts of the phone. Finding exploits is painstaking work consisting of decoding thousands of raw, fine-grained instructions to various unfamiliar chips, tracing them step by step, and trying to see how they work. It took almost six months for hacks in the 3G iPhone baseband to be discovered and exploited for unlocking.

Many exploits have been developed for jailbreaking phones: unlocking is a more difficult task. Jailbreaking simply changes some settings on the flash drive to allow unsigned third-party applications, but unlocking requires sophisticated alteration of the baseband software, and requires an understanding of cellular protocols, baseband programming, and the security layers added to the equation with Apple's iTunes-based phone activation system.

How Does It Work?

As described in **[Hack #2.01]**, there are two "brains" in the iPhone: the baseband, and the iPhone ARM CPU. The baseband is the "cell phone brain" of the iPhone (Figure 7-4), and it is this chip and its associated code that prevents or allows communication with the SIM card.

Figure 7-4.
iPhone baseband boot sequence and CPU boot sequence

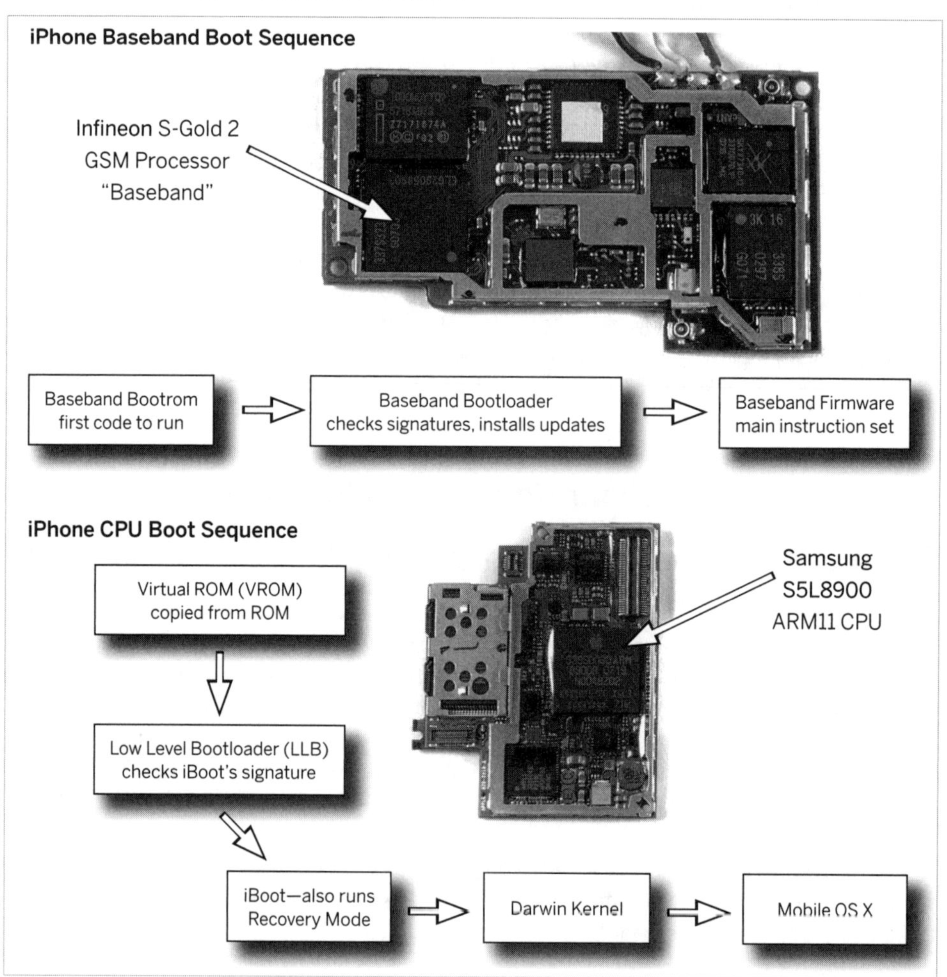

In a sanctioned unlock **[Hack #7.01]**, there is a section of the baseband called the "seczone" where the lock state (unlocked or locked, and associated information) is stored on the phone. In the seczone is stored a token, a combination of information unique to every phone, including its IMEI (International Mobile Equipment Identity) number and a unique device ID. When an iPhone is activated, or unlocked through sanctioned means, this token is sent to Apple's servers, and Apple uses encryption technology to digitally sign a "permission slip" for this token that is sent back to the phone to activate or unlock. iTunes sends this information to the iPhone, and the iPhone obeys the unlock or activation only if the token is properly signed by Apple.

Because encryption technology is a strong defense, no one has been able to crack Apple's code directly and create an authentic Apple signature. Rather, they have taken the approach of making the iPhone ignore these instructions from the mothership. And every time that the iPhone is updated, these "don't listen to Apple" instructions inserted by hackers tend to be erased or overwritten, and the phone made more resistant to these breaches of loyalty.

For the original iPhone, several major software unlocking techniques were developed.

- anySIM (http://code.google.com/p/devteam-anysim): anySIM (Figure 7-5) was originally available only in a paid application, but once alternative unlocking methods became available, it was open sourced. The first anySIM technique simply disabled signature checks in the baseband so that any attempt to verify an Apple signature would say "success." This achieved the goal of unlocking, but was sensitive to restores, in that each time a new baseband firmware was released by Apple, it would undo the effects of this hack and the hack would need to be reapplied. An unfortunate side effect of this hack was that it irreversibly altered part of the baseband (the *locktable*, a section relating to lock status), and this resulted in temporary bricking when new basebands were installed. Virginization software was developed—this software could write virgin, locked locktables back to the device. An improved version of anySIM changed the baseband (but not the seczone portion of the baseband or the locktables) so that any MCC/MNC pair (Mobile Country Code/Mobile Network Code, used to identify a cell network) would appear to be valid.
- iphoneSimFree (www.iphonesimfree.com): Often abbreviated as IPSF, iphoneSimFree was a software unlock that works differently from anySIM—it is able to survive firmware updates. This hack changed the lockstate table in the seczone to unlocked, and then exploited several bugs: one in the RSA decryption parsing in the 3.9 bootloader and one in a data validation check, resulting in a token that appeared validly signed. Because the token itself is stored in the seczone, which is not updated by baseband updates, this particular hack survived firmware upgrades.

Figure 7-5.
anySIM

BootNeuter (for Original iPhone)

A very stable method of unlocking the original iPhone was developed by the iPhone Dev Team and incorporated into the Pwnage software. This incorporates the various hacks mentioned previously, including repairs for common ravages of earlier unlocking techniques. BootNeuter can be installed in Cydia (Figure 7-6) or can be automatically installed when you create a jailbreak firmware image [Hack #1.03] and apply it to your phone (Figure 7-6). BootNeuter allows you to switch between the 3.9 or 4.6 bootloader. "Neutering" your bootloader allows a modified bootloader to be considered valid by the iPhone. From there it is a simple operation to unlock the phone. FakeBlank is a modified version of the 3.9 bootloader (a 4.6 FakeBlank is also available) that "blanks" a section of memory so that advanced bootrom hacking can be done and if trouble arises, the hacker can "roll back" their bootloader. If you aren't experimenting with bootloader patches (you'll know if you are) and just want an unlock, then you can leave the default settings.

Figure 7-6.
BootNeuter

YellowsnOw (for iPhone 3G)

The iPhone 3G was released in the summer of 2008, but it took until New Year's Eve of that year to unlock it via software. This unlock was far more difficult to accomplish than the first-generation unlock because more signature checking and software verification were added (specifically, the bootrom checks to see whether the 3G bootloader has been altered at boot). YellowsnOw gets around this problem by loading an in-memory process that, after booting, tricks the phone into thinking it is unlocked.

Because the unlock is simply a startup item, you can toggle the unlocked state with applications like BossPrefs (available on Cydia) or simply uninstall the program when you don't need it. Like BootNeuter for first-generation iPhones, YellowsnOw can be installed with Pwnage or via Cydia (Figure 7-7).

Figure 7-7.
YellowsnOw

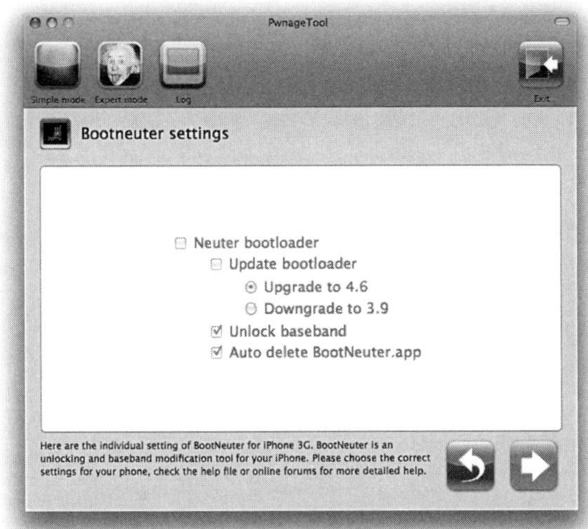

HACK 7.03: Unlock Your iPhone with a SIM Hack

You can use a locked phone on a different carrier with a physical hack to the SIM card.

As mentioned in **[Hack #7.02]**, the second method of the anySIM software hack changed the baseband so that any MCC/MNC pair (used to identify a cell network) portion of the phone's IMSI (International Mobile Subscriber Identity) would appear to be a valid pair. Even if you can't successfully hack the baseband—for instance, on a 3G iPhone—there is a hardware method for doing the same thing.

As there already existed a large market for unlocking phones prior to the iPhone, many companies were already producing solutions for hacking SIM cards. Bladox, a Czech Republic–based SIM test tool manufacturer, introduced the Turbo-SIM in 2004. This clever device consisted of a thin circuit board shaped like a SIM card, and a tiny microcontroller (Figure 7-8). By cutting a tiny square out of the plastic casing of the SIM card (which did not affect the SIM card's normal functioning), the Turbo-SIM could piggyback the SIM card, intercept its communication with the phone, and mediate between the two to make sure they "agreed."

SIM card sandwich hacks of this nature were some of the most consistently effective for first-generation iPhones, and are currently the only effective solutions for iPhone 3G hacking. As with many hacking solutions, a game of cat-and-mouse has ensued, and many of these SIM piggyback cards ceased to work when firmware 2.2 was released for the iPhone. Because the piggyback SIM has a reprogrammable microcontroller, they can be upgraded with new firmware (with the right programming equipment) to work around new problems.

Example: i3gSim

All this unlocking method requires is that you purchase the unlocking tool, and sandwich it with your non-AT&T SIM card. This tool works by tricking your iPhone into thinking that the proper AT&T

SIM (or whatever network your iPhone is locked to) is inserted, even though a SIM card from a different GSM provider is inserted.

To do this and unlock your iPhone, first turn off your iPhone, and then remove its SIM card tray. Now take a look at the i3gSIM tool. You'll notice a black chip that sticks out from the card in the top left corner of Figure 7-8. To get the tool to sandwich with your SIM card, you will need to cut a notch out of the SIM. The portion of the SIM card that you will be cutting out will not affect its performance in any way. A sharp knife such a razor blade is perfect for this job. Figure 7-9 shows a SIM card with the proper-sized notch cut out of it.

Figure 7-8.
The i3gSIM unlocking tool

Notice the black chip in the top left that sticks out of the tool.

Figure 7-9.
A SIM card with a notch cut out of it in the top right so that it can accommodate the i3gSIM unlocking tool

Once you've got your SIM card properly cut, get the i3gSIM tool, your SIM card, and the SIM card tray ready to put into your iPhone (Figure 7-10). Lay the i3gSIM tool on top of the SIM card so that the black chip is resting inside the notch, and place them into the SIM card tray, as in Figure 7-11.

Figure 7-10.
SIM card tray, notched SIM card, and i3gSIM unlocking tool (left to right)

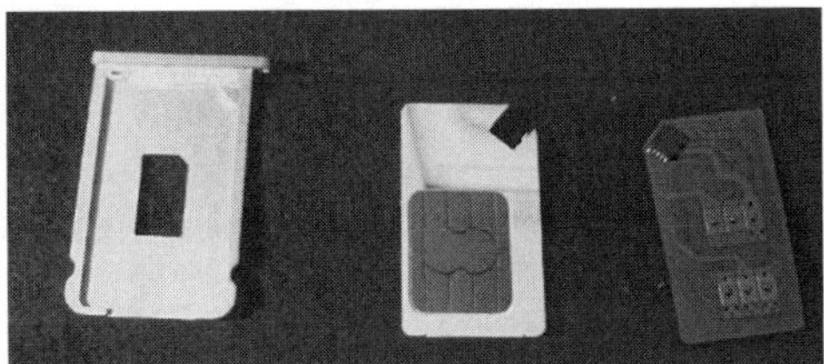

Figure 7-11.
SIM card and i3gSIM tool

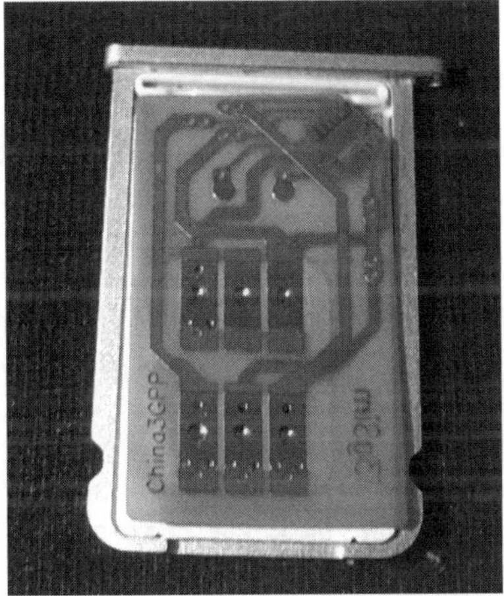

Now just slide the SIM card tray back into your iPhone, and turn it on. Once it's started up, the carrier name at the top left of the screen will change to the name of the SIM card's provider, as shown in Figure 7-12.

Figure 7-12.
An iPhone using the i3gSIM unlocking tool. Notice how the carrier name at the top left has changed to T-Mobile!

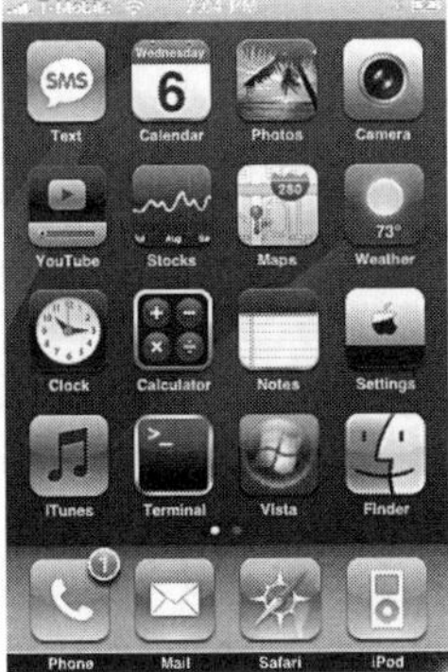

Vendors and Caveats

There are drawbacks to these solutions. Because they are hacking the phone+network combination, instead of the phone alone, there can be poor implementations:

- Some cards work only with 2G (not 3G) networks.
- Some cards get banned from the cell network.

The reason for cell phone banning is that the hacks used violate network policies by looking like a "cloned" SIM card, which is a common method of stealing cell service. Even though the only SIM being "cloned" is your own, in an extreme case, this could cause the SIM to be banned from the network, requiring another SIM.

Despite these caveats, a unit purchased from a reputable vendor is very likely to work on the networks and firmware versions they specify, and many such products are in successful use.

Also of note:

- Several vendors (such as i3gSim and RebelSim) make cards that do not require any SIM-trimming, by moving the microcontroller or producing custom trays for the phone.
- Most vendors recommend that you put tape on your SIM card as a ripcord so that you can pull it out later. The small force exerted by the paperclip in the hole is insufficient to push out the wedged pair of cards.

A few vendors are active in the iPhone unlocking market and update their products frequently to deal with new firmware. They all have a mysterious quality to them—no mailing address, all communication through the website—but perhaps this is to be expected of gray market phone hacking vendors. You should definitely check the community sites [Hack #2.06] and check references—and verify phone compatibility—before you send your money. These vendors are:

www.any-network.com
www.iphone-sim-unlock.com
www.i3gsim.com
www.rebelsimcard.com

It's worth noting that companies like www.yessim.com and www.rebelsimcard.com provide the programming tools (Figure 7-13) and bulk sets of 3G cards (in case you're running a mobile phone unlock shop) and even lets you private-label your SIM sandwiches, in case you're the entrepreneurial type. The programming tool lets you specify what network you want it to spoof for your phone (which varies by country) so that you can log onto the cell network successfully with your iPhone.

Figure 7-13.
Yessim programming tool for 3G SIM

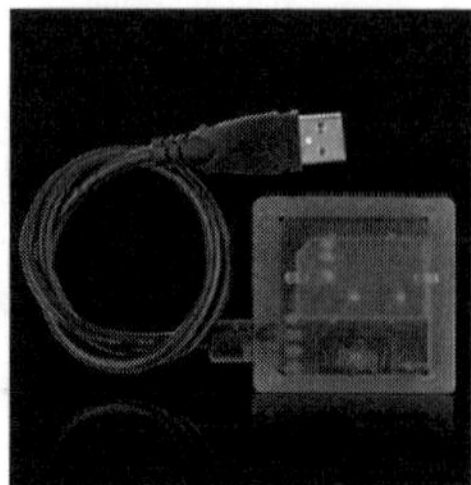

HACK 7.04: Configure Your iPhone After Unlocking

Because Apple didn't intend for the iPhone to be used with alternative mobile carriers, some of its functions may not work correctly after you finish an unlock. Luckily, you can fix them and get your iPhone working like it should.

Fix Cellular Data Settings

Once you've unlocked your phone via any of the methods described in previous hack, phone calls should work, but your cellular networking may not. On the first-generation iPhone with 1.x.x firmware, this was easy to do via Settings→Network→EDGE Settings (Figure 7-14). Nowadays, with 2.x firmware and 3G phones, it's just a little bit harder.

Figure 7-14.
Edge settings

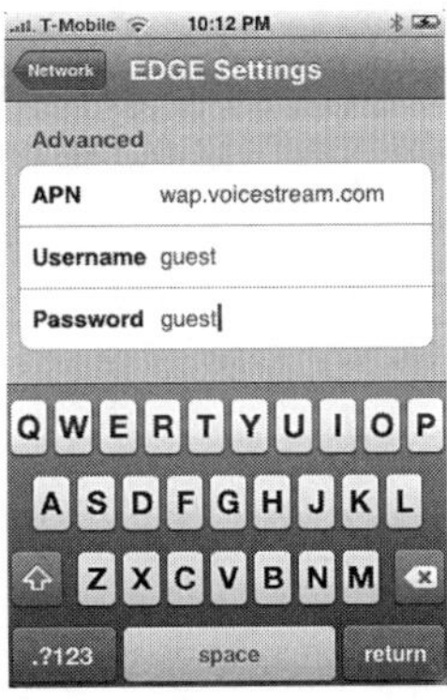

There are just a few steps to fixing your networking:

1. Find out the Access Point Name (APN), username, and password for your network.
2. Enter this data in the phone manually with a configuration utility or with a downloaded carrier bundle.

Step 1: Learn your APN.

Find out the APN, username, and password for the network you want to connect to. You can find these settings by calling your carrier or looking online. A list of common APNs by carrier can usually be found on popular iPhone or BlackBerry forums such as www.pinstack.com/carrier_settings_apn_gateway.html.

Step 2: Edit your APN settings.

With the information, you can edit the settings on your phone. To accomplish this you can either enable APN editing, use the iPhone Configuration Utility, or download a carrier pack from Cydia.

Enable APN editing on the iPhone

On older firmware, you could go to Settings→General→Network, but this does not work on 2.x firmware. To reenable this feature, you'll need to edit the binary *carrier.plist* **[Hack #11.02]** corresponding to your carrier. Find the file */System/Library/Carrier Bundles/<carrier>* where *<carrier>* is the carrier for your SIM card (Figure 7-15).

Figure 7-15.
Carriers

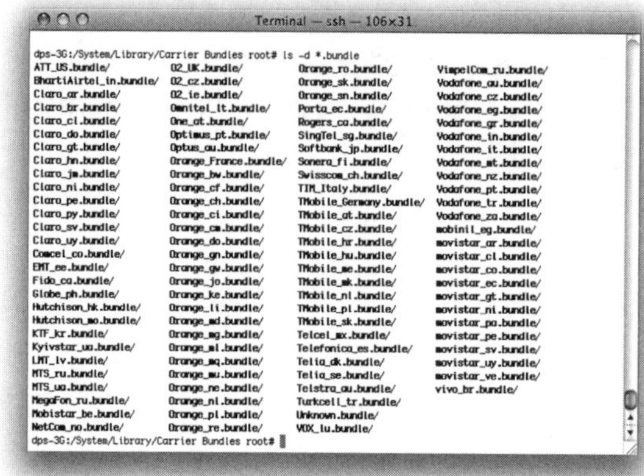

If you're on a Mac, you can mount your iPhone with AFP **[Hack #9.06]** and double-click the *.plist* file to edit it (Figure 7-16).

Figure 7-16.
Editing the carrier *plist*

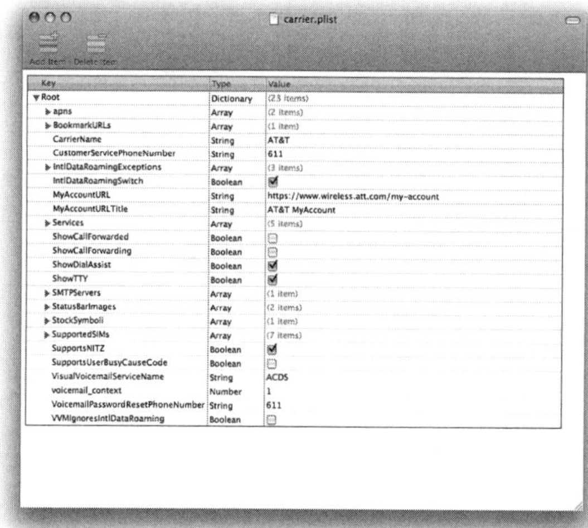

Add the following text (if you're editing the *plist* as a text file) or add the following key as a boolean (Figure 7-17):

```
<key>AllowEDGEEditing</key>
<true/>
```

Figure 7-17.
Setting AllowEDGEEditing to true

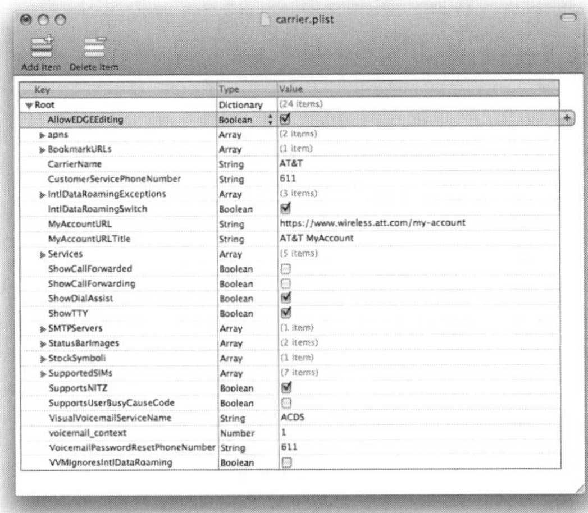

Now, the settings for that carrier will be editable in Settings→General→Network→Cellular Data Network (Figure 7-18).

Figure 7-18.
Editable carrier settings

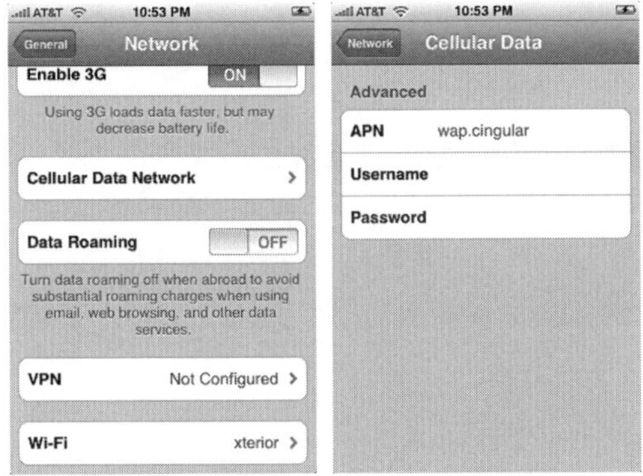

iPhone Configuration Utility

If you have an Apple-unlocked phone **[Hack #7.01]** on 2.x firmware, you can also use the iPhone Configuration Utility (Figure 7-19) from www.apple.com/support/iphone/enterprise to create a profile—an XML file with the needed settings—that you email to your iPhone.

You can find versions here:

http://support.apple.com/downloads/iPhone_Configuration_Utility_1_1_for_Windows
http://support.apple.com/downloads/iPhone_Configuration_Utility_1_1_for_Mac_OS_X

Once you get it running, you'll need to connect your phone, create a new configuration profile, and enter some information about it (Figure 7-19).

Figure 7-19.
iPhone Configuration Utility

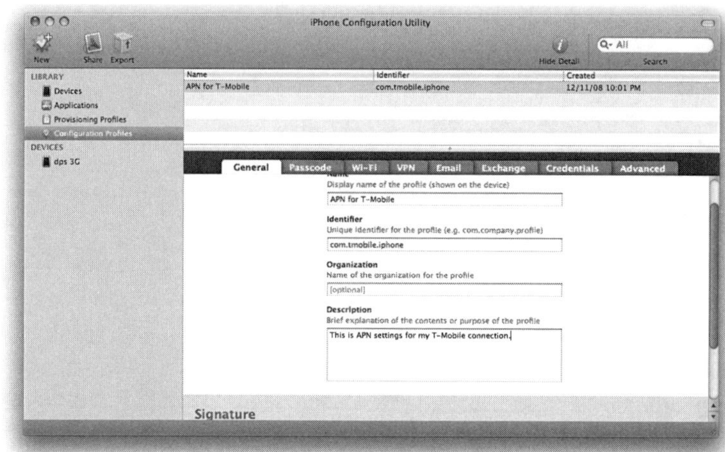

The network settings are found under the Advanced tab. As an example, we'll enter T-Mobile's APN wap.voicestream.com, and enter *guest* for both username and password (Figure 7-20).

Figure 7-20.
The Advanced tab

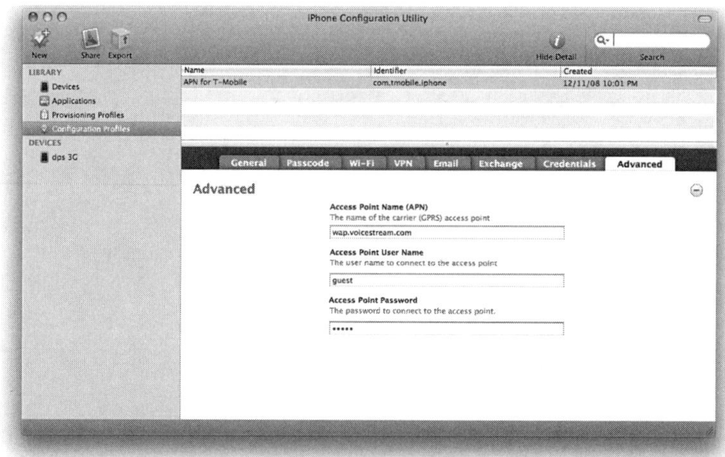

Once you've set all this and exported it, you'll have a *.plist* file **[Hack #11.02]** that looks like Figure 7-21.

```
<?xml version="1.0" encoding="UTF-8"?>
<!DOCTYPE plist PUBLIC "-//Apple//DTD PLIST 1.0//EN" /www"http:/.apple.com/DTDs/
PropertyList-1.0.dtd">
<plist version="1.0">
 <dict>
 <key>PayloadContent</key>
  <array>
   <dict>
   <key>PayloadContent</key>
    <array>
```

```
      <dict>
      <key>DefaultsData</key>
      <dict>
      <key>apns</key>
       <array>
        <dict>
        <key>apn</key>
        <string>wap.voicestream.com</string>
        <key>password</key>
         <data>
          Z3Vlc3Q=
         </data>
        <key>username</key>
        <string>guest</string>
        </dict>
       </array>
      </dict>
      <key>DefaultsDomainName</key><string>com.apple.managedCarrier</string>
      </dict>
     </array>
    <key>PayloadDescription</key>
    <string>Provides customization of carrier Access Point Name.</string>
    <key>PayloadDisplayName</key>
    <string>Advanced Settings</string>
    <key>PayloadIdentifier</key>
    <string>com.tmobile.iphone.apn</string>
    <key>PayloadOrganization</key>
    <string></string>
    <key>PayloadType</key>
    <string>com.apple.apn.managed</string>
    <key>PayloadUUID</key>
    <string>E5B5A7BA-2AB1-4946-899E-B39E318510B2</string>
    <key>PayloadVersion</key>
    <integer>1</integer>
    </dict>
   </array>
  <key>PayloadDescription</key>
  <string>This is APN settings for my T-Mobile connec-tion.</string>
  <key>PayloadDisplayName</key>
  <string>APN for T-Mobile</string>
  <key>PayloadIdentifier</key>
  <string>com.tmobile.iphone</string>
  <key>PayloadOrganization</key>
  <string></string>
  <key>PayloadType</key>
  <string>Configuration</string>
  <key>PayloadUUID</key>
  <string>A339F026-0C7A-4B2F-9A97-25E62FF76C53</string>
  <key>PayloadVersion</key>
  <integer>1</integer>
   </dict>
</plist>
```

Figure 7-21.
Exported network settings

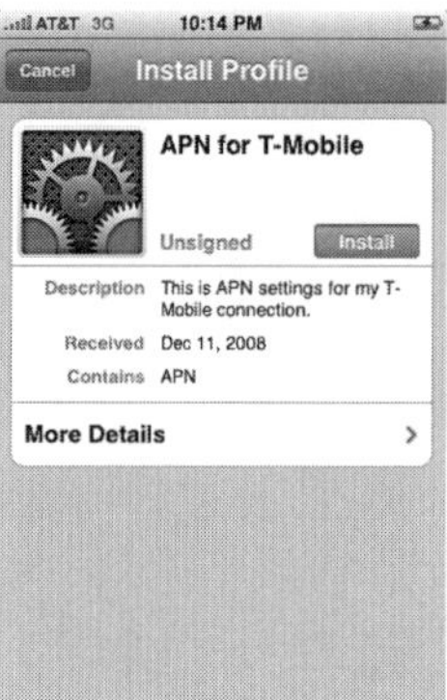

Email this file to your iPhone and open it on the iPhone. Click the attachment and you'll see the screen shown in Figure 7-22.

Figure 7-22.
Installing a profile

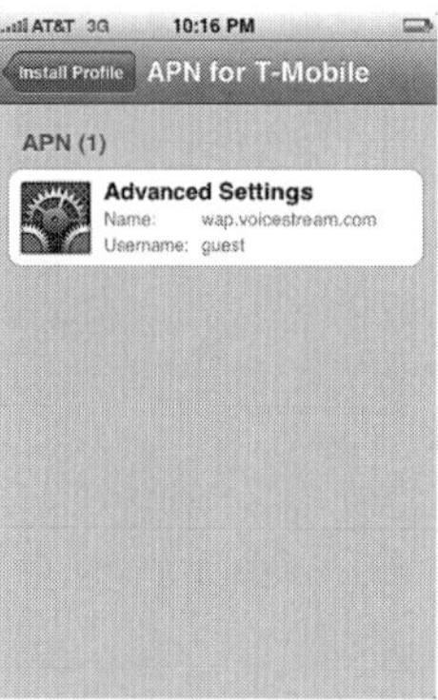

Download a Carrier Bundle from Cydia

A simple way to get carrier bundles for some popular carriers is via Cydia. Search for the word "bundle," or the name of your carrier, and you will get a list of carriers (Figure 7-23). You may need to add some sources **[Hack #1.04]** to find additional bundles.

Figure 7-23.
Downloading carrier bundles

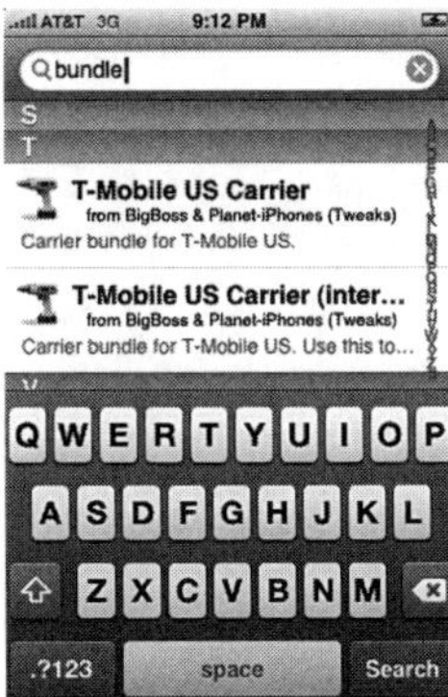

One More Thing: YouTube Fix

On some phones where YouTube has not been "activated," it will give an error message and not function after being unlocked on another carrier. If you can't seem to get YouTube to connect, there is a straightforward fix for this:

1. Download Pwnage or Winpwn. If you used these to do a software unlock, you should already have them. If you are doing a new unlock, you can simply check the "Activate YouTube" option when you create the image.
2. With Pwnage, you will find the necessary files by viewing package contents on *PwnageTool.app*, then going to *PwnageTool.app/Contents/Resources/CustomPackages/YoutubeActivation.bundle*, and viewing package contents again. On Winpwn look in */Program files/Winpwn/bundles/YouTubeActivation.tar*. Extract the three files: *data_ark.plist*, *device_private_key.pem*, and *device_public_key.pem*.
3. Put the files in */private/var/root/Library/Lockdown* **[Hack #1.05]**, replacing the files that are there.
4. Change the ownership and permission of the files **[Hack #9.04]** at the command line: *chmod* to owner=root, group=wheel, permissions = 0644.
5. Create a folder called *activation_records* in */private/var/root/Library/Lockdown/* if one does not already exist.
6. If there is a folder called *pair_records in /private/var/root/Library/Lockdown/*, delete its contents.
7. Reboot the iPhone, connect to a Wi-Fi network, and try out YouTube. It should now work.

With EDGE and YouTube properly working, your unlocked iPhone should be as good as new.

08 CUSTOMIZATION

People like to personalize and customize their phones. The multibillion-dollar ringtone market is a testament to that fact. And although Apple has provided a few ways to rearrange icons and change a background picture, there are dozens of other aspects of the phone that people want to change—but ordinarily can't.

The simplest example is ringtones. Although you can make ringtones out of any song you've bought online, iTunes doesn't provide a way to make them with the songs you already have. With the techniques described in this chapter, that's easy to remedy. System-wide skinning, system sounds, boot screens, and even the words that your iPhone recognizes are all susceptible to change once you know how. And if you want, you can even go beyond software and make skin-deep changes to the color scheme of your phone.

With almost 10 million iPhones sold at the time of this writing, you may no longer feel unique in having an iPhone. In some circles, just about *everyone* has one. But before mourning your complete loss of social cachet, it's worth noting that according to Gartner Research (www.gartner.com/it/page.jsp?id=612207), about a *billion* mobile phones ship each year.

If you're still feeling like a lemming after that reassurance, remember that performing the hacks in this chapter will help you ensure that *your* iPhone is unequivocally one of a kind.

HACK 8.01: Add Custom Ringtones to Your iPhone

The iPhone comes with several preinstalled ringtones when you first purchase it, but if that isn't enough, there are a couple ways in which you can add your own ringtones.

Apple has provided a method for creating ringtones from songs in iTunes to sync to your iPhone. However, the downside of using iTunes is that you can create ringtones only from songs that you've purchased from the iTunes store. Furthermore, after you create the ringtone, you have to purchase it again from the iTunes store. You have to purchase the same song twice!

If you would rather customize your ringtone for free, and be able to choose any sound you want, then you're in luck. There are several different ways to go about doing this.

Custom Ringtones via iTunes

Although iTunes may be infamous for trying to sell you ringtones for your iPhone, it can also be used as a tool to create custom ringtones from songs in the music library:

1. Open the Preferences menu on iTunes, click the Advanced tab, and click the Importing subtab. Make sure that the Import Using box is set to AAC Encoder, as in Figure 8-1.
2. Close the Preferences menu, right-click the song in your iTunes library that you'd like to make a ringtone from, and select Get Info from the context menu, as shown in Figure 8-2.
3. Click on the Options tab, check the Start and Stop Time boxes, and enter custom times, as in Figure 8-3. Once you have custom start and stop times, click OK at the bottom right to close the song info window.
4. Right-click the song again, and select Convert Selection to AAC, as in Figure 8-4. iTunes will convert it, and place the custom song back in your music library, as in Figure 8-5.
5. Right click the newly created clip and click "Show in Windows Explorer/Finder." Drag this file to the desktop and delete the entry from your iTunes Library.
6. Change the *.m4a* file extension to *.m4r*.
7. Double click on the renamed song, and iTunes will automatically place it in the Ringtones library, as in Figure 8-6. Now the ringtone can be synced to your iPhone (Figure 8-7).

Figure 8-1.
Setting the import preferences to use AAC Encoder

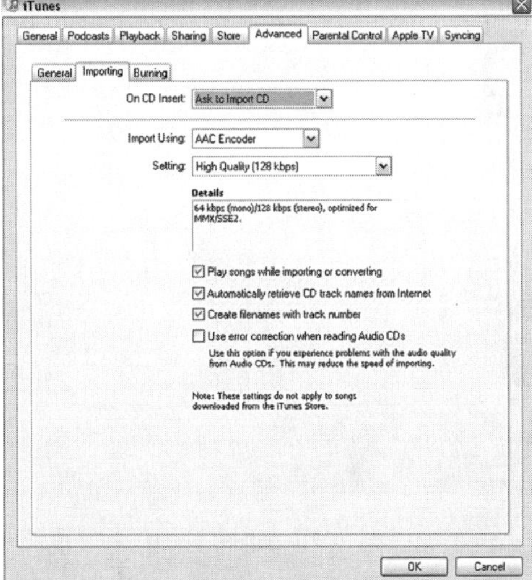

Figure 8-2.
Selecting Get Info

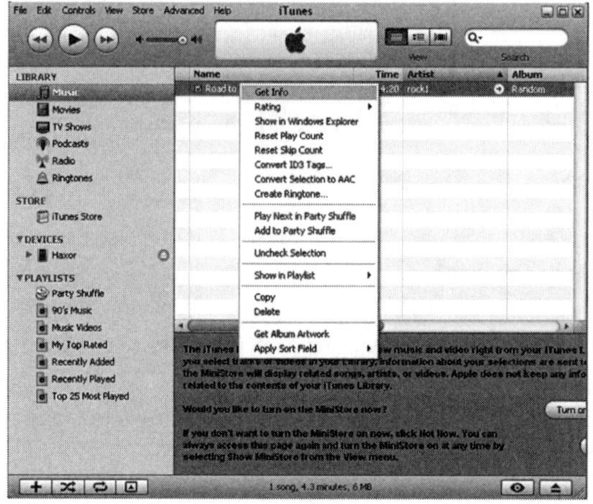

Figure 8-3.
Setting custom start and stop times

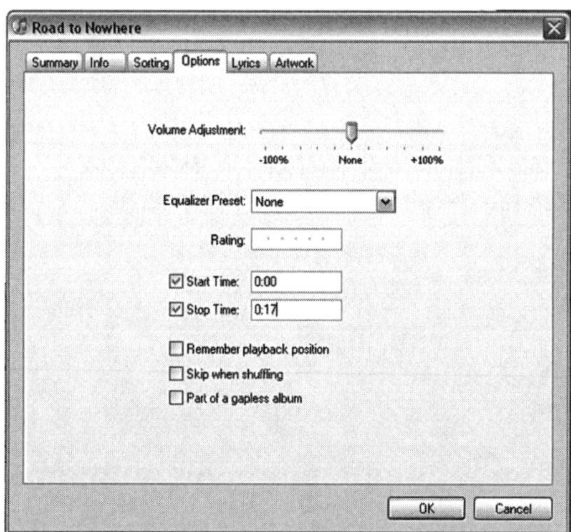

Figure 8-4.
Converting the song to AAC format

Figure 8-5.
After converting, the custom song will appear in the library

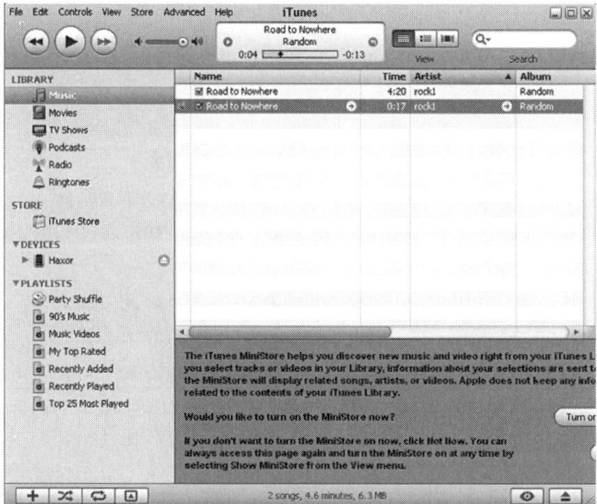

Figure 8-6.
The renamed *.m4r* song shows up in the ringtones library

Figure 8-7.
Syncing the custom ringtone

Custom Ringtones via Other Applications

GarageBand

If you're the creative type, you can make tracks in GarageBand and import them directly to iTunes as ringtones.

1. Open GarageBand and either compose a song or open one you've already made.
2. Select Share→Send Ringtone to iTunes. A dialog box will tell you that you need to select a looping portion of your song, less than 40 seconds, and will show you the cycle button that you need to press (Figure 8-8).
3. Press the Cycle Region button, which lets you highlight a section of the song to loop above your track. Pick a section of up to 40 seconds to use as a looping ringtone (Figure 8-9).
4. Select Share→Send Ringtone to iTunes again. Your song will appear on the ringtone list and, if you've set iTunes up to sync ringtones, it will be sent to your iPhone the next time you sync.

You don't have to compose a song in GarageBand for this to work—you could drop any unprotected music file or audio clip in GarageBand and turn it into a ringtone.

Figure 8-8.
Send Ringtone to iTunes

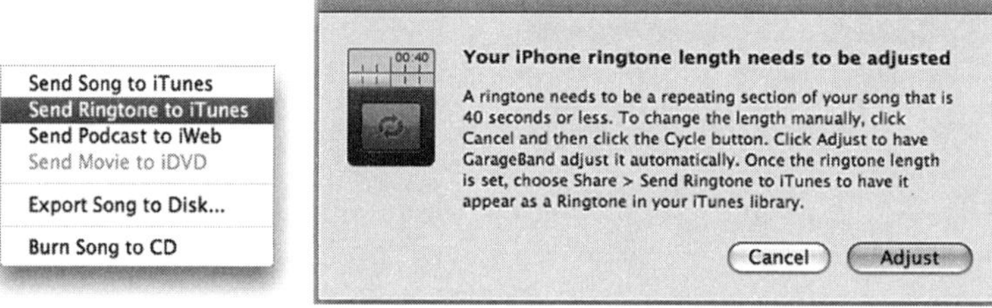

Figure 8-9.
Making a ringtone with GarageBand

The App

If you want a faster, easier method of transferring ringtones, try iToner, available from www.ambrosiasw.com/utilities/iToner (Figure 8-10). iToner is designed to put sound files onto the iPhone for use as ringtones. It has a very simple-to-use interface and reasonable price tag (a $15 one-time fee can end up costing you less than paying $1–$3 per song).

1. Make sure that your iPhone is plugged into your computer. Download, install, and run iToner. A window resembling an iPhone will pop up.
2. Drag and drop the files you want to add onto the window to add them to the list.
3. Press the Sync button on the bottom of the window. iToner will add the files on the list to your phone's ringtone menu.

And you're done. iToner is easily worth it if you want to halve the number of steps and quarter the amount of time necessary to put ringtones on your phone from the alternative method presented earlier.

Figure 8-10.
iToner

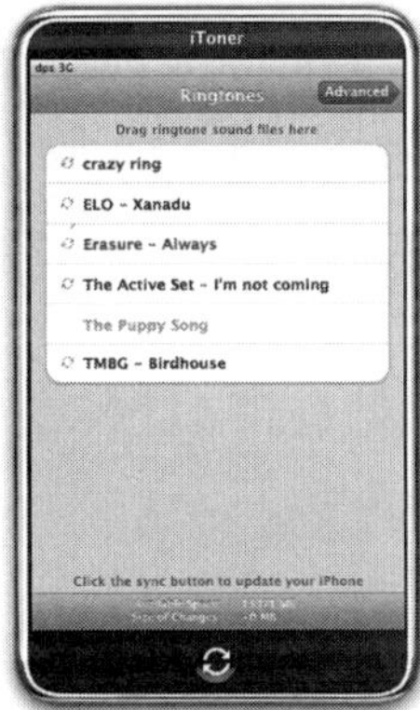

If iToner isn't your thing, there's iPhoneRingToneMaker (www.efksoft.com/products/iphoneringtonemaker/index.htm). This app also does MP3s, WAVs, and OGGs. It also works on Windows.

The iPhone App

iDrum **[Hack #10.01]** allows you to create ringtones based on the iDrum songs you make. All you need is the iDrum Ringtone Sync app from www.izotope.com/products/audio/idrum/iphone, and you're golden. Run iDrum on your phone, and iDrum Ringtone Sync on your computer. Follow the instructions on iDrum Ringtone Sync, and before you know it, your handcrafted tunes will be ripped into iTunes and available to sync as ringtones onto your phone.

The Directory

If you've SSHed into your iPhone **[Hack #9.04]** or have an AFP connection on your phone **[Hack #1.05]**, then this hack will be the simplest ever.

If for some reason you can't get the iTunes hack at the top of this chapter working, try this method. Follow the steps as listed previously, but once you have your ringtone converted to AAC and renamed as a *.m4r*, navigate to */var/stash/Ringtones/* on your iPhone and drop the file straight in there. It will appear on the list on your phone with all the standard ringtones, no restart or sync needed.

Whether you're using a Mac or a PC, there is always a custom ringtone solution that doesn't rely on the expensive iTunes Store method. What will you do with all the money you save?

 HACK 8.02: Skin Your iPhone and Change System Sounds

You can change the skin of your iPhone in nearly limitless ways using WinterBoard.

The iPhone has a very carefully designed user interface, handcrafted to the last pixel by designers at Apple. Though that's admirable, it does nothing to reduce people's urge to customize every aspect of their GUI with their own graphics. On a jailbroken phone, this is possible.

Introduction to Themes

On its main screen, the iPhone runs an application called SpringBoard (Figure 8-11), which is the global launcher for applications. It can be thought of as a stripped-down mobile version of similar tools such as the Finder in OS X, the file browsers on Gnome and KDE in Linux, or Explorer in Windows.

Figure 8-11.
The SpringBoard

The first approach to skinning was simply to find where all the images were stored and manually replace them. Eventually the paths for all the images contained in a skin (the black "wallpaper," the application icons, etc.) were discovered, and the people rejoiced and made full collections of skins to replace these images. This functionality was soon simplified into an application named SummerBoard. SummerBoard—whose name is based on the seasonal definition of Spring (get it?)—allowed users to install skin packages from Installer and toggle them at will. Its power was limited, however, and there were several icons that it was not programmed to change. Some examples are the signal and Wi-Fi indicators, the battery icon, and SMS chat bubbles. Other applications such as Customize were available to change these.

With the arrival of Version 2.0 firmware, the closed source and rarely updated SummerBoard was usurped by WinterBoard (Figure 8-12), and there was again much rejoicing (and much skinning, of course).

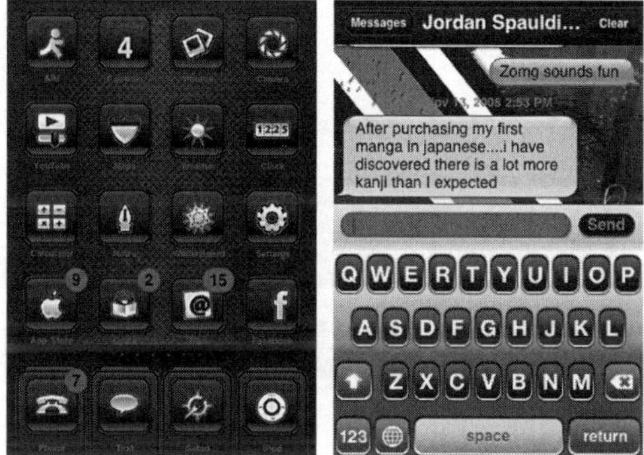

Figure 8-12.
Left: A reskinned SpringBoard with the KillSignCarbonRed skin by KillSign. **Right:** SMS screen reskinned with the Abstract Racing Stripe skin by poetic_folly and Chromium Keyboard skin by Allen from planet-iphones.com.

Using WinterBoard

WinterBoard can be found on Cydia **[Hack #1.04]**, and a wealth of skins can be found there too. We mean it: there are hundreds. As you scour the categories on Cydia and accumulate skins, they will appear on the WinterBoard menu (Figure 8-13). See Figure 8-14 for an example of what skins can do for your device.

Figure 8-13.
The WinterBoard menu with some skins downloaded

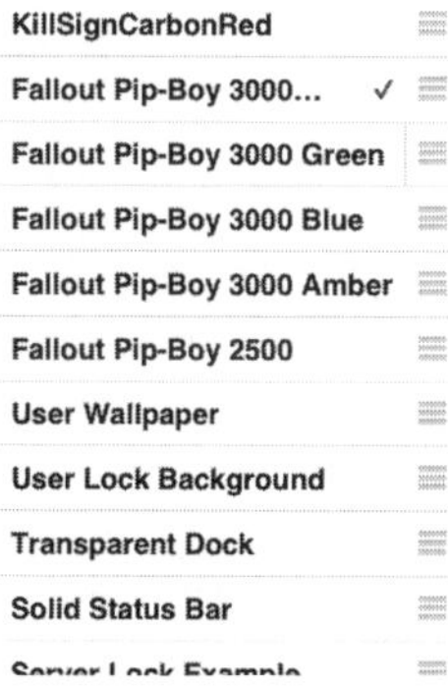

A checkmark indicates the package that's been chosen to skin your phone (Figure 8-14).

Figure 8-14.
A richly skinned phone, with an animated background

WinterBoard skins "stack," so that the highest skin in the stack will override any icon below it. Thus, if there are smaller additions you want to install over a larger skin, arrange them so that the smaller packages are above the larger packages (incidental icons higher on the list than full skins). This makes them replace the redundant images in the larger package (Figure 8-15).

Figure 8-15.
The skinned signal and Wi-Fi bars: no longer the package defaults

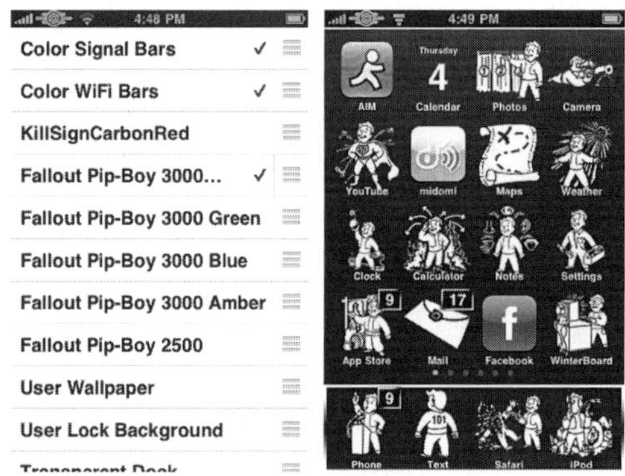

WinterBoard can also support sound packages, allowing you to change various UI sounds. It's hard to take a screenshot of those, however, so you'll have to take my word for it!

Understanding WinterBoard

WinterBoard works by having named folders for each theme, containing picture and/or sound files that are used to replace files located elsewhere while the theme is enabled.

Theme creation consists of making a folder in */Library/Themes/*, named whatever you want the theme to be called, then placing files in this folder with specific names and subdirectories in order to replace other files. The folder */Library/Themes/* is actually a link to */var/stash/Themes.WA77b5/*. If for some reason you can't work with */Library/Themes/*, use */var/stash/Themes.WA77b5/* instead.

If you download an old theme that is for SummerBoard and not WinterBoard, it will still work, but the files will be located in */var/mobile/Library/SummerBoard/Themes/*.

Ideally, you should give your folder a *.theme* file extension (i.e., */mycooltheme.theme/*). You can still work with it as a folder, but it'll be more of a tidy package and easier to identify.

Now that you know where the themes go, what sorts of things can you put in them?

- *Themes/**themename**/Wallpaper.png* will change the wallpaper on your SpringBoard that sits behind the applications.
- *Themes/**themename**/Icons/* is an easy way to change the images used to represent applications. Place an appropriately sized *.png* named after the application (e.g., *WinterBoard.png* or *App Store.png*) in it. This is useful if your theme entirely remakes the color scheme or icon style of the interface, and the standard candy-colored rounded square icons of most applications don't fit any longer.

To change deeper, more interesting images, you'll need to make folders for each application based on its bundle name. This is a string in the format `com.authorname.appname`. For example, *com.apple.calculator* is the bundle name of the default Apple calculator application. Therefore, if you want to make a custom skin for the calculator, you'll need to make a folder called *Themes/**themename**/com.apple.calculator* and put files in it corresponding to the files in the application itself.

How do you find out the names of the files you want to replace, as well as the package name? Go to */Applications/* (or */var/mobile/Applications/*, for App Store apps) on the iPhone, and open the *.app* package like a folder. (On a Mac, control-click for View Package Contents.) This will have all the images in the proper subdirectories that you need to mirror in your theme (Figure 8-16). Any image you put in your theme that matches an image in the application will take precedence and replace it while your theme is enabled. To find out the bundle name, you'll need to open the *Info.plist* file and find the entry for `CFBundleIdentifier`. It will be in the `com.authorname.appname` format. For more information on plists, see [Hack #11.02].

Figure 8-16.
The calculator buttons in file format within the app itself

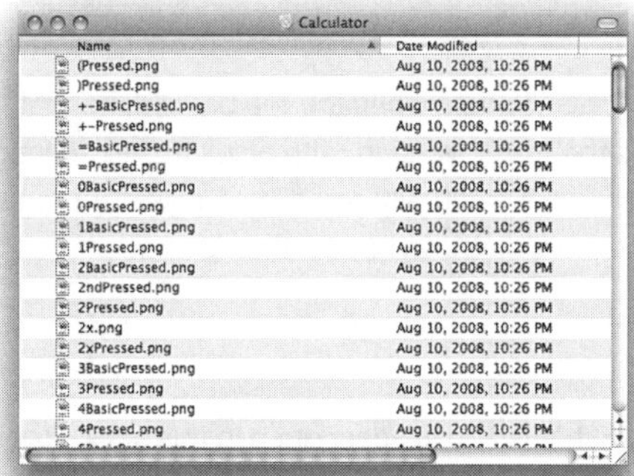

One common application you'll want to edit is the SpringBoard itself. This is what you want to work with if you want to change the icons on the top bar, the dock background, and so on.

Changing Sound Files

These files are AIFF format audio files with the extension *.caf* instead of *.aif*. To put sound files in a theme, put them in *Themes/**themename**/UISounds/* with a subdirectory structure matching that of */System/Library/Audio/UISounds/*.

Changing Carrier Logos

Sometimes the cleverest statements are made with hacked carrier logos. Instead of a boring text string, replace the carrier's name with their iconic logo. Or change it to something from left field (Figure 8-17).

Figure 8-17.
Live in denial or live in the past with a hacked carrier logo

To change your carrier logo, the directories you'll need to know are */System/Library/Carrier Bundles/* and *Themes/**themename**/Bundles/*. The first one is the directory where all the bundles containing pictures and other data for the different available carriers are located. The second directory is where you must put the directory corresponding to the carrier you'd like to change. For example, */Bundles/com.apple.ATT_US/* is where AT&T modifications go. Just like for applications, you'll need to find the *Info.plist* in the bundle to see what to name your folder. The folder structure for the LA Cellular logo theme is shown in Figure 8-18.

Figure 8-18.
/Bundles/com.apple.ATT_US/ is where AT&T modifications go

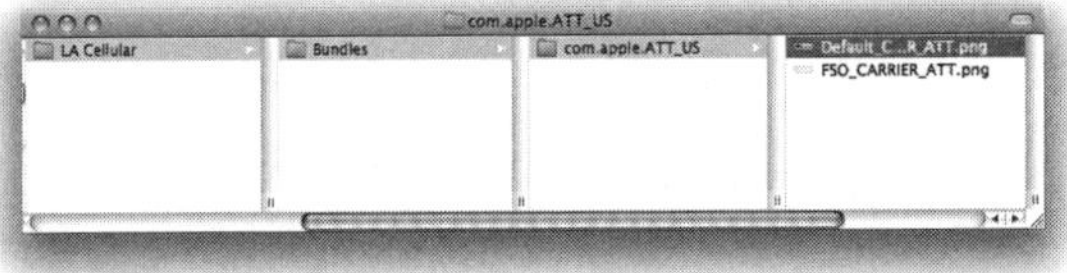

FSO_CARRIER_xxxxx.png is the "light" version of the image, for use when the top bar is dark, that is, on the SpringBoard. *Default_CARRIER_xxxxx.png* is the "dark" version, with black text for when the top bar is silver, that is, in an application. The other files are actually somewhat important to the carrier's operation, so you probably don't want to try to include those in your theme.

And More

If you find a theme that does something different than what is already described in this hack, you can always do an autopsy on the theme directory and see what it did. It may involve custom files or special *.plist* editing **[Hack #11.02]**.

For more insight and advanced feature details, check out www.saurik.com/id/9 for a full-featured rundown on more to do with WinterBoard.

HACK 8.03: Change Your Boot Screen

Don't forget the boot screen and restore logos when you're customizing your device.

You can use WinterBoard **[Hack #8.02]** to change practically every image and sound on your phone. Everything on your phone reminds everyone how much you like the Raiders/World of Warcraft/the color blue/*Star Wars*/trucks, except for when you restart your phone (Figure 8-19). Unfortunately, the graphics for the boot screen are not stored on the filesystem and aren't susceptible to mere file replacement. This hack will show you how to finish customizing your iPhone's graphics.

Figure 8-19.
The ubiquitous boot screen

There are much more interesting graphics that you could display when booting your phone, and several ways to achieve this.

Via Pwnage

The simplest way is to do it is when you first hack your phone. When using the PwnageTool **[Hack #1.03]**, you'll want to be in expert mode. After choosing a package to modify, click the Custom Logos button (Figure 8-20).

Figure 8-20.
The Pwnage Custom Logos screen

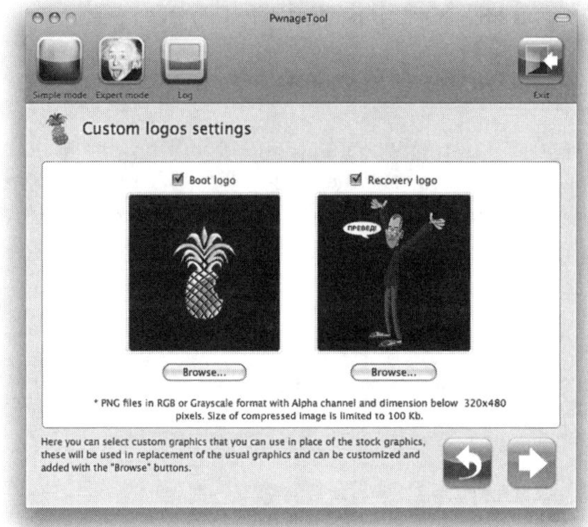

The image on the left represents what your "silver apple" will become, and the one on the right represents what the "Connect to iTunes" screen will be, that is, the one that appears on a phone in Recovery mode.

You can find, create, or edit images to fit the dimensions specified in the app, then select them for your custom restore package. Whenever you restore your phone with that package, the images that you selected will be used for your boot and/or restore logos.

Via the LogoMe App

If you've already hacked your phone and don't want to re-restore and lose your changes, there is another procedure that you can use. The application LogoMe (Figure 8-21) allows you to change your boot screen without restoring your phone.

Figure 8-21.
LogoMe

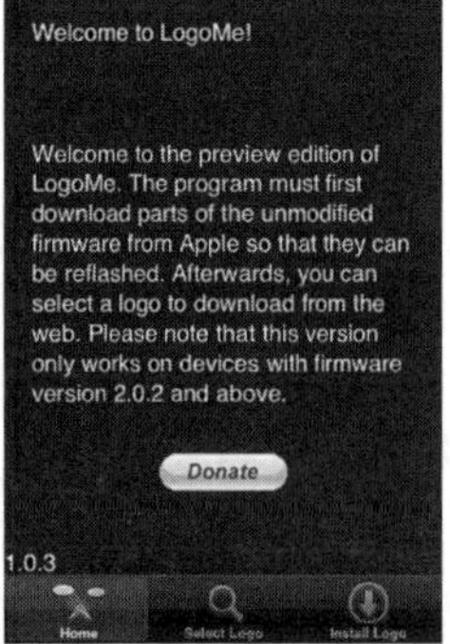

When you start LogoMe, it will download a portion of unmodified firmware in order to edit and reflash it. Find a *.png* somewhere online that you want to use as your boot screen, type the URL into the next screen in LogoMe, and download it. On the Install Logo tab, you can preview the image (Figure 8-22) to make sure that it's downloaded properly, and finally install it. Your boot screen is changed quickly and simply.

Figure 8-22.
Image from eff.org

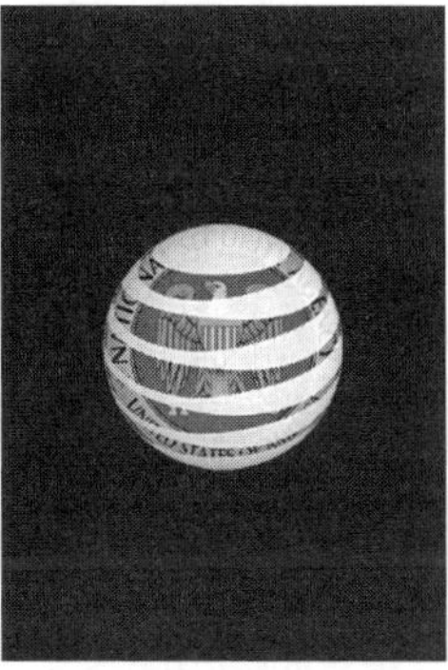

HACK 8.04: Enhance Autocorrection with Address Book Entries

Teach your iPhone your favorite words.

The iPhone and iPod touch's autocorrection can be very helpful when typing messages. It reduces the amount of legitimate typos and grammatical errors (Figure 8-23).

Figure 8-23.
Thank you, iPhone/iPod!

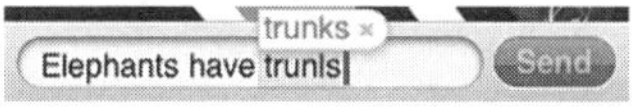

Problems ensue when you try to use words that are outside the built-in dictionary (Figure 8-24).

Figure 8-24.
No thank you, iPhone/iPod!

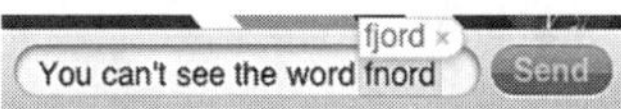

Supposedly the iPhone will learn after three instances of your correcting its correction (by tapping the x on the autocorrect popup), but this does not always work, for some mysterious reason. The most noticeable issue is with swear words. The iPhone assumes that you want to say, "I'm not taking your shot anymore, it ducking posses me off," but what does that even mean? Are we playing basketball?

Fortunately, there's a more reliable, visible way to make your device remember useful words. If you put these words in an address book entry, the iPhone will give them linguistic priority (Figure 8-25).

Figure 8-25.
Your words may vary

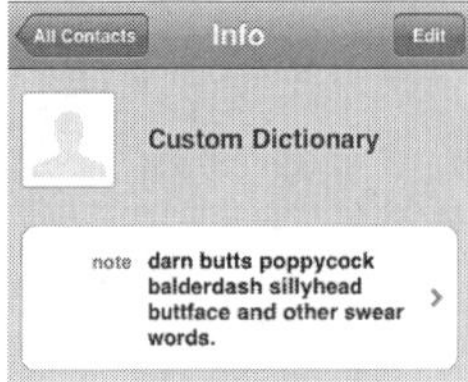

Put the words you want to use into a custom address book entry in the Note section. You could also put these in existing address book entries, if you want to put obscene secret messages that (hopefully) only you know about on your family's and/or co-workers' entries.

HACK 8.05: Skin Your iPhone Externally

ColorWare can color-code your iPhone to fit your color cravings.

Setting the Scene

You've made your own custom skin and boot screen, but it bothers you that your iPhone isn't personalized at all when it's lying there with the screen off (and you've tried custom cases; they aren't your thing).

If only that dull metal/shiny white/shiny black back of your phone could be made more interesting and colorful.

ColorWare (www.colorwarepc.com; see Figure 8-26) is a company that has been doing colorization of various devices since 2000.

Figure 8-26.
ColorWare

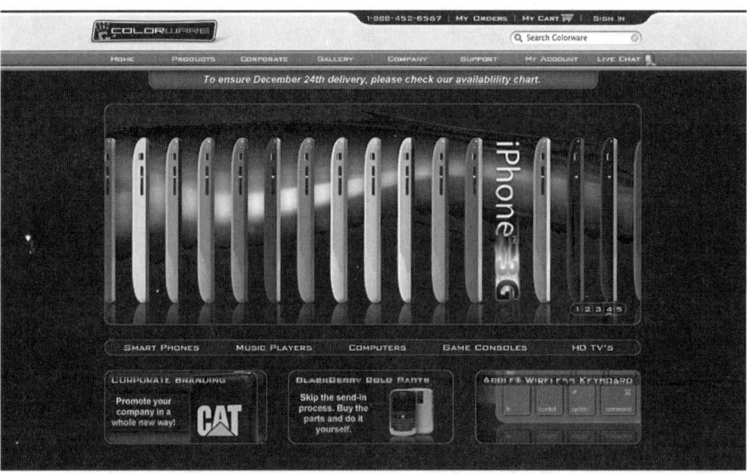

They can help you paint the exterior of your iPhone to fit your wishes. Maybe you miss your old U2 edition iPod, and wish you could have a red-tinted U.S. edition U2 iPhone (Figure 8-27)?

Figure 8-27.
U2 2.0

Or a slick blue iPod touch, with a dock and headphones to go with it (Figure 8-28)?

Figure 8-28.
Color me blue

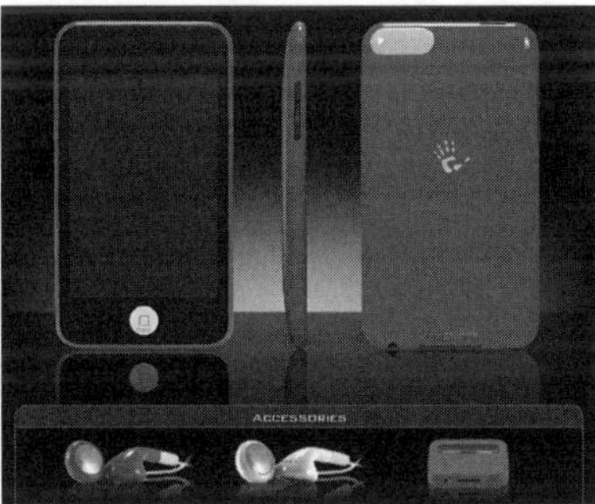

It costs a pretty penny, but it could very well be worth it to add that extra personalization you crave.

 HACK 8.06: Hide Unwanted Applications

BossPrefs and an app launcher will keep your apps out of sight, but there if you need them.

Are you one of the many iPhone or iPod touch users for whom the Stocks app is pointless? Do you find the Notes app so useless as to be offensive to your sight? Are there some apps that you simply wouldn't like others to see or mess with? You've tried to throw your unsightly apps on to another SpringBoard page, but they're still there, wasting real estate. And you don't want to delete them, because you know at some point they might be useful—and if they're gone, you're left kicking yourself.

Your solution is simple: BossPrefs, available from Cydia. It has an app that used to be known as Poof! integrated into it. What does Poof! do? It gives you a list of toggle switches (Figure 8-29) for all the apps currently on your phone (from the App Store or elsewhere). If you don't want to see an app, just set the slider next to it to Off, and it will vanish from the SpringBoard. If you change your mind, you can flip it to On. There when you want it; not there when you don't—simple as that.

Figure 8-29.
Hide iTunes to prevent impulse buying; hide Vonagent to prevent voicemail snooping, and so on

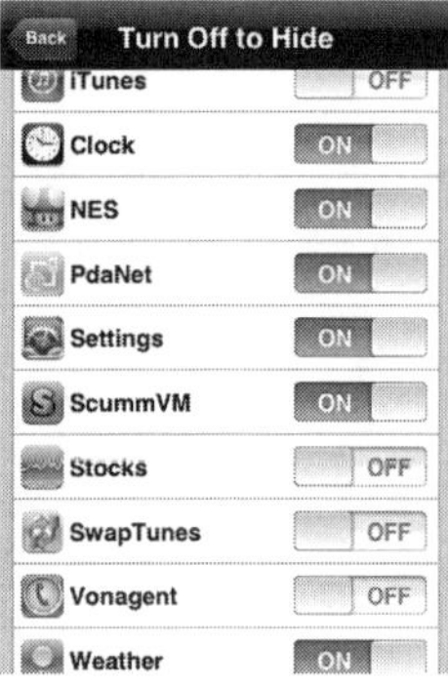

Now, if you just don't want it on the SpringBoard, but want to be able to access it more quickly than it would take to constantly rinse and repeat the previous instructions, all you need is an app launcher...app. Several come up when you type "launcher" into the search bar in Cydia, and they should all work equally well. Here we use AppFlow by Erica Sadun as an example, because it is pretty. These launchers will indiscriminately list all the apps on your phone, hidden or not (Figure 8-30). You can tap any of them and get going quickly and easily. AppFlow even features a landscape Cover Flow mode (Figure 8-31).

Figure 8-30.
Keep apps out of sight until you need them

Figure 8-31.
Stocks, how are you doing? I haven't seen you in a while.

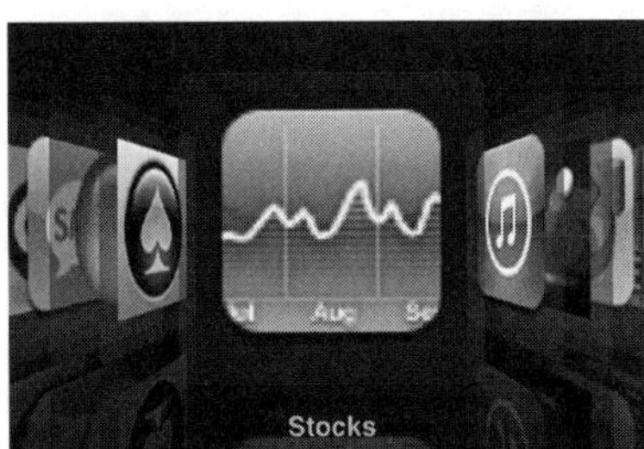

09 NETWORK HACKS

The iPhone and iPod touch both shine at networking. Because there's Unix inside them, there's an almost limitless supply of open source networking software available to recompile for use on the iPhone. Shortly after the iPhone was jailbroken and development tools were developed for it, all the usual suspects—web servers, file servers, scripting languages—were ported over to the iPhone. After Apple opened up the iPhone to developers, some tools appeared in the App Store as well.

To an end user, this may not seem like much. But to power users and developers, the iPhone is a tool of unparalleled flexibility. You can SSH into your servers. You can use it as a remote control for your media center—or your desktop PC. You can surf the Web with remarkable fidelity, download files, upload files, and generally do anything that you could want to with a desktop computer running Mac OS X, Windows, or Linux.

This chapter presents a sampling of some useful networking features of the iPhone and iPod touch. Many of the staple applications for server administration are available in the App Store, and even more are available for a jailbroken phone. Because of ongoing development, new network apps appear constantly, so keep searching for your favorite protocol or utility in Cydia and the App Store.

HACK 9.01: Use Your iPhone or iPod touch as a Trackpad

Upgrade your several-hundred-dollar device to a several-hundred-dollar wireless trackpad.

Many people connect computers to their flat-screen TVs in order to watch movies. But it's not always that easy to remotely control media player software that was designed to be used with a mouse. For instance, if you have a Mac Mini hooked up to your television, the Apple Remote won't control VLC, QuickTime, or the DivX player. A Bluetooth mouse won't work well on the arm of your couch, and a wireless keyboard with integrated trackpad is a pretty bulky remote. What device do you own that can talk to other computers, and has a touch screen? Hmm...

There are several apps at several different price points that allow your iPhone and iPod touch to control your PC or Mac. The price point ranges from free to $9.99. Let's take a look at the free RemotePad to get a feel for how these applications work.

RemotePad (http://tenjin.ics.es.osaka-u.ac.jp/RemotePad) is your free solution. It comes in two parts: a desktop server and an App Store app. With these two parts, it takes mere moments to set up.

Make sure that your two devices are in the same wireless network. Start the server on the desktop, and the app on the iPhone/iPod. Your computer's name should show up on your device (Figure 9-1). Tap it, and you should be good to go. Your new screen will be black with buttons, and you can start trackpadding around your computer (Figure 9-2). You'll have to try it for yourself to see it in action, as a screenshot could never do it justice.

Figure 9-1.
The server selection screen

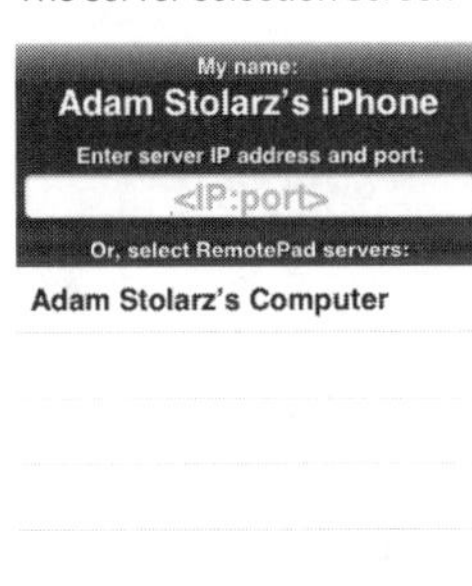

Figure 9-2.
Making a real connection

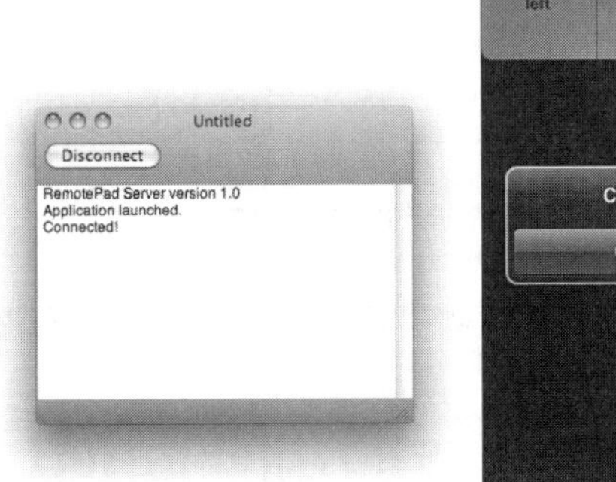

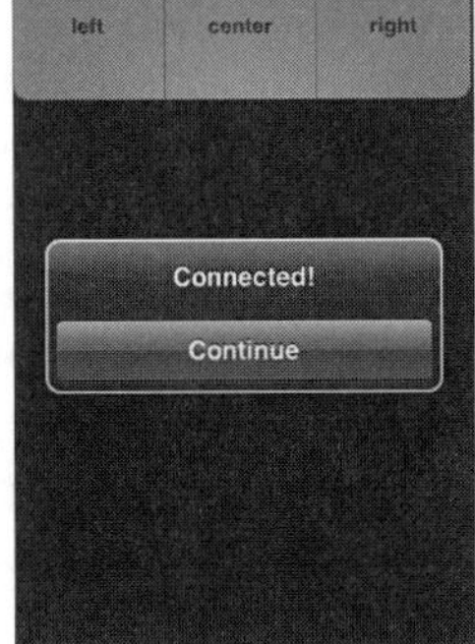

The other apps will have different layouts and features: look for them in the App Store or Cydia and give them a try if RemotePad doesn't cut it.

HACK 9.02: Control Your Desktop or Laptop with Your iPhone or iPod touch

Control your whole PC from your iPhone or iPod touch.

Are all the remotes [Hack #4.03], [Hack #10.06], [Hack #12.23] in this book not enough? Is something not covered? With this hack you can type responses to instant messages, open new applications, check file transfer status, and start and stop your media player—the possibilities are endless!

First, install a server on your desktop PC, if you haven't already done so. RealVNC is a good, free server for Windows. For Mac you can either use Vine (www.redstonesoftware.com), or you can go into your Sharing settings in System Preferences and enable VNC, as shown in Figure 9-3.

Figure 9-3.
The easy way to VNC into your Mac

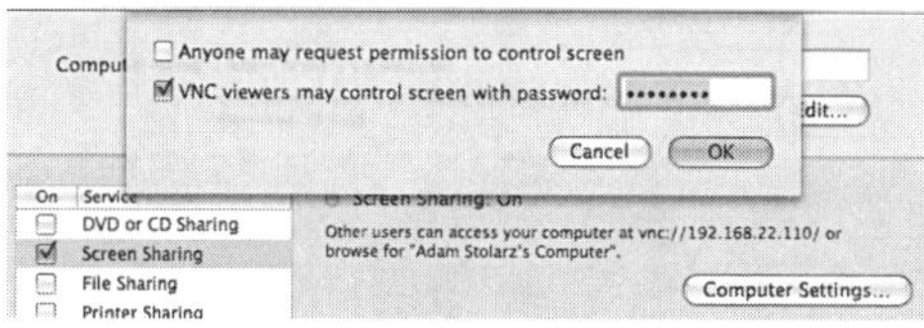

Before firmware 2.0 [Hack #1.02], there were a number of jailbroken VNC clients for the iPhone. Now that we have Mocha VNC (Figure 9-4) in the App Store, its predecessors have vanished.

Figure 9-4.
Mocha VNC controlling a Mac

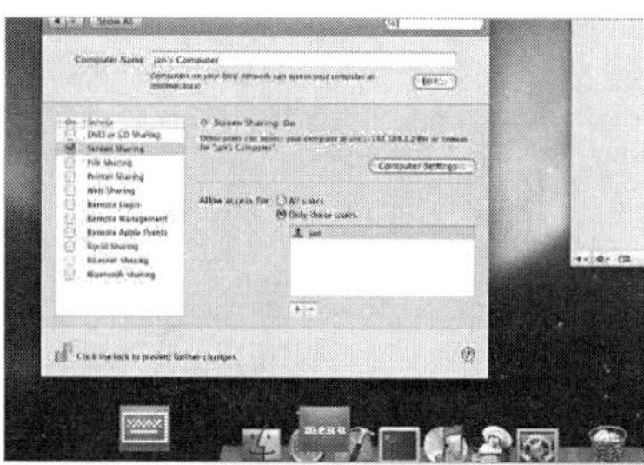

To use VNC, install one of the servers listed earlier onto your machine (or configure Remote Desktop, also as described previously). Then configure and launch the server, and enter your desktop's internal IP into Mocha VNC. You can zoom using two-finger multitouch, and control your computer just as if you were there!

For Windows Remote Desktop users there is an app called Remote Desktop (Figure 9-5). It works essentially like Mocha VNC, but with special support for Windows Remote Desktop.

Figure 9-5.
Remote Desktop

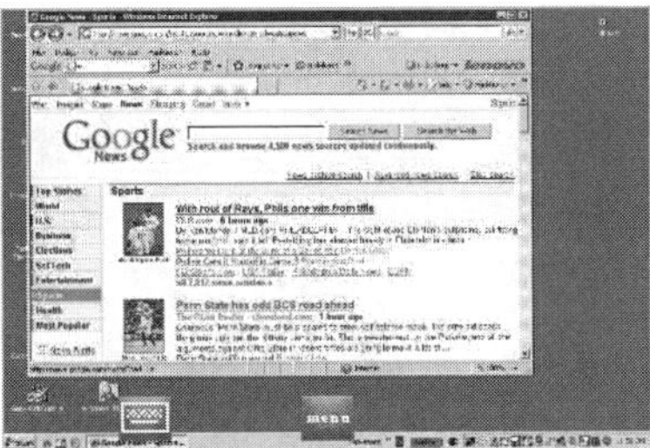

Another solution, if you run software from LogMeIn, is their release of LogMeIn Ignition (https://secure.logmein.com/products/ignition/iphone), a version of their client software for the iPhone (Figure 9-6).

Figure 9-6.
LogMeIn Ignition

HACK 9.03: Control Your iPhone or iPod touch with Your Desktop or Laptop

You can control a jailbroken phone right from your desktop.

Reaffirming the fact that the strong can control the weak, here comes the jailbroken app Veency. Veency is a VNC server for your iPhone/iPod touch, as opposed to Mocha VNC, which is a VNC client. What does that mean for you? It means you can do something akin to Figure 9-7.

Figure 9-7.
That is not an iTunes control widget—that is an iPhone!

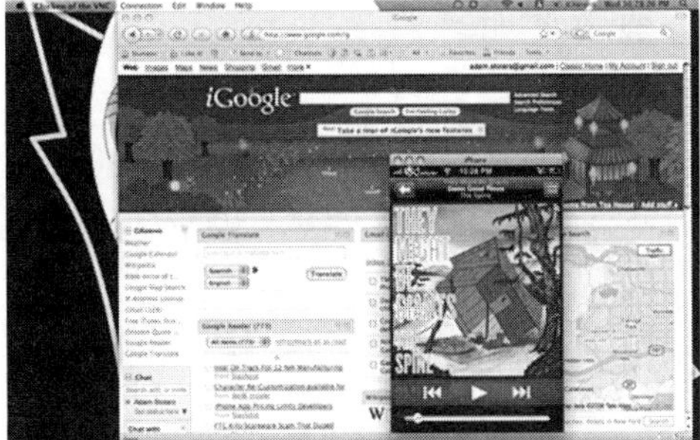

Just download a client onto your computer, like RealVNC's VNCViewer for Windows or Chicken of the VNC for Mac. Put your computer and device on the same network, and put your iPhone/iPod's local IP into your desktop's VNC client. As there is no password option yet, a confirmation screen will show up on your device (Figure 9-8). An iPhone-sized screen will pop up and you will be in control.

Figure 9-8.
Big Brother computer knows what's best

Left-click taps, right-click (Control-click on Macs) presses the Home button, and middle-click locks the phone.

If you want to take this and **[Hack #9.02]** to create an infinite loop of remote control, that's your decision—please just don't make the universe swallow itself.

> **QUICK HACK**
>
> **SAVE TIME WHEN TYPING IN THE TERMINAL**
>
> Tab autocomplete is performed by entering "Control+I" while in the mobile terminal. Because there is no Control key, the large dot symbol is used instead. To enter a dot, select ".?123", then press "#+=". The dot should be on the right side of the keyboard, above the backspace.

HACK 9.04: Connect to Your iPhone with a Secure Shell (SSH) Terminal Program

You can use a terminal program to connect to the iPhone, copy files to and from it, manipulate the filesystem, and run programs.

Contrary to the corny virtual-reality-in-cyberspace-VR-glove user interfaces depicted in contemporary Hollywood movies, most "hacking" is actually done with text commands on a simple monochrome screen. As it turns out, a lot of system administration is done this way, too.

Secure Shell, or SSH, is a network protocol that creates a secure connection between two computers and allows them to exchange data. It has replaced the venerable but insecure Telnet, and is the universal way to "log on" to a Unix or Linux machine remotely.

Although this book tries to provide links to GUI-based "hacking" tools whenever available, the reality is that almost every hack in this book was initially performed by SSHing (that's the verb form) into the iPhone and executing the necessary commands. In fact, if you aren't a programmer, but you like to try out the most bleeding-edge hacks, you'll need to know how to use a terminal.

Installing an SSH Server

There have been various versions of SSH installed by the various jailbreaking tools on the iPhone, but as of this writing the stable SSH is provided by Cydia. When you run Cydia, you can find SSH on the main screen, or you can search for OpenSSH and install it (Figure 9-9).

Figure 9-9.
Installing SSH

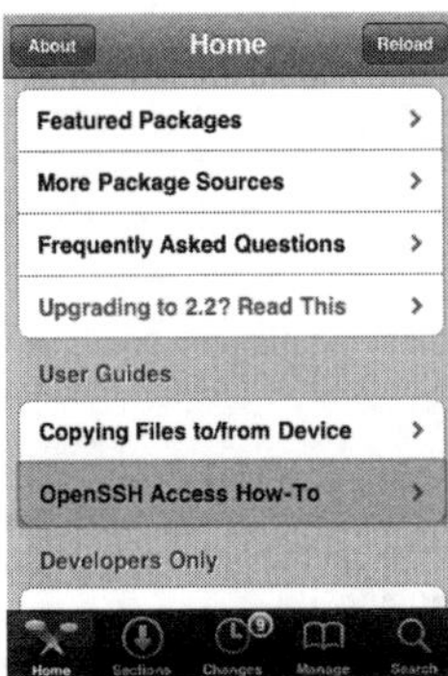

The SSH server works only over a Wi-Fi network. It probably would work over 3G, but usually the network operator blocks incoming services and does not provide mobile phones with a public IP address. Usually the iPhone connects to a Wi-Fi network and gets a dynamic (temporary) IP address. To SSH into the phone, you'll need to get a terminal program, and you'll need to know your iPhone's IP address. You can find the IP address by going to Settings→General→Network→Wi-Fi and then clicking the arrow next to the network you're connected to. You'll see DHCP selected in blue, and your IP address (Figure 9-10).

Figure 9-10.
Finding out your dynamic IP address

If you find yourself connecting to your iPhone a lot, looking up the IP address all the time will become annoying, so you may want to set a static (unchanging) IP address for connection to your Wi-Fi network. To do this, note down the information for your DHCP address, then go to the Static tab and enter it all in, but set the last digit of the IP address to something that you can remember (Figure 9-11). Your iPhone will remember this IP address and will use it whenever it connects to this Wi-Fi network again (i.e., at your home or work).

Figure 9-11.
Setting a static IP

Whenever you use SSH to connect to your iPhone, you'll be required to enter a username and firmware-specific password. Although late-model firmware added a second user, `mobile`, the superuser, `root`, has access to the entire filesystem and can change things more easily:

- User name: `root`
- Password for firmware 1.0.2 and earlier: `dottie`
- Password for firmware 1.1.1 to 2.2: `alpine`

Once you have SSH installed and know your IP address, the next step is to get connected.

SSH Client Software for Windows

If you're a Windows user, there are two main programs that you should have on your computer to connect via SSH with your iPhone: PuTTY and WinSCP.

PuTTY is a terminal client for PCs that allows you to connect to SSH servers and enter commands. It can be downloaded from www.chiark.greenend.org.uk/~sgtatham/putty. When you start the program, you'll see a configuration window (Figure 9-12). Enter your iPhone's IP address in the Host Name box, choose SSH for the Connection type, enter 22 in the Port box, and then click Open. When you connect to your iPhone for the first time, you'll be asked to "permanently add the RSA key fingerprint." RSA is a method of encryption, and adding the fingerprint indicates that you trust the remote machine (your iPhone), so just select Yes (Figure 9-13). If you ever connect to a different machine with that same IP address with SSH, the program will let you know that the key has changed, as a safety precaution, so that you can verify which machine you're connecting to. You may have to wait a while the first time you connect, while the iPhone generates an encryption key. A new black window will open, and prompt you to log in and enter a password. Type `root` as your login name, and use the appropriate password for your iPhone's firmware (see the previous section). Upon entering the correct password, your session will start, and you can start typing commands (Figure 9-14).

Figure 9-12.
PuTTY configuration

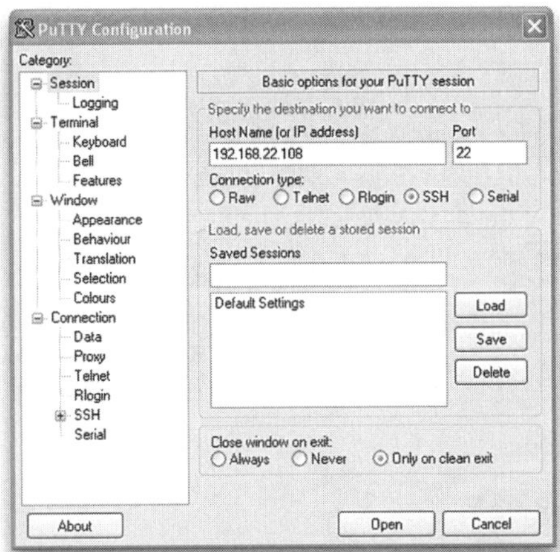

Figure 9-13.
Accepting the host key

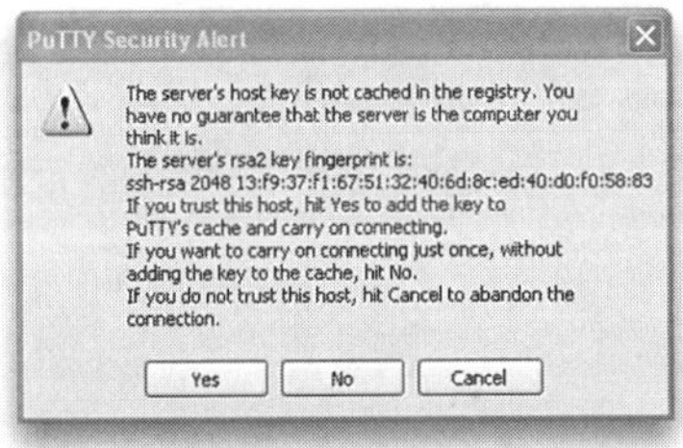

Figure 9-14.
After login, you can enter terminal commands into PuTTY's window

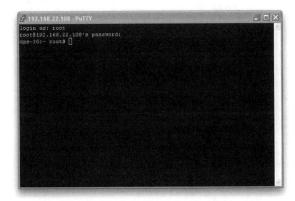

Now you're connected to your iPhone and ready to type commands.

WinSCP is SSH client that features a graphical user interface to the files on an SSH server. It can be downloaded from http://winscp.net. WinSCP functions similarly to file browsing programs such as iPhoneBrowser **[Hack #1.05]**. In addition to its file browsing capabilities, WinSCP also has PuTTY built in.

When you start WinSCP, you'll see the login window, as in Figure 9-15. Click New in the top-right corner, which produces a new window (Figure 9-16). Enter your iPhone's IP address in the Host Name box, and enter 22 in the Port Number box. Enter the appropriate username/password combination, according to your firmware version (see the earlier section in this hack), and then click Login and type "yes" when prompted.

Figure 9-15.
WinSCP login window

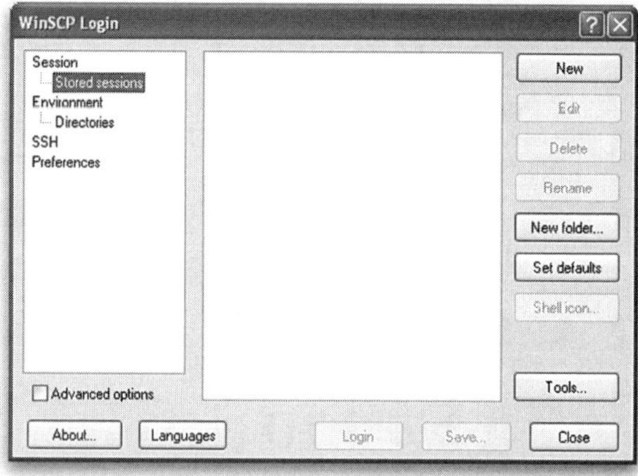

Figure 9-16.
Connecting via WinSCP

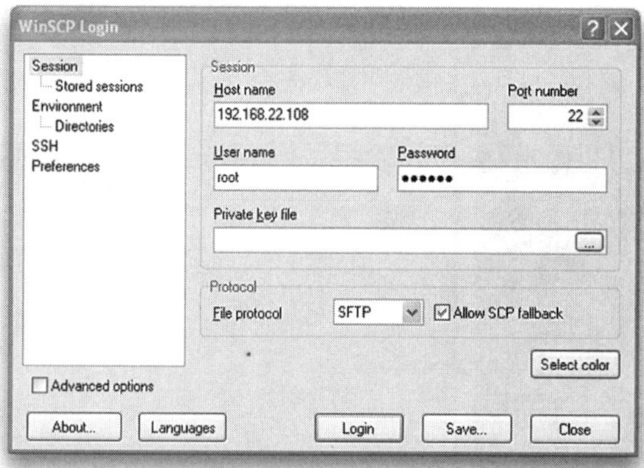

A window will open displaying the */private/var/root/* directory of your iPhone on the right, as in Figure 9-17. You can navigate through your file directory, and upload and download any files to and from your iPhone. If you need to run terminal commands, just click the Commands tab at the top, as shown in Figure 9-18, and you can open PuTTY conveniently.

Figure 9-17.
The */private/var/root/* directory of the iPhone is shown on the right side of the WinSCP window

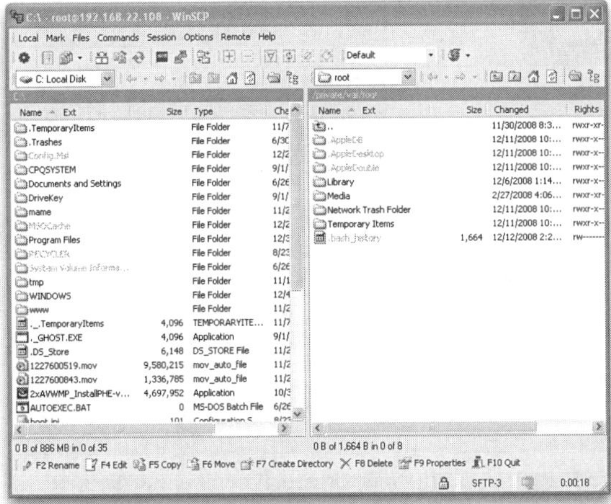

Figure 9-18.
Clicking on the Commands tab

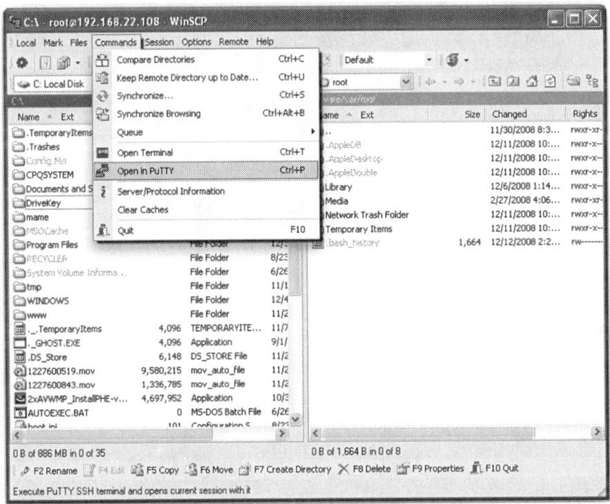

SSH Client Software for Mac Users

Mac computers feature a built-in SSH client that can be accessed by opening Terminal, which is found in Applications→Utilities→Terminal. In the Terminal window type `ssh root@` followed immediately by your iPhone's IP address, as shown in Figure 9-19. When you connect via SSH to your iPhone for the first time, you'll be asked to permanently add the RSA key fingerprint. RSA is a method of encryption, and adding the fingerprint indicates that you trust the remote machine (your iPhone), so just select Yes. If you ever connect to a different machine with that same IP address with SSH, the program will let you know that the key has changed, as a safety precaution, so that you can verify which machine you're connecting to. Once you log in, you can now enter commands.

Figure 9-19.
Connecting to the iPhone's SSH server in Terminal

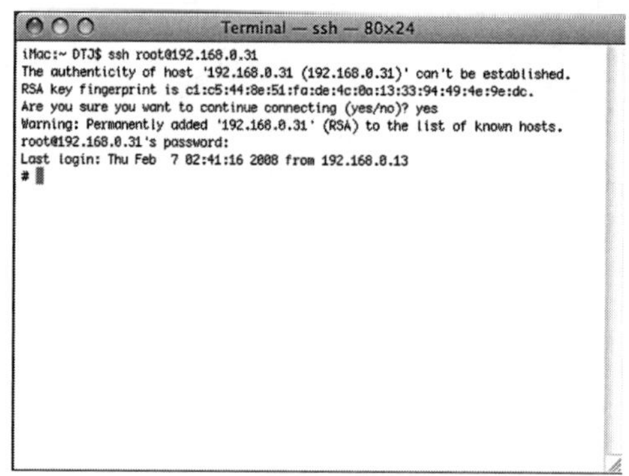

If you need a good SSH file browsing program, then Cyberduck is for you. It can be downloaded from http://cyberduck.ch. When you start the program, click Open Connection at the top left of the window. A new window like the one in Figure 9-20 will open. Select SFTP for the protocol, enter your iPhone's IP address in the Server box, and enter the standard SSH login and password for your firmware version (see the earlier section in this hack). Finally, click Connect—Cyberduck will display your iPhone's file directory so you can make any necessary changes, as shown in Figure 9-21.

Figure 9-20.
Configuring the connection settings on Cyberduck

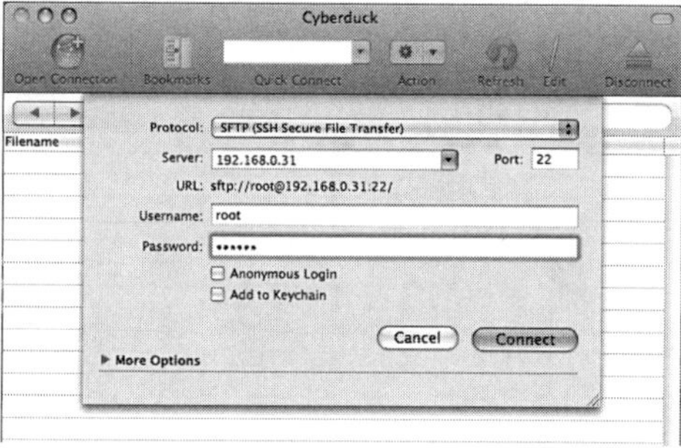

Figure 9-21.
Browsing the iPhone's file directory with Cyberduck

What Do I Do Now?

If you're new to Terminal, there are plenty of resources to help you learn the Unix shell on Mac OS X.

If you've logged in to your iPhone in order to run through the steps of some online walkthrough, it's worth learning a tiny bit about the shell—the text environment you're logged into—so you can feel more comfortable with what you're doing.

For a gentle introduction to the Unix shell used by Mac OS X, see *Learning Unix for Mac OS X Tiger*, by Dave Taylor (O'Reilly).

A good online resource for learning the command line is http://linuxcommand.org/index.php. Linux, you say? Well, the command-line tools are pretty much equivalent across Unix and Unix-like machines.

Hacking the Hack: SSH with no passwords

When you're doing development work or copying files to and from your iPhone from a command line, it can get somewhat tiring typing in your passwords over and over. Especially when you're developing on your computer using the toolchain **[Hack #11.06]** and testing on the phone, you probably want your *make* script to automatically copy the application you build over to the phone without demanding a password.

Another reason to eliminate the shell is scripting on the phone. If you want to write scripts to back up files to the Internet, i.e., to your web server, you're going to need a secure channel between your iPhone and the server that doesn't require passwords.

SSH is secure because it uses a pair of encryption keys, a public and a private one. Each key can decode data that is "locked" by the other key. Thus, to "pair" two computers, you need to create a pair of keys, put the public key on the destination computer, and keep the private key only on the source computer. To make this clearer:

- If you want to log into your iPhone from, say, your desktop, you create a private/public key pair on your desktop and copy the public key to your iPhone
- If you want to log into a server from your iPhone, you create a private/public key pair on the iPhone and copy the public key to the server

The following walkthroughs will show you how to do this:

SSH with no passwords

In this example, the author's computer is dps17 (a 17" Mac Book Pro) and the author's iPhone is dps-3G. Since my iPhone has been set to a static IP address I'm going to create an alias to it in */etc/hosts* (Figure 9-22), which will allow me to access it by name. You can type in the bolded commands to duplicate the steps.

Make an alias and edit the file as shown in Figure 9-22:

```
dps17-2:~ $ sudo pico /etc/hosts
```

FIND MISSING DIRECTORIES AND FILES

A FEW COMMANDS WILL GET YOU GOING:

- `cd` changes directory, so you can type, for instance, `cd /var/mobile/Media/`
- `ls` lists what files are there.
- `pwd` tells you what directory you are in.
- Several hacks in this book reference specific directories or files that need to be modified. However, depending on your phone's firmware version, you may have a different directory structure. In this case, find the new directory by entering the following command in the mobile terminal, or an SSH session: `find / -name "<file name>"`

Figure 9-22.
editing */etc/hosts*

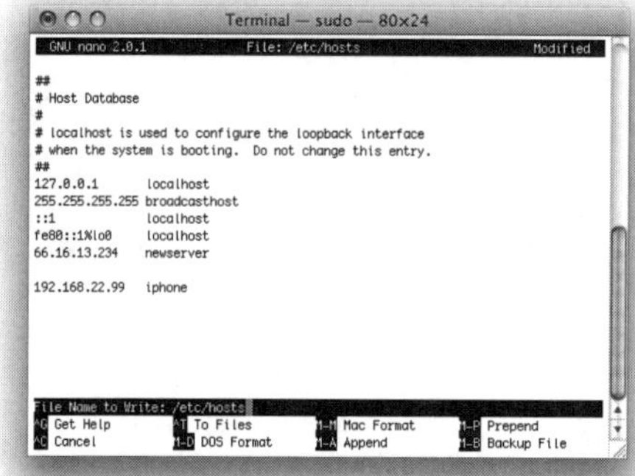

Ping the iPhone:

```
dps17-2:~ $ ping iphone
PING iphone (192.168.22.99): 56 data bytes
64 bytes from 192.168.22.99: icmp_seq=0 ttl=64 time=328.536 ms
64 bytes from 192.168.22.99: icmp_seq=1 ttl=64 time=85.387 ms
^C
--- iphone ping statistics ---
2 packets transmitted, 2 packets received, 0% packet loss
round-trip min/avg/max/stddev = 85.387/206.962/328.536/121.575 ms
```

To generate the private/public key pair on the computer:

```
dps17-2:~ $ ssh-keygen -t rsa
Generating public/private rsa key pair.
Enter file in which to save the key (/Users/dstolarz/.ssh/id_rsa): <press enter>
Enter passphrase (empty for no passphrase): <press enter>
Enter same passphrase again: <press enter>
Your identification has been saved in /Users/dstolarz/.ssh/id_rsa.
Your public key has been saved in /Users/dstolarz/.ssh/id_rsa.pub.
The key fingerprint is:
f1:d7:1a:aa:d9:f3:7c:1b:66:17:05:05:a7:ca:ce:90 dstolarz@dps17-2.local
The key's randomart image is:
+--[ RSA 2048]----+
|              ooo|
|               + |
|        .     . .|
|         o o o  .|
|        S E = .. |
|           * o  .|
|          . + + .|
|         +.. o.o |
|        o .oo... |
+-----------------+
dps17-2:~ dstolarz$ ssh root@iphone mkdir -p .ssh
root@iphone's password: alpine
```

```
dps17-2:~ $ cat .ssh/id_rsa.pub | ssh root@iphone 'cat >> .ssh/authorized_keys'
root@iphone's password: alpine
dps17-2:~ $ ssh root@iphone
dps-3G:~ root#
```

iPhone→server with no passwords

In this example, the author's computer is dps17 (a 17" MacBook Pro), and his iPhone is dps-3G. The following assumes that a user named iphonehacks exists on the server (perceptdev.com):

Let's test this new user. Here are the commands we typed from a Terminal on the iPhone, just to make sure we can actually connect from the iPhone:

```
dps-3G:~ # ssh iphonehacks@perceptdev.com
The authenticity of host 'perceptdev.com (208.97.133.135)' can't be established.
RSA key fingerprint is da:86:84:d0:c0:66:20:17:58:da:b8:86:a1:3b:1f:72.
Are you sure you want to continue connecting (yes/no)? yes
Warning: Permanently added 'perceptdev.com,208.97.133.135' (RSA) to the list of known
hosts.
Password: <type password here>
Linux perceptdev 2.6.24.2-grsec-p4-peon-1.1.2-grsec #1 SMP Wed Feb 20 15:30:29 PST
2008 i686 GNU/Linux

[perceptdev]$ exit
logout
Connection to perceptdev.com closed.
```

Our goal is to be able to upload files from the iPhone to the perceptdev.com shell account automatically from a script. First we log into the iPhone from the computer (you could do this from a Terminal on the iPhone, but it's easier from a computer), then we create and copy our public key to *perceptdev.com*, and finally we log in without requiring a password.

```
dps17:~ $ ssh root@iphone
dps-3G:~ # ssh-keygen -t rsa
Generating public/private rsa key pair.
Enter file in which to save the key (/var/root/.ssh/id_rsa): <press enter>
Enter passphrase (empty for no passphrase): <press enter>
Enter same passphrase again: <press enter>
Your identification has been saved in /var/root/.ssh/id_rsa.
Your public key has been saved in /var/root/.ssh/id_rsa.pub.
The key fingerprint is:
e6:68:35:95:ac:7e:d0:e4:27:5a:08:e2:01:4b:1b:59 root@dps-3G
The key's randomart image is:
+--[ RSA 2048]----+
|  +oE            |
| ..=      . .    |
|  o o .    =     |
|    . o . B      |
|     .   S = .   |
|        * = o    |
|       o + .     |
|      .   .      |
+-----------------+
```

```
dps-3G:~ # ssh iphonehacks@perceptdev.com mkdir -p .ssh
Password:
dps-3G:~ # cat .ssh/id_rsa.pub | ssh iphonehacks@perceptdev.com \
  'cat >> .ssh/authorized_keys'
Password: tsXE9Z3J
dps-3G:~ # ssh iphonehacks@perceptdev.com
Last login: Sun Feb 15 13:34:27 2009 from 24.24.166.171
Linux perceptdev 2.6.24.2-grsec-p4-peon-1.1.2-grsec #1 SMP Wed Feb 20 15:30:29 PST
2008 i686 GNU/Linux

                              --

[perceptdev]$
```

See? No password required!

Test

As a test, we'll execute a one-line upload to see if we can back up a file easily. We'll look in */private/var/mobile/Library/* for something we don't want to lose:

```
dps-3G:~ # ls /private/var/mobile/Library/
AddressBook/              Carrier\ Bundles/       Maps/
SafeHarbor/
Application\ Support/     ConfigurationProfiles/  MobilePhone/                Stocks/
BossPrefs/                Cookies/                Notes/                      Voicemail/
Caches/                   Cycorder/               Operator\ Bundle.bundle@    Weather/
Calendar/                 Keyboard/               Preferences/                WebClips/
CallHistory/              Logs/                   SMS/                        WebKit/
Carrier\ Bundle.bundle@   Mail/                   Safari/                     YouTube/
```

Let's back up the Address Book. First we'll find out what it's named:

```
dps-3G:~ # ls -l /private/var/mobile/Library/AddressBook/
total 1512
-rw-r--r-- 1 mobile mobile 1119232 Feb 14 18:09 AddressBook.sqlitedb
-rw-r----- 1 mobile mobile 423936 Feb 15 12:16 AddressBookImages.sqlitedb
```

Then we'll upload it to *perceptdev.com* using scp:

```
drwx------  5 iphonehacks pg233143 4096 2009-02-10 15:43 Maildir
dps-3G:~ # scp /private/var/mobile/Library/AddressBook/ \
  AddressBook.sqlitedbiphonehacks@perceptdev.com:~/
AddressBook.sqlitedb                              100% 1093KB 218.6KB/s   00:05
```

And just to make sure it's there:

```
dps-3G:~ # ssh iphonehacks@perceptdev.com ls -l
total 1108
-rw-r--r--  1 iphonehacks pg233143 1119232 2009-02-15 15:34 AddressBook.sqlitedb
dr-xr-x---  2 iphonehacks dhapache    4096 2009-02-10 15:24 logs
drwx------  5 iphonehacks pg233143    4096 2009-02-10 15:43 Maildir
```

Now that you've got scripting down, you can build your script into an application **[Hack #11.02]** or a background task **[Hack #11.03]**.

`root` and `mobile`

It's important to note that although you may log in to your iPhone as `root` for convenience, iPhone applications run as the user `mobile`. Thus, if you're going to be making script-based applications **[Hack #11.01]**, you'll need to repeat this procedure logged in as `mobile`. To do this, follow the same instructions above, but on the step where you log into the iphone, log in as the user `mobile`.

— Damien Stolarz & Mathias Kettner

HACK 9.05: Administer Remote Servers with a Terminal Program

Your iPhone can help you hack it with a terminal program on board. If you have to manage Unix/Linux servers with your iPhone, a professional terminal client for the iPhone is an indispensable tool.

The sophisticated Mac OS X operating system that powers the iPhone is based on the Unix operating system. Because of this, some of the hacking that you do to your iPhone may require the use of Unix terminal commands.

In the early jailbreak days, a simple native terminal program appeared. It was very helpful for hacking and tweaking the iPhone without having to use a computer. But it also quickly showed how difficult command-line manipulation can be on a software keyboard.

Since the launch of the App Store, almost a dozen terminal programs have appeared. Most of these are still similar to conventional terminal programs, but some developers have added features that use the multitouch features of the screen.

TouchTerm

TouchTerm (Figure 9-23) was the first SSH/terminal client to be released for the iPhone. It has a basic and a pro version. Both versions provide a translucent keyboard, so you can use the full screen for viewing while typing. You can pinch and zoom in for a larger virtual screen size, and switch to landscape mode (Figure 9-24). The pro version adds a deep layer of customizability, providing a large number of touchscreen gestures that can be used to paste in commonly used commands (Figure 9-25).

Figure 9-23.
TouchTerm with dimmed-out keyboard

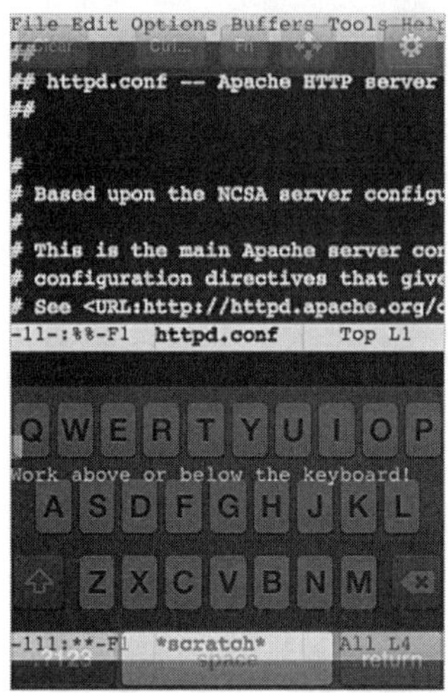

Figure 9-24.
TouchTerm (landscape)

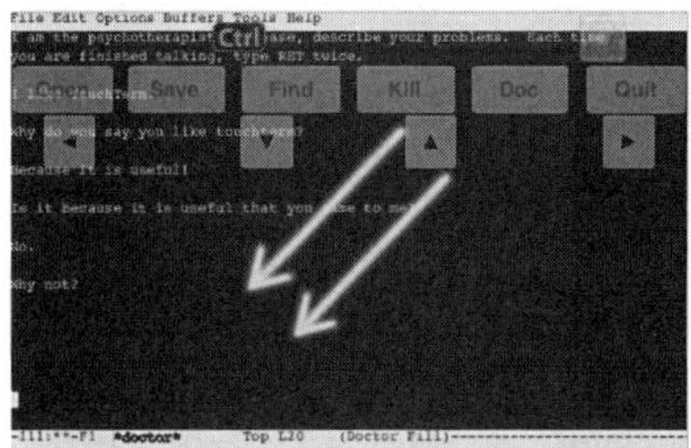

Figure 9-25.
Double-stroke gesture

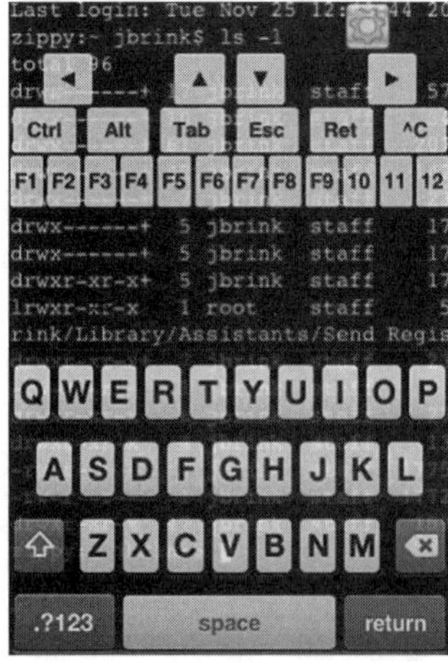

You can tap twice to hide and show the keyboard, tap the left side of the screen to bring up various key palettes (Figure 9-26), and tap the right side of the screen to bring up autocompletion features, so that you rarely have to type a complete word. You can customize the gesture actions to perform your most common server tasks with a minimum of keystrokes.

Figure 9-26.
TouchTerm Pro keyboard

 To connect to the iPhone itself, you should connect to "localhost" or 127.0.0.1 and login **[Hack #9.04]**.

iSSH

iSSH is another popular terminal client application. It supports a wider variety of terminal emulations than TouchTerm, including T100, VT102, VT220, ANSI, xterm, and xterm-color, so if you need compatibility with full-screen editors and programs beyond the basic text editor, this client may be a better option.

iSSH makes clever use of left/right/up/down strokes in different areas of the screen to emulate the arrows, one of the most commonly needed keys for full-screen applications. Figure 9-27 shows three areas—swiping in area ❶ emulates arrow keys in the direction you swipe; swiping in area ❷ scrolls into the back buffer, and swiping in area ❸ switches between active open terminals, as shown in Figure 9-28.

Figure 9-27.
Swipe areas in iSSH

Figure 9-28.
Switching between open sessions in iSSH

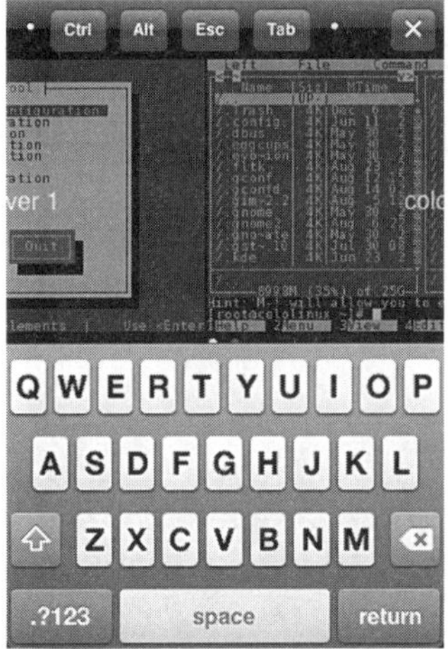

Other Options

If you have to connect to venerable mainframe or minicomputers with glowing green terminal screens, there are several other specific programs available. TN3270 (Figure 9-29) can emulate a mid-1970s, form-input-based IBM3278 terminal.

If you're a manager at your local DMV, then TN5250 (Figure 9-30) can help you connect to your AS/400 server. Put all your staff in jeans and matching T-shirts, let them mingle with the customers and handle transactions on their iPhone, and run your DMV like an Apple store!

Figure 9-29.
Using TN3270

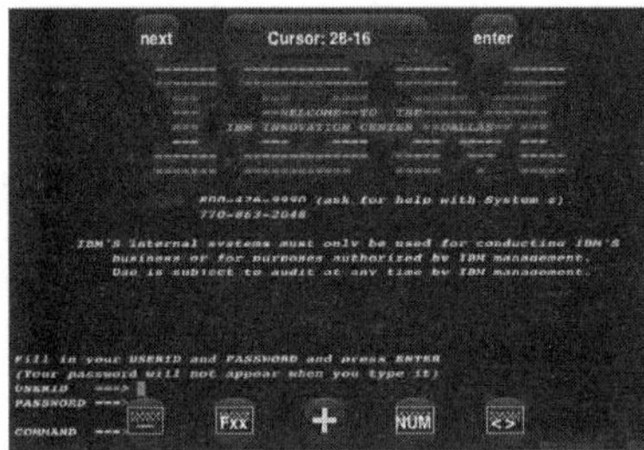

Figure 9-30.
Using TN5250

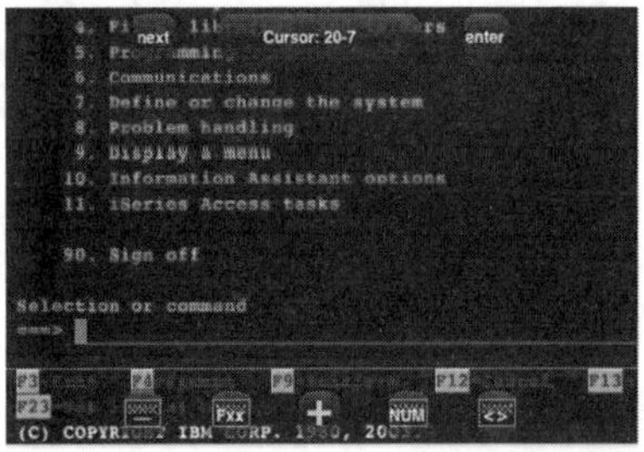

HACK 9.06: Mount the iPhone Filesystem on Your Mac with AppleTalk or SSH

View your entire iPhone filesystem in Finder!

[Hack #1.05] discussed several ways to get files to and from your iPhone. But having to run a program to copy the files can slow you down when you're trying to develop software or tools on the iPhone. This hack discusses a more convenient way to edit files on your iPhone—by mounting the filesystem.

AFP

Apple Filing Protocol, or AFP, is a network-based filesystem that can be used by Mac computers. Setting up AFP on your iPhone will allow its entire filesystem to be viewed and modified over Wi-Fi from the convenience of Finder in Mac OS X.

To get AFP working, your device must be on the same network as your Mac. For the actual AFP application, we will use Netatalk from Cydia. It's not an app in the traditional sense, as it won't appear on the SpringBoard, but it works in the background to broadcast an AFP server whose network name is based on your phone's name.

If your phone and Mac are both on, you should see your phone listed under Shared in any Finder window (Figure 9-31).

Figure 9-31.
The easy way to connect

If you don't see that listing, you'll have to go to choose Go→Connect to Server (Command-K) and connect to `afp://IP_ADDRESS` (replace *`IP_ADDRESS`* with your iPhone's IP address). Once you've connected, it will ask for a username and password. The default login for an iPhone or iPod touch is username `root`, password `alpine` (try password `dottie` if your iPhone is running very old firmware). You should probably change this at some point with the `passwd` command over SSH if you plan on having your device broadcast an AFP server wherever you go.

After entering the correct name and password, you'll have a choice of the root folder or the home folder (Figure 9-32). The home folder is simply */var/root/*, which is far less exciting than your real root directory. (Your real root directory, */*, is a dangerous place to be. Don't go poking around deleting files you don't know well, or you may render your phone unusable.) You can now do any modifying or browsing that you need. Once you're done using AFP, just hit the Eject button next to the server name in the left side of the Finder window.

Figure 9-32.
Browsing an iPhone over AFP

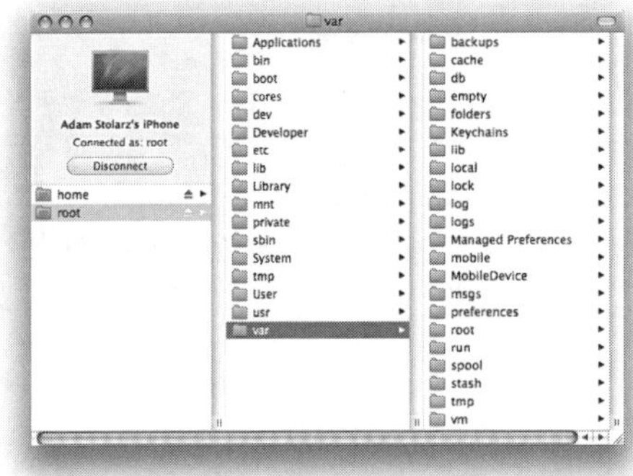

MacFUSE

MacFUSE is a program that allows the Mac to mount various filesystems—both on disk and over networks or the Internet—that Mac OS X doesn't support natively. One of the "filesystems" it is able to mount is SSH—which is convenient because all jailbroken phones support SSH **[Hack #9.04]**. The installer for MacFUSE can be found at http://code.google.com/p/macfuse (Figure 9-33).

Figure 9-33.
MacFUSE's gallery of supported filesystems

After installing MacFUSE, you can use the command line to mount your iPhone, but an even easier GUI way to do it is to install Macfusion (www.macfusionapp.org). Once you've installed both MacFUSE and Macfusion, you'll be able to add your iPhone and mount it as either the `root` or `mobile` user (Figure 9-34).

Figure 9-34.
Macfusion launch screen

To find out your iPhone's IP address, you can go to Settings→Wi-Fi, and select the network name of your currently connected network.

If you usually mount your iPhone on a home/office network, you can set a static (fixed) IP address in the Wi-Fi networks settings. In this case, we've given the iPhone the address 192.168.22.99 on our network so that it will always have the same address when we try to mount it.

With most iPhones, as of this writing, the default username/password combinations for the `root` and `mobile` users are *root/alpine* and *mobile/alpine* **[Hack #9.04]**. Enter these settings, along with the part of the iPhone filesystem you'd like to mount in *path*, by clicking the + sign on the bottom and then selecting SSHFS. You can then edit the settings (Figure 9-35).

Figure 9-35.
Macfusion edit screen

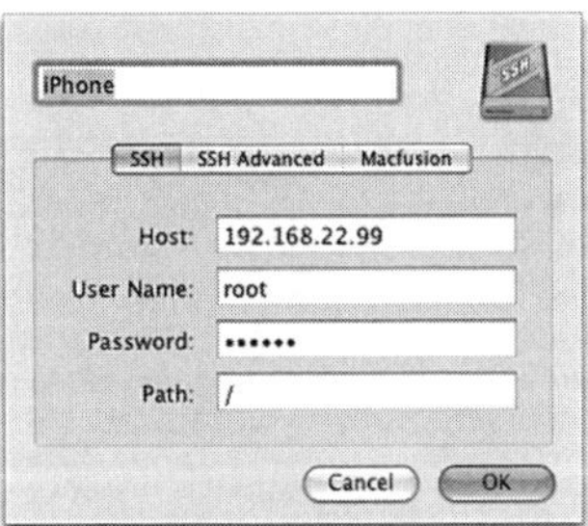

Once mounted, the Macfusion screen will show green mounted disk icons, and you'll see the filesystems in Finder (Figure 9-36).

Figure 9-36.
Mounted devices

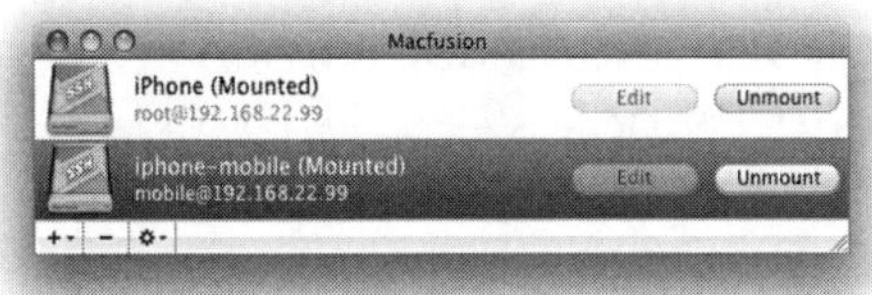

Now that your iPhone root filesystem and mobile folder are mounted as disks, you can customize your phone more easily. You can directly edit plist files (Figure 9-37) using the plist editor, text files using the text editor of your choice **[Hack #11.02]**, and even directly view and edit iPhone database files **[Hack #11.04]**.

Figure 9-37.
Opening a *.plist* file

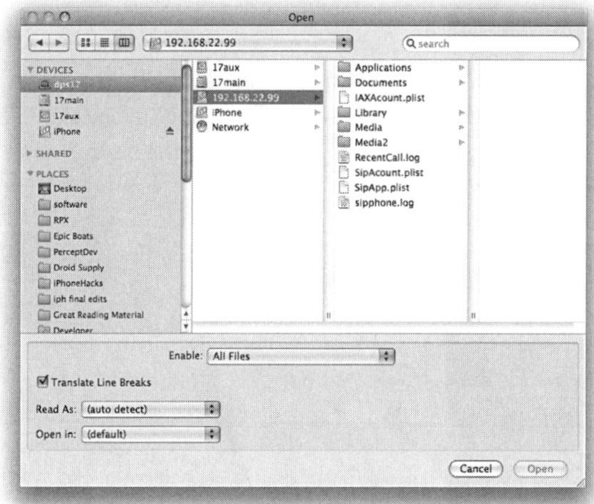

Linux, Windows, and other OSs

The MacFUSE system is actually inspired by the original FUSE system (FUSE stands for Filesystem in USEr space) from Linux, so you can use FUSE on Linux instead. As of this writing, the authors are unaware of a stable working method of mounting SSH as a filesystem on Windows.

HACK 9.07: Easily Manage All the Network Services on Your iPhone

Running lots of network services on your phone consumes resources and opens up possible security holes.

If your iPhone is running several network services such as SSH **[Hack #9.04]**, AFP **[Hack #9.06]**, an HTTP server **[Hack #9.10]**, and so on, then you most likely will need a good way to manage them all. At certain times, you may not want to be running every single service. You could manually enter long commands into Mobile Terminal **[Hack #9.05]** to start and stop these services. But there's a much easier way to do this.

SBSettings is your solution to managing your network services. It can be downloaded from Cydia, along with many add-ons for every toggleable service you can imagine. To open SBSettings, slide your finger across the status bar on top of the screen. This will work in any app or on the SpringBoard. A window will pop down, as in Figure 9-38, with up to 12 toggle buttons for services that you have selected and installed (and have the add-on for). Tap More to configure and select which toggles to show.

Another alternative is BossPrefs **[Hack #8.06]**, which can also hide unused applications.

Figure 9-38.
SBSettings, dropping down from the top of the screen

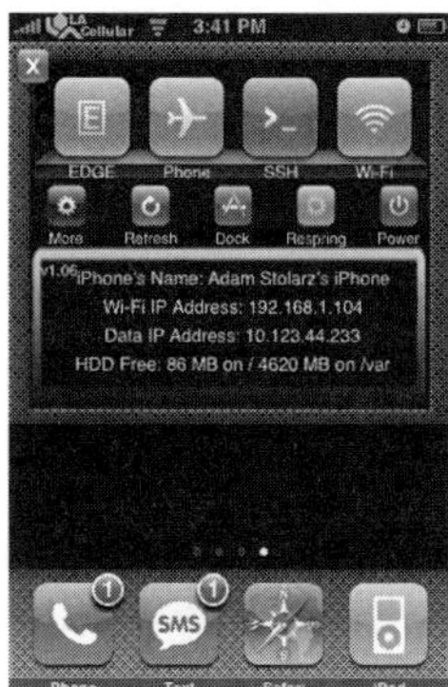

HACK 9.08: Track and Recover Your iPhone

With findme, you can track your phone.

No cell phone owner wants their phone stolen or lost, but sometimes even with all the precautions in the world, you may still manage to lose track of it. It's during times like these that you want your iPhone to "call home" regularly in case of such a loss, or—let's be more realistic—theft. That's what findme addresses. When run, it tells you the tower ID, plus its latitude and longitude courtesy of Google Maps.

Still, how to get the location report to a place you can get it, but nobody else can...and without receiving a zillion SMS messages? For this part of the puzzle, enter Twitter. You can set up a private account that allows your iPhone to phone home but keeps the location data relatively private.

To do this, create a new Twitter account just for your iPhone (it will need its own unique email address, separate from your main account, so have one handy). Open the Settings panel, and look for the "Protect My Updates" checkbox. It's towards the bottom of the page, just above the Save button. Check this and click Save. With protected updates, only the Twitter users that you approve will see the updates for this iPhone-only account (Is it just you? You and a spouse? You, a spouse, kids, and "special friends?" It's up to you).

After creating your phone's Twitter account, you're ready to set up your iPhone to tweet in on a regular basis. Here's how:

1. **Install `findme`.**
   You can download findme as part of the Erica Utilities package available on Cydia **[Hack #1.04]**. `findme` will be installed to */usr/bin*.
2. **Make sure you have `curl` and `sed`.**
   `Curl` is a command-line utility that can be used to GET and POST URLs, and `sed` helps edit text streams **[Hack #11.01]**, such as trimming the XML that `findme` produces. Both can be installed via Cydia **[Hack #1.04]**.
3. **Create a tweet shell script.**
   Copy the following text into a new text file called tweet, and add it to your binaries folder:

```
curl --basic --user username:password --data status=`/usr/bin/findme \
| sed "s/.*<Latitude>/<Latitude>/" \
| sed "s/<\/Longitude>.*/<\/Longitude>/"` \
http://twitter.com/statuses/update.xml
```

 Those single quotes are "`" (grave accents), which should be on the same key as "~" (tilde).

Use the proper path to `findme` and substitute your actual username and password. Make the file executable with the command `chmod 755 tweet`.

4. Create a launch daemon. (You can find more extensive explanation of recurring launch daemon tasks in **[Hack #11.03]**.) In */System/Library/LaunchDaemons*, you'll find a simple daemon that runs once a day, called *com.apple.daily.plist*. Copy this to *com.sadun.tweet.plist*, and edit it as follows:

   - Update the Label to com.sadun.tweet.
   - Delete the two lines that relate to "nice." You don't want your script to be usurped by other processes.
   - Change the program arguments to */var/root/bin/tweet/*.
   - Change the start interval from 86400, according to your needs. 86400 is once a day (60 seconds x 60 minutes x 24 hours). You can set it to launch every 10 minutes (600) while you check whether the launch daemon is functioning properly.

```
<?xml version="1.0" encoding="UTF-8"?> <!DOCTYPE plist PUBLIC "-//Apple//DTD PLIST
1.0//EN" "http://www.apple.com/DTDs/PropertyList-1.0.dtd">
<plist version="1.0">
  <dict>
    <key>Label</key>
    <string>com.sadun.tweet</string>
    <key>ProgramArguments</key>
    <array>
      <string>/var/root/bin/tweet</string>
    </array>
    <key>StartInterval</key>
    <integer>600</integer>
   </dict>
 </plist>
```

5. Reboot. This allows the iPhone to restart, loading your new launch daemon. Your actual tweets should look like this:

```
<Latitude>39.711611</Latitude><Longitude>-104.902137</Longitude>"
```

 If you're traveling across the country, and want to share, change your start interval to 15 minutes or half an hour and use a public Twitter account. (Remember to reboot after making changes to the launch daemon.)

Enjoy your newfound location awareness!

— Erica Sadun

 HACK 9.08: Track, Recover, and Control Your iPhone

iLocalis lets you monitor your iPhone's location and discreetly control it.

If you want to know where your phone is, have a selection of tools to help get it back, don't want to mess with the command line **[Hack #9.08]**, and don't mind passing your location data through his server, Antonio Calatrava's iLocalis service (http://ilocalis.com) is the thing for you.

You can download iLocalis from Cydia **[Hack #1.04]**. When you first run the application, it will ask you to create a username and password for your new account. After your account is created, you can access it online by logging in to http://ilocalis.com, which allows you to view your iPhone's location and control it to some extent, through the easy-to-use website interface (Figure 9-39).

Figure 9-39.
iLocalis's Google Maps display of my iPhone's location

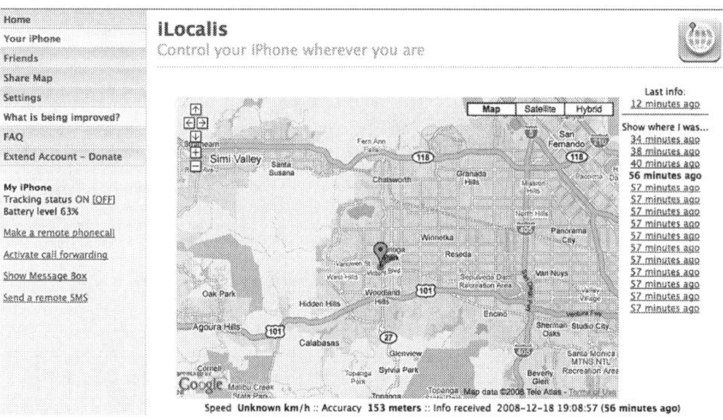

You can customize how often your iPhone will post updates, the default being every 15 minutes. Also, you can see a number of other options along the side. You can set commands for your phone to carry out the next time it synchronizes. You can make it discreetly call a number, so that you can listen to the ambient noise and play detective. You can set a message to pop up, either as a note to yourself or to startle and confuse the new "owner" of your phone. You can make your phone send an SMS that can let you know whether they've swapped SIM cards, and provide you with the new number.

You can also track nearby friends who use iLocalis and send them messages through the service.

You can see examples of how to confuse and demoralize ne'er-do-wells in Figures 9-40 and 9-41.

Figure 9-40.
Sending the message online

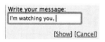

Write your message:
I'm watching you,
[Show] [Cancel]

Pending commands to send to iPhone on next connection:
[Cancel] **Show Message Box [phelan] I'm watching you, you scoundrel.**

Figure 9-41.
The hunter becomes the hunted. Well, not exactly.

There are a few other commands that you can set from the iPhone only (Figure 9-42). You can have it update your location status to a Twitter account, similar to use of findme in **[Hack #9.08]**. You can also configure keywords that you can send in SMS form to trigger responses (they are case-sensitive). The "locate" command results in a text back with latitude and longitude information. The "callback" command forces the phone to send a call to the number you texted it from.

Figure 9-42.
Extra settings for the iPhone

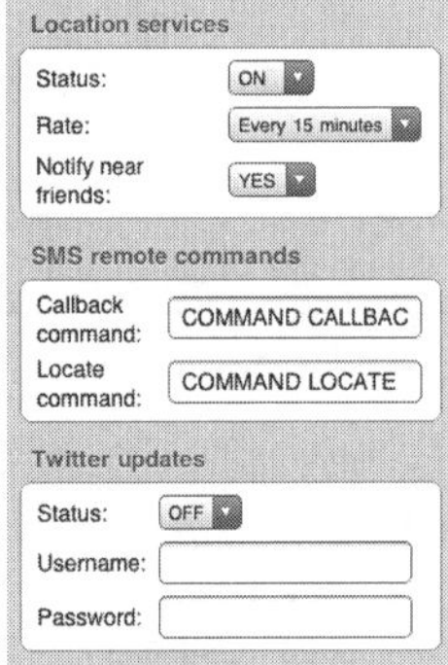

If your phone is simply misplaced, there's a call forwarding feature: you can forward all your calls to a new number until you get your phone back.

iLocalis is easy to use and affordable. After the 10-day trial, a small donation extends your account for a whole year. You could of course donate more, if you really enjoy this app.

There is another service for jailbroken phones called Findmyi (www.findmyi.org) that can also help with tracking and retrieval—and certainly more to come.

HACK 9.10: Make Your iPhone or iPod touch a Web Server

With lighttpd you can host a web server on your iPhone.

lighttpd is a lightweight HTTP server package that's been ported to the iPhone. It is available as a tiny package on Cydia, but requires slightly more setup than most other apps. We'll let the description speak for itself for once, in Figure 9-43.

Figure 9-43.
That's how it is

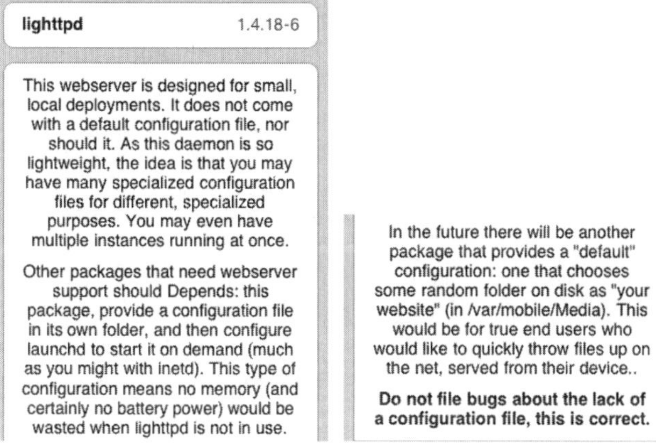

So, as you can see, once lighttpd is installed, you'll need to create a configuration file before it will run. SSH to your phone, either from your computer or on the iPhone itself [Hack #9.04]. Navigate to */etc/* and type `nano lighttpd.conf`, then press Enter. This step opens up a new file in the nano editor.

All you really need to put in this configuration for it to work are the following lines:

```
    dir-listing.activate = "enable"
    server.document-root = "/Library/WebServer/"
mimetype.assign = (
  ".html" => "text/html",
  ".txt" => "text/plain",
  ".jpg" => "image/jpeg",
  ".png" => "image/png",
  ".mp3" => "audio/mpeg"
)
```

Also make sure to create */Library/WebServer* (`mkdir -p /Library/WebServer`).

The document root, inside the quotes, can be any directory you want. We're using "*/Library/Webserver/*" as an example. A better choice might be */var/mobile/Media* or some other directory that you want to make public, so that you could easily access your music and other media from any computer on the same network. There are plenty of other options that you can set for your web server as well; check out the documentation here: http://redmine.lighttpd.net/wiki/lighttpd/Docs.

You'll probably want to use your favorite text editor to make a sample *index.html* to dump into the */Library/WebServer/* directory (or wherever you chose to put the files).

To start up your web server, type `lighttpd -f /etc/lighttpd.conf` and make sure that there are no error messages. If you want it to start up automatically, you'll want to create a startup daemon **[Hack #11.03]**.

Even if you don't have an HTML page on your server yet, pulling it up should yield a rewarding screen, such as shown in Figure 9-44.

Figure 9-44.
The phone is telling the computer that something is in this directory. Yay!

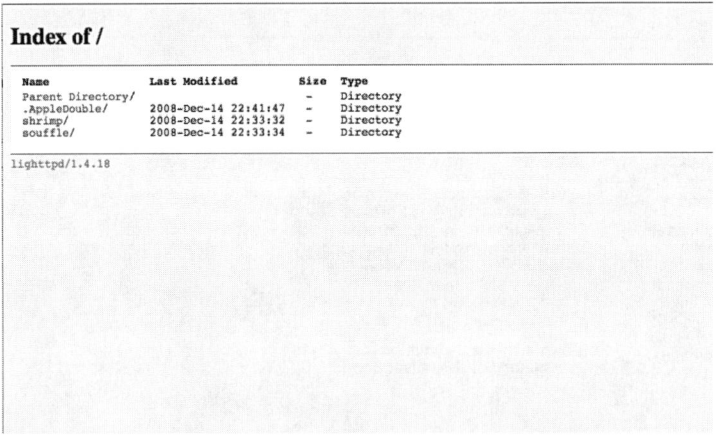

Index of /
Name Last Modified Size Type
Parent Directory/ - Directory
.AppleDouble/ 2008-Dec-14 22:41:47 - Directory
shrimp/ 2008-Dec-14 22:33:32 - Directory
souffle/ 2008-Dec-14 22:33:34 - Directory
lighttpd/1.4.18

HACK 9.11: Connect to Your iPhone or iPod touch from Outside Your Home/Office Network

You can configure your home or office router to allow connections to your iPhone.

The iPhone and iPod touch are capable Unix servers. You can run web services, terminal services, and file sharing, and connect to these servers from any computer. But unfortunately, most cellular providers have fierce firewalls that prevent your phone from permitting connections to any of these services via EDGE or 3G.

There are various reasons, besides the novelty of serving your web page from your pocket, why you'd want to allow external connections. If you've gotten tech support for your iPhone hacking **[Hack #2.06]** and your assistant needs to SSH into your phone, you'll need to provide a way for them to get through the firewall to do so.

> The AT&T mobile network, and probably other mobile networks, have firewalls that severely restrict incoming connections to your phone. Therefore, you won't be able to serve web pages when you aren't on a Wi-Fi network.

If you still want to set up an iPhone-powered web server at your home or office—then read on.

IP Addresses

Public IP addresses are IP addresses like 128.97.128.1 or 206.13.29.12. You can connect to them from any device connected to the Internet; they're unique on the Internet, and aren't hidden deep in a private network. Private IP addresses are reserved groups of addresses like 192.168.x.x or 10.0.x.x —addresses reserved for inside a company or home that aren't unique.

Static IP addresses are private or public IP addresses that are assigned to a specific machine and don't change. Dynamic IP addresses are private or public IP addresses handed to the computer when it boots up. DHCP stands for Dynamic Host (computer) Configuration Protocol, and when you select "DHCP," it means, "get a dynamic IP address from a router on the network."

The most common configuration for home Internet is to have a device called a router (a.k.a. NAT, firewall; see Figure 9-45 for an example) that is connected to a cable modem or DSL modem. The router gets a dynamic, public IP address, and provides dynamic, private IP addresses to machines inside the network behind the router.

Figure 9-45.
A Linksys router

In order for someone to connect to your iPhone from the Internet, the iPhone needs a public IP address. Because you can't connect the iPhone directly to a cable modem or DSL connection, you'll have to do the next best thing: port forwarding from your network router to your iPhone.

Port Forwarding

The trick of port forwarding is simple: you set a static internal IP address for your phone, and then forward the ports of whatever services you want your iPhone to serve.

To set a static internal IP address, find out the IP addresses that your router gives out (serves via DHCP). Then choose one in the same subnet—but outside the range of addresses that the router will use. For instance, if your Linksys router starts at 192.168.22.100, you could choose 192.168.22.99 for your iPhone (Figure 9-46). Set the router address to the IP address of your router: usually this is the same as your device's IP but with a .1 at the end instead of .99 or whatever you used.

Figure 9-46.
Checking on your IP

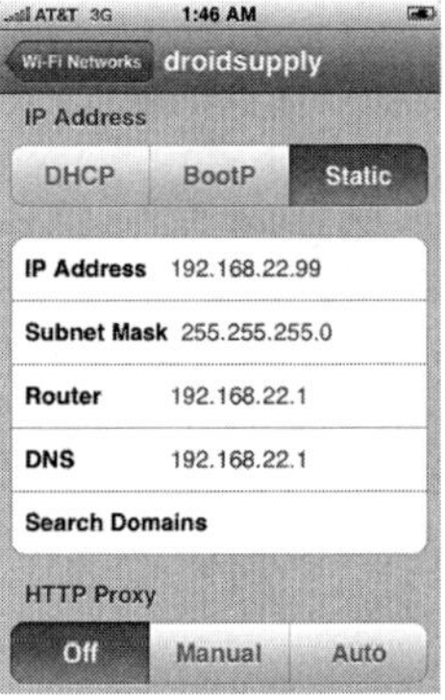

Now you need to choose which protocols you want to support. For example, the HTTP protocol (the protocol used for serving web pages) uses port 80. If you're running a web server on your iPhone **[Hack #9.10]**, then you can forward to any port—not just 80—to the IP of your iPhone. If you need to let someone SSH into your phone, simply forward any port you choose to port 22 on your phone. The same rule applies for services that you want to enable and forward to your phone (Figure 9-47).

Figure 9-47.
Forwarding ports

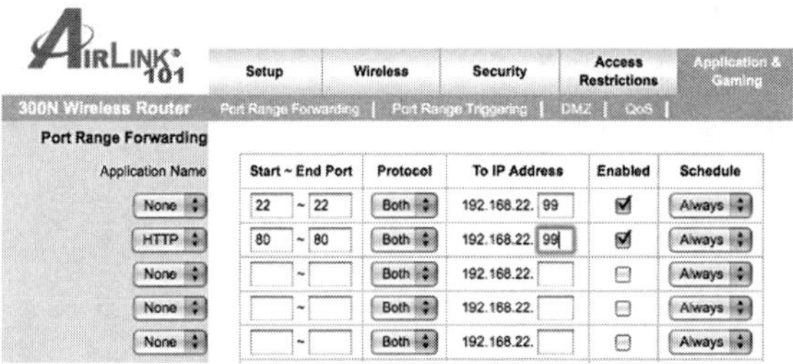

If you want to open up *all* of the services on your iPhone (on a temporary basis with no firewall) you can put your iPhone into the "demilitarized zone" or DMZ, a place where there is no firewall protection between the Internet and your device (Figure 9-48). Entering your iPhone's IP address as the DMZ server will direct any incoming traffic to your iPhone. Some malicious users routinely run port scanners, which look for open services on random IP addresses. This hack opens any network service you have running on your iPhone to the network at large, and makes it a cracking target, so do this with caution.

Figure 9-48.
Demilitarizing your iPhone

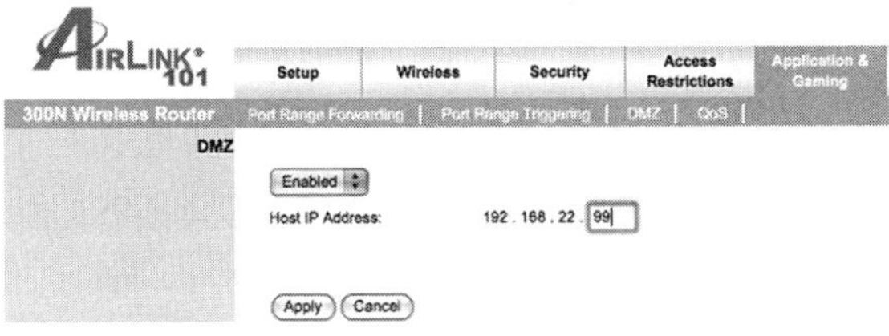

Dynamic DNS

There's one more trick that makes things even easier. Because most home IP addresses are dynamic, they change frequently and can't be counted upon, making it difficult to get back to that website you're trying to serve from your iPhone. In this case, you need a dynamic DNS service—such as that provided by DynDNS (dyndns.org)—to point a domain name at your ever-changing cable modem IP address.

Dynamic IP addresses can be used with your own domain name, but the usual quick and effective way is to sign up for a free dyndns.org account (Figures 9-49 and 9-50) and then enable the dynamic DNS feature in the router (Figure 9-51). Whenever the IP address changes, your router will inform dyndns.org, and the name that you've mapped to your router will keep sending traffic your way.

Figure 9-49.
Creating a domain with DynDNS

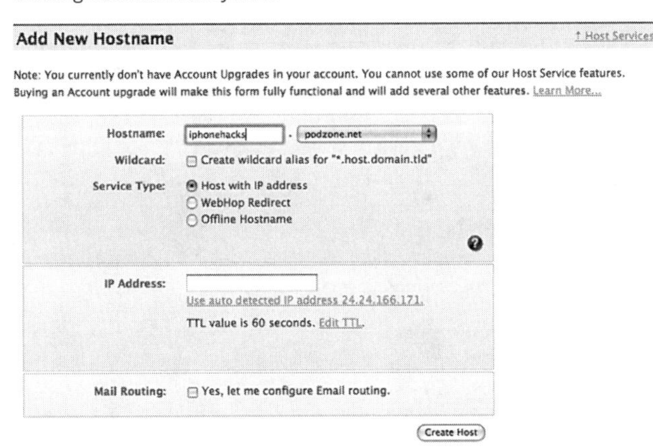

Figure 9-50.
List of domains on DynDNS

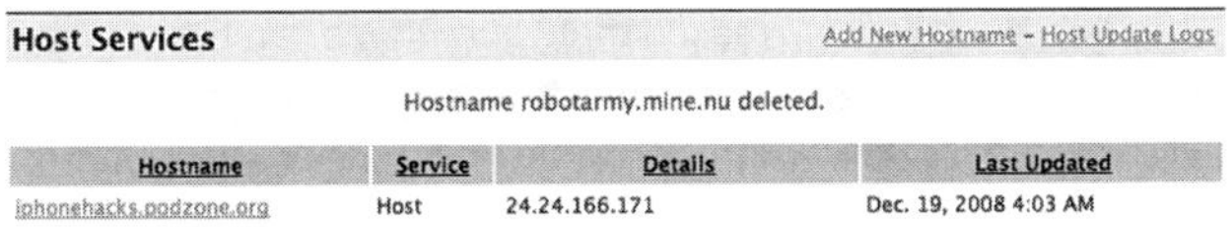

Host Services — Add New Hostname - Host Update Logs

Hostname robotarmy.mine.nu deleted.

Hostname	Service	Details	Last Updated
iphonehacks.podzone.org	Host	24.24.166.171	Dec. 19, 2008 4:03 AM

Figure 9-51.
DynDNS on the router

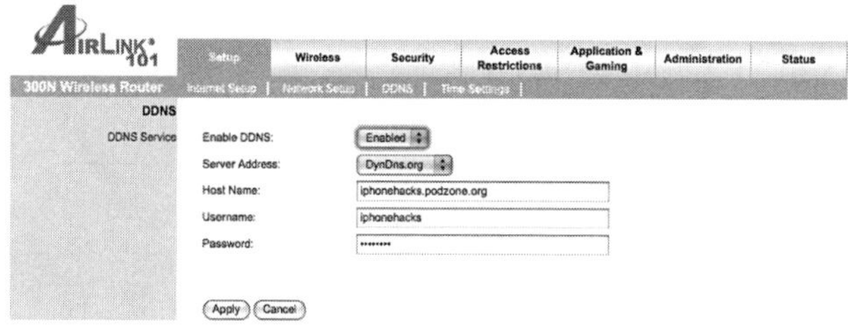

Once it's set up, you can test, or ping, your new domain name (Figure 9-52). Don't be too worried if the ping doesn't work: some ISPs and routers have network filters that disable pings. Just try another service that you know is running, like SSH.

Figure 9-52.
Ping results for the new domain name

```
dps17-2:~ dstolarz$ ping iphonehacks.pozone.org
PING iphonehacks.pozone.org (24.24.166.171): 56 data bytes
64 bytes from 24.24.166.171: icmp_seq=0 ttl=64 time=0.944 ms
64 bytes from 24.24.166.171: icmp_seq=1 ttl=64 time=1.122 ms
```

Your iPhone hacking helper can now SSH into your iPhone remotely by domain name (Figure 9-53).

Figure 9-53.
SSHing into your phone

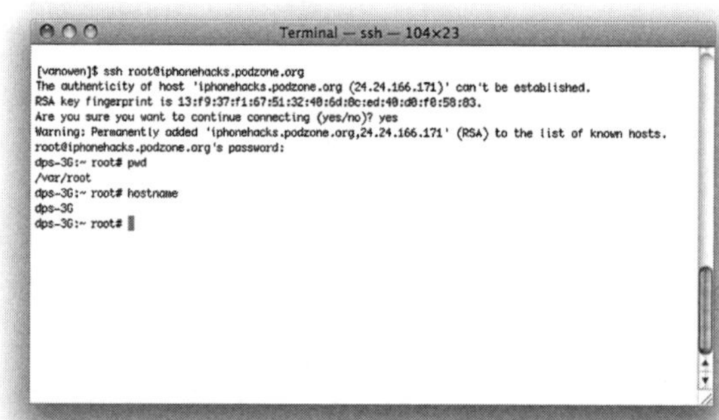

One More Thing

If you have a set of fixed, external IP addresses, there's no reason that your iPhone can't be directly on the Internet. All you need to do is connect a wireless router that acts as a bridge, instead of putting the iPhone behind a private set of IP addresses. If your router doesn't have this feature, an easy way to do it is to connect the Ethernet with all the IP addresses to the LAN port of your router instead of the WAN port. Then assign one of your fixed IP addresses in the iPhone network settings when you connect to the router. As long as your phone is on, you should be able to use that fixed IP directly, and you can even assign a domain name to it.

 If you're serving from your iPhone, make sure to disable Auto-Lock under Settings→Auto-Lock or run Insomnia [Hack #9.15] to keep your phone connected to the wireless network.

 There are many different routers and possible network configurations, and this hack is just a start. Comprehensive instructions on how to configure a static IP and port forwarding can be found at www.portforward.com.

HACK 9.12: Print from Your iPhone to Any Fax Machine

You can print from your iPhone—as long as you have a fax machine nearby.

No matter how digitally you'd like to live your life, there are many times when you need to print something out. Often you've already left the house and forgot to print some directions you need to hand to someone else. Or you're at a conference and you need to print out registration information. Or you're at an out-of-town business meeting and want to print a new draft of the contract.

Although it seems easy, adding print support to the iPhone is not that simple. There are thousands of printers to support, and dozens of different protocols. Even though work may be in progress to bring printing to the iPhone, and to mobile devices in general, you need to print now.

Fortunately, you can solve the problem of impromptu printing right away with our good old friend the fax machine.

Fax Technology

Fax machines are a black-and-white printing technology that outputs between 100 and 200 dots per inch (dpi). Specifically, standard resolution is 203x98 dpi, and fine resolution is 203x196 dpi. This means that a fax print will never look fantastic, but as you know, faxes are entirely adequate for printing text documents and simple illustrations.

Now, the iPhone doesn't have any built-in fax software. However, because the iPhone has great Internet connectivity, you can use an email-to-fax service to print out your documents.

Email-to-Fax Services

There are a variety of services to choose from that allow email-to-fax. Generally, these services are bundled with an incoming fax line, which can cost from a few dollars to perhaps $20 a month. But if your purpose is only to be able to print—and not to receive faxes—then you can use a pay-as-you go service.

Because these faxes are an outgoing call, they do cost a little bit. Depending on the service, you pay around ten cents per page, which is debited from money on your account like a prepaid calling card.

Here are a few services to try (we've tested most of them):

www.faxaway.com
www.faxpipe.com
www.popfax.com
www.fax1.com/send_faxes.html
www.greenfax.com/sendonlyplan.php

Printing on the Go

A very common scenario is that someone mailed you a document and you need to print it out. Getting someone to print something out for you may be more of a favor than you wish to ask for, and this approach is complicated by needing to forward the email to them and hoping that they can read the attachment.

However, it's much easier to simply ask, "Do you mind if someone faxes me at your number?"

The process is simple:

1. Before you need to do this, sign up for one of these services. You can do it from your phone if you have to.
2. Find out the fax number.
3. Launch your mail program.
4. Find the email that has the attachment that you want to print.
5. Forward the email, including the attachment (Figure 9-54).
6. If there is more than one attachment, delete all but the attachment you want to print by moving your cursor to the right of unwanted attachments and pressing delete (Figure 9-55).
7. Address the email to <fax number>@<fax service you chose>.com (Figure 9-56) and send it.
8. Within a few minutes, your document should print out on the printer.

Figure 9-54.
Include the ones you want.

Figure 9-55.
Delete the ones you don't.

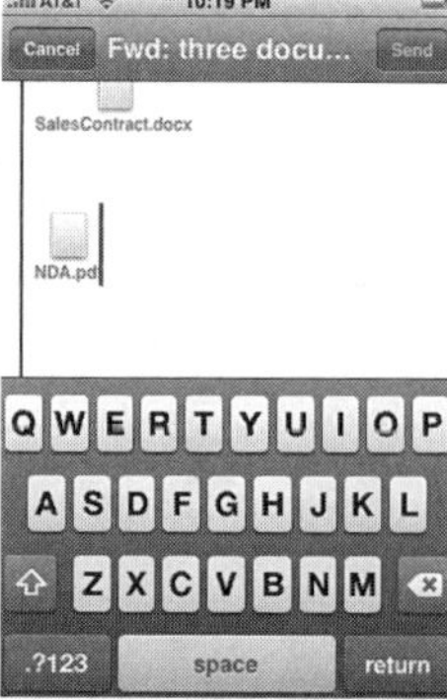

Figure 9-56.
Forward it to a fax machine.

Depending on the service that you use, you may get a confirmation email (Figure 9-57).

Figure 9-57.
Text of the confirmation email

```
Hello from Faxaway, the world's easiest E-Mail to Fax service!

CONFIRMATION OF YOUR FAX TRANSMISSION
FAX STATUS: SUCCESSFUL TO 13105551212
COUNTRY: 1-NORTH AMERICA
TRANSMISSION: 01-Jun-2009 22:27:06 GMT.
1 Page(s).
DURATION: 1.8 Minute
TOTAL COST: $0.20
YOUR FAXAWAY ACCOUNT BALANCE: $8.62.
```

Thus, if you need to print something out—such as at a hotel—you just fax your document to their fax machine, it's printed out—and they might even deliver it to your room.

You'll need to read the instructions for whatever fax vendor you select. Some can accept multiple attachments; some can take only one attachment. Some of them use the subject line and the body of the email as the cover sheet for your fax. They also vary in what documents they support. In our testing, Faxaway was a very inexpensive option ($12/year), had excellent support, and supports a wide range of documents for fax printing.

Receiving Faxes

If you have a lot of business on the go that involves having to print out documents, sign them, and fax them back, you might as well sign up for an incoming fax number at the same time that you set up this hack. [Hack #6.07] explains how to set up a voice mail service that forwards voice mails to your email. Many of those same services—including some of those listed earlier in this hack—allow you to receive faxes that get sent as attachments.

Make sure that your services supports PDF, as the iPhone will be able to display those. The TIFF format used by these services does not work. Of those listed previously, greenfax.com and faxpipe.com offer a PDF receive option; other services such as eFax.com can as well, but they may not have an email-to-fax service.

You can print out the faxes you receive through the same approach as shown previously, if you need a hard copy. Otherwise, simply view them on your phone.

HACK 9.13: Tether Your iPhone's EDGE/3G Network to Your Laptop

Bring your iPhone's anywhere-Internet to your laptop with iPhone Modem or PdaNet.

For some time, cell phone users have been able to tether their phones to their laptops and use them as Bluetooth modems, utilizing their data plan to power their laptop's browsing. For a time, this ability was not available on iPhones. People were unable to use their mighty EDGE or 3G for nonphone browsing. Jailbroken apps changed this.

There are a few tethering apps to be found on Cydia. The two covered here will be iPhone Modem (www.iphonemodem.com) and PdaNet (www.junefabrics.com). For either one, download them from Cydia.

iPhone Modem also has a desktop app for you to use that streamlines the process of tethering and that works on either Mac or Windows. To connect your Mac to the PdaNet, you'll need to make an ad hoc network.

If you chose the iPhone Modem route, just launch the desktop app and press Connect. It will do the following step for you.

To do this on a Mac, go to the drop-down menu of your Airport status icon and click Create Network. Name the network whatever you wish, and include a password if you so choose. On a PC, go to the Network and Sharing control panel, and select "Set up a connection or network." Specify that it should be a wireless ad hoc network, and click through to create it. Again, name it whatever you want, and choose a level of security. Check "Save" if you want to use this network sometime in the future for the same purpose.

Now connect your iPhone to the network you just made, and start up your app. On iPhone Modem, press connect. On PdaNet, turn on the Wi-Fi Router.

When your app shows a happy connection screen (Figure 9-58), you should be connected. Most apps should work fine over your tethered connection. EDGE is fine for browsing and anything that the iPhone feels safe doing over EDGE. 3G is even strong enough to handle Skype. It can even, for those so inclined, handle World of Warcraft (Figure 9-59).

Figure 9-58.
iPhone Modem connected with an EDGE iPhone, and PdaNet connected with an iPhone 3G

Figure 9-59.
~300ms ping can get some quests done just fine.

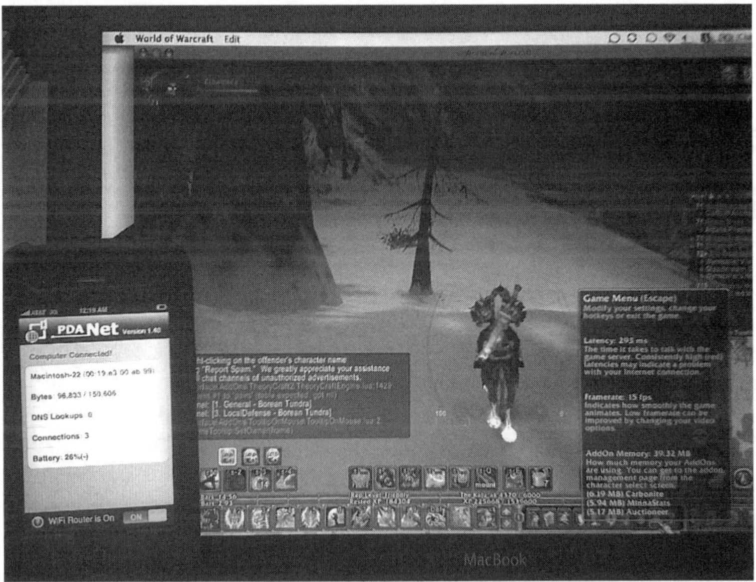

HACK 9.14: Run Applications in the Background

Keep your apps going with Backgrounder.

Only a handful of Apple's standard apps will keep updating when they aren't open—things like SMS, Mail, and the alarms. This means that apps like AIM and Yahoo!Messenger will function and receive IMs only when the phone is unlocked (screen on) and the app is running (on screen). This almost defeats the purpose of their convenient messaging.

With Backgrounder running, you can leave these applications running in the background while you do other things, or while your phone is in your pocket. You can use it to more quickly boot up an application that you use frequently, or keep it running for background updates (like the instant messenger apps).

Download Backgrounder from Cydia. It won't have an icon on the SpringBoard—it will simply be hooked onto your device's apps. When you want something to keep running in the background, open it up and then hold the Home button for a second or two. A window like th256e one in Figure 9-60 will show up, and your app will stay open after you return to the home screen. IMs will still beep, thus you'll know when someone sent you an instant message...instantly.

Some apps of note: if you use this on Ocarina, it will continue to respond to microphone stimuli, and resound its standard note. Lightsaber Unleashed will continue to hum in the background, but it will not respond to motion, unfortunately.

Figure 9-60.
Backgrounding AIM

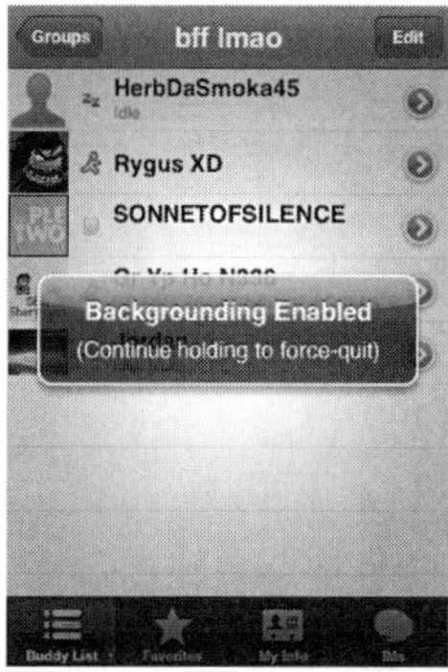

HACK 9.15: Keep Your Wi-Fi Running All the Time on Your iPhone

You can keep your iPhone connected to Wi-Fi when it goes to sleep with this hack.

The iPhone has remarkable networking capabilities, in that it rather seamlessly switches between EDGE, 3G, and Wi-Fi connections. But sometimes what the iPhone wants to do is not what you want it to do. Often if you're at home or at work, and you need to access files on your iPhone, you'd like it just to stay online instead of sleeping and locking itself. Normally, 30 seconds after the screen shuts off, the iPhone sleeps.

The fix is easy. Insomnia (Figure 9-61), an application that has existed for years for Mac notebooks and is now available for the iPhone, keeps things running when the phone sleeps, including Wi-Fi networking. You can find Insomnia in Cydia [Hack #1.04].

Figure 9-61.
Keep your iPhone awake with Insomnia

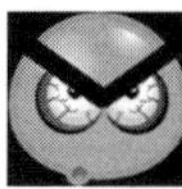

Insomnia has no real user interface except for a bloodshot-eyed blue guy (Figure 9-62). Tapping the icon toggles Insomnia on or off.

Figure 9-62.
Insomnia active

Note that leaving Wi-Fi on all the time will reduce battery life. However, if you're usually on Wi-Fi and you have an iPhone 3G, you can disable your 3G network to get some of that idle energy back.

Programming

You can download the source code for iPhone Insomnia and learn how to incorporate the Insomnia code into your own application at http://code.google.com/p/iphone-insomnia.

[Hack #11.01] shows how you can develop your own script-based application similar to Insomnia.

 HACK 9.16: Trick Your Wi-Fi Apps into Working Over 3G

Using VoIPover3G, you can download apps and make VoIP calls *without* Wi-Fi.

Although the 3G network has completely acceptable speeds—even for demanding network services such as the App Store, iTunes Store, and VoIP—these apps stop working when not used over Wi-Fi. But if you need an app, song, or need to make a VoIP call and there's no open Wi-Fi to be found, what do you do? You trick the apps into thinking that you do have Wi-Fi, so that they'll happily chug along.

There's one simple step to do this: download VoIPover3G from Cydia. You may now use the App Store, iTunes Store, Fring, and Truphone—all over 3G.

If those are not all the apps that you wish to trick into thinking you're connected to Wi-Fi, you will need to do something a bit more in depth. Find the file */Library/MobileSubstrate/DynamicLibraries/VoIPover3G.plist* on your iPhone [Hack #1.05]. This plist file contains the list of apps that VoIPover3G will attempt to pull a fast one on. You'll need to add the bundle identifier that is contained in the *Info.plist* file [Hack #11.02] (e.g., `com.apple.mobilestore`) to this plist just like the other ones that sit there. Or, for a really bad idea, you can delete the entire *VoIPover3G.plist* file, and all apps will be bamboozled into thinking that they have Wi-Fi—under any circumstances. Some apps do not like being tricked like this and will react poorly, because of the slower network performance.

Now go out there and make some VoIP calls!

BETTER WIRELESS WEB PERFORMANCE ON AN ORIGINAL IPHONE

GET OUT OF THE WAY OF YOUR WIRELESS ANTENNA SO YOU CAN SURF FASTER

If you have a first-generation iPhone, you can noticeably increase your network performance simply by moving your hand away from the antenna! In fact, page 105 of your official *iPhone User's Guide* states that the antenna must be kept at least 5/8" from your body to avoid potentially harmful radiation from the cellular wireless signals. When your body intercepts these signals, besides purportedly being bad for you, it is also decreasing the speed of the EDGE network. On the 3G iPhone, the antenna has been changed, so this tip applies only to the first-generation iPhone.

Good iPhone handling

10 APPLICATION HACKS

The iPhone has shown us more clever things to do with a smartphone than ever before.

It seems like the whole world has finally realized a couple of things:

1. Mobile phones are computers.
2. You can never install enough programs on your computer.

This brief chapter provides a grab bag of hacks that weren't included in earlier chapters, but we felt just had to be included. From music, measurement, and media management to the conspicuously missing ability to cut and paste, and even a BitTorrent client, we round out the capabilities of the iPhone with an eye to the future.

HACK 10.01: Create Music with the iPhone and iPod touch

A variety of programs lets you create and play music on your iPhone.

The iPhone is many things to many people, and for many it is a musical instrument. Its multitouch screen allows for multiple notes to be played at the same time in a number of simulated instruments—guitars, bass, piano—as well as a real ocarina-inspired wind instrument.

In this hack, we show you a brief sampling of some of the clever musical tools available in the App Store.

The Basics: Silly Instruments

The novelty of the iPhone's accelerometer wears off after a while, but not until you've had the opportunity to try out a silly instrument like iMaracas (Figure 10-1).

Figure 10-1.
iMaracas

Although it's fun, the musical quality of iMaracas probably won't lure you into spending more on other music programs in the App Store. You need a real "gateway drug" such as one of the dozens of chord-capable piano programs to show you the potential of the iPhone as a real instrument.

MiniPiano

The iPhone has more CPU power and memory than many conventional electric keyboard synthesizers, so it seems natural that it would be able to emulate a piano well. Because of the limited screen space, you won't be able to get 88 keys on the screen, but you will find some remarkable sound coming out of MiniPiano (Figure 10-2). If you want more octaves, you'll need to upgrade to their pro app, FingerPiano.

Figure 10-2.
MiniPiano

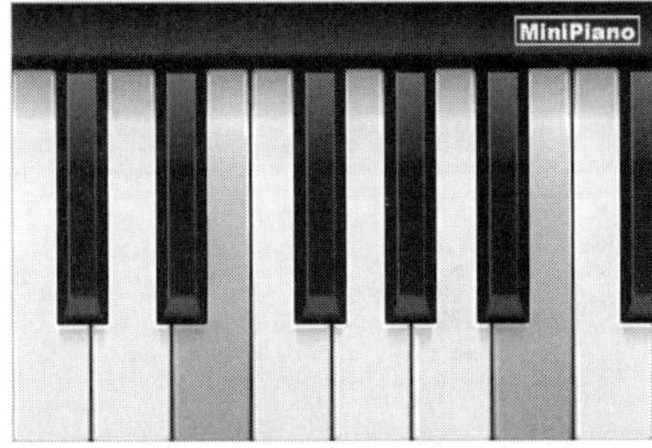

There are dozens of other piano applications on the App Store, competing on sample quality, blending, and ability to switch to different octaves quickly. But because the iPhone can't replace a real piano, perhaps a better use of the iPhone is as a musical learning tool.

Learning

A number of promising music education applications have popped up to exploit the combination of interactivity and sonic fidelity that the iPhone provides.

PianoChordy (Figure 10-3) is essentially a flash card application for piano chords. But unlike your dusty stack of cards on the piano shelf, this one is interactive, and it has a reward payoff: you get to hear the chord when you get it right. This feedback reinforces both keys and sounds for a beginner, and is a great way to pass idle moments constructively.

Figure 10-3.
PianoChordy

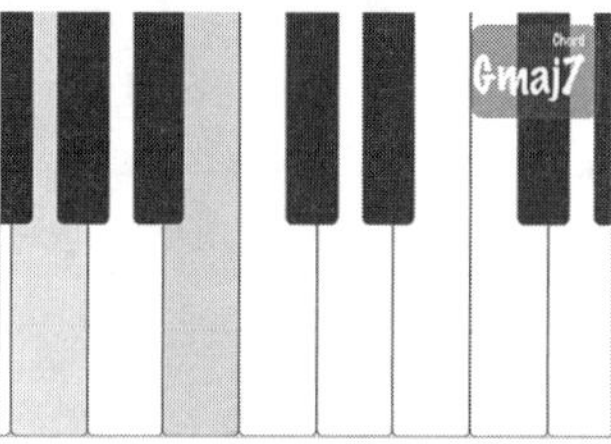

PianoChords (Figure 10-4) takes a different approach, allowing a piano player to look up chords in any key by choosing a root note and then choosing a chord derived from that note.

Figure 10-4.
PianoChords

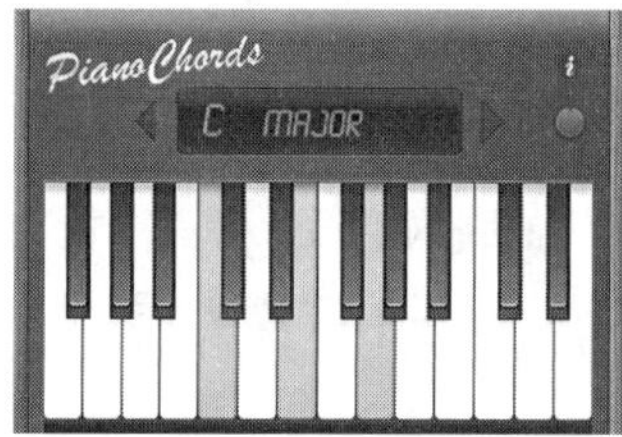

If it's guitar you're learning, chord charts are the handiest thing to have. The 7-Chords (Figure 10-5) application offers a quick list of chords—in tab—with sound! Flash cards never sounded this good.

Figure 10-5.
7-Chords

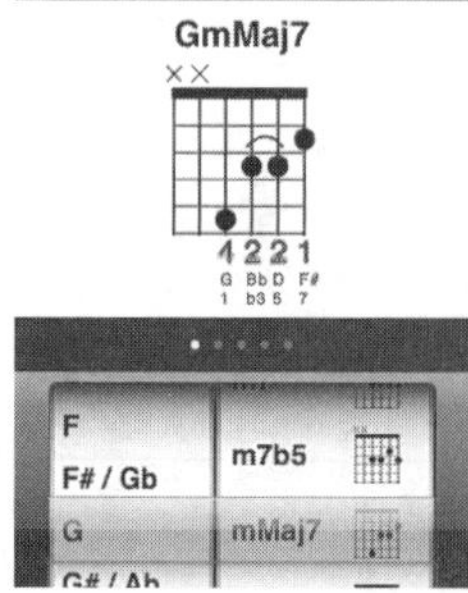

Tuning Your Instrument

Whether you're a beginner or you've been playing all your life, you never escape tuning. The iPhone offers an orchestral range of options when it comes to tuning. Cleartune (Figure 10-6) and Tuner 440 (Figure 10-7) are two instrument tuners. Using the microphone built into the iPhone, these apps can tune dozens of instruments. The free Tuner 440 can tune a variety of string instruments, and the inexpensive Cleartune can even tune a wide variety of wind instruments. Just remind your orchestra to mute their iPhones before the concert starts.

Figure 10-6.
Cleartune

Figure 10-7.
Tuner 440

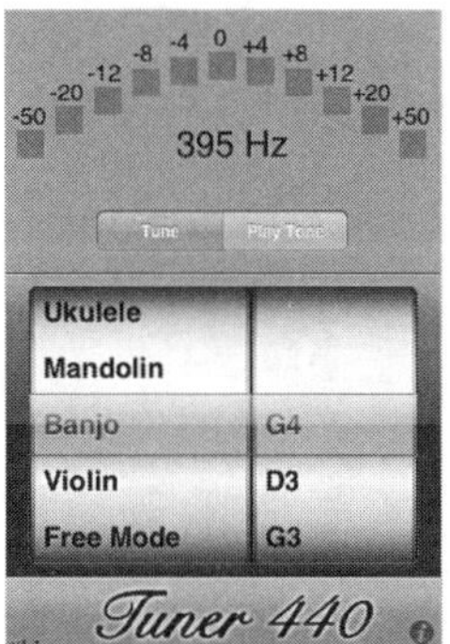

Recording Your Performances

Once you're ready to start recording songs, there are a number of options for you. If you like the one-man-band approach, then the aptly named Band (Figures 10-8 and 10-9) application incorporates a drum, a bass, and an innovative keypad that allows you to play blues guitar backing and solos. Entire compositions can be built up by flipping through the various screens.

Figure 10-8.
Band's intuitive Funky Drummer and Bassist interfaces

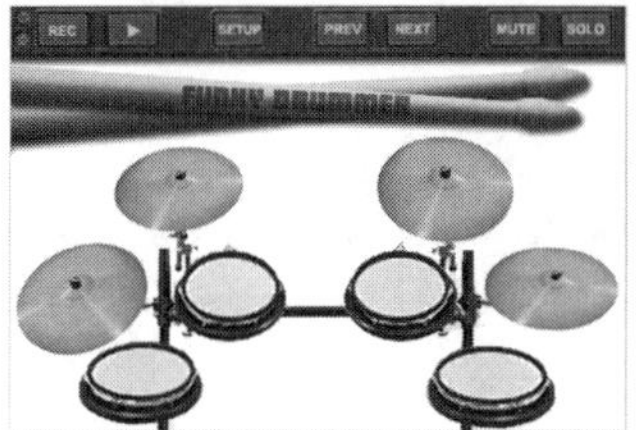

Figure 10-9.
Band's unique 12 Bar Blues keypad interface

If you're interested in recording your own analog instruments with the iPhone, 4-track (Figure 10-10) is a four-track recorder. It's worth noting that the Beatles produced some fantastic albums on a four-track recorder—recording one track at a time, then layering on more accompaniments while listening to the first tracks.

Level indicators keep your recording from clipping, and a built-in compressor-limiter fattens the sound. The app will record off the built-in mic of the iPhone, or the mic on the stereo headphones, or whatever mic you want if you build a mic input **[Hack #12.01]**. You can export your recordings using Wi-Fi and continue to edit them in GarageBand.

Figure 10-10.
4-track

Mixing and Synthesis

If your musical talents lie in the area of synth and DJing, there are even more applications to create with. You can emulate a Roland TB-303 with Bassline (Figure 10-11) and a range of TR-x0x synths (such as a 707, 808, or 909) with IR-909 (Figure 10-12).

Figure 10-11.
Bassline, inspired by the Roland TB-303

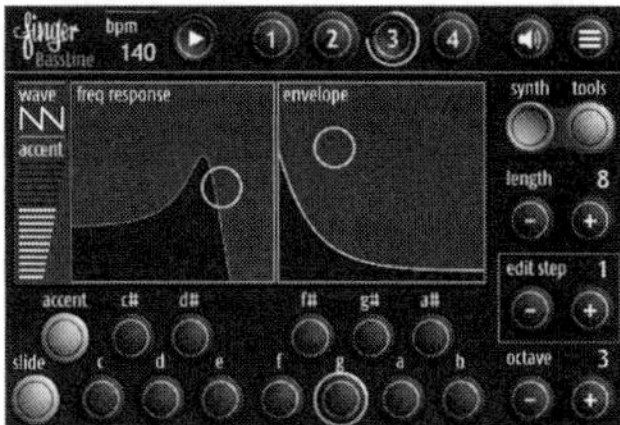

Figure 10-12.
IR-909

If you're focused on tapping out drum rolls, digidrummer (Figure 10-13) lets you do just that.

Figure 10-13.
digidrummer

But if you're looking to create drum loops, iDrum (Figures 10-14 through 10-16) is the app of choice. It comes in several varieties, including a Hip-Hop edition, a Club edition, and even a Deep House and Techno edition made in partnership with the London-based Ministry of Sound (www.ministryofsound.com). Even for a beginner, it's very easy to learn. Each square represents an instrument, and each of the blocks within that square represents a 16-beat pattern. By zooming into the patterns, you can turn off that instrument or sample for that beat. And you can easily turn your mix into a ringtone.

Figure 10-14.
iDrum Hip Hop edition detail

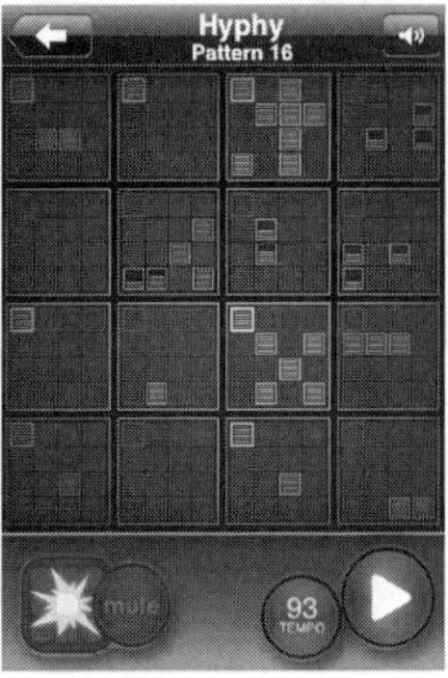

Figure 10-15.
iDrum Deep House and Techno edition detail

Figure 10-16.
iDrum Deep House and Techno edition load screen

Ocarina

Last but far from least, probably the coolest iPhone-based music-making application is Smule's Ocarina. This is a top-form application and qualifies as an actual instrument, not just a simulator. You blow into the microphone on an iPhone, and press one of the four "stops" on the screen (Figure 10-17), either on your own or with the helpful tablature they provide (Figure 10-18).

But it doesn't stop there. The moment you start playing, you're actually part of a global concert of Ocarina players, and using the location and Internet features of the iPhone, your performances go onto a server and out to the world. You can go into a section of the app where notes float up to the sky from a 3D globe, and leave it there, part of a gentle serenade by Ocarinists everywhere (Figure 10-19).

Figure 10-17.
Smule's intuitive Ocarina interface

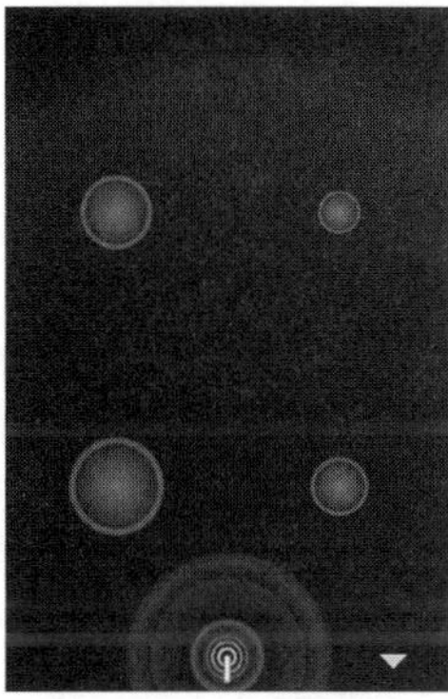

Figure 10-18.
Ocarina tablature for "Twinkle Twinkle Little Star"

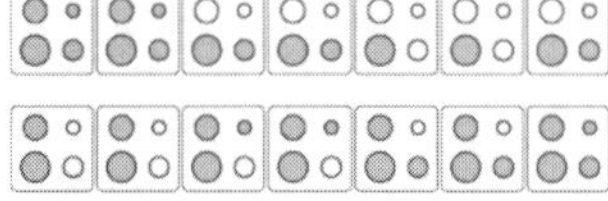

Figure 10-19.
Ocarina's interactive 3D globe

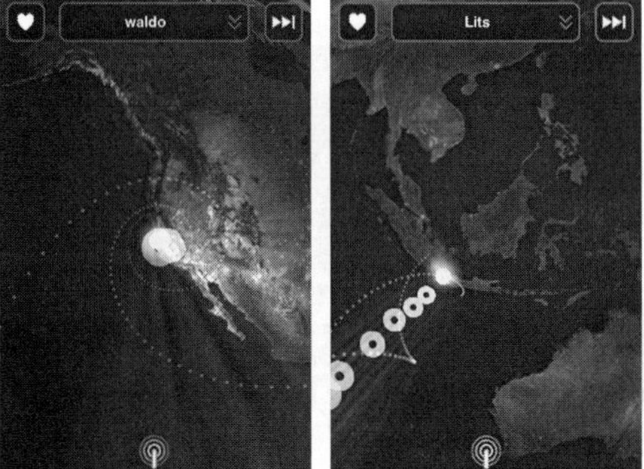

Going on Stage

With so many options to create music, it's only logical that iPhone quintets and pop orchestras will be coming together. When you're playing these instruments, the built-in speakers or headphones just don't do these instruments justice. You can hook them up to a pair of desktop speakers, or better yet, hook up a wireless audio transmitter to plug into your pro mixing board.

HACK 10.02: Triangulate Distances with Your Built-in Camera and GPS

Using trigonometry and your digital camera, it is possible to determine sizes or distances of objects with better precision than eyeballing.

You probably learned how to use trigonometry in high school for such tasks as measuring the height of a tree or other exercises that may or may not have turned out to be too useful to you. However, there are some times when you want to be able to measure the size of an object, or the distance to it, and the iPhone's combination of camera and GPS bestows some unique benefits.

Let's take a common example. While playing golf, how far is the hole? Most golf flagpoles are 7 feet tall (some are 8 or 9 feet). If you photograph the flagpole with your camera, holding the phone sideways so the screen is wider than it is tall, then you'll be able to tell how far the flagpole is using this simple formula:

```
10 / f = distance
```

where `f` is the fraction of the screen that the flag occupies. So if the flagpole is 1/5 the height of the screen, then you are 50 feet or just under 17 yards from the flag.

Usually, the flag will be very small, so you'll want to zoom in by clicking on the camera roll and using your two-finger zoom to make the flag larger. It turns out that if you zoom in as far as you can while keeping the phone on its side, then the formula becomes:

```
45 / f = distance
```

In this case, 1/5 the height of the screen leads to a distance of 225 feet, or 75 yards.

That's useful!

How does it work?
First we'll have to assume that you remember those trigonometry functions: sine, cosine, and tangent. Next, you need to note what the specifications are for the iPhone camera: the image resolution of the EDGE and 3G iPhones is 1200 x 1600 pixels (1,920,000 pixels)

- Angular resolution: 2 arc minutes/pixel (+/– 1/2 arc seconds/pixel)[1]
- Field of view: 38 x 50 degrees

This means that the total view of the camera is 40 degrees wide by 50 degrees tall, roughly speaking. You could photograph the entire 360 degree view around yourself with about nine photos, assuming they aligned end to end. Note that 57 degrees is about a radian,[2] so the camera's angular resolution is about one radian.

The next thing you should know is that the tangent of an angle less than about 20 degrees is close to the angle itself. For example, 20 degrees is about 1/3 radian, and tan (1/3) is equal to 1/3,

1. Remember, an arc minute is a 60th of a degree, where 360 degrees makes a circle.
2. In case you don't remember what a radian is: here's your cheat sheet. It is an angle of 57 degrees (ignoring decimals). This turns out to be $1/2\pi$ of a circle, which means that a circle has 2π radians in it.

accurate to within a couple percent. For larger angles, this isn't true—so what we are about to say works *only* for measuring heights that are about half of a screen width.

You have probably used a formula like `h/d = tan(a)`, where `h` is the height of the tree, `d` is your distance from it, and `a` is the angle. However, because of the iPhone's camera characteristics, anything less than 1/2 the width of the screen is less than 20 degrees, which means that angle `a`'s tangent is roughly equal to its size in radians, so you can just call the formula `h/d = a`. This makes life much simpler.

Next, if you know the height of your object (such as 7 feet for the flagpole), then you know `h`. So you can rearrange the equation: `h/a = d`. And you can determine `a` from what fraction of the width the photograph occupies.

If the object you are looking at is 1/4 of the width of the screen, then it is roughly 10 degrees, because 10 degrees is close to 1/4 of 38 degrees—the screen width. If it is 1/8 of the width of the screen, then it is 5 degrees. Now, the tricky part is `a`, because the equation uses radians. What you really want is a fraction of the screen. So use the fact that:

```
a = (πf)/(38x180)
```

`38` is the number of degrees in the screen width, `π/180` is the conversion from degrees to radians. Then:

```
a = 0.66f
```

Plug this into `h/a = d` and you get:

```
7/(0.66f) = d
10.55/f = d
```

or good enough:

```
10/f = d
```

You can play this trick for any object you commonly use. For example, if you live on a farm, you can determine your distance from a silo using a similar formula if you know the height of the silo.

Most people don't want to be doing math while out on a jaunt with their iPhone (well...most people don't; I might be one of the few who actually do!). Therefore, you need some rough simple formulae that are easy to remember. For most purposes, an accuracy of 5 percent is generous, so this is what we get:

`d = 1.5h / f` when you are viewing an image in the camera roll.

`d = 6h / f` when you are viewing an image in the camera roll and you have zoomed to maximum zoom using the pinch gesture.

As before, `d` is the distance to the object, `h` is the height of the object, and `f` is the fraction of the screen the object occupies.

These work only when the object to be measured is viewed vertically, and the camera is on its side (as if you were watching video). If you want to measure something horizontal like the diameter of the world's largest pizza at the festival you are attending, then turn the camera vertically so that the home button is closest to your feet. In this case, the height, `h`, is now the width, `h`.

Is that all you can do? NO! If you have a 3G iPhone, then you have GPS. There is a cheap application from the App Store called Tape Measure (Figure 10-20) that allows you to measure distances on your GPS.

Figure 10-20.
Tape Measure

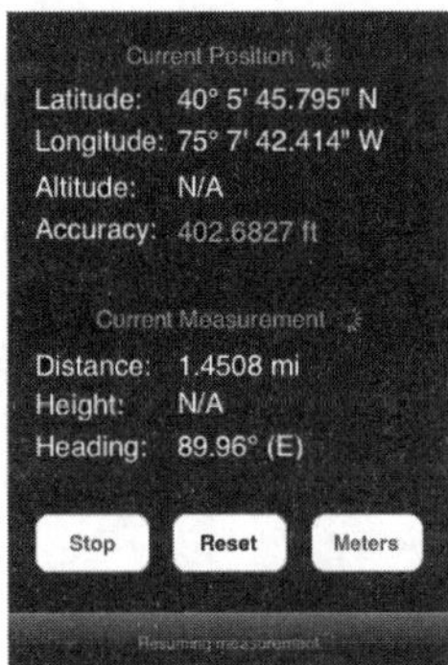

Because your GPS is accurate only to within a few meters, you can measure only distances that are larger than about 10 meters to any real accuracy. However, you can measure the heights of mountains easily by walking a distance toward the mountain with your GPS (good for exercise) and photographing the mountain before and after. The difference in angle is proportional to the distance you walked. Therefore, the distance you walked is `d`, and the difference in angle is `a`. You just plug these values into the formula given previously.

Likewise, you can use Google Maps to locate your distance from a landmark like the Seattle Tower. Knowing `d`, you can measure the height easily with just a photo from your iPhone.

Applying the Hack

Here we have an example with the Campanile tower (Figure 10-21) at the University of California, Berkeley. We'll use meters as our units for this example. We don't know yet exactly how tall it is, but Figure 10-21 shows a photo taken from 435 meters away (with an accuracy of plus or minus 30 meters) based on GPS coordinate differences.

As you can see in the photo, the Campanile is `y` fraction of the width of the camera view, which means that we can rearrange `d=1.5h/f` to be `fd/1.5 = h`.

The measured values are:

```
f = 360 pixels / 1200 = 0.3
d = 435 +/- 30 meters (between 405 and 465).
```

Thus, calculating the height:

```
h= fd/1.5 = 0.3 (405m to 465m)/1.5 yields:
h = 87 meters +/- 6 meters (i.e., between 81-93 meters)
```

The actual height of the tower is 93.6 meters (according to Wikipedia). So this reflects the accuracy of the method ~15% as promised if one assumes h = 87 meters.

Figure 10-21.
Picture of Campanile tower

Fun projects:

- Measure the altitude of a helicopter.
- Go sailing and measure your distance to shore.
- Using the fact that the distance to the moon is 384,000 km, measure the diameter of the moon.
- Measure the height of the Matterhorn at Disneyland.

— Zack Gainsforth

HACK 10.03: Add More Ways to Sync

With these apps, you can get data from your iPhone or iPod touch to your computer.

You can put all sorts of wonderful things on the iPhone. But if you lose the original data on your computer, it's somehow gone forever, trapped in the iPhone vault. What if you could sync the other way, and get files back off your iPhone? Of course, this is not a new idea. It's as old as the iPod itself. It is good to know, however, that the systems have been upgraded to support new iPhone data such as SMS and call logs.

From Your iPhone to Your Computer

Ecamm's PhoneView (www.ecamm.com/mac/phoneview) provides access to your call and SMS logs, as well as all the media, contacts, calendars, and so on, that are stored on your iPhone. You can also use it to store non-syncable data on the iPhone. You can see screenshots of it at work in Figure 10-22.

Figure 10-22.
Disk use, call log, and SMS

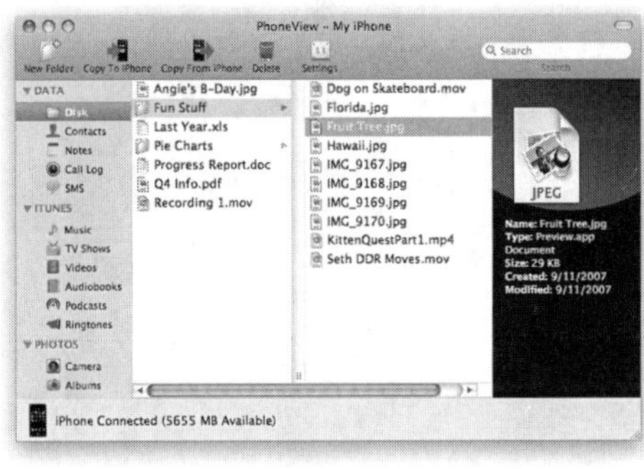

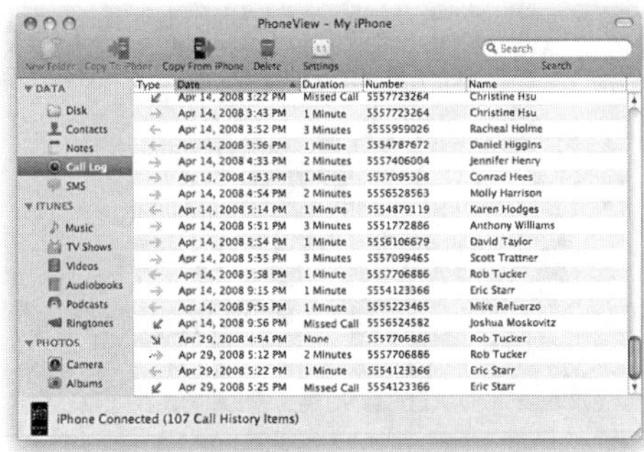

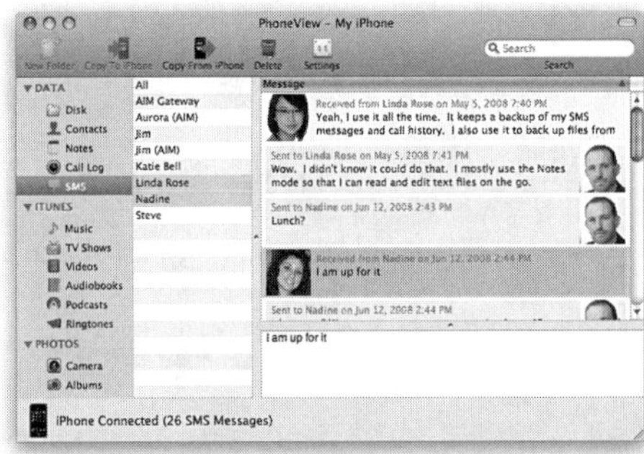

Senuti (www.fadingred.com/senuti) has a simple interface and is dedicated to copying music off an iPod or iPhone—it can even automatically add the songs to iTunes (Mac only).

TouchCopy (www.wideanglesoftware.com/touchcopy) is available for Mac OS and Windows, and has a feature set similar to PhoneView, only without SMS and call log.

Migrating from Smartphone to iPhone

The Missing Sync (www.markspace.com/missingsync_iphone.php) is a combination file transfer and migration assistant. That is, it can help get your contacts and other data from your old BlackBerry, Palm, or Windows Mobile device to your iPhone.

HACK 10.04: Alter Your Voice and Outgoing Caller ID on the iPhone

With iSpoof you can make iPhone calls in disguise.

iSpoof allows you to fake your caller ID, alter your voice, and optionally record the resulting conversation (by default, it notifies the person you're recording). You could use it as part of a practical joke, a con, an elaborate hoax, or for security purposes. iSpoof is available from Cydia **[Hack #1.04]**.

If you're willing to sit through a voice ad, you don't need to sign up. If you do sign up, input the PIN that you're given into the Settings section of the iSpoof app (Figure 10-23). You'll now be able to use the minutes you buy and add more minutes on the Replenish screen in the app.

iSpoof saves the credit card information you enter, and although it encrypts the transaction itself, there's no password to input while purchasing the minutes through the app. This means that someone who has possession of your phone could buy minutes using your credit card without your consent. It doesn't display any usable credit card information in the app, however, so that's all they'd be able to buy.

Figure 10-23.
The settings screen and the minute replenishment screen

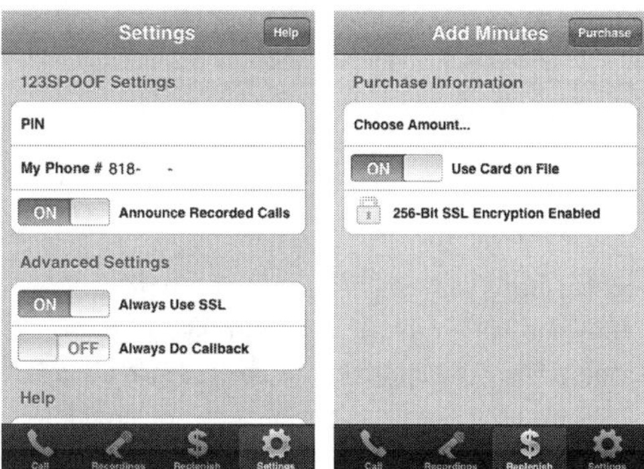

The fun part of this app is in Figure 10-24. The Call tab lets you make spoofed calls. You can (of course) change your caller ID, but you can also put on a voice filter to sound deep and bassy or oddly high-pitched, record the call (with or without a legally required notice), or even go straight to voicemail to leave frightening messages or tell your boss you're sick without a burdensome actual conversation.

Figure 10-24.
iSpoof call screen

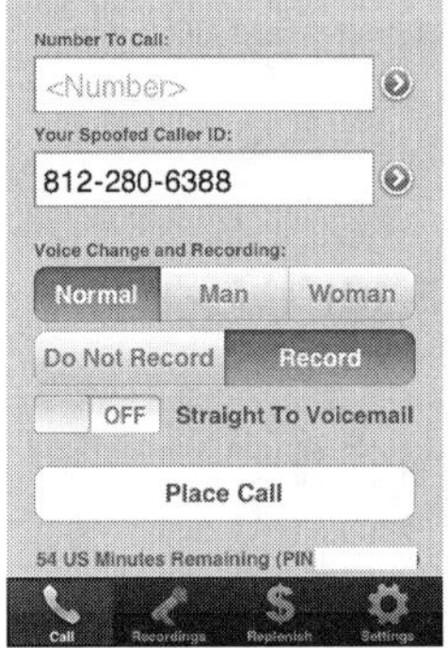

iSpoof has many practical and frivolous uses, and is definitely worth checking out.

HACK 10.05: Use Your iPhone as a Media Remote Control

You can use your iPhone as a remote control for your computer and media center.

If you've ever seen a top-of-the-line home theater installation connected to a multiroom sound system, you might have been impressed by the programmable touchscreen controls embedded in the walls near the light switch. And most home theater aficionados eventually get upsold on some sort of super-ultra programmable remote with software programmable buttons.

Well, those days may be coming to a close, as iPhones and iPod touches become the future of home theater control.

Apple TV & iTunes

Apple set the standard for iPhone remote media control apps with their release of Remote, which is available from the App Store. This app allows your iPhone or iPod touch to control your iTunes or Apple TV just as seamlessly as it controls its own media. You may think that the pictures in Figure 10-25 are that of the iPod's own controls, but how else would a seamless remote control app look?

Figure 10-25.
Apple's Remote for iTunes and Apple TVs

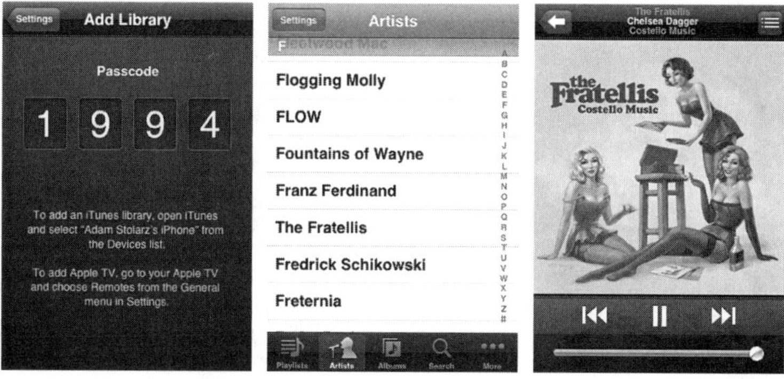

If you have a Sonos music system, they provide a Sonos Controller application for iPhones you can use: www.sonos.com/whattobuy/controllers/iphone. The same is true for media systems available from Savant: www.savantav.com/products.php?navigationitem=1&subnavigationitem=2&item=0.

Web-based Controls

Back before the App Store, when all that was available for iPhone development was the web-based SDK, network-based remote controls were some of the coolest tricks in town. Because the iPhone can render web pages that look somewhat like a real iPhone app, it seems like everyone was (and still is) putting easy-to-use iPhone-oriented web pages into their already web-server-enabled devices.

Remote Buddy (www.iospirit.com; see Figure 10-26) is one of the first and best implementations of this sort of remote. Using your unjailbroken iPhone, connecting to only a web application, you can control your desktop fully—using the iPhone as a remote trackpad (Figure 10-27), and even automatically launching DVD movies stored on your computer (Figure 10-28).

Figure 10-26.
Remote Buddy configuration

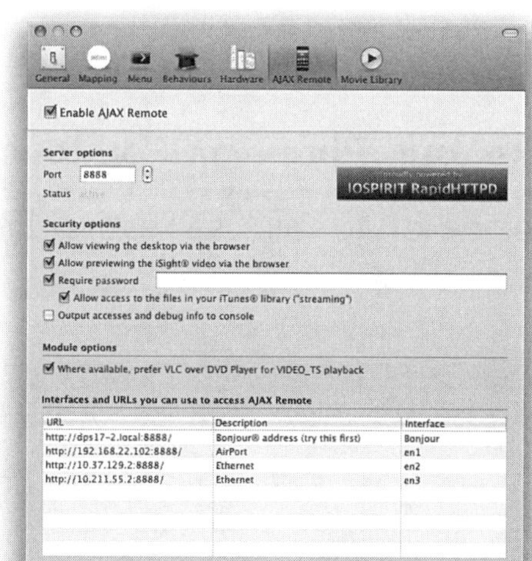

Figure 10-27.
Remote Buddy iPhone trackpad

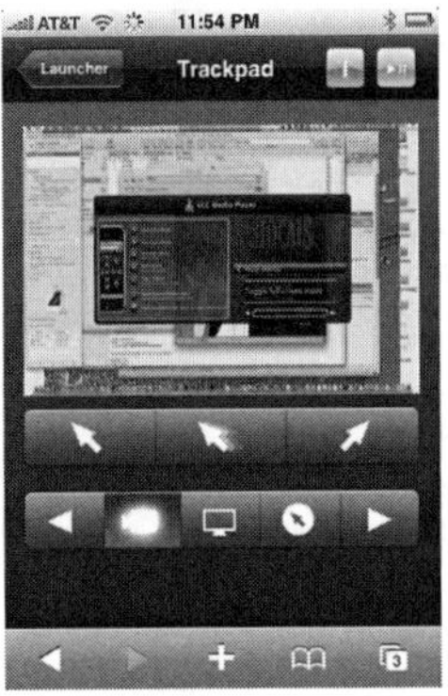

Figure 10-28.
Remote Buddy DVD interface

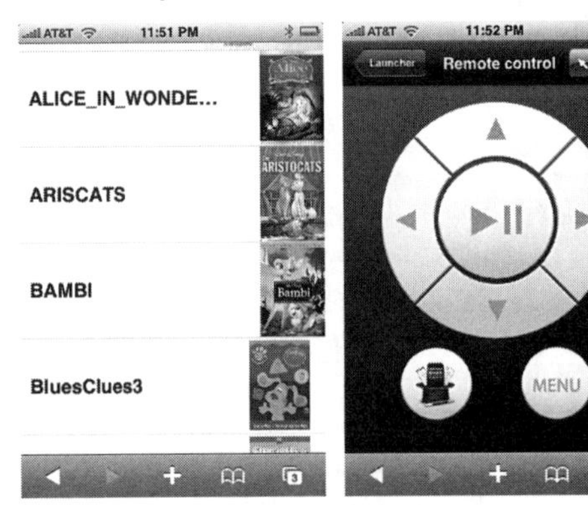

Combine a Mac Mini and an iPod touch, and you can build yourself a DVD jukebox system. Pull the DVD *VIDEO_TS* folder onto your Mac Mini as in **[Hack #4.02]**, then install Remote Buddy and you can watch any DVD you want at full quality, with all the DVD menus—no conversion required!

The iPod touch and iPhone are bringing the high-end, configurable-touchscreen remote control experience into the mainstream.

 HACK 10.06: Make Your iPhone or iPod touch Talk

When you have no one left to call, use Festival-Lite to make your iPhone talk to you.

With the utilities in this hack, you can add a text-to-speech engine to your phone, allowing you to turn text into speech! This can be implemented in an existing app or used on its own for various comedic or practical purposes.

To get started teaching your phone how to talk, fire up Cydia **[Hack #1.04]** to find and install the Festival-Lite and Erica Utilities packages (and Mobile Terminal, if you don't have that yet). See Figure 10-29. Festival is a port of a Unix-based TTS engine, and the Erica Utility is called play, a simple command-line player of audio files.

Figure 10-29.
The two utilities and how to find them

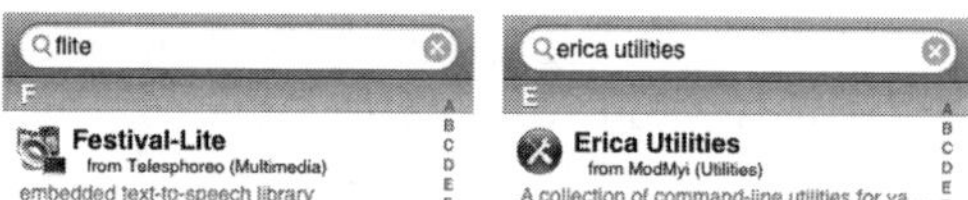

As these are just command-line utilities, that's all the setup you need. Once those are installed, connect to your iPhone via SSH **[Hack #9.04]**. Type in the following commands, with your own content where necessary:

```
flite "This is text to speech" -o filename.wav
play filename.wav
```

You can see what that would look like in Figure 10-30.

Figure 10-30.
iPhone ventriloquism

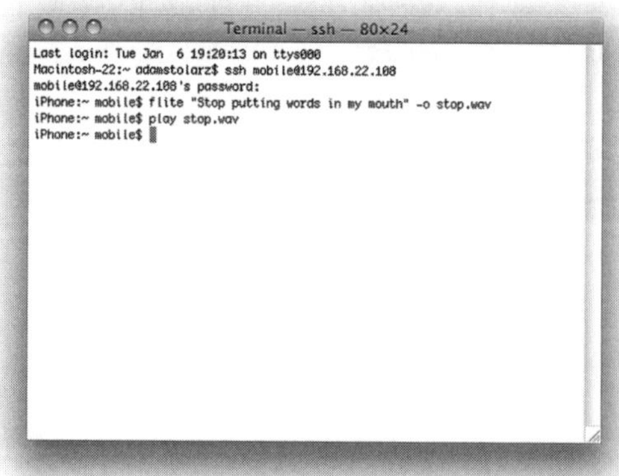

If all went well, you should be hearing your iPhone or iPod touch say the sentence in its new voice.

You can even do this directly on your iPhone **[Hack #9.05]** by connecting to your phone (server IP 127.0.0.1) as the user "mobile" and typing the same commands as shown previously.

HACK 10.07: Copy and Paste Between Applications

Clippy (and friends) add copy and paste to the iPhone and iPod touch.

Copy and paste. Until iPhone OS 3.0, it was the most glaring feature missing from Apple's otherwise killer device. It's present on practically every other smartphone on the market, and has infinite applications of convenience, as any journeyman computer user has discovered. So why go without it on a portable master communication device? The Clippy application gives us the copy and paste that iPhone OS 1.x/2.x owners had been clamoring for. Clippy is available from Cydia **[Hack #1.04]**.

Once it's installed, Clippy morphs the dragging text cursor movement present in all editable text boxes into a text highlighting tool. Tapping and dragging over a section of text highlights it. To bring up the commands for Clippy, go to the numbers and symbols page of the keyboard (the one reached via the ".123" button in the bottom left). The command buttons will be along the top of the keyboard, as in Figure 10-31.

Figure 10-31.
The command buttons for Clippy

Copying a phrase adds it to Clippy's "Stack," which is there so that you can copy and paste multiple things at a time. You can use it to keep a list of things you type frequently, saving keywords or things such as email addresses or simple stock SMS messages. The stack is shown in Figure 10-32. As can be expected, you can drag and delete the items, just like you would on any other list.

Figure 10-32.
The Stack: tap an item in it to paste it where your cursor lies

Clippy will work between most applications that support text entry. It has a few quirks, but it's the next best thing to the official Apple copy and paste mechanism.

With Clippy, your efficient communication device is a little more efficient—unless you use it for something like Figure 10-33.

Figure 10-33.
The time-wasting aspect of Clippy in action

Pardon my redundancy. Pardon my redundancy. Pardon my redundancy. Pardon my redundancy. Pardon my redundancy. Pardon my redundancy. Pardon my redundancy. Pardon my redundancy. Pardon my redundancy. Pardon my redundancy. Pardon my redundancy. Pardon my redundancy. Pardon my redundancy.

HACK 10.08: Download YouTube Videos Instead of Streaming

With MxTube, you can store YouTube videos on your phone.

The default iPhone YouTube application is useful, but lacking. It lacks access to your YouTube account, and the ability to download videos that you watch frequently. (Admittedly, YouTube itself lacks this feature.) The MxTube application by MxWeas (www.mxweas.com) lets you download videos from YouTube in high quality (for example, off the Wi-Fi in your office) and then watch them later (for example, on your flight to Jamaica, when you get away from your office). It's so simple once it's implemented that you'll wonder how you ever went without it. MxTube is available from Cydia **[Hack #1.04]**.

With MxTube, you can even force YouTube to serve you up Wi-Fi-quality video over EDGE or 3G. In Figures 10-34 through 10-36, you can see me finding a video, downloading it, and finally watching it in high quality—and this is off of the slower EDGE cellular network.

Figure 10-34.
A choice for video files

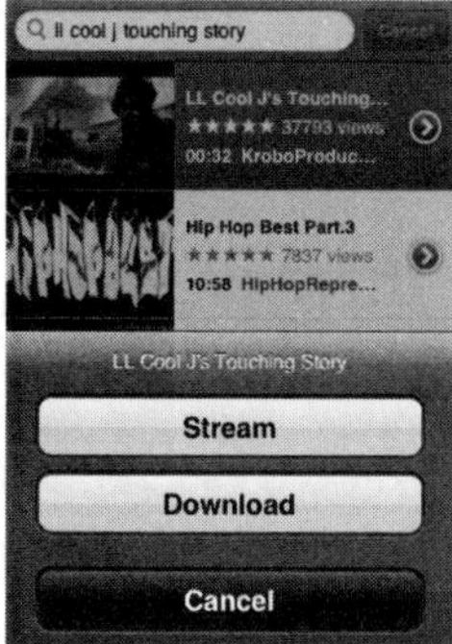

Figure 10-35.
Download one or more videos at once

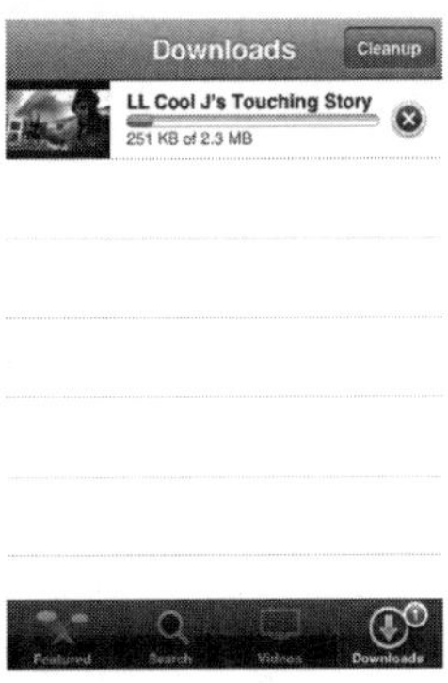

Figure 10-36.
No buffering and no waiting!

HACK 10.09: Acquire New Media with dTunes

Stream and download songs, videos, and torrents to your iPhone or iPod touch.

Is an obscure song that you want immediately not available from the iTunes Store? Do you want to share a YouTube video with your off-the-grid friend who lives beyond the reach of any cell signal or Wi-Fi? Or do you just want to make the most out of your unlimited data plan by filling the "phone tubes" with multigigabyte torrent files? dTunes solves all those problems. It works as a portal to different media search websites, allowing you to download files from them easily.

Music

The music download section uses www.seeqpod.com (Figure 10-37) to trawl the Internet in search of downloadable MP3s.

Figure 10-37.
Downloading a song with dTunes

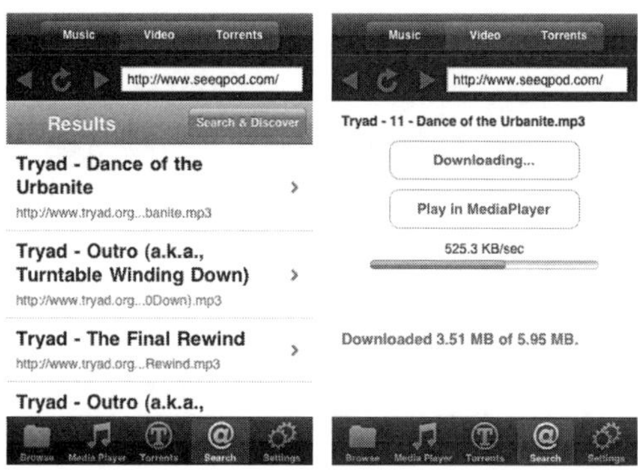

Video

The video tab uses www.tinytube.com, a mobile-friendly frontend for YouTube to access videos. You can either stream them or download them (Figure 10-38).

Figure 10-38.
Downloading a movie with dTunes

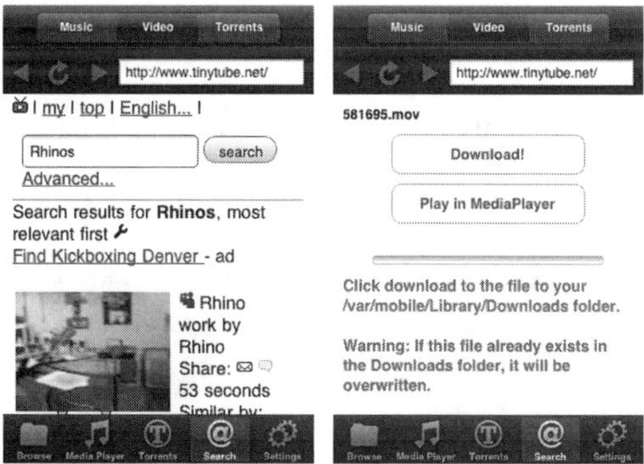

Torrents

dTunes allows you to download BitTorrent files from any of the popular torrent websites.

Just use the browser to search for a torrent you want to download, and download the file.

 For the torrent downloading to work, you'll need both Enhanced Ctorrent and Mobile Terminal. Both of these are available from Cydia **[Hack #1.04]**.

Go to Browse and click on the torrent file you just downloaded to prepare it for downloading through the command line. Now go into Mobile Terminal and type `./gettorrent`. If you get an error, make sure that you went into dTunes on the Browse tab and tapped the torrent you wanted to download. More information is in dTunes itself, as shown in Figure 10-39.

Figure 10-39.
More information about torrenting, with a helpful diagram straight from dTunes

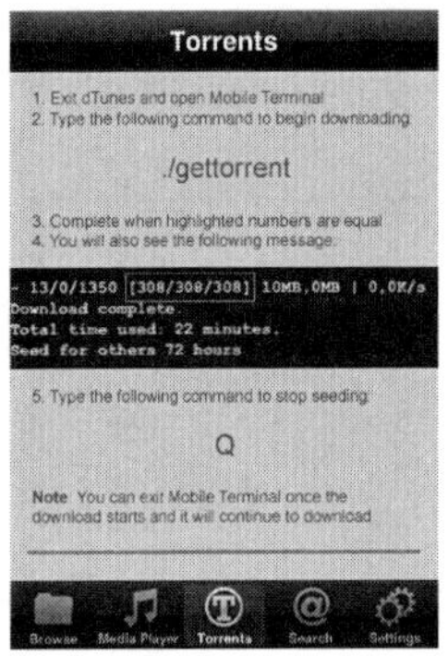

When your torrent is done downloading (and you're done seeding), open up Mobile Terminal again and input the command `Q`. That will quit the torrent app.

If the files you downloaded are compatible media files, you can view them in dTunes under Browse.

Now your iPhone or iPod touch is free to download the world.

HACK 10.10: Back Up Your Jailbroken Apps

With AptBackup, you can protect your jailbroken app library from firmware updates.

One major inconvenience with jailbreaking is that after a new firmware update comes out and is made completely safe and jailbroken, the unofficial apps you have installed are still erased after installing it. It's a painful process trying to remember each app and reinstall them one by one, but fortunately AptBackup exists to take care of all that.

When you press the Backup button in AptBackup, it creates a list of all the jailbroken apps you've downloaded and saves them as part of your backup package, so that when you back up in iTunes (Figure 10-40), they will be saved as well.

Figure 10-40.
Backing up

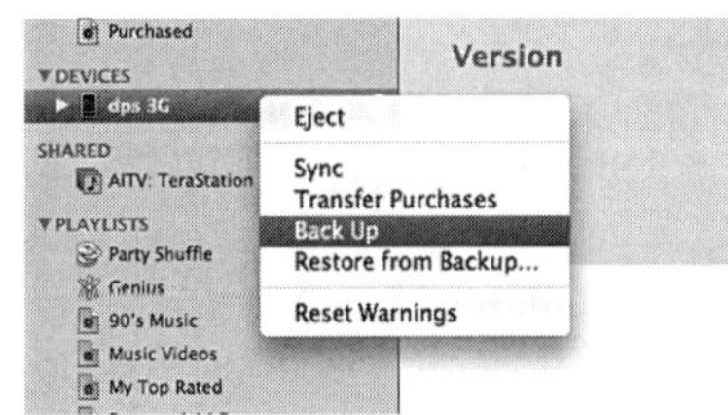

So when you do install the firmware update and restore from backup (Figure 10-41), that list gets put back onto your phone.

Figure 10-41.
Restore from Backup

Then you just have to reinstall AptBackup from Cydia (after jailbreaking your phone again, of course) and hit the Restore button to reinstall them all.

The caveat with this program is that it *doesn't* back up settings or anything added as a result of those apps (downloaded movies, and the like), but anything downloaded from Cydia is reclaimed. That includes, for example, WinterBoard skins.

Fortunately, many settings for jailbroken apps get saved during regular syncing anyway. You should still check each application you use (e.g., Cycorder) to see whether there's data, recorded media, or other information that hasn't been saved. Backups are always your friend.

This utility definitely helps those who rejailbreak with every iPhone firmware release.

11 DEVELOPMENT HACKS

When Objective-C was chosen to be the primary development language for Nextstep, no doubt its reflective features and dynamic late-bound messaging system were cited as significant advantages. Although the language's quirky syntax is a turn-off for some, its uneasy marriage between a Smalltalk-inspired object model and the raw low-level power of C is what gives the language its own unique strengths. That Objective-C heritage, carried through as Nextstep, became Mac OS X, and more recently spawned the iPhone OS.

How ironic that this powerful dynamic language also helped to thwart Apple's efforts to lock down the iPhone.

Dynamic languages with reflection data compiled into their binaries are unusually vulnerable to reverse-engineering. All that metadata, so instrumental to runtime binding and reflective analysis, is also visible to anyone who can decipher your compiled binary format. So when the iPhone Dev Team **[Hack #2.06]** set themselves to the task of creating an iPhone SDK, Objective-C's reflective metadata made the job a whole lot easier.

The first part of this chapter will show how far you can go with Unix scripting: using command-line tools to build solutions and wrapping them in push-button applications. The next section will show you how to take advantage of the iPhone APIs—both their developer-friendly features and their hacker-friendly internals. We'll explore some of the development environments that you can use, and how to customize them for your own needs. And along the way, you'll learn about some handy tools and techniques for your iPhone hacking and development arsenal.

HACK 11.01: Turn Command-Line Scripts into iPhone Apps

You can write complex utility applications for the iPhone in almost any scripting language.

Because Mac OS X is a Unix operating system, the bountiful riches of Unix programming are available on the iPhone. If you're familiar with any command-line programming tools, from languages like C to the dozens of scripting languages such as Python and Ruby (available on Cydia), Java, and even shell programming, you can write utility applications that perform useful functions, and wrap them in a push-button icon on your iPhone.

Writing Scripts

The first step to writing a script, as opposed to a full-blown iPhone application, is to SSH **[Hack #9.04]** into your phone. If you've mounted your iPhone in the filesystem **[Hack #9.06]**, then you can edit text files more easily. At the command line, you'll find a familiar set of Unix shell tools. Some useful packages to install can be found in Development, Networking, Java, and Scripting under "Sections" in Cydia. You should browse around and search for the tools that you're most comfortable with.

In any event, you'll need to install a variety of useful command-line utilities from Cydia.

Core Utilities

A key set of GNU Unix shell utilities:

gawk

An implementation of the awk tool for manipulating text

sed

A tool to edit text streams using patterns

gzip

File compression utility

inetutils

Includes a command-line FTP utility, ping, and telnet

nano

A command-line text editor that's easier to use than *vi*

netatalk

Support for the Apple File Protocol; also contains a very useful timeout command for watching runaway scripts

rsync

A bandwidth-conservative network backup utility

network-cmds

Contains traceroute and netstat, both useful for network debugging

shell-cmds

Gives you the time, which, and killall commands, that are useful for script debugging

Erica's Utilities

A collection of great command-line tools (more info at http://ericasadun.com/ftp/EricaUtilities)

SQLite v3

An application that can manipulate the database used by the phone

OpenSSH and *bash* are required. Both should be installed by default when you jailbreak the phone **[Hack #1.03]**.

Hello World

First, let's get our feet wet. SSH into your iPhone **[Hack #9.04]** and log in as *root* (default).

Now create a test script. (# represents the root prompt, which is where you type commands. In these examples don't type the #. Another thing to look out for is `^D`. Instead you should press Control-D. Don't type `^D` literally.)

```
# cat > test.sh
echo "Hello World"
^D
# chmod 777 test.sh
# ./test.sh
Hello World
#
```

We just created a file using the `cat` command; it's a bit easier to use a command-line text editor such as nano, which you can invoke with:

```
# nano test.sh
```

Figure 11-1 shows the nano editor in action.

Figure 11-1.
The nano editor in action

As mentioned in **[Hack #9.06]**, you can edit text files from your computer by mounting the iPhone filesystem, if you prefer.

Backup Locally

Now let's test a more useful script. Perhaps you want to back up your call log? It's located here:

/private/var/mobile/Library/CallHistory/call_history.db

You can make a one-line script using the *gzip* and *date* commands to make a time-stamped backup. Create a file called *calllogbackup.sh* with:

```
gzip -c /private/var/mobile/Library/CallHistory/call_history.db > \
/private/var/mobile/Library/CallHistory/call_history_`date +%Y%m%d_%H%M%S`.db.gz
```

Now you can test this backup:

```
# chmod 777 calllogbackup.sh
# ./calllogbackup.sh
# ls -l /private/var/mobile/Library/CallHistory/
total 136
-rw-r--r-- 1 mobile mobile 101376 Feb 15 12:17 call_history.db
-rw-r--r-- 1 root   mobile  36619 Feb 15 12:46 call_history_20090215_124637.db.gz
```

Back Up to a Server

In **[Hack #9.04]** we showed how to upload a file to a server from your iPhone. We'll build on that now by creating a time-stamped backup of your call log and uploading it to the server. Edit *calllogbackup.sh* and replace its contents with the following (changing the username and domain to match your system):

```
backup=/private/var/mobile/Library/CallHistory/call_history_`date +%Y%m%d_%k%M%S`.db
cp /private/var/mobile/Library/CallHistory/call_history.db $backup
echo backing up call_history.db to $backup.gz
gzip $backup
echo uploading $backup.gz to the server
scp $backup.gz username@yourdomain.com:~/
```

Now test it:

```
# ./calllogbackup.sh
backing up call_history.db to /private/var/mobile/Library/CallHistory/call_
history_20090215_170737.db.gz
uploading /private/var/mobile/Library/CallHistory/call_history_20090215_170737.
db.gz to the server
call_history_20090215_170737.db.gz                         100%   36KB  35.8KB/s
00:00
```

Great! We've got a one-line script that backs up the call log. You could run this from MobileTerminal **[Hack #9.05]** on your phone, but it would be more convenient to have an iPhone application simply run your script.

Wrap the Backup in an Application

We don't want to do a bunch of development (we're scripting here), so we're going to take an existing application, copy it, and put our script inside. On the iPhone, applications are stored in bundles, which are simply folders, usually with an *.app* extension.

We'll use the application *respring* **[Hack #11.12]** (Figure 11-2) from Cydia as our template. *respring* is also how we'll make our new application show up in SpringBoard.

Figure 11-2.
respring

SSH over to your iPhone and you'll be able to see *Respring.app* in */Applications/*:

```
# cd /Applications
# ls
AppStore.app/     FieldTest.app/          MobileSMS.app/        Stocks.app/
BootNeuter.app/   Insomnia.app/           MobileSafari.app/     TVOut.app/
BossPrefs.app/    Installer.app/          MobileSlideShow.app/  Weather.app/
Calculator.app/   Maps.app/               MobileStore.app/      Web.app/
CallBackup.app/   MobileAddressBook.app/  MobileTimer.app/      YouTube.app/
CallLog.app/      MobileCal.app/          PdaNet.app/           biteSMS.app/
Cycorder.app/     MobileMail.app/         Podcaster.app/        iCallBR.app/
Cydia.app/        MobileMusicPlayer.app/  Preferences.app/      siax.app/
DemoApp.app/      MobileNotes.app/        Respring.app/
Documents/        MobilePhone.app/        ScreenSplitr.app/
```

Make your own app bundle using the *Respring.app* bundle:

```
# cp -R Respring.app/ CallBackup.app
# cd CallBackup.app
# ls -l
total 124
-rw-r--r-- 1 root staff 97332 Feb 15 17:19 Default.png
-rw-r--r-- 1 root staff   778 Feb 15 17:19 Info.plist
-rw-r--r-- 1 root staff  6770 Feb 15 17:19 icon.png
-rwxr-xr-x 1 root staff 13616 Feb 15 17:19 respring*
```

Inside the bundle are four files. If you've mounted your iPhone on your computer, you can "Show Package Contents" (Figure 11-3) on CallBackup (Figure 11-4) to see what's inside. On Windows, just open the directory.

- *Default.png* is the image you'll see when you launch the app.
- *Info.plist* defines the name of the application.
- *icon.png* is the icon that shows up in SpringBoard.
- *respring*, in this case, is the executable.

Figure 11-3.
Show package contents

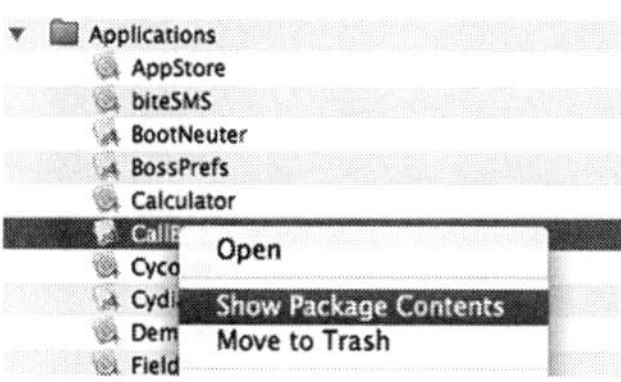

Figure 11-4.
Contents of CallBackup

The minimum necessary changes are to replace the executable and edit the text-based plist. Copy your calllogbackup script into the *CallBackup.app* directory and delete the file named *respring*:

```
# cp ~/calllogbackup.sh .
# rm respring
```

Next, edit the plist using a plist editor or a text editor **[Hack #11.02]**. (On a Mac, choose "open hidden" to open the plist from inside an application bundle, or drag the files out of the bundle to edit them.)

Minimal necessary changes are bolded:

```
<?xml version="1.0" encoding="UTF-8"?>
<!DOCTYPE plist PUBLIC
"-//Apple Computer//DTD PLIST 1.0//EN" "http://www.apple.com/DTDs/PropertyList-
1.0.dtd">
<plist version="1.0">
<dict>
        <key>CFBundleCopyright</key>
        <string>Perceptive Development</string>
        <key>CFBundleDevelopmentRegion</key>
        <string>English</string>
        <key>CFBundleExecutable</key>
        <string>calllogbackup.sh</string>
        <key>CFBundleIdentifier</key>
        <string>com.perceptdev.calllogbackup</string>
        <key>CFBundleInfoDictionaryVersion</key>
        <string>6.0</string>
```

```
        <key>CFBundlePackageType</key>
        <string>APPL</string>
        <key>CFBundleSignature</key>
        <string>????</string>
        <key>CFBundleVersion</key>
        <string>0.1</string>
</dict>
</plist>
```

We need to run *respring* to make our new application appear in SpringBoard. Let's run it (Figure 11-5). As there's no application name in this plist, the application name that shows up in SpringBoard will be the name of the bundle/folder, without the *.app*: *CallBackup*.

Figure 11-5.
Resprung *CallBackup*

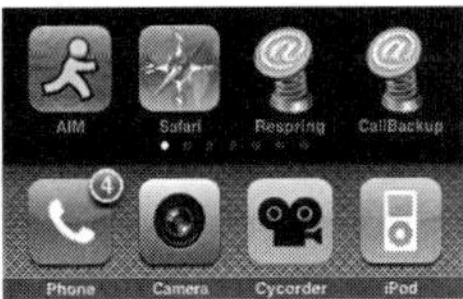

Set the Icon and Picture

To distinguish your application, you can change the background picture and icon. Simply copy the *Default.png* and *icon.png* from the *CallBackup.app* directory to your computer, edit them, and put them back in the application bundle/folder (Figure 11-6). We're editing the files in Adobe Photoshop, then choosing "Export for Web and Devices" to create small PNG files of less than 100K in size.

Figure 11-6.
Editing *Default.png* and *icon.png* in Adobe Photoshop

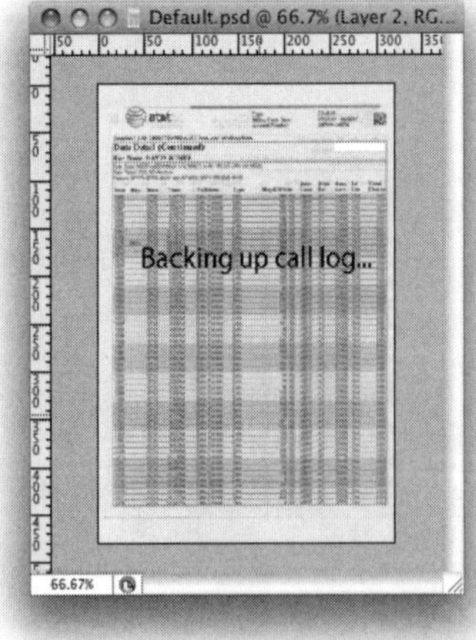

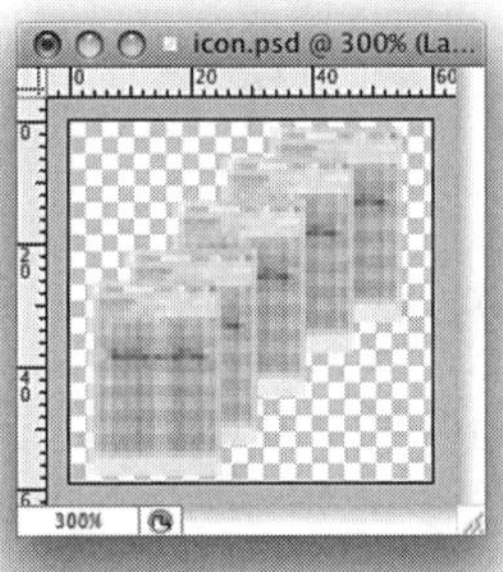

When these have been edited and added to the bundle, you can run *respring* again to see them (Figure 11-7).

Figure 11-7.
Final CallLogBackup icon and screen (AT&T bill courtesy of David Winer)

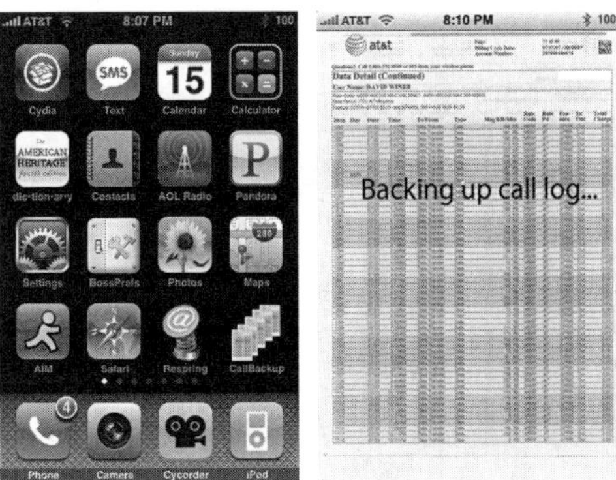

Handle Timeouts Gracefully

One thing you will quickly learn is that if you write bad scripts, your script-based iPhone application will hang. You can terminate it by holding down the Home button for a while **[Hack #2.02]**, but better yet, you can put some error handling in your script.

A useful utility called *timeout*, found at */usr/bin/timeout*, is installed as part of netatalk **[Hack #9.06]**.

```
# /usr/bin/timeout
Usage: /usr/bin/timeout [-s signal] seconds program [args]
```

You can use a numerical signal, or one of these (if you don't supply a signal, it defaults to TERM):

```
HUP   INT   QUIT  ILL   TRAP  ABRT  IOT    EMT
FPE   KILL  BUS   SEGV  SYS   PIPE  ALRM   TERM
URG   STOP  TSTP  CONT  CHLD  TTIN  TTOU   IO
XCPU  XFSZ  VTALRM      PROF  WINCH INFO   USR1    USR2
```

If you put `timeout 5` before another command, it will run that command, and then kill it in 5 seconds if it hasn't already completed. For example:

```
# timeout 5 cat > hang
Terminated
#
```

(`cat > hang` waits for input and would therefore go on forever until the user entered Control-D).

So to improve our backup script, we'll add timeouts to hold our backup script. We'll copy our working script to *backup.sh*:

```
# cp calllogbackup.sh backup.sh
# chmod 777 backup.sh
```

Then we'll replace the contents of *calllogbackup.sh* with the following, which uses `` `dirname $0` `` to find the directory of the script that was launched by the application:

```
script=`dirname $0`
/usr/bin/timeout 60 $script/backup.sh
```

The bundle should now contain the following files:

```
# ls -l
total 108
-rw-r--r-- 1 root staff 94206 Feb 15 20:09 Default.png
-rw-r--r-- 1 root staff   809 Feb 15 17:46 Info.plist
-rwxrwxrwx 1 root staff   334 Feb 15 20:27 backup.sh*
-rwxr-xr-x 1 root staff    21 Feb 15 20:27 calllogbackup.sh*
-rw-r--r-- 1 root staff  2267 Feb 15 20:04 icon.png
```

Now we know that our app will eventually quit (after 60 seconds) if it doesn't succeed.

Display Result Codes

As our final trick, we'd like to know whether our last backup succeeded. In the Erica Utilities is a program called "badge" that puts a label on the application icon.

You can try it out—you should get the result shown in Figure 11-8:

```
# badge
badge application-name (badge)
# badge CallBackup hello
attempting to badge com.perceptdev.calllogbackup
```

Figure 11-8.
Badge

To find out what badge to put on our backup application, we need to know whether our backup succeeded. We'll add several more lines to check the success of our script using the script variable `$?`, which should contain a zero (0) if our upload was successful. We'll also add a line to delete any files that are left over from the backup process.

The final contents of *backup.sh* are (new lines in bold):

```
backup=/private/var/mobile/Library/CallHistory/call_history_`date +%Y%m%d_%H%M%S`.db
cp /private/var/mobile/Library/CallHistory/call_history.db $backup
echo backing up call_history.db to $backup.gz
gzip $backup
echo uploading $backup.gz to the server
scp $backup.gz iphonehacks@perceptdev.com:~/
if [ $? = 0 ] ; then
    echo "yes"
    /usr/bin/badge CallBackup Yes
else
    echo "no"
    /usr/bin/badge CallBackup No
fi
rm /private/var/mobile/Library/CallHistory/call_history_*
```

The results of a successful (left) or failed (right) backup are shown in Figure 11-9.

Figure 11-9.
Indicating script results with an application badge

You can find the code and applications listed in this hack at www.perceptdev.com/labs/iphonehacks.

 HACK 11.02: Edit Mac OS X Property Lists (plists)

You can edit iPhone configuration settings stored in property lists.

The basic way to change many settings on iPhone is to edit property lists, or plist files. Often they're stored in an easy-to-edit text format, but sometimes they're stored in a smaller binary format.

To edit a plist file, you need to copy the file from your iPhone **[Hack #1.05]**, or mount your iPhone on your computer **[Hack #9.06]**. If you're using Windows and not using a shell, then just copy the file over to your computer using your preferred method.

For this example, we're going to edit a common iPhone preference file by copying it to our desktop using scp in a terminal program on Mac OS X:

```
$ scp root@192.168.1.109:/User/Library/Preferences/com.apple.Preferences.plist .
com.apple.Preferences.plist              100%  214     0.2KB/s   00:01
```

(You'll need to replace 192.168.1.109 with your iPhone's IP address.)

If you've installed the developer tools on Mac OS X, there is a program in */Development/Application/Utilities/* called Property List Editor. For binary plists such as *com.apple.Preferences.plist*, this is the only way to edit the file. If you've done registry editing on a Windows PC, the concept is similar; preferences are stored in hierarchical lists of labeled data. You can see the *com.apple.Preferences.plist* file being edited in Property List Editor in Figure 11-10.

Figure 11-10.
Property List Editor

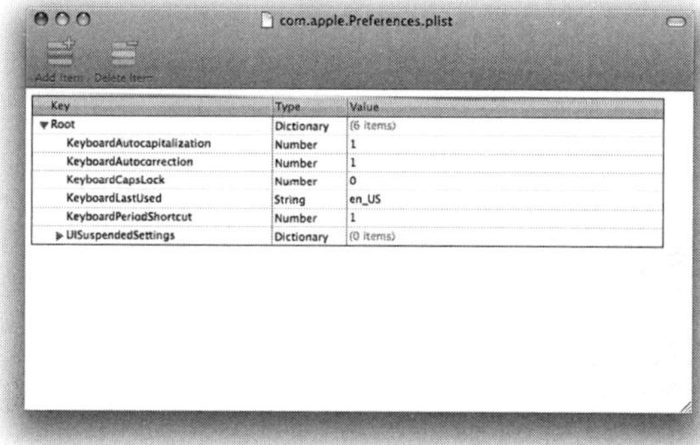

Tweaking a Property List

As an example of changing a feature, we're going to enable *emoji*—Japanese emoticons for chat—by adding a preference key.

Click Add Item and add a key called KeyboardEmojiEverywhere, make it a boolean, and check the box next to it (Figure 11-11). Next, change KeyboardLastChosen to *emoji*.

Figure 11-11.
Enabling *emoji* with Property List Editor

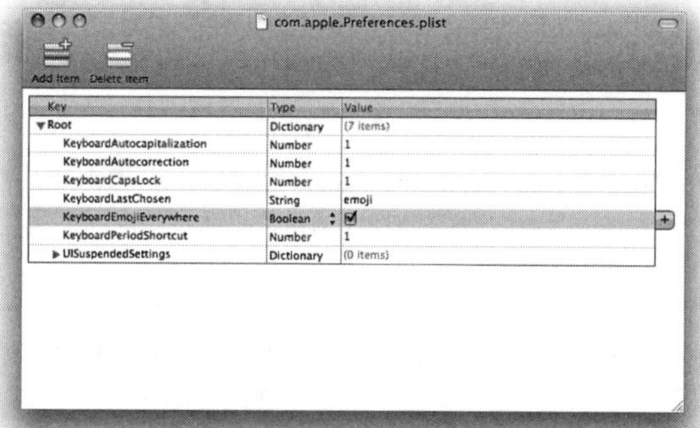

Once you're done, copy it back to the iPhone (you can type the command all on one line, but you must omit the backslash, \). Also be sure to replace 192.168.1.109 with your iPhone's IP address:

```
$ scp ~/Desktop/com.apple.Preferences.plist \
root@192.168.1.109:/User/Library/Preferences/com.apple.Preferences.plist
100%  244     0.2KB/s   00:00
```

Editing on Non-Mac Platforms

If you're on Windows, Linux, or the iPhone itself, you won't have Property List Editor. But there are still some solutions.

There is a command-line utility called *plutil* that is part of Erica's Utilities **[Hack #11.01]**, and can convert back and forth between binary and text formats. You can convert the *.plist* you want to edit to XML format, edit it in the text editor of your choice (even on the iPhone), then convert back to binary for use. It overwrites the original file, but nondestructively; you can convert it back.

To do this, you need to learn the syntax of plist files, but they're not too hard to figure out. To convert a binary *.plist* to XML format for editing, type this in the Terminal on the iPhone:

```
# plutil -cxml1 /User/Library/Preferences/com.apple.Preferences.plist
Converting /User/Library/Preferences/com.apple.Preferences.plist to XML
```

Here are the contents of */User/Library/Preferences/com.apple.Preferences.plist*:

```
<?xml version="1.0" encoding="UTF-8"?>
<!DOCTYPE plist PUBLIC "-//Apple//DTD PLIST 1.0//EN"
 "http://www.apple.com/DTDs/PropertyList-1.0.dtd">
<plist version="1.0">
<dict>
        <key>KeyboardAutocapitalization</key>
        <integer>1</integer>
        <key>KeyboardAutocorrection</key>
        <integer>1</integer>
        <key>KeyboardCapsLock</key>
        <integer>1</integer>
        <key>KeyboardEmojiEverywhere</key>
        <true/>
        <key>KeyboardLastChosen</key>
        <string>emoji</string>
        <key>KeyboardPeriodShortcut</key>
        <integer>1</integer>
        <key>UISuspendedSettings</key>
        <dict/>
</dict>
</plist>
```

To convert an XML plist file to binary so that the iPhone will recognize it:

```
# plutil -cbinary1 /User/Library/Preferences/com.apple.Preferences.plist
Converting /User/Library/Preferences/com.apple.Preferences.plist to binary
```

If you want to edit binary plist files on Windows, you can find Windows-based plist editing utilities such as *pledit.exe* (http://iphone.cazisoft.com/?p=569, Figure 11-12) and Plist Editor for Windows (www.ipodrobot.com, Figure 11-13).

Figure 11-12.
pledit.exe

Figure 11-13.
Plist Editor for Windows

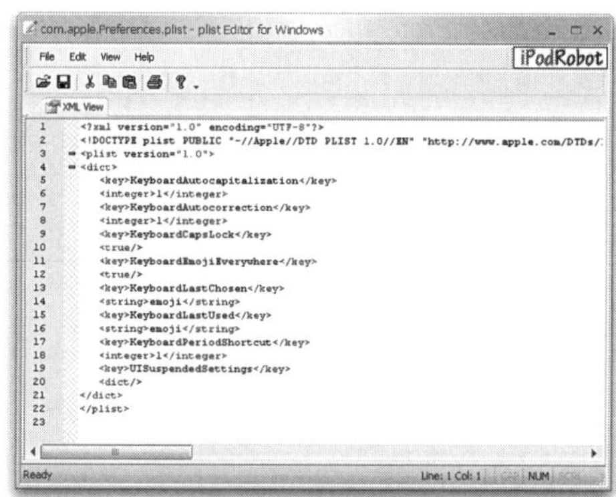

HACK 11.03: Create Periodic Tasks that Run in the Background

Your iPhone and iPod touch can execute programs on a schedule or when triggered by certain events.

Every operating system has a method of running "daemon" tasks in the background, as well as running scheduled tasks. If you want to turn an iPhone into a simple webcam, upload your position to a web server, or automatically back up some of your iPhone files to the cloud, you'll need to know how to schedule tasks on Mobile Mac OS X.

On Unix/Linux, the rc.d scripts, inetd, and cron systems run startup scripts, network services, and recurring tasks, respectively. On Microsoft operating systems, the Windows registry enumerates

Services and Scheduled Tasks, both of which can be managed by control panels of the same name. On Mac OS X, and thus on the iPhone, these functions are gathered together under a system managed by *launchd*.

Getting to Know *launchd*

Naturally, background tasks, like background processes, are not a user-accessible feature of the iPhone without jailbreaking. Once you've jailbroken your iPhone or iPod touch, you can SSH in or mount the filesystem, and take a look at the various launch system-wide *daemons* and per-user *agents*.

Apple provides decent documentation on *launchd*:

- http://developer.apple.com/technotes/tn2005/tn2083.html provides an excellent overview and good definitions of terms.
- http://tinyurl.com/launchd2 describes how to create a *launchd* plist file.
- http://tinyurl.com/launchd documents the *launchd* plist file structure, which lists the paths in Table 11-1.

Table 11-1
launchd paths, from the launchd.plist(5) *man* page

/System/Library/LaunchDaemons	Mac OS X system-wide daemons
/Library/LaunchDaemons	System-wide daemons provided by the administrator
/System/Library/LaunchAgents	Mac OS X per-user agents
/Library/LaunchAgents	Per-user agents provided by the administrator
~/Library/LaunchAgents	Per-user agents provided by the user

LaunchDaemons are run during boot, and LaunchAgents run after a specific user logs in. While technically */System/Library/* is reserved for the system, you can put your *launchd* scripts in there and they will work. In this hack, we'll store them in */Library/LaunchDaemons*, just because it's less crowded in that directory.

You can connect to your iPhone and check out the existing LaunchDaemons:

```
$ cd /System/Library/LaunchDaemons
$ ls
com.apple.AOSNotification.plist
com.apple.graphicsservices.sample.plist
com.apple.AddressBook.plist                  com.apple.iapd.plist
com.apple.BTServer.plist                     com.apple.itunesstored.plist
com.apple.CommCenter.plist                   com.apple.locationd.plist
com.apple.CrashHousekeeping.plist            com.apple.mDNSResponder.plist
com.apple.DumpBasebandCrash.plist            com.apple.mDNSResponderHelper.plist
com.apple.DumpPanic.plist                    com.apple.mediaserverd.plist
com.apple.MobileFileIntegrity.plist          com.apple.mobile.lockbot.plist
com.apple.ReportCrash.DirectoryService.plist com.apple.mobile.lockdown.plist
com.apple.ReportCrash.Jetsam.plist           com.apple.mobile.obliteration.plist
com.apple.ReportCrash.SafetyNet.plist        com.apple.notifyd.plist
com.apple.ReportCrash.SimulateCrash.plist    com.apple.powerlog.plist
```

```
com.apple.ReportCrash.plist
com.applc.SCHelper-embedded.plist
com.apple.SpringBoard.plist
com.apple.aslmanager.plist
com.apple.chud.chum.plist
com.apple.chud.pilotfish.plist
com.apple.configd.plist
com.apple.daily.plist
com.apple.dataaccess.dataaccessd.plist
com.apple.datamigrator.plist
com.apple.fairplayd.plist
com.apple.securityd.plist
com.apple.stackshot.server.plist
com.apple.syslogd.plist
com.apple.tcpdump.server.plist
com.apple.update.plist
com.apple.usbptpd.plist
com.jft.pn.plist
com.saurik.Cydia.Startup.plist
com.saurik.afpd.dns-sd.plist
net.sourceforge.netatalk.afpd.plist
org.iphone-dev.yellowsn0w.plist
```

Creating a Recurring Task with *launchd*

launchd provides for both background-service daemons and repeating tasks; they differ only in how you write the plist. The easiest way to see how this works is to create a simple script and run it. For this example, we'll assume you have Erica's Utilities installed (using Cydia), so you can invoke the play command. Connect to your iPhone and type:

```
$ /usr/bin/play /System/Library/Frameworks/UIKit.framework/Tink.aiff
```

You should hear a "tink" sound. If so, create a text file called *com.perceptdev.tink.plist* (either run nano on the command line, or create the file on your computer and copy it over) and enter the following script, which you can download from www.perceptdev.com/labs/iphonehacks.

```
<?xml version="1.0" encoding="UTF-8"?>
<!DOCTYPE plist PUBLIC "-//Apple//DTD PLIST 1.0//EN"
 "http://www.apple.com/DTDs/PropertyList-1.0.dtd">
<plist version="1.0">
<dict>
	<key>Disabled</key>
	<false/>
	<key>Label</key>
	<string>com.perceptdev.tink</string>
	<key>ProgramArguments</key>
	<array>
		<string>/usr/bin/play</string>
		<string>/System/Library/Frameworks/UIKit.framework/Tink.aiff</string>
		<string></string>
	</array>
	<key>RunAtLoad</key>
	<true/>
	<key>StartInterval</key>
	<integer>10</integer>
	<key>WatchPaths</key>
	<array/>
</dict>
</plist>
```

Save this file in */Library/LaunchDaemons/*. Now load it into *launchd* by running the following command:

```
launchctl load /Library/LaunchDaemons/com.perceptdev.tink.plist
```

You should now hear a tink every 10 seconds. Hurray! You've created a background task.

To turn off the task, unload it:

```
launchctl unload /Library/LaunchDaemons/com.perceptdev.tink.plist
```

Protect Your Tasks with Timeout

As mentioned in **[Hack #11.01]**, the */usr/bin/timeout* utility acts as a monitor to kill a hung or runaway process. If a background task ever hangs, *launchd* may not run it any more. Thus, your recurring task must be responsible for shutting itself down without hanging. We'll put a timeout before our task (as shown in bold):

```
<?xml version="1.0" encoding="UTF-8"?>
<!DOCTYPE plist PUBLIC "-//Apple//DTD PLIST 1.0//EN" "http://www.apple.com/DTDs/
PropertyList-1.0.dtd">
<plist version="1.0">
<dict>
        <key>Disabled</key>
        <false/>
        <key>Label</key>
        <string>com.perceptdev.tink</string>
        <key>ProgramArguments</key>
        <array>
                <string>/usr/bin/timeout</string>
                <string>3</string>
                <string>/usr/bin/play</string>
                <string>/System/Library/Frameworks/UIKit.framework/Tink.aiff</string>
                <string></string>
        </array>
        <key>StartInterval</key>
        <integer>10</integer>
        <key>WatchPaths</key>
        <array/>
</dict>
</plist>
```

Save this file in */Library/LaunchDaemons/*. Now load it by running the following command:

```
launchctl load /Library/LaunchDaemons/com.perceptdev.tink.plist
```

Make sure you hear your tink every 10 seconds again. If you don't, verify that the exact */usr/bin/play* command you have in the script works on the command line. Try launching the *launchd* script again manually. Then, you can test if it comes up automatically on reboot. Power down your phone, power it up, and listen. The tink sound should start after the phone fully boots.

As before, you can turn it back off with:

```
launchctl unload /Library/LaunchDaemons/com.perceptdev.tink.plist
```

Debugging *launchd* scripts

If you're testing many different versions of your script, it's sometimes easier to put all the commands in a script in */var/root/* and call this script in your *launchd* task. So we'll put in this:

```
<?xml version="1.0" encoding="UTF-8"?>
<!DOCTYPE plist PUBLIC "-//Apple//DTD PLIST 1.0//EN" "http://www.apple.com/DTDs/
PropertyList-1.0.dtd">
<plist version="1.0">
<dict>
        <key>Disabled</key>
        <false/>
        <key>Label</key>
        <string>com.perceptdev.tink</string>
        <key>ProgramArguments</key>
        <array>
              <string>/var/root/tink.sh</string>
              <string></string>
        </array>
        <key>StartInterval</key>
        <integer>10</integer>
        <key>WatchPaths</key>
        <array/>
</dict>
</plist>
```

If your script isn't working correctly, you can do rudimentary debugging by adding `print` statements to a log file you create. This is done by "echoing" into your logfile., as shown in */dev/root/tink.sh*:

```
echo starting script >>/var/root/debug.log
date >>/var/root/debug.log
/usr/bin/timeout 3 /usr/bin/play /System/Library/Frameworks/UIKit.framework/Tink.aiff
```

Don't forget to make *tink* executable:

```
# chmod 777 /var/root/tink.sh
```

Then you can check out your logfile:

```
# cat debug.log
starting script
Mon Feb 16 22:04:19 PST 2009
starting script
Mon Feb 16 22:04:29 PST 2009
starting script
```

```
Mon Feb 16 22:04:39 PST 2009
starting script
Mon Feb 16 22:04:49 PST 2009
#
```

While developing and testing scripts, you may want to set a high update frequency, such as once a minute, and then look in the filesystem to read your logfile to see how things are going. Once you have your script working how you want it, you may want to monitor it for a few days to make sure that it survives phone reboots, phone calls, and various other conditions. A simple way to know whether your script is running is to have it play a unique sound whenever it runs. You can upload any sound you want to into */var/mobile/Media/* and use Erica's play utility to play it from your script:

```
/usr/bin/timeout 3 /usr/bin/play /var/mobile/media/Unique.aiff
```

When you hear your sound, you know your script has at least run.

If your script ever stops running inexplicably, chances are that the script, or one of the commands in it, has hung. To check this out, type the following:

```
launchctl list | grep name of your launchd without the plist at the end
```

such as:

```
# launchctl list | grep com.perceptdev.tink
-       0       com.perceptdev.tink
```

If the result starts with a dash -, you're fine. But if the process is hung, it will have a process ID as the first number:

```
# launchctl list | grep com.perceptdev.tink
679     -       com.perceptdev.tink
```

You can kill this process, and the script should unstick and start working again. You should also then add any appropriate */usr/bin/timeout* commands to your script, or figure out why it's hanging, to prevent this in the future. Here's the kill command:

```
# kill 679
```

Easy *launchd* Plist Editing

This hack showed you how to edit plists. However, if you're still learning the *launchd* syntax, there is an easy graphical utility available for Mac OS X called Lingon (http://tuppis.com/lingon) by Peter Borg (Figure 11-14). It can be used to view the many example *launchd* plists on your Mac, and create valid plist files for your iPhone.

Figure 11-14.
The Lingon plist editor

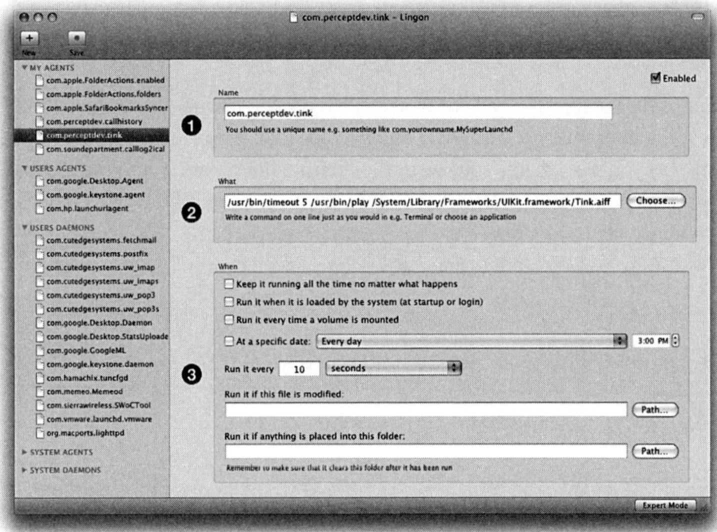

After you've added the basic functions that you want performed and specified how you want to trigger them, you can click Expert Mode on the bottom left of Lingon's editing panel to see the plist XML that it produces (Figure 11-15).

Figure 11-15.
Lingon Expert Mode

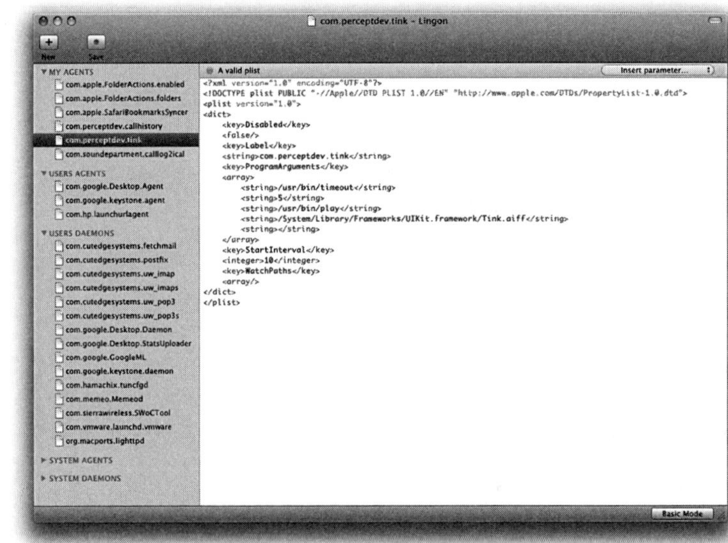

This output code can be easily copied and pasted into a plist file for your iPhone or iPod touch.

Create Periodic Backups with *launchd*

The backup script from **[Hack #11.02]** can be triggered on a schedule so that you don't have to remember to run your backup program. In this example, create */var/root/backup.sh*, and add timeouts in it for safety:

```
backup=/private/var/mobile/Library/CallHistory/call_history_`date +%Y%m%d_%H%M%S`.db
/usr/bin/timeout 10 cp /private/var/mobile/Library/CallHistory/call_history.db $backup
/usr/bin/timeout 20 gzip $backup
/usr/bin/timeout 60 scp $backup.gz iphonehacks@perceptdev.com:~/
```

Create the appropriate repeating task in Lingon (Figure 11-16). Select a 24-hour repeat (you could also choose "every day" from the specific date checkbox and choose a time of day), and check the box to run it at login.

Figure 11-16.
Creating a repeating task in Lingon

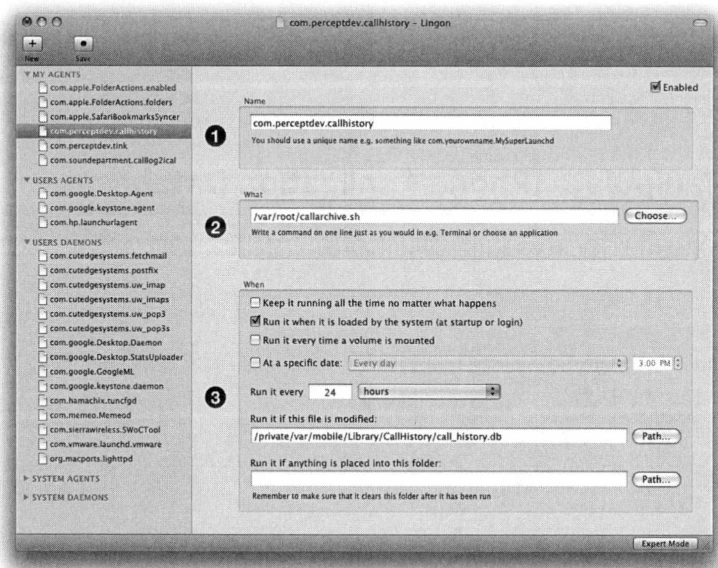

Then save the resulting plist file as */System/Library/LaunchDaemons/com.perceptdev.callhistory.plist*:

```
<?xml version="1.0" encoding="UTF-8"?>
<!DOCTYPE plist PUBLIC "-//Apple//DTD PLIST 1.0//EN"
  "http://www.apple.com/DTDs/PropertyList-1.0.dtd">
<plist version="1.0">
<dict>
        <key>Label</key>
    <string>com.perceptdev.callhistory</string>
    <key>ProgramArguments</key>
```

```
        <array>
            <string>/var/root/callarchive.sh</string>
        </array>
        <key>RunAtLoad</key>
        <true/>
        <key>StartInterval</key>
        <integer>86400</integer>
        <key>WatchPaths</key>
        <array>
            <string>/private/var/mobile/Library/CallHistory/call_history.db</string>
        </array>
    </dict>
    </plist>
```

Load it by running the *launchctl* load command:

```
launchctl load /System/Library/LaunchDaemons/com.perceptdev.callhistory.plist
```

Or simply reboot your phone. Either way, you'll now get an automatic backup of your call history whenever it is modified.

HACK 11.04: Manipulate iPhone Application Databases

You can back up and modify built-in iPhone application databases with SQLite.

Although preferences are usually stored in plists, many iPhone apps store their application data in SQLite database files (Figure 11-17).

Figure 11-17.
call_history.db

SQL, or Structured Query Language, is a database language developed by IBM in the early 1970s. It is now the de facto, universal standard for client-server databases worldwide. SQLite is a high-performance, local database engine that stores its data in files on disk or flash memory. It has become a standard tool for storing relational data on Mac OS X and is used by most of the built-in iPhone applications, such as Mail, Calendar, iTunes, Phone, and Address Book. Here is a list of some of the SQLite databases and their locations on the iPhone:

```
/Private/var/mobile/Library/CallHistory/call_history.db
/Private/var/mobile/Library/AddressBook/AddressBook.sqlitedb
/Private/var/mobile/Library/AddressBook/AddressBookImages.sqlitedb
/Private/var/mobile/Library/Calendar/Calendar.sqlitedb
/Private/var/mobile/Library/Notes/notes.db
/Private/var/mobile/Library/SMS/sms.db
```

A basic tutorial on using *sqlite3*, a command-line utility for manipulating sqlite databases, can be found at www.sqlite.org/sqlite.html.

Learning SQL

If you've ever worked with databases such as Oracle, Microsoft SQL, or MySQL, SQLite is very similar. It has a smaller subset of commands, because it isn't designed to serve files to millions of users over a network—just to a few programs on the same machine. SQL is a simple language used to ask for information from a database.

If you haven't worked with SQL before, it's okay—it's not that hard to pick up. For beginners, there's *Head First SQL*, by Lynn Beighley (O'Reilly, 2008). A good programmer's book on SQLite in particular is *Inside SQLite*, by Sibsankar Haldar.

Running SQLite

Even if you don't know SQL, you can follow these steps, and you'll pick up most of what's going on. First, install *sqlite3* in Cydia **[Hack #1.04]** Then log into your iPhone **[Hack #9.04]** and type:

```
# sqlite3 /private/var/mobile/Library/CallHistory/call_history.db
sqlite>
```

You can type `.help` to get a list of commands. `.table` shows you what tables (in SQL, data is organized into tables, which are tabular collections of data consisting of rows and columns) are in this database, and `.dump` will give you several screens worth of information showing the SQL commands to create the whole database, tables, and data entries from scratch.

The most common command you'll need is *select*, which shows you the contents of tables. You can see what is in each table with `select * from <table name>`:

```
sqlite> .tables
_SqliteDatabaseProperties  call
sqlite> select * from _SqliteDatabaseProperties;
call_history_limit|100
timer_last|420
timer_outgoing|220260
timer_incoming|193800
timer_all|414060
timer_lifetime|414060
timer_last_reset|0
data_up_last|101.5009765625
```

```
data_down_last|1145.037109375
data_up_all|31542.912109375
data_down_all|299468.912109468
data_up_lifetime|31542.912109375
data_down_lifetime|299468.912109468
data_last_reset|0
_ClientVersion|3
_UniqueIdentifier|571721D0-F5CA-46F7-A3D1-CC73EB96EE22
__CPRecordSequenceNumber|2644
sqlite> select * from call;
1351|3232544000|1231266047|0|5|3480
1352|3235541000|1231266052|0|5|4280
1353|13233812000|1231266056|0|5|2975
1354|32390880000|1231266061|0|5|2906
1355|3233812000|1231266066|0|5|2975
1356|3235541000|1231266071|0|5|4280
1357|3235541000|1231266266|0|5|4280
1358|8189088000|1231266271|0|5|2906
1359|8189088000|1231266452|0|5|2906
1360|3105541000|1231266456|0|5|4280
1361|3105541000|1231266461|0|5|4280
...
```

Browsing Databases with a GUI Application

If you've mounted your iPhone drive on your computer's filesystem **[Hack #9.06]**, or copied a *.db* file over to your computer, then you can use a SQLite file browser such as MesaSQLite (www.mesamysql.com/?realmesa_home) to view the iPhone files (Figure 11-18).

Figure 11-18.
Opening a Database File

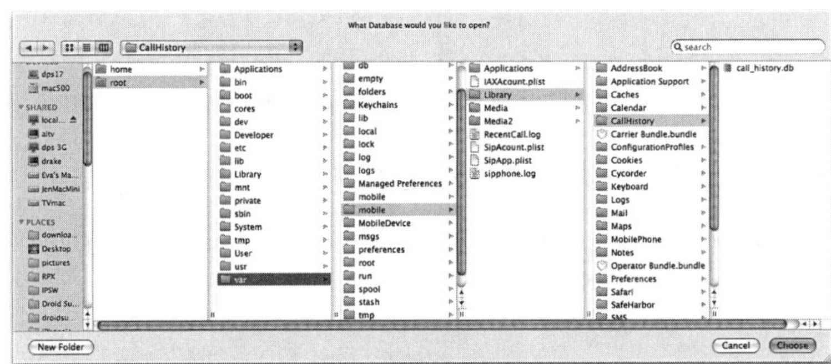

You can view all the entries of the call database by selecting *call* from the drop-down table menu, and clicking Show All (Figure 11-19). This executes the SQL query, shown in the bottom left, which is `select * from call`.

Figure 11-19.
`Select * from call` in MesaSQLite

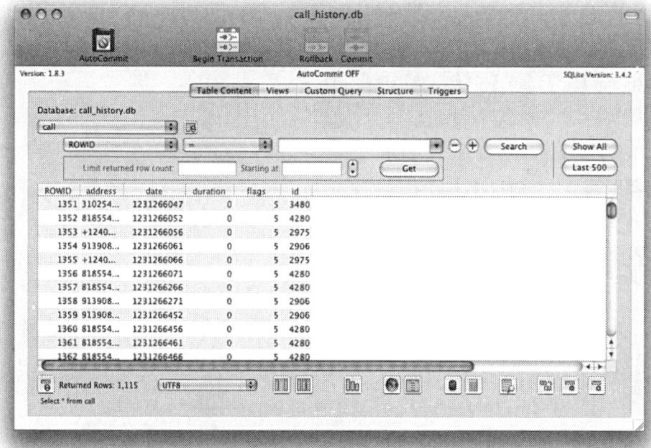

Extending the iPhone Call Database

The example `SQL` command showed us all the entries of the call database. Unfortunately, the iPhone trims this database to the last 50 entries, including dropped calls. Thus, for some heavy phone users, the log goes back only a day or two.

The following hack extends the call record so that it keeps all the calls. Even though the iPhone keeps trimming, this hack will save the deleted entries and reinsert them into the call table. Here's how it works:

1. Each time the */private/var/mobile/Library/CallHistory/call_history.db* is changed, trigger a script using *launchd* **[Hack #11.03]**.
2. In this script, create a new table called *archive* if it doesn't already exist, and copy all the new call records to *archive*.
3. If desired, copy the full *archive* table back over the *call* table, so that the whole list can be displayed.

The SQL commands to accomplish these steps are straightforward. You can download these scripts from www.perceptdev.com/labs/iphonehacks.

Here is the file that you should save as */var/root/callarchive.sh*:

```
# This script and associated SQL commands are released to the Public Domain
# this script runs a sqlite command to copy the most recent entries from the
# 'call' table to the 'archive' table
# the call_history.db must already have an 'archive' table with the same
# structure as 'call'
# you can do this by typing
#     sqlite3 /private/var/mobile/Library/CallHistory/call_history.db
#     create table if not exists archive as select * from call;
#
timeout 20 sqlite3 \
  /private/var/mobile/Library/CallHistory/call_history.db < \
  /var/root/archive.sqlcmds
timeout 5 play /var/mobile/Media/Tock.aiff
```

Here is the file that you should save as */var/root/archive.sqlcmds*:

```
create table if not exists archive as select * from call;
insert into archive select * from call
  where ROWID > (select max (ROWID) from archive)
  and ROWID <= (select max (ROWID) from call);
insert into call select * from archive
  where ROWID < (select min (ROWID) from call);
```

To test the script, simply run it at the command line. You should hear the "tock" sound:

```
# ./callarchive.sh
```

This will create the *archive* table (if it does not already exist) and make a backup of whatever is currently in your call history. Now, dial/hangup/dial/hangup a few times (you don't have to wait for the call to connect) to stuff the database full of entries.

Now run it again:

```
# ./callarchive.sh
```

Because the phone application may already have a cache of what is in the call database, you may need to run it, then hold the Home button for 10 seconds to force quit it **[Hack #2.02]**. Then launch it again. Now, if you dial a few numbers beyond the limit (50) you can scroll down and see that they are being retained.

You can create a background task **[Hack #11.03]** that is triggered whenever */private/var/mobile/Library/CallHistory/call_history.db* is modified to make sure that the archive table captures every call that is made. Then, even if the iPhone trims the main call table, *archive* will have a complete record. To do this, create a *launchd* file and put it in */Library/LaunchDaemons*:

Here is the file that you should save as */Library/LaunchDaemons/com.perceptdev.callarchive.plist*:

```
<?xml version="1.0" encoding="UTF-8"?>
<!DOCTYPE plist PUBLIC "-//Apple//DTD PLIST 1.0//EN" "http://www.apple.com/DTDs/
PropertyList-1.0.dtd">
<plist version="1.0">
<dict>
    <key>Label</key>
    <string>com.perceptdev.callarchive</string>
    <key>ProgramArguments</key>
    <array>
        <string>/var/root/callarchive.sh</string>
    </array>
    <key>StartInterval</key>
    <integer>86400</integer>
    <key>WatchPaths</key>
    <array>
        <string>/private/var/mobile/Library/CallHistory/call_history.db</string>
    </array>
```

```
    <key>RunAtLoad</key>
    <true/>
</dict>
</plist>
```

This script launches based on three different triggers: at load (RunAtLoad), every 24 hours (StartInterval), and whenever the database file is written to (WatchPaths).

To test it, you can dial a number and hang up quickly. Whenever you finish a call, the phone should "tock." You may need to occasionally restart the phone application as described previously to get the list to show up, but each tock means that the archive is being faithfully kept. You should be able to scroll a very long call list.

— Damien Stolarz & Devananda Van Der Veen

 HACK 11.05: Sync Your Call Log with iCal on Mac OS X

Using a script on your Mac OS X machine, you can import your call log records into iCal.

If you're one of those people who like to keep track of everything in your calendar program, you may have wondered why the iPhone doesn't put the call log right into iCal. The call log database is stored separately and differently than the calendar database on the phone, and there's nothing there to keep them in sync.

One way to approach the problem would be to create a script that runs on the phone and does all the necessary syncing. However, someone has already tackled the problem.

iphonelogd

There's a great Ruby script developed by Jamie Hardt available at http://code.google.com/p/iphonelogd called *calllog2ical.rb*. It accomplishes the laudable goal of importing call records from an iPhone backup by iTunes, into iCal, on Mac OS X 10.5.

This approach is great, but it has some drawbacks. First, if you have a lot of different devices that sync to your Mac, then the script doesn't always know which one to grab the call records from. Second, and through no fault of the script, the iPhone tends to delete records much more frequently than many people sync to iTunes.

The elements of a solution, however, have already been discussed. [Hack #11.02] showed you how to back up the call log. And [Hack #11.03] showed how to do it on a schedule. If you've implemented those hacks, your call log should be very long and safely stored somewhere. Now we just need to import it!

To import the call logs, we're going to:

1. Upload the Address Book and call logs from the iPhone to a web server.
2. Download the Address Book and call logs from the server to the Mac.
3. Import them into iCal.

iPhone to Server

In order to properly show the name of who called—instead of just the phone number—it's necessary to get a copy of */Private/var/mobile/Library/AddressBook/AddressBook.sqlitedb* from the iPhone as well. We'll update our script from **[Hack #11.01]** to add uploads for both these files. For cleanliness, we'll create two files: *callarchive.sh* and *callarchive-do.sh*. That way we can call them from an app, or a task, and the parent script will take care of timeouts.

Here's what needs to go into */var/root/callarchive.sh* (edit with nano **[Hack #11.04]** or on your computer):

```
/usr/bin/timeout 60  /var/root/callarchive-do.sh
```

Here is the contents of */var/root/callarchive-do.sh*:

```
# This script and associated SQL commands are released to the Public Domain
# this script runs a sqlite command to copy the most recent entries from
# the 'call' table to the 'archive' table
# the call_history.db must already have an 'archive' table with the same
# structure as 'call'
# you can do this by typing
#     sqlite3 /private/var/mobile/Library/CallHistory/call_history.db
# create table if not exists archive as select * from call;
sqlite3 /private/var/mobile/Library/CallHistory/call_history.db < \
  /var/root/archive.sqlcmds
scp /private/var/mobile/Library/CallHistory/call_history.db \
  iphonehacks@perceptdev.com:~/
scp /private/var/mobile/Library/AddressBook/AddressBook.sqlitedb \
  iphonehacks@perceptdev.com:~/
```

The *callarchive-do.sh script* can be launched manually from an application **[Hack #11.01]** or a *launchd* task **[Hack #11.03]**:

```
# ./callarchive.sh
call_history.db                100%  103KB 103.0KB/s   00:00
AddressBook.sqlitedb           100% 1093KB 182.2KB/s   00:06
```

In our testing, the call log was over 100K and the Address Book was over a megabyte—not something you want to upload from an original iPhone over EDGE. If you're going to automate this in a *launchd* task, you may want to upload the Address Book once, and then only upload the *call_history.db* on a schedule.

Server to Mac

You'll need to choose a working directory on the Mac to which you'll download the files and run your import script. Copy the relevant files down to your Mac with the following commands in Terminal:

```
# scp iphonehacks@perceptdev.com:~/call_history.db .
Password: ********
call_history.db           100%  103KB 103.0KB/s   00:00
# scp iphonehacks@perceptdev.com:~/AddressBook.sqlitedb .
Password: ********
AddressBook.sqlitedb        100% 1093KB   1.1MB/s   00:00
```

If you don't want to bother with copying it to the server first, you can simply copy it directly from your iPhone to your computer. However, as our earlier hacks made a convenient way to back it up to the server, you could automate the rest of the task and have the call records in iCal automatically.

Import to iCal

The only parts of the original *icalllog2ical.rb* Ruby script that have been changed are the pieces that load and extract the call log database from the iPhone backup. The other parts that do the import and iCal feeding are unmodified.

Our modifications to *calllog2ical2.rb*, change the script so that it loads the call log and Address Book from the same directory it's run in, instead of from the iPhone backups made by iTunes. The modified script can be found at www.perceptdev.com/labs/iphonehacks. The original import script and our modifications are licensed under GPL v2.

Put the databases you just downloaded and *calllog2ical2.rb* in the same folder. Then launch the iCal application and create a new calendar named "iPhone." You will use this command as the argument to *calllog2ical2.rb*.

Go back to terminal, and run the import.

```
$ ./calllog2ical2.rb iPhone
```

You can switch back to iCal and watch as it fills in the calls (Figure 11-20). Depending on the length of your call log, this will take several minutes. The script is somewhat smart about starting where it left off last. You should not add any other entries to this calendar manually, as that will confuse the script.

Figure 11-20.
Call logs in iCal

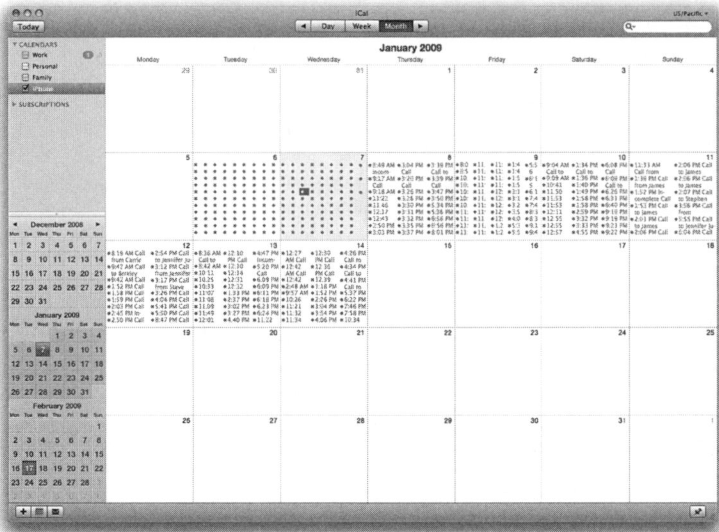

The script has some additional options: you can exclude specific phone numbers ("I didn't call her, I swear!") and eliminate zero-duration calls (like calls that failed, or accidental dial/hangups). You can see some of the options when you run the script with the help (`-h`) argument:

```
$ ./calllog2ical2.rb -h
Usage : calllog2ical.rb [options] [CALENDARNAME]
    -v, --verbose                    Run verbosely
    -l, --leave-db                   Leave the extracted working sqlite files
                                     in their temporary location instead of
                                     deleting.
    -e, --exclude-number NUMBER      Exclude calls from the given number
    -x, --exclude-file EXCLUDE-FILE  Exclude calls listed in EXCLUDE-FILE.
                                     EXCLUDE-FILE should contain a whitespace-
                                     separated list of telephone numbers.
    -f, --force DATE                 Force calendar to be updated with all call
                                     log events since DATE, deleting all events
                                     after DATE before going through the normal
                                     read process
    -0                               Don't copy events with zero duration.
                                     (Incomplete/Unanswered calls)
    -h, -?                           Show this message.
```

If you zoom into specific days, you can see where all that time goes. Maybe it's time to sign up for an unlimited all-you-can-talk plan (Figure 11-21).

Figure 11-21.
Call log database visualized in iCal by week

Figure 11-22 shows a day view. You can uncheck the calendar titled "iPhone" if you want to remove all the clutter (Figure 11-23). You can stop making so many phone calls if you *really* want to remove all the clutter.

Figure 11-22.
Day view

Figure 11-23.
Call log off

HACK 11.06: Choose Between the Apple SDK and Open Tools for iPhone Development

Despite what Apple would like you to believe, the official SDK is not the only game in town.

So you have an idea for an iPhone application. One of the first decisions you must make as a would-be iPhone developer is which SDK to use. This decision has lasting implications, because it determines what frameworks you can access, what features your application is allowed to have, and ultimately who can install it on their phones.

It seems unfair to have to make such an important decision so early, particularly if you've never written an iPhone application before. Fortunately, you can reverse your decision later—nothing is set in stone—but as you'll see, switching SDKs may require some significant code changes if you don't plan ahead. Also, using the Apple SDK requires you to sign a licensing agreement. So it's important to make the right choice early on.

The Contenders

The *iPhone open toolchain* (generally just referred to as the "toolchain") was the first development kit released for the iPhone. It was pieced together from a variety of open source projects, with a lot of modifications and original code written by a dedicated group of coders and hackers. Apple didn't make it easy—once the phone was jailbroken [Hack #1.03] to allow access to the filesystem so that files could be added and modified, there was also the problem of Apple's modified compiler based on an outdated version of `gcc`, for which the modified source code had not yet been released. Herculean efforts were required to circumvent these problems and create working tools (for further details you can read Jay "**saurik**" Freeman's detailed account of the process at www.saurik.com/id/4). The result of all this work is a suite of tools that are both incredibly powerful and incredibly complex.

Apple's *iPhone SDK* entered beta testing in March 2008, after the open toolchain had enjoyed months of success, and many thousands of iPhones were already jailbroken and running applications. The SDK features a variety of useful tools and a fairly simple install process, as well as a thorough set of documentation. The streamlined APIs are more accessible and easier to understand. But the SDK also imposes strict limits on developers, and deliberately restricts access to some of the more powerful aspects of the iPhone's firmware.

Choosing one development environment over the other is not a clear-cut decision, and there are several factors to consider.

Cost

The open toolchain is open source and completely free. The iPhone SDK is also free to download, but you are required to sign up (for free) as a Registered iPhone Developer, which means you are subject to the terms of Apple's developer agreement. The Official SDK also does not allow you to test applications on the phone without a code signing certificate. Apple provides these certificates only to members of the iPhone Developer Program. (The program also provides other benefits, including distribution on the iTunes App Store and access to prerelease firmware.) Membership costs $99 for the Standard program. The Enterprise program, targeted at businesses wishing to develop proprietary in-house software, costs $299.

Documentation

When the open toolchain was first reverse-engineered from the iPhone firmware, all of the iPhone's internal frameworks were exposed. The API headers that were generated were functionally complete but lacking in documentation, and some of the original names and data types could not be recovered from the compiled binaries. Because the iPhone OS is based on Mac OS X, some of the APIs were already familiar to developers on the Mac platform. But many frameworks specific to the iPhone, even though they are available through the toolchain, are difficult to use, because they simply haven't been fully explored and documented.

This issue was particularly problematic before the release of Apple's official SDK, because the Version 1.x firmware was significantly different from 2.x. Its APIs were not intended for public use, so they were not as carefully designed as one might hope, and sometimes difficult to grasp based solely on the class interfaces. Even one of the most essential frameworks, UIKit (which provide the

GUI for iPhone apps) was not completely understood in firmware Version 1.x, and documentation was sparse. Developers wishing to use any but the most common classes were in for a struggle.

With the release of the iPhone SDK, official documentation is now available for the public frameworks and classes in firmware v2.x. (However, many of these classes have changed significantly from their 1.x counterparts, including those in the UIKit framework, so the SDK offers little insight for those targeting older 1.x firmware versions.) For developers targeting jailbroken 2.x firmware via the toolchain, the SDK documentation can be quite helpful—at least as a starting point.

Features and Limitations

The SDK includes an iPhone simulator (Figure 11-24), and an integrated debugger that works with apps running on either the simulator or the device. The toolchain has neither. However, if you are targeting the Version 2.x firmware, you may still be able to test your toolchain code on the simulator, as long as the code uses mainly the unrestricted frameworks of the SDK. (Some of the frameworks are too difficult to simulate without cell phone hardware, and are therefore understandably absent.) The toolchain can also be integrated into Xcode, allowing toolchain apps to be debugged on jailbroken devices using the integrated debugger.

Figure 11-24.
The iPhone Simulator

The iPhone SDK also comes with Interface Builder, a graphical layout application for user interfaces. It is a powerful tool, though it has a bit of a learning curve for those accustomed to a fully integrated interface designer like the one in Microsoft's Visual Studio. Using it can be a great boon to those who plan to distribute through the App Store, but those who are considering unofficial distribution should beware. The toolchain has no way to compile Interface Builder's *.xib* files, which forces you to use Xcode for at least part of the build process. If you're contemplating the option of targeting jailbroken phones, you should therefore consider creating your user interface programmatically (Apple's APIs are quite capable in this regard) rather than using Interface Builder.

The iPhone SDK exposes many of the frameworks that are present on the iPhone, but several frameworks are private, and third-party (that's you) applications are forbidden to use them. Some examples include:

- BluetoothManager—interface to the iPhone's Bluetooth hardware
- Celestial—a streaming audio framework
- CoreSurface—access low-level graphics buffers directly
- CoreTelephony—interface to the iPhone's cellular telephony hardware
- LayerKit—layer-based graphics compositing
- WebKit—the web browsing and rendering framework that powers Safari

There are workarounds that can expose these APIs—usually by splicing **[Hack #11.15]** toolchain headers into the SDK—but Apple has stated that applications that use private frameworks will not be distributed on the iTunes App Store. To be fair, many of these functions can be accessed at a higher level of granularity through public frameworks, and some developers will not miss them. Still, certain applications requiring fine-grained control of these functions will be severely hampered by this restriction.

Many classes and even individual class methods have also been left out of the official headers, even when the overall framework is made public. Some of these hidden objects and methods can also be accessed by splicing toolchain headers into the SDK, or by using the `class-dump` tool to generate new headers. It is not clear whether Apple would prohibit this use of undocumented classes and methods in public frameworks, nor is it clear whether they are capable of detecting it. Google, for example, has successfully published an application that clearly uses undocumented functions—but not prohibited ones—and so far Apple has not chosen to remove the app from the store.

Toolchain applications are completely unrestricted, and can use any known framework—but again, many of the private frameworks are poorly documented.

Official SDK applications are also subject to certain technical restrictions due to Apple's sandboxing security model. Applications have limited file access rights, except in their own dedicated folders. They cannot access the iTunes library content stored on the phone, or any data stored by other applications, unless a public framework exposes it (like the Address Book). They are also unable to run as background processes; the application is forced to close when it loses focus. All of these are deliberate design choices and Apple is unlikely to reverse their decision in the future. Toolchain applications running on jailbroken phones have no such restrictions.

There are additional terms-of-use restrictions on the App Store that some developers will find onerous:

- Applications cannot use excessive bandwidth, especially on the cellular network (the precise threshold which constitutes "excessive" is not known).
- Applications cannot execute other program code (e.g., emulators, VMs, and other runtime engines like Flash or .NET).

Also note that Apple's licensing terms may conflict with certain open source licenses. For example, Apple's code signing policies would seem to violate the terms of GPLv3. If you plan to bring an open source project to the iPhone and distribute it through official channels, you should make sure that your open source license is compatible with Apple's terms.

As for toolchain applications, *Installer.app* and Cydia distributors will probably accept any kind of application except malware.

A final note on software license issues: although the binary tools in the toolchain, such as the compiler and linker, are based on open source projects and are compliant with their licenses, it is important to realize that the header files may not be so unencumbered. Current versions of the toolchain depend on headers that must be copied from the official SDK, which means they are subject to licensing restrictions. For now it is common practice to ignore this hiccup, but in order to achieve greater legitimacy, the open toolchain development community may need to put some effort into reverse-engineering their own header files, using tools like `class-dump-x`, so that the Apple SDK can be avoided entirely if so desired.

Distribution

Developing an application for the Official iPhone SDK gives you the opportunity to distribute your application through the iTunes App Store. If you choose to charge for your application, Apple's cut of the purchase price is 30%; free apps are distributed without any additional charge. (This is in addition to the $99 membership fee for the Developer Program.) In return, you get to use Apple's considerable digital sales and distribution muscle, including payment processing, server hosting for your app's installation bundle, and a store listing, all handled for you automatically. Your widest possible audience encompasses anyone who has firmware Version 2.0 or later—an audience that is increasing over time as the iPhone 3G is being sold with 2.x preinstalled.

Toolchain applications on 1.x firmware were most often distributed through Installer.app. Since the debut of 2.0 jailbreaking methods, a new premier player in this space has emerged, the aforementioned Cydia, which is a user-friendly front end for Debian's APT package manager. The two differ in their implementation of packaging schemes, list formats, and other details, but the essential purpose and features are similar. Because many software jailbreaks load one or both of these installers onto the phone automatically, this is the best-known and most popular method for obtaining third-party applications outside of the App Store.

Lag Time

Developer Program members targeting the Official SDK have access to prerelease versions of the firmware and matching development kits before the firmware is made available to the public. This means that you have a chance to update your application to take advantage of the new firmware, and hopefully you can have the new version ready for release as soon as the firmware goes public.

Toolchain developers, on the other hand, must wait for the new firmware to be jailbroken (which may take some time after the public release) and for the toolchain to be updated with any new APIs. Clever hackers may find ways to gain access to the upcoming firmware and prepare for it ahead of time, but unless you can access the prerelease firmware yourself and test against it, you may still experience significant lag time before you can release your updated application. The lag is particularly noticeable when significant API changes occur, such as during the transition from v1.x to v2.0 firmware. It leaves toolchain developers stuck in a waiting game, knowing that new documentation and classes are available that would make their lives easier, but being unable to take advantage of those upgrades until after the firmware is released and jailbroken.

On the other hand, developers who use the App Store sometimes run into a different kind of lag. Apple's manual approval process can cause a significant delay between the time you submit your app (or an updated version of it) and the time it is accepted and made available through the store. Though Apple insists that it is making great efforts to streamline the process, there are still horror stories circulating around the Internet. The unpredictability of this phenomenon can wreak havoc with outside marketing schedules, not to mention inducing a lot of indigestion, as hapless victims anxiously await judgment from the fickle gods at Apple's approval department.

To Each His Own

Ultimately, the choice of Apple's official SDK vs. the open toolchain is one that you have to make for yourself, based on your application's needs and your intended audience. You may need total access to the phone's filesystem; you may need the infrastructure of the App Store; or you may simply prefer the independent spirit of the toolchain developers. Whatever you decide, there is a whole community of iPhone users out there waiting to see what you have to offer.

— George Dean IV

> **QUICK HACK**
>
> **SEE MORE DEVICE INFORMATION IN ITUNES**
>
> The Summary screen in iTunes can be used to get more information about your device. Click on the Capacity bar at the bottom to see how many items are on the phone, the length of existing playtime, or the amount of memory used. Click on the words "Software Version," "Serial Number," or "Phone Number" at the top to see additional technical information. This can be an easy way to get the phone identifier if you need to send it to a developer.

HACK 11.07: Develop iPhone Applications with Apple's SDK

The most comfortable way to develop iPhone apps is with Xcode.

Apple's SDK is based on the Xcode suite, which is the primary development kit for Mac OS X. Under the hood, the Xcode IDE is simply invoking Apple's version of the GCC compiler. Regardless of whether you're developing for the open toolchain or the App Store, there is strong incentive to use these official tools, particularly for simulation and debugging.

Downloading and Installing the SDK

If you don't have the SDK already, you can get it from Apple at http://developer.apple.com/iphone. You'll have to register for a developer account and agree to some licensing terms, but it's free of charge.

The SDK is packaged as a disk image file (*.dmg*), which Finder will mount as a virtual disk. To install the SDK, launch the package installer located in the virtual disk (Figure 11-25).

Figure 11-25.
Apple's iPhone SDK installer

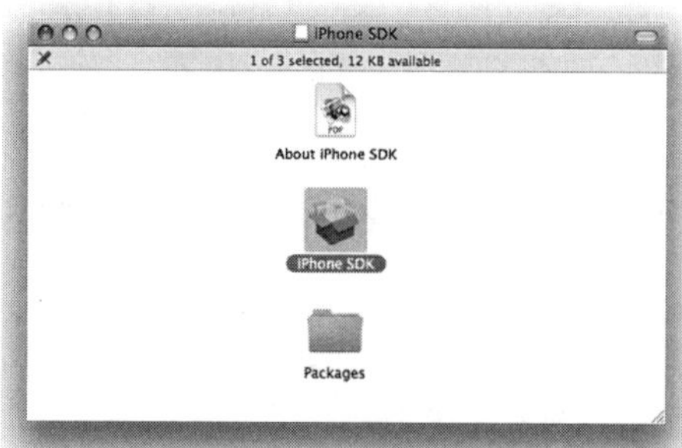

Once the SDK is installed, you will find the suite of applications and tools in */Developer/Applications*. Xcode, the main IDE, is the one you will use most often, and you'll probably want to drag it to your Dock right away (Figure 11-26).

Figure 11-26.
Xcode

Building the UICatalog Sample

Let's build one of Apple's sample applications. The one we'll use in this example is UICatalog, which is a demonstration of just about every built-in user interface element that's available on the iPhone, as well as some of the configuration options that you can use to customize their appearance and behavior. It has also been ported to the iPhone open toolchain already, and can be built on both Linux **[Hack #11.10]** and iPhone **[Hack #11.11]**, so it will be our universal example for all three platforms.

In Xcode, open the Documentation window by choosing Help→Documentation from the menu (or you can press Command-Option-Shift-?) (Figure 11-27).

Figure 11-27.
Documentation window

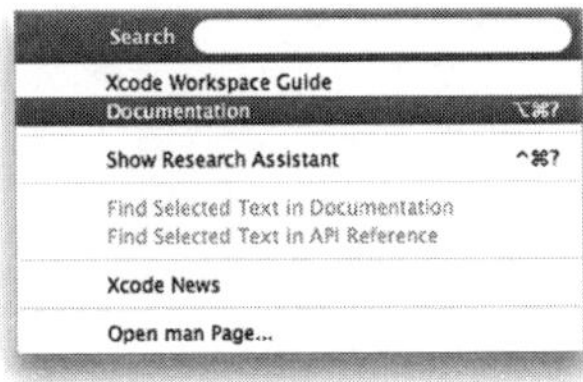

In the Documentation window, type UICatalog into the search box and press Enter. The first entry in the results list should be the UICatalog sample application. Choose that result, and scroll down the page to the "Download Sample" links (Figure 11-28).

Figure 11-28.
Download sample

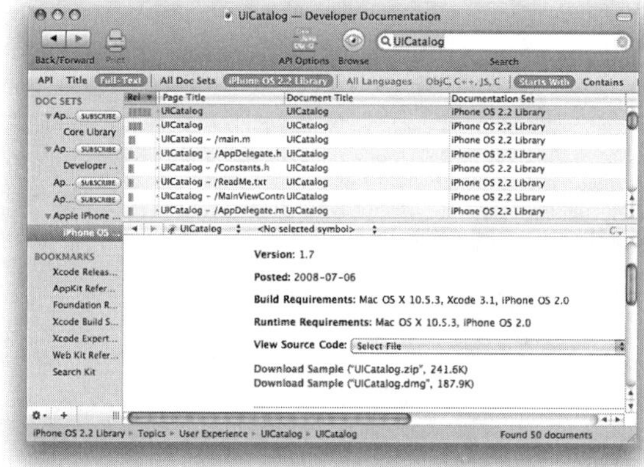

Alternatively, you could visit the iPhone Dev Center at http://developer.apple.com/iphone and download the sample directly from the website.

You can get the sample code as either a DMG or a ZIP archive. Download and unpack the contents to a new folder.

One of the files in the archive is an Xcode project file called *UICatalog.xcodeproj*. Open this. The Xcode project window will appear (Figure 11-29).

Figure 11-29.
Xcode project window

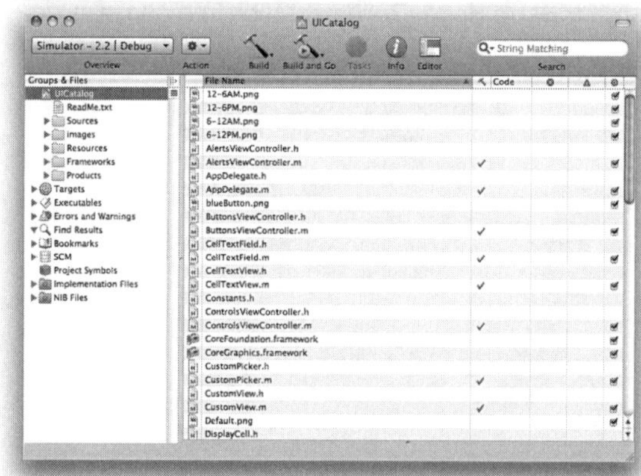

Open the Build Configuration drop-down list in the upper-left corner of the project window, and make sure that the Active SDK is Simulator—iPhone OS 2.2, or whichever the most recent SDK version is (Figure 11-30).

Figure 11-30.
Choosing the Active SDK

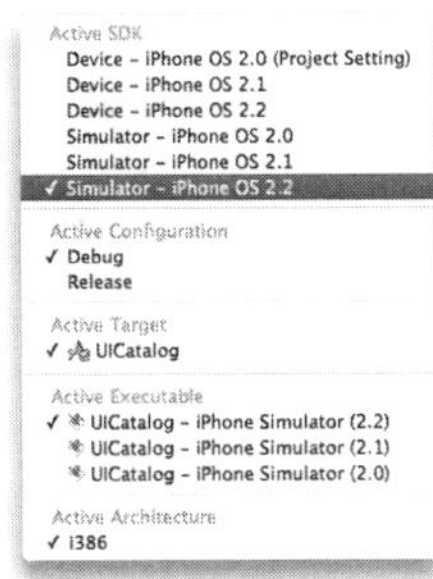

Now you can click Build and Go (or press Command-Enter), and the project will be compiled and launched in the iPhone Simulator (Figure 11-31).

Figure 11-31.
The iPhone simulator

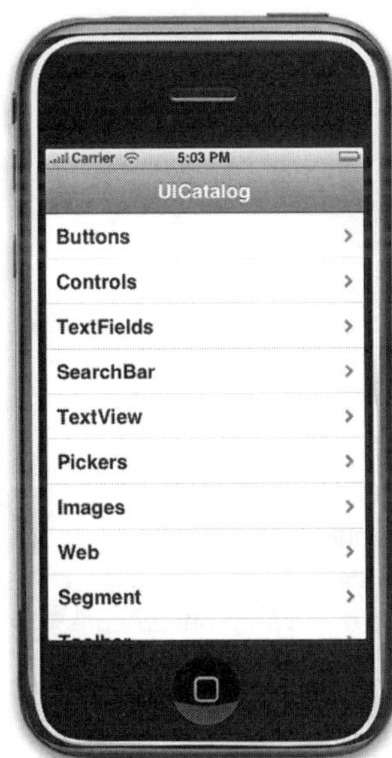

The iPhone simulator is a convenient tool for testing your applications before installing them on the actual device. It has faster turnaround than a full deployment to the phone (which can take several seconds to complete over USB), so it is well suited to testing rapidly iterated changes that require many rebuild cycles. It also has no provisioning requirements, so it is easier to set up than a real deployment. However, the simulator is not an emulator, so the performance characteristics and memory footprint of your simulated application will bear little resemblance to the actual conditions on the device. Also, although most of the frameworks function identically in both the simulator and the real firmware, there are some major and minor differences (in both public and private APIs) that will cause problems if you depend too heavily on the simulator for testing. Ultimately, you will need to go beyond the simulator and deploy your application to a real device.

Install the UICatalog Sample on the Device

In order to install your applications to the iPhone with the Apple SDK, you must have a valid *provisioning profile*. This profile combines your code-signing identity with a list of *unique device identifiers* that determines which devices are allowed to install and run your application. In order to create a provisioning profile, you must be a member of one of Apple's paid developer programs, either Standard ($99) or Enterprise ($299). Creating this profile is a lengthy process that is spelled out in the How To tab of the Provisioning section of the Developer Program Portal, accessible at http://developer.apple.com/iphone.

If you don't have a provisioning profile, there are ways to work around the requirement, as described in **[Hack #11.08]**.

Once the provisioning situation is taken care of, you're ready to build and install the UICatalog sample to the device. You simply need to select Device → iPhone OS 2.2 (or the most recent SDK version) as the active SDK from the Build Configuration drop-down list. Then click Build and Go to build, install, and launch the application on your iPhone.

— George Dean IV

 HACK 11.08: Self-Sign Your SDK Projects

You can build and deploy SDK apps to your jailbroken phone with your own code certificate.

With the Apple SDK, you usually have to provision a device to test your code on it. If you have SDK-based code working and you want to test it on your jailbroken iPhone or iPod touch, you can self-sign the code and skip the provisioning.

The iPhone uses three basic security restrictions to keep unauthorized code from running on the platform. The first restriction, the *chroot jail*, keeps the user from making any significant modifications to the filesystem, and it is overcome by jailbreaking **[Hack #1.03]**. The second restriction, *code signing*, ensures both file integrity and authentication of the program author's identity. Jailbreaks eliminate the authentication check, but they leave the integrity checking intact (because the integrity information is easy to generate and the checks for it are widespread and difficult to disable). The third restriction, *provisioning*, determines whether the application is authorized to run on a particular device. This restriction is overcome by modifying the MobileInstallation framework.

You need to install and run at least one app from the App Store before you try this, or these workarounds may fail. It can be a free or paid app—it just needs to be from the real App Store.

Code Signing with Self-Signed Certificates

There are two main ways to self-sign your code. When using Xcode, the simplest method is to set a *self-signed certificate* as your signing identity. Xcode will use this certificate to sign your executables, with the result that all the integrity-checking information is properly generated but the rest of the signature is invalid. On a jailbroken phone, this is fine, because the rest of the signature will be ignored anyway.

To generate a self-signed certificate, you can follow the steps in Apple's guide at http://developer.apple.com/documentation/Security/Conceptual/CodeSigningGuide/Procedures/chapter_3_section_2.html. When creating the self-signing identity, take careful note of the name you used when creating the certificate, because you'll need it in the next step.

Next, open up your Xcode project in order to set the new code signing identity. With the project open, go to Project→Edit Project Settings. Find the setting called Code Signing Identity: Any iPhone OS Device, click the value field, and select Other from the menu that pops up. Now change the value to the exact name you used when creating the self-signing identity (Figure 11-32), and hit OK to save the new setting. This should configure the project to use the new identity.

Figure 11-32.
Self-signing certificates in Xcode

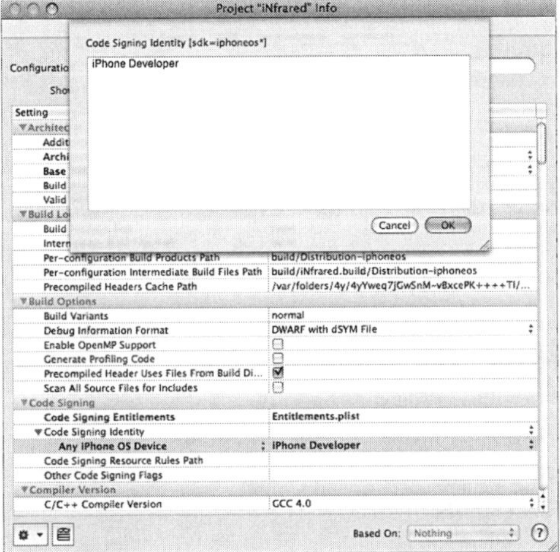

You may have to restart Xcode or reboot your computer after these changes.

Code Signing with *ldid*

Self-signed certificates solve the code signing problem only when you're running Xcode. For other platforms, there is a program called *ldid* that is used to create fake code signing data from scratch. You can get it from Cydia under the name Link Identity Editor. To sign an unsigned binary, invoke it with the `-S` parameter:

```
$ ldid -S <program file>
```

Most Makefiles for iPhone projects already invoke *ldid* in this way during the install phase. If you're creating your own Makefile for a project, or porting a project from another platform, you'll probably want to add this step in order to save yourself some typing, otherwise you would have to invoke *ldid* yourself after every make.

Disable Provisioning in Xcode

The automated install process on the iPhone relies on provisioning profiles to determine whether the application is authorized. Because Xcode is designed to use this automated process, it requires a valid provisioning profile when building an app for the device. You can disable this requirement, however, by editing a certain property list [Hack #11.02]:

```
/Developer/Platforms/iPhoneOS.platform/Info.plist
```

Be sure to back up the original before you make any changes. Open the file in a text editor or plist editor and add the highlighted entries shown here:

```
<key>NATIVE_ARCH</key>
<string>armv6</string>
<key>PLIST_FILE_OUTPUT_FORMAT</key>
<string>binary</string>
<key>PROVISIONING_PROFILE_ALLOWED</key>
<string>NO</string>
<key>PROVISIONING_PROFILE_REQUIRED</key>
<string>NO</string>
<key>SDKROOT</key>
<string>iphoneos2.2</string>
```

Save it, and restart Xcode. You should be able to build your project in device mode without setting a provisioning profile.

Disable Provisioning Checks on the iPhone

When iTunes or Xcode attempts to automatically install an application, the phone uses the MobileInstallation framework to verify that the device is authorized to run the application based on the provisioning profile. Disabling this check, so that any application can be installed by iTunes or Xcode, requires a modification to the MobileInstallation binary file.

Fortunately, iPhone developer **javacom** of http://iphonesdkdev.blogspot.com provides an automated patcher that can be installed through Cydia. First, add the correct server to your Cydia source list:

Once the source is added to Cydia, you can install the package named MobileInstallation Patch, which will apply the patch and disable the provisioning checks.

A new MobileInstallation patch must be issued for each firmware release, but so far the updates have been prompt. You can check for the latest news at the blog URL given earlier in this hack, or at this post on the Hackint0sh forums [Hack #2.06], which is kept up to date with the latest MobileInstallation patch announcements: http://hackint0sh.org/forum/showpost.php?p=340693&postcount=14.

— George Dean IV

HACK 11.08: Manually Install Applications

The Xcode "Build and Go" method isn't the only way to install your applications on the iPhone.

Once you've built your application (or if you've manually downloaded an app from someone else), you'll need some way to get it onto the phone. If you're using the Official SDK, and all your provisioning ducks are in a row, this would be a job for Xcode or iTunes. But there is an alternative to this automated process, using a Unix tool called `scp`.

First, find out what your phone's IP address is. You can get this from the built-in Settings app, or from another control panel app like BossPrefs.

Your computer and your iPhone should be on the same Wi-Fi network. You'll also need to make sure that SSH is installed and enabled on your phone, as `scp` uses the SSH protocol to communicate with the phone. You can check this in BossPrefs as well.

Next, open a Terminal window on your computer, and navigate to the parent directory that contains the *.app* bundle you wish to install. Now it's time to invoke `scp` (which is short for "**s**ecure **c**o**p**y"). The command looks like this:

```
$ scp -r YourApplication.app root@192.168.0.101:/Applications/
```

where *`YourApplication`*`.app` is the name of your application bundle, and *`192.168.0.101`* is the IP address of the phone. Just substitute the correct values for your application and phone. Be ready to type in the root password, which by default is *alpine* **[Hack #9.04]**.

Once the copy is complete, the final step is to reinitialize SpringBoard (the iPhone application launcher) so that it will detect your application and show its icon. You could turn off your phone and reboot it, but that takes some time. Fortunately you can soft-reset SpringBoard with *respring*, which you can invoke from the command line or through the UI. For details on how to install and use *respring*, see **[Hack #11.12]**.

Once SpringBoard restarts, your application icon should be visible, and you're ready to run.

Although it's important to understand these steps in principle, usually this process will be automated in your Makefiles, when you invoke the `install` target on your development computer:

```
$ make install
```

The `install` target typically uses scp to copy the files, *ldid* to fake the code signing, and finally *respring* to restart SpringBoard. But if `make install` fails, or you need to customize your Makefile, you'll need to know what the steps are.

— George Dean IV

HACK 11.10: Use a Virtual Machine for Building iPhone Apps

You can develop jailbroken apps for the iPhone, even if you don't own a Mac.

Apple's official SDK requires Mac OS X; developers who exclusively use other platforms are out of luck. But there are still ways to do the bulk of your coding on other platforms. For example, you could use a portability layer to hide the platform-specific details, like developer Chad W. Randall of Just Kissed Games. He wrote his own framework to simulate the iPhone on Windows so that he could develop in the familiar environment of Microsoft Visual Studio. (The resulting game, Beseigement, can be found in the App Store; the official website is at www.beseigementgame.com.)

Still, even with a portability framework, you must ultimately move the code over to a Mac in order to build the app with the SDK. But if you're thinking of creating apps with the open toolchain, the possibilities are practically endless. The open source tools that make up the toolchain are highly portable and can be built on a variety of platforms, including Linux.

If you want to work through the entire process of building the toolchain on Linux, you can find a complete walkthrough on Jay "saurik" Freeman's website at www.saurik.com/id/4. However, this is a slow and painstaking process, involving many of the sort of command-line machinations that Unix geniuses consider expedient, but that baffle the rest of us.

There is a much easier solution, if you have the ability to run virtual machines. (VMware has some excellent free tools for both Linux and Windows at www.vmware.com.) Some clever toolchain developers have created preconfigured virtual machines that contain a working toolchain running on a Linux guest OS. As these are updated frequently, links change. An Internet search for "vmware iphone toolchain" will reveal sites like http://hackint0sh.org/forum/showthread.php?t=26548, which has instructions and links for obtaining one of these images as of this writing. You can also appeal to the iPhone community **[Hack #2.06]**, which will direct you to the latest tools.

Downloading and Configuring the VM

This particular VM is hosted at http://iphonefix.de. You'll have to visit the website first to get a login/password for their FTP server—the site's administrators have disabled anonymous access for security and performance reasons. Once you have the session-specific username and password, you can download the image by navigating to the iPhone Toolchain VMware Image.

You may want to use a dedicated FTP program (Figure 11-33), as the file weighs in at more 1.2 GB, so that downloads can be resumed if they get interrupted.

Figure 11-33.
Using an FTP program to download the toolchain

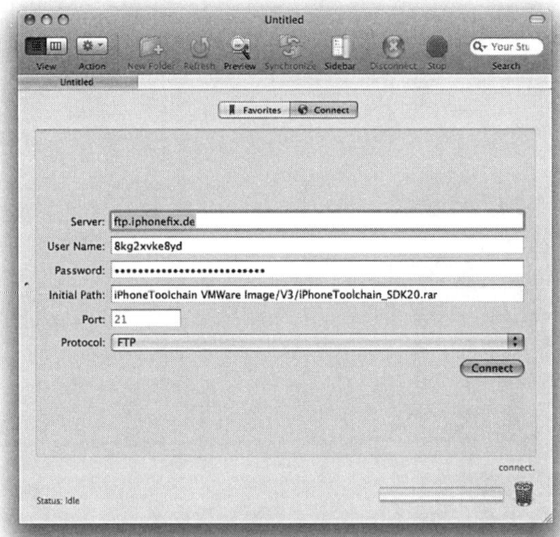

Once you have the iPhone Toolchain VMware image, launch it (Figure 11-34). It contains a command-line-only Ubuntu Linux installation. The root password is *toolchain*.

Figure 11-34.
VMware launch screen

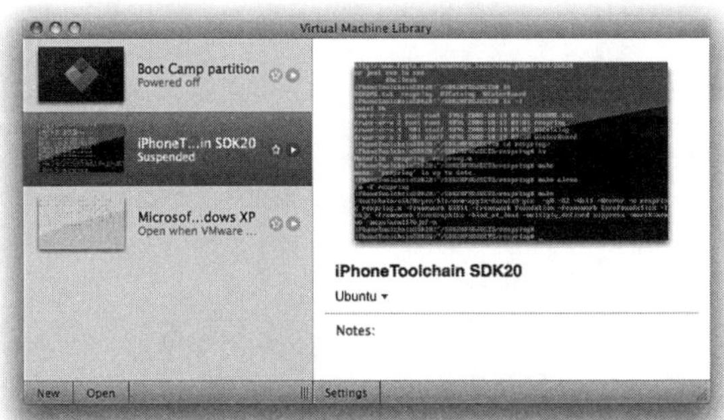

Next, configure networking. In VMware's network settings, configure this machine to use shared networking (NAT) or bridged networking. You can use this command to examine your VM's network adapters:

```
$ ifconfig -a
```

Inside the guest OS, your Ethernet adapter may come up as `eth0`, or `eth4`, or some other `eth` device. Cloning a VMware image can cause a new device to be detected, so if you're having trouble you can delete the file */etc/udev/rules.d/z25_persistent-net.rules* (which stores the various detected Ethernet devices) and reboot, and it should let Linux find your `eth0` device.

If your VM's Ethernet device does not list an IP address, you can try to enable DHCP by running `dhclient` (Figure 11-35). If this approach successfully obtains an IP address for the network adapter, you can check it by running `ifconfig` again.

Figure 11-35.
Running `dhclient`

```
iPhoneToolchain SDK20
64 bytes from localhost (127.0.0.1): icmp_seq=1 ttl=64 time=0.062 ms
64 bytes from localhost (127.0.0.1): icmp_seq=2 ttl=64 time=0.112 ms

--- localhost ping statistics ---
2 packets transmitted, 2 received, 0% packet loss, time 1003ms
rtt min/avg/max/mdev = 0.062/0.087/0.112/0.025 ms
iPhoneToolchainSDK20:/toolchain/sdk20# dhclient
Internet Systems Consortium DHCP Client V3.0.4
Copyright 2004-2006 Internet Systems Consortium.
All rights reserved.
For info, please visit http://www.isc.org/sw/dhcp/

eth4: link up
Listening on LPF/eth4/00:0c:29:45:9c:57
Sending on   LPF/eth4/00:0c:29:45:9c:57
Listening on LPF/eth5/00:0c:29:45:9c:61
Sending on   LPF/eth5/00:0c:29:45:9c:61
Sending on   Socket/fallback
DHCPDISCOVER on eth4 to 255.255.255.255 port 67 interval 8
DHCPOFFER from 192.168.53.254
DHCPREQUEST on eth4 to 255.255.255.255 port 67
DHCPACK from 192.168.53.254
Reloading /etc/samba/smb.conf: smbd only.
bound to 192.168.53.129 -- renewal in 863 seconds.
iPhoneToolchainSDK20:/toolchain/sdk20#
VMware Tools is out of date. Choose the Virtual Machine > Install VMware Tools menu.
```

Once you have an IP address, you no longer have to work with VMware's screen directly—instead, you can use your favorite SSH program **[Hack #9.04]** on the host to connect one or more terminal sessions to the server (Figure 11-36):

```
# ssh root@<IP address>
```

Figure 11-36.
SSH connection to the VMware Ubuntu Toolchain Server

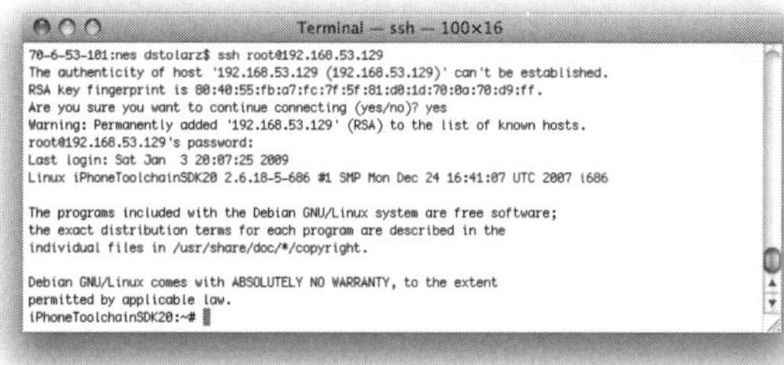

To gain access to various codebases available online, you'll want to install CVS. The easiest way to do so is by invoking the APT package manager that's included with all Debian Linux distributions (Figure 11-37).

```
# apt-get install cvs
```

Figure 11-37.
Installing CVS

Building the Samples

There are some goodies in the root account's Home directory, */root*. Most notable are the sample projects found in */root/SDK20PROJECTS/*, where you will find:

```
-rw-r--r-- 1 root root  1951 2008-10-19 09:46 README.txt
drwxr-xr-x 2 root root  4096 2008-12-28 09:45 respring
drwxr-xr-x 4  501 staff 4096 2009-01-04 00:10 UICatalog
drwxr-xr-x 2  501 staff 4096 2009-01-03 20:41 WinterBoard
```

respring, a command-line utility, will restart the SpringBoard application launcher and rebuild its cache. For further details see **[Hack #11.12]**. UICatalog is a sample application that demonstrates a variety of UI elements available in the UIKit framework. WinterBoard is an open source skinning application by the aforementioned Jay "saurik" Freeman, and it also serves as an example of how to combine Objective-C with C++.

Unless you already have a command-line version of *respring* installed on your iPhone, you should build and install *respring* first. The other sample, UICatalog, tries to execute *respring* in its Makefile in order to display its application icon after installation. The easiest way to make sure that this will work is to build and install the included version of *respring*.

The Makefiles of both *respring* and UICatalog have lines near the top that look like this:

```
IPHONE_IP=192.168.0.11
```

You'll need to edit the Makefile, replacing that IP address with the correct IP for your phone, so that the Makefile can automatically install the app to the correct location.

If you're not already accustomed to the popular text editors in Linux, like *vim* or an Emacs clone, you may find their unusual editing keystrokes rather offputting and difficult to learn. Fortunately, there are many text editors available, including my personal favorite, JOE (Joe's Own Editor), which uses a mishmash of WordStar and Emacs key mappings. It can also emulate Emacs, WordStar, or Pico. But most importantly, it has a handy onscreen key reference. If you're interested in installing JOE, you can once again take advantage of Debian APT:

```
# apt-get install joe
```

Once JOE is installed, you can run it to edit the Makefile:

```
# cd /root/SDK20PROJECTS/respring
# joe Makefile
```

Now that the IP address has been corrected, all you have to do is build and install the app:

```
# make
# make install
```

You can follow the same basic procedure for the UICatalog sample. Change the IP address in the Makefile, build, and install. When you install UICatalog to the phone with `make install`, your SpringBoard should restart and then the UICatalog icon should appear.

UICatalog is a port of Apple's sample application to this build environment. The major difference, other than adding a Makefile to support Unix-style builds, is the fact that Interface Builder files (XIB and NIB) are not used here. As Interface Builder is available only on the Mac platform, there is no way to compile the XIB source files into loadable NIB files without using a Mac. To avoid this problem, the user interface elements that would have been loaded from the NIB are instead created programmatically in this version of the app. Almost all toolchain apps create their interfaces programmatically in order to avoid Interface Builder dependencies.

Even in its original form, UICatalog already creates almost all of its controls programmatically, so it provides an excellent resource for learning how to create and configure the various UI controls in your code. This version simply takes it one step further, by converting the remaining few elements that were created in the XIB.

Ready to Go

You now have all the tools you need to get started developing toolchain apps in Linux. This open source software stack will enable you to explore the vast possibilities of the jailbroken iPhone platform.

— George Dean IV

 HACK 11.11: Develop iPhone Applications on Your iPhone

It's almost poetic: build your iPhone application right there on your iPhone.

The power of the iPhone's Unix-based OS really begins to sink in when you realize that it can run `gcc`, and therefore *build its own applications*. Granted, there's no possibility of installing an IDE, so this method isn't likely to become an overnight sensation. But for those who feel at home on a Unix command line, there is a certain appeal to developing apps *in situ*.

Installing the Toolchain

Installing the tools themselves is easy, because they are available as Cydia packages. You simply use the Search feature to find the proper packages and install them:

GCC
  The GNU Compiler Collection

Make
  The standard command-line tool for dependency-based build scripts (Makefiles)

Link Identity Editor (ldid)
  An application that simulates code signing

OpenSSH (ssh)
  For remote terminal access

Getting the appropriate headers installed is a bit more complicated. Putting together a set of headers from their original sources is a long, laborious process that involves extracting the framework headers from the iPhone SDK, reorganizing their path structure (Apple places the headers in nonstandard locations) and copying them over to the phone is detailed here: www.saurik.com/id/4. Alternatively, you may be able to get help from the community **[Hack #2.06]** or from someone who has already gone through the process (http://antirez.com/page/iphone-gcc-guide.html). Either way, you can install the headers to `/usr/include` on your iPhone.

Building an Open Source Program on the iPhone

Now you have everything you need to build something, let's try it out. Since there aren't any sample projects included, you'll have to download something. How about the JOE editor mentioned in **[Hack #11.10]**? You'll have to edit Makefiles and other text files fairly frequently, so it might be nice to have a terminal-oriented text editor installed. This will also get you acquainted with some of the issues you may face when building other projects on the iPhone.

First, you'll need to download the source code tarball, named *joe-3.7.tar.gz*, from the official JOE website: http://joe-editor.sourceforge.net. Then you'll need to copy it over to the phone and extract the contents:

```
# scp joe-3.7.tar.gz root@<iPhone IP address>:/var/root
# ssh root@<iPhone IP address>
# tar xvzf joe-3.7.tar.gz
# cd joe-3.7
```

The JOE website claims that you should be able to run three commands: `./configure`, `make`, and `make install`, and that will be it. Unfortunately, that doesn't work correctly on the iPhone platform, so there are additional steps to be taken.

The first command, `./configure`, runs the *configure script* for the project, which autodetects certain attributes of your system and creates a customized Makefile that takes your platform's idiosyncrasies into account. But if you simply run `./configure`, it will fail, because one of the tests tries to execute the output of a build. This test fails because the iPhone requires code signing, and the configure script knows nothing about code signing. The workaround is tricky to figure out but simple to perform. Fortunately, the execution check is skipped if the configure script is told that it is *cross-compiling* for a different platform, instead of compiling natively for the current platform. So even though we are compiling for the native platform, we just tell the script that it's a cross-compile by explicitly specifying the `--host` parameter:

```
# ./configure --host=arm-apple-darwin
```

Even though this is the same platform descriptor as the one you're running on, the script takes us at our word and assumes we are cross-compiling. In this configuration, the script no longer attempts to execute the test program that it builds, and it should complete without error.

At this point, the configure script has generated a proper Makefile, but there is one more unexpected problem with this project. JOE has built-in expression evaluation capabilities, including a lot of math functions. Unfortunately, for unknown reasons, some of the functions from the C math library *math.h* are missing on the iPhone. In particular, the Bessel functions, j0, j1, y0, and y1, are missing. But the source file *umath.c* attempts to use them, which will lead to link errors if you try to build this program in its current form. The solution is to remove all references to the missing functions. Fortunately there are only eight such references, and you can delete the entire line in each case. This makes the edit so simple that you can run it as a single command using `sed`, the Unix Stream EDitor:

```
# sed -i.old '/[jy][01]/ d' umath.c
```

Let's break down this command line briefly so that you'll know what it's doing. The first argument `-i.old` tells `sed` to edit the file in place, and back up the old version with the extension *.old*. The last argument, `umath.c`, is the name of the file that we want to edit. That leaves the second argument, `'/[jy][01]/ d'`, which does all the work, is a `sed` command that will be run on each line of the file. The first part of the command is a regular expression that each line is matched against. If a line matches, then the `d` at the end of the command tells `sed` to delete the line. So `sed` will delete any line containing `j0`, `j1`, `y0`, or `y1`. (That also includes larger identifiers that contain these sequences, like `m_j0`. Fortunately, that's what we want, in this specific case.) This example barely scratches the surface of `sed`. It's a complex and rich tool, and you would be well served to learn more about it.

With that fix to the source code, the project is now ready to build. The `make` command does the job:

```
# make
```

Once you've built it, though, you can't just install it right away; you need to fix the code signing problem first, or it won't run. That's where *ldid* comes in. It adds fake code signing blocks to your executable so that it will pass muster. Once it's fake-signed, you can proceed with the install step.

```
# ldid -S joe
# make install
```

And that's it! You've successfully built an open source project on the iPhone. You can now invoke JOE just as you would on other platforms:

```
# joe README
```

You may find some of these workarounds useful in the future. The configure script issue is one that you may face once in a while, and the `--host` fix should work in most of those cases. And of course the *ldid* code-signing step has to be performed on every executable you build. (Fortunately, a lot of Makefiles for iPhone projects already include this step, so you don't always have to type it in.)

Build the UICatalog Sample

Now let's try building the UICatalog sample on the iPhone. First, you should make sure you have a command-line version of *respring* installed, as described in [Hack #11.12], because the Makefile for UICatalog will try to invoke it.

As the UICatalog sample isn't preloaded, we'll need to download it. An iPhone toolchain-compatible version is hosted on Google Code, but you'll need a subversion client to get the source code. Fortunately subversion has been ported to the iPhone already. You can get it from Cydia, or install it from the command line:

```
# apt-get install subversion
```

Once subversion is installed, you can check out the code using the `svn co` command:

```
# cd ~
# svn co http://apiexplorer.googlecode.com/svn/trunk/UICatalog UICatalog
```

The source code includes three different Makefiles so that you can build the same code on Mac, Linux, or iPhone toolchains. The one we want to use is named `Makefile.iphone`. Let's rename it to `Makefile`, so that the `make` command will pick it up automatically. Then it's just a matter of running `make` and `make install`:

```
# cd UICatalog
# mv Makefile.iphone Makefile
# make
# make install
```

After the SpringBoard restarts, the UICatalog application should now be available.

— George Dean IV

HACK 11.12: Restart Your SpringBoard to Reveal Newly Installed Applications

Restarting the SpringBoard is a small but critical step in the deployment process.

There are several different ways to restart your SpringBoard, through both the UI and the command line, and they each have their own merits.

One application that can restart the SpringBoard is BossPrefs. Recent versions have a "Fast Respring" button on the Power management screen (Figure 11-38). Touching the button will immediately quit BossPrefs and restart the SpringBoard.

Figure 11-38.
BossPrefs power management screen

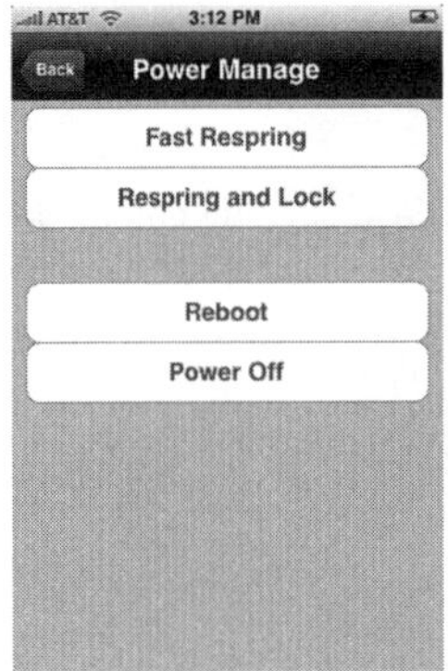

respring allows you to restart the SpringBoard directly from the Home screen. Just touch the *respring* icon (Figure 11-39) and you're good to go.

Figure 11-39.
respring ready to restart SpringBoard

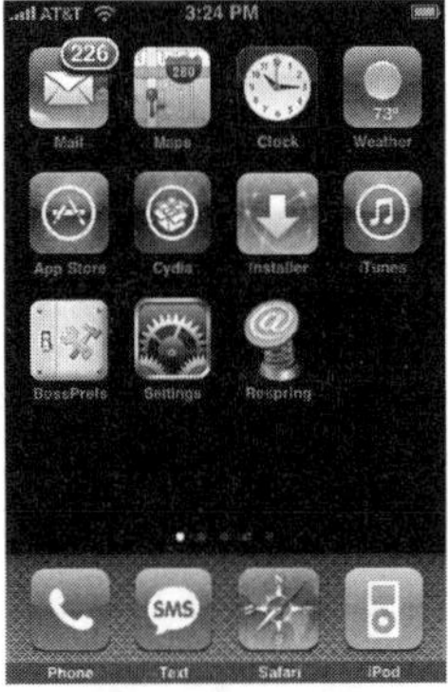

Both BossPrefs and *respring* are available from the BigBoss source in Cydia **[Hack #1.04]**.

When you want to automatically restart SpringBoard (such as in the install phase of a Makefile) you'll need a command-line version of *respring*. There are two basic ways to approach this. One way is to download a command-line *respring* package, which is available from the Cydia repository at www.iphone.org.hk/apt. (If you haven't already added that source, you'll have to add it manually, but it contains several useful utilities discussed in this chapter.) The *respring* package (notice the lowercase r in Figure 11-40) installs a *respring* program in */usr/bin*, so that you only need to type "respring" on the command line to trigger it.

Figure 11-40.
Download *respring* package from Cydia (notice lowercase r)

Alternatively, if you already have BossPrefs or *respring* installed, you can copy the program to */usr/bin/* yourself, and avoid downloading a separate package:

```
# cp /Applications/BossPrefs.app/Respring /usr/bin/respring
```

or

```
# cp /Applications/Respring.app/respring /usr/bin/respring
```

Alternatively, you could make a symbolic link in */usr/bin/* instead of copying the file:

```
# ln -s /Applications/BossPrefs.app/Respring /usr/bin/respring
```

or

```
# ln -s /Applications/Respring.app/respring /usr/bin/respring
```

Whichever method you choose, the result is that a simple *respring* command will restart your SpringBoard.

— George Dean IV

HACK 11.13: Create a UI Without Interface Builder

Though it lacks Interface Builder's drag-and-drop simplicity, hand-coding an iPhone UI is fairly straightforward.

Typical iPhone projects, including most of Apple's sample apps, rely on Interface Builder's NIB files for at least some portion of their UI. This presents a problem when trying to build those projects on other platforms, because Interface Builder is available only on Mac OS X. Currently the only way to overcome this is to create the desired UI elements programmatically, thereby eliminating the need for the NIB files.

The UICatalog sample serves as an invaluable resource for hand-coding your UI. For one thing, most of the controls are hand-coded even in Apple's original version of the code; and also, the sample has already been converted to be NIB-free. You can examine the changes yourself in detail, by visiting the project's Google code repository at http://code.google.com/p/apiexplorer/source/detail?r=17. (The NIB removal was done in revision 17, and that page shows you every edit made in that revision.)

A variety of changes were required in order to allow UICatalog to break free of Interface Builder. But don't think that this only applies to projects that started out using Interface Builder; most of these steps must be fulfilled in any NIB-free application, even if it's written from scratch.

Also keep in mind that if you're converting your UI from an existing Interface Builder XIB document, you must be intimately familiar with its contents in order to do the conversion. You either need to have the document open in Interface Builder, or attempt to decipher the convoluted XML format that makes up the XIB file itself.

Specify the Application Delegate Class

The NIB file typically specifies which class should be loaded as the application delegate. When you remove the NIB, this association is lost. It's up to you to explicitly provide the class name as a parameter to `UIApplicationMain`, which is called from the `main` function:

```
int retVal = UIApplicationMain(argc, argv, nil, @"AppDelegate");
```

Create the Main Window and Root Views

Now that you know the application delegate will be loaded properly, let's make sure that it is fulfilling its responsibilities. In general, an object should create the UI objects it owns. That has special meaning when Interface Builder is involved, because Interface Builder allows you to attach NIB-created objects to *outlets* provided by your classes. When the NIB is gone, you must not only create the UI objects, but also make sure that they are referenced by the correct outlets. To determine which class should own each UI object, follow these guidelines:

- If the object is referenced by exactly one of your classes, that class owns it.
- If the object is referenced by more than one of your classes, you must choose the best one to own it (usually the class that is higher in the UI hierarchy).
- If the object is not referenced by any of your classes, then it should be created by whatever class creates its parent object.

The application delegate class typically owns the main window and the root portions of the view controller hierarchy. The logical time to create these root UI elements is when the application first launches, which is indicated by the `applicationDidFinishLaunching:` method in the modified, NIB-free UICatalog:

```
// create window
window = [[UIWindow alloc] initWithFrame:[[UIScreen mainScreen] bounds]];
window.backgroundColor = [UIColor blackColor];
// set up main view navigation controller
MainViewController *mainViewController = [[MainViewController alloc] init];
// create a navigation controller using the new controller
navigationController = [[UINavigationController alloc]
 initWithRootViewController:mainViewController];
[mainViewController release];
// add the navigation controller's view to the window
[window addSubview: navigationController.view];
[window makeKeyAndVisible];
```

In this example, the primary view controller at the root of the hierarchy is a `UINavigationController`. It contains a `MainViewController` instance as the root of its navigational structure. Some applications choose `UITabBarController` as the primary controller; others use custom view controllers when the application is not suited to the standard navigational models of the iPhone. But whatever the right root view is for your application, this is where it gets created and added to the main window.

Create Subviews for Your Custom View Controllers

This part varies greatly between projects, because it is highly dependent upon what type of subviews are needed for each custom view controller. Rather than get bogged down in the specific implementation details of the UICatalog sample, let's focus on the key points.

There are two broad categories of initialization that must take place to fully instantiate a custom view controller: data initialization, and the actual creation of subviews. When a view controller is loaded from a NIB, the data initialization typically is done in response to one of two load-time messages: `initWithCoder:`, the special initializer that gets called during loading from a NIB, or `awakeFromNib`, the notification message that is sent right after a NIB loading operation completes. But neither of these calls will be made when a new instance is created explicitly, which means any data initialization that's buried in one of those methods must be moved to a standard initializer. The default initializer `init` is a good choice.

The actual creation of views typically constitutes the bulk of the new code that you'll have to write. When loading from a NIB, of course, all this is done for you; but when creating a new instance from scratch, the correct place to create subviews is in the `loadView` method. This is called when the view controller needs to be displayed. Finally, when the hierarchy of subviews is created, you simply need to assign the top-level parent view to the view controller's `view` property.

This code snippet from UICatalog's `MainViewController loadView` method illustrates the creation of a simple top-level container view:

```
UIView *contentView = [[UIView alloc]
 initWithFrame:[[UIScreen mainScreen] applicationFrame]];
self.view = contentView;
[contentView release];
self.view.autoresizesSubviews = YES;
```

By setting the `autoresizesSubviews` property, this view will automatically resize its contents to adjust for other screen elements like toolbars and navigation bars.

Other, more specialized views are then added as subviews of this generic parent container. In this example, the only subview is a `UITableView` that fills its parent. Here are the key lines that accomplish that:

```
myTableView = [[UITableView alloc] initWithFrame:self.view.bounds
 style:UITableViewStylePlain];
myTableView.autoresizesSubviews = YES;
myTableView.autoresizingMask =
  (UIViewAutoresizingFlexibleWidth | UIViewAutoresizingFlexibleHeight);
[self.view addSubview: myTableView];
```

The `initWithFrame:` initializer is common to all `UIView` subclasses. (In this case, we're using the class-specific `initWithFrame:style:`, but it serves the same function.) It allows you to set the frame coordinates of your view as you're creating it, so that you can place it in the desired screen location right from the start. You will use some variant of `initWithFrame:` for most of your hand-coded subviews.

The `autoresizingMask` property determines which dimensions will be adjusted when its parent tries to automatically resize it. Views intended to fill their parents should set `UIViewAutoresizingFlexibleWidth | UIViewAutoresizingFlexibleHeight` so that both width and height are adjusted. You could also allow the margins to be adjusted—that is, the distance between an edge of the subview and the corresponding edge of its parent—by specifying one or more of `UIViewAutoresizingFlexibleTopMargin`, `UIViewAutoresizingFlexibleBottomMargin`, `UIViewAutoresizingFlexibleLeftMargin`, or `UIViewAutoresizingFlexibleRightMargin`.

Finally, the subview is added to the parent view by sending the `addSubview:` message:

```
[self.view addSubview: myTableView];
```

By combining these basic ingredients—`initWithFrame:`, `autoresizesSubviews`, `autoresizingMask`, and `addSubview:`—you can create arbitrarily complex adjustable layouts for your application's views.

Removing the NIB from Your Project

Once you've converted all your UI elements to be created programmatically, you should go ahead and remove the XIB file from the Xcode project (if you have any intention of being able to build the project in Xcode in the future). You also need edit the *Info.plist* file to remove the `NSMainNibFile` key, which refers to the NIB file. Both the key name and the string value need to be deleted.

While you have *Info.plist* open, you should also replace all those unexpanded variables, like `${PRODUCT_NAME}` and `${EXECUTABLE_NAME}`, with appropriate values for your project. Xcode fills in these variables for you, but other build environments won't.

There are also references to `IBOutlet` scattered throughout the code. These are textual tags added to the code for the benefit of Interface Builder. Because `IBOutlet` is `#defined` to be an empty macro, these occurrences of `IBOutlet` should be harmless. But if you ever want or need to get rid of them, you can safely delete these references now that Interface Builder is no longer in use. Similarly, `IBAction` is `#defined` to be `void`, so you can feel free to substitute `void` anywhere `IBAction` appears.

Explore More UIKit Controls

UICatalog's wide array of programmatically created controls should be able to help guide you in creating almost anything you might find in a XIB document. I highly recommend perusing the program to familiarize yourself with all the styles and choices available. And of course the SDK documentation has more to say about UIKit than just about any other framework.

— George Dean IV

HACK 11.14: Use API Explorer to Peek into Built-in Frameworks

See what classes are really available on your iPhone.

API Explorer is a useful utility that lets you examine all the classes in all the frameworks that it's linked to. The prebuilt version is linked to CoreGraphics, Foundation, and UIKit. But if you download the source, you can rebuild it and link it to almost any frameworks you want!

The prebuilt version of API Explorer is available from this Cydia repository: www.iphone.org.hk/apt. You'll need to add this source to Cydia if you haven't already done so, and then install the package called API Explorer. The icon will then appear on your SpringBoard (Figure 11-41).

Figure 11-41.
API Explorer

Launching the program presents you with a list of class names (Figure 11-42). These are all the classes currently loaded by the Objective-C runtime in this program; effectively, all the classes in all the frameworks that it was linked with at build time. (For this build, that's CoreGraphics, Foundation, and UIKit, as mentioned earlier; but as CoreGraphics and UIKit rely on other frameworks, such as QuartzCore and WebKit, they are silently linked in as well.)

Figure 11-42.
Class names in API Explorer

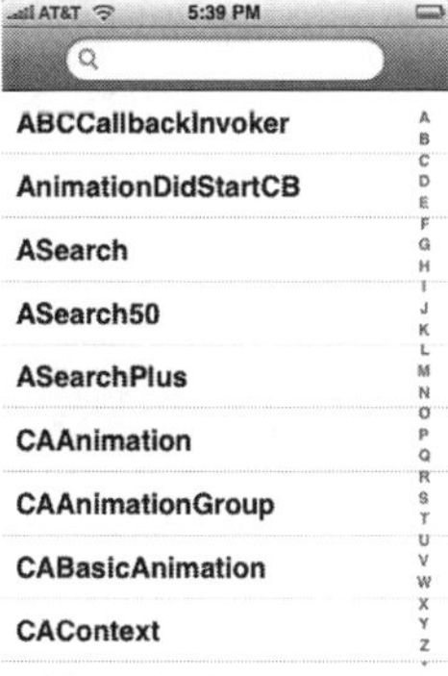

You can use the search box at the top to enter all or part of a class name, and API Explorer narrows down the results list to only the class names that contain that substring (Figure 11-43).

Figure 11-43.
Filtering class names

When you select a class from the list, you will be presented with some pertinent information regarding that class: its superclass, any formal protocols it implements, its instance variables, class methods, and instance methods (Figure 11-44).

Figure 11-44.
Class information

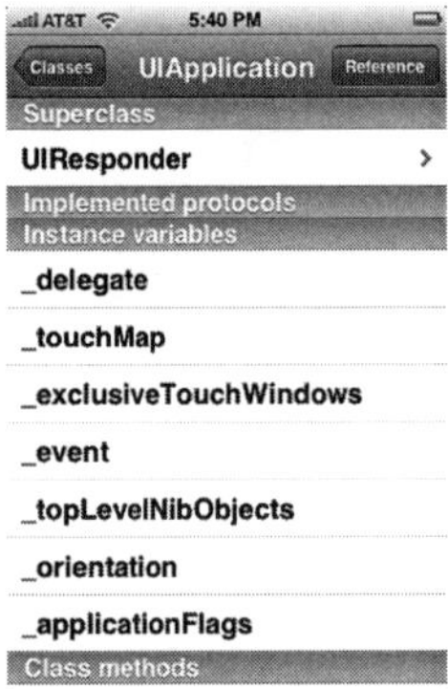

You can also click the Reference button to visit the reference page for this class on Erica Sadun's website. Her extensive collection of class-dumped header files and cross-referenced code analysis can help you discover even more about the classes you are interested in (Figure 11-45).

Figure 11-45.
Class reference pages

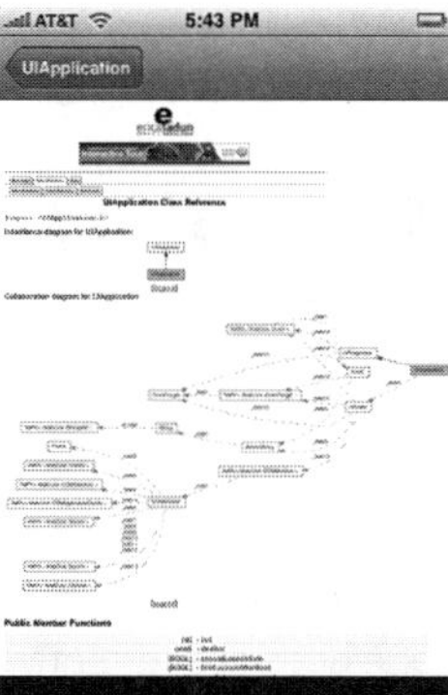

But the three frameworks linked to this build of API Explorer are just the tip of the iPhone iceberg. To explore more frameworks, you need to download the source code and build your own version. It's designed for Xcode and the Apple SDK, so if you're running on Linux or some other toolchain-based environment, you'll have a bit of a porting adventure on your hands.

The project is hosted on Google Code at http://code.google.com/p/apiexplorer. You can check out the code from the subversion repository at http://apiexplorer.googlecode.com/svn/trunk/apiexplorer using your favorite subversion GUI or with this terminal command:

```
$ svn checkout http://apiexplorer.googlecode.com/svn/trunk/apiexplorer apiexplorer
```

When the download completes, open the Xcode project. You'll need to change the code signing settings: in the main menu, choose Project→Edit Project Settings. When the Project "Explorer" Info window comes up, go to the Build tab, and select your preferred code signing identity in the Code Signing section. (You can read more about code signing identities in **[Hack #11.08]** and **[Hack #11.09]**.) Now you should be able to click Build and Go and successfully test the application.

Once you've got everything up and running, you can add whatever frameworks you see fit (except for a few dummy frameworks like IOKit, which will cause link errors if you try to use them). See **[Hack #11.15]** to learn how to add frameworks. Even though the private frameworks don't have headers, you can still link them to API Explorer, and the application will use Objective-C's runtime information to explore every class in the framework. And if the framework has been class-dumped by Erica Sadun, you can jump to the online reference pages as well.

— George Dean IV

HACK 11.15: Access Private APIs

Private doesn't necessarily mean inaccessible.

Apple's SDK only exposes a small fraction of the iPhone's frameworks. Even in those frameworks that are public, only a tiny fraction of the classes in each framework are documented and have official header files. And in those classes for which header files are provided, only a small percentage of each class's methods are declared in the headers. All those other classes and methods are hidden, waiting to be accessed—and you can use them in your jailbroken applications. All you need to know is how to tell the compiler about those hidden APIs.

In order to tell the compiler what's there, of course, you have to know about it yourself. You can do a simple examination with the API Explorer application [Hack #11.14], but that app does not currently display type information, such as variables or methods, so you won't get very far that way. You'll need a more powerful tool.

class-dump

The ultimate source of hidden API information is class-dump, a utility that dumps all the type information from an Objective-C framework and creates header files for every class it finds. Some type information is lost; Objective-C does not store the static types of object references, so they all show up as the generic type `id`. But the type information expressed in the generated headers is complete enough to allow you to use the framework successfully.

A large set of doxygen-generated reference pages, based on class-dumped headers, is maintained by Erica Sadun at her website, http://ericasadun.com. The pages for firmware Version 2.2 are found at http://ericasadun.com/iPhoneDocs220. These pages contain both annotated source code for the headers and cross-linked reference pages.

The Linux virtual machine referred to in [Hack #11.11] already has a full set of class-dumped headers. For other development platforms, you can use class-dump to generate your own headers. It's available for the iPhone and can be installed through Cydia or with the following iPhone terminal command:

```
# apt-get install class-dump
```

Let's say you want to dump the Celestial framework so you can use its media playback capabilities. At the iPhone command line, type these commands:

```
# mkdir -p ~/dump/Celestial
# class-dump -H -o ~/dump/Celestial \
  /System/Library/PrivateFrameworks/Celestial.framework/Celestial
# cd ~/dump/Celestial
```

Unfortunately, the generated headers are not perfect. They frequently start with `#import "NSObject.h"`, which doesn't exist, thus causing compilation errors when you try to use the headers. You can fix this by removing these lines, because most Objective-C programs will `#import NSObject.h` from the Foundation framework very early in each file. The `sed` command to do this removal is:

```
# sudo sed -i.old '/NSObject\.h/ d' *.h
```

You may encounter other bad header references when using these files. Be prepared to occasionally hand-edit the `#import` statements to get them to point to the correct locations.

Now you need to place these headers in the correct location for your dev environment. For iPhone development, just move the generated files to a subdirectory of */usr/include/*:

```
# mv ~/dump/Celestial /usr/include
```

For the Linux toolchain, you already have a full set of headers, as mentioned earlier, but if you need to redump later (for example, if you need to update for a newer firmware version), you can replace the existing set (replace *iPhoneIP* with your iPhone's IP address). At the Linux prompt type:

```
$ cd /toolchain/sdk20/sys/usr/include/
$ mv Celestial Celestial.220
$ scp -r root@iPhoneIP:~/dump/Celestial .
```

If you're using Xcode, placing the headers is a lot more complicated. Xcode relies on each version of a framework having its own dedicated folder, which contains both the binary file (for use by the linker) and the headers for that version of the framework (if they are provided). Unfortunately, this means that for Xcode to automatically pick up the headers, there must be redundant copies of the header files for each version of the framework. As of SDK Version 2.2, there are six different versions of each framework: separate copies of the frameworks are stored for simulator versions 2.0, 2.1, and 2.2, and there are corresponding copies for each version of the device firmware.

Each of the six platform- and version-specific copies of the SDK build files comes with a *Library* folder located as follows:

/Developer/Platforms/
  iPhoneOS.platform/Developer/SDKs/
    iPhoneOS2.0.sdk/System/Library/
    iPhoneOS2.1.sdk/System/Library/
    iPhoneOS2.2.sdk/System/Library/
  iPhoneSimulator.platform/Developer/SDKs/
    iPhoneSimulator2.0.sdk/System/Library/
    iPhoneSimulator2.1.sdk/System/Library/
    iPhoneSimulator2.2.sdk/System/Library/

Within each *Library* folder there are two folders called *Frameworks* and *PrivateFrameworks*. *Frameworks* contains the dedicated folders for all the public frameworks, and *PrivateFrameworks* contains all the dedicated folders for the private frameworks. So, for example, the framework folder for the private framework *Celestial*, for builds targeting the device, in Version 2.2, is found at this location:

/Developer/Platforms/
  iPhoneOS.platform/Developer/SDKs/
    iPhoneOS2.2.sdk/System/Library/
      PrivateFrameworks/Celestial.framework

Finally, within each dedicated framework folder, you will find the binary file (named after the framework, in this case, *Celestial*) and a *Headers* folder, if headers are provided. Private frameworks don't come with a *Headers* folder, but if you create one, Xcode will use it, just like a public framework.

So, to install the Celestial header files, you'll need to create six `Headers` folders, one for each occurrence of `Celestial.framework`. To make things a little easier, I've created a *bash* script that installs private framework headers to all six SDK locations automatically:

```
#!/bin/bash
for PLAT in OS Simulator; do
  for VER in 2.0 2.1 2.2; do
    fwpath=/Developer/Platforms/iPhone${PLAT}.platform/Developer/SDKs\
/iPhone${PLAT}${VER}.sdk/System/Library/PrivateFrameworks/$2.framework
    echo "Copy to framework: ${fwpath}"
    cp -R $1 "${fwpath}/Headers"
  done
done
```

Save that script as *~/install-framework-headers.sh* using your favorite text editor. Then enable execution privileges on it:

```
$ chmod 755 ~/install-framework-headers.sh
```

The script takes two arguments: the first argument is the path that you want to copy the headers from, and the second argument is the bare name of the framework.

Suppose, for example, that you want to install the Celestial headers that you dumped earlier on your iPhone. First, you need to copy the headers to a local directory, then you can invoke the script to copy those files out to the six install locations. At the OS X terminal command line (replace *iPhoneIP* with your iPhone's IP address):

```
$ mkdir ~/dump
$ scp -r root@iPhoneIP:~/dump/Celestial ~/dump/Celestial
$ sudo ~/install-framework-headers.sh ~/dump/Celestial Celestial
```

Notice that you must preface the script invocation with `sudo`. This is because the framework directories are write-protected for nonroot users. `sudo` will ask for your password, and then execute the six-way copy script as `root` to overcome the permissions problem. If all goes well, you should have six well-placed sets of header files ready for consumption by Xcode.

Add a Private (or Public) Framework to Your Application

Whether the framework you want to use is public or private, the procedure for adding it to your project is the same. On Linux and iPhone, linking to a framework is a matter of adding an additional command-line parameter for the linker. Most Makefiles use an `LDFLAGS` variable to store linker parameters, so adding a framework simply means adding a line like this:

```
LDFLAGS += -framework Celestial
```

To add a framework in Xcode, right-click on the *Frameworks* folder in the project window (Figure 11-46), and choose Add→Existing Frameworks.

Figure 11-46.
Add existing frameworks in Xcode

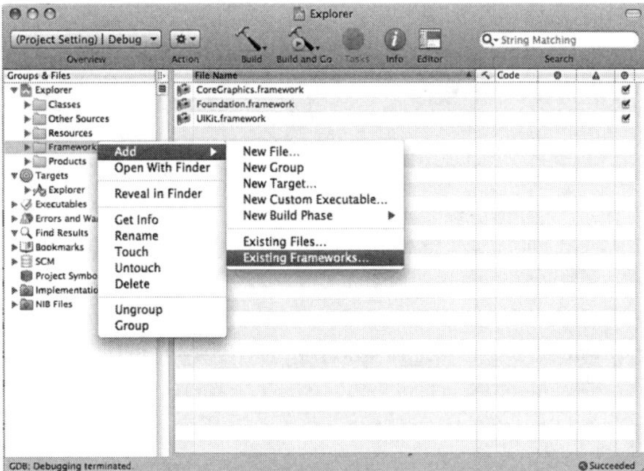

Use the file browser to navigate to the *Frameworks* or *PrivateFrameworks* folder. (You don't have to worry too much about which platform- and version-specific directory you load the framework from; Xcode should automatically redirect to the correct location based on which platform and SDK version you choose in the project's Build Configuration drop-down.) Select the dedicated folder for your desired framework, and choose Add (Figure 11-47).

Figure 11-47.
Selecting a framework in Xcode

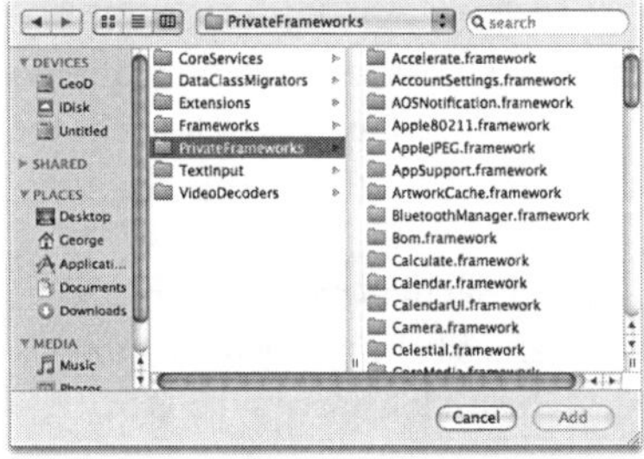

Add a Private Class to Your Application

If you want to use a class from a private framework, you can just add the framework to your project and `#import` the appropriate header, and you're good to go. But what if the class you want is a hidden class in a public framework? You have headers for the public classes already installed, but not for the hidden classes. There are several approaches to solving this problem.

You could replace the entire set of official SDK headers for that framework with your class-dumped versions. Unfortunately, as class-dumped headers don't have complete type specifications for a lot of message parameters and instance variables, you'll lose some valuable information this way—not to mention that class-dump can't retrieve C function specifications, and most C structures are either lost entirely or given arbitrarily generated names.

One approach you might take is to copy just the one header file for the class you're trying to use, and add it to the official headers. Think of it as "splicing" classes into your SDK headers. Note that you may also need to copy headers for the subclasses of your dumped class, if they are also hidden classes.

Also keep in mind that if you're replacing or splicing your official headers, there are multiple copies of the official headers—and you will have to modify all of them.

One other option is to add the header directly to your project, and just keep a local copy with the rest of your source files. Once again, keep in mind that you may need to add subclasses as well. You also won't be able to use the typical `#import <Framework/Header.h>` formulation to import the file; depending on where you put it, you'll need to use either `#import "Framework/Header.h"` or `#import "Header.h"`. Also, the header itself may use incorrect paths when importing dependencies from its own framework, so you may have to tweak some import statements there as well.

Add a Private Method to Your Application

If you want to call a method on a private class, you need to import the class as described earlier. But what if you want to call a private method on a class that's already declared in the official SDK? Once again, there are a few different ways to approach this.

The first option is to replace the official class header with a class-dumped version. This is just like splicing a class-dumped class into your official headers as described previously, except that this time, you're replacing one that already exists. For one thing, you'll have to do it in multiple places. And you'll also be discarding a lot of valuable type information about message parameters that was provided in the official header.

You could also splice the additional method declarations from the class-dumped header into the official header, creating a merged header. This gets complicated, because you will have to find all the duplicates from the class-dumped section and delete them, and they will probably be scattered throughout the list and difficult to locate. And once again, you have to copy the merged file to all the other locations.

But there's a useful hack that allows you to call a private method without modifying headers and without causing compiler warnings. Because Objective-C allows classes to be augmented through the category mechanism, you can fool the compiler into letting you call additional methods by creating a fake category.

Suppose that you want to be able to set your application's icon badge to contain some arbitrary text. You can set the badge using the UIApplication class (Figure 11-48), but the only public method for setting the badge takes an unsigned integer, which is very limiting. A little digging in API Explorer **[Hack #11.14]** reveals that there is a private method, `setApplicationBadge:`, that looks more promising.

Figure 11-48.
Set the badge using the UIApplication class

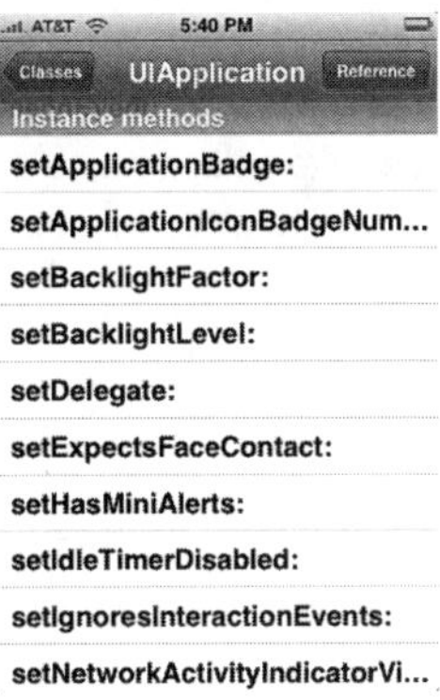

Checking the class dump for the UIKit framework, we can see that it takes an `id` and returns `void`:

```
- (void) setApplicationBadge:(id)fp8;
```

A little web searching will make you confident that the argument is supposed to be an (`NSString*`). Unfortunately the limited type information stored in the compiled binaries makes it difficult to know in general what the expected object types are for private messages. You will have to rely on forum discussions and trial-and-error to figure it out.

Armed with this knowledge of the method declaration, we can now write a fake category declaration to convince the compiler that this method really does exist:

```
@interface UIApplication (FakePrivateMethods)
- (void) setApplicationBadge:(NSString*)text;
@end
```

The name of the category doesn't matter, because you won't be providing an implementation; as long as the name doesn't conflict with any existing category name on that class, you'll be fine. (You will seldom find real categories with the name `FakePrivateMethods`, so that should be a good choice.) And best of all, the compiler will never complain about the fact that your fake category has no implementation.

So now the compiler is convinced that this method exists, and you can call it freely anywhere that it's declared. (I suggest creating a header file for your project called `PrivateMethods.h`, and putting all your fake categories there so that you can `#import` your declarations easily in multiple files.) At runtime, when you invoke the call, the Objective-C runtime will look for an implementation that matches that selector—and it will find the implementation that already existed in the framework. Success!

— George Dean IV

RUN LINUX ON YOUR IPHONE

BECAUSE SOME PEOPLE JUST CAN'T HELP THEMSELVES

Even though most of Apple's proprietary iPhone OS has been cracked open like an egg, there is still a strong desire in some circles to install a truly open OS on the iPhone. Enter the most popular open source kernel: Linux.

It boots! But that's about all it does right now (Figure 11-49).

Figure 11-49.
openiboot

This effort has a long way to go—their own progress chart (Figure 11-50), at www.iphonelinux.org, tells the story.

Figure 11-50.
iPhoneLinux.org's progress chart

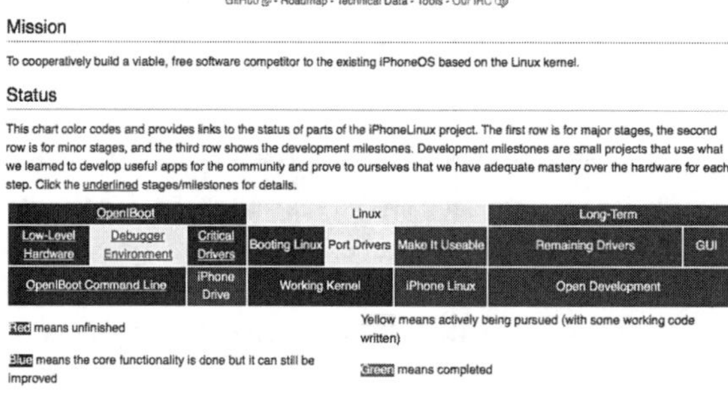

Welcome to iPhoneLinux

GitHub - Roadmap - Technical Data - Tools - Our IRC

Mission

To cooperatively build a viable, free software competitor to the existing iPhoneOS based on the Linux kernel.

Status

This chart color codes and provides links to the status of parts of the iPhoneLinux project. The first row is for major stages, the second row is for minor stages, and the third row shows the development milestones. Development milestones are small projects that use what we learned to develop useful apps for the community and prove to ourselves that we have adequate mastery over the hardware for each step. Click the underlined stages/milestones for details.

<table>
<tr><td colspan="3">OpenIBoot</td><td colspan="3">Linux</td><td colspan="2">Long-Term</td></tr>
<tr><td>Low-Level Hardware</td><td>Debugger Environment</td><td>Critical Drivers</td><td>Booting Linux</td><td>Port Drivers</td><td>Make It Useable</td><td>Remaining Drivers</td><td>GUI</td></tr>
<tr><td colspan="2">OpenIBoot Command Line</td><td>iPhone Drive</td><td colspan="2">Working Kernel</td><td>iPhone Linux</td><td colspan="2">Open Development</td></tr>
</table>

Red means unfinished

Yellow means actively being pursued (with some working code written)

Blue means the core functionality is done but it can still be improved

Green means completed

The "Make It Useable" work item is color-coded red, meaning that it's unfinished and *not yet even being actively pursued.*

Still, the work continues. It's a huge challenge, because of all the hardware drivers that have to be reverse-engineered. It's more of a proof-of-concept at this point (Figure 11-51).

RUN LINUX ON YOUR IPHONE, CONT'D 

Figure 11-51.
Image courtesy of Salvatore Iovene, www.geekherocomic.com

Maybe you're wondering why anyone would bother, when there's already a generally well-liked OS on the device.

It's like Mount Everest. Somebody has to do it—because it's there.

— George Dean IV

12 HARDWARE HACKS

In the future, everyone will have a personal computer with all their information on it, and they will carry it around in their pocket. That future is now, and the computer is called the iPhone.

But just because all our data is on a little pocket computer doesn't mean we can access it the way we want to. To a large degree, we're relying on cloud connectivity—our data pushes up from our PCs or Macs, to the cloud, and down to our iPhone. We're untethered, but still dependent upon the network and our home PC. What we need is a way to finish the transformation, and make it so we don't even need a personal computer—make it so that everything is in the phone.

That's what the future holds—if you look.

This chapter will go over the dozens of things you can do to enhance your iPhone-centric lifestyle with hardware and accessories. You'll learn how to view your iPhone media on your home TV, in the car, and in the hotel room when you're traveling, and how to keep it charged as you go. If you're handy with a screwdriver and a spudger, this chapter will show you how to disassemble and reassemble all the iPhones and iPod touches. And if you're the circuit builder type, you'll learn methods for connecting and controlling almost any device—serial or otherwise—to your iPhone, without having to jailbreak it!

HACK 12.01: Adapt Existing Headphones to Work with the Original iPhone

You can easily adapt hard-to-fit 3.5 mm plugs into a first-generation iPhone.

If you're using an original iPhone, you know that the headphone jack is recessed, making it harder to plug devices into it. There are countless adapters and splitters you can purchase to let you pull this recessed jack out and plug normal devices into it. Figure 12-1 shows an example from Boxwave (www.boxwave.com/products/iphoneheadsetadapter/index.htm).

Figure 12-1.
Boxwave iPhone 3G headphone adapters (picture courtesy of Boxwave.com)

Hacking the Wire

To make other 3.5 mm plugs work, you simply need to hack away at the plastic sleeve to make enough room around them so they'll fit in the hole.

The technical problem that normally prevents most headphones from connecting is the plastic sheath at the base of the plug. The girth of this plastic piece is too wide to fit in the narrow recess surrounding the iPhone's headset port. If you compare the plug of the iPhone headset to that of a standard set of headphones, you'll notice the difference in thickness. To get the 3.5 mm plug of almost any standard pair of headphones to fit in your iPhone, you will need to shave off about 5 mm of the plastic sheath, as shown in Figure 12-2.

Figure 12-2.
Hacked old iPhone headphones

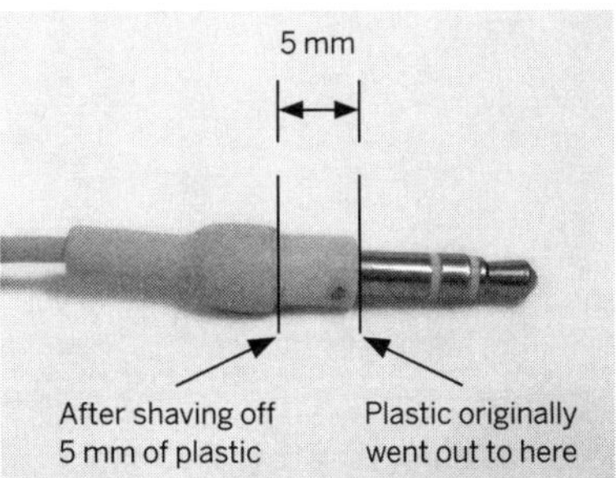

Some headphones and cables have a large metal disk at the base of the plug, making it impossible to shave down without a metal grinder. Check for this before you start gouging the plastic cover.

Although the alteration to your headphones is cosmetically irreversible, none of their functionality will be compromised. They still will work perfectly with any other device.

HACK 12.02: Make the Original iPhone Dock Work for the iPhone 3G

Even though the iPhone 3G didn't come with a dock, you can shave an old dock to work.

You can modify the iPhone dock that comes with the original iPhone to be compatible with and fit the iPhone 3G.

Here are the tools you'll need:

1. Clear packing tape
2. Sharp tool (I used a cheap utility knife)
3. Small flathead screwdriver
4. 100-grit aluminum oxide sandpaper (found in the paint aisle of any home improvement store for about $2.50)

Step 1

Cover the male (inside cradle) and female (on back of dock, along with the line out plug) dock connectors with tape to insulate them. You don't want plastic shavings to ruin the connectors!

Step 2

Start carving out the inner sides and back of the dock with the sharp tool of your choice. Cover your desk with something to make it easy to dispose of all the shavings. Carve for 5 minutes at a time, and then take the tape off the male dock connector to test out your progress as you go. You can use the small flathead screwdriver to help take the tape off of the male dock connector. Don't forget to recover the connector with tape after each test. Don't worry about making your carvings even or smooth. (That will be addressed in the final step.)

Step 3

Once you think the iPhone sits nicely, test out the connection to make sure that your iPhone 3G syncs (taking the tape off of the connectors, obviously).

Step 4

Reapply the tape to the connectors.

Step 5

Sand down your carvings with the 100-grit aluminum oxide sandpaper. This is pretty messy, so you may want to do this part over a trash can while you're wearing safety glasses.

Overall, this entire process should take around an hour, including the time going to the hardware store to get the sandpaper—depending on how far away your hardware store is! Figures 12-3 and 12-4 show the results.

Figure 12-3.
Original iPhone dock modified to accept iPhone 3G

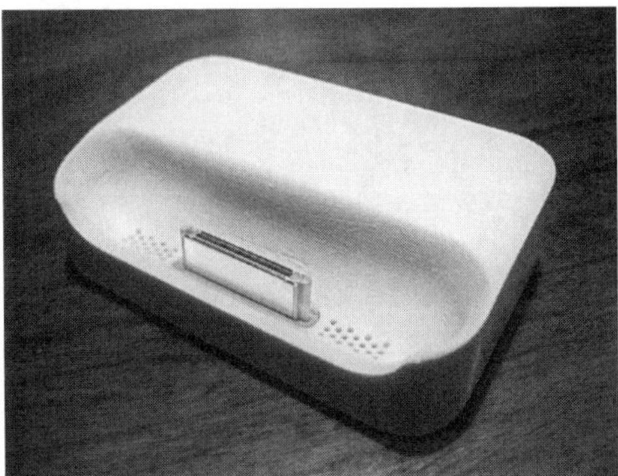

Figure 12-4.
iPhone 3G resting in modified iPhone dock

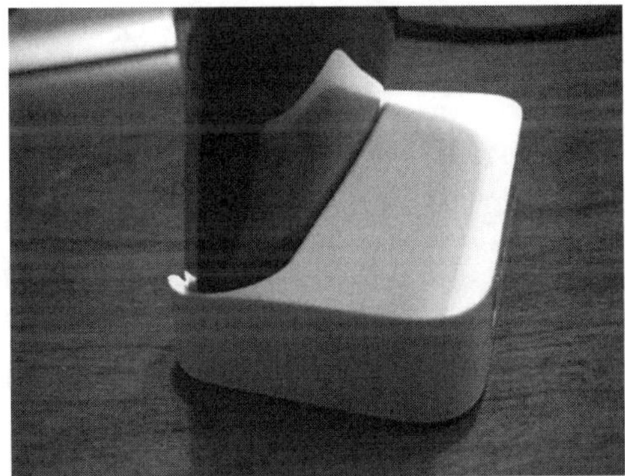

Hopefully, this hack will help save the money it would require to purchase the new 3G dock!

— Matthew Drengler

HACK 12.03: Make Noise-Cancelling iPhone Headset

You can use existing noise-cancelling headphones with your iPhone—or, better yet, improvise with the ones you have.

Sometimes the person you're calling can hear you just fine, due to the well-designed microphone, but you just can't hear what he or she is saying because of the noise around you (Figure 12-5).

You could always use a pair of noise-cancelling headphones (Figure 12-6). If you have an original iPhone you'll have to either modify the plug **[Hack #12.01]** or use an adapter.

Figure 12-5.
What was that?

Figure 12-6.
Bose QuietComfort headphones with an iPhone microphone adapter

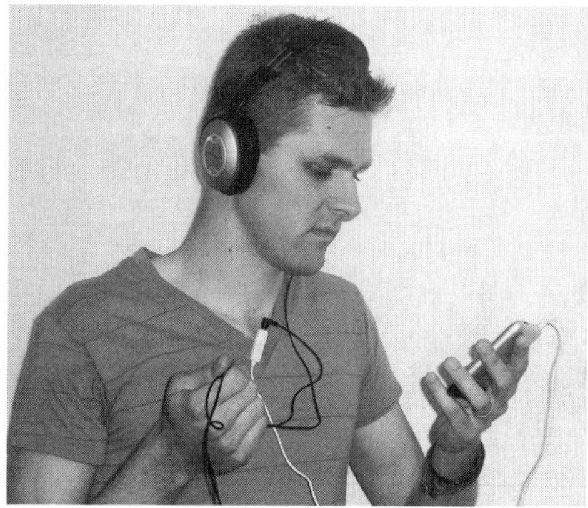

There are many brands of noise-cancelling headphones on the market today. What you may not know is that over-the-ear noise-cancelling headphones work just fine over the headphones that come with your iPhone. If you own an original iPhone you'll get the benefit of noise-cancellation, without having to buy an adapter (Figure 12-7).

Figure 12-7.
Noise-cancelling headphones over the iPod headphones

Now if you want that quiet stillness but you don't have noise-cancelling headphones, there's a very low-tech solution: ear protection gear from a hardware store. Any Home Depot or similar store should carry them (Figure 12-8).

Figure 12-8.
Ear protection

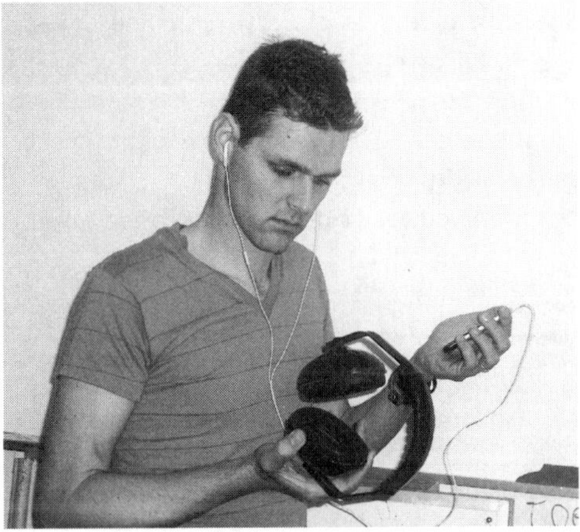

Figure 12-9 shows a happy improviser understanding the other party, now that the distracting noises have been eliminated.

Figure 12-9.
Improvised noise-cancelling headphones

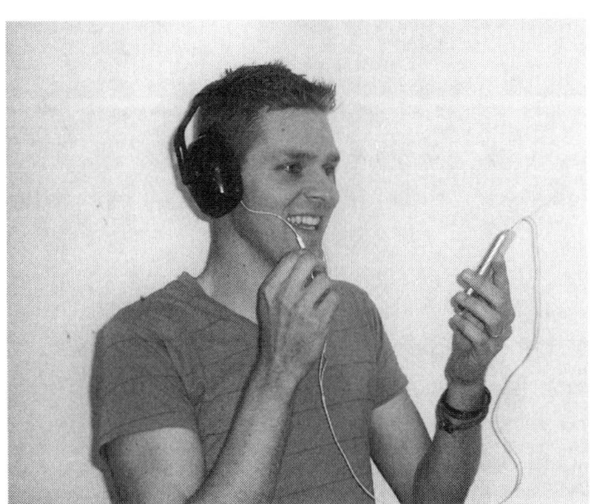

— Damien & Matthew Stolarz

HACK 12.04: Use the iPhone Camera for Close-Ups

With the right lens, you can take sharp close-ups with your iPhone's camera.

The iPhone camera has a modest yet respectable 2 megapixel resolution, but no integrated optical zoom capabilities. It was designed for point-and-click simplicity with very little variability left to the user. As there is no user-adjustable focus, the iPhone is set at "infinite" focus, which is fine for just about anything but close-ups.

Close-ups are important for a number of reasons. If you're trying to use your iPhone to document fine details of objects that you're working on, or scan bar codes on products to look up prices, or even to take a picture of a business card you've been given, you need close-up focus (often called *macro mode*), which the iPhone lacks.

Fortunately, a number of pre-existing, new, and improvised products and tools can help alleviate this problem.

Physically Adjust the Focus of the iPhone's Camera

If you want to use your iPhone only for close-up shots, and you don't want anything attached to your iPhone, then you can try the surgical approach: open the iPhone and change the focus. The process entails opening the phone up, isolating the camera unit, and using pliers to break the glue seal that holds it in the "infinite focus" position. You can see more details on this process as performed by Daniel Forsythe at www.eastrain.com/?p=73. You can see examples of a photo taken with this adjustment at www.flickr.com/photos/defor/sets/72157606981066775.

You can learn about disassembling your iPhone in [Hack #12.10] and [Hack #12.11].

Use Camera Viewfinders

Patrick Ng, a photography and gadget enthusiast used the viewfinders from Lomo cameras (available from http://shop.lomography.com) to achieve some interesting artistic effects, which he details here:

> I use my iPhone camera mostly for shooting objects, but I'm not going to limit my options by modifying the built-in camera as described earlier. So I decided to try using viewfinders from Lomo cameras to see what I could achieve (Figure 12-10).

Figure 12-10.
Lomolized iPhone camera

All these Lomo camera lenses have add-on viewfinders and they have great effects on the iPhone! The Diana+ wide-angle lens, LCA+ wide-angle lens, and Fisheye each create unique imagery. I carry my Diana+ wide-angle viewfinder with me all the time because I love the way I can hold it in front of my iPhone using its viewfinder holder (Figure 12-11).

I can play with numerous analog effects: adding a prism in front, creating a pack film effect by painting/printing on a transparent film as filter, etc. I'm trying to find an easier way to put dozens of filters in front of the viewfinder so that I will be carrying only one gadget for a lot of different effects (Figures 12-12 and 12-13).

By the way, the Diana+ viewfinder holder can actually hold any of these viewfinders.

Figure 12-11.
Lomolized iPhone holding position

Figure 12-12.
Lomolized iPhone Camera—Diana+ wide-angle viewfinder and painted film

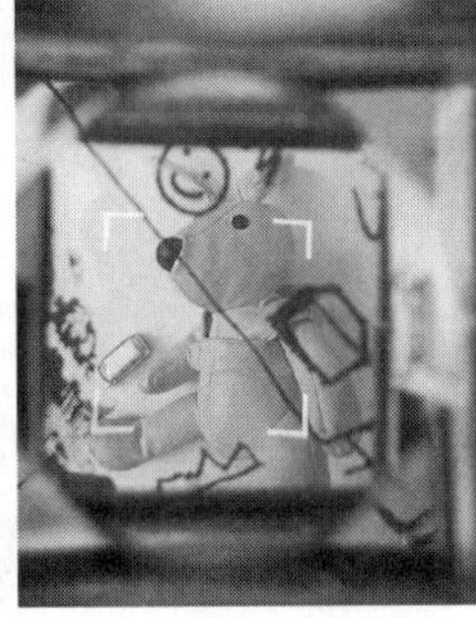

Figure 12-13.
Lomolized fisheye shots

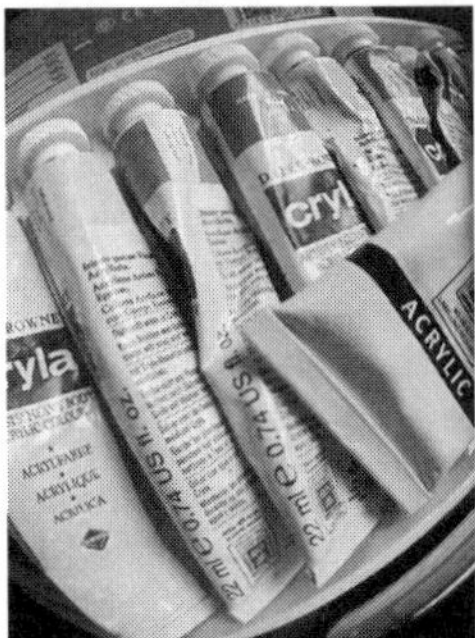

In addition to "Lomolizing" your iPhone, using the Diana+ wide-angle viewfinder as an iPhone add-on lens not only improves close-up quality, but also even allows you to create a double-exposure effect (Figure 12-14) as well as a kaleidoscope effect.

Figure 12-14.
Double-exposure effect

If you look at the Diana+ viewfinder closely, you'll see a top window collecting light for the cross-hair seen through the viewfinder. By prying open the top window, you will be able to remove the cross-hair film and replace it with anything you like, such as some negative/positive film or a painted transparent film, thereby creating an overlay or double-exposure effect when the viewfinder is used to take shots.

Mobile Phone lenses

There are several close-up lenses designed specifically for mobile phones—and the iPhone specifically. The eyeMobile KC-1 (Figure 12-15) is available at http://store.mouse.ne.jp/?language=en. The lens attaches to the iPhone with a wide circle clip. You can carry it on a keychain when you aren't taking close-ups.

Figure 12-15.
eyeMobile KC-1 close-up lens

For the second-generation iPhone, Griffin has created the Clarifi case, which includes an integrated, switchable overlay lens (Figure 12-16). See www.griffintechnology.com/products/clarifi.

Figure 12-16.
Griffin Technology's Clarifi 3G Case

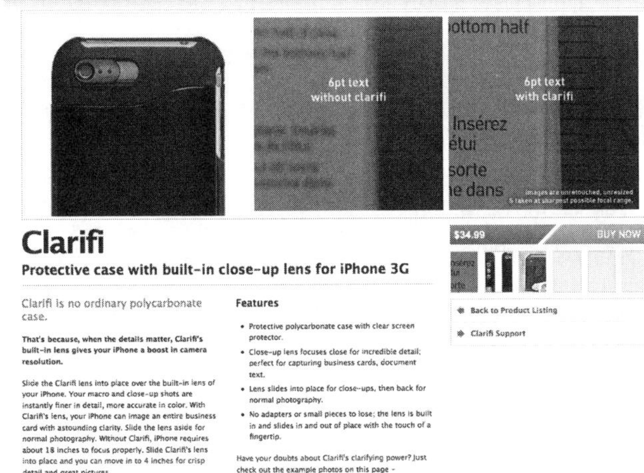

Improvise a lens

If you don't want to break open your phone or buy viewfinders, you can get by with a simple magnifying glass. Figure 12-17 shows some of what Richard Dodd achieved with the magnifying glass from a Swiss Army knife. You can see the rest of the set at www.flickr.com/photos/cellodick/sets/72157601804979593/detail.

Figure 12-17.
Close-ups using an iPhone and a small magnifying glass (pictures courtesy of Richard Dodd)

 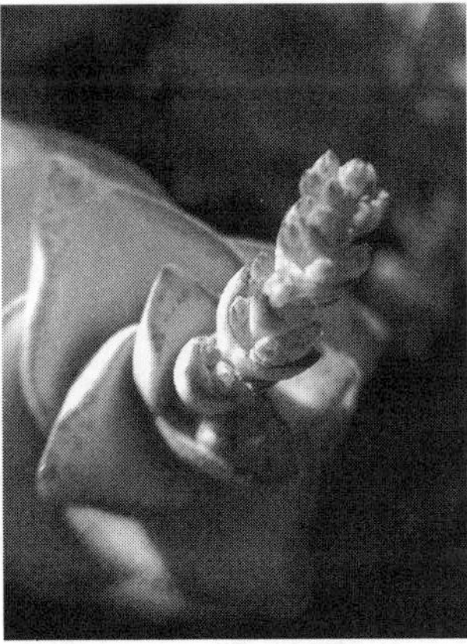 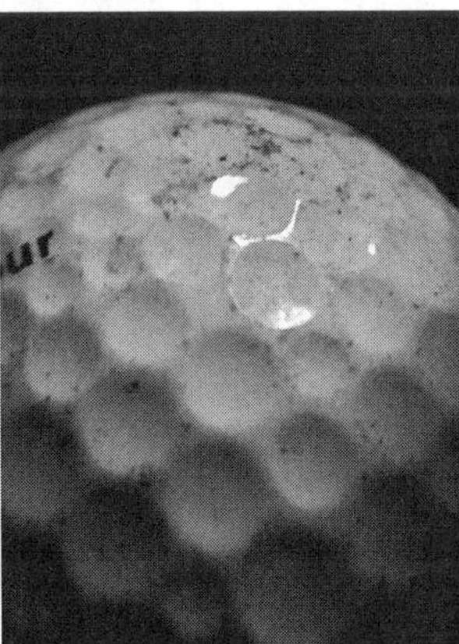

— Damien Stolarz & Patrick Ng

HACK 12.05: Watch Your iPhone or iPod touch on a TV

Don't pay $11.99 to rent a bad movie when you have your own personal entertainment already on your iPhone.

If you've spent any time on the road, you know that hotels charge unconscionable fees for simple little things like ordering a movie. But you know that if you crack open your laptop, you're likely to get distracted, not watch the movie, and thus tragically fail to chill out. And even if you get the movie started, the excessive lap heat generated by the whole laptop-in-bed thing might limit your reproductive life (depending on your gender, of course).

So you try to catch up on that science fiction series on your iPhone screen, but your neck gets sore, your hands don't want to hold anything, and you're just not getting the relaxing audiovisual experience you needed.

Luckily, there is a solution.

Before you try this hack, check the television for audio (red and white) and video (yellow for NTSC or red/green/blue for component video) inputs. If the TV has those, then you can plug your iPhone directly into the TV (with the appropriate iPhone video cable or dock). See "Swanky Hotels," at the end of this hack.

RF Modulation

An RF modulator, or radio frequency modulator, is a very geeky term for a simple device: it makes the yellow-red-white audio/video output wires show up on channel 3 or 4. It's that simple. If you had an Atari, Nintendo, or other video game systems of yore, with a correspondingly antique television, you may vaguely recall a little box that screwed into the back of the television and plugged into your game console.

Well, amazingly, your video source is now smaller than the little box, but you can still buy those things and "hack" into the hotel television.

What you'll need:

1. RF modulator (Figure 12-18)
2. Pliers and/or hands
3. Apple composite A/V cable (Figure 12-19)
4. Composite extension cables, so you can keep your iPhone right next to you and use headphones to listen (optional)
5. Spare coaxial cable (to connect the RF modulator to the TV)

Figure 12-18.
RF modulator

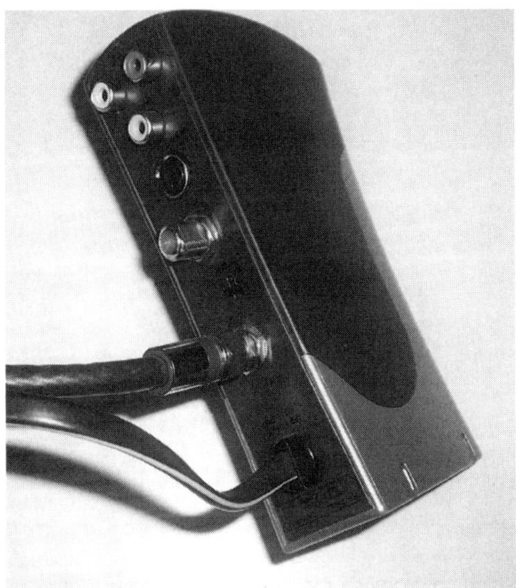

Figure 12-19.
Apple composite AV cable

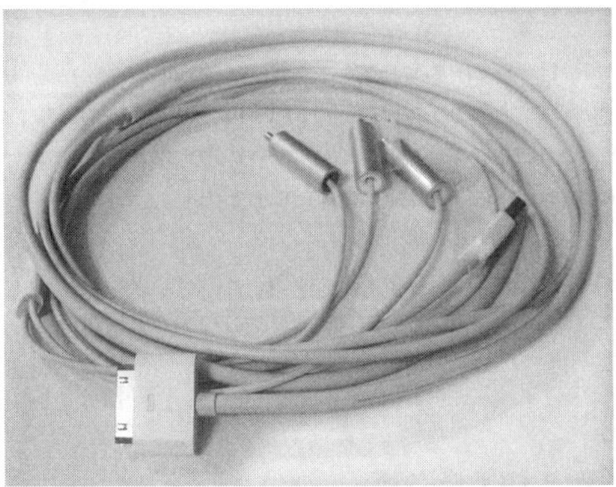

Figure 12-20 shows the coaxial jack that you might find on the back of your hotel TV. If you can't unscrew it from the TV, try finding the other end, where it comes out of the cable box or proprietary hotel-video-rental guest-exploitation-unit. Once you've unscrewed one end or the other, connect the TV to the output of the RF modulator. Note how everything was before you start, so you can put everything back the way you found it when you're done outsmarting "the man."

Figure 12-20.
Cable input on TV

Once you've got this connected, you'll be able to watch any movie or video podcast in your hotel room. And if you have an iPhone 3G or an available Wi-Fi connection, you can probably *buy* a movie via iTunes for the price that it would cost to *rent* it from the hotel!

Swanky Hotels

If you're staying in a hotel that has a high definition flat-screen, chances are that the video inputs work—and chances are that you're not trying to go cheap on the entertainment options, anyhow. But if the content on your iPhone is all you want to watch, you can also purchase Apple's component A/V cable, which gives you the red-green-blue RCA cables for analog HD.

Of course, video is not all you can do with your TV-out connection on an iPhone. And no, we're not talking about viewing PowerPoint presentations **[Hack #4.03]**. You can use almost any iPhone application on the TV—see **[Hack #12.06]**.

HACK 12.06: Mirror or Output the iPhone Screen with TV-Out

ScreenSplitr and TVOut do just what they say—to great satisfaction.

Apple makes lovely cables (Figure 12-21) that plug into the bottom of the iPhone and iPod touch with the ubiquitous red-white-yellow RCA connectors on the end. They let you play movies on screens larger than 3 inches, and output audio to speakers. (There's even a component version of the adapters if you want HD output.)

Figure 12-21.
Pretty white Apple cables

But what if you wanted to give a Steve Jobs–style demonstration of a new app you made, with your iPhone screen mirrored on the monitor behind you? The iPhone won't do this out of the box, but with the following two applications available on Cydia **[Hack #1.04]** you'll be able to mirror your iPhone screen with TV-Out.

ScreenSplitr

ScreenSplitr is a workaround (available via Cydia) that, when enabled, mirrors the video output of your entire device and all its applications. It has a simple one-button operation (Figure 12-22); tap the icon to toggle video-out. This app will transmit anything on the screen over the wire to your TV, and the image will stay on the iPhone's screen so that you can control it easily. The disadvantage is that the frame rate on the external feed is noticeably lower than normal.

Figure 12-22.
ScreenSplitr's only real interface: the icon

TVOut

TVOut, also available on Cydia, lets you toggle video output for each individual application (Figure 12-23). When an application is being sent to an external monitor with TVOut, it is not shown on the iPhone itself. Because of this, it can be hard to control (you can't see the screen, which makes tapping/touching difficult), but the advantage is that it displays at full frame rate.

Figure 12-23.
TVOut's list of application toggles

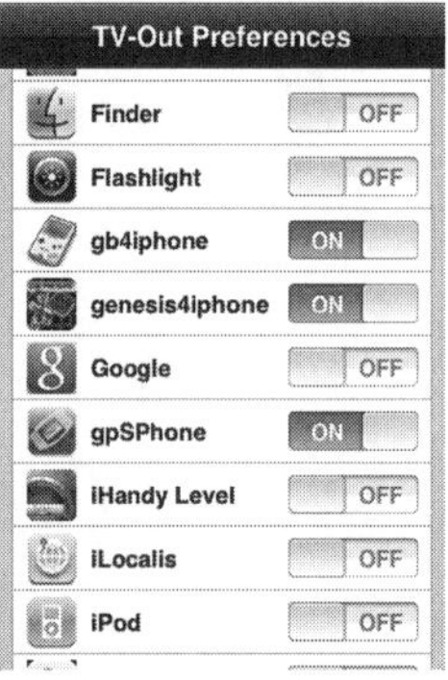

The high frame rate of TVOut allows you to easily play game emulators on external displays, with the iPhone as a controller. You can see an example of this in Figure 12-24.

Figure 12-24.
Playing NES on a screen with an iPhone

HACK 12.07: Connect the iPhone to a Car

There are many ways to enhance your drive with the iPhone.

For the past hundred years, almost every type of audiovisual entertainment has eventually made it into the vehicle. Sure, the phonographs tended to skip a lot, but with tapes and CDs and DVDs, it's worked out pretty well. So it was only a matter of time before iPod integration became a standard feature in the car. And because the iPhone honors its iPod heritage, many of the solutions for earlier iPods still work for the iPhone. And those few features that don't work are remediable.

Front-Seat Entertainment

Connecting your iPhone or iPod touch to the vehicle is relatively easy and very satisfying. There are four basic ways to get iPhone audio to play through your car's speakers:

1. Tape adapter
2. Radio adapter
3. Car stereo auxiliary input
4. iPhone dock integration

The first two solutions are widely available at any big-box retailer, electronic store, RadioShack, or Apple Store: just connect them via the iPhone's 3.5 mm headphone plug, and you're up and running. The third, auxiliary input (if your car has it), is a fortunate development in automotive manufacturing, and simplifies the process greatly. All you need is a 3.5 mm male-to-male extender (the same cable that connects most PC speakers to the PC), and your iPhone can plug right in.

The fourth option (Figure 12-25), an iPhone or iPod dock connector, is the slickest one, especially if you can get a car with it preinstalled.

Figure 12-25.
iPod integration in a Lexus 400h

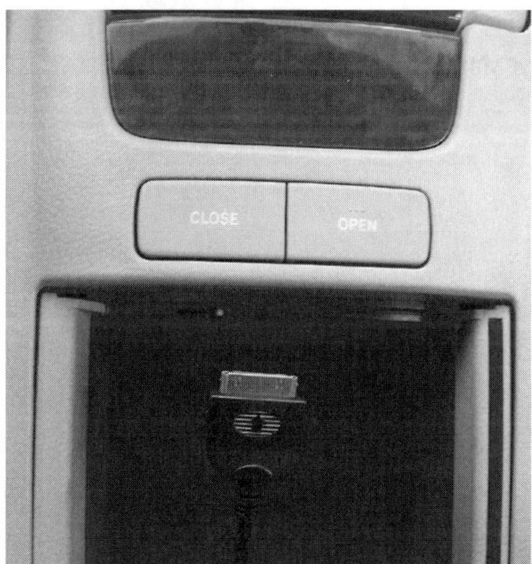

iPod/iPhone Integration

One of the problems with iPod integration is that iPhone integration isn't perfect. For one thing, the iPhone 3G won't charge via many of the iPod integration systems, because they provide 12V to the FireWire pins **[Hack #12.17]** instead of 5V. Figures 12-26 and 12-27 show two adapters that solve this problem: one by Scosche (www.scosche.com/products/productID/1667) and the other by CableJive (http://cablejive.com/chargeconverter.html).

Figure 12-26.
Scosche passPORT 12V to 5V charging adapter

The CableJive adapter also has a mini-USB output if you have to charge some other device (your Zune, maybe).

Figure 12-27.
12V to 5V charging adapter

Even if you've adapted the power, you may not have enough reach to keep your iPhone accessible. As you can see in Figure 12-26, you now have a rigid, somewhat unwieldy 4-inch protrusion from the bottom of your iPhone. And unlike a traditional iPod, whose sole purpose in life is to play music, your iPhone also wants to make phone calls, and you may need it within reach to answer or place a call, or just to see who's calling. For this, CableJive makes a dock extender (Figure 12-28).

Figure 12-28.
CableJive's dock extender

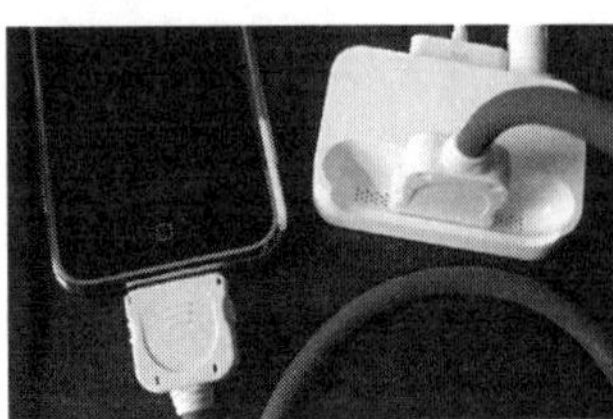

[Hack #12.17] shows you a couple more adapters that you can use to charge your iPhone—and even how to build your own.

Adding iPod integration

If your car didn't come with auxiliary input or iPod integration, don't despair: there are hundreds of aftermarket options available that might match your car. Some leading aftermarket vendors of iPhone-car integration are www.pac-audio.com, http://peripheralelectronics.com, and www.pie.net. You can go to their sites and browse lists of their applications (i.e., a kit for a specific car).

One unique product worth mentioning is iSimpleSolutions iPhone integration system (Figure 12-29). It works with any late model car that is satellite radio–ready (which is a lot of them) and tricks the radio into thinking the iPhone is a satellite radio. You can browse the music collection, see track and artist names, and of course charge the iPhone while it's plugged in (www.isimplesolutions.com/CES/Gateway.asp).

Figure 12-29.
iSimple Gateway iPhone car stereo integration

Controlling Your iPhone/iPod touch

The name of the game in driver safety is keeping your eyes on the road, hands on the wheel. Scosche also makes a clever device for controlling your iPod (Figure 12-30), which, though in this sense unsupported by Scosche, also happens to work for the iPod touch and iPhone (www.scosche.com/products/sfID1/210/sfID2/324).

Figure 12-30.
Scosche IPNRFC iPod remote control

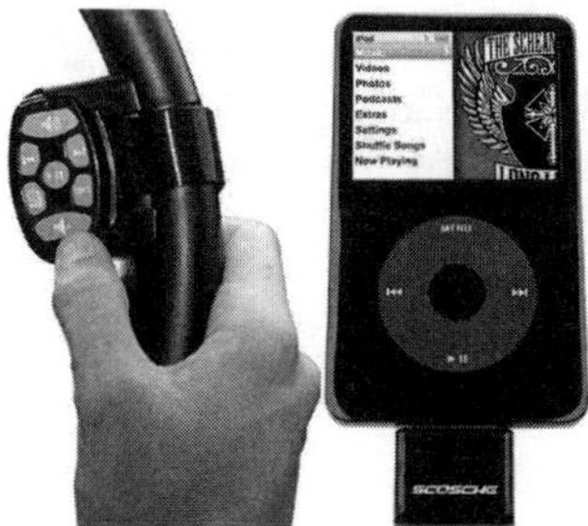

Rear-Seat Entertainment

If you've got kids who ride in the car with you, you probably have learned about the "electric babysitter." Putting screens in the rear headrests of your vehicle is the humane thing to do on long drives (unless you were thoughtful enough to buy a car just for its integrated DVD player).

The Apple composite A/V adapter **[Hack #12.05]** easily plugs into the composite input of almost any in-vehicle screen (Figure 12-31), and can even drive multiple screens with a simple RCA jack splitter (Figure 12-32). Vizualogic (www.vizualogic.com) created the screens for this Dodge Caravan, and they sell screens to match the vinyl, leather, or fabric of almost any modern vehicle for a factory-integrated look. If you don't want to permanently install rear screens, you can get a pair that install quickly by hooking to the rear headrests at stores like Target, Wal-Mart, or Best Buy (in the United States).

Figure 12-31.
Dual Video display from an iPhone

Figure 12-32.
RCA splitter

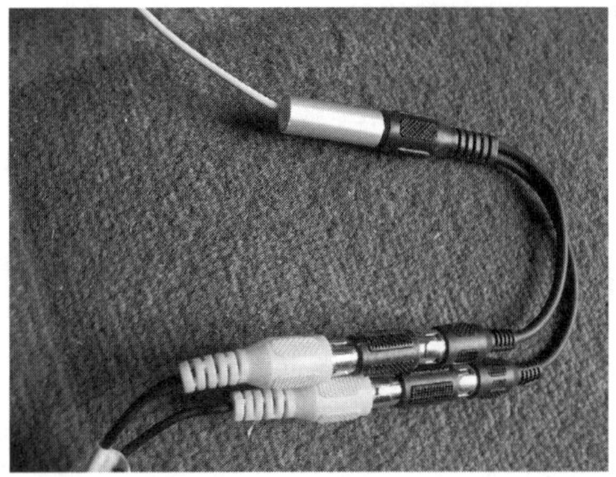

Because the adapter has a USB plug as well, you can charge while playing. Automotive USB power adapters are available for $5–$10 at many electronics retailers. The one in Figure 12-33 is a double-headed adapter, so you can charge two devices at once.

Figure 12-33.
Auto 12V power socket to USB adapter

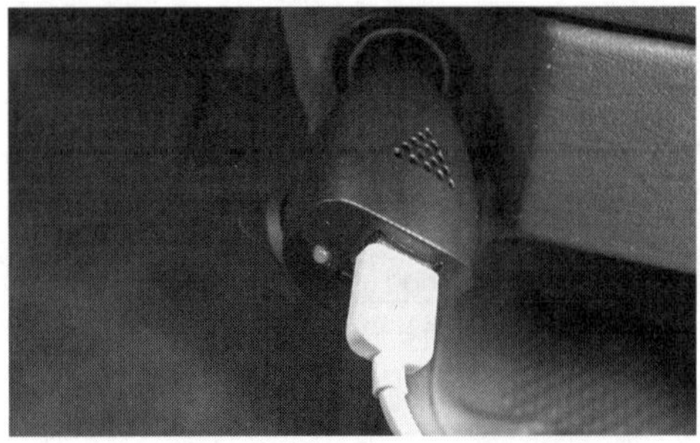

If your screens in headrests come with wireless headphones, you can connect the white and red (left- and right-channel) RCA connectors to the headrest input. But if you want the sound to go through the stereo system, you may need to use an adapter (Figure 12-34) to convert the RCA back into a 3.5 mm stereo output.

Figure 12-34.
RCA to 3.5 mm adapter

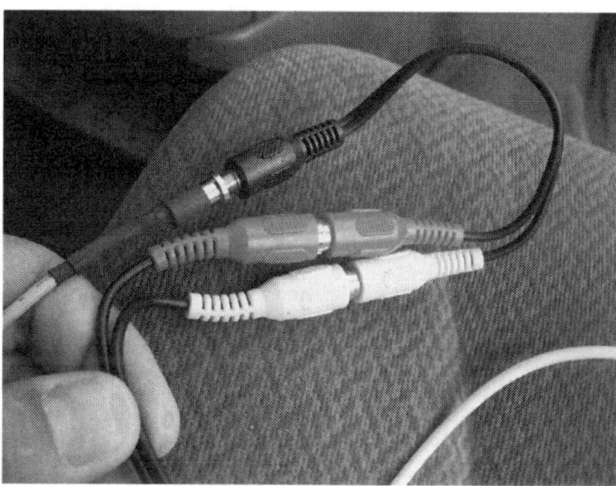

If your vehicle comes with a center console, you can do a clean, hidden install, where the iPhone or iPod touch is accessible to the front seat, and the power, audio, and video cables are tucked away (Figure 12-35).

Figure 12-35.
Hidden away in your center console

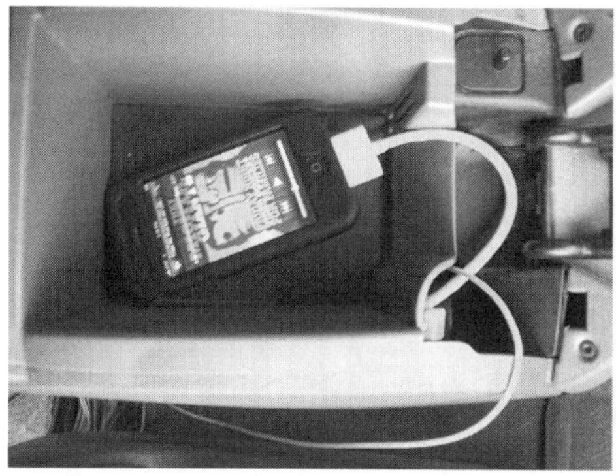
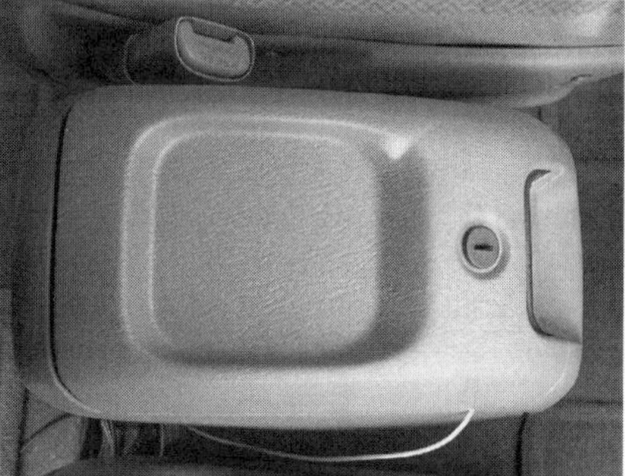

There's one issue that occasionally comes up that creates an annoying buzz in the sound. This is caused by signals from the car looping back through the ground connection of the device. A *ground loop isolator* (available from RadioShack and www.crutchfield.com), as shown in Figure 12-36, goes between the audio outputs and stereo input, and eliminates this noise.

Figure 12-36.
Ground loop isolator

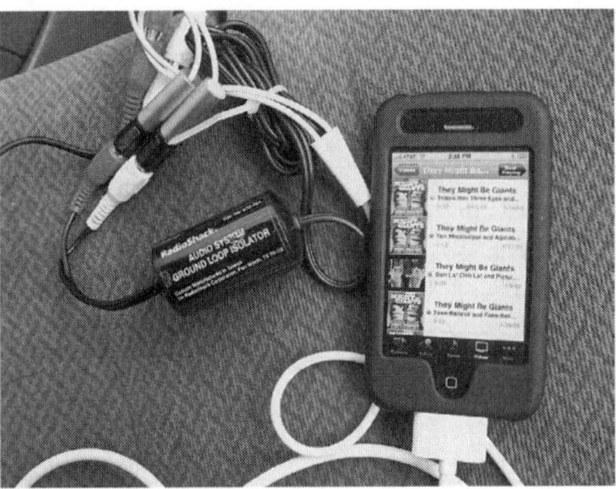

In-Vehicle Internet

If you have an iPhone 3G, then you already have near-broadband speeds in areas that are served by AT&T's 3G network. But if you have an iPod touch or an original iPhone, you may feel out of touch on the road, unable to play network games and download movies. But there's a solution to that, too.

There are several devices that can help make your vehicle into a Wi-Fi hotspot. Portable wireless routers, such as the Kyocera KR-1, turn a Verizon or Sprint EV-DO mobile broadband card into a wireless hotspot (Sprint sells a portable router for $140 as well). CradlePoint (www.cradlepoint.com) also makes portable wireless routers (Figure 12-37). You can find a full list of similar devices at www.evdoinfo.com.

All of these products provide Wi-Fi to any device you've got, so if you're trying to make sure that you're almost always online, these are an essential addition to your arsenal of gadgets.

Figure 12-37.
CradlePoint portable wireless router

HACK 12.08: Use Your iPhone with Gloves On

You can keep your hands warm and still use your iPhone.

The iPhone has a capacitive touch screen. That means it's registering the presence of a conductive object, such as your finger, and not the pressure of your touch as you might expect. If you're curious, get a piece of carrot and try to use your phone with that. You will find that it works just as well as your finger.

When you're wearing mittens or gloves in colder climates, it's uncomfortable and inconvenient to keep taking them off and on in order to operate a touch device like the iPod. While some gloves have fingertip caps that you can open, it is at times too cold to comfortably do this. What you need is a way to make your fingers work right through the glove.

There are several approaches to making the fingertips of your gloves conductive:

- Put conductive glue on the fingertips
- Sew conductive thread into the fingertips
- Attach rivets
- Buy ready-made conductive gloves

DIY Conductive Glue

To make conductive glue, grind mechanical pencil leads (Figure 12-38) into a fine powder and mix the graphite powder with a minimal amount of Elmer's rubber cement (Figure 12-39). Glue should be added one drop at a time while stirring, until you get a paste-like consistency. At first you just get gooey balls of graphite, but as soon as you've added enough glue, it turns into a black sludge. Then put the glove on your hand, and dip your thumb and index finger in the bowl. You have to be moderately quick, because it will dry quickly. Also, it's pretty messy. You *will* get graphite on your hands, and probably any surface you are working on. It goes without saying that although graphite isn't poisonous like lead, you probably don't want to use your nice cooking pestle and mortar set to do the grinding.

Surprisingly, this actually works, and it works well. It gives a natural feeling, and good control. You don't have to layer it on too thickly for it to work; you might just try a dot of glue, or a thin coating. The drawback of this solution is that sometimes you may leave graphite smudges on things, but these can be wiped off.

Figure 12-38.
Mechanical pencil lead, ready for grinding with a pestle

Figure 12-39.
Rubber cement mixed with powdered pencil graphite

Rubber cement costs about $5 and you'll probably spend another $5–$10 for the pencil lead. So at $15, the glue option is the cheapest, easiest, and quickest to apply, and gives the best control over the phone. The price of pencil leads is usually the same regardless of the thickness of lead, so you get slightly more for your money if you buy the thickest pencil lead you can.

Conductive Thread

Conductive thread (Figure 12-40) works well, and can be made to look nice, depending on your sewing skill levels. Both finger and thumb work fine, but the stitching on the index finger (Figure 12-41) gives more control than the thumb. Although more thread works better, experimentation showed that a minimal amount of thread was still functional (Figure 12-42).

Figure 12-40.
Conductive thread

Conductive thread can be purchased from SparkFun Electronics (www.sparkfun.com, part number DEV-08549). In this hack, 4-ply thread was used, but 2-ply would probably also work well, and might be more attractive. The price is currently about $20 a spool plus shipping, but one spool could easily do multiple pairs of gloves and be used for other projects.

Figure 12-41.
Conductive thread stitching on the index finger

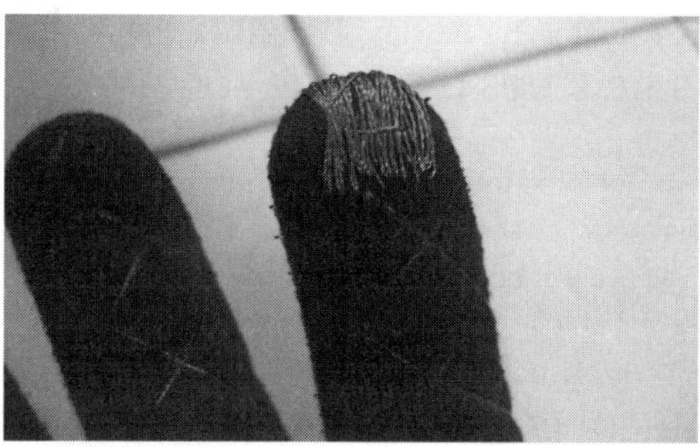

Figure 12-42.
It works just fine!

Premade Solutions

An inexpensive, already conductive solution for the problem of cold hands and iPhones is made by DOTS (Figure 12-43): the iPhone Glove.

Figure 12-43.
DOTS iPhone Gloves

— Christopher Kurpinski

HACK 12.08: Peek Inside Your Device

Whether you're replacing the battery or replacing the screen, this hack will introduce you to the delicate steps of iPhone surgery.

There is a wonderfully macabre portion of the iPhone and iPod touch community that can't help but recklessly disassemble and document each new model as soon as they come out. They revel in unveiling the inner workings and most secret physical components of each soap-bar-like device. This process is often very well documented and of great help to anyone who wishes to modify, repair, or simply torture their device. This hack will focus on modifications and repair, with images helpfully provided by our disassembler friends over at iFixit (www.ifixit.com), which is also a great source for any of the parts you might need in the repair of your device.

Most disassembly instructions for devices will drop a bomb on you right at the end of the instructions that "reassembly is the opposite of disassembly" or "reverse these steps to reassemble." At that point, you may suddenly realize that you haven't exactly been keeping track of which screw goes where, or even taking care not to lose the screws. Here we'll warn you ahead of time. So find some shotglasses or plastic food storage containers, such as ice cube trays, to save the screws (Figure 12-44), and pay attention to the steps, thinking about them backward as well as forward so that reassembly will be as easy as possible. If you keep a camera handy to take photos of your work at each critical step, it will make it way easier to backtrack.

Figure 12-44.
Screws saved in a shotglass

Tools

Spudgers are the most generic-seeming yet most crucial tool for disassembly of tightly constructed devices such as the iPhone (Figure 12-45). They're sticks of plastic or metal with different tips. Often they have wedges, hooks, or points. Devices like the iPhone aren't like toy guns, in that they don't have lots of loose plastic that can simply be screwed together. They use systems of internal clips and wedging, the disassembly of which requires specific spudgers if you want it done right—and without serrated butter-knife marks on your casing. The steps in the this hack will reference specific kinds of spudgers, as well as a special tool called the *iPod Opening Tool*. Next is a rundown on the specific spudgers and other tools.

Figure 12-45.
Using a metal spudger to remove the screen from an iPod touch

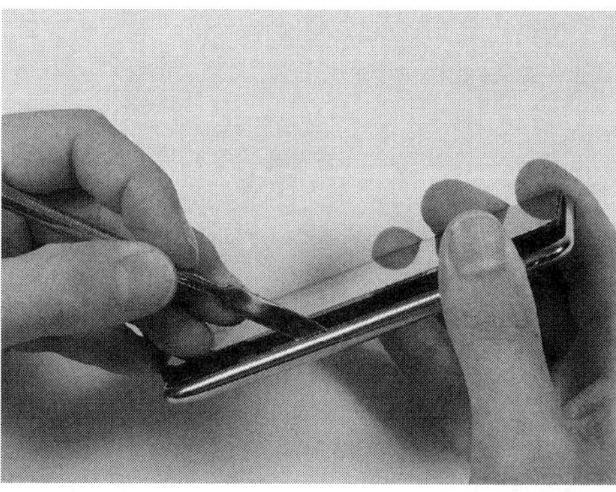

The simple spudger (Figure 12-46) has a wedge with a hook on one end, and a pencil-like point on the other end. It's made of tough and antistatic plastic. It is used in prying, lifting up connectors, and at one point in this disassembly, scraping away glue.

Figure 12-46.
The spudger

The heavy-duty spudger (Figure 12-47) has a thicker wedge and thicker point. It does the "heavy lifting" as it were. It is plastic, like the regular spudger.

Figure 12-47.
The heavy-duty spudger

The metal spudger (Figure 12-48) is even sturdier, because it is metal. It's used in the prying of certain edges as well as in the removal of the original iPhone's antenna cover.

Figure 12-48.
The metal spudger

The iPod Opening Tools (Figure 12-49) are specially made for prying up the edges of iPods and iPhones without damaging them. They are made of a lighter material than that of the iPod, and thus are prone to damage if not used properly. Too many failures could result in them being unusable, in which case a thin metal blade or guitar pick would work as a replacement.

Figure 12-49.
The iPod opening tools

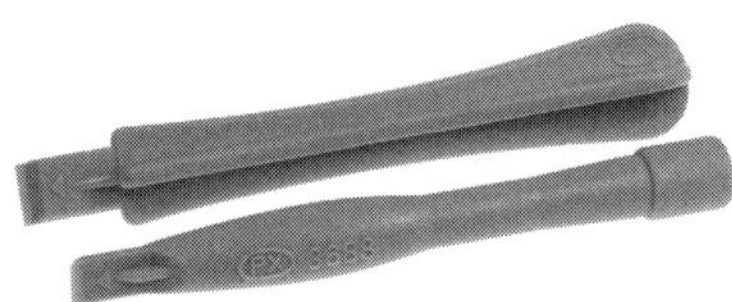

The #00 Phillips screwdriver (Figure 12-50) is a very small screwdriver, used for the kinds of tiny screws that you'll find in small precision devices like iPhones.

Figure 12-50.
The Phillips #00 screwdriver

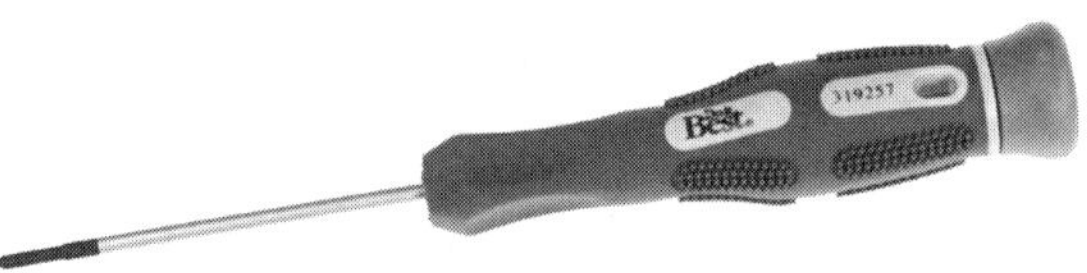

To whet your appetite for disassembly fun, here are four grand reveals of iPhone and iPod touch insides. Figure 12-51 shows a disassembled original model iPhone—the same model that is pictured partially nude on the cover of this book as a teaser.

Figure 12-51.
You can tell it's the original iPhone from the black plastic antenna cover portion.

Figure 12-52 shows a dismembered iPhone 3G, with all the fixins.

Figure 12-52.
The iPhone 3G, which comes with all that you see here

Figure 12-53 shows a filleted original iPod touch. It looks simpler than the iPhone, because it is: no SIM card, camera, or microphone.

Figure 12-53.
The original iPod touch

Figure 12-54 shows a splayed iPod touch 2G. It's like the original version, but rounder.

Figure 12-54.
The opened-up original iPod touch

The following four hacks will give you disassembly instructions for both generations of iPhone and iPod touch. By the time you're done reading, you'll feel like you could disassemble anything.

HACK 12.10: Disassemble and Reassemble Your Original iPhone

Master the skill of disassembling and reassembling your iPhone.

Taking apart the first-generation iPhone is quite different from taking apart the iPhone 3G.

 The advanced stages of this hack require soldering experience. If you don't have experience soldering, check out the Learn to Solder Bundle from MAKE, available at www.makershed.com/ProductDetails.asp?ProductCode=MSBUN1.

The first thing you'll want to do before you start taking apart your phone is to remove the SIM card tray by inserting a paper clip into the hole on top of the iPhone and sliding the tray out (Figure 12-55). If you don't do this, you'll likely bend or break your SIM card tray at some point in disassembly.

 For tips on reassembling the device, as well as an overview of the tools used here, see [Hack #12.09].

Figure 12-55.
Popping out the SIM card tray

The next part necessary in any iPhone disassembly is removing the black plastic antenna cover (Figure 12-56). It has four tabs that you need to pop open with a metal spudger and an iPod opening tool. First, release the tabs near the dock connector by sliding a metal spudger in-between the dock connector and the antenna cover (Figure 12-57). Make sure that you're actually sticking it between those two pieces and not simply sticking it in the dock connector. Next, insert the wedge of the iPod tool between the front metal bezel and the antenna cover (Figure 12-58). The wedge should be facing the antenna cover. Slide the iPod tool up and around the corner to unhook the side tabs. Do this once for each side. Next, grab the panel by the sides, lift it away, and slide it off the iPhone (Figure 12-59). This might take some force. If it doesn't seem to be coming off, make sure you're lifting it out from the iPhone before you slide it off down the bottom.

Figure 12-56.
The antenna cover

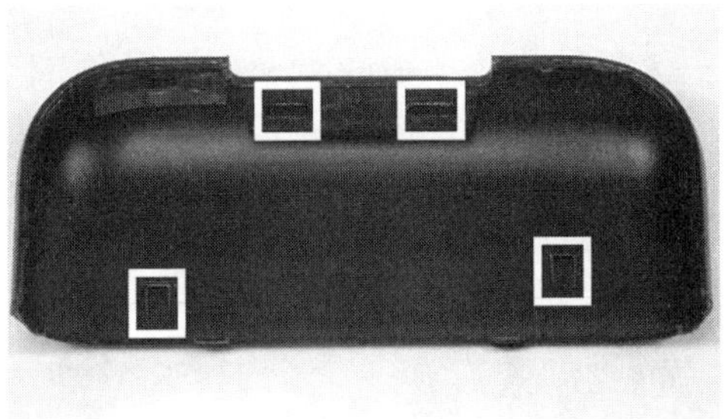

Figure 12-57.
Putting a metal spudger in-between the dock connector and antenna panel

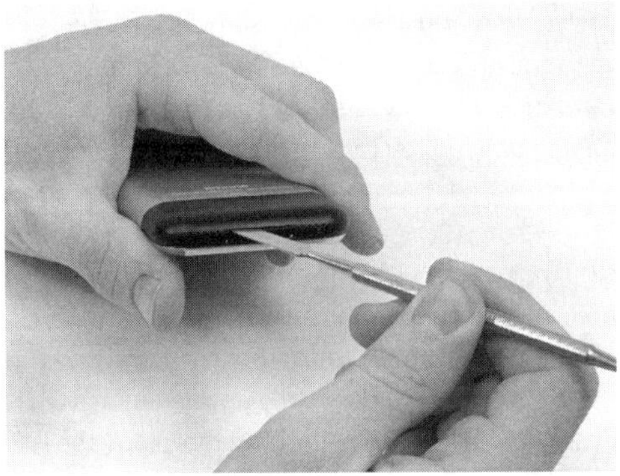

Figure 12-58.
Sliding an iPod tool between the metal frame and antenna panel

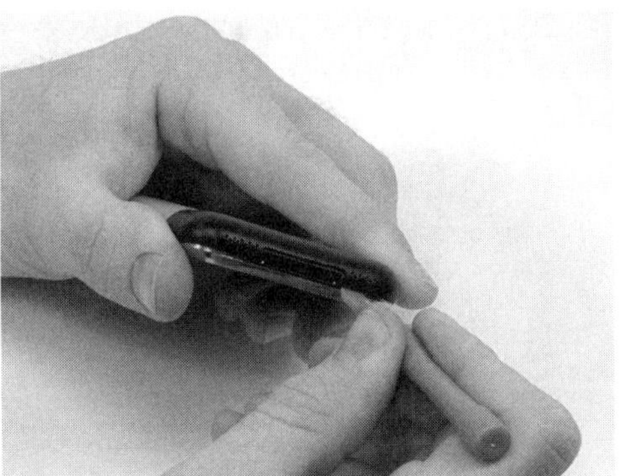

Figure 12-59.
Removing the antenna panel

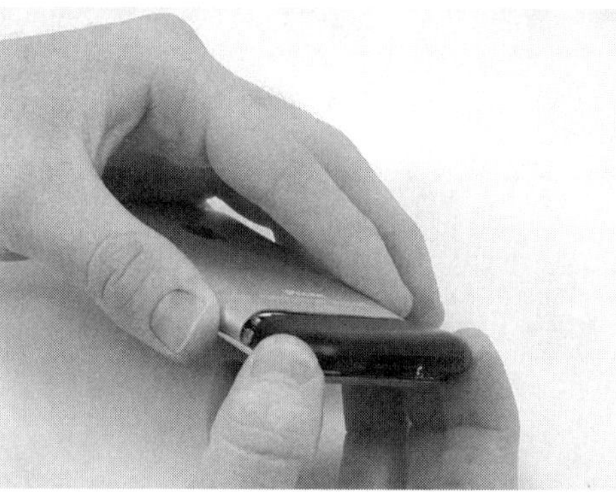

Next, the metal rear panel is the object of our deconstruction. You'll want to unscrew the three Phillips #00 screws that attach the panel to the rest of the phone (Figure 12-60). Make sure to note where these were (check the photograph for help) and tuck them away safely. Now, this panel is rather hard to remove, so don't get discouraged or angry at it, or you may damage it more than you intended to.

Now you'll need to do more prying. Start with the side that doesn't have the volume buttons, as whichever side you tackle first is going to be the hardest to get, and then you won't risk damaging those buttons. Insert the point of a heavy-duty spudger into the gap between the rear panel and the area around where you removed the screw (Figure 12-61). Gently pry the frame upwards until you can insert an iPod tool in the gap between the bezel and rear panel. Slide the iPod tool along the side of the case and pop the four tabs open (Figure 12-62).

Make sure during the remaining steps that you don't squeeze the case and repop the tabs back into place. Now repeat the same pry-and-pry procedure on the button side (Figure 12-63), which only has 3 tabs. Now you can lift off the rear panel. But don't yank it off, as you still need to use a spudger to disconnect the headphone jack cable from the logic board (Figure 12-64).

Figure 12-60.
Unscrew three Phillips #00 screws

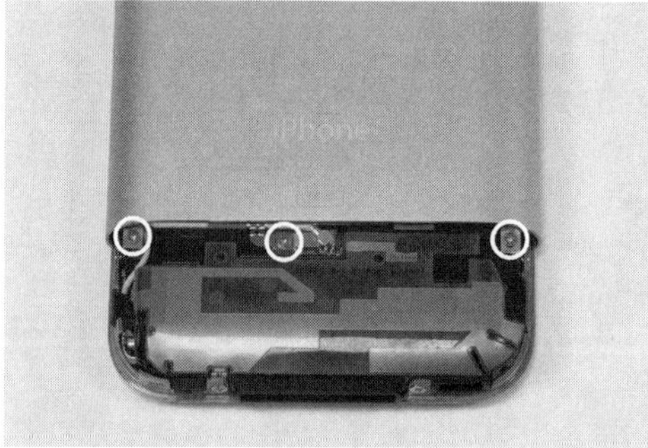

Figure 12-61.
Insert heavy-duty spudger

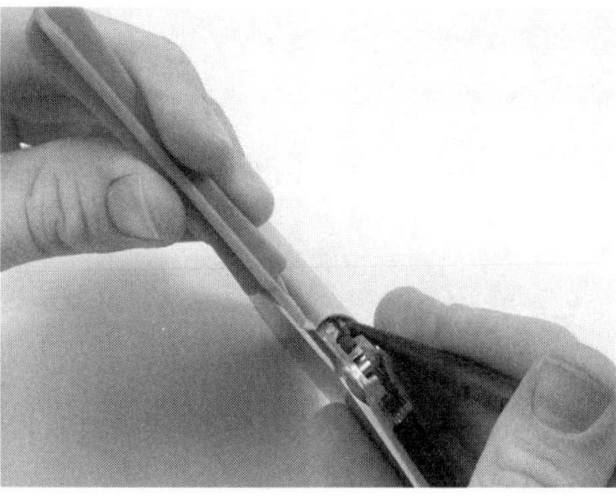

Figure 12-62.
Slide iPod tool along case

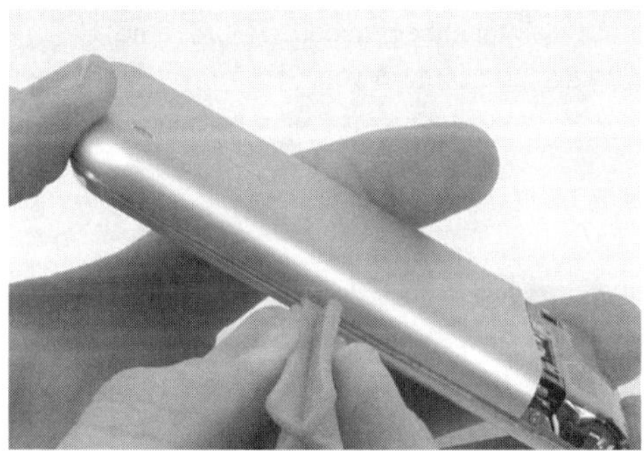

Figure 12-63.
Slide iPod tool along other side of case

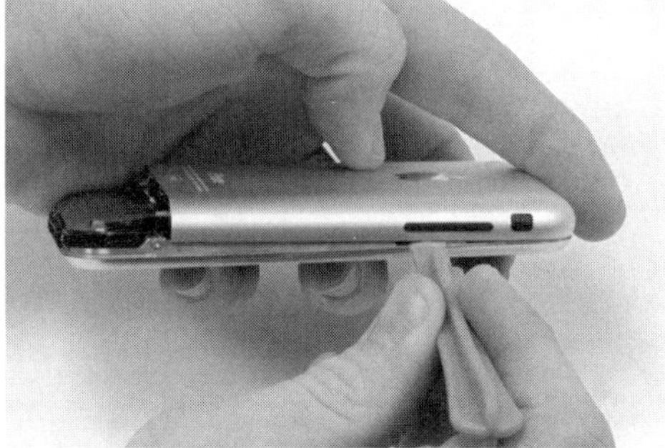

Figure 12-64.
Disconnect the headphone jack cable from the logic board

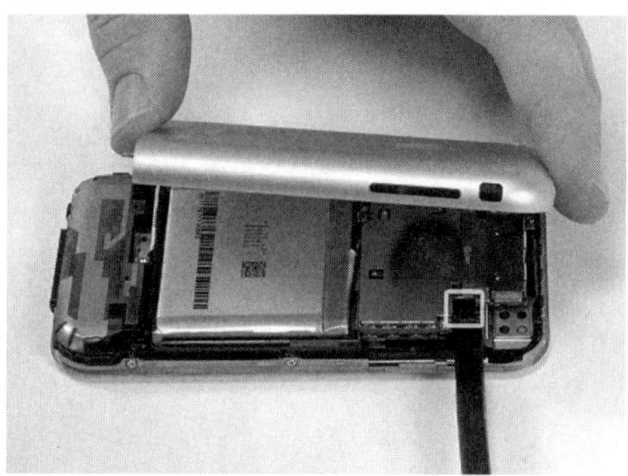

It's Open!

Now your iPhone is opened up, and you can access nearly everything from this point. The rest of this section will cover removing the battery, a common maintenance procedure. More removal instructions can be found by poking around with spudgers and screwdrivers yourself, or through the guides available on www.ifixit.com.

Removing the Battery

Use the tip of a spudger to remove the cloudy white glue covering the battery contacts, as shown in Figure 12-65.

Figure 12-65.
Remove glue from contacts

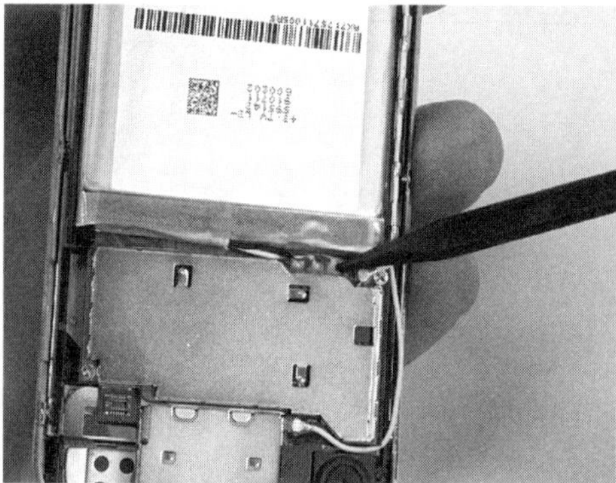

Working from the edge opposite the battery connectors, insert a spudger between the battery and the plastic frame and pry up (Figure 12-66). The battery is attached to the casing with an adhesive, but should slowly come free.

Figure 12-66.
Pry up battery

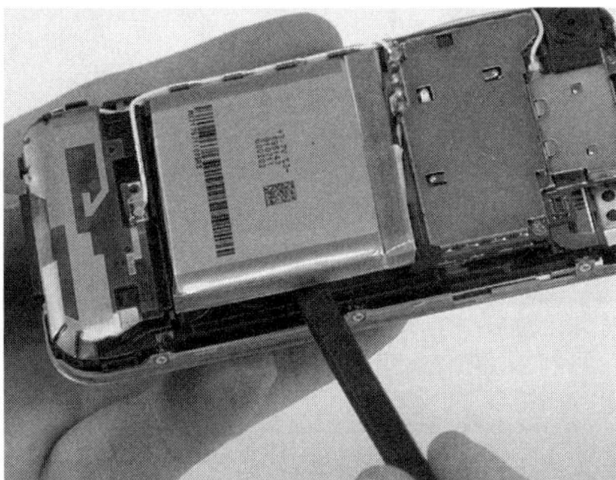

We're now ready to begin the soldering process. You'll need a soldering iron, solder, and desoldering wick. You should be able to find these items at a RadioShack, if you don't already have them.

Clean the soldering iron by melting a small amount of solder directly onto the soldering iron's tip (as shown in Figure 12-67) and then wiping the tip of the soldering iron on a damp sponge.

Figure 12-67.
Cleaning soldering iron tip with solder

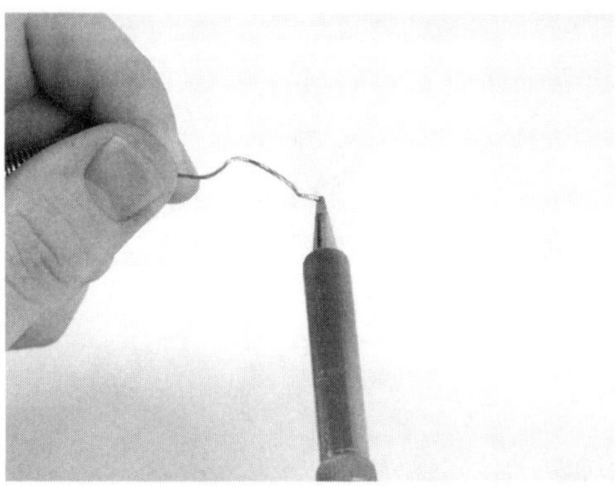

Now, you need to disconnect the battery:

1. Place the desoldering wick on top of the solder ball as shown in Figure 12-68.
2. Place the soldering iron on top of wick above the solder ball.
3. Hold the soldering iron in place until the solder melts into the wick.

Repeat this procedure on the remaining two connectors.

Lift the old battery out of the iPhone. Be sure that all the solder has been removed before pulling the wires away from the board. The wires should come free with little to no resistance.

Figure 12-68.
Desoldering the battery from the board

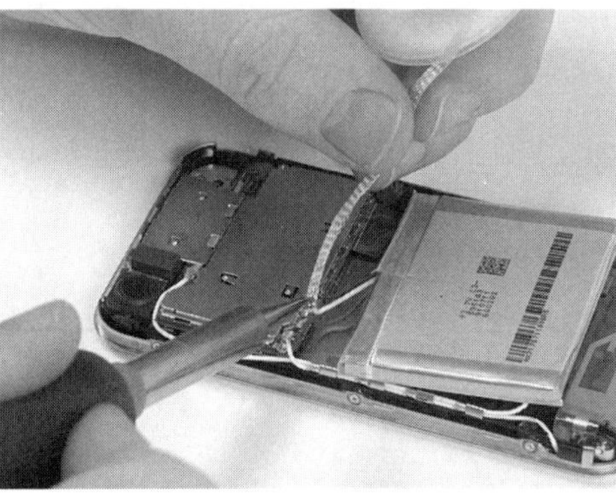

Clean the exposed surface of the board with a soft lint-free cloth or sponge and a small amount of rubbing alcohol.

Replacing the Battery

Melt a small solder bead directly onto the metal connector on the board by placing the soldering iron onto the metal connector and then pressing solder against the tip and the board. Once a small amount of solder has melted onto the board, lift the solder away first and then the soldering iron. See Figure 12-69.

Figure 12-69.
Prepare soldering area

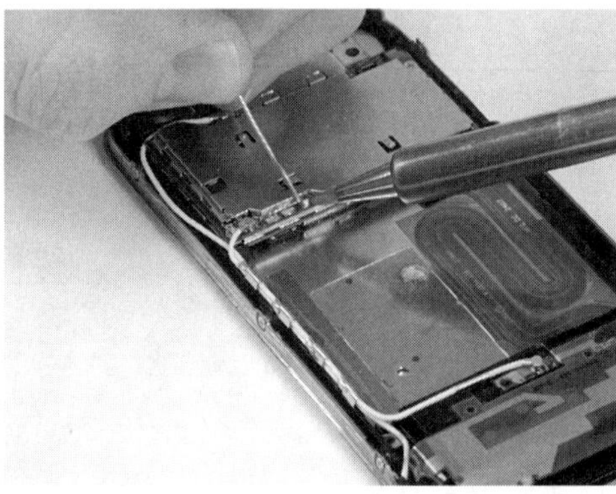

The solder bead should look like a small dome or hemisphere (Figure 12-70). If it is flat or jagged, simply place the soldering iron back on the solder to remelt it and then pull the soldering iron away. It may require a little more solder if this does not work.

Figure 12-70.
Good solder beads

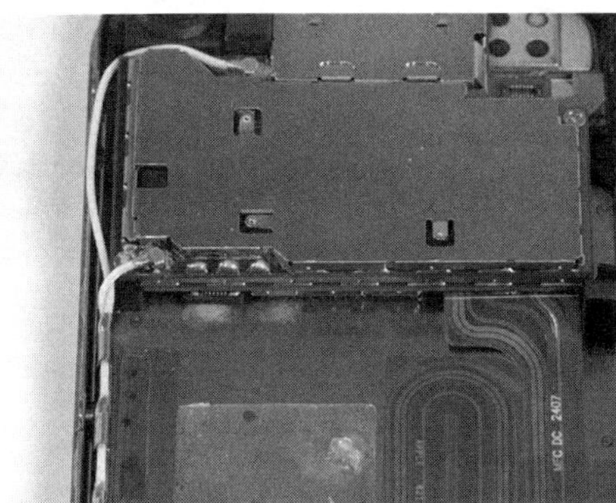

Place the wire from the new battery onto the new solder bead. Press the tip of the soldering iron onto the solder bead until it melts, as shown in Figure 12-71. Slide the wire lead into the liquid solder until it is in the center of the bead, then remove the soldering iron.

Continue with the other two connections the same way, taking special care not to solder two of the connectors together. That would make for major iPhone sadness.

Figure 12-71.
Soldering a battery wire

If you've successfully followed all these steps, congratulations! You've taken apart the most complex of the four devices covered in this chapter. The more Apple has redesigned these soap bars, the better the insides have become to dig around in.

— iFixit.com & Adam Stolarz

HACK 12.11: Disassemble and Reassemble Your iPhone 3G

Master the skill of disassembling and reassembling your iPhone.

The iPhone 3G is quite an upgrade from the original iPhone. The case is made of fewer parts, and all in all, the device is easier to deconstruct. Apple has even included numbered stickers to indicate what order to detach various cables.

To get started, remove the two Phillips #00 screws from the dock-connector end of the iPhone, as shown in Figure 12-72.

 For tips on reassembling the device, as well as an overview of the tools used here, see **[Hack #12.09]**.

Figure 12-72.
Remove the two Phillips #00 screws from the dock connector

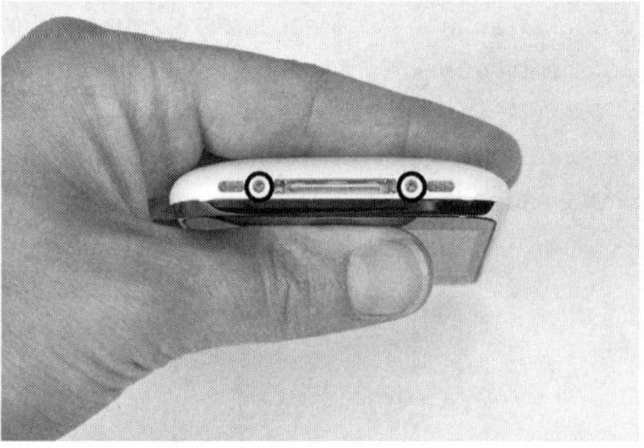

There is a fragile rubber gasket between the silver front bezel and black display assembly. Keep your tool as close to the silver front bezel as possible to prevent damaging the gasket.

A metal spudger is recommended for this task (Figure 12-73), but an X-Acto knife should also work—just be careful not to slip.

Insert a metal spudger into the seam between the silver front bezel and the black display assembly on the edge closest to the home button. Gently pry the display assembly up from its bezel.

Figure 12-73.
Opening the bezel with a metal spudger

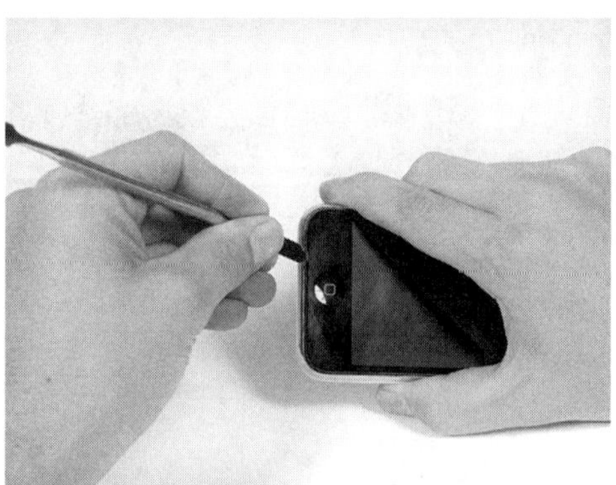

If necessary, insert the metal spudger in the same manner on the side of the iPhone and continue to pry up gently, as shown in Figure 12-74. Stop using the metal spudger once the display assembly is up enough that you can lift it up with your fingers.

Figure 12-74.
Going along the side

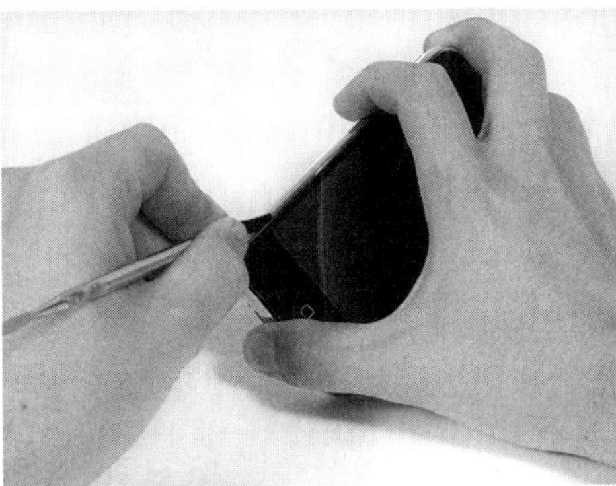

The display assembly is still connected to the iPhone by several cables, so don't try to remove it entirely just yet.

Lift the free edge of the display assembly up until it is at an angle of approximately 45 degrees, as shown in Figure 12-75.

Figure 12-75.
Lifting the display

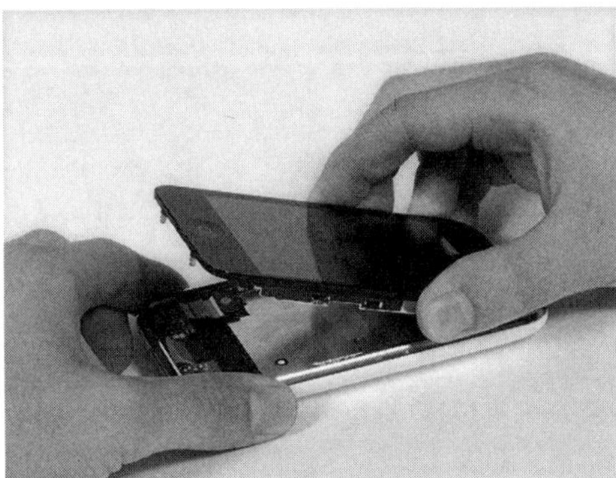

Continue to hold the display assembly with one hand, and use your other hand and a spudger to disconnect the black ribbon cable labeled "1" inside the iPhone, as shown in Figure 12-76.

Figure 12-76.
Detaching cable 1

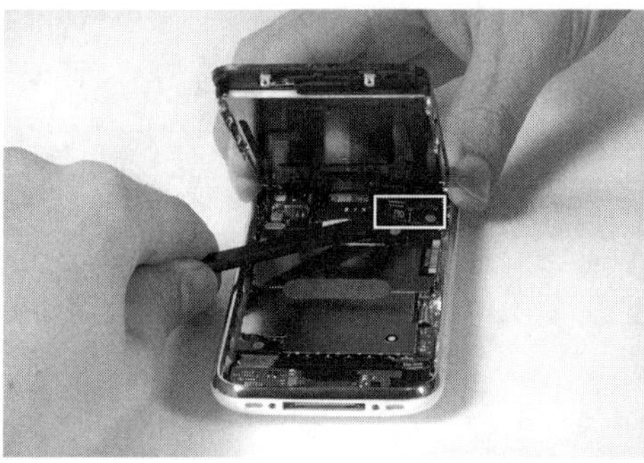

Lift the display assembly up until it is roughly vertical. This will allow you easier access for disconnecting the remaining cables.

Use a spudger to disconnect the black ribbon cable labeled "2" inside the iPhone, as shown in Figure 12-77.

Figure 12-77.
Detaching cable 2

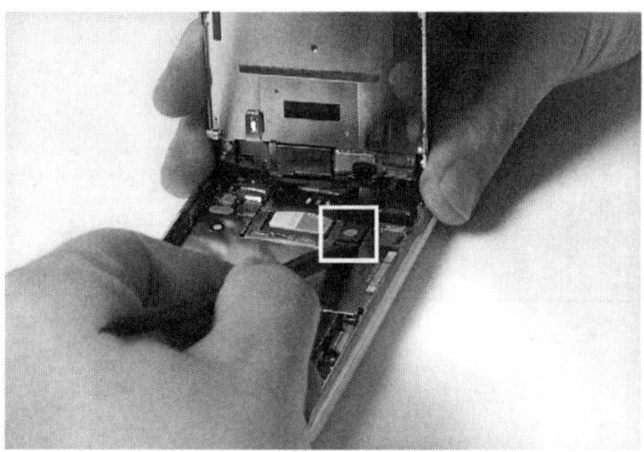

Use a spudger to flip up the white plastic tab holding the third ribbon cable in place, as in Figure 12-78. The white tab will rotate up 90 degrees, releasing the ribbon cable.

Slide the black ribbon cable out of its connector, and remove the display assembly from the iPhone.

Figure 12-78.
Detaching cable 3

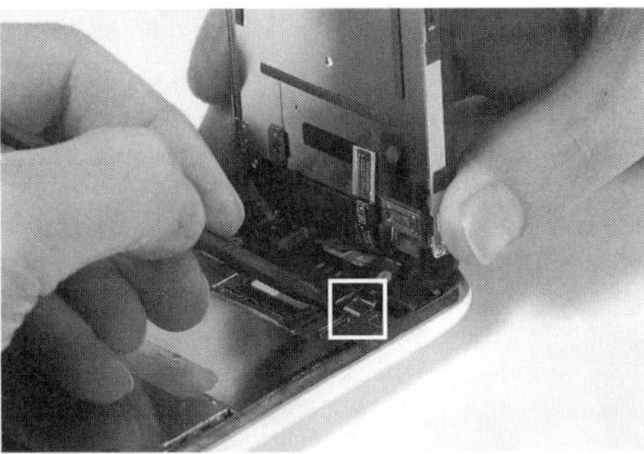

Insert your SIM eject tool or a paper clip into the hole next to the headphone jack as shown in Figure 12-79. Press down on the tool until the SIM card tray pops out.

Grasp the SIM card tray and slide it out of the iPhone.

Figure 12-79.
Removing the SIM tray

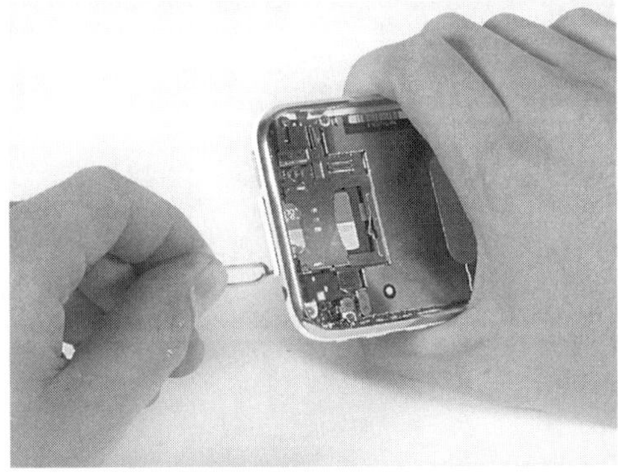

Use a spudger to disconnect the ribbon cable that is labeled "4" inside the iPhone (Figure 12-80).

Figure 12-80.
Detaching cable 4

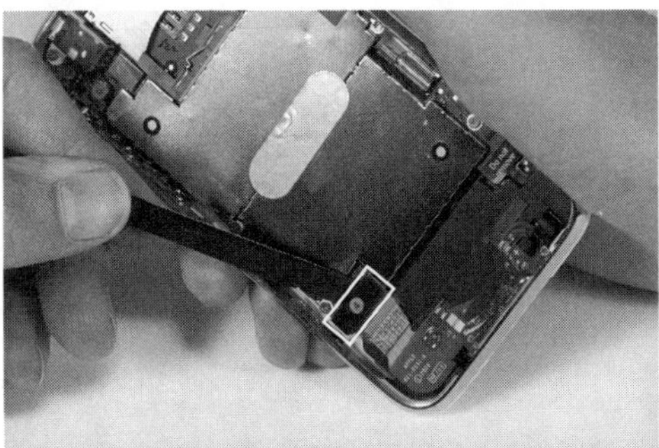

Use a spudger to disconnect the ribbon cable that is labeled "5" inside the iPhone, as shown in Figure 12-81.

Figure 12-81.
Detaching cable 5

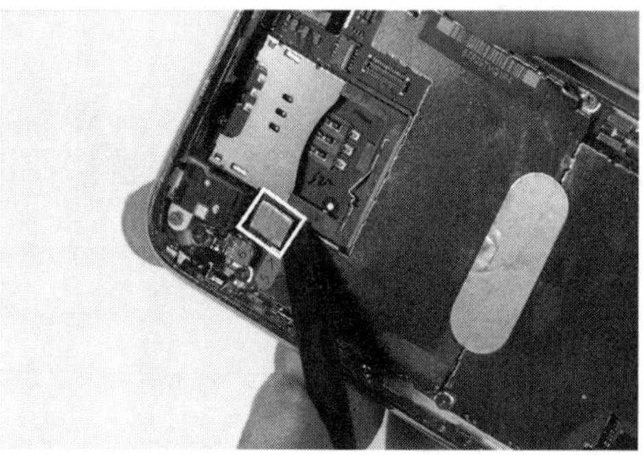

Use a spudger to disconnect the ribbon cable labeled "6" (Figure 12-82).

Figure 12-82.
Detaching cable 6

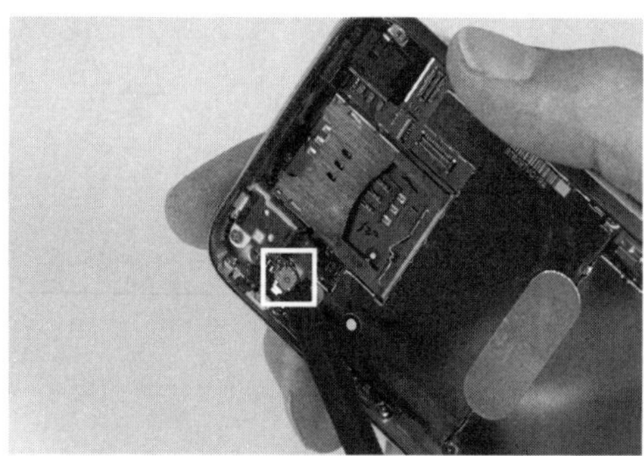

Carefully peel up the small sticker labeled "Do not remove." Isn't Apple nice? They tell you exactly what to do and then tell you to turn around and go home. See Figure 12-83.

Figure 12-83.
Removing the sticker

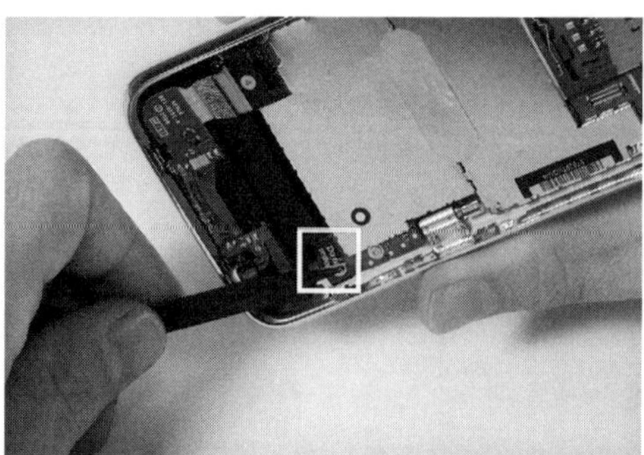

Next, remove the following eight screws, which are circled in Figure 12-84:

- Five 2.3 mm Phillips #00 screws with partial threads securing the logic board to the rear panel.
- Two 2.3 mm Phillips #00 screws with full threads securing the logic board and camera.
- One 2.9 mm Phillips #00 screw from beneath the "Do not remove" sticker.

Figure 12-84.
The screws

Use a spudger to gently pry the camera up and out of its housing in the rear panel, as shown in Figure 12-85. The camera cannot be removed entirely yet, because it's connected to the bottom of the logic board.

Figure 12-85.
Prying up the camera

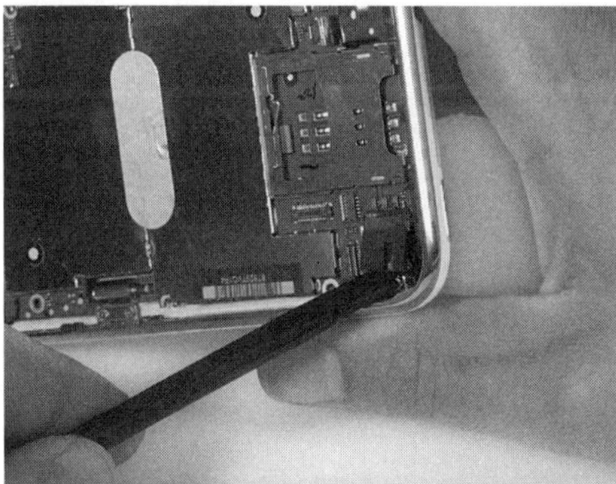

Use a spudger to gently pry up the end of the logic board closest to the dock connector as shown in Figure 12-86. If the board won't lift up, double check to make sure that all the screws securing the logic board have been removed.

Figure 12-86.
Spudging the logic board

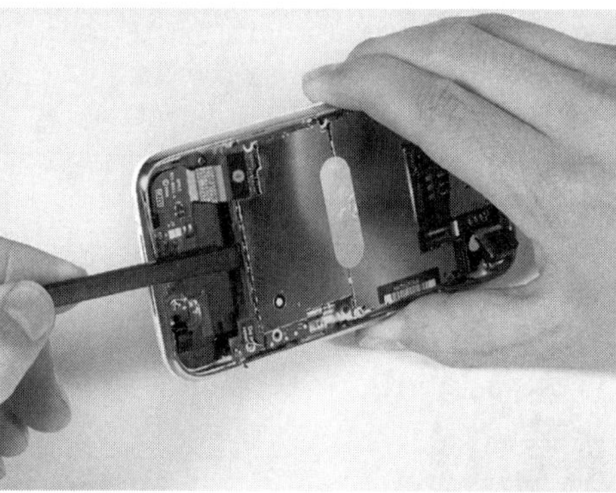

Slide the logic board toward the dock connector and out of the iPhone (Figure 12-87).

Figure 12-87.
Sliding it off

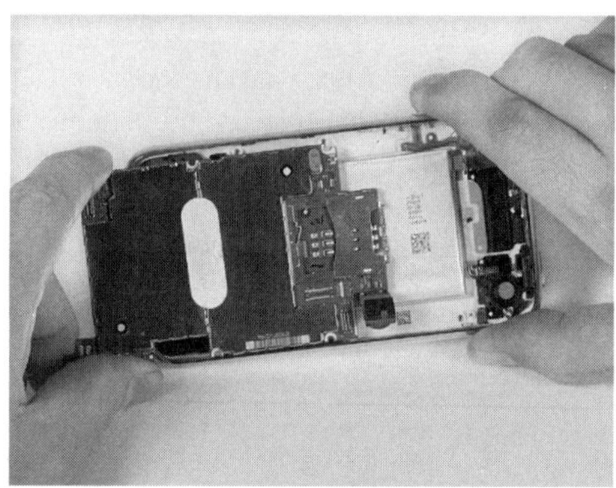

At this point, you are within a few steps of taking out anything in the phone. Whatever you can identify should be a few screws away from being uninstalled.

Replacing the Battery

For those replacing their battery, here's the best way to remove it. The battery is attached with an adhesive strip around the perimeter of the battery. Use a spudger (Figure 12-88) to pry the battery up from the rear panel (to prevent the battery from bending during the removal process, we recommend against using just the plastic pull-tab). Honestly, it is that easy. As you can see, it is not soldered on like the early iPhones **[Hack #12.10]**.

Figure 12-88.
Prying the battery

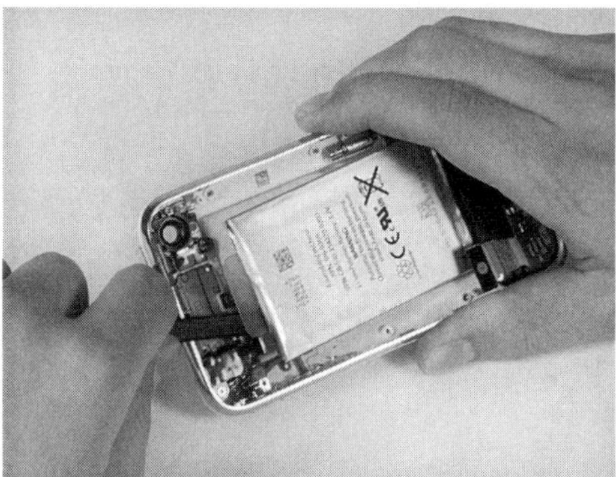

Now your phone is open, as shown in Figure 12-89, and you can mess with it as you see fit. You shouldn't have any problems from here on out, particularly if you remember that the labeled wires should be reassembled in reverse order: 6-5-4-3-2-1.

Figure 12-89.
The nonwire battery connector

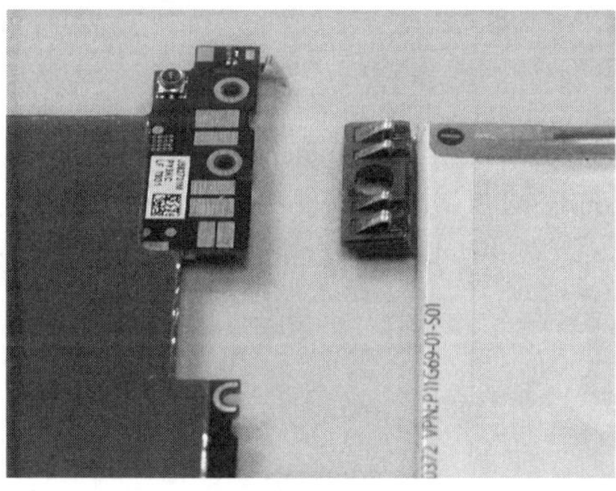

— iFixit.com & Adam Stolarz

HACK 12.12: Disassemble and Reassemble Your Original iPod touch

Master the skill of disassembling and reassembling your iPod touch.

The iPod touch's interior was clearly designed for ease of maintenance. Some lessons were learned in designing the iPhone that make the first-generation iPod touch simpler inside. And it helps that it doesn't have as much stuff crammed in it as the iPhone does.

For tips on reassembling the device, as well as an overview of the tools used here, see **[Hack #12.09]**.

Opening the iPod touch is similar to opening an iPhone **[Hack #12.10]** and **[Hack #12.11]**. Run a metal spudger along the sides and separate the metal tabs.

The iPod touch doesn't need a large speaker or microphone, so the battery occupies a larger portion of the internal space than the iPhone's battery, as shown in Figure 12-90.

Figure 12-90.
The cracked-open iPod touch case

There are no wires connecting the rear panel to the iPod. Apple used an elegant contact connection to make assembly and disassembly easier, as shown in Figure 12-91.

Figure 12-91.
The contact connector

The large battery is soldered to the logic board, like the early-model iPhone and many of Apple's recent iPods. You can lift it up using a simple spudger, however, as shown in Figure 12-92.

Figure 12-92.
Lifting up the battery

The huge touchscreen lies beneath the battery. The logic board is beneath the metal shield (Figure 12-93).

Figure 12-93.
Under the battery

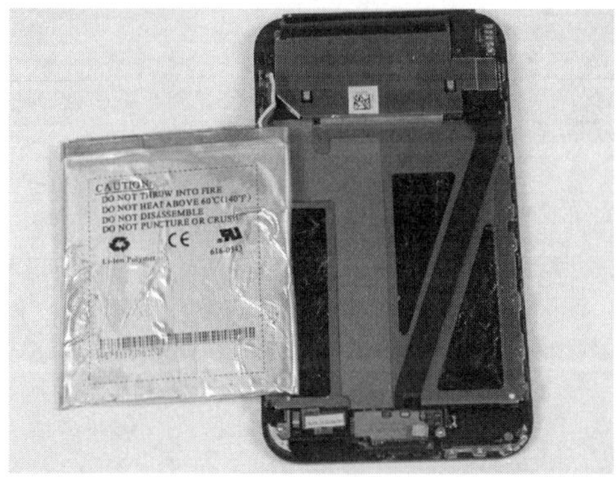

The metal case opens easily by prying the right side, which reveals the logic board (Figure 12-94).

Figure 12-94.
The logic board

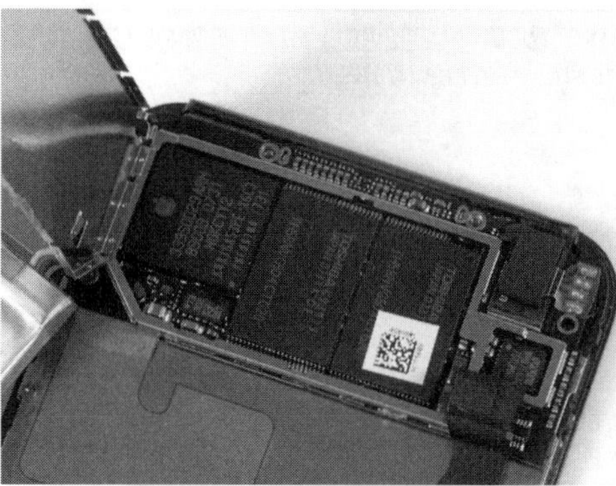

Nearly everything in the iPod touch lifts up easily (Figure 12-95).

Figure 12-95.
Lifting out the board

You can pry the logic board up and off fairly easily with a spudger (Figure 12-96).

Figure 12-96.
Prying the logic board

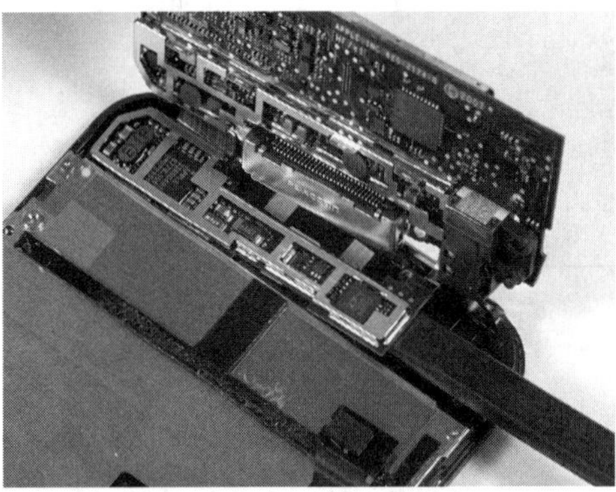

The display attachment is completely different from the iPhone's. The display is attached to the front of the iPod by 16 Phillips #00 screws. On the iPhone, the display and front bezel are fused together with very strong adhesive, which makes it impossible to separate the display from the glass. But the iPod's design is better for repairs, as removing the display is very doable. The LCD just comes right out after you remove the screws, as shown in Figure 12-97.

Figure 12-97.
Removing the plate

As you can see in Figure 12-98, compared to the early-model iPhone, the first-generation iPod touch is a dream to disassemble. Self-repair and part replacement is relatively easy compared to other models.

Figure 12-98.
Detached bezel and screen

— iFixit.com & Adam Stolarz

HACK 12.13: Disassemble and Reassemble Your Second-Generation iPod touch

Take apart the easiest iDevice yet.

As with the first generation of the iPod touch **[Hack #12.12]**, the second-generation iPod touch benefits from a similar ease of disassembly. The second-generation iPod touch does not have a two-piece shell like the first generation. Instead, you start by prying up the glass screen cover itself. In Figure 12-99, a metal spudger is shown. Of course, be careful not to damage the edge of the glass or the case.

Figure 12-99.
Prying the display

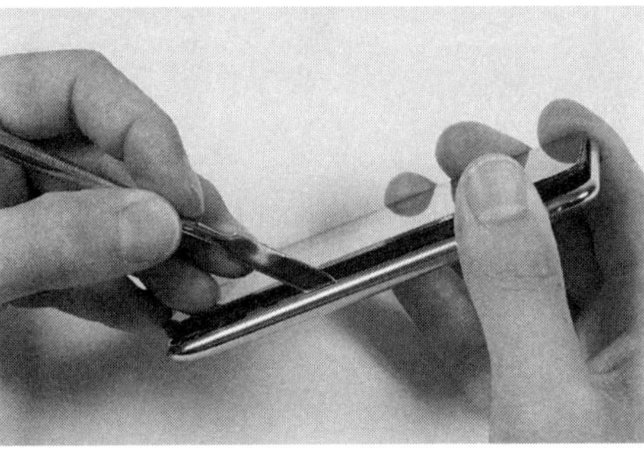

There are no screws securing the LCD (Figure 12-100). Instead, it's held in place with a little double-sided tape.

Figure 12-100.
Screen without covering bezel

Lifting it up reveals a metal plate hiding the goods (Figure 12-101), but that's nothing a #00 screwdriver won't solve.

Figure 12-101.
Lifting off the screen

The battery is held to the plate with two strips of light adhesive, but peels off easily, as shown in Figure 12-102.

Figure 12-102.
Under the metal

Disconnect the display data cable with some simple spudging as demonstrated in Figure 12-103. Note the residue from the glue holding the battery to the metal backing.

Figure 12-103.
Prying off the battery connector

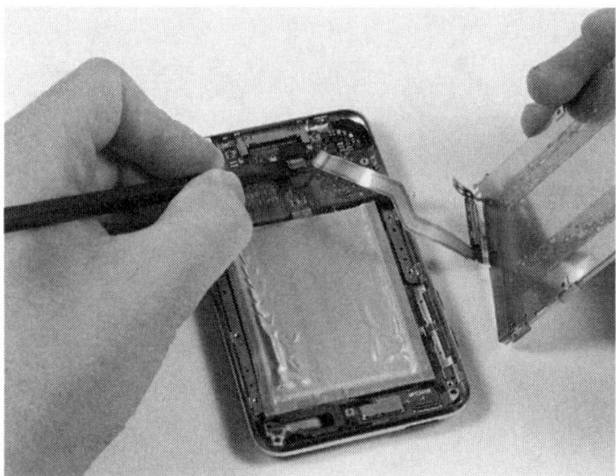

The battery and all the remaining parts can be lifted out easily now (Figure 12-104).

Figure 12-104.
The remaining pieces

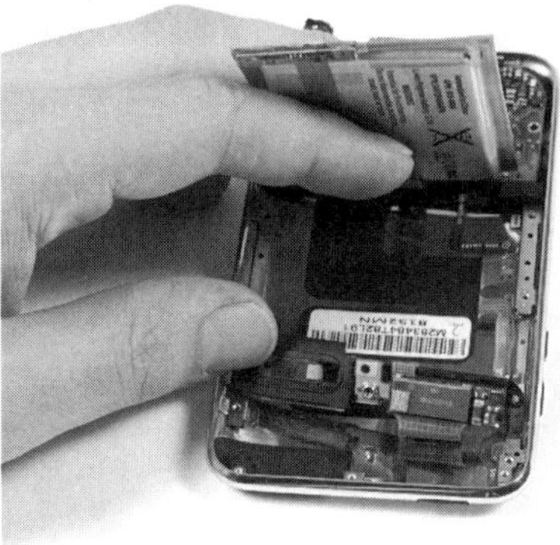

Simplicity of design, with little guesswork and a small handful of screws to remove means that you can easily replace anything in the second-generation iPod touch (Figure 12-105).

Figure 12-105.
The touch, splayed

— iFixit.com & Adam Stolarz

HACK 12.14: Learn the Pinouts of the iPhone and iPod touch

To connect hardware to your iPhone, you need to know its interfaces.

The iPod created a whole aftermarket and third-party industry around its dock connector standard. This standard has made its way into countless speakers, charging kits, and automotive integration systems.

In addition to the dock connector, though, Apple has continually experimented with various interfaces on the top of the device. The early iPods had a wired remote control connector on the top, with which you could play, fast forward, and rewind while the iPod was in your pocket. The latest family of devices (the iPhone and iPod touch) have continued this experimentation, and have added a 4-wire or "4-pole" connector for microphones and headphones.

Because many computer wires and plugs have traditionally involved many pins plugging into some sort of receptacle, the term for a chart showing what wire goes to which pin is called a *pinout*. In order to hack new devices into communication with the iPhone, we need to know the pinouts—the purpose of each wire or physical electrical contact—and thus what we can and cannot connect to it.

The Headphone Connector Pinouts

The iPhone headphone system is pretty clever. Most audio-type jack plugs (male connectors) have a convention for naming the contacts called the "tip-ring-sleeve" (TRS), as shown in Figure 12-106. In most headphones, the three contacts are (from the tip to the sleeve) left-right-ground. The ground contact is twice as long as the right channel, and the jacks (female sockets) that receive them have three poles, or contacts. Many jacks have a feature that allows the computer or device to detect when something is plugged in or not.

Figure 12-106.
Tip-ring-sleeve conventional 3.5 mm headphone jack. The iPhone jack is slightly different.

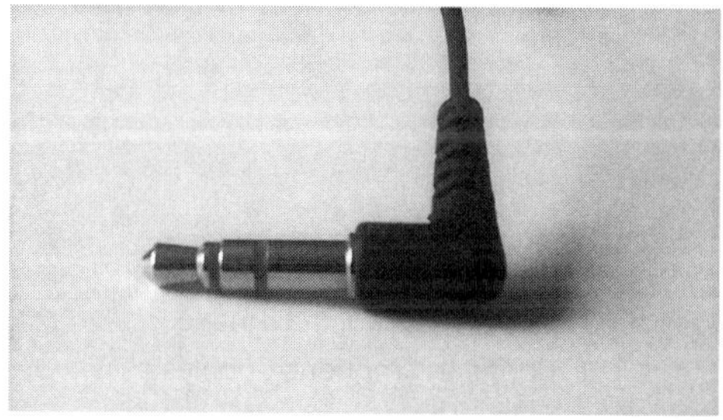

In the iPhone headphone, there are two rings (TRRS). The very tip of the iPhone headphone connectors is the left audio channel, and the ring after this is the right audio signal. The next ring is the conventional "ground" or return wire, and those three pins alone constitute the listening part of the headphones. In addition, there is a fourth contact, the sleeve, which is connected to the iPhone microphone (Figure 12-107).

Figure 12-107.
The iPhone headphone jack plug pinout

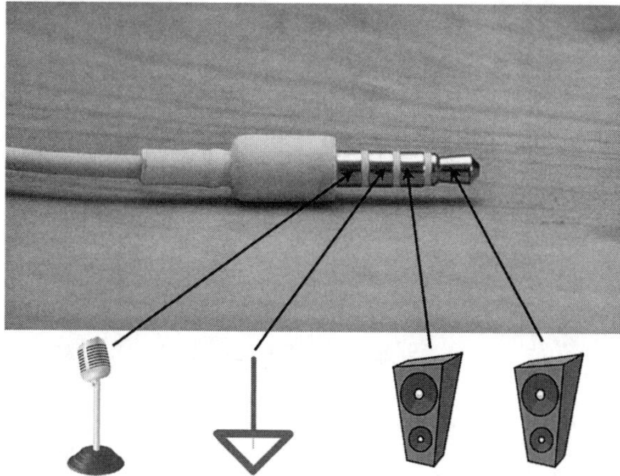

The microphone has a resistance of about 1K (1 kilo-ohm), which is used by the iPhone to detect whether a microphone is plugged in. If conventional headphones are plugged in, you can see that the sleeve would bridge both the microphone and ground pins. Thus, the iPhone senses zero ohms, indicating that only headphones are connected. If it senses 1K, it means that microphone is present as well. You can see an opened-up 4-pole connector in Figure 12-108.

Figure 12-108.
Freshly soldered iPhone 4-pole plug

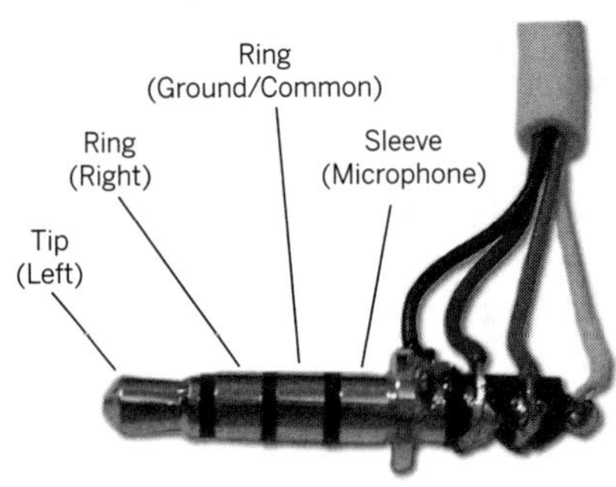

Because of this ability to sense the resistance of the ground-mic connection, the iPhone headphones also do a couple of additional clever things. The iPhone microphone doubles as a switch (Figure 12-109) that can play and pause music, and answer or hang up a call. If you "double click" (squeeze two times fast) during music playback, the iPhone or second-generation iPod touch will skip to the next song. Monster makes an adapter that adds a microphone and switch to existing headphones, which you can see cracked open in Figure 12-110.

Figure 12-109.
The iPhone microphone-switch

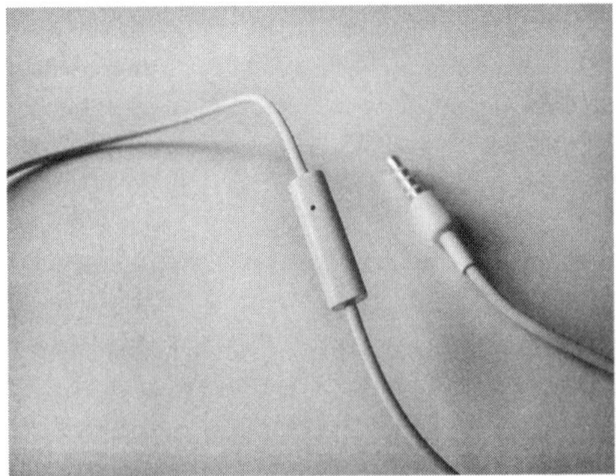

Figure 12-110.
Inside the Monster adapter

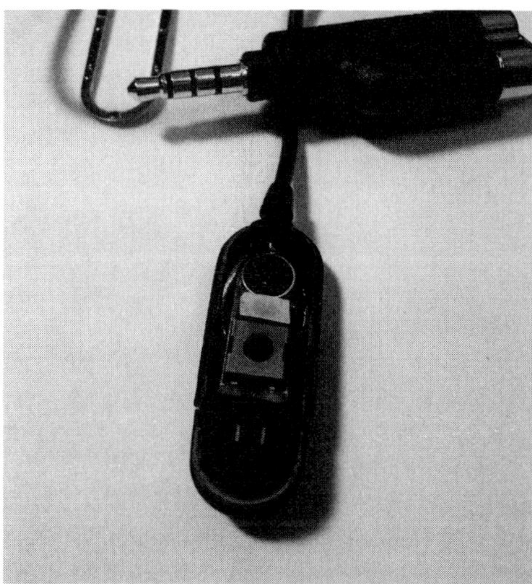

Using the Headphone Jack

Because we know how the iPhone microphone circuit works, we can now begin to attach our own devices. Here's some things we can build:

1. An auxiliary audio input port, so we can plug in things we want to record instead of using the microphone
2. Hands-free car integration via a wired microphone, and a button that shorts out the mic/ground so that we can skip songs **[Hack #12.07]**
3. Nonaudio devices—such as microcontrollers, serial devices, or keyboards—that we can "listen" to by transforming their output into audio pulses **[Hack #12.21]** and **[Hack #12.22]**

Figure 12-111 shows two views of an iPhone microphone and headphone splitter. It separates out a pair of microphone and audio jacks so you can record directly from another audio device. You can see it in action with a pair of headphones and an in-vehicle microphone **[Hack #12.07]** in Figure 12-112.

Figure 12-111.
An iPhone jack input/output splitter

Figure 12-112.
An iPhone jack input/output splitter in use

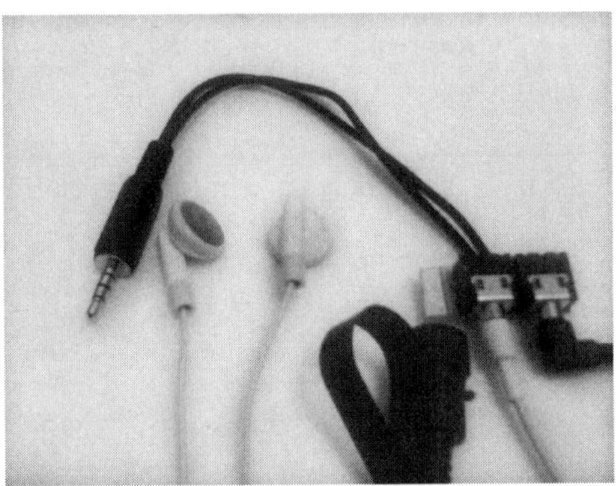

Finding a source for the 4-pin jack plugs, especially small ones that fit in the original iPhone recessed jack, can be challenging. You can purchase 4-pole plugs (Figure 12-113) from Maplin (www.maplin.co.uk/module.aspx?moduleno=29686). You can also scavenge them from the 4-pole cables used for camcorders from vendors like www.allelectronics.com (part number CB-218 is shown in Figure 12-114).

Figure 12-113.
Maplin 4-pole plug

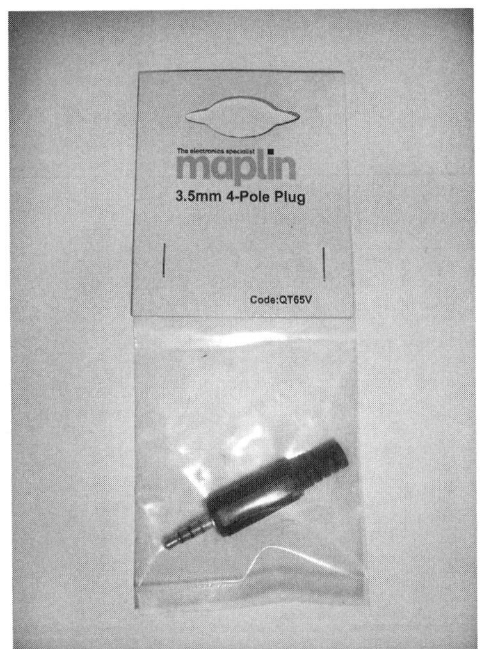

Figure 12-114.
AllElectronics.com 4-pole cable part number CB-218

One of the better sources of a 4-pole adapter plug is a 4-pole Y-splitter from Radtech (part number 13757 from http://radtech.us/products/iPhoneCables.aspx), the ProCableAudio Y Cable Splitter 3.5 mm. This cable can be cut and spliced so that you can connect to the headphone port (Figure 12-115). When you cut the wires, you'll see that they are coated in colored insulating paint. Sometimes you can just solder it and the coating will melt off, but to make sure that your connection is good, you can lightly sand this paint off (including the clear copper wire) without ripping the wire. Figure 12-116 shows a quick-and-dirty splice to heavier-duty wires that was used as we worked on **[Hack #12.20]**.

Figure 12-115.
Radtech 4-pole Y-splitter

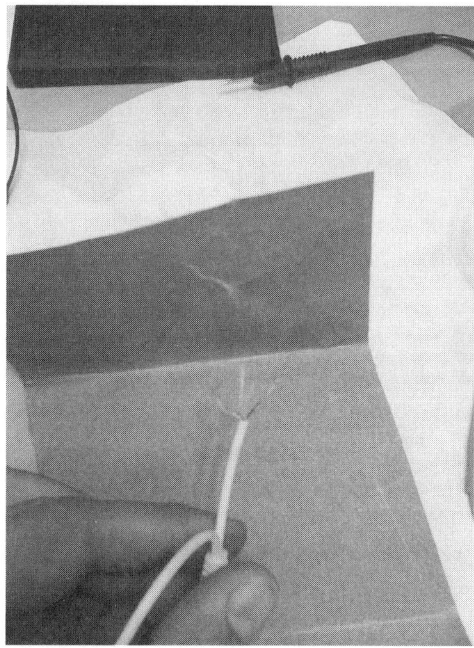

Figure 12-116.
Radtech 4-pole splice

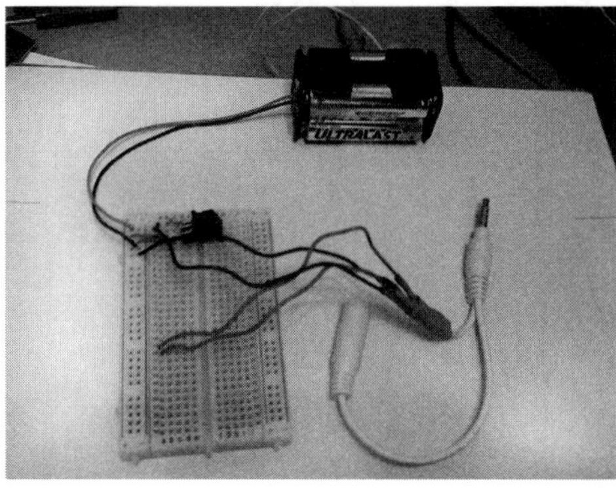

The Dock Connector Pinouts

The bottom dock connector has changed over time in terms of the features that it exposes. Video out, audio in and out, 12V charging, 5V charging, FireWire and USB syncing, and various custom communication protocols have come and gone over the years. But because the iPhone remains the flagship iPod, it retains compatibility with the majority of in-market iPod dock–based hardware. Figure 12-117 shows a PodBreakout from SparkFun Electronics (www.sparkfun.com, part number DEV-08295) that is available for less than $20. Figure 12-118 shows the dock connector close up.

Figure 12-117.
PodBreakout (picture from sparkfun.com)

Figure 12-118.
iPod dock breakout cable: pin 1 is on the far right, pin 30 on the left (picture from sparkfun.com)

The pinout of the iPod dock connector has been pretty consistent since it was released; some pins get repurposed, or dropped, depending on the device and the accessory in question. A recent change between the first-generation iPhone and the iPhone 3G is that support for FireWire charging (pins 19, 20, 29, and 30) was dropped. A selected list of pins relevant to the iPhone is shown in Table 12-1. Additional pins for all models of iPod and iPhone can be found at http://pinouts.ru/PortableDevices/ipod_pinout.shtml and http://datacables.ws/iphone.

Table 12-1.
Interesting iPhone pins

Pin	Description
1	Video ground
2	Audio ground
3	Right channel audio out
4	Left channel audio out
8	Video out (composite, yellow plug) or Pb channel (component, blue plug)
9	Video Y channel (component, green plug)
10	Video Pr channel (component, red plug)
11	3.3V TTL (not RS232) serial ground **[Hack #12.18]**, **[Hack #12.19]**
12	3.3V TTL (not RS232) serial transmit (TX)
13	3.3V TTL (not RS232) serial receive (TX)
15	Ground
16	USB ground
18	3.3 volt power output
21	Accessory indicator. Depending on the resistor connected between ground and this pin, the iPhone or iPod touch will believe that a certain device is connected, such as a car interface, dock, photo dock, and so on. For an example, see **[Hack #12.19]**
23	5V USB power input
24	USB data (minus connection)
27	USB data (plus connection)

Although pins 8, 9, and 10 provide video output, the iPhone requires the proprietary iPhone cable **[Hack #12.06]** to enable the video, so you can't just make your own dock.

Pins 11, 12, and 13 support the serial protocol that can be spoken by the iPhone to devices via the iPod dock protocol **[Hack #12.19]**, such as in-vehicle integration. Although it is a serial connection, it isn't the relatively high-voltage 12V to –12V RS-232 serial connection on the back of many older computers, but rather a TTL (transistor-transistor logic) connection that goes from 0V to 3.3V to indicate ones and zeros. **[Hack #12.18]** shows how to adapt between 3.3V TTL and RS232 serial (as well as USB) so that you can communicate with your iPhone via a serial port.

Pin 21, the accessory connector, is part of how the iPhone detects what is connected. With various resistor settings, you can trick the iPhone into different modes, and a few of the hacks such as **[Hack #12.17]** and **[Hack #12.19]** will demonstrate this.

If you're trying to make a device to connect to the dock connector, you don't have to buy a breakout card. In fact, with the proliferation of under-$10 iPhone connectivity gadgets, you can probably find a hackable donor dock connector from a device that you already own and don't need, or something at your local electronics store. For instance, in **[Hack #12.15]** an iPhone flashlight is scavenged from a charging cable (Figure 12-119).

Figure 12-119.
Old iPhone/iPod dock connector

The item you're most likely to have already is a USB sync cable, so we'll show how you can adapt this connector to your needs. However, if you plan to do a lot of dock connector hacking, you'll find the PodBreakout cable from SparkFun (www.sparkfun.com; part #DEV-08295, Figure 12-125) very useful.

The first task is to rewire the USB sync cable so it uses the pins you want, rather than the USB pins. Not all the pins are populated, so you'll need to move them around for the ones you use. To do this, you will have to open up the iPhone plug using a spudger (Figure 12-120). Inside the plastic layer, you will find an additional metal layer for shielding radio frequency emissions. It should look like Figure 12-121.

Figure 12-120.
Opening the connector

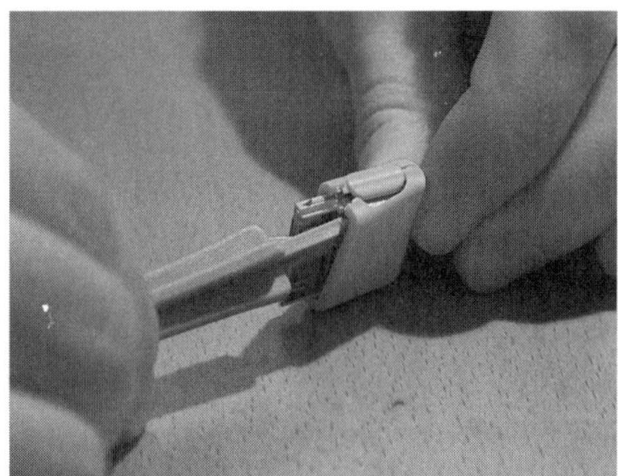

Figure 12-121.
Opening an iPhone dock connector plug

You attack this layer from the side. There are two little tabs that catch at the rear. Pry them out, as shown in Figure 12-122.

Figure 12-122.
Removing the iPhone plug shielding

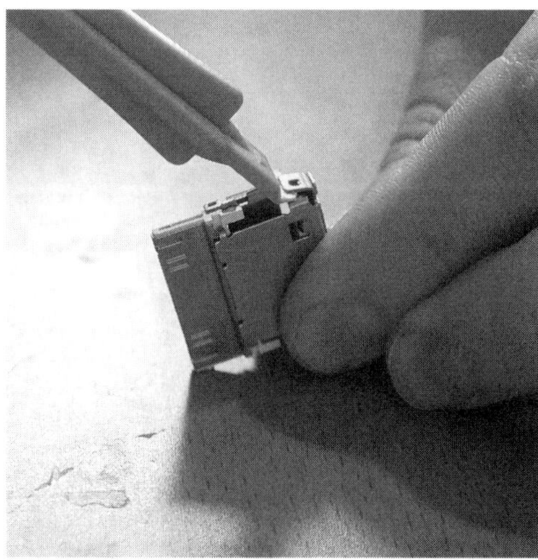

Eventually you will remove all the metal shielding and will wind up with just the plastic plug, wires, and pins, as shown in Figure 12-123.

Figure 12-123.
Shields off

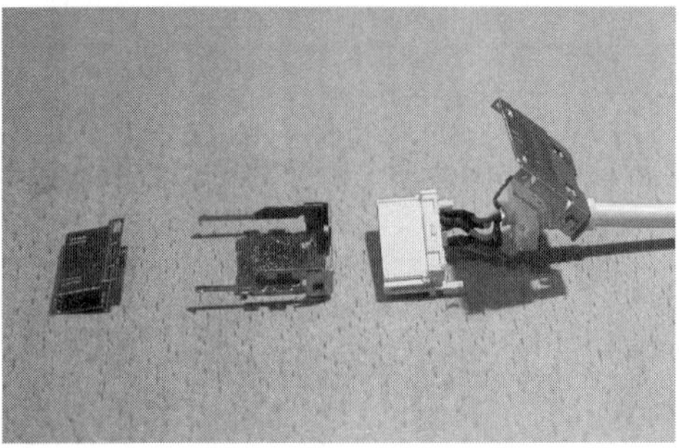

Leave the shielding wire soldered if you can, but if it comes off, you may find that your cable leaks some radio noise. Some places sell cables that have the wires glued into the connector. If you bought one of these, you need to purchase them from another vendor; otherwise, you will have a lot of difficulty trying to pull the pins out and reinsert them (http://allelectronics.com sells suitable connectors, part #IPD-3). Speaking of which, your next step is to use a pair of needle-nose pliers to remove the pins from their existing seats and push them back into the pins that you need to access—see Table 12-1.

Pins can be pulled and reinserted with your fingers, or with needle-nose pliers, as shown in Figure 12-124.

Figure 12-124.
Rearranging the pins

Once you've rewired and double-checked all your pins to make sure that they're correct, you can reassemble the shielding and plastic casing.

Finding Pins

It's important in any electronics, especially with a $300 iPhone, to get the pins right. Figure 12-125 illustrates the position of the dock pins on an iPhone. Looking at Figure 12-125, pin 1 is the farthest to the left. You can find pin 1 by holding your iPhone in your left hand face up. The pin closest to your left hand is pin 1. Pins 2, 3, and so on are found by counting away. Pin 30 is the farthest to the right.

Figure 12-125.
Pin 1 is on the left, pin 30 is on the right

There's a lot you can do with the dock connector. **[Hack #12.15]** shows you how to make a flashlight, **[Hack #12.17]** shows you how to build an iPhone charger, and **[Hack #12.18]** shows how you can turn a USB-to-dock connector iPhone cord into a serial-to-dock connector by rearranging its pins as shown in this hack.

— Damien Stolarz & Zack Gainsforth

HACK 12.15: Make an External Camera Illuminator for Your iPhone

An iPhone-powered LED flashlight can help you take better photos.

Getting your iPhone to take a good picture in a badly lit area is nearly impossible, especially as the iPhone has no built in flash. So the next best thing is to make your own external illuminator, as shown in Figure 12-126!

Figure 12-126.
External Camera Illuminator

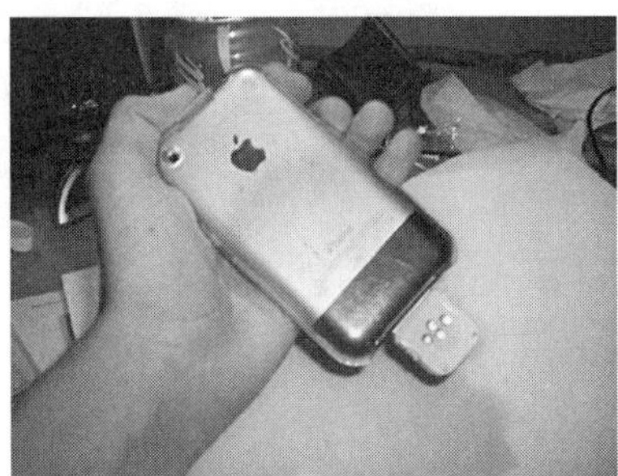

When the iPhone's initial specs were released by Apple, many users complained about its lack of a camera flash. Using a USB connector, four white LEDs, and a tactile switch, you can build a removable flash unit.

The parts you'll need to make a camera flash are:

- An old iPhone/iPod dock connector **[Hack #12.14]**
- A couple of LEDs (3 mm or 5 mm super-bright white LEDs are preferable), SparkFun part COM-00531 (www.sparkfun.com), RadioShack part 276-017
- Insulated wire that can handle a 3.3V current such as 30-gauge wire
- Tactile switch (Figure 12-127), SparkFun part COM-00097, RadioShack part 275-002
- 10 ohm resistor (optional, but if you want to play it safe you should use it), RadioShack part 271-1301
- Soldering iron and solder
- Dremel or similar rotary tool
- Super Glue

Figure 12-127.
Tactile momentary switch

First, pop open the dock connector, and examine the wires connected to its pins. You should review **[Hack #12.14]** to familiarize yourself with the dock connector's 30 pins and their functions. There should be a black ground wire attached to pin 29 or 30. Cut all the other wires, except the ground, as close to the pins as possible. Then cut the ground wire at a farther point so a portion of it is still hanging from the dock connector pin that it's attached to.

Now attach one end of an insulated wire to pin 18. Some dock connectors don't have pins in all 30 positions, so you will have to slide a pin out from a different place, and insert it into position 18. To configure the remainder of the flash refer to Figure 12-128, using solder to connect each wire to its appropriate component.

Figure 12-128.
Schematic for LED Illuminator

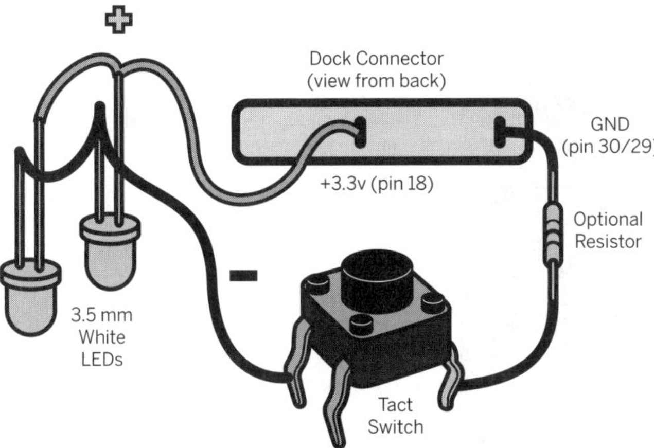

With the guts of the flash assembled, use your Dremel to drill holes in the dock connector's shell for the LEDs to stick through. Once the LEDs are in place use some Super Glue to secure them. Next, Super Glue the tactile switch to the bottom of the dock connector shell where the wires used to be. Solder everything together. Finally, Super Glue the dock connector back together.

Your custom light is complete! Plug it into your iPhone's dock and press the tact switch on the bottom of the connector (Figure 12-129) to turn the LEDs on whenever you need some extra lighting for a picture (Figure 12-130)

Figure 12-129.
Light plugged into bottom of iPhone

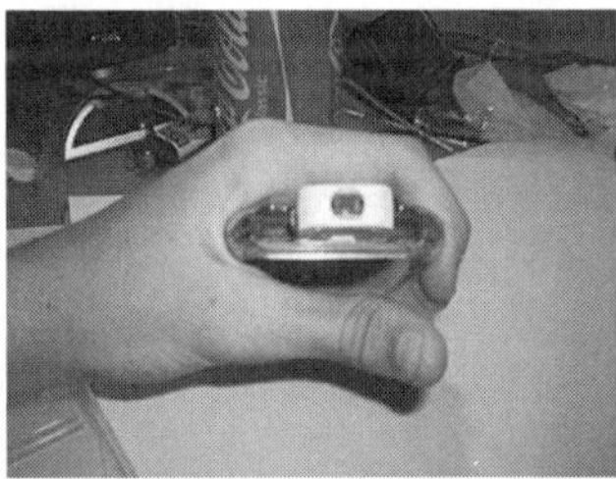

Figure 12-130.
Bright light

Figure 12-131 shows a pair of before and after shots with the illuminator.

Figure 12-131.
Before (top) and after (bottom) pictures using the iPhone flashlight

— Joe Vennix

HACK 12.16: Control the Physical World from Your iPhone

By combining an iPhone app, Arduino, and a few transistors, you can control lights—and even an R/C car—with your iPhone.

By plugging an Arduino electronics prototyping board into a network-connected computer, installing an app from the App Store, and wiring things up, you can turn your iPhone into a remote control for the physical world.

This hack sounds complex, but it's not that hard. Once you've gotten all the parts, it only takes about two hours to make—and the results, as shown in Figure 12-132—are worth it.

Figure 12-132.
iPhone-controlled R/C Car

In this hack, you'll start out simple: using the iPhone to make an LED blink. From there, you'll move up to controlling a remote control (R/C) car. The system for this is pretty simple. The iPhone sends data (button presses and the iPhone's accelerometer data) over Wi-Fi to your computer, where you can perform some computations and finally send data to an Arduino board, which controls the car's remote control (which, in turn, controls the car's motors).

First, you have to get data from your iPhone to your computer. The easiest way to do this is an application that is normally intended to be used by a DJ or musician, such as TouchOSC or OSCemote. Both of these applications use the OSC (Open Sound Control) protocol, which is pretty easy to work with. You can emulate button presses with it and even send accelerometer data.

After data is transmitted to your computer over Wi-Fi, you have to write a simple application to process it. I chose to use the rapid prototyping tool Max/MSP (www.cycling74.com). The free PureData (http://puredata.info) would also have worked. Both of these can handle the OSC protocol.

The output of this application will be a few commands such as "Turn right," "Turn left," "Go forward," "Go backward." It's completely up to you what commands you implement, as it depends on the type of your R/C car (see "Hacking into the R/C Controller," later in this hack). In this hack, we used a continuous track (steers like a tank) R/C car. You also have a choice as to how you want to drive the car: button presses or the motion of the accelerometer.

The application will need to send its commands to a microcontroller. I chose an Arduino controller, which is very popular and has a large community for support. To talk to Arduino, the application uses a USB connection and sends commands as strings using a USB serial port protocol.

The Arduino program (called a "sketch") then sets voltage on some of its pins, depending on which command it receives. For example, the Arduino program has a variable named "Go forward," which corresponds to a particular pin on the microcontroller. If "Go forward" is set to true, the microcontroller will set the associated pin to HIGH (+5V). If it is false, the pin will be set to LOW (0V).

Using this with a transistor, we can emulate button presses on the R/C car's controller. Even though there are joysticks on many R/C controllers, joysticks are nothing more than a set of buttons. For example, left and right are simply controlled by a pair of buttons (as are forward and backward).

Here's the list of parts you'll need:

- Cheap R/C car (we used an old Tyco Rebound 4x4)
- Arduino USB board such as the Duemilanove (available from MAKE at www.makershed.com/ProductDetails.asp?ProductCode=MKSP4 or from http://arduino.cc)
- Wi-Fi-enabled PC or Mac
- 4 NPN transistors (we used C547C)
- A few wires

Make sure that your iPhone and your computer are on same Wi-Fi network. Download the OSCemote (Figure 12-133) application from the App Store ($5). Run OSCemote, tap More, then Settings, and enter your computer's IP address (its Bonjour hostname may also work) as the OSC Host, and 7000 as the port (Figure 12-134).

Figure 12-133.
OSCemote

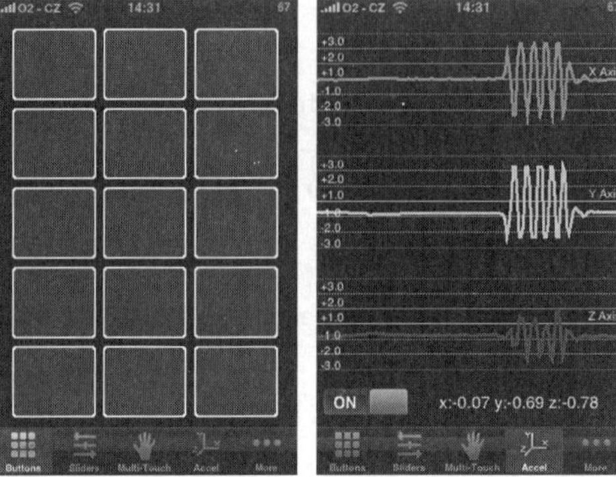

Figure 12-134.
OSCemote settings

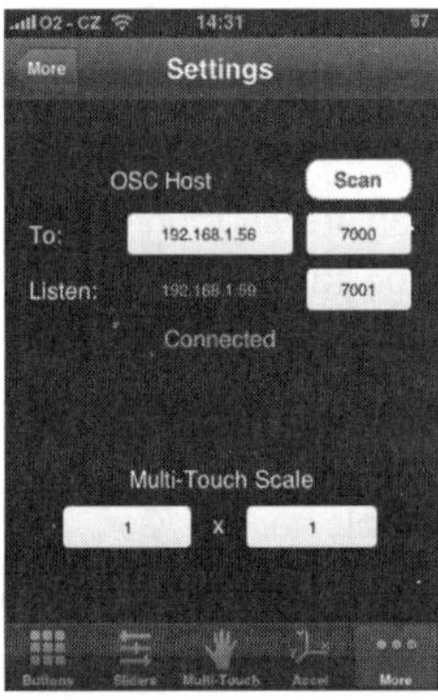

To run the sample application, you'll need the latest Max5 Runtime, which is available for free (http://cycling74.com/downloads/max5) for your platform. Go to http://code.google.com/p/iphonerccar/downloads/list and download and unzip the latest copy of the remote control software. Run either *Continuoustrack.maxpat* or *Standarttype.maxpat*, depending on the type of your R/C car. *Continuoustrack.maxpat* is for tank-style cars, where each side is independently controlled, and *Standarttype.maxpat* is for cars that have steering and acceleration.

 While you are playing with this hack, you might want to disable Auto-Lock on your iPhone (otherwise, it will keep switching off and dropping the connection between OSCemote and Max/MSP). Go to the iPhone Settings, tap General, then Auto-Lock, and set it to Never. You probably want to re-enable Auto-Lock when you are done using OSCemote.

Set the input port to the same value that you set in OSCemote (7000). Now you should see some movement in the accelerometer area.

You can test it by switching to the Buttons screen on OSCemote and tapping buttons. The symbols in the lower-left corner will blink, based on how you move the controls. You can also switch to the Accel screen, toggle the accelerometer on, and then wiggle the iPhone. The control scheme is shown in Figure 12-135.

 If you tried out the accelerometer feature, please turn it off for now, as it will interfere with the input messages coming from the buttons.

Figure 12-135.
Controller scheme

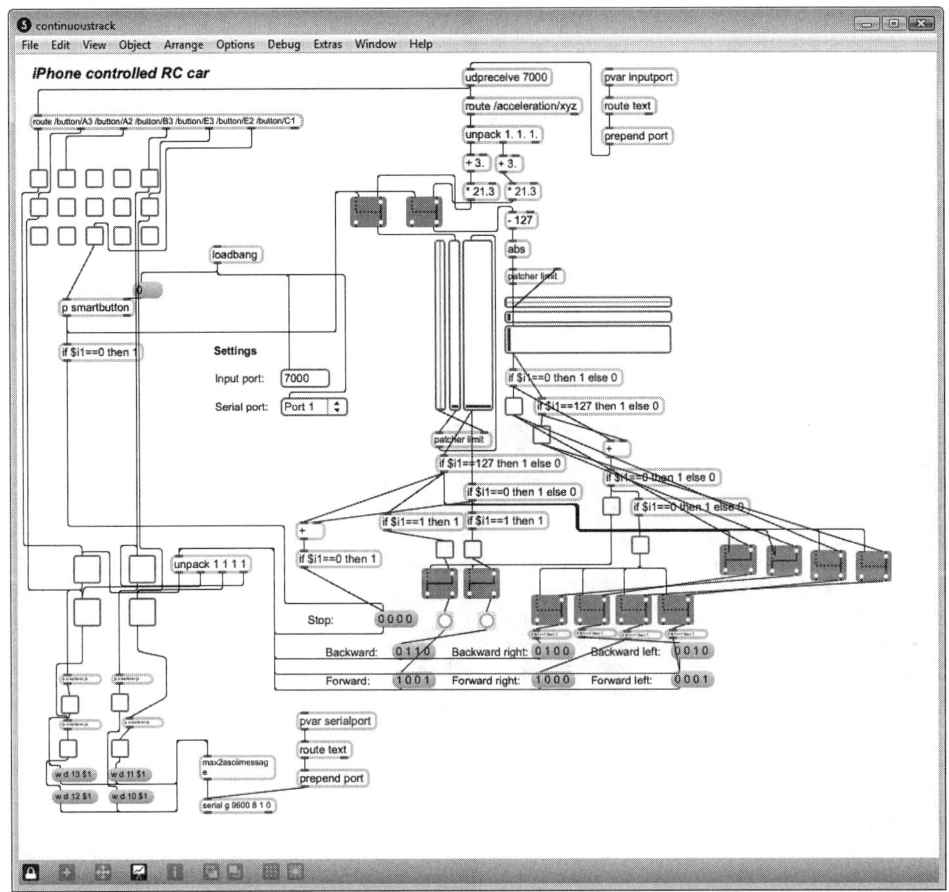

Now you need to download SimpleMessageSystem for Arduino. It's available from www.arduino.cc/playground/Code/SimpleMessageSystem. Download it and install it. Note that the *read_me.pdf* file included with the download is out of date. Instead of copying the SimpleMessageSystem folder into the *lib/targets/library/* subdirectory of the Arduino installation, put it into *hardware/libraries/*.

After you've installed SimpleMessageSystem, open the *Arduino.pde* sketch in the Arduino Integrated Development Environment (IDE). Upload the sketch to your Arduino over USB.

Close the Arduino IDE, but leave the Arduino connected to your computer. Return to Max/MSP and choose the serial port to connect to your Arduino (Figure 12-136).

Figure 12-136.
Set the serial port (Windows shown to the left, Mac OS X to the right)

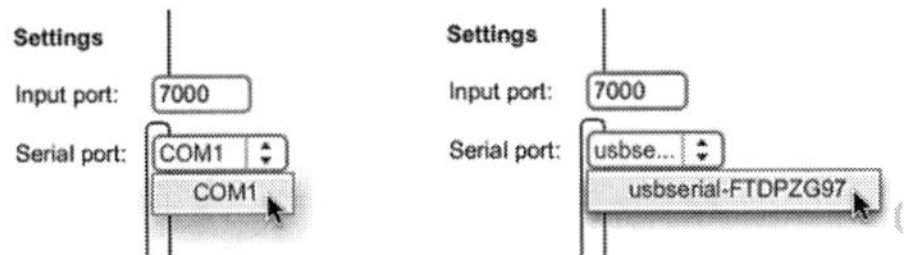

Now, rotate the iPhone so that the Home key is to your right and the top of the phone to your left (look ahead to Figure 12-141). Using OSCEmote, switch to the Buttons view, and tap the upper-left button.

You should see the LED next to pin 13 blink on the Arduino. If it blinks, you're good (Figure 12-137). If you want to see more light, slide an LED into the Arduino: short lead (negative, cathode) goes to GND, long lead (positive, anode) goes to pin 13. If it does not blink, make sure that the Arduino is really communicating with Max/MSP (blinking RX and TX). Make sure that you closed the Arduino IDE (because it locks the port for its own use) and try reselecting the serial port in the Max/MSP patch. If you still have problems, you can open a ticket on Google code at http://code.google.com/p/iphonerccar.

Figure 12-137.
LED near pin 13

Hacking into the R/C Controller

Prepare all four NPN transistors by soldering 10-inch wires to their base pins (this is the center pin labeled "B" that's bent up, as shown in Figure 12-138). Use 22 AWG wire (often called *hook-up wire*), because you need it to slip securely into the Arduino pins. Strip the other end of the wires, leaving about 3/4 of an inch exposed.

 If you don't have an R/C car, you might be tempted to use LEDs for all four pins just to try this hack out. If you do that, be sure to put a resistor (220 ohms or more should be fine) in series between the LED and either the GND or the pin you are using. You do not need a resistor for pin 13 because one is built in to the Arduino board.

Open your R/C car's remote controller and find switches that are triggered by the joystick controllers. Now, you're basically going to replace the original switches with transistors. In fact, you don't have to replace them: it's possible to have both the transistors and original switches working in parallel, but that depends on you and how clever you feel like being. In the pictures that follow, you can see that I opted to just replace the buttons.

The collector pin of each transistor should be soldered to negative (ground) and the emitter pin to positive side of each switch (Figure 12-139).

Figure 12-138.
NPN transistor pinout

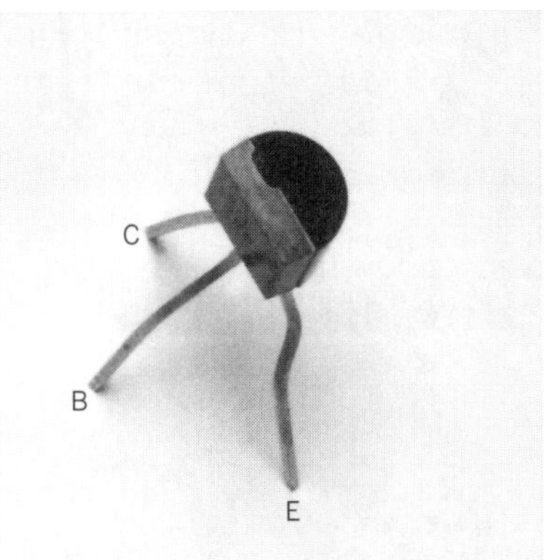

Figure 12-139.
NPN transistor

Find a suitable place to solder one wire to the controller's ground, because we need a common ground between Arduino and the controller. Because this will go into the Arduino, use a 22 AWG wire that is at least 10 inches long and strip the other end to about 3/4 inch.

You can see the four transistors soldered to replace the switches in Figure 12-140, along with one wire coming from each switch (you will connect these to the Arduino digital pins shortly). The wire at the top is the antenna, and the wires at the bottom are the connection to 9V battery (red and black wires), with one wire (white-brown) to make a common ground with the Arduino.

Figure 12-140.
Transistors replacing each button

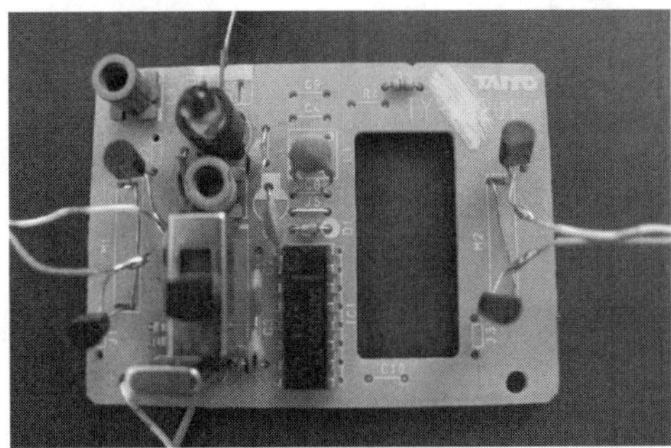

Now, connect the Arduino, with the ground wire going to the ground pin on the Arduino. Again, your choice of pins depends on the type of remote you have (continuous track, on which the left and right motors are controlled independently to steer) or standard (which has a steering control and a forward/reverse control).

Figures 12-141 and 12-142 show the two controller configurations for OSCremote.

Here's how to hook the Arduino to a continuous-track controller:

- Left side, forward—Arduino pin 13
- Left side, backward—Arduino pin 12
- Right side, backward—Arduino pin 11
- Right side, forward—Arduino pin 10

Figure 12-141.
OSCremote—continuous control

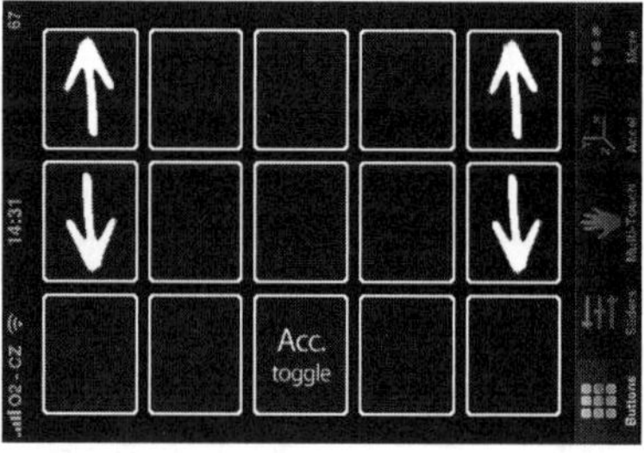

Here's how to hook the Arduino to a standard controller:

- Turn left—Arduino pin 13
- Turn right—Arduino pin 12
- Go forward—Arduino pin 11
- Go backward—Arduino pin 10

Figure 12-142.
OSCremote—standard control

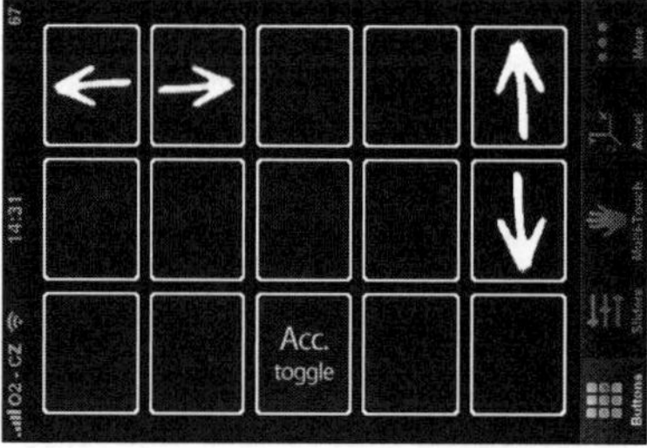

Figure 12-143 shows the final continuous-track circuit wired to the Arduino microcontroller board.

Figure 12-143.
Completed wiring

You are ready to power on the remote controller and power on your car. You should be able to control it by your iPhone!

Hacking the Hack

Now it's up to you what you can do with it. If your car supports changing shape or some other button-press function, you can add one more transistor to the original remote control, then change the Max/MSP patch slightly, and you can control that, too.

If you're a more experienced hacker, you can see possibilities other than just controlling an R/C car. If you use relays instead of transistors, you can control lights in your house, or whatever you want. I've tried to make the software for the computer as simple as possible—this is just a small taste of what you can do. You can upload your modifications to Google Code for others, if you want, too.

You can see videos of the car and other projects using the iPhone at http://josef-prusa.eu/obsah/blog/iphone-controlled-rc-car-eng.html.

HACK 12.17: Charge Your iPhone from (Almost) Any Source

Charge your iPhone and iPod touch with any USB port.

You may have noticed that some older iPhone chargers (particularly the cheaper models) won't work with the iPhone 3G. If your charger used the FireWire pins, you'll be disappointed to know that FireWire has been discontinued in the iPhone 3G and your charger will not work (unless you hack it; read on). This is commonly the case with car chargers, because the car battery supplies a voltage very close to the voltage needed by FireWire, which greatly simplifies the charging electronics.

If yours was a USB charger and it now fails to charge your iPhone, it probably wasn't built to use the signaling protocol that Apple requires from USB chargers, starting with the iPhone 3G. You might think there's a standard USB charging specification: all chargers should have certain characteristics so that any device built to spec should work with any charger built to spec. While such a specification exists, don't waste your time on it. The fact is that most device developers do not follow the specification, but instead design their own protocols—and this includes Apple.

The first-generation iPhone was very forgiving: if there was power on the USB cable, it charged. The iPhone 3G is more discerning. The pins typically used for transferring data (D+ and D–) **[Hack #12.14]** need to have specific resistors attached that tell the iPhone that this is an Apple-compliant charger.

If you are stuck with one of the old incompatible chargers, you still have a few choices, which are conveniently described in this hack.

Buy a Universal Charger with a Dock Connector Passthrough

The Kensington 4-in-1 universal charger and Ridax Dock Connector both provide a way to charge from USB while providing a passthrough to the dock connector for the audio and control connections (Figure 12-144).

Figure 12-144.
Kensington 4-in-1 universal charger

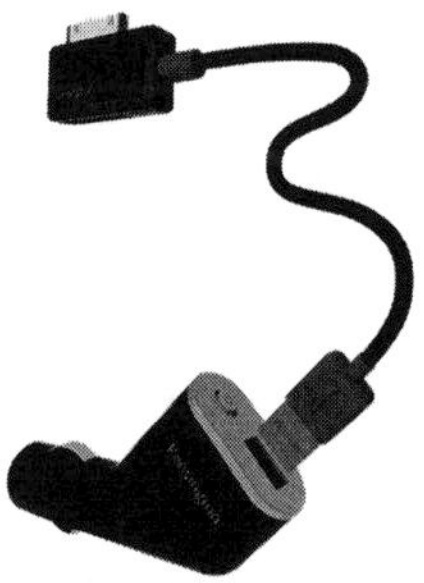

Buy an Adapter for Your Existing Charger

Iogear and Boxwave both make USB adapters that allow the iPhone to charge from any source (Figure 12-145). Scosche makes an adapter that connects to the iPhone dock and accomplishes the same thing **[Hack #12.07]**. Just add these adapters between your charger and your iPhone, and you should be able to use your charger again. They aren't too expensive.

Figure 12-145.
Boxwave iPhone charging adapter

Build Your Own Adapter

You can build your own adapter using a few resistors and a touch of USB cable splicing.

The way you charge the iPhone is to feed it 5V on pin 23, ground on 16, and resistors to D– (25) and D+ (27). D+ and D– are the pins that normally carry the USB data transmission **[Hack #12.14]**. There are two valid voltage dividers that you can connect to D+ and D–, depending on how much current you want your iPhone to draw from your charger:

1. Two resistors, 500 mA (0.5 ampere)
2. Four resistors, 750 mA (0.75 ampere)

Method 1 is the cheapest, easiest, and most compact. It only requires two resistors set up in the network as shown in Figure 12-146. This method gives you a current of 500 mA.

Figure 12-146.
500mA sense resistors

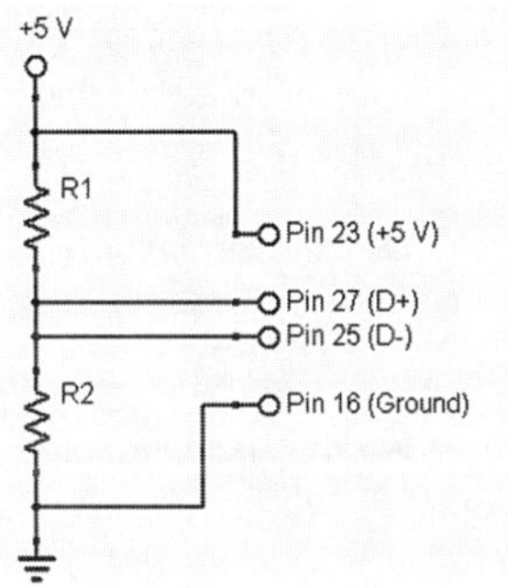

You need to choose values for R1 and R2 between 50K to 100K (50 to 100 kilo-ohms—each, not combined). Varying resistor sizes will work, as long as R1 and R2 are the same—and if the resistance is not too great or to small, you should be OK.

Method 2 is to use a four-resistor network configured as shown in Figure 12-147, which gives you a current of 750 mA.

Figure 12-147.
750mA sense resistors

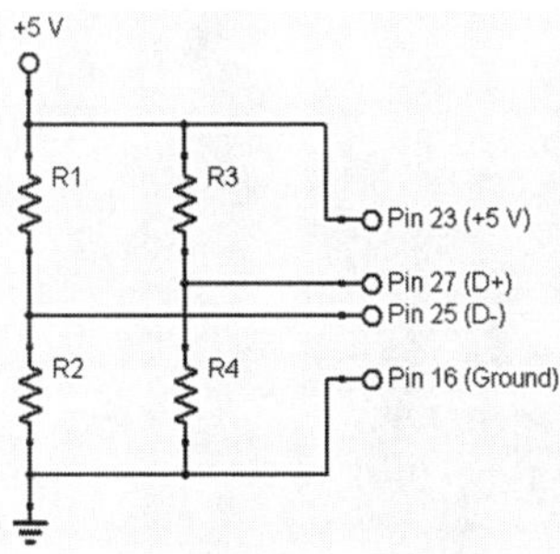

In this case, R1 and R2 must be 50K, R3 must be 150K, and R4 must be 100K. This tells the iPhone to draw up to 750 mA amps of current from your charger. If your charger cannot handle that much current, then you may want to use the first method, which consists of two resistors.

But what if your charger doesn't supply 5V? (You'd have this problem with a FireWire charger.) Read on for a solution.

Make a 3G Adapter Cable to Charge via FireWire

The goal of adapting the FireWire cable is to convert the FireWire voltage (often 12 volts) to the 5 volts needed for USB. This technique works for many chargers and power sources, including battery backups and the like. Your goal is to obtain a smooth and stable 5-volt source, and then add the resistor network described previously to the end of it.

Voltage regulator chip

By far, the simplest and easiest method is to use the LM7805 chip. Available from any electronics supplier, including RadioShack, it can take any voltage up to 35V and reduce it to a very steady stable 5V. It will supply up to 1 amp of current, which is more than enough for the iPhone. It's a dream, right? Well, there is a catch. The 7805 wastes all the extra juice: if you feed it 12–15V from a car battery through the cigarette lighter adapter, that means 1/3 of the juice goes to your iPhone, and 2/3 goes into heat. This also means your 7805 chip can get *very* hot, to the point of becoming a fire hazard. To avoid that danger, you'll have to install a heat sink to dissipate the heat. You'll also need to ensure that your chip never gets above 150°C (300°F), and it would be best to stay below 100°C (212°F). That might mean quite some heat sink.

This is a quick and dirty source of power and isn't really practical, but it does make a great demonstration. The circuit is shown in Figure 12-148, using the iPod breakout board to demonstrate. If you don't have a breakout board handy, you can use an iPod dock connector if you have one lying around [Hack #12.14].

Figure 12-148.
Charging the iPhone 3G with 12V

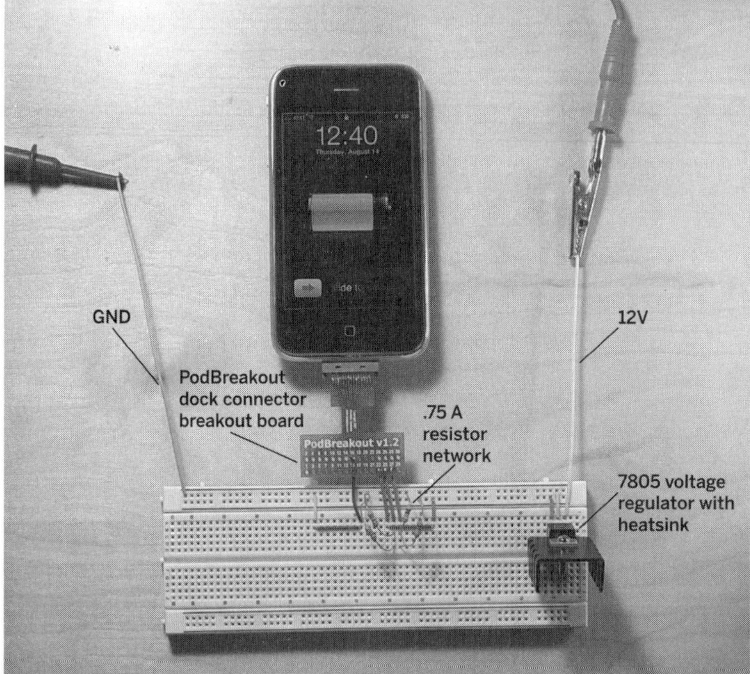

Hacking the Hack

Once you have the tools described in this hack under your belt, there are myriad combinations you can apply in order to power your iPhone in any environment—even from solar cells.

We'll run through one last example of crossing a "wall wart" FireWire charger with a 3G USB car charger to create a wall wart charger for your iPhone 3G.

This hack will require some soldering skill and isn't for the faint of heart. You'll need the following:

- A soldering iron and some solder.
- A USB car charger. Make sure that it works before beginning by charging your iPhone in the car. You might want to use a charger that provides multiple USB outlets. You can modify one output for the dock cable, and keep the other outlet for charging other USB devices.
- A dock extender cable. A number of companies produce dock extender cables. CableJive and Ridax both sell dock extender cables on their websites. Make sure that the cable you order has all the connections you want. For example, the CableJive cable doesn't provide audio inputs to the phone. If you need only audio out and iPod control, both cables should be fine. We'll use the Ridax cable for this example, because it has all the connections we want; plus, the flat-pack cable will make it easier to determine which wires to cut.

The basic idea here is to take the 12V source from the original FireWire pins and run it through the USB charger to produce a 5V output. (Internally, the USB charger most likely has a switched-mode power supply.) We can then run the 5V power to the USB pins on the output side. Essentially, we're going to hard-wire the USB conversion into our adapter cable, while making sure not to change the audio or control wires. It's probably a good idea to remove the cable before attempting any data transfers or sync operations.

First, find and cut the following wires:

- FireWire power (pins 19 & 20)
- FireWire ground (pins 29 & 30)
- USB power (pin 23)
- USB Data + (pin 27)
- USB Data – (pin 25)
- USB Ground (pin 16)

 More pinout information can be found at: http://pinouts.ru/Devices/ipod_pinout.shtml and **[Hack #12.14]**

Open the casing on your USB charger, then follow these steps:

1. Desolder the original power wires, noting which spot was connected to power (the tip of the charger) and which was connected to ground (the side prong). For now, we'll reuse the charger casing, but you may want to put it in a different housing if it's too bulky.
2. Cut the FireWire power (19, 20) wires on the dock cable.
3. Solder the wires coming from the female end to the 12V input on the charger.
4. Cut the FireWire ground wires (29,30) on the dock cable.
5. Solder the wires coming from the female end to the ground input on the charger.
6. Make sure that the USB charger power and ground are connected to the female dock connector. At this point, you might want to test your cable. Connect the female end to your iPod connector, and attach your iPhone or a USB device to the charger output. Make sure that the USB output is working properly, and recheck your work if it isn't.

If necessary, add the USB voltage divider described earlier in this hack to the USB output of the charger. You may need to remove the USB connector to make room for the new wires.

7. Cut the USB power (23) and ground (16) wires on the dock cable
8. Solder the wires coming from the male ends to the USB power (1) and ground (4) pins on the charger.
9. Cut the USB D+ (27) and D- (25) wires on the dock cable
10. Solder the wires coming from the male end to the D+ (3) and D- (2) pins on the charger USB output.

Now you need to seal the USB wires coming from the female dock connector, making sure that none of them are touching each other. If you plan on using your cable year 'round, or in a humid environment, you might want to use something that will form a watertight seal.

Optional: ground the remaining FireWire wires coming from the male connector. This will ensure that the iPhone doesn't see any floating signals on the unused FireWire pins. If you chose not to ground these pins, make sure that they are sealed.

Now it's time to wrap it up:

11. Close the charger case, making sure not to crimp the new wires.
12. Secure the new wires to the connector to make sure that they do not get pulled out, and make sure that there are no exposed connections.

Plug the adapter into your original dock connection, and connect your iPhone to the other end. Verify that it is charging, and that your audio and control connections still work. If you used a dual-outlet USB charger, you should be able to charge other USB devices from your adapter cable as well.

— Zack Gainsforth & Christopher Kurpinski

HACK 12.18: Connect Your iPhone to a Serial Port Using a Dock Connector

With the right adapter, your iPhone can talk to serial devices via the dock connector.

Serial has been the staple low-speed communications protocol for decades. Because the iPhone is the new overlord of connectivity, obviously you'll want to add RS-232 to its repertoire (or USB-Serial if your computer does not have legacy ports). The problem is that the iPhone has only a 3V TTL connection built into the base. However, a bit of fancy adaptation allows you to conjure up a serial connection anyway. You'll need your wire strippers as well as a converter cable. If your serial device doesn't draw too much power, you can even power it from the iPhone!

The parts you'll need are:

- A 3.3V TTL-to-RS-232 cable, part number MCU-026-172 from www.superdroidrobots.com or a 3.3V TTL-to-USB cable, such as part number 768-1016-ND from www.digikey.com. If you're connecting to another 3.3V TTL device—such as a microcontroller—this is not needed.

- An iPod USB sync cable, such as part number IPD-3 from All Electronics www.allelectronics.com or the PodBreakout from SparkFun Electronics (www.sparkfun.com, part number DEV-08295)
- Spudgers for opening the cable plug **[Hack #12.09]**

The first task is to rewire the USB sync cable so that it uses the iPhone's serial pins rather than the USB pins **[Hack #12.14]**. To do this, you will have to open up the iPhone plug using a spudger, as shown back in. There you'll also see the process of rearranging the pins in a dock connector. Once you have completed the steps in **[Hack #12.14]**, your next step is to use a pair of needle nose pliers to remove the pins from their existing seats and push them back into the pinout, as listed in Table 12-2.

Table 12-2
iPhone serial and power pins

Pin Number	Color	Purpose
1	White/Yellow	Ground
12	Black	iPhone Serial TX
13	Green	iPhone Serial RX
18	Red	iPhone 3.3V power

Pin 1 is the pin farthest to the left. You can also find pin 1 by holding your iPhone in your left hand face up, and then plugging in the cable with your right hand. The pin closest to you is pin 1. Pins 2, 3, and so on are found by counting away. Pin 30 is the farthest to the right.

Pins are pulled and reinserted with your fingers, or with needle-nose pliers, as in Figure 12-149.

Figure 12-149.
Rearranging the pins

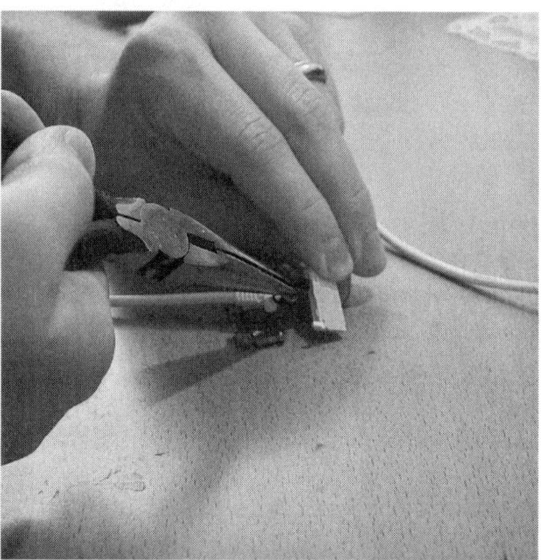

Next, snip the USB end off the sync cable and strip the wires. Then snip the end off the RS-232 cable (if you are using the USB/TTL cable, it should come with stripped ends) and place a section of heat-shrink tubing over one of the cables. Next, solder the cables together, matching wires by color. Note that yellow matches with white. If you have any doubt about which wire goes with which, you can consult the datasheet for the RS-232 or USB/TTL cable.

It is helpful to snip the RS-232 or USB/TTL cable at the very end, as you may encounter unused wires (with different colors), which can be mildly confusing.

After soldering, wrap each wire with electrical tape so that they don't short out against one another. Pull the shrinkwrap over the joint, and heat it up with a hot air gun. Your final result should look like Figure 12-150.

Figure 12-150.
iPhone serial to RS232

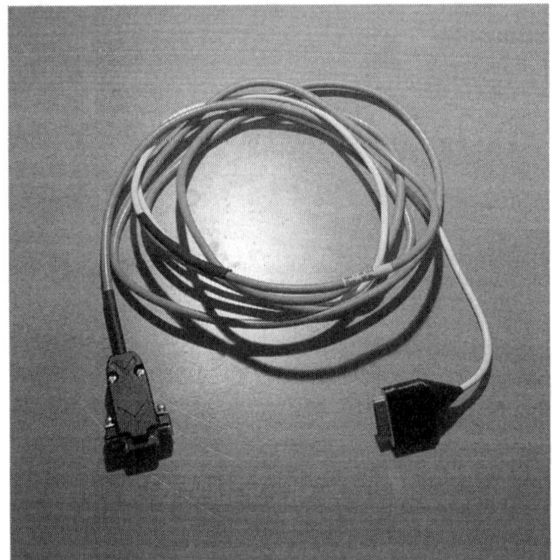

Talking to the iPhone

Once you've done all this, you're going to need some software to talk to it. To write programs to work with the serial port on an iPhone, you'll need the source code at http://devdot.wikispaces.com/Iphone+Serial+Port+Tutorial, which you can build with one of the development environments in Chapter 11.

HACK 12.19: Remote Control Your iPhone or iPod touch with the Dock Connector

Make an iPhone- and iPod-compatible docking station.

Ever since the second generation of iPods, there has been the option to control the iPod through an external interface so that you could remotely skip songs and use other functions. This feature still exists in today's iPhone.

In order to control your iPhone externally, we're going to use the serial port pins that you learned about in [Hack #12.14] and [Hack #12.18] in the dock connector. This time, though, we're going to emulate one of those iPhone docking stations that you find in boomboxes or cars. The iPhone is smart, in that it detects when it is being controlled serially, and switches the audio output from the headphones to the bottom plug. This feature is useful for docking stations, because you just set your iPhone on the station and it handles both communication and audio (and charging too).

If you want to try adapting this hack for use with a microcontroller, be careful that you match voltages correctly, or something will fry. Because the iPhone exposes TTL serial, you could bypass the TTL-to-RS-232 or TTL-to-USB adapter entirely if you connect the iPhone directly to your microcontroller. However, the iPhone uses 3.3V signaling, so if you are using a microcontroller that uses 5V (or 1.8V), you'll need a level shifter such as the $1.95 Logic Level Converter from SparkFun Electronics (www.sparkfun.com), part number BOB-08745.

You'll need the following:

- An PodBreakout breakout board, part number DEV-08295 from www.sparkfun.com
- A 3.3V TTL-to-RS-232 cable, part number MCU-026-172 from www.superdroidrobots.com, or a 3.3V TTL-to-USB cable, such as part number 768-1016-ND from www.digikey.com
- An audio jack such as part number 274-141 from RadioShack, www.radioshack.com, or part number PRT-08032 (3.5 mm jack) and PRT-08827 (audio jack breakout board) from SparkFun
- A breadboard.
- A 500K (500 kilo-ohms) resistor, or multiple resistors that add up to 500K
- 22-gauge wire
- A soldering iron
- Serial debugging software, such as wSHDCOM on Windows (http://wshdcom.exor.hr); you can use any serial comm/modem program, as long as you can paste and send binary strings.

You are going to assemble the setup shown in Figure 12-151.

Figure 12-151.
iPod dock remote control

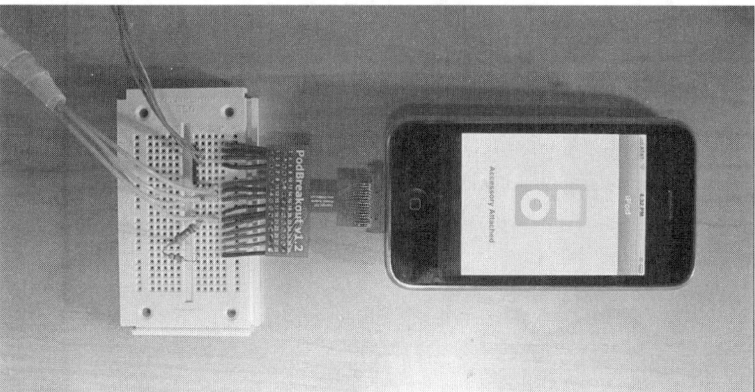

The first step is to solder up your PodBreakout board. Using 22 gauge wire, strip 1/2 inch or so from each end, and solder one end into pins 1-4, 11-13, 18, 21, and 30. You can also solder other pins if you wish to use the same PodBreakout for other projects such as the USB charger **[Hack #12.17]**. As an alternative to making your own wires, you can purchase breadboarding jumper wires and use them instead. These are just 22 gauge wires, precut and prestripped.

Now you need to connect everything on the breadboard, as shown in Figure 12-151. Connect the serial ground to the iPhone breakout ground (pins 1 and 11). Leave pin 2 separate, as that is audio ground and does not need to match the other grounds. You will obtain better audio quality this way.

Connect the serial cable into pins 11–13 and 18. The pinout for the RS-232 and USB TTL cable is shown in Table 12-3.

Table 12-3
Cable pinouts

PodBreakout Pin Number	USB/TTL Cable Color	RS-232 Cable Color	Purpose
11	Black	White/Yellow	Ground
12	Yellow	Black	iPhone Serial TX
13	Orange	Green	iPhone Serial RX
18	No Connection	Red	iPhone 3.3V power

Audio

The audio jack connects to pins 2–4. You will need to open up your jack and solder 22 AWG wire to it. Then you can plug these wires into the breadboard according to the pinout in Table 12-4.

Table 12-4
Audio pinout

Pin	Purpose
2	Audio ground
3	Audio left ear
4	Audio right ear

Old iPods know when they are connected to a docking station, because of a 500K resistor placed between pins 21 and 30. This resistor is not strictly necessary for your iPhone, but if you add this, then your docking station will be fully backward-compatible with iPods, too. If you don't have a 500K resistor, you can usually find a combination of two resistors that produce the required value.

Because this is an iPhone and not an iPod, as soon as you plug it in, you will get the message shown in Figure 12-152. You can choose "Yes" or "No" as you see fit. Rest assured: the protocol works fine on the latest iPhones. We usually select "No;" it will still work.

Figure 12-152.
Just say "No"—it will still work

Schematic

Putting everything together, this is the electrical schematic you should build (Figure 12-153). Note that the TX and RX are from the perspective of the iPhone; you can verify the pinouts at **[Hack #12.14]**. Thus, TX (pin 12) goes to the RX of the PC or device you're connecting to, and RX (pin 13) goes to the TX of the PC or device you're connecting to.

Figure 12-153.
iPhone dock remote schematic

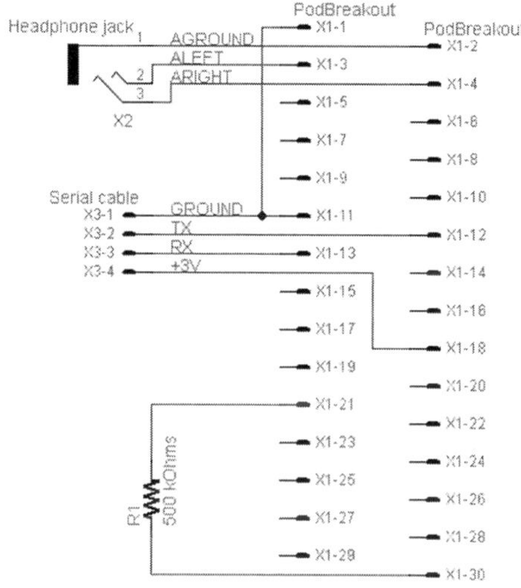

Serial commands

OK, so now you've built it. How do you control it? First, you need a serial program that allows you to send hexadecimal sequences to your serial port. One example is wSHDCOM, which works under Windows. Next, configure it to run at 9600 baud, 8N1.

Now you're going to use serial commands to control it. The protocol is nicely documented at http://stud3.tuwien.ac.at/~e0026607/aap/ipod_aap.html, but just to get you started, we'll give you here the sequence to start playing whatever music happens to be on your iPhone.

First, switch to accessory mode:

```
FF 55 03 00 01 04 F8
```

You should get no apparent response from the iPhone except that if the screen is still lit, you will see a display that says "Accessory Attached." So, just to make sure everything is working, ask for the iPhone name:

```
FF 55 03 04 00 14 E5
```

You should get a response containing an ASCII string with your iPhone name in it. In my case:

```
FF 55 0A 04 00 15 69 53 6D 61 73 68 00 78
```

(Bonus points: What's my iPhone name?)

If that passes, you now give it a command to select playlist #0, which contains all songs on the iPhone:

```
FF 55 08 04 00 17 01 00 00 00 00 DC
```

You should get a response:

```
FF 55 06 04 00 01 00 00 17 DE
```

Now tell it to switch to the playlist that you selected and start playing:

```
FF 55 07 04 00 28 00 00 00 00 CD
```

You should get a response:

```
FF 55 06 04 00 01 00 00 28 CD
```

And music should start playing!

One last command you might want is the play/pause command:

```
FF 55 04 04 00 29 01 CE
```

Now that you've made the connection, you can write programs on your computer—or microcontroller—that control the iPhone by sending commands like these over the serial port.

HACK 12.20: Read Signals from an Infrared Remote Control—Without Jailbreaking!

You can receive infrared input on your iPhone without jailbreaking, using the audio input jack.

Although numerous one-off hacks connecting all sorts of devices to the iPhone have been posted on blogs and YouTube, the problem with these approaches is that they usually use the dock connector **[Hack #12.18]** and thus cannot be reduced to commercial products until the iPhone 3.0 operating system is released.

However, there is an I/O (input/output) port on the iPhone just waiting to be used: the headphone/microphone port **[Hack #12.21]**. If you think about it, people have been squeezing over 50Kbps (kilobits per second) out of phone lines, and they have far less fidelity than the iPhone's sound chip. And Apple's SDK works fine with audio input and output...no jailbreaking required!

You can find the source code for the application as well as the schematic at http://perceptdev.com/labs/iphonehacks.

For this demonstration hack, we've wired up a simple circuit that takes infrared pulses and converts them to a sound wave. Then we've written code to recognize the signals from a well-known remote: the IR (infrared) remote that comes bundled with most Macs.

What you'll need:

- A 38kHz infrared receiver (Figure 12-154), part number PCM-1 from www.allelectronics.com
- A 1K (1 kilo-ohm) resistor (color code: brown-black-red)
- A 220K resistor (color code: red-red-yellow)
- One electrolytic (cylinder) capacitor in the 47–220uF range
- One electrolytic capacitor around 10uF
- One 4-AA battery holder
- Four 1.2V AA rechargeable batteries

Figure 12-154.
A 38kHz infrared receiver

Figure 12-155 shows the pinouts of the IR receiver. It is quite simple: you connect it to 5V (pin 2) and ground (pin 3), and it will output a signal on pin 1.

Figure 12-155.
IR pinout

Figure 12-156 shows a close-up of the breadboarded circuit for this hack. Pins 2 and 3 of the IR receiver are connected to 5V and ground, respectively. A capacitor (I used 10uF) is put across ground and 5V to stabilize the input from the batteries.

When you point a remote at the IR receiver and press its buttons, this creates a signal in the 5V range on pin 1 of the IR receiver, which is much too hot for the iPhone microphone circuit. So we pass pin 1 (row 2) of the IR receiver through a 220K resistor (rows 2 and 8), to the 1K resistor (rows 8 and ground), which then goes to ground. Where these two resistors meet (shown as row 8 in Figure 12-156), they join a 47uF capacitor. The other side of the 47uF capacitor provides the lowered signal that can be safely put into the microphone port of the iPhone.

Figure 12-156.
Close-up of the breadboarded infrared circuit

You'll need an audio splitter [Hack #12.14] and a battery pack (four 1.2V rechargeables will give you 4.8V, which should work). You can see the complete circuit in Figure 12-157.

Figure 12-157.
The completed IR circuit

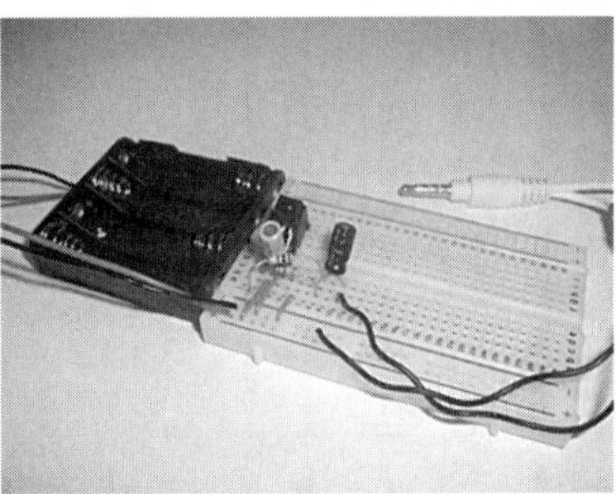

Figure 12-158 shows the demo application. The source code for this application and libraries that you can incorporate in your own application can be found at http://perceptdev.com/labs/iphonehacks. When you press any button on the IR remote while it's aimed at the IR receiver, the corresponding button will light up (Figure 12-158).

Figure 12-158.
Pressing the middle button

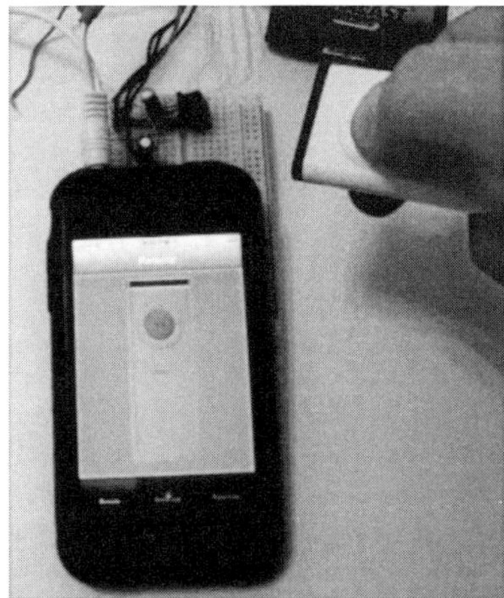

If you click the pulse log button shown in Figure 12-159, you'll see a numerical readout of the different pulses. If you use a different remote control, you can watch those numbers to "learn" new remotes and alter the source code to recognize your new remote (Figure 12-160).

Figure 12-159.
Pulse log

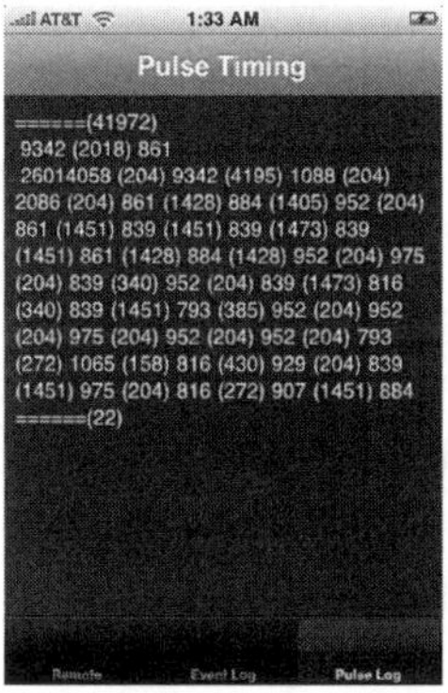

Figure 12-160.
Pressing middle button

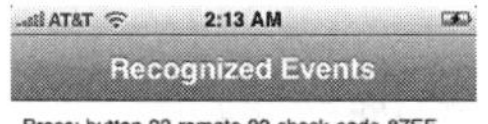

 You can find out more ways to capture signals in the world with the microphone from similar hacks at:
http://wiki.laptop.org/go/Measure
http://wiki.laptop.org/go/Measure/Start#How_to_connect_sensors_.28

HACK 12.21: Connect a Serial Device to Your iPhone—Without Jailbreaking!

Connect all kinds of hardware to an iPhone using the headphone jack as a serial port.

The iPhone has a modem. Did you know that? Well, not quite, but when you're done with this hack, it will. With a little hardware wrangling, you can build a device that interfaces with your iPhone via the microphone/audio jack and can send 1200 baud serial data both ways.

Although there are a number of ways to get data into and out of the iPhone—the dock connector, Bluetooth, the camera and screen, and Wi-Fi—none of these are well suited for simple, low-speed bidirectional communication with inexpensive components. Plus, several of these are simply inaccessible from Apple's SDK. The audio port, however, is accessible from the SDK—both playing audio and recording it—and thus does not require a jailbreak. The demo applications and source code for this hack can be downloaded from www.perceptdev.com/labs/iphonehacks and built by any registered iPhone developer.

We start with a souped-up microcontroller, the Cypress PSoC (Programmable System on a Chip). It exposes a UART (serial port) on one side, and talks to your iPhone using FSK (frequency-shift keying), the same technique used on some of the first modems (like the old 300 baud modems).

Frequency shift keying is a system that uses alternating analog signals to send information: for example, in binary FSK, a tone of 8000 Hz (hertz) might signify a digital 1, and 4000 Hz digital 0. We chose these two frequencies for this project because:

1. Our sound must be easily played and recorded through the iPhone audio circuitry.
2. If we choose harmonic frequencies (8000 Hz = 2 * 4000 Hz), then we can use a simple method to decode the signals and make this a weekend hack instead of a weeklong hack.

The Circuit

You'll need the following electronic components. Most of the components cost less than $20; the 5V UART is the most expensive part, at around $30:

- Cypress PSoC: CY8C29466-24PXI (http://mouser.com or www.digikey.com part #428-1586-ND)
- Cypress PSoC MiniProg USB programmer: CY3217 (http://mouser.com or www.digikey.com)
- Breadboard (a solderless breadboard would work)
- Three 1K resistors (color code: brown-black-red)
- One 220 K resistor (color code: red-red-yellow)
- One 0.1 uF (microfarad) ceramic capacitor (should be labeled "104")
- One 0.2 uF capacitor; two 0.1uF (104s) in parallel will work
- A pair of iPhone headphones that you don't mind destroying
- 5–9V power source (a 9V battery is fine)

- LM7805 voltage regulator, unless you are using a steady 5V power source (Digikey part# LM340T-5.0-ND)
- 5-pin male 0.100 K.K. header (Digikey part # WM4203-ND)
- A 5V UART such as the TTL-232R cable (www.ftdichip.com/Products/EvaluationKits/TTL-232R.htm)

Build the circuit pictured in Figure 12-161. You should get the results shown in Figures 12-162 through 12-165, which show the project from several angles.

Figure 12-161.
FSK circuit schematic

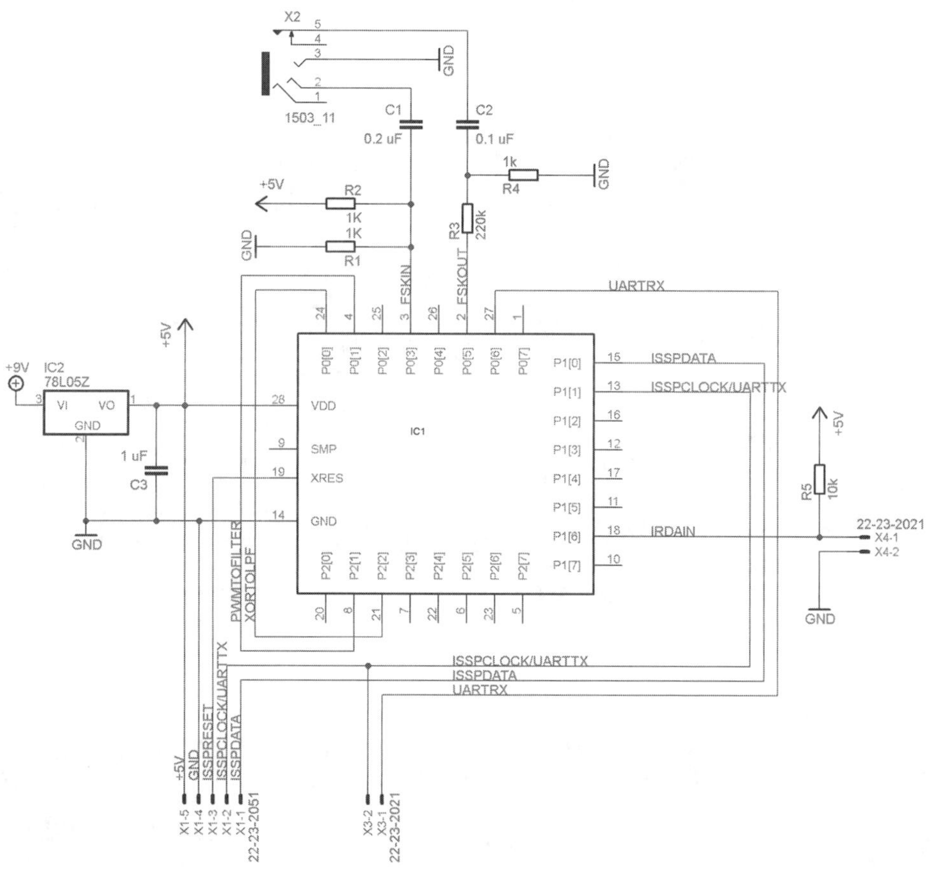

If you look at Figure 12-161, you'll see two inputs. X3-1 and X3-2 connect to a UART (the FTDI USB to TTL serial cable) that you can talk to over a serial connection, such as a PC running HyperTerminal or another serial terminal program (such as *screen* on Mac OS X/Linux or *minicom* on Linux). You may need to download a driver for the FTDI cable from www.ftdichip.com/FTDrivers.htm.

X4-1 and X4-2 on the right side of the circuit are for the next hack **[Hack #12.22]**. The same basic circuit is used for both hacks, just with different firmware. The top of the schematic shows the wiring that connects to the headphone jack to plug into the iPhone. The bottom left of the schematic shows the header pins that connect to the UART programmer itself.

Figure 12-162.
FSK circuit—top view

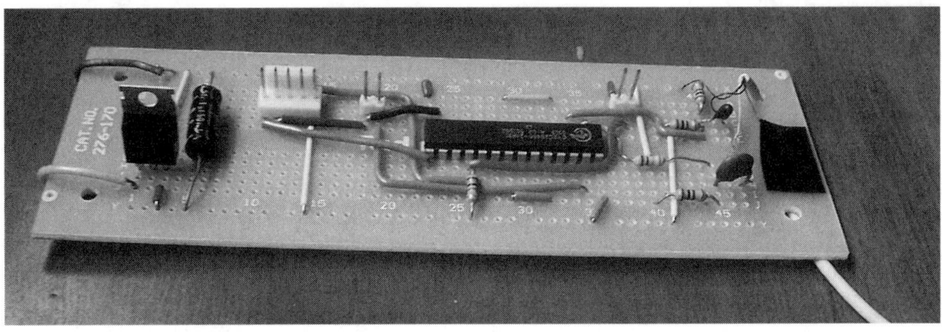

Figure 12-163.
FSK circuit—top down

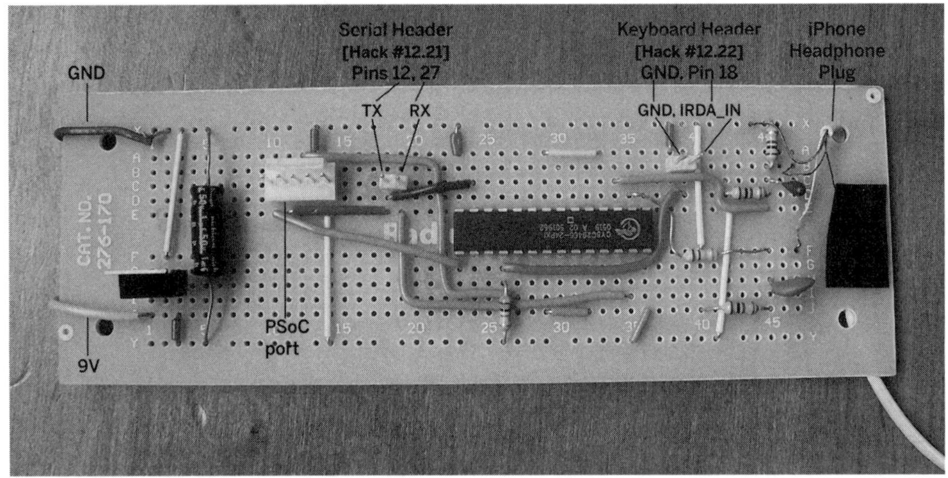

Figure 12-164.
FSK circuit—isometric view

Figure 12-165.
FSK circuit—bottom

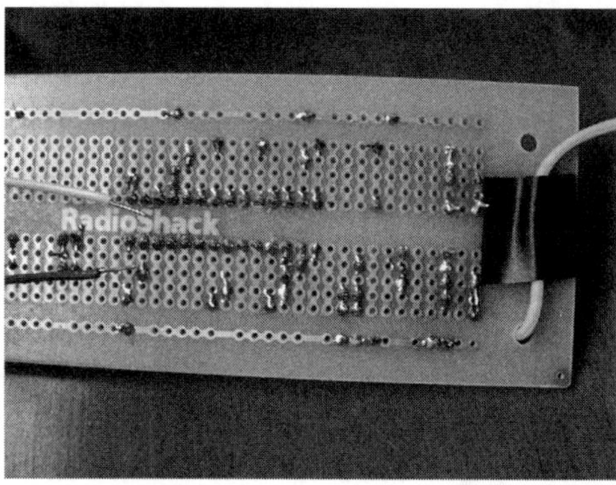

Figure 12-166.
FSK circuit, with PSoC programmer and battery attached

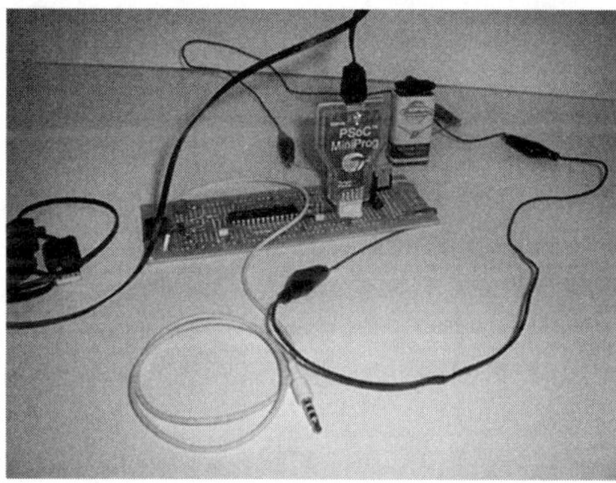

You will find it easiest to make the connection to your audio/microphone jack by cutting up an old pair of iPhone headphones and wiring the plug direct to your breadboard.

Programming the Cypress Chip

You will need a Cypress programming system. The baseline, simplest programmer is the CY3217 part listed earlier in this hack (Figure 12-166). If you are really interested in spinning projects of your own with this processor family, you'd be better off dropping the greenbacks to purchase an ICE (in-circuit emulator) that allows to you debug the hardware. It is a must for development, but overkill for simply programming a chip. You can find information about the ICE and how do develop your own projects at www.psocdeveloper.com/getting-started.html.

You will also need the PSoC Designer software at: www.psocdeveloper.com/tools/psoc-programmer.html (Figure 12-167). You can then download the source code for this hack, both for the iPhone application and for the PSoC from http://perceptdev.com/labs/iphonehacks.

Figure 12-167.
PSoC Programmer software

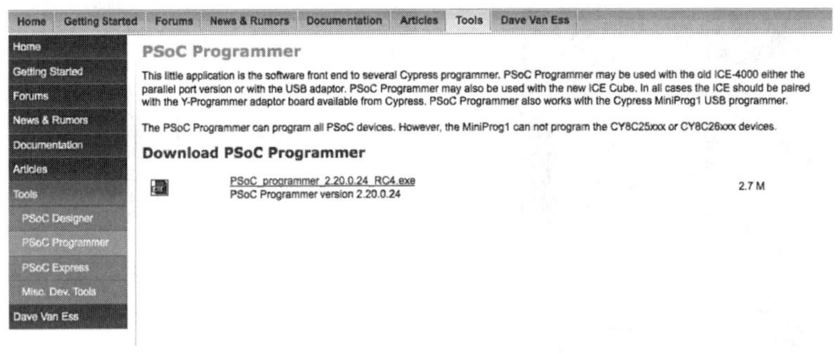

Unfortunately, the Cypress PSoC development environment is Windows-only. However, it is free to download. It includes its own C compiler, which is also free (but limited in functionality: you will need to spend a lot of money to obtain the fully optimized version). This hack was actually developed on a Mac using Windows running under Parallels Desktop as well as VMware Fusion, so you could run it on your Mac if you don't mind purchasing VMware or Parallels as well as a Windows license.

There are few devices on the market like the Cypress chip. It's not just a microcontroller. It is a combination microcontroller, FPGA (Field Programmable Gate Array), and analog device. Cypress calls it a "mixed signal array." Whereas an FPGA has software configurable *digital* hardware, the Cypress chip also has software configurable *analog* hardware. An equivalent design to this application would have about 10 op-amps, and a bunch of other discrete components on the board, as well as an FPGA that you would have to program.

Incidentally, this is the reason why the Cypress is so good for analog audio processing: it really allows you to squeeze a whole circuit board onto one chip. For example, this hack (UART to FSK) was converted to keyboard-to-FSK **[Hack #12.22]** in about a day. The hardware for both is *exactly* the same, requiring you to just upload a different program to the chip.

To flash the chip, you'll need to use the PSoC Programmer, shown in Figure 12-166. You'll also need the firmware for this hack, which you can download from www.perceptdev.com/labs/iphonehacks.

Plug the USB end into your computer. If not already installed, install the PSoC drivers, and the PSoC Programmer software (Figure 12-168).

Figure 12-168.
PSoC Programmer software

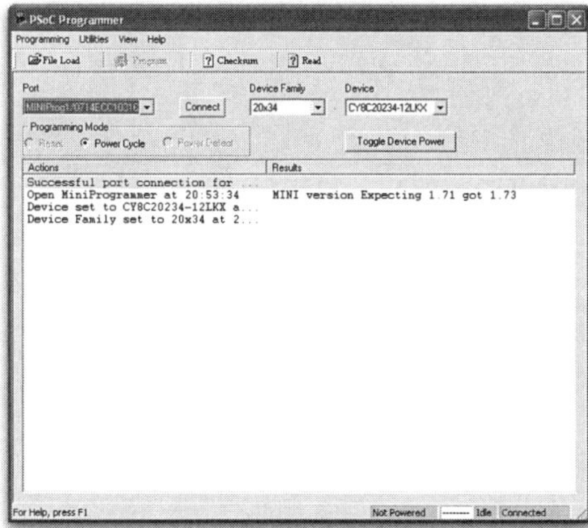

After you start it up, select the correct chip family, the 29x66, CY8C29466 (Figure 12-169). You should see "connected" on the bottom right of your screen if the software and chip are communicating. You can test the connection by clicking Toggle Device Power, and you should see a red LED light up or turn off on the PSoC programmer hardware, and the words "Not Powered" on the bottom of the screen will change to "Powered."

Figure 12-169.
Choose the correct family

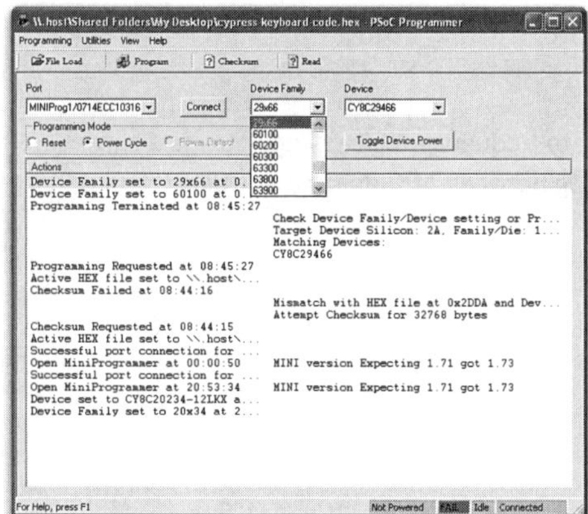

Click "file load" to load the firmware file that you downloaded from http://perceptdev.com/labs/iphonehacks, and then click Program, which will flash the chip (Figure 12-170).

Figure 12-170.
Programming the PSoC

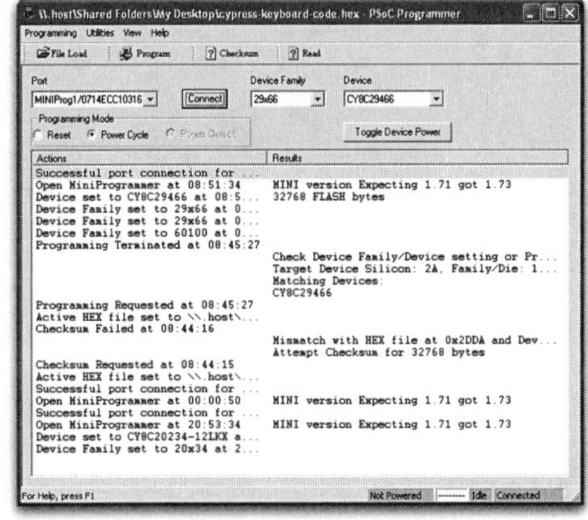

How it Works

To build the FSK to UART converter shown in this hack, we used the method described in two papers:

- FSK Generator, Application Note AN2098: www.psocdeveloper.com/docs/appnotes/an-mode/detail/an-pointer/an2098/an-file/122.html, which describes how to take digital bits and turn them into an FSK audio signal.
- FSK Detector, Application Note AN2336: www.psocdeveloper.com/docs/appnotes/an-mode/detail/an-pointer/an2336/an-file/124.html, which describes how to decode the FSK audio signal back into digital bits.

The circuit takes serial from the computer, converts to frequency-shift keying. It takes a carrier signal, such as a sine wave, and modulates it, toggling between 4000Hz and 8000Hz (Figure 12-171).

Figure 12-171.
4kHz to 8kHz frequency-shift keying

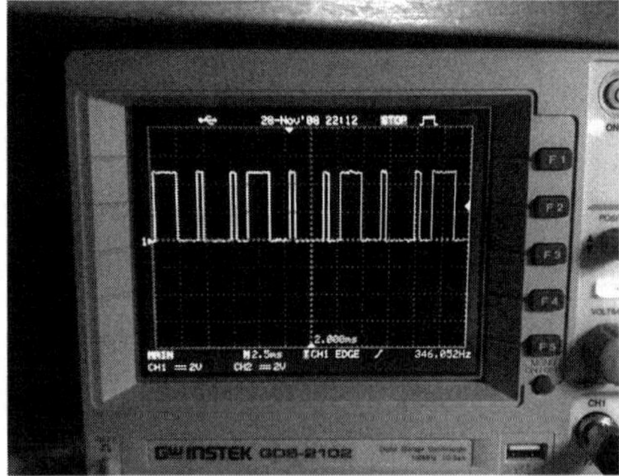

You can find the source code used to program the Cypress chip at www.perceptdev.com/labs/iphonehacks. There you will also find audio files that are canned recordings of serial data modulated with the FSK method presented here.

As a test, you can play these audio files out of your computer, and pipe the audio into your iPhone using the microphone splitter from [Hack #12.14]. One of the audio files has a canned message: "If you can read this, then your system is working!" Like a player piano, you can even see the speed and cadence of the original typing as it plays.

The iPhone can even be acoustically coupled—a fancy word for holding the iPhone near a speaker using the microphone on the bottom, without using a microphone splitter. You can simply play some of the sample FSK files from your laptop or desktop speakers, and hold the iPhone, running the FSK application, near the speakers. You'll have to hold it just right to get a clean decoding, as you can see in Figure 12-172.

Figure 12-172.
PC Speakers <--> FSK Application demo

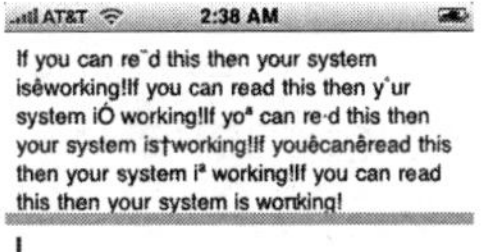

The FSK specifications are:

- 1200 baud 8-N-1
- Bit 1: 8kHz
- Bit 0: 4kHz

The baud rate to the iPhone is 1266 exactly (intended to leave a little buffer so that a 1200 baud device connected to the FSK circuit never gets jammed). If you treat TX as 1200 baud, you'll be fine, because the chip will never send anything at a rate faster than 1200 baud.

The bytes are sent as ASCII little-endian (LSB/MSB). So for example, "U" is sent as the following 9 bits:

```
bit 0: 4 kHz start bit
bit 1: 8 kHz
bit 2: 4 kHz
bit 3: 8
bit 4: 4
bit 5: 8
bit 6: 4
bit 7: 8
bit 8: 4
```

Standby is at 8kHz. That is, if you're not sending data, then emit a constant 8kHz tone.

You can decrease the sample rate of this audio file significantly in an audio editing program, even compressing it to an MP3, and it will still work. It has been tested to 20kHz at 16 bits, and it was just fine. Theoretically, you could go to 16kHz and retain the information.

Hacking the Hack

If you've read this far, you probably already have ideas for how to apply this. **[Hack #12.22]** jumps right into applying this circuit to the holy grail of iPhone device connectivity: an iPhone keyboard.

— Zack Gainsforth, George Dean IV & Damien Stolarz

HACK 12.22: Connect a Keyboard to Your iPhone—Without Jailbreaking!

Adapt an infrared keyboard for PDAs and type on your iPhone.

A number of industrious hackers have achieved what to some is the holy grail of iPhone accessories: a physical iPhone keyboard. But most have done it in a very hard-to-repeat manner, and few have shared the methods they used.

This hack attempts to solve both of these problems. For one, it uses the audio port, an Apple-SDK supported method of communicating with an iPhone or second-generation iPod touch. And for another, the source code for the hardware used—both to program the chip, and to run on the iPhone—are publicly available. You can download schematics, code, plans, and a parts list from http://perceptdev.com/labs/iphonehacks.

Furthermore, you can purchase new and used infrared keyboards online for less than $10 USD. Thus, with everything needed from **[Hack #12.21]**, you're looking at potentially less than $75 USD to build a keyboard, chip programmer included (Figure 12-173).

Figure 12-173.
Typing on a Targus PDA keyboard into the iPhone

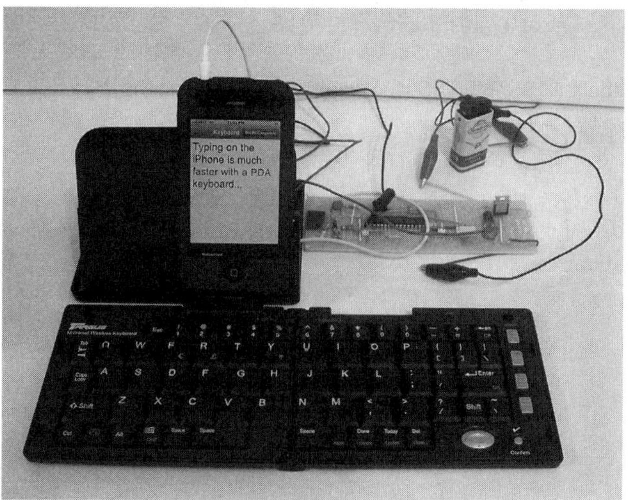

Using a modified version of the iPhone modem Cypress firmware from **[Hack #12.21]**, you can attach an external portable keyboard to your iPhone. We implemented support for two keyboards: a MicroInnovations IrDA Palm keyboard, which had an unusual binary protocol ("scan codes"), due to its unusual keyboard layout (Figure 12-174); and a Targus keyboard, whose scan codes matched a standard PC keyboard. Both were designed for use with a PDA and use a form of infrared called IrDA to send keypresses to a device.

Figure 12-174.
MicroInnovations keyboard hooked to Cypress circuit

Rather than worry about building an IrDA receiver, we just wired the IrDA signal directly by soldering leads to both terminals of the IrDA transmitter. This gave us a cleaner signal and simplified development (Figure 12-175). If you wish, you can certainly add an IrDA receiver to the modem and obtain the same functionality.

Figure 12-175.
Soldering onto both sides of the IrDA transmitter LED

The schematic for the keyboard hack is the same one described in **[Hack #12.21]**, except now we're using the header for keyboard in. It is shown again in Figure 12-176 for ease of reference.

Figure 12-176.
The iPhone FSK adapter schematic

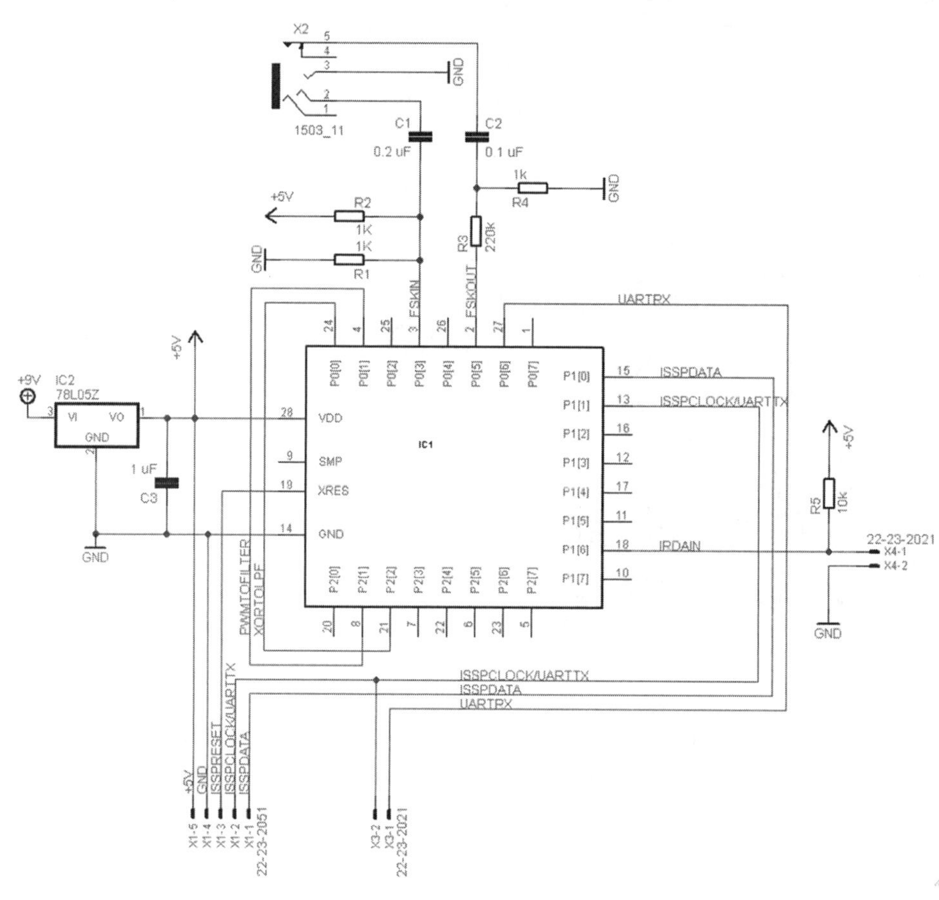

To connect the Targus keyboard, you need to snip the red and white wires that lead to the IR transmitter (Figure 12-177).

Figure 12-177.
Finding the IR red and white wires

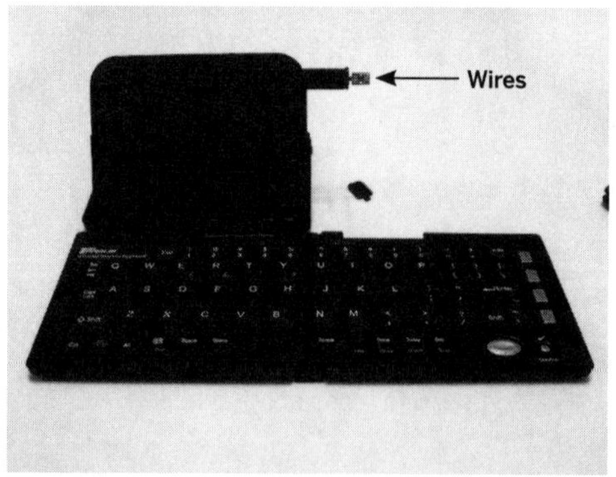

Then clip these two wires. The white wire from the Targus IR keyboard (not shown) clips to the IRDA_IN pin on the circuit. The red wire from the Targus IR keyboard (not shown) clips to any convenient ground (Figure 12-178).

Figure 12-178.
Connecting the keyboard to the FSK circuit

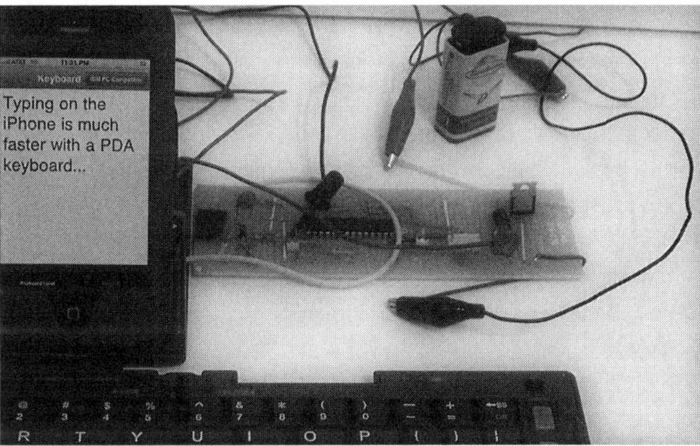

How It Works

The IrDA signal on the keyboard essentially "shorts" a voltage (brings it down to zero), which you provide via a 5K (5 kilo-ohm) pull-up resistor. Thus, the standby voltage is 5V (in our case) and the value goes to 0V (short) for brief, 5 microsecond pulses as the keyboard shorts the line. A series of pulses (or lack thereof) indicates what data is being transmitted. (Figure 12-179 shows a single byte sent over the channel.)

Figure 12-179.
One byte (start bit + 10001100)

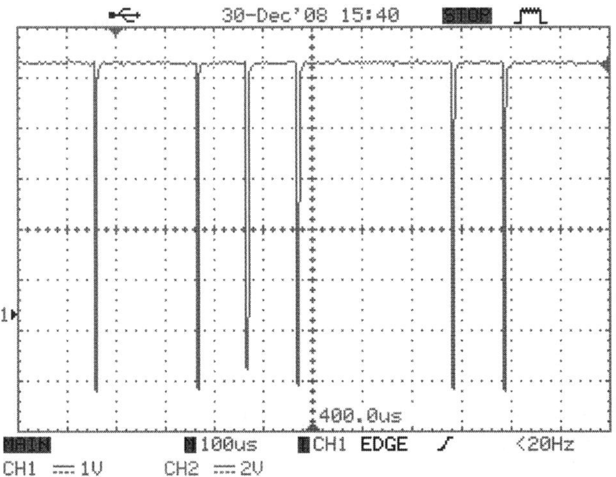

In Figure 12-179, the leftmost bit is the start bit (logic 0, voltage 0). The 8-bit sequence following is 10001100. The absence of a pulse implies logic 1, the presence of a pulse implies logic 0. This is the first byte (first half of the scan code) sent in response to a keypress "u."

In this configuration, the presence of a pulse indicates a logic 0, and the absence indicates a logic 1. The pulses are sent at 9600 baud. Therefore, in order to read the data sent by the keyboard, you have to do the following:

1. Using a DigInv block on the Cypress chip, use an interrupt to call a function in your code each time a negative pulse (zero) arrives.
2. Wait for a first pulse. This is your start bit, which signifies the start of a byte. Your function will start a timer that goes for 3/2s of a 9600 baud period (150 microseconds).
3. If subsequent pulses arrive during the timer period, your function notes them. If no pulse occurs, your function is not called.
4. When the timer is up, check to see if the interrupt function was called. If not, that would mean the last bit was a logic 1 (no pulse). If it was called, then the bit was logic 0. Reset the timer for a single 9600 baud period (100 microseconds).
5. Repeat step 4 seven more times.
6. On the last bit (now you have 8), write the byte to the FSK system—which is identical to what you did in **[Hack #12.21]**. Also turn off the timer, and have your interrupt function wait for another start bit.
7. At this point, you will be in the middle of a stop bit, which is always logic 1, (no pulse, signifying the end of the byte.

Because the keyboard sends data at 9600 baud, the circuit has to buffer data to some extent, even though nobody can seriously type faster than 1200 baud. This is because key presses generate multiple bytes: they're scan codes, not ASCII. And, because scan codes vary from keyboard to keyboard, you are best off figuring out what they are by pressing keys. Note that both the press and release of a key generate a scan code, as do modifier keys like shift, alt, and control. So a single character typed could generate 6 or more bytes of data. With stop bits, it could be up to over 50 bits for a single keypress. A 120 words per minute typist can type 10 characters per second. Yet even with overhead, 500 bits per second fits into our 1200 baud bandwidth budget.

When the keyboard firmware is loaded onto the Cypress chip, it replaces the bidirectional serial firmware from **[Hack #12.21]**. There is only enough memory on the Cypress to do one-way communication (keyboard to the iPhone) in the current code, but if you optimized it further or used a larger Cypress chip, it would be possible to have keyboard input simultaneously with some sort of serial output to a device.

It's also worth noting that the keyboard uses only the microphone input. Thus, using a simple Y-splitter **[Hack #12.14]**, you should be able to listen to audio while typing.

Hacking the Hack

The source code for the Cypress firmware for reading the keyboard is available from www.perceptdev.com/labs/iphonehacks.

Because the source code is available, and because kits with the keyboard preassembled are straightforward to produce, the library that adds keyboard support can be integrated into any iPhone application.

Thus, a programmer could create terminal programs, note-taking programs, and even full-screen text editors with arrow controls. Given that some old serial mice originally ran at 1200 baud, it's entirely conceivable that an improved circuit could be produced with both mouse and keyboard support.

But with the iPhone being such a nice computer...with a keyboard...it seems like we're only a few steps away from a mobile PC revolution **[Hack #12.23]**.

— Zack Gainsforth, George Dean IV & Damien Stolarz

HACK 12.23: Use Your iPhone to Go Back in Time

The iPhone is a portable personal computer.

Everyone with a smartphone has a personal computer in their pocket. But if the iPhone is such a great computer, why are we still carrying around a laptop?

There are wireless technologies coming around the corner, such as UWB ("ultra wideband"), that promise to connect devices to screens wirelessly. But until that time, we have **[Hack #12.06]** to enable our iPhones to connect to monitors.

Using **[Hack #12.06]** combined with **[Hack #12.22]**, we've finally "demobilized" the iPhone, taking portable computing to its illogical conclusion (Figure 12-180).

Figure 12-180.
The iPhone as a desktop personal computer

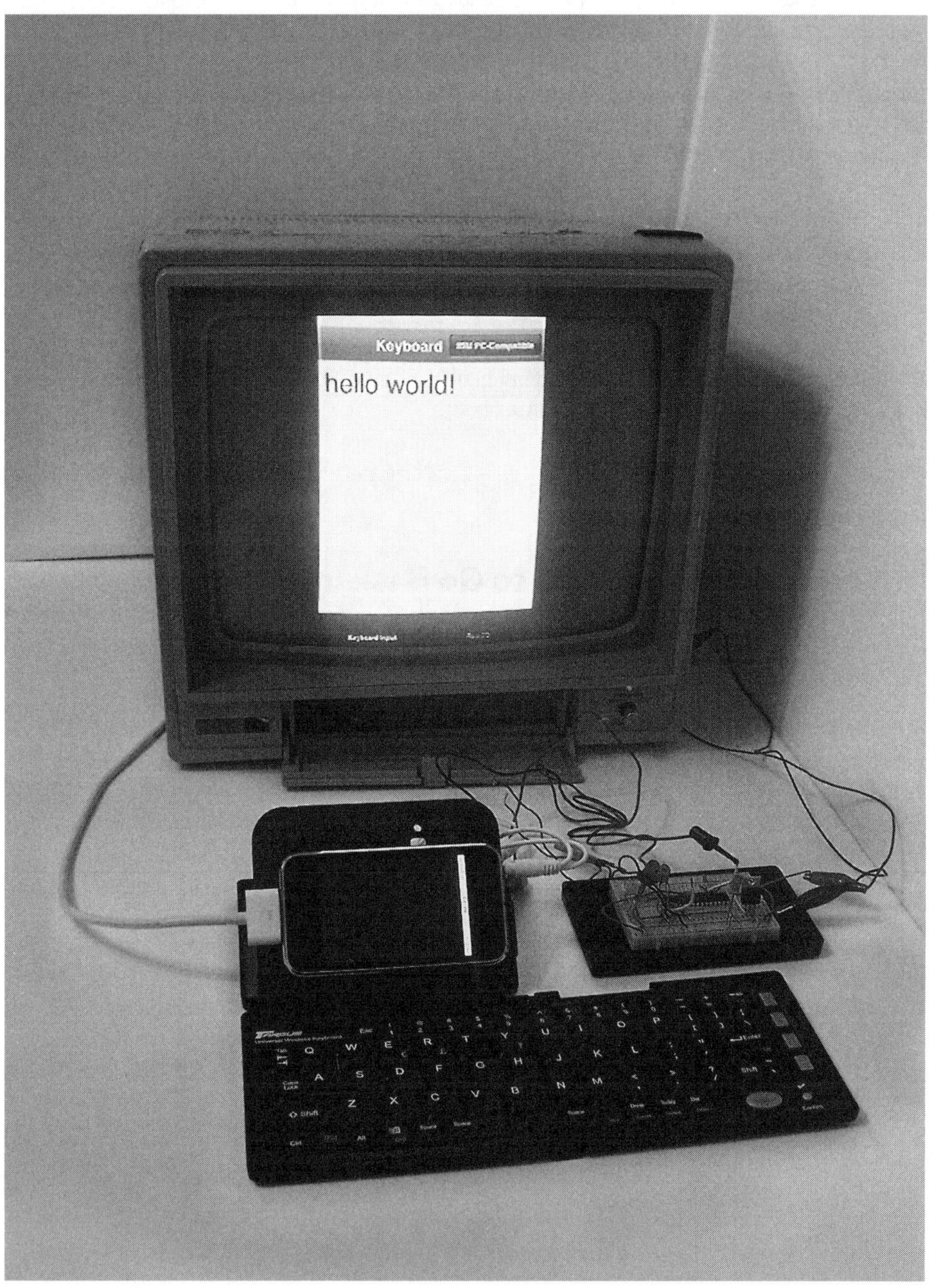

Enjoy hacking your phone!

INDEX

D

N

O

P

T